2nd Edition

Marketing Theory

Edited by
Michael J. Baker
& Michael Saren

Marketing Theory

A Student Text

2nd Edition

Edited by

Michael J. Baker
& Michael Saren

SAGE

Los Angeles | London | New Delhi
Singapore | Washington DC

Preface and editorial arrangement © Michael J. Baker
and Michael Saren 2010

Chapter 1 © Michael J. Baker 2010
Chapter 2 © Michael Saren 2010
Chapter 3 © D.G. Brian Jones 2010
Chapter 4 © Patrick E. Murphy 2010
Chapter 5 © Richard Varey 2010
Chapter 6 © Allan J. Kimmel 2010
Chapter 7 © Kjell Grønhaug and Ingeborg Astrid
    Kleppe 2010
Chapter 8 © Kam-hon Lee and Cass Shum 2010
Chapter 9 © Walter van Waterschoot and Thomas
    Foscht 2010
Chapter 10 © Robin Wensley 2010

Chapter 11 © Sally Dibb and Lyndon Simkin 2010
Chapter 12 © R.W. Lawson 2010
Chapter 13 © Susan Hart 2010
Chapter 14 © Kristian Möller 2010
Chapter 15 © Gerard Hastings, Abraham Brown
    and Thomas Boysen Anker 2010
Chapter 16 © Christopher Moore 2010
Chapter 17 © William E. Kilbourne 2010
Chapter 18 © Roderick J. Brodie and Mark S.
    Glynn 2010
Chapter 19 © Evert Gummesson 2010

First published 2010
Reprinted 2013

SAGE Publications Ltd
1 Oliver's Yard
55 City Road
London EC1Y 1SP

SAGE Publications Inc.
2455 Teller Road
Thousand Oaks, California 91320

SAGE Publications India Pvt Ltd
B 1/I 1 Mohan Cooperative Industrial Area
Mathura Road
New Delhi 110 044

SAGE Publications Asia-Pacific Pte Ltd
3 Church Street
10-04 Samsung Hub
Singapore 049483

Library of Congress Control Number: 2009935057

British Library Cataloguing in Publication data

A catalogue record for this book is available from the British Library

ISBN 978-1-84920-465-1
ISBN 978-1-84920-466-8 (pbk)

Typeset by C&M Digitals (P) Ltd., Chennai, India
Printed and bound by CPI Group (UK) Ltd, Croydon, CR0 4YY
Printed on paper from sustainable resources

Contents

List of Contributors

Thomas Boysen Anker trained as a philosopher, is currently doing his PhD in marketing ethics at the University of Copenhagen. His research covers topics such as ethics in branding, marketing communications and autonomy, commercial social marketing and the societal impact of commercial health branding. His interest in the social aspects of marketing led him to the Institute for Social Marketing, University of Stirling, which he is currently working with on various projects.

Michael J. Baker is Emeritus Professor of Marketing at the University of Strathclyde where he founded the Department of Marketing in 1971. Author/ Editor of more than 50 books, most recently 'Business and Management Research', 3rd Edition 2009 with Anne Foy. He is the Founding Editor of the Journal of Marketing Management and currently Editor of the Journal of Customer Behaviour.

Roderick J. Brodie (PhD) is Professor in the Department of Marketing at the University of Auckland Business School, New Zealand. His publications have appeared in leading international journals including; *Journal of Marketing, Journal of Marketing Research, International Journal of Research in Marketing, Management Science, Journal of Service Research*. He is an area editor of *Marketing Theory* and on the Editorial Boards of the *Journal of Marketing*, the *International Journal of Research in Marketing*, the *Journal of Service Research*, and the *Australasian Journal of Marketing*.

Abraham Brown is a research fellow at the Institute for Social Marketing, University of Stirling. He completed his PhD in Social Marketing in July 2009 at the University of Stirling. Abraham's research interests include tobacco control, social norms, and the application of statistical modelling to change health behaviour. He is a member of the International Tobacco Control Policy Evaluation Project, a collaboration of over 70 researchers from 20 countries who are conducting research to evaluate the impact of national-level tobacco control policies of the Framework Convention on Tobacco Control, the first-ever international treaty on health.

Sally Dibb   is Professor of Marketing and joint Head of the Marketing and Strategy Research Unit at the Open University Business School, Milton Keynes, UK. She was awarded her PhD (Marketing) from the University of Warwick, where she was previously Associate Dean. Sally's research interests are in marketing strategy, segmentation and consumer behaviour, areas in which she has published and consulted extensively. Sally is currently involved in social marketing research with the Institute for Social Marketing, examining targeting strategies, and research examining consumer behaviour in China. She has co-authored nine books and her journal publications include articles in the *Journal of the Academy of Marketing Science, European Journal of Marketing, Industrial Marketing Management, Services Industries Journal, Long Range Planning, Journal of Marketing Management* and *OMEGA*, among others. Sally is co-chair of the Academy of Marketing's Special Interest Group in Market Segmentation.

Thomas Foscht   studied business administration at Karl-Franzens-University Graz, Austria, where he also earned his PhD and his habilitation degree. He was an assistant and associate professor of marketing at Karl-Franzens-University Graz, Austria before he became full professor of marketing at California State University, East Bay (San Francisco), USA. Currently he is a full professor of marketing and chair of the marketing department at Karl-Franzens-University Graz, Austria. He was also a visiting professor at Johannes-Kepler-University, Linz, Austria. As a guest speaker he lectured amongst others at Columbia University, New York, Temple University, Philadelphia, USA, and ETH Zurich (Swiss Federal Institute of Technology). He co-authored a textbook on consumer behaviour, which is written in German and in its third edition and also the book 'Reverse Psychology Marketing', which has been published in English, Spanish and Korean. His papers have been published in leading international academic journals like International Journal of Retail & Distribution Management, Journal of Retailing and Consumer Services, International Journal of Bank Marketing, Journal of Product and Brand Management, Journal of Fashion Marketing and Management, Journal of International Food & Agribusiness Marketing as well as in a number of German Journals.

Mark S. Glynn   is a Senior Research Lecturer in the Faculty of Business and Law at Auckland University of Technology, Auckland, New Zealand. He has a Master of Commerce degree with first class honours and a PhD in Marketing from the University of Auckland. Prior to his academic career, Mark had fifteen years business experience in marketing and brand management. His research experience is in the areas of branding, relationship marketing, business-to-business marketing, and retail channels. In 2006, Mark won the Emerald/EFMD best thesis award for outstanding doctoral research in the category of Marketing Strategy. Mark has published in the Australasian Marketing Journal, Industrial Marketing Management, International Journal of Retail & Distribution Management, Journal of Product and Brand Management, Journal of Business & Industrial Marketing, as well as Marketing Theory. Mark is also co-editor of Business-to-Business Brand Management: Theory, Research and Executive Case Study Exercises which is Volume 15 of the Advances in Business Marketing and Purchasing Series. He reviews for several international journals and serves on the editorial boards of Industrial Marketing Management and Journal of Business & Industrial Marketing.

Kjell Grønhaug is Professor of Business Administration at the Norwegian School of Economics and Business Administration, Bergen-Sandviken. He holds an MBA and a PhD in marketing from the School, an MS in sociology from the University of Bergen, and did his postgraduate studies in quantitative methods at the University of Washington. He has been Visiting Professor at the universities of Pittsburgh, Illinois at Urbana-Champaign, California, Kiel and Innsbruck and several other European institutions. Grønhaug is also Adjunct Professor at the Helsinki School of Economics and associated with the Institute of Fishery Research at the University of Tromsø. He is honorary doctor at Turku School of Economics and Business Administration, and the recipient of the prize for excellence in research at his own institution awarded every fifth year. He has acted as a consultant to business and governmental institutions both in Norway and abroad. Over the years he has been involved in a number of research projects related to a variety of marketing problems, corporate strategy, industry studies and multiple evaluation studies. His publications include 18 authored and co-authored books, and numerous articles in leading American and European journals and contributions to many international conference proceedings. His present research interests relate to cognitive aspects of strategy, creation and use of knowledge, marketing strategies in novel, hi-tech markets and methodological issues.

Evert Gummesson is Emeritus Professor of Marketing and Management at the Stockholm University School of Business, Sweden; Honorary Doctor of the Hanken School of Economics, Helsinki, and a Fellow of Tampere University, Finland. His interests especially embrace service, relationship marketing and CRM, and a network approach to marketing, reflected in his latest book *Marketing as Networks: The Birth of Many-to-Many Marketing*. His book *Total Relationship Marketing* was published in its 3rd and revised edition in 2008. In 2000 he received the *American Marketing Association's (AMA) Award for Leadership in Services*, and his article (with Christopher Lovelock) 'Whither Services Marketing?', in the *Journal of Service Research*, won the *AMA Award for Best Article on Services in 2004*. He is one of the 50 most important contributors to the development of marketing included in the guru list of the *Chartered Institute of Marketing (CIM)*, UK. Dr Gummesson also takes a special interest in research methodology and the theory of science. He has spent twenty-five years as a business practitioner and is a frequent speaker at conferences, business meetings and universities around the world.

Professor Susan Hart (BA Hons., PhD, DipMRS, FRSE) is Dean of Strathclyde Business School. Formerly Professor of Marketing and Head of Department at Strathclyde (2002–2004), and Vice Dean for Research (2005-2008). Previous posts held were Professor of Marketing and Head of Department at the University of Stirling from 1995-98, and Professor of Marketing at Heriot Watt University from 1993-95. In addition, Susan Hart has worked for a variety of private sector companies, ranging from multinational to small manufacturers in consumer and industrial enterprises.

Professor Hart's research areas of interest include innovation and product-service development, marketing and competitive success and marketing performance measurement. She has been awarded research grants by The Leverhulme

Trust, Economic and Social Research Council, Science and Engineering Research Council, Design Council Scotland, the Chartered Institute of Management Accountants and Scottish Enterprise. Journal articles have appeared in the *Journal of Product Innovation Management and Industrial Marketing Management* and two recent books include *Product Strategy and Management* and *The Marketing Book*. A member of the Executive Committee of the Academy of Marketing and the Senate of the Chartered Institute of Marketing, as well as a Fellow of the Marketing Society. Recently elected to the Royal Society of Edinburgh. She edits the *Journal of Marketing Management*, an international, peer review journal. Professor Hart is a Director of The Royal Scottish National Orchestra and a member of the Universiti Putra Malaysia Advisory Board.

Gerard Hastings is the first UK Professor of Social Marketing and founder/director of the Institute for Social Marketing and Centre for Tobacco Control Research at Stirling and the Open University. He researches the applicability of marketing principles such as consumer orientation, relationship building and strategic planning to the solution of health and social problems. He also conducts critical marketing research into the impact of potentially health damaging marketing, such as alcohol advertising, tobacco branding and fast food promotion.

Prof Hastings teaches and writes about social and critical marketing both in the UK, where he has run Masters and Honours level programmes, and internationally in North America, South East Asia, the Middle East and Europe. He has published over a hundred refereed papers in major journals such as the *European Journal of Marketing*, the *International Journal of Advertising*, the *Journal of Macromarketing*, *Psychology and Marketing*, *Social Marketing Quarterly*, the *British Medical Journal*, the *British Dental Journal*. His book *Social Marketing: Why Should the Devil have all the Best Tunes?* was published by Butterworth Heinemann in May 2007. In 1997 Prof Hastings became the first Andreasen Scholar in Social Marketing and in 2009 was awarded the OBE for services to health care.

Brian Jones is Professor of Marketing at Quinnipiac University. He is Editor of the *Journal of Historical Research in Marketing* and serves as Treasurer and Past President of the Conference on Historical Analysis & Research in Marketing (CHARM) Association. His research has been published in the *Journal of Marketing, Journal of the Academy of Marketing Science, Journal of Historical Research in Marketing, Journal of Macromarketing, Marketing Theory, Journal of International Marketing, Psychology & Marketing, Accounting History*, and other publications. He is also co-editor, with Mark Tadajewski, of the (2008) three-volume set of readings titled *The History of Marketing Thought*.

William E. Kilbourne (PhD) received his degree from the University of Houston in 1973. He is a Professor of Marketing at Clemson University, and his research interests are in materialism, globalization, and environmental issues in marketing. Most recently, his attention has been directed to developing, both theoretically and empirically, the role of a society's Dominant Social Paradigm in environmentally relevant consumption behaviour and in materialistic values. The research agenda entails the cross-cultural comparison of both environmental and materialistic values. He has published 40 articles in refereed journals and more than 100 papers in national and international conferences. He is currently the Global Policy and Environment section co-editor for the Journal of Macromarketing.

Allan J. Kimmel   is Professor of Marketing at ESCP Europe in Paris, France. He holds MA and PhD degrees in social psychology from Temple University (USA). He has served as a visiting professor at Université Paris IX-Dauphine (Paris), TEC de Monterrey (Mexico), Universidad de San Andrés (Buenos Aires, Argentina), Turku School of Economics (Finland), and the University of Vaasa (Finland). He has research and writing interests in marketing and research ethics, deception, consumer behavior, marketing communication, commercial rumors, and connected marketing and word of mouth. He has published extensively on these topics, including three books on research ethics, and articles in the Journal of Consumer Psychology, American Psychologist, Psychology & Marketing, Journal of Behavioral Science, Business Horizons, Ethics & Behavior, Journal of Marketing Communications, and European Advances in Consumer Research, among others. His latest books are *Rumors and Rumor Control: A Manager's Guide to Understanding and Combatting Rumors* (2004), *Marketing Communication: New Approaches, Technologies, and Styles* (2005), and *Connecting With Consumers: Marketing for New Marketplace Realities* (2010). Kimmel is an ad hoc reviewer for several research journals and currently serves on the editorial board of The Open Ethics Journal.

Ingeborg Astrid Kleppe   is Associate Professor at the Norwegian School of Economics and Business Administration, Bergen, Norway. She holds an MBA and a PhD in marketing from the School, and MS in sociology from the University of Bergen. Kleppe has extensive international experience from universities in the USA, Sweden, and Australia. In her current research she collaborates with researchers from School of Economics, University of Gothenburg; University of Sydney; Schülich School of Business York University, Toronto; and Leeds University Business School. She has also worked in the World Bank doing poverty research in sub-Saharan Africa. Kleppe has taken her interdisciplinary and international experience into her research on different topics in consumer behaviour. Currently she is doing research on consumer communities in the social media and consumers' adoption to public health interventions in developing countries. Kleppe has also published on country-of-origin and national images in tourism and international marketing journals.

Rob Lawson   is Professor of Marketing at the University of Otago, where he has worked for over 20 years. Rob's education and early career were at the universities of Newcastle and Sheffield in the UK and, though he has published over 100 papers across a wide range of topics in marketing, his main area of interest is consumer behaviour. Much of his current work looks at household energy behaviours and understanding the adoption of energy efficient practices and technologies. Most of Rob's teaching is now at graduate level, including extensive PhD supervision. He is the immediate past-president of ANZMAC and was granted Distinguished Membership of the Academy in 2007. He has also worked as research dean at the University of Otago and was a member of the PBRF Business and Economics assessment panel for research quality New Zealand in both 2003 and 2006.

Professor Kam-hon Lee   is Professor of Marketing and Director, School of Hotel and Tourism Management at The Chinese University of Hong Kong, Shatin, Hong Kong. His research areas include business negotiation, cross-cultural marketing, marketing ethics, social marketing and tourism marketing. He obtained his B.Com. and M.Com. at The Chinese University of Hong Kong, and his PhD in Marketing at Northwestern University in Evanston, Illinois, USA. Professor Lee has taught in executive programs or rendered consulting services to different institutions including the World Bank, Hang Seng Bank, Giordano, K-Wah, Ryoden, Coca-Cola (China), Procter & Gamble (Guangzhou), Digital Equipment Corporation, Du Pont Asia Pacific Ltd., Dentsu Advertising Agency, Chinese Arts & Crafts (H.K.), Hong Kong Tourism Association, Hong Kong Hotels Association and Hong Kong Travel Industry Council. Professor Lee has also served on various government and social service committees, including Advisory Committee on Social Work Training and Manpower Planning, Tourism Strategy Group, Advisory Committee on Travel Agents and Steering Committee on MICE. Professor Lee has published in *Journal of Marketing, Journal of International Business Studies, Journal of Management, Journal of Business Ethics, European Journal of Marketing, International Marketing Review, Psychology and Health, The World Economy, Cornell HRA Quarterly* and other refereed journals.

Kristian Möller   is a Research Professor and Director of the Business Networks Domain at the Aalto School of Economics (formerly the Helsinki School of Economics). He chairs the executive board of the Finnish Doctoral Program in Business Studies. Formerly the President of the European Marketing Academy and the Head of the Marketing and Management Department of the HSE, Dr. Moller is an active member of the international research network. He has been a visiting research scholar at Penn State, Aston Business School, University of Bath, and the European Institute for Advanced Studies in Management in Brussels. His current research is focused on business and innovation networks, competence-based marketing, and marketing theory. His work has been published in *California Management Review, European Journal of Marketing, Industrial Marketing Management, International Journal of Research in Marketing, Journal of Business Research, Journal of Management Studies, Journal of Marketing Management, and Marketing Theory.*

Christopher M. Moore   is Vice-Dean and Chair in Marketing & Retailing at Glasgow Caledonian University, Glasgow. Previously, he was Professor in Retail Marketing at the George Davies Centre for Retail Excellence, at Heriot Watt University, Edinburgh. A graduate of Glasgow and Stirling universities, his doctoral research was in the area of fashion retailer internationalisation. Current research interests include luxury brand marketing, fashion retailer internationalisation, country-of-origin impact on luxury branding and buying & branding strategies within the fashion sector. Professor Moore has provided consultancy support to a wide range of international fashion retailers, luxury brands companies, as well as consumer-facing organisations within the financial services, transport and public service sectors.

Patrick E. Murphy   is Professor of Marketing at the University of Notre Dame in Indiana, USA. He specializes in marketing and business ethics issues. His recent work has focused on normative perspectives for ethical and socially responsible marketing, distributive justice as it relates to marketing decision making, emerging ethical concerns in advertising, and the ethical foundations of relationship marketing. His research has appeared in leading academic journals in the US and Europe. Professor Murphy's articles have won 'best paper' awards from the *Journal of Advertising, Journal of Macromarketing* and the *European Journal of Marketing.* He served as editor of the *Journal of Public Policy & Marketing* and is now a member of four editorial review boards. Professor Murphy teaches courses in business ethics, marketing ethics and corporate sustainability. He has taught previously at Marquette University and spent sabbaticals at the Federal Trade Commission, University College Cork in Ireland and University of Lille 2 in France. His PhD is from the University of Houston, MBA from Bradley University and BBA from Notre Dame.

Michael Saren   is Professor of Marketing at the School of Management, University of Leicester, UK and holds a PhD from the University of Bath. He previously held Chairs in Marketing at the Universities of Stirling and Strathclyde. He was a founding editor in 2001 of the Sage journal *Marketing Theory* and co-editor of *Rethinking Marketing,* (Brownlie et al, 1999, Sage), *Marketing Theory,* Volumes I, II & III, Sage Library in Marketing Series (Maclaran et al, 2007), *Critical Marketing: Defining the Field* (Saren et al, 2007, Elsevier) and the *Sage Handbook of Marketing Theory* (Maclaran et al, 2010). His introductory text is *Marketing Graffiti (*2006, Butterworth Heinemann). He has also published many articles in academic journals including the International Journal of Research in Marketing, Marketing Theory, Consumption, Markets and Culture, Industrial Marketing Management, British Journal of Management, Australasian Marketing Journal, Journal of Business Ethics, Journal of Macromarketing, European Journal of Marketing, Journal of Business and Industrial Marketing, the Service Industries Journal and the Journal of Management Studies.

Cass Shum   is a PhD student in the Department of Management at the Hong Kong University of Science and Technology. She graduated from the School of Hotel and Tourism Management at The Chinese University of Hong Kong and she formerly served as a project officer at the Center for Hospitality and Real Estate Research at The Chinese University of Hong Kong. Her research interests are flexible workforce, strategic human resources management and social exchange theory.

Lyndon Simkin   is Professor of Strategic Marketing at Oxford Brookes University. Previously he was at Warwick Business School, where he was Director of the MSc in Marketing & Strategy and versions of Warwick's MBA Programme. In addition to many journal articles, Lyndon has authored numerous books, including two addressing the theme of this chapter, market segmentation. Lyndon is consultant to many blue chip corporations, including QinetiQ, GfK, Fujitsu, Raytheon and IKEA, plus he is a recognised High Court expert witness in cases of marketing and business planning litigation. He is also co-chair of the Academy of Marketing's Special Interest Group in Market Segmentation. Lyndon has published in many journals, including the *European Journal of Marketing, Industrial Marketing Management, Services Industries Journal, Journal of Marketing Management, Journal of Industrial & Business Marketing, Journal of Strategic Marketing* and the *International Journal of Advertising.*

Dr Richard Varey is Professor of Marketing at The Waikato Management School, Hamilton, New Zealand. He inquires on society and marketing, human interaction in commercial situations, and systems of managed communication. His scholarly project is "marketing for sustainable prosperous society". He is Associate Editor (Asia-Pacific) for the Journal of Customer Behaviour, and a member of the editorial boards of Marketing Theory, the European Journal of Marketing, the Journal of Communication Management, the Journal of Marketing Communications, the Australasian Marketing Journal, the Corporate Reputation Review, the Journal of Management Development, the Journal of Business Ethics (sustainability panel), and the Atlantic Journal of Communication. He is Book Reviews Editor for Prism: The Online Public Relations Journal, and former Editor of the Australasian Marketing Journal. He is a member of the Expert Panel of the TechCast virtual think tank on technology futures. Richard was a Principal Investigator on the FRST-funded "Socially & Culturally Sustainable Biotechnology in New Zealand" research programme. He was Secretary of ANZMAC in 2006-7, and is a Fellow of the Academy of Marketing Science. Richard's research interests are marketing as a social interaction system, the political economy of market systems, and participatory and ethical communication and information systems management.

Walter van Waterschoot was a doctoral student at the Catholic University of Leuven and served as assistant in the European Marketing Programme of Insead/Cedep before earning his PhD at Saint-Ignatius University (Antwerp). Currently he is professor of Marketing and Channel Management at the University of Antwerp. He is a vested author of marketing textbooks written in Dutch. The general marketing management textbook he co-authored is currently in its twelfth edition. He has also contributed numerous chapters in international monographs, including the Oxford Textbook of Marketing (2000). He prepared entries for several encyclopedias, including the International Encyclopedia of Marketing (2000). He published papers in leading academic journals including the Journal of Marketing, the Journal of Retailing, the Journal of Retailing and Consumer Services, the International Journal of Research in Marketing, and Health Marketing Quarterly. His paper on the classification of the marketing mix ('The 4P classification of the marketing mix revisited' with Christophe Van den Bulte, Journal of Marketing 46(4)) was included in the compilation of the most influential articles in the history of marketing published by Routledge (2000).

Robin Wensley (BA (Cambridge), MSc, PhD (London) is Professor of Policy and Marketing at the Warwick Business School and has been Director of the

ESRC/EPSRC Advanced Institute of Management Research based in London since 2004. He is a member of the Sunningdale Institute and was Chair of the Warwick Business School from 1989 to 1994, Chair of Faculty of Social Studies from 1997 to 1999, and Deputy Dean from 2000 to 2004. He was also co-editor of the *Journal of Management Studies* from 1998 to 2002. He is also Dean of the Senate of the Chartered Institute of Marketing, and was a Board member of the ESRC Research Grants Board from 1991 to 1995 and a council member from 2001 to 2004. His research interests include marketing strategy and evolutionary processes in competitive markets, investment decision making, the assessment of competitive advantage and the nature of choice processes and user engagement in public services. He has published a number of articles in the *Harvard Business Review*, the *Journal of Marketing* and the *Strategic Management Journal* and has twice won the annual Alpha Kappa Psi award for the most influential article in the US *Journal of Marketing*.

Preface

The first edition of *Marketing Theory: A Student Text* first appeared in 2000 in order to fulfil the need for an advanced text to be used in capstone courses in marketing by students who had studied the subject in some depth, to pull together and consolidate the principal ideas, concepts and theories that underpin the discipline. A selection of 18 chapters was seen as meeting this need and proved to be very successful, with numerous reprints since its first appearance.

While many of the key ideas and core concepts remain unchanged, the discipline of marketing has continued to evolve and for this reason we have produced a new, revised and extended second edition of this successful text. The authors of some chapters contributed to the original edition, whereas others are completely new.

Our perspective is that marketing does not depend on a 'pure' or single disciplinary base. Instead it may be regarded as an applied social science or *synthetic* discipline in the original sense of the process or result of building up separate elements, especially ideas, into a connected whole, especially into a theory or system. It follows that if one wishes to be qualified to practice the profession of marketing then one should know and understand the sources of the original ideas and theories on which it is founded.

For students following a marketing degree programme, marketing theory as a distinct subject or module is generally taught at the final-year level of undergraduate marketing degrees and on taught postgraduate programmes such as the MBA and MSc in Marketing, often as part of the methodological and theoretical preparation for students undertaking marketing dissertations.

Marketing Theory, second edition, is intended as an authoritative overview of the theoretical foundations and current status of thinking on topics central to the discipline and practice of marketing. It comprises original contributions from an international panel of experts on their individual subject areas. In doing so it brings together in a single text a comprehensive review of the major sub-fields of the discipline which otherwise could only be found by specific reference to the literature of those sub-fields or from major reference texts written for advanced academics and

PhD level scholars, involving considerable effort and expense. While clear and concise in its presentation, every chapter is supported by extensive references enabling further in-depth research into the subject matter of the individual chapters.

Taken together we hope that this text will provide the reader with an accessible, authoritative and broad introduction to the topic.

Michael J. Baker and Michael Saren

Section A

Overview of Marketing Theory

1

Marketing – philosophy or function?
Michael J. Baker

Chapter Topics

Overview

This opening chapter seeks to define what might be considered the true essence of marketing: that it is the establishment of mutually satisfying exchange relationships. The modern marketing concept would appear to have undergone at least three major phases of evolution – the emergence of the mass market, the articulation of the modern marketing concept, and the transition from an emphasis upon the transaction to the relationship.

The chapter concludes with a review of specific definitions of marketing to document how these have changed over time and to speculate as to the possible nature and direction of future change in order to ponder the question, what is marketing?

Introduction

On first introduction to a subject it is understandable that one should seek a clear and concise definition of it. If nothing else, this definition should enable one to distinguish the domain of that subject from others whilst also giving an indication of its scope and nature. Of course, none of us expect that a short definition will be able to encompass the complexity of a subject as extensive as marketing. That said, it does seem reasonable that persons who profess or claim expertise on the subject should be able to define it.

In this introductory chapter it will become clear that there is no scarcity of definitions of marketing and we will review a number of them. In doing so it will also become clear that views as to the scope of the subject tend to polarize in the manner implied by the title of this chapter between those who perceive marketing as a philosophy of business, or state of mind, and those who regard it as a managerial function responsible for particular activities, in much the same way as production, finance or human resource management.

To throw light on this dichotomy it will be helpful first to review what is seen to be the true essence of marketing – mutually satisfying exchange relationships – and its evolution over time in parallel with stages of economic growth and development. On the basis of this review it will be argued that marketing has always been an intrinsic element of the commercial exchange process but that its importance has waxed and waned with shifts in the balance between supply and demand. Without anticipating unduly Brian Jones' discussion of historical research in marketing it will be suggested that we can detect at least three major phases in the evolution of the modern marketing concept – the emergence of the mass-market circa 1850, the articulation of the modern marketing concept circa 1960, and the transition from an emphasis upon the transaction to the relationship circa 1990. In conclusion we review specific definitions of marketing to document how these have changed over time and speculate as to the possible nature and direction of future change in order to answer our opening question, marketing – philosophy or function?

Exchange and economic growth

Since time immemorial humans have had to live with scarcity in one form or another. In its most acute form scarcity threatens the very existence of life itself, but, even in the most affluent and advanced post-industrial societies its existence is still apparent in the plight of the homeless and the poor. Indeed, in some senses it is doubtful whether mankind will ever overcome scarcity, if for no other reason than that there appears to be no upper limit to human wants.

The use of the noun 'wants' is deliberate, for early on in any study of marketing it is important to distinguish clearly between 'needs' and 'wants'. Needs have been classified as existing at five levels by Abraham Maslow (1943) and his 'hierarchy of human needs' (Figure 1.1) is a useful starting point for discussion of the nature of marketing. As can be seen in Figure 1.1, Maslow's hierarchy conceives of human needs as resting on a foundation of physiological needs, essential to existence, and ascending through a series of levels – safety, love and esteem – to a state of self-actualization in which the individual's specification of a need is entirely self-determined. According to this conceptualization one can only ascend to a higher

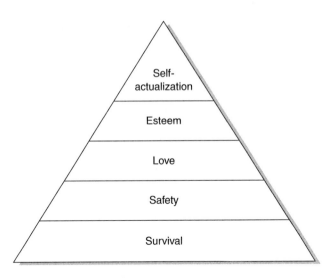

Figure 1.1   Maslow's hierarchy of human needs (Maslow, 1943: 370–96)

level once one has satisfied the needs of a lower level, and the inference may be drawn that scarcity would only cease to exist once every individual has attained the highest level of self-actualization.

From this description it is clear that 'needs' are broadly based and defined and act as a summary statement for a whole cluster of much more precisely defined wants which reflect the exact desires of individuals. In a state of hunger the Westerner may want bread or potatoes but the Easterner is more likely to want rice. Both of these wants are fairly basic. While they have the ability to satisfy the need 'hunger', they offer little by way of variety. The desire for variety, or choice, is another intrinsic element of human nature and much of human development and progress may be attributed to a quest for variety – for new ways of satisfying basic needs. Indeed, the process appears to be self-sustaining which prompted us to propose that a maxim of marketing is that 'the act of consumption changes the consumer' (Baker, 1980). In other words, each new experience increases and extends the consumer's expectations and creates an opportunity for a new supplier to win their patronage by developing something new and better than existing solutions to the consumers need.

Faced with an apparent infinity of wants the challenge to be faced is in determining what selection of goods and services will give the greatest satisfaction to the greatest number at any particular point in time. Indeed, the purpose of economic organization has been defined as 'maximising satisfaction through the utilisation of scarce resources'. Marketing is a function which facilitates achievement of this goal. To understand how it does this, it will be helpful to review the process of economic development. Rostow's (1962) Stages of Economic Growth model provides an excellent basis for such a review.

Rostow's model is shown in Figure 1.2 and proposes that human societies progress from the lowest level of subsistence or survival in a series of clearly identified

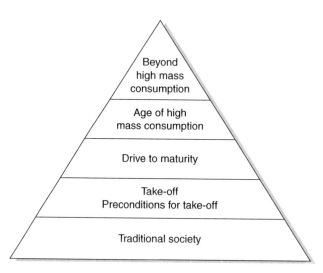

Figure 1.2   Rostow's Stages of Economic Growth model (Rostow, 1962)

stages until they achieve the sophistication and affluence of the modern post-industrial state. In grossly simplified terms, certain key events appear to be associated with the transition from one stage to the next.

At the lowest level of all is the subsistence economy based upon hunting, gathering and collecting. Such economies are nomadic and entirely dependent upon nature for their survival. While members of such nomadic tribes may share food and shelter, and band together for safety, they are societies which are devoid of any recognizable form of commercial exchange.

With the domestication of animals and the development of primitive agriculture man begins to exercise a degree of control over his environment. At the same time new activities create new roles and the potential for the first step towards increased productivity and economic progress – task specialization. Once it becomes recognized that some people are better suited to some tasks than others then the potential for task specialization exists. For it to be realized, however, an agreed system of exchange must be developed. Indeed, it seems likely that the creation of a system of exchange was a necessary prerequisite for task specialization to flourish.

A fundamental law of economics is that beyond a certain point each additional unit of any good or service becomes worth progressively less and less to its owner (the law of diminishing marginal utility). Given a surplus of any specific good the owner will be able to increase their overall satisfaction by exchanging units of their surplus for another good which they want. Thus hunters can exchange meat for vegetables with farmers to their mutual and enhanced satisfaction.

For an exchange to occur there must be at least two persons, each with a surplus of one good which is desired by the other. Once contact has been established between the two persons they can then negotiate an exchange which will increase their overall satisfaction by swapping units until the marginal utility of the two goods is equal (i.e. one would receive less satisfaction by acquiring one additional unit of the other person's surplus than by retaining a unit of one's own output). While this concept is easy to understand in principle, especially when discussing only one exchange, its implementation in practice poses numerous problems. To reduce these problems three additional developments are called for.

First, in order that those with services to exchange can be brought together it will be helpful to set aside a specific place for the purpose – a market. Second, one needs an accepted store of value that will act as a universal medium of exchange – money. Third, because marketing is a separate task from production it will further increase productivity and add value if specialist intermediaries – merchants and retailers – come into existence to perform these functions. Clearly, markets, money and intermediaries have existed since the earliest civilization. Indeed, it would be no exaggeration to claim that the development of formal commercial exchange relationships was the foundation for civilization as we know it today. It would seem that marketing is perhaps not such a recent phenomenon as many believe it to be!

The creation of markets and the development of exchange provides preconditions for take-off

> '... take-off consists, in essence, of the achievement of rapid growth in a limited number of sectors, where modern industrial techniques are applied'. (Rostow, op. cit. 317)

For take-off to occur task specialization has to be taken a stage further, to what economists call the division of labour. One of the earliest and best known examples of the division of labour is provided by Adam Smith's description of the pin-making industry.

> To take an example, therefore, from a very trifling manufacture; but one in which the division of labour has been very often taken notice of, the trade of the pin maker; a workman not educated to this business (which the division of labour has rendered a distinct trade), nor acquainted with the use of the machinery employed in it (to the invention of which the same division of labour has probably given occasion), could scarce, perhaps, with his utmost industry, make one pin in a day, and certainly could not make 20. But in the way in which this business is now carried on, not only the whole work is a peculiar trade, but it is divided into a number of branches, of which the greatest part are likewise a peculiar trade. One man draws out the wire, another straights it, a third cuts it, a fourth points it, the fifth grinds it at the top receiving the head; to make the head requires three distinct operations; to put it on is a peculiar business, to whiten the pins is another; it is even a trade by itself to put them into the paper; and the important business of making a pin is, in this manner, divided into about 18 distinct operations, which, in some manufactures, are all performed by distinct hands, though in others the same man will sometimes perform two or three of them. I have seen a small manufactury of this kind where 10 men only were employed and where some of them consequently performed two or three distinct operations. But though they were very poor, and therefore but indifferently accommodated with

the necessary machinery, they could, when they exerted themselves, make among them about 12 pounds of pins in the day. There are in a pound upwards of 4000 pins of the middling size. These 10 persons therefore, could make among them upwards of 48,000 pins in the day. Each person, therefore making a tenth part of 48,000 pins, might be considered as making 4800 pins in a day. But if they had all wrought separately and independently, and without any of them having been educated to this peculiar business, they could certainly not each of them have made 20, perhaps not one pin in a day; that is, certainly, not the 240th, perhaps not the 4800th part of what they are at present capable of performing, in consequence of a proper division and combination of their different operations. (Smith, [1776] 1970)

It seems reasonable to assume that under conditions of craft industry, where each craftsman was responsible for all the tasks associated with the production of a particular good, the number of craftsman in a community would be approximately sufficient to satisfy the demands of that community. Indeed, the medieval craft guilds (and, more recently, trade unions) strictly controlled the number of apprentices that could be trained in a craft to ensure that a satisfactory balance between supply and demand be maintained. Clearly, the enormous increase in productivity associated with the division of labour destroyed this control and flooded the market with the product in question, driving the price down and making many craftsmen redundant. One new pin factory employing 10 pin makers could match the output of 240 craftsmen and so service the needs of 240 times as many customers. As a result production became concentrated in locations possessing natural advantages associated with the product – sources of power and raw material, labour, good channels of communication – and it became necessary to employ salespersons to help sell the output into a greatly enlarged market.

Because of the enormous increase in output associated with factory production, standards of living improved substantially with a consequential increase in life expectancies and the numbers of children surviving infancy. As the size of the market is determined ultimately by the size of the population, an expanding population represented an expanding market and further fuelled the rapid economic growth associated with take-off. This growth was to receive an even greater impetus with the spate of scientific and technological innovation of the eighteenth century, which gave birth to what has become known as the industrial revolution and form the foundation for Rostow's fourth stage of economic growth – the age of high mass consumption.

In his original conceptualization Rostow (1962) perceived that some of the more advanced and affluent industrialized economies were approaching the limits of mass consumption. While population growth had slowed to a near steady rate, further improvements in productivity had created saturated markets and the potential for excess supply. John Kenneth Galbraith (1958) designated this the post-industrial society while Rostow merely termed it the age beyond high mass consumption. Eight years later, in 1970, Rostow revised his model and designated the final stage, the 'search for quality' – the inference being that if a static population could not physically consume more, then the only way growth could be sustained would be to consume 'better'.

Elsewhere (Baker, 1994) we have discussed the way in which the stages in Maslow's need hierarchy correspond closely to the stages in Rostow's economic stages model, for example, subsistence economies are concerned primarily with physiological needs; the search for quality with self-actualization, etc. Clearly, human needs (demand) motivates supply creation and the matching of supply and demand is achieved through a process of exchange and marketing. It is also clear that these processes have existed for a very long time indeed, so why is marketing often represented as a twentieth-century phenomenon? We turn to this question in the next section, but, before doing so, will summarize some of the key points that have emerged from a greatly simplified account of economic development.

First, exchange adds value and increases satisfaction. It also encourages variety and improves choice. Second, the parties to a commercial exchange are free agents so that for an exchange to occur both parties must feel that they are benefiting from that exchange. It is from these observations that we derive our basic definition of marketing as being concerned with mutually satisfying exchange relationships. Third, task specialization and the division of labour greatly enhance productivity and increase the volume of goods available for consumption. In turn this increased supply results in an improved standard of living and growth in the population, thereby increasing demand and stimulating further efforts to increase supply. Fourth, the concentration of production and the growing size and dispersion of the market increases the need for specialized channels of distribution and other intermediaries to service and manage them. Fifth, improved standards of living in the advanced industrialized economies lead to a stabilization of population growth and absolute market size (demand), but accelerating technological innovation continues to enhance our ability to increase supply. It was this which was to lead to the 'rediscovery' of marketing.

The rediscovery of marketing

As we have seen, markets and marketing are as old as exchange itself yet many people regard marketing as a phenomenon which emerged in the second half of the twentieth century – to be precise about 1960 when Professor Ted Levitt published an article entitled 'Marketing myopia' in the *Harvard Business Review* in which he addressed the fundamental question of why do firms, and indeed whole industries, grow to a position of great power and influence and then decline. Taking the American railroad industry as his main example, Levitt showed that this industry displaced other forms of overland transportation during the nineteenth century because it was more efficient and effective than the alternatives it displaced. By the beginning of the twentieth century, however, development of the internal combustion engine, and the building of cars and trucks, had provided an alternative to the railroads for both personal and bulk transportation. In the early years this challenge was limited because of the high cost of the substitute product, its lack of sophistication and reliability and low availability. However, its potential was clear to see – if you owned a car or truck you had complete personal control over your transportation needs and could travel from door to door at your own convenience. Henry Ford perceived this market opportunity, invented the concept of mass assembly and began to produce a reliable, low-cost motor car in constantly increasing numbers. From this time on the fortunes of the railroad began to decline so that, by the 1950s, this once great industry appeared to be in terminal decline.

What went wrong? Levitt's thesis is that those responsible for the management of the railroad were too preoccupied with their product to the neglect of the need that it served, which was transportation. Because of their myopia, or 'production orientation', they lost sight of the fact that the railroad product had been a substitute for earlier, less attractive products, so that, offered a choice, consumers have switched from the old to the new to increase their personal satisfaction. It should have been obvious, therefore, that if a new, more convenient mode of transportation was developed then consumers would switch to it too. Thus, if the railroad management had concentrated on the need served – transportation – rather than their product, they might have been able to join the infant automobile industry and develop a truly integrated transportation system. In other words the railroads failed because they lacked in marketing orientation.

At almost the same time as the appearance of Levitt's seminal paper, Robert Keith (1960) published an article in which he described the evolution of marketing in the Pillsbury Company in which he worked. In Keith's view the company's current marketing approach was a direct descendant of two earlier approaches, or eras, which he termed production and sales. This three eras, or stages, model – production, sales, marketing – was widely adopted by what has come to be known as the marketing management school whose ideas dominated the theory and practice of marketing for 30 years or more.

The essence of the production orientation – a preoccupation with the product and the company – and the marketing orientation – a focus on the consumer's needs and the best way to serve it – have already been touched on in reviewing Levitt's 'Marketing myopia'. Keith's contribution then was to propose an intermediate or transitional phase he termed the 'sales era'. In the sales era firms were still largely production orientated but, as demand stabilized supply, continued to grow, resulting in fierce competition between suppliers. One aspect of this was that producers committed more effort to selling their products with an emphasis on personal selling, advertising and sales promotion – hence the 'sales orientation'.

Chronologically the production era dated from the mid-1850s and lasted until around the late 1920s, at which point the sales era was born, which lasted to around the mid-1950s, when the marketing era commenced. This conceptualization is now seen to be seriously flawed in terms of its historical accuracy but nonetheless remains a useful pedagogical device for reasons we will return to. First, however, it will be helpful to set the record straight.

As we have noted on several occasions there has been a tendency to date the emergence of marketing to the late 1950s and early 1960s. In an article entitled 'How modern is modern marketing?' Fullerton (1988) provides a rigorous analysis based on historical research.

At the outset it will be helpful to summarize the three key facets of the historical approach. First, there is a 'philosophical belief that historical phenomena such as markets are intrinsically rich and complex; efforts to simplify or assume away aspects of such phenomena are deeply distrusted' (Fullerton, 1988: 109). Second, the historical research tradition emphasizes 'systematic and critical evaluation of historical evidence of accuracy, bias, implicit messages, and now extinct meanings' (1988: 109). The third facet of historical research is the process itself through which the researcher seeks to synthesize and recreate what actually happened in the past.

While there is considerable evidence that supports the existence of a production era there are also strong arguments to support a contrary view. Fullerton summarizes these as follows:

1. **It ignores well-established historical facts about business conditions – competition was intense in most businesses, overproduction, and demand frequently uncertain.**
2. **It totally misses the presence and vital importance of conscious demand stimulation in developing the advanced modern economies. Without such stimulation the revolution in production would have been stillborn.**
3. **It does not account for the varied and vigorous marketing efforts made by numerous manufacturers and other producers.**
4. **It ignores the dynamic growth of new marketing institutions outside the manufacturing firm. (Fullerton, 1988: 111)**

Each of these arguments is examined in detail and substantial evidence is marshalled to support them. A particularly telling point concerns the need for active demand stimulation and the need for production and marketing to work in tandem.

> **Some of the famous pioneers of production such as Matthew Boulton and Josiah Wedgwood were also pioneers of modern marketing, cultivating large-scale demand for their revolutionary inexpensive products with techniques usually considered to have been post-1950 American innovations: market segmentation, product differentiation, prestige pricing, style obsolescence, saturation advertising, direct mail campaigns, reference group appeals, and testimonials among others. (Fullerton, 1988: 112).**

In Fullerton's view 'demand enhancing marketing' spread from Britain to Germany and the USA. In the USA it was adopted with enthusiasm and Americans came to be seen as 'the supreme masters of aggressive demand stimulation', a fact frequently referred to in contemporary marketing texts of the early 1990s. Numerous examples support Fullerton's contention that producers of the so-called production era made extensive use of marketing tools and techniques as well as integrating forward to ensure their products were brought to the attention of their intended customers in the most effective way. That said, the examples provided (with one or two possible exceptions) do not, in my opinion, invalidate the classification of the period as the 'production area' in the sense that it was the producer who took the initiative and differentiated his product to meet the assumed needs of different consumer groups based on economic as opposed to sociological and psychological factors. In other words, producers inferred the consumer's behaviour but they had not yet developed techniques or procedures which would enable them to define latent wants, and design, produce and market products and services to satisfy them.

Similarly, while the period from 1870 to 1930 saw the emergence and development of important marketing institutions in terms of physical distribution, retailing, advertising and marketing education, which are still important today, it does not seem unreasonable to argue that all these institutions were designed to sell more of what was being produced. This is not to deny the 'rich marketing heritage' documented by Fullerton, but to reinforce the point that the transition to a 'marketing era' was marked by a major change in business philosophy from a producer-led interpretation of consumer needs to a consumer-driven approach to production.

As to the existence of a sales era (rejected by Fullerton) this seems as convenient a label as any to give to the transitional period between a production and marketing orientation. In addition to the reality of a depressed world economy in the 1930s, which required large-scale producers to sell more aggressively to maintain economies of scale, the period saw the migration of many behavioural scientists from a politically unstable Europe to the safety of the USA. In retrospect it appears that it was this migration that led to the more rigorous analysis of consumer behaviour which was to underpin the emergence of a new 'marketing era'.

Combined with its greater insight into consumer behaviour was a period of great economic growth and prosperity following the Second World War, together with a major increase in the birth rate, which was to result in a new generation of consumers brought up in a period of material affluence (the baby boomers). It was this generation which sought to reassert consumer sovereignty and so initiated the change in the balance of power between producer and consumer which heralded the 'marketing era'.

Fullerton's argument that the production–sales–marketing era framework is a 'catastrophic model' 'in which major developments take place suddenly, with few antecedents' (1988: 121) is not without merit. Certainly, it could and has had the effect of disguising the evolutionary nature of marketing thought and practice. In place of a catastrophic model, or indeed, a continuity model which tends to observe differences over time, Fullerton suggests a 'complex flux model'. Such a complex flux model has the ability to incorporate dramatic changes but it also 'stresses that even dramatic change is based on and linked to past phenomena' (Fullerton, 1988: 121). It is also neutral in the sense that it does not automatically equate development or evolution with 'improvement', leaving such judgements for others to make.

Fullerton's complex flux model embraces four eras:

1. *Setting the stage: the era of antecedents.* A long gestational period beginning around 1500 in Britain and Germany, and the 1600s in North America. The period of low levels of consumption in which '75–90% of the populace were self-sufficient, rural and viscerally opposed to change' (1988: 122). Commerce was generally discredited but its standing improved as the benefits of trade became apparent.

2. *Modern marketing begins: the era of origins.* Britain in 1759; Germany and the USA circa 1830. 'This period marked the beginning of *pervasive* attention to stimulating

and meeting demand among *nearly all of society'* (1988: 122). Precipitated by the Industrial Revolution, and the mass migration from the countryside to an urban environment, potential markets had to be created through marketing techniques and activities.

3. *Building a superstructure: the era of institutional development.* Britain in 1850; Germany and the USA circa 1870 until 1919. 'During this period most of the major institutions and many of the practices of modern marketing first appeared' (1988: 122).

4. *Testing, turbulence and growth: era of refinement and formalization.* From 1930 to the present day. 'The era's most distinguishing characteristic, however, has been a further development, refinement, and formalization of institutions and practices that were developed earlier' (1988: 122).

Fullerton's analysis reflects a growing interest in the history of marketing thought and confirms that 'modern marketing has a rich heritage worthy of our attention' (1988: 123). Whether one should substitute his conceptualization as contained in his complex flux model for the widely accepted production–sales–marketing era's model is not seen as an either/or choice. Indeed, Fullerton's emphasis on the origins and evolution of marketing thought and practice reflects the historical research approach and merits attention in its own right. By contrast the 'era's model' is seen, at least by this author, as serving a different purpose in that it seeks to distinguish between marketing as a practice clearly present in both the production and sales eras, and marketing as a philosophy of business which shifts the emphasis from the producer's pursuit of profit as the primary objective to the achievement of customer satisfaction which, in the long run, is likely to achieve the same financial reward.

In other words the three eras model provides a convenient framework for summarizing changes in the dominant orientation of business management. Thus it is a useful, albeit oversimplified, model of the evolution of modern marketing, or what I prefer to designate 'the rediscovery of marketing' (Baker, 1976). In truth, marketing has been around since the very first commercial exchange but there can be little doubt that until comparatively recently it has been of secondary or even tertiary importance to other more pressing imperatives in terms of increasing supply to meet the needs and wants of a rapidly expanding population. The objective of authors and teachers in using the three-stage evolutionary model has been to highlight the major changes in the dominant orientation of business rather than to analyse in detail the much more complex processes which underlay and resulted in these changes. What is beyond doubt is the fact that from around 1960 onwards marketing thinking and practice has been dominated by the marketing management school of thought.

The marketing management school

The marketing management school which evolved in the late 1950s and early 1960s is inextricably linked with the concept of the marketing mix and an analytical approach to marketing management following the positivist sequence of Analysis, Planning, Control. As with most major paradigms shifts, no single author/researcher can claim sole credit for the new phenomenon. Among those who contributed significantly to the new school of thought were Joel Dean (1951), Peter Drucker, Ted Levitt, E. Jerome McCarthy, Neal Borden and Philip Kotler. Dean and Drucker writing in the early 1950s paved the way but it was McCarthy's *Basic Marketing* (1960) which first promoted what came to be known as the four Ps of marketing – the idea that the marketing manager's task was to develop unique solutions to competitive marketing problems by manipulating the four major marketing factors – product, price, place and promotion. This idea of a 'marketing mix' (the four Ps) was elaborated on by Neil Borden (1964) building on an earlier idea of James Culliton (1948), and confirmed by the appearance in 1967 of the first edition of Philip Kotler's bestselling *Marketing Management: Analysis, Planning and Control*. Levitt's contribution in distinguishing the essence of the marketing orientation/concept – a focus on customer needs – has already been referred to.

An authoritative view of the marketing management school is to be found in Frederick E. Webster Jr's 1992 article in the *Journal of Marketing* ('The changing role of marketing in the corporation'). In his own words,

> **the purpose of this article is to outline both the intellectual and the pragmatic roots of changes that are occurring in marketing, especially marketing management, as a body of knowledge, theory, and practice and to suggest the need for a new paradigm of the marketing function within the firm. (Webster, 1992: 1)**

While Webster's article recognized the need for 'a new paradigm of the marketing function within the firm', in the opinion of many European scholars a much more radical reappraisal was called for which challenged the very roots of the marketing management school.

The European perspective

One of the leading critics of the marketing management school was French professor Giles Marion. Marion's views are contained in a paper 'The marketing management discourse: what's new since the 1960s?' (1993), which is 'an attempt to describe the formalisation of ideas which make up marketing management as a school of thought' (1993: 143), based upon the content of the most popular marketing textbooks (American and European).

Marion argues that 'marketing as a discipline, should show greater humility by presenting its prescriptions in a more prudent manner, and by describing more systematically the interaction between supply and demand and the organisational consequences that follow' (1993: 166). In conclusion he expresses the view that, while the normative theory of marketing management may well have had a useful impact on managerial thinking and practice 'there has been nothing new since the 1960s or even well before' (1993: 166).

While Marion's critique struck at the very heart of the marketing management school promoted in the USA it was comparatively mild compared with the trenchant criticism expressed by Evert Gummesson, a leading member of the Scandinavian School. In Gummesson's view 'the traditional textbooks do not satisfactorily reflect reality' and he proposed six objections to support his thesis (1993):

1. Textbook presentations of marketing are based on limited real-world data – specifically, they are largely concerned with mass marketed, packaged consumer goods.

2. Goods account for a minor part of all marketing, but the textbook presentations are focused on goods; services are treated as a special case.

3. Marketing to consumers dominates textbooks, while industrial/business marketing is treated as a special case.

4. The textbook presentations are a patchwork; new knowledge is piled on top of existing knowledge, but not integrated with it.

5. The textbooks have a clever pedagogical design; the form is better than the content.

6. The Europeans surrendered to the USA and its marketing gurus and do not adequately promote their own original contributions.

In sum, Gummesson argues that US textbooks represent the colonization of thought and that this thought excludes or ignores much of the development in marketing thinking which had occurred in the fields of industrial and services marketing in Europe during the 1970s and 1980s, and even before. To some extent the blame must rest with the Europeans for failing to promote their ideas in the USA but the dismissive, not-invented-here attitudes of American academics who act as gatekeepers to US-based publications must also bear some of the blame.

Many of the views expressed by Marion and Gummesson are echoed in the works of Christian Grönroos (another leading member of the Scandinavian school). In Grönroos' view (1994) the majority of marketing academics and textbooks treat marketing as a subject which emerged in the 1960s and is founded upon the concept of the marketing mix and the four Ps of product, price, place and promotion (McCarthy, 1960) which comprised it. As a consequence 'empirical studies of what the key marketing variables are, and how they are perceived in use by marketing managers have been neglected. Moreover structure has been vastly favoured over process considerations' (Kent, 1986).

While McCarthy's simplification of Borden's original conceptualization of the marketing mix has obvious pedagogical attractions, its application appears best suited to mass markets for consumer packaged goods, underpinned by sophisticated distribution channels and commercial mass media. Indeed, this is the context or setting of many marketing courses and texts, but it is clearly representative of a limited aspect of the domain and process of marketing.

However, the concept of the marketing mix is more seriously flawed. To begin with, the paradigm is a production-oriented definition in the sense that its approach is that customers are persons *to* whom something is done rather than persons *for* whom something is done (see Dixon and Blois, 1983; Grönroos, 1989, 1990.)

A second deficiency is that while McCarthy recognized the interactive nature of the four Ps, 'the model itself does not explicitly include any interactive elements. Furthermore, it does not indicate the nature and scope of such interactions' (Grönroos, 1994).

However, perhaps the major deficiency of the four Ps approach is that it defines marketing as a functional activity in its own right and so creates the potential for conflict with other functional areas, discourages persons from becoming involved in marketing because it is the preserve of the marketing department, and, as a result, can frustrate or compromise the adoption of the marketing concept.

Grönroos sees the four Ps as a direct development from the microeconomic theory of imperfect competition developed by Robinson (1933) and Chamberlin (1933) in the 1930s, but argues that the separation of the four Ps model from its theoretical foundations left it without roots. Indeed, Grönroos goes even further and argues that 'the introduction of the four Ps of the marketing mix with their simplistic view of reality can be characterised as a step back to the level of, in a sense equally simplistic, microeconomic theory of the 1930s'. This observation is largely prompted by the apparent failure of marketing academics in the USA to detect the evolution of the Copenhagen School's parameter theory. Building upon the work of Frisch (1933), Von Stackelberg (1939), Kjaer-Hansen (1945) and Rasmussen (1955), Gosta Mickwitz observed:

> When empirically based works on marketing mechanisms show that the enterprise uses a number of different parameters markedly distinct from each other, the theory of the behaviour of the enterprise in the market will be very unrealistic if it is content to deal only with ... [a few] ... of them. We have therefore tried throughout to pay attention to the presence of a number of different methods which firms employ to increase their sales. (Mickwitz, 1959: 217)

Grönroos (1994) explains further: 'The interactive nature of the marketing variables was explicitly recognised and accounted for in parameter theory by means of varying market elasticities of the parameters over the life of the product life cycle.'

At the same time that the four Ps was becoming the established 'theory' or normative approach to marketing in the USA, and many other countries, new theories and models were emerging in Europe – specifically, the interaction network approach to industrial marketing and the marketing of services (1960s), and, more recently, the concept of relationship marketing.

The interaction/network approach originated in Uppsala University in Sweden during the 1960s and was subsequently taken up in many countries following the establishment of the IMP (Industrial Marketing and Purchasing) Group. As Grönroos explains:

> Between the parties in a network various interactions take place, where exchanges and adaptation to each other occur. A flow of goods and information as well as financial and social exchanges takes place in the network. (See, for example, Håkansson 1982, Johanson and Mattson 1985, and Kock 1991). In such a network the role and forms of marketing are not very clear. All exchanges, all sorts of

interactions have an impact on the position of the parties in the network. The interactions are not necessarily initiated by the seller – the marketer according to the marketing mix paradigm – and they may continue over a long period of time, for example, for several years. (1994: 353)

The interaction/network model recognizes that exchanges are not the exclusive preserve of professional marketers and may, indeed, involve numerous other members of the interacting organizations, some of whom may well have more influence and impact on the relationship than the functional specialists.

In the 1970s interest in the marketing of services developed simultaneously in the USA and Europe. But, while the four Ps framework continued to prevail in the USA, in Scandinavia and Finland the Scandinavian School of Services saw the marketing of services as an integral element of overall management. Grönroos and Gummesson have been strong proponents of the school and have written extensively on the subject.

The interaction and network approach to industrial marketing and modern service marketing approaches 'clearly views marketing as an interactive process in a social context where *relationship building* and *management* is a vital cornerstone' (Grönroos, 1994: 353). He argues that this approach is similar to the system-based approaches to marketing of the 1950s (e.g. Alderson, 1957) and contrasts strongly with the clinical approach of the four Ps paradigm which makes sellers active and buyers passive. As noted earlier, the latter emphasis tends to put exchange relationships into the hands of professional marketers which may psychologically alienate other members of an organization from becoming involved. This is a far cry from Drucker's (1954) observation that the sole purpose of the business is to create customers!

As a consequence of rapid advances in both manufacturing (flexible manufacturing, CAD, CAM) and information technology, the mass consumer markets suited to the four Ps approach have become fragmented and call for flexible and adaptable marketing approaches. In the 1980s *relationship marketing* emerged in response to this need. Grönroos refers to his own (1990) definition of relationship marketing: 'Marketing is to establish, maintain and enhance relationships with customers and other partners, at a profit, so that the objectives of the parties involved are met. This is achieved by mutual exchange and fulfilment of promises'. While more extended and explicit, this definition is essentially similar to that proposed by Baker (1976) a number of years earlier: 'Marketing is a process of exchange between individuals and/or organizations which is concluded to the mutual benefit and satisfaction of the parties' (4). Similarly, Baker (and other authors) have argued consistently for the need to regard marketing both as a philosophy of business and a business function. As a business function responsible for coordinating and executing the implementation of a marketing plan, marketing is likely to continue to find the marketing mix model a useful one, albeit that the four Ps is an oversimplified version of the original concept. It is, of course, important to emphasize that continuing to use such an organizational and planning framework is in no way inimical to the emphasis on relationship marketing as contrasted with the prior emphasis on a transactional model.

Today, relationship marketing is widely accepted as reflecting the essence of the marketing concept. In reality, this has always been the case in the majority of buyer–seller interactions since commercial exchanges were first initiated. Buyers have always looked for reliable sources of supply at a fair price as this reduces the dissonance and uncertainty of having to consider every single transaction as an entirely new decision. Similarly, sellers recognize that there are increased opportunities for long-term survival and profit if they can establish a customer franchise and repeat purchasing behaviour. That said, there can be no doubt that there exist two radically different interpretations of capitalism and the market economy, one of which emphasizes long-term relationships, the other the one-off transaction.

It was perhaps only with the collapse of the centrally planned and controlled command economies of Eastern Europe and the Soviet Union that the existence of two models of capitalism came into sharper relief and focus. Based on a book by Michel Albert (1991), Christian Dussart (1994) highlighted the differences between the Anglo-Saxon model of capitalism, as practised in the UK and USA, which is essentially short-term and transactionally based, and the Alpine/Germanic model, which also embraces Scandinavia (and Japan), that emphasizes long-term relationships as a source of buyer satisfaction and seller profitably.

So what is marketing?

At the 1993 UK Marketing Education Group conference a group of researchers from the Henley Management College (Gibson et al., 1993) presented their findings of a content and correspondence analysis of approximately 100 definitions of marketing in an attempt to answer the question 'What is marketing?' Specifically, the authors set out to 'shed some light on the nature of the process of defining marketing, to identify strong and emerging themes, and to develop a map of the territory'. By using content analysis to evaluate the definitions collected, and using these findings as an input to a correspondence analysis, the authors provided both a qualitative and quantitative analysis of how scholars had defined marketing over the years and up to that time.

To begin with, a collection of approximately 100 explicit marketing definitions were collected from textbooks, journals and institutes/association publications spanning the twentieth century. The majority of these definitions were academic and originated in the USA, UK and Europe. Themes were selected as the unit of assessment and five clusters were established as:

1. Object of marketing

2. Nature of the relationship

3. Outcomes

4. Application

5. Philosophy or (versus) function.

The authors describe in some detail how each of these themes was derived and how definitions falling within them have changed in approach and emphasis over time. However, 'in order to simplify the definitions of various authors, and give more relevance to the five themes identified earlier, some of the definitions gathered and analysed for content were subjected to a process of correspondence analysis' (Gibson et al., 1993). In essence, correspondence analysis is a graphical technique which enables one to develop a two-dimensional plot indicating the degree of similarity or correspondence between rows or columns of data which have similar patterns. Using the authors as rows and their perspectives on the themes as columns the map reproduced here as Figure 1.3 was produced.

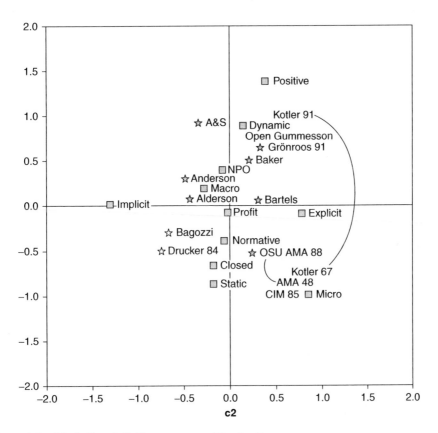

Figure 1.3   Marketing definitions: a map of the territory

They explain:

the authors' perspective on the original themes were constructed as dichotomies and include, first 'profit and non-profit', which related to the outcomes and application themes; secondly, 'micro and macro', which translated across to philosophy or function; thirdly, 'static and dynamic' and 'open and closed' which referred

> to the relationship theme and to some extent provided some insight into the content and nature of the whole definition; and finally, two additional dichotomies were included, 'positive and normative', namely, whether the definitions described what exists or prescribed what 'ought' to happen, and whether the definition was 'explicit or implicit'. (Gibson et al., 1993)

Based upon both qualitative and quantitative analyses certain conclusions were derived.

'1. Changes have occurred across all five content themes indicating significant evolution in the concept of marketing since its earliest definition.

2. The greatest change has occurred in the 'nature of the relationship' (i.e. between provider and user), from one-way narrow, discrete transactions to the recognition and positioning of relationships as a key strategy resource'. This change is also reflected in the other themes, particularly 'philosophy or function', and marks the moderation of economic explanations of consumption behaviour through the admission of concepts derived from psychology and sociology.

3. Changes in the marketing environment have resulted in a broadening and softening of the original concept and its transfer to other domains – services, not-for-profit, etc.

4. 'Marketing' has shown itself to be adaptable, flexible, international and open. But Gibson et al. warn that 'this latitude has allowed ambiguity to creep into its definition and cause confusion. Definitional clarity is essential in the future'.

In conclusion, Gibson et al. (1993) offer three further points prompted by their analysis:

'1. Marketing and its guardians continue to foster its open and innovative culture.

2. A single definition is not aimed for, as its existence would probably discourage future development of the subject.

3. Nonetheless, greater rigour should be given to the formulation of definitions in future.'

Marketing's mid-life crisis

In the turbulent and recessionary environment which characterized the early 1990s Webster's call for a new approach to the practice of marketing cited earlier was widely echoed, particularly in practitioner publications. Among the more influential of these was Brady and Davis' (1993) observation that marketing was experiencing a 'mid-life crisis'. In simplified terms the argument ran that if exchange was concerned with relationships between individuals and organizations then marketing must be everybody's business and not the preserve of a privileged few to be found within a formal marketing department. This perception was probably magnified by the fact that several important developments in managerial thinking such as benchmarking, total quality management, strategic alliances, globalization and strategic thinking might properly be considered the primary concern of marketers. These fields had been pre-empted by others.

In the new millennium marketers appear to have recovered some of their confidence and are able to take a more balanced view of their discipline. It is now generally accepted that the relationship marketing approach has effectively extended the marketing concept into areas such as services and business-to-business marketing, which were poorly served by the marketing management model, based as it was upon concepts of mass production, mass distribution and mass marketing, essentially of packaged consumer goods. At the same time, it has also been appreciated that many marketing exchanges are based upon low involvement and transactions and that the two distinct approaches can co-exist together. Simultaneously, a clearer distinction is being drawn between the philosophy of marketing which is encapsulated in a marketing orientation that can be held by everybody, both internal and external to an organization, and the market-oriented organization which is customer oriented and market driven. The former marketing-orientated organization is committed to the philosophy of mutually satisfying exchange relationships while the latter market-oriented company is focused on how to achieve this through the professional practice and management of the marketing function.

A new model of marketing?

In 2004 the *Journal of Marketing* published an article by Stephen Vargo and Robert Lusch that prompted extensive debate about the need for a new model, or paradigm, of the domain of marketing. The article that precipitated this debate is entitled 'Evolving to a new dominant logic for marketing'. In the abstract the authors write:

> The purpose of this article is to illuminate the evolution of *marketing* thought toward a new dominant logic ... Briefly, *marketing* has moved from a goods-dominant view, in which tangible output and discrete transactions were central, to a service-dominant view, in which interchangeability, exchange processes, and relationships are central. (Vargo and Lusch, 2004: 2)

The authors then stress that their interpretation of 'service-centred' should not be equated with current conceptualizations of services as a residual, that is not a tangible good; something to add value to a good – value-added services; or service industries like healthcare and education. They state:

> Rather, we define services as the application of specialised competences (knowledge and skills) through deeds, processes, and performances to the benefit of another entity or the entity itself ... Thus, the service-centred dominant logic represents a reoriented philosophy that is applicable to all *marketing* offerings,

> including those that involve tangible output (goods) in the process of service
> provision. (ibid.)

In effect Vargo and Lusch are arguing that we move away from a model of exchange inherited from economics with a focus on 'goods' in which intangible services are treated as a residual or special case. One consequence of the economic model is its emphasis upon the management and allocation of scarce resources. This, in turn, results in a focus on the supply side and the marketing management model which is concerned with advising suppliers how to manipulate demand in order to dispose of the supply which they have created. This is not to say that suppliers do not take into account the needs and wants of customers in determining what goods and services to create, but rather that their interpretation could be much improved through closer collaboration with their intended customers.

While some would point to the emergence of customer relationship management as recognition by the supply side of a need to engage more closely with the customer, my own, more cynical, view is that this is paying lip service to the notion of 'relationships'. Relationships are interactions that have to be worked at by both parties; as soon as one party believes that they can 'manage' or manipulate the relationship to their advantage – the objective of most CRM schemes I have come across – then it would seem to be doomed to failure.

Elsewhere (Baker, 2007) I review the arguments deployed by Vargo and Lusch in some detail (2007: 533–6). At the heart of their argument is the distinction between what they term operand and operant resources. Operand resources are those on which some actual operation has to be performed to produce an effect, while operant resources are those that produce effects. Put another way operand resources are equivalent to the economist's 'scarce resources' while operant resources may be equated with the actions that transform these into goods and services. Clearly it is decisions with regard to the latter which are the more important, and I agree with Vargo and Lusch when they claim:

> Operant resources are often invisible and intangible; often they are core competences or organisational processes. They are likely to be dynamic and infinite and not static and finite, as is usually the case with operand resources. Because operant resources produce effects, they enable humans both to multiply the value of natural resources and to create additional operant skills. (Vargo and Lusch, 2004: 3)

In light of this it is then argued that a 'service-centred logic' is necessary to reflect this change of emphasis. This proposal is based on the view that traditional marketing is seen as focusing on operand resources, is goods centred and concerned with the notion of utility(ies). By contrast, service-centred marketing is grounded in and largely consistent with resource advantage theory and is customer centric and market driven.

In the original article (it has been revisited by the authors and many others since) Vargo and Lusch (2004) develop their arguments through a comparison between traditional and service-centred marketing and conclude that the latter is the model to be followed in future. For my part I tend to agree with Evert Gummesson (2007) that 'Their logic opened up an international dialogue on the output of marketing as value propositions rather than as goods or services'. He goes on to say: 'The *service-dominant logic* suggests *service* (in the singular) as the core concept replacing both goods and services. A supplier offers a *value proposition*, but *value actualisation* occurs in the usage and consumption process. Thus value is the outcome of *co-creation* between suppliers and customers' (2007: 117).

In the final chapter of this new edition, Gummesson develops these ideas in some detail. Initially, he was asked to revisit his contribution to the first edition on the 'Marketing of services'. However, as will rapidly become apparent when you read this chapter, the debate initiated by Vargo and Lusch is prompting a radical reappraisal of the nature of marketing and its theory. While all marketing academics would not subscribe to the proposition that service-dominant logic has displaced or superseded alternative theorizations, there can be little doubt that it has become a major focus of attention. In light of this the editors decided that it would form an effective postscript to the contributions to this book and have positioned it accordingly.

It is my view that an emphasis on value as opposed to 'service' is more consistent with the original conceptualization of marketing as a philosophy of exchange focused upon 'mutually satisfying relationships'. This view is supported by a subsequent definition offered by Lusch and Vargo (2006) to the effect that 'marketing is the process in society and organisations that facilitates voluntary exchange through collaborative relationships that create reciprocal value through the application of complementary resources' (p. 5). Somewhat lengthier, but very much in the spirit of my own (Baker, 1976) definition.

By contrast, stressing 'service' may merely prolong the goods versus services debate; but the reader will need to consult current marketing journals to determine how this debate is developing. What is clear to my mind is that the concept or 'philosophy' of marketing remains the same – it is the implementation of the function through marketing practice that continues to evolve to better achieve the intention and objectives of the philosophy.

Summary

In this chapter we have endeavoured to shed some light on the nature and scope of 'marketing'. As we have seen, marketing is a large and complex subject which covers a multitude of economic and social activities. Many of these are described in some detail in the chapters which follow. That said, the practice of marketing is founded on a very simple philosophy, that of 'mutually satisfying (commercial) exchange relationships'.

In the 1990s relationship marketing became the dominant theme almost everywhere, despite its somewhat belated recognition in the USA. As my review has attempted to show, it was ever thus, but, depending upon the existing balance between supply and demand at any point in time, one or other of the parties to an exchange is likely to exercise more control over the relationship than the other. If this is the producer/seller it does not necessarily mean that they are production or sales oriented and insensitive to customer needs. Indeed, it is a truism that all successful businesses are marketing orientated – if they were not meeting and satisfying customers' needs profitably they would not be successful. What matters is the state of mind of the producers/sellers – their philosophy of business. If this philosophy includes a concern for the customer's needs and wants, and appreciation of the benefits and satisfactions which are looked for, together with a genuine effort to establish a dialogue and build a long-term relationship, then this is the marketing philosophy irrespective of whether or not the organization possesses any personnel or function designated as 'marketing'.

In the chapters which follow many facets and aspects of the subject are examined and explored by internationally recognized experts. Taken together these provide an extensive overview and introduction to the underlying theories and principles which underpin both the theory and practice. While personal perspectives may vary, the core proposition remains – marketing is concerned with the identification, creation and maintenance of mutually satisfying exchange relationships.

References

Albert, Michel (1991) *Capitalisme contre Capitalisme*, Paris: Seuil, L'Histoire Immédiate.

Alderson, W. (1957) *Marketing Behavior and Executive Action*, Homewood, IL: Irwin.

Baker, Michael J. (1976) 'Evolution of the marketing concept', in Michael J. Baker (ed.) *Marketing Theory and Practice*, London: Macmillan.

Baker, Michael J. (1980) 'Marketing maxims', *Advertising* 66: Winter.

Baker, Michael J. (ed.) (1994) *The Marketing Book*, 3rd edn, Oxford: Butterworth Heinemann Ltd.

Baker, Michael J. (2007) *Marketing Strategy and Research*, 4th edn, Handmills: Palgrave Macmillan.

Borden, Neil H. (1964) 'The concept of the marketing mix', *Journal of Advertising Research*.

Brady, J. and Davis, I. (1993) 'Marketing's mid-life crisis', *The McKinsey Quarterly* 2: 17–28.

Chamberlin, E.J. (1933) *The Theory of Monopolistic Competition*, Cambridge, MA: Harvard University Press.

Culliton, James W. (1948) *The Management of Marketing Costs*, Andover, MA: The Andover Press Ltd.

Dean, Joel (1951) *Managerial Economics*, Englewood Cliffs, NJ: Prentice-Hall.

Dixon, D.F. and Blois, K.J. (1983) 'Some limitations of the 4 Ps as a paradigm for marketing', *Proceedings*, Marketing Education Group Conference, Cranfield.

Drucker, Peter (1954) *The Practice of Management*, New York: Harper & Row.

Dussart, Christian (1994) 'Capitalism versus capitalism', in Michael J. Baker (ed.) *Perspectives on Marketing Management*, Vol. 4, Chichester: John Wiley & Sons.

Frisch, R. (1933) 'Monopole–Polypole – la notion de la force dans l'économie', *Nationalokonomisk Tidskrift*, Denmark.

Fullerton, Ronald A. (1988) 'How modern is modern marketing? Marketing's evolution and the myth of the production era', *Journal of Marketing* 52, January: 108–25.

Galbraith, J. K. (1958) *The Affluent Society*, Harmondsworth: Penguin.

Gibson, Helen, Tynan, Caroline and Pitt, Leyland (1993) 'What is marketing?: a qualitative and quantitative analysis of marketing decisions', *Proceedings*, Marketing Education Group Conference, Loughborough.

Grönroos, C. (1989) 'Defining marketing: a market-oriented approach', *European Journal of Marketing* 23: 52–60.

Grönroos, C. (1990) *Service Management and Marketing. Managing the Moments of Truth in Service Competition*, Lexington, MA: Free Press/Lexington Books. p. 138.

Grönroos, Christian (1994) 'Quo vadis marketing? Toward a relationship marketing paradigm', *Journal of Marketing Management* 10(5): 347–60.

Gummesson, E. (1993) 'Broadening and specifying relationship marketing', invited paper, Monash Colloquium on Relationship Marketing, Monash University, Melbourne, Australia, 1–4 August.

Gummesson, Evert (2007) 'Exit *services* marketing – enter *service* marketing', *Journal of Customer Behaviour* 6(2): 113–41.

Håkansson, H. (ed.) (1982) *International Marketing and Purchasing of Industrial Goods*, New York, NY: Wiley.

Johanson, J. and Mattson, L.-G. (1985) 'Marketing investments and market investments in industrial networks', *International Journal of Research in Marketing* 2: 185–95.

Keith, R.J. (1960) 'The marketing revolution', *Journal of Marketing* 24: 35–8.

Kent, R.A. (1986) 'Faith in 4 Ps: an alternative', *Journal of Marketing Management* 2(2): 145–54.

Kjaer-Hansen, M. (1945) *Afsaetningsokonomi* [Marketing], Copenhagen: Erhvervsokonomisk Forlag.

Kock, S. (1991) *A Strategic Process for Gaining External Resources through Long-lasting Relationships*, Helsingfors/Vara, Finland: Swedish School of Economics and Business Administration.

Kotler, Philip (1967) *Marketing Management: Analysis, Planning and Control*, Englewood Cliffs, NJ: Prentice-Hall.

Levitt, T. (1960) 'Marketing myopia', *Harvard Business Review* July-August.

Lusch, R.F. and Vargo, S.L. (2006) (eds) *The Service-Dominant Logic of Marketing: Dialog, Debate, and Directions*, New York: M.E. Sharpe.

McCarthy, E. Jerome (1960) *Basic Marketing: A Managerial Approach*, Homewood, IL: Irwin.

Marion, G. (1993) 'The marketing management discourse: what's new since the 1960s?', in Michael J. Baker (ed.) *Perspectives on Marketing Management*, Vol. 3, Chichester: John Wiley & Sons.

Maslow, A.H. (1943) 'A theory of human motivation', *Psychological Review* July: 370–96.

Mickwitz, Gosta (1959) *Marketing and Competition*, Helsingfors, Finland: Societas Scientarium Fennica.

Rasmussen, Arne (1955) *Pristeori eller parameterteori – studier ombring virksomhedens afsaetning*, Copenhagen: Erhvervsokonomisk Forlag.

Robinson, Joan (1933) *The Economics of Imperfect Competition*, London: Macmillan.

Rostow, W. W. (1962) *The Process of Economic Growth*, 2nd edn, New York: W.W. Norton.

Smith, Adam (1776) *The Wealth of Nations*, Andrew Skinner (ed.) (1970), Harmondsworth: Pelican Books.

Stackelberg, H. von (1939) 'Theorie der Vertreibspolitik and der Qualitatsvariation', *Schmollers Jahrbuck* 63/1.8

Vargo, S.L. and Lusch, R.F. (2004) 'Evolving to a new dominant logic for marketing', *Journal of Marketing* 68(1), January: 1–17.

Webster, Frederick E., Jr (1992) 'The changing role of marketing in the corporation', *Journal of Marketing* 56: 1–17.

2

Marketing theory

Michael Saren

Why we need theory in marketing

The evolution of theory is essential for any discipline. This assertion is taken for granted in sciences but has to be re-emphasized in an applied social science like marketing. All academic disciplines build their own bodies of theory and apply their own unique lens to particular phenomena. In this way marketing is a bit like a magpie in that it takes many of its theories from other disciplines, such as psychology and economics (Baker, 1995b) The challenge for marketing as a relatively young discipline is to build its own distinct body of theory (Murray et al., 1997).

One of the main reasons why marketing scholars cannot agree on a common definition for theory is because, depending on philosophical orientation, scholars will have different views of what constitutes theory. The term theory is sometimes used to refer to a set of propositions or an abstract conceptualization of the relationship between entities. At other times it can be a general principle that is used to explain or predict facts or events. Often 'theory' conveys verification of facts, systems of organization, lawlike generalizations and tested hypotheses. Consequently, it is frequently associated with the production of scientific knowledge and the notion of an objective, explanatory lens upon the world.

Hunt (1991) states that the purpose of theory, more broadly, is to increase scientific understanding through a systematized structure capable of both explaining and predicting phenomena. If we look to the role of theory in the management literature, Bacharach (1989: 496) defines theory as 'a statement of relations among concepts within a set of boundary assumptions and constraints'. He goes further to argue that theory is no more than a linguistic device used to organize a complex empirical world. Van de Ven (1989) maintains that it is the use of theory that matters. As Kurt Lewin is reputed to have put it: 'nothing is so practical as a good theory'. Llewellyn (2003) argues that the value of qualitative empirical research lies in its 'conceptual framing' of organizational actions, events, processes and structures, and the possibilities for conceptual framing extend beyond the highly abstract schema generally considered as 'theories' by academics.

There is common agreement from all sides, however, that theory offers explanations of the physical and social worlds around us that can reveal deeper understandings of how and why things happen. Essentially, theory is really an organized way to think about a topic. The various views above also illustrate that theory is by no means value free. For example, some marketing theorizing implicitly adopts a machine metaphor to characterize human behaviour that is also inherently gendered in its assumptions. This metaphor has for a long time privileged the mind and cognitive activity (assumed male) over the (female) body and emotions (Campbell et al., 2009). Many other types of power relationships, such as those implicated by the Cold War, have also influenced the development of marketing theory (Tadajewski, 2006). As Maclaran et al. (2009) argue, this is why we also need to be suspicious of theory. Just like the use of metaphor, theory can both broaden our minds and tie us into particular ways of thinking, skewing our perspectives in ways that often go unquestioned and unrecognized

An essential aspect in developing marketing theory is the understanding of its historical evolution, the current knowledge base, its relative strengths and weaknesses, potential dangers and future direction. Providing an introduction and review of these topics is the objective of this chapter.

Debates about theory in marketing

Debates around the best way of seeking knowledge about marketing phenomena are long standing. These can be traced all the way back to the philosophy of science debates that began at the turn of the twentieth century between the laissez-faire oriented scholars versus their German historical counterparts (Jones and Monieson, 1990). Serious discussion of the scientific nature of marketing began to appear in late 1940s (Alderson and Cox, 1948; Bartels, 1951; Converse, 1945). The reasons for the emergence of this interest in theory at that time were explained by Alderson and Cox (1948) as partly intellectual curiosity and partly 'follow-the-leader': 'When some people become avidly and outspokenly interested in anything, others will take a look and see what is going on' (1948: 138) More fundamentally, they argue that the underlying foundations of this interest in theory consisted of two core elements: (1) students of marketing, for all their efforts, have produced very few accurate, comprehensive and significant generalizations, principles or theories;

and (2) the belief that they have achieved little, even in setting themselves fundamental problems, and less still in developing procedures for solving such problems. They complain, 'the multitude of facts thus far assembled seems to add up to very little' (Alderson and Cox, 1948: 138). A sound theory is needed, not simply to produce immediate generalizations, but because it helps marketers to better initiate and direct their inquiries.

Alderson and Cox's fundamental rationale for their call in 1948 for better theory was that it would help identify salient problems to be solved and thus direct the researcher to understand which facts to assemble and how to analyse them. 'Only a sound theory of marketing can raise the analysis of such problems above the level of an empirical art and establish truly scientific criteria for setting up hypotheses and selecting the facts by means of which to test them' (1948: 139). This reasoning was subsequently endorsed by Baumol (1957: 160) who stated succinctly that 'facts are silent' and therefore theory is needed to describe and explain the workings of facts.

The Marketing Science Institute (MSI) was established in 1961 to 'create knowledge that will improve business performance' (Lehman and Jocz, 1997: 141). They established four 'position studies', which went some way to setting out the 'fundamental problems' that Alderson and Cox cited, and one of these was to conduct long-term research on marketing theory and its application in order to provide the 'concepts, methods and opportunities for more creative and imaginative solutions for more difficult and important problems' (Lehman and Jocz, 1997: xiv). Several reasons for the importance of this effort to improve the theory were presented in the 1965 report by Michael Halbert, as follows.

1. Theoretical rules are a prerequisite for learning. 'It is said that we learn by experience, but we really learn only by the analysis of experience … But without a theoretical base, we cannot analyse, for the rules of proper analysis are theoretical rules; we cannot be selective about which experiences are relevant, for the criteria of relevance are theoretical criteria' (1965: xiv). There are a great deal of data and knowledge available about the operation of the marketing system but theory is needed to provide a formal structure for organizing, analysing and evaluating this knowledge. Adequate theories would also help present a much more 'coherent, understandable and useful picture' of the entire marketing process.

2. Practitioners need theory in order to make better decisions. As well as facts, the executive's informational needs also include marketing theory 'because it can reduce the cost and uncertainty of decision making while increasing the productivity and assurance of decision makers' (Halbert, 1965: xxii). Examples given here are theory concerning how pricing affects distribution and what happens if advertising spend doubles.

3. Marketing cannot rely on borrowing from other disciplines. Not all borrowing is bad, but one must distinguish between three classes of borrowing: (i) of content, which presents few problems; (ii) the adaptation of techniques and methods from other subjects, which is acceptable if properly applied; and (iii) the borrowing of theories and concepts from other disciplines which is 'dangerous at best and larceny at worst … often semantic

similarity is mistaken for formal appropriateness' (Halbert, 1965: xxvi). It is seldom that a theoretical structure from one area is directly applicable to another and the many problems associated with marketing's reliance at that time on borrowing particularly from economics, behavioural sciences and law are examined in the report.

In his influential text, *Marketing: Theory and Practice* (1995) Michael Baker devotes a whole chapter to 'The need for theory in marketing'. Taking a marketing-as-exchange position along with Bagozzi (1978), he presents the core reason as '... the recognition and acceptance of the need to improve our understanding of the manner in which the [marketing] system works which underlies the need to develop a workable theory of exchange' (Baker, 1995b). The benefits resulting from this he agrees with Halbert (1965), will be; (i) the satisfaction of intellectual curiosity; and, (ii) improved operational performance. By solving immediate operating problems, the latter would permit marketing academics to concentrate on the more fundamental problems underlying them. This would also liberate marketing practitioners from 'fire-fighting' activities in order to concentrate on anticipating and avoiding marketing problems in an increasingly complex business world.

The need for marketing theory is now largely accepted (Kerin, 1996). In order to summarize all the arguments put forward above, they can be grouped into four main categories – practical, knowledge, academic and intellectual needs.

1. *Practical value*. Better theories will improve managerial decision making and problem solving.

2. *Knowledge creation*. Theory provides direction and structure to academic inquiry and helps 'make sense of facts'.

3. *Academic status*. Marketing as an academic discipline requires its own theory. It cannot rely on borrowing from other disciplines.

4. *Intellectual curiosity*. Only theory can provide the basis for understanding how the marketing system works and explaining the underlying foundations and forces.

In true demand–pull fashion, the early identification of a need for theory stimulated the start of its production by academics such as Alderson himself (1957), McGary (1953) (both functionalist), Bartels (1968) (general theory), and McInnes (1964) (systems model), which, as we shall see in the next sections, spawned over 50 years of debate as to what marketing theory should be like and, indeed, whether it is possible at all.

_____ Can we have scientific theory in marketing?_____

Marketing would appear to be primarily an area for application of findings from the sciences (primarily the behavioral sciences) and not a science in itself. Should then the attempt to make it a science be abandoned as a wild-goose chase? (Buzzell, 1963: 34)

So Robert Buzzell in his 1963 *Harvard Business Review* article, 'Is marketing a science?', expressed the question over which marketing theorists have been locked in debate (in one form or another) ever since Alderson and Cox made their 'call to arms' 60 years ago. Indeed only six months after their article appeared Roland Vaile published a direct commentary on it in the *Journal of Marketing*, in which he took the contrary view that 'marketing will remain an art' (1949: 522). Thus began the 'marketing as science versus art' controversy that filled the journals up to the mid-1960s and still echoes today. Those who began the need for theory tended to recommend a scientific approach to its development and evaluation, at least along the positive lines of the social sciences, if not akin to the physical sciences (Alderson & Cox, 1948; Bartels, 1951). Those who responded from the managerial, normative perspective regarded marketing as a vocation, an application of scientific principles, like engineering or medicine (Vaile, 1949). Managers certainly don't regard marketing as scientific 'The businessman's practical wisdom is of a completely different character than scientific knowledge. While it does not ignore generalities, it recognizes the low probability that given combinations of phenomena can or will be repeated … In place of scientific knowledge, then, the businessman collects lore' (Ramond, 1962, quoted in Buzzell, 1963: 34).

Few would disagree with this today, especially given the recent anthropological attention to management behaviour, but adducing the paucity of managers' use of marketing models and theories is not sufficient to refute the possibility of the development of scientific theories in marketing. To do so requires detailed attention to exactly what constitutes a theory. Vaile (1949) raised this issue initially in his critique of Alderson and Cox (1948), who proposed that a systematic theory of marketing can and should be developed and that it may become scientific. 'Useful discussion of the propositions just stated requires definition of the term "theory". This the authors do not undertake' (Vaile, 1949: 521). Vaile suggests a dictionary definition of theory as 'a coherent group of general propositions used as principles of explanation for a class of phenomena' (ibid.). Marketing theory cannot exist he argues because; (i) marketing has many, not one, coherent groups of propositions; and (ii) marketing must do more than explain, it also must make judgements about marketing policies.

Buzzell (1963) also argued that marketing is not a science because it does not meet his definition. In order to qualify as a distinct science in its own right, marketing will have to meet some rather stringent requirements. For example, it is generally agreed that a science is:

> **a classified and systematized body of knowledge, organized around one or more central theories and a number of general principles, usually expressed in quantitative terms, knowledge which permits the prediction and, under some circumstances, the control of future events. Few believe that marketing now meets these criteria. (Buzzell, 1963: 33)**

Shelby Hunt, the leading proponent of the 'marketing-is-science' school, argued that these definitions are over restrictive, and, following Rudner (1966), proposed that: 'Theories are systematically related sets of statements, including some law-like generalizations, that are empirically testable. The purpose of theory is to increase scientific understanding through a systematized structure capable of both explaining and predicting phenomena' (Hunt, 1971: 65). This avoids the central theory requirement, which, even today, for marketing is clearly untenable and by 1983 Hunt was able to assert that 'both philosophers of science and marketing theorists agree on the nature of theory' (p. 10). He cited the definitions adopted by many of the marketing-is/not-science writers such as Alderson (1957), Zaltman et al. (1973), Bagozzi (1980), Ryan and O'Shaunessy (1980) and even Keat and Urry (1975), to demonstrate that both advocates and critics 'basically concur as to the general characteristics of theory' (Hunt, 1983: 10).

In reviewing the *Journal of Marketing*'s 60-year pursuit of the 'ideal' of advancement of science and practice in marketing, Roger Kerin argues that by 1965 marketing literature had become more scientific, particularly in terms of quantitative analysis being an integral element. 'Marketing phenomena, originally addressed by intuition and judgement, were increasingly studied with fundamental tenets of the scientific method' (Kerin, 1996: 5)

The debate about whether it is possible to have scientific theories in marketing then moved on from the 'definition' issue to the question of what marketing theory should be like.

What form should marketing theory take?

The Fall 1983 edition of the *Journal of Marketing* began the next 'round' in the contest about the nature of marketing theory (Kavanagh (1994) likens the debate to a boxing match). In that edition Paul Anderson questions particularly Hunt's positivistic concept of the scientific method: 'Despite its prevalence in marketing, positivism has been abandoned by these disciplines [philosophy and sociology of science] over the last two decades in the face of overwhelming historical and logical arguments that have been raised against it' (1983: 25). Thus, the debate moved from whether marketing can have scientific theory to what form of scientific theory is appropriate. It is argued that there is no longer one 'correct' method for evaluating theory and different research disciplines will adopt different methodologies, ontologies and epistemologies. These marketing theorists draw on Kuhn's (1962) revolutionary view of scientific progress in terms of competing paradigms (see Dholakia and Arndt, 1985), which within any discipline are 'incommensurable' – that is scientists of each persuasion have different 'worldviews' and are unable to agree on salient problems, theories or terminologies to be employed, and thus could never agree on any 'experiments' or data that would resolve their differences. In marketing, Anderson (1983) cites theory of consumer behaviour and theory of the firm as incommensurable. With no agreed or agreeable 'demarcation criterion' between theory and non-theory, or even science and non-science, in marketing, Anderson concludes that a relativistic approach is the only viable one.

As Kavanagh (1994) notes, Hunt (1984) was quick to counter-attack Anderson's naive relativist advocacy, which can easily be forced to its (il)logical conclusion of nihilism, ontological solipsism (death of the *object*) and epistemological anarchy (can't know anything or can know everything). Interestingly, both Hunt and Anderson moved their positions somewhat after each other's attack in this 'round' in order to defend their 'weak flanks'. Hunt moved from logical empiricism to scientific realism, in which he accepts a critical realist position that some of our perceptions may be illusions and certainly some are more accurate than others (thus moderating pure empiricism). Therefore the job of science is to develop theories that have 'long-run predictive success' (Hunt, 1990) in explaining behaviour, 'even if we cannot finally "know" whether the entities and structure postulated by the theory actually exists' (McMullin, 1984: 26).

Anderson meanwhile was adopting critical relativism which accepts the possibility of a single pre-existing 'reality', but rejects the notion that it can be discovered via the scientific method (1986: 157). So, it seemed for a while that boxing had brought them closer together. This debate between realism and relativism in marketing theory mirrors debate which had been going on in the social sciences (see Burrell and Morgan, 1979) about how we can *know* the world; is reality out there or a product of one's mind? As Kavanagh rightly observes, epistemology and ontology tend to be conflated in all these debates – that is, 'being is reduced to knowledge and knowledge is reduced to being' (1994: 31). Although this certainly all follows from the Cartesian dictum *cogito ergo sum*, the question for marketing theory is that we need to be able to know more about reality beyond one's own existence.

Hunt (1976) refutes of all forms of relativism, arguing that the knowledge claims of any theory must be *objective* in the sense that 'its truth content must be intersubjectively certifiable' and that 'requiring that theories, laws and explanations be empirically testable ensures that they will be intersubjectively certifiable since different (but reasonably competent) investigators with differing attitudes, opinions and beliefs will be able to make observations and conduct experiments to ascertain their truth content' (Hunt, 1976: 27). He challenges all those academics in what he calls marketing's 'crisis literature' who have questioned the very possibility of objective marketing research, for example, 'Objectivity is an illusion' (Peter, 1992: 77), 'objectivity is impossible' (Mick, 1986: 207)), 'Researcher objectivity and intersubjective certifiability are chimeras – they cannot be achieved' (Fullerton, 1986: 433). Hunt categorizes and articulates the five 'primary arguments' which marketing writers have employed 'ostensibly implying the impossibility of objective marketing research' (1993: 80). He summarizes these along with their original philosophical sources (see Table 2.1) and then refutes each argument from a scientific realist perspective, often asserting that the marketing authors have misconstrued, misunderstood or misapplied the ideas from the philosophy of science literature.

Following the discussion above of the influence on marketing theory of Kuhnian ideas about the progress of science (see also Dholakia and Arndt, 1985), take, for example, Hunt's refutation of argument 2 in Table 2.1, which had been used by Anderson *inter alia*, that 'objectivity is impossible because the paradigms that

Table 2.1   Arguments against objectivity

1. Objectivity is impossible because the language of a culture determines the reality that members of that culture see.
2. Objectivity is impossible because the paradigms that researchers hold are incommensurable.
3. Objectivity is impossible because theories are undermined by facts.
4. Objectivity is impossible because the psychology of perception informs us that a theory-free observation language is impossible.
5. Objectivity is impossible because all epistemically significant observations are theory-laden.

Source: Adapted from Hunt (1993) *Journal of Marketing* 57, April: 76–91. Reprinted with permission from the *Journal of Marketing*, published by the American Marketing Association.

researchers hold are incommensurable'. Countering it Hunt (1993: 82) makes two points; firstly that it is 'simply incoherent' to compare and contrast different paradigms in marketing and then to claim that they are incommensurable because they are 'non-comparable', and secondly, that for incommensurability to bar objective choice between two paradigms implies that they are *rival*, but most of the so-called paradigms identified by marketers are simply *different*, not necessarily putting forward conflicting knowledge claims. Going on to counter all five arguments, Hunt concludes that 'there is nothing, absolutely nothing, in modern philosophy of science or psychology that makes objectivity either impossible or undesirable' (1993: 87).

Whether Hunt is correct or not about 'rival' or different' paradigms in marketing there certainly are a lot of them. Carmen (1980) identifies six (microeconomic, persuasion/attitude change, conflict resolution, generalist system, functionalist and social exchange paradigms), Fisk and Meyers (1982) classify another six (network flow, market scarcity, competitive marketing management, evolutionary systems change, general systems and dissapative structures paradigms). Sheth et al. (1988) list 12 'schools of thought' in marketing (commodity, functional, functionalist, regional, institutional, managerial, buyer behaviour, activist, macromarketing, organizational dynamics and social exchange schools). Kerin (1996) chooses six 'metaphors' which characterized marketing science and practice in each of the six decades since the launch of the *Journal of Marketing* in 1936. – marketing as applied economics, a managerial activity, a quantitative science, a behavioural science, a decision science and as an integrative science. Wilkie and Moore (2003) identify '4 eras' of thought development, which are: 1900–1920, 'Founding the Field'; 1920–1950, 'Formalizing the Field'; 1950–1980, 'A Paradigm Shift – Marketing, Management, and the Sciences'; 1980–present, 'The Shift Intensifies – A Fragmentation of the Mainstream'.

Of course, taking Hunt's point about interpreting Kuhn's ideas correctly, many of the above are not strictly 'paradigms' and it can be seen that they are by no means all posited as such. Indeed, as so often happens with even the supposedly technical language of science (cf. argument 1 in Table 2.1 above), a term loses its 'original' meaning in the noise of academic discourse. The 'paradigm' is (adopting the vernacular) an excellent paradigm of this phenomenon. Even those who take an 'alternative paradigm' approach to marketing theory recognize this. 'It is commonly agreed that the paradigm concept itself remains somewhat vague and unclear. This is partly because [it] has taken on different meanings over time' (Arndt, 1985: 19). Even in

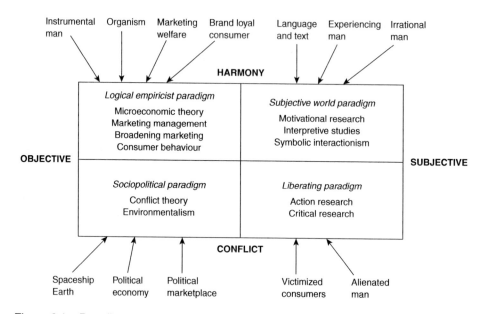

Figure 2.1   Paradigms and metaphors in marketing (Arndt, 1985)

Source: Arndt (1985) *Journal of Marketing* 49, Summer: 18–23. Reprinted with permission from the *Journal of Marketing*, published by the American Marketing Association.

its original formulation the notion was ambiguous and Kuhn has been accused of using the paradigm notion in many different ways (Morgan, 1980).

Arndt (1985) attempts to make sense of the concept for use in marketing theory by adapting Morgan's (1980) hierarchy, which distinguishes paradigms (alternative realities or world views) at the second level from *orientations* (perspective of the researcher relating to the role of data, theory and values) above it at level 1 with *metaphors* (basis for schools of thought) at level 3 and *puzzle-solving* (based on specific tools or procedures) at level 4. Using Morgan's framework, Arndt analyses and categorizes the different paradigms and metaphors in marketing theory, identifying four main paradigms based on different (and indeed one would have to say *conflicting*) world views. These contain 'different metatheoretical assumptions about the nature of science, the subjective – objective dimension and the explicitness of long-term conflicts in society. There are also assumptions about the nature of the marketing discipline and the study of marketing phenomena' (Arndt, 1985: 15). These are shown in Figure 2.1. classified along two dimensions – objective/subjective and harmony/conflict. He thus classifies four paradigms in marketing along these dimensions: (i) logical empiricist; (ii) sociopolitical; (iii) subjective world; and (iv) liberating paradigms.

The *Logical empiricist paradigm* emphasizes measurability and intersubjective certification. It takes a mechanistic approach, assuming that marketing relations have a real existence independent of the observer and a systematic character resulting in regularities in marketing behaviour and equilibrium-seeking marketing systems. Neoclassical economics provides the basis for many of its typical metaphors such as *instrumental man* with rational decision-making and the *organism metaphor* for the organized behaviour and environmental learning of the marketing system.

The *sociopolitical paradigm* is similarly based on the assumption of a real and measurable world of marketing phenomena and predictable uniformities in marketing behaviour. Unlike the value-free and equilibrium assumptions of logical empirical theories however, this paradigm explicitly recognizes conflicts of interests, resources and relations in marketing exchanges and systems. The metaphors of this paradigm constitute the *political markets and economies* and even spaceship *Earth*, the global, ecological approach of much of what would nowadays be called green marketing.

The *subjective world paradigm* rejects the existence of social reality in any verifiable or concrete sense. It is the product of the subjective experiences and inter-experiences of individuals and therefore marketing phenomena cannot be understood from the perspective of an external observer, but must be studied from the viewpoint of the participant. It thus incorporates the interpretive and social constructionist approaches and adopts the motivational and psychology-based metaphor of *irrational man*, the phenomenological metaphor of *experiencing man*, with an existential and semiological basis, and the *language and text* metaphor for understanding the behaviour of marketing actors from stories, myths, rhetoric and discourse.

The *liberating paradigm* also takes a social constructionist perspective regarding the ontological status of reality but focuses on the social, economic and techno-logical processes that constrain and control human beings in the marketing system. The role of theoretical inquiry is to identify and analyse the conflicts and contradictions in the system and point the way to emancipation. Critical theory adherents within this paradigm often take *alienation* and *victimization* as metaphors for the oppressed groups in modern mass consumer society.

A strong case is made by Arndt (1985) that marketing has been dominated by one paradigm – that is, logical empiricism.

> **Even a cursory perusal of scholarly articles in marketing journals is bound to confirm the dominant status of logical empiricism. The principles of empiricism appear to be treated synonymously with the scientific method as such ... The control technology and instrumentalist of the logical empiricist paradigm may well be compatible with the problem solving needs and pragmatism of marketing practitioners. (Arndt, 1985: 19)**

This is directly opposed by Hunt's contention that to even ask the question

> **'what philosophy dominates marketing?'** *presumes* **that marketing is** *dominated* **(which carries pejorative overtones) by one view or another and that in any case, on the contrary, 'the marketing discipline has been amazingly eclectic' and 'the most accurate answer is: 'No single philosophy dominates marketing. (Hunt, 1991: 398)**

Arndt makes a strong case for pluralism in orientations and paradigms for the development of marketing theory: 'by limiting itself to the empiricist orientation and logical empiricist paradigms such as instrumental man, marketing has remained essentially a one-dimensional science concerned with technology and problem solving'. (Arndt 1985: 21). Adopting other paradigms and metaphors will result in the asking of quite different research questions. 'The *notion* of paradigms should be viewed as an argument for paradigmatic tolerance and pluralism'

(Arndt, 1985: 21). Perhaps this explains one reason why Hunt goes to such great effort to reject the notion itself for marketing theory?

Despite the length and intensity of the debate regarding the appropriate characteristics of and scientific underpinning for the development of marketing theories, and despite the coalescence of key positions around the two poles of relativism and realism, there is no consensus as to what marketing theory should be like. We do have several competing schools of thought, if not exactly 'paradigms'. Attempts at constructing 'general/generic' theories of marketing (Alderson, 1957; Bartels, 1968; Kotler, 1972) have not led to any shared, let alone agreed theoretical basis for the discipline. Worse still, whether it is because of over-emphasis on empirical research at the expense of theory generation by positivists (Deshpande, 1983; Peter, 1992: 72–79) or because of the advocacy of loosely thought out epistemological 'anarchy' by relativists (Hunt, 1994), the one thing that most authors on both sides agree about is that, since Alderson and Cox's call 60 years ago, marketing theory has not advanced as well as it should have done – or even satisfactorily. The next question then is: 'What's gone wrong?'

What's gone wrong?

The American Marketing Association (AMA) set up a task force in 1984 to investigate the development of marketing thought. Its report (AMA, 1988) recognized that 'the marketing discipline has come a long way since 1959. Nevertheless the task force believes that our self-evaluation of how marketing develops, disseminates and utilizes marketing knowledge indicates that, as a discipline, we still have a long way to go' (AMA, 1988: 24). An earlier commission set up under the auspices of the AMA and the MSI to assess the effectiveness of research and development for marketing management had concluded that marketing research 'has had relatively little impact on improving marketing management practice' (Myers, et al., 1980: 280). The AMA task force identified six principle barriers:

1. Insufficient resources devoted to marketing knowledge and development
2. Too few people generating and disseminating knowledge
3. The premature end to too many research careers at pre-tenure and post-tenure stages
4. Senior faculty do not devote sufficient time to knowledge generation
5. Restrictions against practical, innovative and long-term projects and reports by journals and doctoral programmes
6. Extremely limited dissemination of knowledge.

Other causes for the discipline's problems have been identified and discussed in the literature, which points to failings in the research approach of the discipline.

Lack of attention to history

Reflecting on the future of marketing, Stephen Greyser (1997) – one of the original AMA/MSI Commission authors – endorses Michael Baker's (1995a) observation that 'what is regarded as history by a new generation was an important element in the education and experience of the old' (Baker, 1995a: 1,004). This carries with it, Baker cautions, a grave danger for the new generation of marketing scholars in their rush to make their own impact that they may overlook or, even worse, ignore the lessons of the past. 'Will our concern for recency blur our vision of what is relevant? In ignoring the past will we reinvent what is already known ...?' (Baker, 1995a: 1,004).

According to Savitt (1980) this may be one reason for the subject's lack of progress in developing marketing theory. He argues for more attention to, and awareness of, the marketing's history and theoretical foundations in order for marketing scholars to gain a better understanding of the discipline's origins and patterns of change. Cunningham and Sheth similarly argue that:

> **Much research in marketing fails because its hypotheses are not well founded in theory. This inevitably leads to ill-defined research and excessively narrow research ideas ... An effective theory paper begins with an exhaustive and critical historical review of past work. Marketing theory is made up of a set of building blocks. Readers of a theoretical paper should be able to see how the new theory builds on past theoretical work. (1982: 11)**

There has recently been much more attention devoted to historical research in marketing which is reviewed elsewhere in this volume. The application of the historical approach has made some significant shifts in academic thinking about the framework of evolution marketing (notably Fullerton's (1988) reassessment of the 'marketing era'). It has also provided an alternative technique for the analysis of practice and potentially for the development of theory. Nevett (1991) emphasizes the advantages of the historical approach to establishing facts, relevance, and causality, which is more impressionistic and intuitive than positivist 'scientific' analysis.

Too much attention to quantitative methods

Venkatesh (1985) presents one reason for the disappointing development of marketing theory in the lack of skills or training in marketing researchers, which was also highlighted by the AMA task force (1988). Training in theory development is not available to most academic marketers who come out of traditional marketing departments, 'where the emphasis is on empirical research, data analysis, and quantitative modeling. These areas offer little potential for theory generation' (Venkatesh, 1985: 62). Deshpande (1983) makes the same point that quantitative methods are more suitable for theory testing than theory generation. He recommends the use of qualitative methods to generate new theory and furthermore advocates them for triangulation in theory testing as well as quantitative methods. In consumer behaviour, Belk (1986) shows how art can be used, in particular, to suggest and inspire hypotheses and theories. Anderson (1994) considers that progress has been impeded by the discipline's 'quantitative bias'. The analytical and empirical 'toolkit' has become ever more sophisticated with far less attention to techniques of theory development. 'Academic research in marketing has been more technique- than theory-driven' (Anderson, 1994: 11).

Armstrong (1982) proposes an 'author's formula' for a successful publication strategy as:

1. Do *not* pick an important problem.

2. Do *not* challenge existing beliefs.

3. Do *not* obtain surprising results.

4. Do *not* use simple methods.

5. Do *not* provide full disclosure.

6. Do *not* write clearly.

Even Shelby Hunt laments the paucity of qualitative research publications:

> **Numerous marketers have pointed out over the last decade that research using qualitative methods could usefully complement our quantitative analyses. I have never heard anyone dispute the potential value of qualitative research – but qualitative works in marketing are few. Why are our major journals almost exclusively devoted to studies using quantitative methods? (Hunt, 1994: 13)**

Following his familiar modus operandi, Hunt proceeds to answer his own question by constructing a step-by-step refutation of the arguments of relativists, constructionists and subjectivists who, according to him, proffer their standard (and to Hunt totally false) reasoning as a basis for advocating the use of qualitative methods. 'Is it any wonder then' he concludes, 'that mainstream marketers have been reluctant to accept qualitative methods when their advocates have explicitly grounded them in relativism, constructionism and subjectivism? How could marketers trust the output of such research methods?'(Hunt, 1994: 21).

There is, then, little disagreement about the *need* for increased and appropriate application of qualitative, as opposed to quantitative techniques for research leading to theory generation in marketing.

_____ Lack of impact on practice _____

In advocating a theory-in-use approach, Heffring asks what accounts for 'this seemingly dismal performance of marketing theory?'(1985: 106). The dismal performance to which he is referring is the conclusion of Myers, Greyser and Massey (1979) that marketing knowledge development, model building and theorizing has had little impact on the practice of marketing: 'There isn't a single problem area with regard to the practice of marketing and management that marketing research or the world of technology and concepts has mastered' (Myers et al., 1979: 280).

Heffring (1985) gives three broad explanations.

1. Marketing theories reflect the realities of the builder, not the user. Managers do have principles and theories that they have acquired over time and use when approaching marketing decisions. They are guided by their own theories-in-use. The trouble is that many of the academic theories do not reflect managers' language nor their business realities.

2. Marketing theory provides complex answers to marketing problems. On the contrary, managers want complex problems to be solved as simplified representations and with clarity. 'Why have concepts like the product life cycle and the product portfolio matrix been adopted so quickly? Primarily because they are simple representations of marketing phenomena that can affect their decisions' (Heffring, 1985: 107)

3. Marketing theories may be logically correct but practically incorrect. Managers have several problems with this: (i) many theories focus on strategy not tactics and do not give guidance for their implementation; (ii) theory is judged by academics by process not relevance of the content; (iii) theory focuses on problem formulation whereas mangers are concerned with problem solving; and (iv) pro-theory bias. It is assumed that theory is good, that it improves manager's decision-making and that to have any theory is better than to have none. Managers in fact are often confused by theories that they find difficult to interpret.

Other authors have blamed the academic system for this state of affairs with its emphasis on research and publication regardless of their significance for managers (Anderson, 1992; Mason 1990). Venkatesh (1985: 63) describes this as the 'Crisis of Relevance' and considers that theories of researchers are not perceived as useful because practitioners want their everyday problems solved and marketing academics *cannot* perform this function.

These problems do not appear to have been overcome. In the July 2009 volume of the *Journal of Marketing*, Reibstein, Day and Wind, in a question remarkably reminiscent of the AMA task force, ask: 'Why do marketing academics have little to say about critical strategic marketing issues and emerging issues ...?', They point to wider concerns regarding wider management education.

> **Criticisms are being leveled at the dominant MBA focus on narrow analytical and cognitive skills, stylized treatment of complex issues by teachers with no direct business experience, self-centred careerism and the declining recognition that management is as much a clinical art as a science. It is further charged that the prevailing paradigm of reductionist, narrowly specified and fragmented research ... cannot address the multi-functional and interconnected problems for managers. Although these concerns loom large for management education in general, *the dilemma is magnified in marketing* – a field that is supposed to be concerned about the connection of the firm with its customers and other stakeholders. (Reibstein, et al., 2009: 1, emphasis added)**

These comments come from authors who are senior established figures in the marketing discipline, not the 'usual suspects' from marketing's perpetual so-called 'crisis literature'. Indeed, some maintain that these are not really problems. Holbrook (1989) argues that managerially relevant applied research tends towards the dogmatic, and basic or pure research is best carried out by the curiosity-driven and self-directed academic, free from the constraints of relevance. The development of theory is necessarily basic and creative in nature, rather than applied research, and therefore the conditions best suited to theory development are those of 'pure' academic freedom. Furthermore, academic theory does not normally produce immediate impact and relevance is itself a problematic construct – try defining it (Wensley, 1995).

There is, nevertheless, a serious issue for marketing theory in this regard and indeed for the academy's understanding of its role. In the recent debate about the 'gap' between the approach and concerns of marketing practitioners and academics, between theory and practice, it is perhaps not surprising that the two 'worlds' are regarded as 'separate'. But the paradox is, as Halbert (1965) put the argument, that the criteria for relevance are theoretical criteria. If we all, academics and managers, need theory (or at least if it is *implicit*, if not explicit) in order to distinguish salient facts and to learn from experience, then what exactly are the reasons for the long-term continuance of this vast gap between the two 'world views'? The answer may be that it has been constructed and maintained by the marketing academy itself (Brownlie and Saren, 1996).

_____ Where to now? _____

It was concluded in the first section here that despite earlier debates the need for marketing theory is now well accepted (Kerin, 1996). As we have seen, however, it has largely failed to live up to its potential to the satisfaction of either academics or practitioners. The need for theory may be even more important today than it was at the time of Alderson and Cox (1948) for two reasons.

First, there has been more emphasis and awareness of 'the power effects of knowledge' (Morgan, 1992: 151) that is, what knowledge *does*. The Foulcauldian synonymity of knowledge and power (Foucault, 1980) implies that 'doing-in-the-world' (after Heideggar, 1962) is inexorably intertwined and embedded in 'knowing-the-world' in a particular way. If theory helps create knowledge, as most marketing academics accept (after Alderson and Cox, 1948), then theory also helps create power. This underlies and reinforces both mangers' and academics' need for marketing theory in order to increase their relative *professional power* over competitors (and colleagues!).

Secondly, in an increasingly information-saturated world, knowledge needs to be firmly rooted in order to be distinctive and meaningful. It has been argued that information is now packaged, mediated and re-presented in various forms and that marketing knowledge has become a 'commodity' to be shaped, packaged, distributed and marketed like any other (Brownlie and Saren, 1995).

Academics are now, not only producers of marketing knowledge, but also merchandisers, retailers and consumers of it as authors, researchers, teachers and consultants. One effect of this process is that the product life-cycle of marketing knowledge is shortening, and thus its velocity of circulation is accelerating. The capital value of marketing knowledge has a shorter shelf life. Under these conditions the need for theory is now even greater in order to provide an anchor and a referent for marketing information and knowledge and to differentiate it and set it in context.

But where are the advances in marketing theory going to come from in the future? There are a number of possibilities.

New general theories

A distinct service marketing sub-discipline has developed along with the rise of service-based economies and markets over the past 50 years. Vargo and Lusch (2004) challenged this view of the key differentiators of services versus goods and proposed a new 'service-dominant logic' (SDL) for *all* marketing that constitutes a general theory of marketing. As a new contender for dominance in marketing theory, in a short time SDL has stimulated much renewed interest and discussion about theory development in marketing (Lusch and Vargo, 2006). The focus of SDL is on marketing as a value co-creation process that is service-based. Marketers can only provide value propositions, embedded in offerings, and their value depends entirely on the experiential evaluation of customers. Service, not goods, is the fundamental basis of exchange and goods are merely 'distribution mechanisms for service provision'. Another key aspect is the role of know-how, capabilities and competencies which are the key 'operant resources' for both creating value propositions and extracting value from them as the primary source of competitive advantage. The corollary is that the role of tangible, finite 'operand resources' is to provide the raw material inputs.

Central to SDL is its distinction from that approach referred to by Vargo and Lusch as the historical and still prevailing, goods-dominant logic (GDL), based on tangible goods and the activities associated with their delivery. The GDL approach is presented as an antithesis to SDL, which provides a '*shift in thinking*'. Vargo and Lusch advocate that SDL should form the basis of a unified theory of marketing. It can be seen more critically, however, in terms of an orientation – that is, a perspective providing guidelines on how certain existing schools of marketing should be utilized in normative fashion in value creation. Further, Schembri (2006) highlights the limitations of SDL and challenges its key foundational premises. She argues that while the service-dominant logic recognizes the emergent service orientation, Vargo and Lusch's analysis of its implications for marketing continues to be founded on the same rationalistic assumptions as the traditional goods-centered logic. Marketers and researchers need to question their underlying assumptions and seek to understand services as constituted in the customer's experience, as opposed to rationalizing the phenomena in terms a foundational 'logic'.

Perhaps consumer behaviour can provide the basis for a general theory since it occupies a unique position in marketing theory development, with the consumer positioned at the centre of the marketing concept, according to Zaltman et al. (1973). They argued that, as opposed to the conflicting and partial explanations of theories in marketing as a whole, the field of consumer behaviour alone contains several grand theories claiming to hold the key to explaining consumer behaviour. The situation today is, if anything, that these approaches are now even *more* divergent in their methodologies and research orientations, making agreement about theories or even core problems less likely. More recently though there has been a movement in consumer behaviour away from an information processing view of the consumer. This has involved more theoretical work from an interdisciplinary perspective based on interpretivist, ethnographic and semiotic methods, which adopt more macro, cultural perspectives to studying the consumer. Some of this is encompassed in the framework of consumer culture theory, as developed by Arnould and Thompson (2005), which maps out the conceptual domain and the theoretical advances in this field.

It may be that the seeds of a general theory are emerging with the adoption of a general integrative approach. Examples of this type of theory-building process in marketing are consumer culture theory (CCT) and service-dominant logic (SDL). Both adopt an integrative process by combining findings and theories from various disciplines, such as economics, political theory, consumer information processing, services marketing and cognitive psychology, thus producing a general theory that is inherently interdisciplinary in nature.

──────────── Networks and relationships ────────────────────

The traditional view of the firm and how managers conduct marketing activities has evolved significantly over the past 20 years or so. The theoretical basis has shifted from the biological analogy of the autonomous organism operating in a changing business environment towards an overlapping network of market actors operating in more or less contingent or strategic modes. In 1982 a research project reported how they had developed an approach that challenged traditional ways of examining industrial marketing and purchasing. In business-to-business settings this Industrial Marketing and Purchasing (IMP) study showed that companies were dominated by long-term business relationships with a limited number of counterparts, within which both marketing and purchasing of industrial goods were seen as 'interaction processes' between the two parties (see Ford, 1990; Håkansson, 1982; Mattsson, 1985). These researchers also observed that interaction in itself included an important content of its own. This concept of interaction in networks challenged the prevailing conceptualizations in B2B marketing in four major respects. Firstly, IMP challenged the narrow analysis of single discrete purchases and emphasized the importance of business relationships. Secondly, the view of industrial marketing as manipulation of marketing-mix variables in relation to a passive market was challenged. The third aspect concerned the assumption of an atomistic market structure where buyers and sellers can easily switch business partners. Fourthly, IMP challenged the separation of theoretical and empirical analysis into either the process of purchasing or the process of marketing.

A range of alternative, broader perspectives of organizations' approach to markets has emerged, which have important implications for the theories regarding firms' relations with markets. Greater emphasis is now placed on marketing organizations' processes, relationships with customers and networks with stakeholders. Araujo, Kjellberg and Spencer (2008), argue that marketing practice and practices influence the operation of markets. They show that the particular definition and understanding of the market that managers adopt itself affects their operations and the outcomes in their chosen, 'enacted market-place'. Reviewing the research undertaken by the Contemporary Marketing Practice (CMP) group, Brodie, Coviello and Winklhofer (2008) develop the case for a multi-theory perspective of the marketing organization. They examine the conceptual foundations of the CMP research and how it evolved to encompass a multi-theory approach. Brodie et al. (2008) also point to the positioning of most marketing theories towards the level of middle-range theory (Merton, 1948; Saren and Pels, 2008).

These approaches all provide potential for the development of a unified general theory of marketing beyond the marketing-as-exchange view (Bagozzi, 1978). In contrast to traditional marketing's microeconomic base, the relational approach emphasizes long-term collaboration as opposed to competition between market and social actors (Webster, 1992). Conceivably all marketing activities, problems, systems and behaviour can be conceptualized and researched taking the unit of analysis as the relationships in which they occur. At the micro-level dyadic relational theory is being developed from social psychology and human relations literature. At the macro-relational level social network theory has been well applied and refined towards a theory of industrial marketing by the IMP group. Relationships and networks may not yet be a new general marketing theory, but as an expanding area of knowledge within the discipline it has considerable potential for providing the basis for a new theory of marketing.

Radical approaches

There are two prominent approaches to marketing that can be classed as 'radical', postmodernism and critical theory. Those marketing academics who have introduced the former to marketing theory make a strong case that marketing is *the* epitome of the postmodern condition (e.g. Brown, 1995; Cova and Badot, 1995; Firat, 1990,1991; Hirschman and Holbrook, 1992; Sherry, 1990; Venkatesh, 1989). 'Marketing has always been a postmodern institution in its fundamental tendencies … it can be expected that marketing, the ultimate postmodern practice, will be the first institution to adapt to postmodernism' (Firat and Venkatesh, 1993: 246). There is no doubt that some of the concepts and ideas of writers who are labelled as postmodern are enormously powerful and directly applicable to marketing. Jean Baudrillard's (1981) notions of 'a system of objects' and 'sign exchange' have made an enormous contribution. One could even envisage all marketing behaviour being conceptualized in terms of semiotic exchanges. Even if it were possible to construct a new marketing theory on this basis, Baudrillard's conceptualization of his 'critique of the political economy of the sign' is in this regard essentially *structuralist* (Marxist even) unlike his later ideas (such as hyperreality, fragmentation, simulation and free-floating signifiers) which can more easily be labelled *postmodernist* . And overall, as Hetrick and Lozada (1999) point out, postmodernism is essentially 'anti-theory' with its denial of the grand narrative. A postmodern marketing *theory* would appear to be an oxymoron (although I suppose its advocates would say that is precisely the point – and I've missed it!) and therefore this is unlikely to be capable of providing a general theory of marketing.

Critical theory attempts to look beneath the explanations and arguments of traditional marketing theories in order to unveil a 'deeper' reality and structures. Based on the Frankfurt school, particularly the ideas of Jürgen Habermas and Herbert Marcuse, this approach has had some impact on theory in marketing communications, consumer behaviour and green marketing in particular. Following Habermas (1971), critical theory distinguishes between: (i) empirical-analytical knowledge concerned with prediction and control; (ii) historical-hermeneutic knowledge, concerned with communicative interpretation in culture and discourse; and (iii) critical-emancipatory knowledge concerned with self-reflection, power relation and liberation. There are many areas of marketing where the critical theory approach can help researchers go beyond the 'one-dimensional' (Marcuse, 1964) perspective of existing theories and methods (Schroeder, 2007) and ask deeper questions, but, like postmodernism, it is unlikely to provide the basis for a complete marketing theory (Saren et al., 2007).

With so many different philosophies, methods and theories in the discipline and yet with so little agreement about marketing research in the academy, it may be that 'better theory' in the subject will inevitably be partial. In any case, several European academics have concluded that with so many new ideas being applied in so many different fields, from consumer behaviour to marketing ethics, there remains a strong case for 'rethinking marketing' again (Brownlie et al., 1999) as another step to realigning research in the future.

_____ **Recommended further reading** _____

Baker, M.J. (1995a) *Companion Encyclopaedia of Marketing*, Routledge, London, pp. 1003–18.
Brownlie, D., Saren, M., Wensley, R. and Whittington, R. (eds) (1999) *Rethinking Marketing: Towards Critical Marketing Accountings*, London: Sage Publications.
Coviello, N.E., Brodie, R.J., Danaher, P.J. and Johnston, W.J. (2002) 'How firms relate to their markets: An empirical examination of contemporary marketing practice', *Journal of Marketing* 66(8): 33–46.
Day, G.S. and Wensley, R. (1983) 'Marketing theory with a strategic orientation', *Journal of Marketing* 47, Fall: 79–89.

Dholakia, N. and Arndt, J. (eds) (1985) *Changing the Course of Marketing: Alternative Paradigms for Widening Marketing Theory* (Research in Marketing Supplement 2), Greenwich, CT: JAI Press.

Grönroos, C. and Gummerson, E. (1985) *Service Marketing: Nordic School Perspectives*, Stockholm: Stockholm University.

Hunt, S.D. (1991) *Marketing Theory: Conceptual Foundations of Research in Marketing*, Homewood, IL: Irwin.

Kjellberg, H. and Helgesson, C. (2007) 'On the nature of markets and their practices', *Marketing Theory* 7(2): 137–62.

Lusch, R. and Vargo, S. (2006a) *The Service Dominant Logic of Marketing: Dialog, Debate and Directions*, New York: M.E. Sharpe.

Maclaran, P., Saren, M. and Tadajewski, M. (eds) (2008) *Marketing Theory*, Volumes I, II & III, Sage Library in Marketing Series, London: Sage Publications.

Mattsson, L.G. (1997) 'Relationship marketing and markets-as-networks approach: A comparative analysis of two evolving streams of research' (Guest Lecture, 20 February, University of Auckland, New Zealand).

Porter, L. and McKibben, L. (1988) *Management Education and Development: Drift or Thrust into the 21st Century?*, New York: McGraw Hill.

Sheth, J.M., Gardner, D.M. and Garrett, D.E. (1988) *Marketing Theory: Evolution and Evaluation*, Wiley: New York.

Zaltman, G., LeMasters, K. and Heffring, M. (1982) *Theory Construction in Marketing*, New York: John Wiley & Sons.

References

Alderson, W. (1957) *Marketing Behaviour and Executive Action*, Homewood, IL: Richard D. Irwin.

Alderson, W. and Cox, R. (1948) 'Towards a theory of marketing', *Journal of Marketing* 13, October: 137–52.

American Marketing Association (AMA) (1988) 'Task force on the development of marketing thought. "Developing, disseminating and utilizing marketing knowledge"', *Journal of Marketing* 52, Fall: 1–25.

Anderson, J.M. (1994) 'Marketing science: where's the beef?', *Business Horizons* January–February: 8–16.

Anderson, M. (1992) 'What! Me teach? I am a professor', *Wall Street Journal* 8 September: 16.

Anderson, P.F. (1983) 'Marketing, scientific progress and scientific method', *Journal of Marketing* 47, Fall: 18–31.

Anderson, P.F. (1986) 'On method in consumer research: a critical relativist perspective', *Journal of Consumer Research* 13, September: 155–73.

Araujo, L., Kjellberg, H. and Spencer, R. (2008) 'Market practices and forms: introduction to the special issue', *Marketing Theory* 8(1): 5–14.

Armstrong, J.S. (1982) 'Barriers to scientific contribution – the author's formula', *Behavioural and Brain Sciences* 5: 197–9.

Arndt, J. (1985) 'On making marketing science more scientific: role of orientations, paradigms, metaphors, and puzzle solving', *Journal of Marketing* 49, Summer: 18–23.

Arnould, E.J. and Thompson, C.J. (2005) 'Consumer Culture Theory (CCT): twenty years of research', *Journal of Consumer Research* 31(4): 868–82.

Bacharach, S.B. (1989) 'Organizational theories: some criteria for evaluation', *Academy of Management Review* 14(4): 496–515.

Bagozzi, R.P. (1978) 'Marketing as exchange: a theory of transactions in the marketplace', *American Behavioral Scientist* 21, March/April: 535–56.

Bagozzi, R.P. (1980) *Causal Models in Marketing*, New York: Wiley.

Baker, M.J. (1995a) *Companion Encyclopaedia of Marketing*, Routledge, London, pp. 1003–18.

Baker, M. (1995b) *Marketing: Theory and Practice*, London: Macmillan Press.

Bartels, R. (1951) 'Can marketing be a science? *Journal of Marketing* January: 319–28.

Bartels, R. (1968) 'The general theory of marketing', *Journal of Marketing* 32, January: 29–33.

Baudrillard, J. (1981) *For a Critique of the Political Economy of the Sign*, New York: Telos Press.

Baumol, W. (1957) 'On the role of marketing theory', *Journal of Marketing* April: 413–8.

Belk, R.W. (1986) Art versus science as ways of generating knowledge about materialism. In Brinberg, D. and Lutz, R.J. (Eds.), Perspectives on methodology in consumer research, pp. 3–17. New York: Springer-Veriag.

Brodie, R.J., Coviello, N.E. and Winklhofer, H. (2008) 'Investigating contemporary marketing practices: a review of the first decade of the CMP research program', *Journal of Business and Industrial Marketing*, 23(2): 84–94.

Brown, S. (1995) *Postmodern Marketing*, London: Routledge.

Brownlie, D. and Saren, M. (1995) 'On the commodification of marketing knowledge', *Journal of Marketing Management* 11(7): 619–28.

Brownlie, D. and Saren, M. (1996) 'Beyond the one-dimensional marketing manager: the discourse of theory, practice and relevance', *International Journal of Research in Marketing* 14: 147–61.

Brownlie, D., Saren, M., Wensley, R. and Whittington, R. (eds) (1999) *Rethinking Marketing: Towards Critical Marketing Accountings*, London: Sage Publications.

Burrell, G. and Morgan, G. (1979) *Sociological Paradigms and Organisational Analysis*, London: Heinemann.

Buzzell, R. (1963) 'Is marketing a science?', *Harvard Business Review* January–February: 32–48.

Campbell, N., O'Driscoll, A. and Saren, M. (2009) 'The posthuman: the end and the beginning of the human', EIASM Workshop on Interpretive Methods in Consumer Research, Milan, April.

Carmen, J.M. (1980) 'Paradigms for marketing theory', in J.N. Sheth (ed.) *Research in Marketing*, Vol. 3, Greenwich, CT: JAI Press.

Converse, Paul D. (1945) 'The development of the science of marketing – an exploratory survey'. *Journal of Marketing* 10, July: 14–23.

Cova, B. and Badot, O. (1995) 'Marketing theory and practice in a postmodern era', in M.J. Baker *Marketing: Theory and Practice*, (3rd edn), London: Macmillan Press.

Coviello, N.E., Brodie, R.J., Danaher, P.J. and Johnston, W.J. (2002) 'How firms relate to their markets: An empirical examination of contemporary marketing practice', *Journal of Marketing* 66(8): 33–46.

Cunningham, W. and Sheth, J.N. (1982) 'From the editor', *Journal of Marketing*, Spring: 11–2.

Day, G.S. and Wensley, R. (1983) 'Marketing theory with a strategic orientation', *Journal of Marketing* 47, Fall: 79–89.

Deshpande, R. (1983) 'Paradigms lost: on theory and method in research in marketing', *Journal of Marketing* 47, Fall: 101–10.

Dholakia, N. and Arndt, J. (eds) (1985) *Changing the Course of Marketing: Alternative Paradigms for Widening Marketing Theory* (Research in Marketing Supplement 2), Greenwich, CT: JAI Press.

Firat, A.F. (1990) 'The consumer in postmodernity', in R.H. Holman and M.R. Solomon (eds) *Advances in Consumer Research*, Provo, UT: Association for Consumer Research.

Firat, A.F. (1991) 'Postmodern culture, marketing and the consumer', in T.L. Childers et al. (eds) *Marketing Theory and Application*. Chicago, IL: AMA.

Firat, A.F. and Venkatesh, A. (1993) 'Postmodernity: the age of marketing', *International Journal of Research in Marketing*, 10(3): 227–49.

Fisk, G. and Meyers, P. (1982) 'Macromarketers' guide to paradigm', in R. Bush and S.D. Hunt (eds) *Marketing Theory: Philosophy of Science Perspectives*, Chicago: AMA.

Ford, I.D. (1990) (ed.) *Understanding Business Markets: Interaction, Relationships and Networks*, New York: Academic Press.

Foucault, M. (1980) *Power/Knowledge: Selected Interviews and Other Writings* (ed. C. Gordon) New York: Pantheon Books.

Fullerton, R. (1986) 'Historicism: what it is and what it means for consumer research', in M. Wallendorf and P. Anderson (eds) *Advances in Consumer Research* 14, Association for Consumer Research, pp. 431–4.

Fullerton, R. (1988) 'How modern is modern marketing? Marketing's evolution and the myth of the production era', *Journal of Marketing* 52, January: 108–25.

Greyser, S. (1997) 'Janus and marketing: the past, present and prospective future of marketing', in D.R. Lehman and K.E. Jocz *Reflections on the Futures of Marketing: Practice and Education*, Cambridge, MA: Marketing Science Institute.

Grönroos, C. and Gummerson, E. (1985) *Service Marketing: Nordic School Perspectives*, Stockholm: Stockholm University.

Habermas, J. (1971) *Towards a Rational Society*, Oxford: Heinemann.

Håkansson, H. (ed.) (1982) *International Marketing and Purchasing of Industrial Goods – An Interaction Approach*. New York: Wiley.

Halbert, M. (1965) *The Meaning and Sources of Marketing Theory*, New York: McGraw Hill.

Heideggar, M. (1962) *Being and Time* (trans. J. McQuarrie and E. Robison), New York: Harper Row.

Heffring, M. (1985) 'A theory-in-use approach to developing marketing theories', in N. Dholakia and J. Arndt (eds) (1985) *Changing the Course of Marketing: Alternative Paradigms for Widening Marketing Theory* (Research in Marketing Supplement 2), Greenwich, CT: JAI Press.

Hetrick, W. and Lozada, H. (1999) 'From marketing theory to marketing anti-theory: implications of ethical critique within the (post) modern experience', in D., Brownlie M., Saren R. Wensley and R. Whittington (eds) *Rethinking Marketing: Towards Critical Marketing Accountings*, London: Sage Publications.

Hirschman, E. and Holbrook, M. (1992) *Postmodern Consumer Research: The Study of Consumption as Text*, London: Sage Publications.

Holbrook, M. (1989) 'Aftermath of the task force: dogmatism and catastrophe in marketing thought', *ACR Newsletter*, President's column, September: 1–11.

Hunt, S.D. (1971) 'The morphology of theory and the general theory of marketing', *Journal of Marketing* 35, April: 65–8.

Hunt, S.D. (1976) 'The nature and scope of marketing', *Journal of Marketing* 40, July: 17–28.

Hunt, S.D. (1983) 'General theories and the fundamental explananda of marketing', *Journal of Marketing* 47, Fall: 9–17.

Hunt, S.D. (1984) 'Should marketers adopt relativism?', in Anderson, P.F. and Ryan, M.J. (eds.) *Scientific Method in Marketing: AMA Winter Educators Conference Proceedings*, Chicago: American Marketing Association, pp. 30–4.

Hunt, S.D. (1991) *Marketing Theory: Conceptual Foundations of Research in Marketing*, Homewood, IL: Irwin.

Hunt, S.D. (1993) 'Objectivity in marketing theory and research', *Journal of Marketing* 57, April: 76–91.

Hunt, S. (1994) 'On rethinking marketing: our discipline, our practice, our methods', *European Journal of Marketing* (special edition on the New Marketing Myopia: Critical Perspectives on Theory and Research in Marketing) 28(3): 13–25.

Jones, D.G.B. and Monieson, D.D. (1990) 'Early development in the philosophy of marketing thought', *Journal of Marketing* 54(1): 102–13.

Kavanagh, D. (1994) 'Hunt versus Anderson: round 16', *European Journal of Marketing* 28(3): 26–41.

Keat, R. and Urry, J. (1975) *Social Theory as Science*, London: Routledge and Kegan Paul.

Kerin, R. (1996) 'In pursuit of an ideal: the editorial and literary history of the *Journal of Marketing*', *Journal of Marketing*, 60(1): 1–13.

Kjellberg, H. and Helgesson, C. (2007) 'On the nature of markets and their practices', *Marketing Theory* 7(2): 137–62.

Kuhn, T. (1962) *The Structure of Scientific Revolutions*, Chicago, IL: University of Chicago Press.

Lehman, D.R. and Jocz, K.E. (1997) *Reflections on the Futures of Marketing: Practice and Education*, Cambridge, MA: Marketing Science Institute.

Llewelyn, S. (2003) 'What counts as "theory" in qualitative management and accounting research? Introducing five levels of theorizing', *Accounting, Auditing & Accountability Journal* 16(4): 662–708.

Lusch, R. and Vargo, S. (2006) *The Service Dominant Logic of Marketing: Dialog, Debate and Directions*, New York: M.E. Sharpe.

Maclaran, P., Saren, M. and Tadajewski, M. (eds) (2008) *Marketing Theory*, Volumes I, II & III, Sage Library in Marketing Series, London: Sage Publications.

Maclaran, P., Saren, M., Goulding, C. and Stevens, L. (2009) 'Rethinking theory building and theorizing in marketing', European Academy of Marketing Conference, Nantes, France.

McGary, E.D. (1953) 'Some new viewpoints in marketing', *Journal of Marketing* XVIII (1), July: 33–40.

McInnes, W.C. (1964) 'A conceptual approach to marketing', in R. Cox, W. Alderson and S. Shapiro (eds) *Theory in Marketing* (2nd Series), Homewood, IL: Richard D. Irwin Inc.

McMullin, E. (1984) 'A case for scientific realism', in J. Leplin (ed.) *Scientific Realism*, Berkeley: University of California Press.

Marcuse, H. (1964) *One-Dimensional Man: Studies in the Ideology of Advanced Industrial Society*, London: Routledge & Kegan Paul.

Mason, J.B. (1990) 'Improving marketing education in the 1990s: a dean's perspective', *Marketing Education Review* November: 10–21.

Mattsson, L.G. (1985) 'An Application of the network approach to marketing', in N. Dholakia and J. Arndt (eds) *Changing the Course of Marketing: Alternative Paradigms for Widening Marketing Theory*, Greenwich, CT: JAI Press.

Mattsson, L.G. (1997) 'Relationship marketing and markets-as-networks approach: A comparative analysis of two evolving streams of research' (Guest Lecture, 20 February, University of Auckland, New Zealand).

Merton, R.K. (1948) 'Discussion', *American Sociological Review* 13: 164–8.

Mick, D.G. (1986) 'Consumer research and semiotics: exploring the morphology of signs, symbols and significance', *Journal of Consumer Research* September: 196–213.

Morgan, G. (1980) 'Paradigms, metaphors and puzzle-solving in organisation theory', *Administrative Science Quarterly* 25, December: 605–22.

Morgan, G. (1992) 'Marketing discourse and practice', in M. Alvesson and H. Willmott (eds) *Critical Management Studies*, London: Sage Publications.

Murray, J.B., Evers, D.J. and Janda, S. (1997) 'Marketing, theory borrowing and critical reflection', *Journal of Macromarketing* 15(2): 92–106.

Myers, J.G., Greyser, S. and Massey, W. (1979) 'The effectiveness of marketing's R & D for marketing management: an assessment', *Journal of Marketing* January: 17–29.

Myers, J.G., Massey, W. and Greyser, S. (1980) *Marketing Research and Knowledge Development: An Assessment for Marketing Management*, Englewood Cliffs, NJ: Prentice Hall.

Nevett, T. (1991) 'Historical investigation and the practice of marketing', *Journal of Marketing* 55, July: 13–23.

Peter, P.J. (1992) 'Realism or relativism for marketing theory research: a comment on Hunt's "scientific realism"', *Journal of Marketing* 56, April: 72–29.

Porter, L. and McKibben, L. (1988) *Management Education and Development: Drift or Thrust into the 21st Century?*, New York: McGraw Hill.

Reibstein, D.J., Day, G. and Wind, J. (2009) 'Is marketing academia losing its way?', *Journal of Marketing* 73, July: 1–3.

Rudner, R. (1966) *Philosophy of Social Science*, Englewood Cliffs, NJ: Prentice Hall.

Ryan, M. and O'Shaunessy, J. (1980) 'Theory development: the need to distinguish the levels of abstraction', in C. Lamb and P. Dunne (eds) *Theoretical Developments in Marketing*, Chicago, IL: AMA.

Saren, M. and Pels J., (2008) 'A Comment on paradox and middle-range theory', *Journal of Business and Industrial Marketing* 23(2): 105–7.

Saren, M., Maclaran, P., Goulding, Elliott, R., C., Shankar, A. and Catterall, M. (2007) (eds) *Critical Marketing: Defining the Field*, London: Elsevier.

Savitt, R. (1980) 'Historical research in marketing', *Journal of Marketing* 44, Fall: 52–8.

Schembri, S. (2006) 'Rationalizing service logic, or understanding services as experience?', *Marketing Theory* 6(3): 281–8.

Schroeder, J.E. (2007) 'Critical marketing: insights for informed research and teaching', in M. Saren, P. Maclaran, C. Goulding, R. Elliott, A. Shankar and M. Caterall (eds) *Critical Marketing: Defining the Field*, London: Elsevier.

Sherry, J.F. Jr. (1990) 'Postmodern alternatives: the interpretive turn in consumer research', in H. Kassarjian and T. Robertson (eds) *Handbook of Research*, Englewood Cliffs, NJ: Prentice Hall.

Sheth, J.N. and Gardener, D.M. (1988) 'History of marketing thought: an update', in R. Bush and S.D. Hunt (eds) *Marketing Theory: Philosophy of Science Perspectives*, Chicago: AMA.

Tadajewski, M. (2006) 'The ordering of marketing theory: the influence of McCarthyism and the Cold War', *Marketing Theory* 6(2): 163–99.

Van de Ven, A.H. (1989) 'Nothing is quite so practical as a good theory', *Academy of Management Review* 14(4): 486–90.

Vaile, R. (1949) 'Towards a theory of marketing – a comment', *Journal of Marketing* 14, April: 520–22.

Vargo, S.L. and Lusch, R.F (2004) 'Evolving to a new dominant logic for marketing', *Journal of Marketing*, 68(1): 1–17.

Venkatesh, A. (1985) 'Is Marketing Ready for Kuhn?', in N. Dholakia and J. Arndt (eds) (1985) *Changing the Course of Marketing: Alternative Paradigms for Widening Marketing Theory (*Research in Marketing Supplement 2), Greenwich, CT: JAI Press.

Venkatesh, A. (1989) 'Modernity and post modernity: a synthesis or antithesis', in T.L. Childers et al. (eds) *Marketing Theory and Application.* Chicago, IL: AMA.

Webster, Frederick, (1992) 'The Changing Role of Marketing in the Corporation', *Journal of Marketing*, 56(1): 1–17.

Wensley, R. (1995) 'A critical review of research in marketing', *British Journal of Management* 6: S63–S82.

Wilkie, W.L. and Moore, E.S. (2003) 'Scholarly research in marketing: exploring the "4 Eras" of thought development', *Journal of Public Policy and Marketing* 22(2): 116–46.

Zaltman, G., Pinson, C. and Angelmar, R. (1973) *Metatheory and Consumer Research*, New York: Holt Rinehart and Winston Inc.

Zaltman, G., LeMasters, K. and Heffring, M. (1982) *Theory Construction in Marketing*, New York: John Wiley & Sons.

3

A history of historical research in marketing

D.G. Brian Jones

Introduction

The purpose of this chapter is to review historical research in marketing. Because of space limitations, this review is more a chronicle of what has been published about historical research in marketing than a critical historical analysis, hopefully providing the reader with a roadmap to further reading on historical topics of interest. Scholars in a wide range of disciplines have published historical research about marketing and have done so in various publications, many outside what would be considered the 'marketing literature'. Except for some overall frequencies of publication reported in this introduction, this review has focused mostly on historical research published in marketing periodicals and in books.

The discipline of marketing emerged early in the twentieth century as a branch of applied economics strongly influenced by the German Historical School and its offspring, the American Institutional School (Jones and Monieson, 1990). Thus, from its beginnings the academic study of marketing was influenced by an historical perspective. However, for economists studying marketing at the turn of the twentieth century, history was a means to an end rather than an end in itself. Marketing economists during that era studied the histories of marketing practices carried out in industries and by firms in order to discover marketing functions and principles.

The earliest university courses in marketing in North America were taught in 1902/03 when the Universities of Illinois, Michigan and California offered the first courses in what was then called distribution (Bartels, 1962). The term 'marketing' was used by economists in a manner consistent with current practice as early as 1897 (Bussiere, 2000) and gradually replaced 'distribution'. A handful of general marketing texts was published by 1920 (Converse, 1933) and the first scholarly journals on the subject appeared in the mid-1930s, merging to form the *Journal of Marketing* in 1936 (Witkowski, 2007). Their sponsoring associations, the American Marketing Society and the National Association of Marketing Teachers, also merged to form the American Marketing Association on 1 January 1937. As the marketing discipline crystallized in the 1930s, scholars began to reflect on their heritage and published what today is considered some of the earliest historical research in marketing.

With some exceptions, historical research about marketing and marketing-related subjects is conducted by two relatively distinct groups of scholars – marketing professors working in business schools, and business history professors who, for the most part, work in history departments. Again, with some exceptions, these two groups tend to present their work at different academic conferences and publish in different journals. Throughout this chapter we'll focus mostly, but not exclusively, on the work of marketing historians publishing in marketing periodicals as well as books.

Marketing historians usually recognize two overlapping, but relatively distinct, general fields within historical research in marketing – 'marketing history', and the 'history of marketing thought'. Marketing history includes, but is not limited to, the histories of advertising, retailing, channels of distribution, product design and branding, pricing strategies, and consumption behaviour – all studied from the perspective of companies, industries, or even whole economies. The history of marketing thought examines marketing ideas, concepts, theories, and schools of marketing thought including the lives and times of marketing thinkers. This incorporates biographical studies as well as histories of institutions and associations involved in the development of the marketing discipline. These two fields or categories of historical research provide one of the two main organizing themes for this chapter. The other theme, of course, is chronological. The history of historical research in marketing is divided here into three eras: (1) 1930–1959; (2) 1960–1979; and (3) 1980–present. Periodization in this case is driven by turning-points in the material being reviewed (Hollander et al., 2005), developments that occurred during the early 1960s and early 1980s.

As detailed below, marketing history as History began to be published during the early 1930s. The 1960s saw a decline of interest in historical research by marketing scholars, probably driven by an increasing pragmatism in business education during that time. Nevertheless, the scope and rigour of individual works published after 1960 was improved considerably over earlier research. During the early 1980s, a number of specialized conferences, collections of readings, and special issues of periodicals fuelled a dramatic growth of interest in historical research in marketing. This growth of interest is illustrated in Table 3.1 which shows the cumulative number of publications on historical research in marketing by decade since 1930, as listed in the Google Scholar database. That database includes peer-reviewed papers, theses, books, abstracts and articles from academic publishers, professional societies, reprint repositories, universities and other scholarly

Table 3.1 Cumulative volume of publications in historical research in marketing, 1930–2009

Search Phrase	Up to:	1930	1940	1950	1960	1970	1980	1990	2000	2009
Retailing history		0	0	2	5	7	17	38	77	147
Advertising history		3	5	8	12	21	67	151	315	553
Marketing history		1	5	6	8	19	33	117	342	837
History of marketing thought		0	0	0	0	1	4	17	49	141
Total		4	10	16	25	48	121	323	783	1,678

Note: All data are end-of-decade count
Source: Google Scholar, accessed 9 June 2009.

organizations. Using the search phrases 'marketing history', 'retailing history' (with 'marketing history' excluded to avoid double counting), 'advertising history' (again, 'marketing history' excluded), and 'history of marketing thought', yielded a cumulative 1,678 publications in historical research in marketing from 1930 through May 2009. These searches probably understate the amount of publishing activity in historical research in marketing since some authors undoubtedly do not use those phrases in their published work. For example, during the 1930s and 1940s there were a number of studies published in the *Journal of Marketing* about the origins of the marketing discipline that do not show up in these searches of the Google Scholar database.

Of course, not all of the publications counted in Table 3.1 were reviewed for this chapter. The relatively smaller number of publications through the 1970s was manageable. However, as Table 3.1 indicates, since 1980 and especially during the past decade there has been dramatic growth of publication activity in this field. For that more recent period this review is more selective, focusing on major publications in the marketing periodical literature as well as the most relevant books.

_____ Recording the facts: 1930–1959 _____

The first scholarly marketing journals, *The Journal of Retailing*, *The American Marketing Journal* and *The National Marketing Review*, began publication in 1925, 1934, and 1935 respectively, with the last two merging in 1936 to form the *Journal of Marketing*. The sponsoring organizations for the two parent journals, the American Marketing Society and National Association of Marketing Teachers, also merged in 1937 to form the American Marketing Association (AMA). These developments provided an important impetus for historical work as they naturally led to reflection about the origins and development of the marketing discipline. At the same time, the *Journal of Marketing* provided a specialized outlet for the publication of such historical reflection. Thus, beginning in the early 1930s there were a number of attempts to put things on the record.

History of marketing thought

From the early 1930s to late 1950s historical research in marketing was dominated by the study of marketing thought. During this period, attention was focused on tracing the earliest literature (Applebaum, 1947, 1952; Bartels, 1951; Converse, 1933, 1945; Coolsen, 1947; Maynard, 1951) and marketing courses taught in American universities (Bartels, 1951; Hagerty, 1936; Hardy, 1954; Litman, 1950; Maynard, 1941; Weld, 1941). The earliest historical study included in this review was Converse's (1933) 'The first decade of marketing literature', published in the *NATMA Bulletin*. Converse's article was typical in its attempt to identify historically significant events. In his opinion the first modern books on marketing were Nystrom's (1915) *The Economics of Retailing* and A.W. Shaw's (1915) *Some Problems in Market Distribution*.

Other early historical studies focused on the individuals and organizations that pioneered the development of the discipline (Agnew, 1941; Bartels, 1951; Converse, 1959b). A series of 23 biographical sketches published in the *Journal of Marketing* between 1956 and 1962 was later reprinted as a collection edited by Wright and Dimsdale (1974) and subsequently reprinted along with other, more recent biographies of other pioneer marketing scholars in Tadajewski and Jones (2008). Bartels' (1951) article titled 'Influences on the development of marketing thought, 1900–1923' was seminal in its attempt to go beyond a simple chronicle of 'firsts'. It drew upon numerous interviews of pioneer scholars in order to examine some of the sources of early marketing ideas. Bartels' article was also the most ambitious historical analysis at that time as it was based on his (1941) doctoral dissertation at Ohio State University, the first such work known.

During the 1950s a trend began towards focusing on the history of marketing concepts (Breen, 1959; Kelley, 1956), theories (McGarry, 1953), and schools of thought (Brown, 1951). Cassels (1936) had earlier examined the influence of significant schools of economic thought on marketing, but it wasn't until the 1950s that marketing *ideas* or *concepts* were developed enough to warrant a retrospective. An important collection of such articles was published in 1951 under the title *Changing Perspectives in Marketing*. It claimed to be 'one of the few, if not the only one, in which a series of papers has been compiled to give historical treatment and perspective to the development of marketing [thought]' (Wales, 1951: v). This included topics such as retailing, sales management, marketing research and marketing theory. Its contributors were eminent scholars in marketing. Most had been recipients of the American Marketing Association's prestigious Paul D. Converse Award.

Marketing history

There was less research done during this early period on marketing history, most of which focused on the history of retailing and wholesaling (Barger, 1955; Emmet and Jeuck, 1950; Jones, 1936; Kirkwood, 1960; Marburg, 1951; Nystrom, 1951; Phillips, 1935). Barger's (1955) book titled, *Distribution's Place in the American Economy Since 1869*, examined the changing role of wholesale and retail sectors in the

American economy from 1869 to 1950. It was a unique study of the cost and output of distribution, and of the relative importance of wholesale and retail sectors as measured by the proportion of the labour force engaged in each. Early books on retailing history included Hower's (1946) history of the R.H. Macy department store; the well-known classic history of mail-order house Sears, Roebuck and Company by Emmet and Jeuck (1950); and histories of the F.W. Woolworth chain store by Phillips (1935) and Kirkwood (1960).

A more general history of marketing, distinctive both for its scope of subject matter and for its breadth of historical perspective, was Hotchkiss' (1938) *Milestones of Marketing*. Using the American Marketing Association's definition of marketing to guide his choice of topics, Hotchkiss traced what he believed to be the most important steps in the evolution of marketing back to ancient Rome and Greece through medieval England to modern North American practices, focusing on retailing, advertising and merchandising.

Another marketing history which complemented the Hotchkiss book in time period by focusing on marketing practices of the early twentieth century was Converse's (1959a) *Fifty Years of Marketing in Retrospect*. This was written as a companion to his (1959b) study of the beginnings of marketing thought cited earlier. Converse described his marketing history book as 'the story of business and particularly of market distribution as I have seen it and as I have studied it' (1959a: vi). In addition to marketing practices such as advertising and promotion, pricing and merchandising, Converse described the changing economic conditions and technological developments during the early twentieth century that influenced such practices.

Throughout this early period, historical research was relatively descriptive as marketers focused on recording the facts of marketing history and the history of marketing thought. The most prolific and perhaps most important contributor during this era was Paul D. Converse whose two monographs published in 1959 are typical of historical research in marketing to that point in time.

Foundations of the new marketing history: 1960–1979

The 1960s was a transition period with fewer, but more ambitious studies of marketing history and the history of marketing thought. A number of significant works and events laid the foundation for the growth of interest in historical research evident today. For example, during the early 1960s successive conferences of the American Marketing Association featured tracks on historical research (Greyser, 1963; Smith, 1964). Most of the papers presented at those sessions called for more historical research and offered justifications for doing such work and, in that way, helped to legitimate subsequent historical research. Although there was a notable decline in the number of publications in the periodical literature (Grether, 1976), several important books were published. Four books in rapid succession were published on the history of marketing thought (Bartels, 1962; Converse, 1959b; Coolsen, 1960; Schwartz, 1963). A wide-ranging collection of work on seventeenth-, eighteenth-, and nineteenth-century marketing practices was also published (Shapiro and Doody, 1968). And finally, a carefully researched, well-documented study of changes in American distribution channels during the nineteenth century provided some foundation for later studies of retailing history (Porter and Livesay, 1971).

History of marketing thought

Converse's (1959b) *The Beginnings of Marketing Thought in the United States* served as a transition, both in time and in depth of analysis, in the study of the history of marketing thought. One of Converse's students, Frank Coolsen, followed with a dissertation on the marketing ideas of four nineteenth-century liberal economists (Edward Atkinson, David Wells, Arthur Farquhar and Henry Farquhar), which was published in 1960 under the title *Marketing Thought in the United States in the Late Nineteenth Century*. According to Coolsen, the writings of those four economists presented a fairly comprehensive view of the scope and importance of marketing in the late nineteenth century. However, their work did not have much influence on the early twentieth century development of the marketing discipline (Jones and Shaw, 2002).

Two other books on the history of marketing thought which complemented each other were Bartels' (1962) *The Development of Marketing Thought* and Schwartz's (1963) *Development of Marketing Theory*. Bartels' book was essentially a chronology of published literature, university courses, and events that had played a role in the development of marketing thought since 1900. Schwartz was more concerned with specific theories in marketing. His was a more concentrated and rigorous follow-up to the 1951 collection edited by Hugh Wales (cited above). In addition to examining the development of well-recognized marketing theories such as retail gravitation, regional theory, marketing functions and Alderson's functionalist theory, Schwartz included chapters examining the potential contribution of fields such as social physics and game theory. That may explain why it has been largely ignored by students of the history of marketing thought. Bartels' book (1962), on the other hand, was twice updated (1976, 1988) and became a staple reading for many doctoral courses in North America. In addition to those general works, there were a few studies of specific concepts and theories during the 1960s. Examples included Hollander's historical analysis of retailing institutions (1960, 1963a, 1966), and historical examinations of marketing management by Keith (1960), Lazer (1965) and LaLonde and Morrison (1967).

During the 1960s some researchers began to integrate marketing history with the history of marketing thought. Such work went beyond the narrower approach of earlier writings by using the history of marketing practice to interpret the development of marketing thought. A good example of this was Hollander's work, cited above, and more recently his re-examination of the origins of the marketing concept (1986). Hollander's distinctive approach to historical research was deconstructed by Rassuli (1988).

_____ Marketing history _____

As the marketing discipline moved away from the traditional institutional and commodity schools of thought and began to popularize marketing functions through the managerial approach, research into marketing history during the 1960s reflected that trend. This included historical research in advertising and promotion (McKendrick, 1960), product innovation (Silk and Stern, 1963), and personal selling (Hollander, 1963b, 1964). A broad range of marketing history, especially in economic development, regulation, institutions and advertising, was covered in Shapiro and Doody's (1968) *Readings in the History of American Marketing: Settlement to Civil War*. As editors of that extensive collection, Shapiro and Doody stated that their objective was to 'awaken the interest of students of marketing in history and historical analysis' (1968: 12). Their book of readings and Bartels' (1962) *Development of Marketing Thought* were probably the most important publications during the 1960s. In both of those books the scope of coverage was unprecedented.

However, as the 1960s drew to a close there seemed to be a decline of interest in historical research in marketing. After the publication of the Gordon and Howell (1959) report, the marketing discipline moved during the 1960s in a more quantitative, scientific direction and historical research may have seemed less rigorous and less relevant.

_____ The new marketing history: 1980–2009 _____

Returning to Table 3.1, the increase in number of publications since 1980 is dramatic. During the 1980s, a number of specialized conferences, collections of readings, and special issues of periodicals fuelled tremendous growth of interest in historical research in marketing. Perhaps most important was the organization of the biennial North American Marketing History Conference. In 1983 the first North American Workshop on Historical Research in Marketing was held at Michigan State University. That conference, now known as the Conference on Historical Analysis & Research in Marketing (CHARM), has been held biennially ever since. At 14 conferences over the past 26 years there have been 487 papers presented and published in the CHARM proceedings. The entire collection of papers is available online at the CHARM website, www.charmassociation.org. A history of the CHARM conference and content analysis of the first 13 conference proceedings is provided by Jones et al. (2009).

In the early 1990s, CHARM became a major contributor of content for the *Journal of Macromarketing* (see Jones and Shaw (2006) for a review of that body of work). From 1994 through 2008 historical research accounted for 72 of the 196 full articles published in *JMM* representing fully 37 per cent of that journal's content. Most of those articles were first presented at a CHARM conference. More recently, the CHARM Association was the driving force behind the new *Journal of Historical Research in Marketing*, which began publication in March 2009.

In 1985 and 1988 the Association for Consumer Research and American Marketing Association respectively held conferences that included a major focus on historical research in marketing. In 1990 the *Journal of the Academy of Marketing Science* published a special issue on the history of marketing thought. Most of those articles were originally papers presented at CHARM. Other journals to feature special issues on historical research in marketing included *Psychology & Marketing* in 1998 and *Marketing Theory* in 2005 and again in 2008. Since its inception in 2000, *Marketing Theory* has regularly published articles dealing with the history of marketing thought. In the UK, the University of Reading hosted conferences in 1991 and again in 1993 on historical research in marketing that resulted in the 1993 publication *The Rise and Fall of Mass Marketing* (Tedlow and Jones, 1993) which includes an interesting selection of papers about British marketing history. Strong interest in historical research in marketing in the UK is further evidenced by the formation in 1998 of the Centre for the History of Retailing and Distribution (CHORD) at the University of Wolverhampton which hosts annual workshops and seminars. Beyond these specialized marketing conferences and periodicals, there is a growing interest in marketing-related history by business historians which is represented by the Business History Conference and in periodicals such as *Enterprise & Society*, the *Business History Review*, *Economic History Review*, and others.

Reflecting on the increased volume, changing focus, and rigour of historical research in marketing since the early 1980s, Hollander and Rassuli described it as the 'new marketing history' (1993: xv). In addition to research on marketing history and the history of marketing thought, one of the important developments in historical research in marketing since 1980 is a growing discussion about the use of historical research methods in marketing.

Historical research methods and historical research in marketing

If one were looking for a single publication that signalled the emergence (or rather, the revival) of history as a 'legitimate' field within the marketing discipline, it might be Savitt's (1980) 'Historical Research in Marketing' published in the *Journal of Marketing*. In substance it was a statement of the rationale and method for historical research, although in the latter, only one of a range of possible approaches. In spirit Savitt's article was both a symbol of the legitimacy of doing historical research by marketing scholars, and a challenge to them to do so. As a statement on method, Savitt's article initiated a much needed discussion in the marketing literature about the theory and methods of historical scholarship.

'Historical Research in Marketing' thus represented an early attempt to articulate some of the methodological issues faced by marketing scholars interested in doing historical research, as well as a rallying cry for more historical research by marketing scholars and, as such, it created a bridge to the mainstream marketing journals. More recently, Savitt (2009) used the format of a memoir to describe what he has learned about doing historical research over the last 30 years, how he learned, and how those lessons can be applied to historical research and teaching in marketing. Admitting that his earlier discussion of historical method was an oversimplified extension of logical positivism, Savitt's more recent work suggests a more interpretive approach to historical research in marketing. As Savitt (2009) concludes:

> **Good marketing history ... recognizes (1) historical events are in the past and cannot be known as contemporary events are known; (2) historical events are unique and unclassifiable; (3) history is about actions, statements, and the thoughts of human beings; and (4) historical events have irreducible richness and complexity. (2009: 198)**

It is important to recognize that history is a discipline or subject, not a singular research method or methodology. There is a wide range of methodological approaches to studying history, from positivistic (e.g. Hempel, 1959) to hermeneutic (e.g. Collingwood, 1974), or from scientific to traditional (Jones, 1993). Like marketing, history is viewed by some as a social science (Golder, 2000; Kumcu, 1987; Savitt, 1980; Smith and Lux, 1993) capable of producing scientific knowledge, and by others as an art or as one of the humanities (Fullerton, 1987; Jones, 1998; Nevett, 1991; Savitt, 2009; Stern, 1990; Witkowski and Jones, 2006). History as social science tends to rely on formal hypothesis testing, development and testing of theory, classification and quantification of data, statistical analysis, and generalization. History as art relies more on unique, qualitative evidence, creative interpretation and descriptive narrative, sometimes described as story-telling. Both of these methodological approaches are used in historical research in marketing, yet even such pluralism is considered inadequate by Brown et al.'s (2001) postmodern critique of historical research methods in marketing.

Fullerton (1987) and Jones (1993) distinguish between the philosophy of history, which is concerned with epistemological and ontological issues, and historical method – the techniques of data collection, analysis, and reporting that follow from the philosophy of history in which one believes. While the philosophical assumptions of most marketing historians may be evident from their work, they are seldom made explicit. Published work rarely includes discussion of research method beyond a description of source materials, if that. And while some of the contributors to this historiographic discussion in marketing acknowledge different points of views (Golder, 2000; Smith and Lux, 1993; Witkowski and Jones, 2008), there is to date no complete discussion of the range of possible methodological approaches to historical research in marketing.

In the echoes of discussions about the philosophy and method of marketing history, there have also been voices calling for more historical research (Fullerton, 1987; Savitt, 1980, 1982), and providing rationales for using marketing history in teaching (Nevett, 1989; Witkowski, 1989a). Nevett (1991) described how historical method relates to marketing decision-making and offered recommendations for applying historical thinking to marketing practice. As well, there are various descriptions of source materials for historical research in marketing (Jones, 1998; Pollay, 1979, 1988a; Rassuli and Hollander, 1986; Witkowski, 1994) and a discussion of various strategies for periodizing marketing history (Hollander et al., 2005).

———————— Marketing history ————————

Until the 1980s, historical research in marketing was dominated by interest in the history of marketing thought. That emphasis has since changed with most research now focusing on marketing history. Of the 487 papers presented at CHARM conferences from 1983 through 2009, 318 focused on marketing history (see Jones et al., 2009 for a content analysis of that body of work), the most popular topics being histories of industry/firm marketing strategies (94 papers), advertising history (74), macro-level consumption behaviour history (67), and the history of retailing and distribution channels (52). From 1981 through 2005, the 75 historical articles published in the *Journal of Macromarketing* included 47 that focused on marketing history (see Jones and Shaw (2006) for an historical review of that literature), with histories of marketing strategies leading in popularity followed by marketing regulation, retailing and channels, macro-level consumption behaviour and marketing systems.

The interest in histories of various aspects of marketing strategy, cited above, was also generally evident in periodicals and books that focused on advertising and promotion history (Beard, 2005; Branchik, 2007; Davis, 2007; De Iulio and Vinti, 2009; Fox, 1984; Gross and Sheth, 1989; Hawkins, 2009; Johnston, 2001; Jones et al., 2000; Kopp and Taylor, 1994; Laird, 1998; Lears, 1994; Marchand, 1985; Meyer, 1994; Mishra, 2009; Nevett, 1982; Pollay, 1984a, 1984b, 1985, 1988a, 1988b, 1994; Pollay and Lysonski, 1990; Pope, 1983; Robinson, 2004; Schudson, 1984; Sivulka, 1998; Stern, 1988; Witkowski, 2003), personal selling (Friedman, 2004), product simplification strategy (Hollander, 1984), product innovation (Keehn, 1994), channel management (Hull, 2008; Marx, 1985), segmentation strategy (Fullerton, 1985; Hollander and Germain, 1992; Tedlow, 1990), branding (Bakker, 2001; Church and Clark, 2001; Duguid, 2003; Golder, 2000; Koehn, 2001; Low and Fullerton, 1994), market research (Fullerton, 1990; Germain, 1994; Ward, 2009), retailing (Benson, 1986; Bevan, 2001; Dixon, 1994; Howard, 2008; Monod, 1996; Stanger, 2008; Witkowski, 2009), and marketing strategies in industries such as the public library system (Kleindle, 2007), and specific companies such as Nestle (Kose, 2007) and Singer (Godley, 2006). It would seem that no matter what your interest in marketing, there is now historical research about it in print.

As evident in Table 3.1, advertising and retailing are two major topics of interest within marketing history. In advertising history, the work of two marketing scholars is noteworthy. One of these was Terence Nevett who published extensively on the history of British advertising (1982, 1985, 1988a, 1988c, 1988d). Much of Nevett's work was comparative and cross cultural, for example, his study with Fullerton of societal perceptions of advertising in Britain and Germany (Fullerton and Nevett, 1986), and of American influences on British advertising (Nevett 1988a), as well as British influences on American advertising (1988c). At times his work has taken on a macromarketing perspective (Fullerton and Nevett, 1986; Nevett, 1985, 1988b) by looking at the impact of advertising on society. Others have also contributed to the study of British advertising history, focusing on specific companies (Ferrier, 1986; Seaton, 1986), professional sales promotion organizations (Leigh, 1986), and self-regulation in the advertising industry (Miracle and Nevett, 1988).

A second marketing scholar whose work on advertising history has been prominent is Richard Pollay. During the late 1970s Pollay observed that there were very few significant sources of advertising history (1979: 8) and those had been written outside the marketing discipline. To address that situation, he outlined an ambitious research programme for advertising history, including the justification, research method, and data sources required for such work (Pollay, 1977, 1978, 1979). Having identified and developed important archival sources (Pollay, 1979, 1988a), Pollay conducted a rigorous content analysis of twentieth-century American print advertising in order to identify the portrayed values (Belk and Pollay, 1985; Pollay, 1984a, 1988b), the extent of informativeness (1984b), and the creative aspects of advertising strategy (1985). Later on, his work, like Nevett's, took on a macromarketing perspective (Pollay and Lysonski, 1990), specifically his work on the history of cigarette advertising and its impact on society. That interest in the history of cigarette advertising is shared by others such as Wilcox (1991) who examined the correlation between advertising and cigarette consumption for the period from 1949 to 1985 and Beard and Klyueva (2010) who provide a detailed account of one of the most controversial advertising campaigns of all time – the 'Reach for a Lucky instead of a sweet' cigarette campaign.

A wide range of methodological approaches to historical research is evident in advertising history. Pollay's use of quantification, content analysis and hypothesis testing is representative of the social scientific approach to historical research. In a similar fashion, Gross and Sheth (1989) performed content analysis of advertisements spanning 100 years in the *Ladies Home Journal* to investigate the use of time-oriented appeals. On the other hand, Stern (1988) has used literary criticism to examine the medieval tradition of allegory in relation to the development of contemporary advertising strategies. Nevett also used biographical data and a qualitative interpretation of advertisements to examine the development of British advertising (1988d).

There is an impressive collection of books about advertising history that has been published since the early 1980s, written by business historians (Fox, 1984; Johnston, 2001; Laird, 1998; Lears, 1994; Marchand, 1985; Norris, 1990; Pope, 1983; Robinson, 2004; Schudson, 1984; Sivulka, 1998). Laird's work is particularly valuable for marketing scholars because of its relatively broad scope in relating changes in advertising during the period from the late nineteenth-century through to the early twentieth century to changes in business culture and consumer marketing practice, and for its relevance to marketing strategy more generally.

Two of the more wide-ranging studies of marketing history focusing on marketing strategy more broadly are Tedlow's (1990) *New and Improved: The Story of Mass Marketing in America* and Strasser's (1989) *Satisfaction Guaranteed: The Making of the American Mass Market*. These are the two assigned readings in the undergraduate course I teach in marketing history at Quinnipiac University. Tedlow's book describes how some of America's most important corporations of the twentieth century, including Coca-Cola and Pepsi, Ford and General Motors, A&P, and Sears and Montgomery Ward, battled for dominance in key consumer product markets during the past 100 years. An emergent theme in Tedlow's work is the evolution of market structure in America from a fragmented market in the nineteenth century, to a mass market, and then to market segmentation. For example, with respect to the soft drink industry Tedlow concludes, 'there was no such thing as the Pepsi Generation until Pepsi created it' (1990: 372). It is that statement which is turned around in the title of Hollander and Germain's (1992) in-depth examination of the history of segmentation practices. Hollander and Germain disagreed with Tedlow's three-phase theory and provided detailed evidence of earlier segmentation practices as well as conceptualizations of segmentation by early marketing scholars.

Like Tedlow, Strasser (1989) covers a wide range of marketing strategies including branding, channel strategy, product development, market research, and advertising and promotion, as well as retailing. Both Tedlow and Strasser make extensive use of archival materials, trade periodicals, ephemera, and available company histories. Both clearly demonstrate that modern, sophisticated marketing practices were in place by the early twentieth century. One of the key differences between these two important studies of marketing history is the class of firm studied: Tedlow clearly focused on large corporations, Strasser on small-scale independent retailers. Another key difference between these two histories is the time period covered, with Strasser's more focused on the late nineteenth and early twentieth centuries. Tedlow covers most of the twentieth century.

Other subcategories of marketing history, more macro in orientation, have attracted considerable attention. First, corporate and industry marketing history has emerged as a popular topic of study (Carlos and Lewis, 2002; Godley, 2006; Hawkins, 2009). Second, the study of the history of marketing systems – whole economies or systems of marketing – also emerged during the 1980s as a significant topic for historical research (Corley, 1987; Fisk, 1988; Fullerton, 1988b; Kaufman, 1987; Kitchell, 1992; Pirog, 1991; Speece, 1990). This is undoubtedly related to the important role played by historical research in the *Journal of Macromarketing*, cited earlier. Pirog's (1991) study of changes in the structure and output of the US distribution system builds on Barger's (1955) seminal work mentioned earlier in this review. Of course, a key issue in the study of marketing systems is the relationship between marketing and economic development (Dixon, 1981; McCarthy, 1988; Savitt, 1988), and that critical role for marketing history has been used as a justification for more historical research in marketing since the late 1950s (Myers and Smalley, 1959).

One other major field of interest that has emerged since the early 1980s is the history of consumption. Some of this work has been carried out by marketing scholars interested in consumer behaviour (Belk, 1992; Belk and Pollay, 1985;

Friedman, 1985; Witkowski, 1989b, 1998, 2004). However, there is a growing body of literature on the history of the 'consumer society' written by business historians (Blaszczyk, 2009; Cohen, 2003; Cross, 2000; Donohue, 2003; Fox and Lears, 1983; McKendrick et al., 1982). The ideology behind much of this work, like that by other business historians writing about advertising history, is more liberal and more critical of marketing's impact on consumer welfare than typical of marketing scholars studying marketing history.

History of marketing thought

Earlier research on the history of marketing thought focused on identifying the first textbooks, university courses, and pioneer teachers. During the 1960s some work began to trace the development of key marketing concepts and theory. During the 1980s and since, there have been much more sophisticated historical studies of influences on the development of marketing thought, of the evolution of schools of marketing thought, and examinations of important theoretical developments over time. As well, there has been renewed interest in biographical research. While the relative volume of work on the history of marketing thought has declined (compared with marketing history) since the early 1980s, there has been important work published including the final edition of Bartels' seminal book (1988), a survey of schools of marketing thought (Sheth et al., 1988), edited collections of readings (Baker, 2001; Hollander and Rassuli, 1993; Tadajewski and Jones, 2008; Wooliscroft et al., 2006) and book-length studies of the history of marketing management (Usui, 2008) and advertising education (Ross and Richards, 2008). There have also been broader studies of the development of the marketing discipline that complement Bartels' earlier work (Jones and Shaw, 2002; Wilkie and Moore, 2003) as well as historical studies of schools of marketing thought (Shaw and Jones, 2005; Sheth et al., 1988).

Since the early 1980s, there has been less research on the history of the marketing literature. Grether's (1976) 40-year review of the *Journal of Marketing* (*JM*) was followed by a 60-year retrospective of *JM* by Kerin (1996) and there is a related, detailed study of the founding of *JM* by Witkowski (2007). There have been retrospectives of other major journals in the field of marketing (Berkman, 1992; Muncy, 1991) and, while somewhat dated now, McCracken's (1987) is a very good review of the consumption history literature. More recently, there has also been less research about the history of marketing teaching (Lazer and Shaw, 1988; Schultz, 1982) but some on the teaching of marketing history (Witkowski, 1989a). There remains a need, however, to examine such developments that occurred outside the United States, such as in Jones' (1992) study of early marketing courses in Canada and Jonsson's history of early marketing education in Sweden (2009).

There is renewed interest in biographical research (Bourassa et al., 2007; Green, 2001; Harris, 2007; Hollander, 2009; Jones, 1994, 1998, 2004, 2007; Kreshel, 1990; Nason, 2009; Shaw and Tamilia, 2001; Wittink, 2004; Wright, 1989;

Wooliscroft et al., 2006) which had dropped from the historical agenda after the early 1960s. In that connection, the third edition of Bartels' (1988) *History of Marketing Thought* is notable for its addition of biographical information about important scholars of the 1960s, 1970s and 1980s. Some 35 short biographies of marketing pioneers are included in a recent three-volume collection of readings on the history of marketing thought (Tadajewski and Jones, 2008) including many from the original *Journal of Marketing* series published between 1956 and 1962, as well as more recent biographical sketches. Stephen Brown has added an interesting dimension to this biographical work by analysing the writing styles of several pioneer marketing scholars, including Theodore Levitt (Brown, 2004), Stanley Hollander (Brown, 2009) and Wroe Alderson (Brown, 2002).

Biographical work is featured in a noteworthy collection of work examining the life and career of Wroe Alderson, considered by many to be the greatest marketing theorist of the twentieth century, in *A Twenty-First Century Guide to Aldersonian Marketing Thought* (Wooliscroft et al., 2006). This encyclopaedic historical study of Alderson and his work is divided into six parts including a biographical sketch of Alderson, selected writings by Alderson about his theory of market behaviour and about marketing management practice, commentaries about Alderson's thinking by other well-known scholars, some fascinating biographical commentaries from other scholars about Alderson, and finally exhaustive bibliographies of Alderson's published work. As one reviewer described it, this collection of readings is 'a fitting tribute to the life, writings, and intellectual legacy of Wroe Alderson ... and a reference work of the first magnitude' (Shaw, 2007). Shortly following the publication of this collection of readings, the *European Business Review* (2007, Vol. 19(6)) published a special issue about Alderson adding to the body of work about this pioneer marketing scholar. And finally, Tadajewski (2009d) documented Alderson's trip to Russia as part of a Quaker-organized visit to comment on US foreign policy. The latter work adds an interesting detail to our knowledge about Alderson.

Alderson was best known as a marketing theorist and the history of ideas and theory in marketing now attracts considerable attention. This work includes historical studies of Reilly's retail gravitation theory (Brown, 1994), spatial theory in retailing (Babin et al., 1994), motivation research (McLeod, 2009; Tadajewski, 2006), service marketing (Vargo and Lusch, 2004; Vargo and Morgan, 2005), channels theory (Wilkinson, 2001), the four utilities concept (Shaw, 1994), and marketing productivity. Both Shaw (1987, 1990) and Dixon (1990, 1991) have done extensive work on the historical development of the concept and measurement of marketing productivity. Shaw's historical review of empirical studies concludes that marketing productivity in the United States during the past century has increased, but he points to the continuing lack of clear concepts and measures of marketing costs and effectiveness (1990: 290).

One theory, in particular, has generated much controversy and considerable interest for marketing historians. It is, in fact, an historical stage theory of marketing's development – the so-called four eras of marketing, first proposed by Keith in 1960. The essential historical question here is when the 'marketing concept' and its closely related notion of relationship marketing emerged, and not just the practice but the articulation of this concept. Hollander (1986), Fullerton (1988a), Gilbert and Bailey (1990), Jones and Richardson (2007) and Tadajewski (2009b, forthcoming) have all published detailed, critical historical accounts of the development of the marketing concept and Church (1999) provides an overview of related historical work. A parallel line of research by Tadajewski examines the history of relationship marketing (Tadajewski, 2008, 2009a, 2009c; Tadajewski and Saren, 2009) building on similar work by Keep et al. (1998). As a body of work, these studies all concluded that serious and sophisticated marketing activities driven by a customer orientation have been practised much longer than conventional wisdom suggests, and that marketers have used a customer or marketing orientation at least since the nineteenth century. With some measure of poetic justice, Tadajewski (forthcoming) uses FBI files to test Keith's own (1960) claims regarding the marketing practices adopted at Pillsbury during the so-called 'marketing' and 'marketing control' eras. Tadajewski documents the participation of Pillsbury in anti-competitive practices beginning in 1958, continuing through the mid-1960s and resulting in Pillsbury being charged and fined for their involvement in a price fixing cartel, behaviour that is hardly consistent with a consumer-friendly, relationship-building, 'marketing orientation'.

Taken together, these studies point to the value, and in some cases the necessity, of historical research in evaluating existing theory, *especially, of course, historical theory*. More importantly perhaps, they have contributed to a more critical perspective and to a rewriting of the history of marketing thought presented by Bartels and other mid-twentieth century marketing historians. This includes an extensive re-evaluation of the schools of thought from which marketing emerged as a discipline (Jones and Monieson, 1990), an extension of our historical perspective beyond the twentieth century (Dixon, 1978, 1979, 1981, 1982) and studies of the development of marketing thought outside North America (Ingebrigtsen, 1981; Jones, 1992; Jones and Monieson, 1990; Jonsson, 2009; Usui, 2000). Ironically, a Japanese scholar has recently taken a much more detailed look at the emergence of marketing management in America between 1910 and 1940 (Usui, 2008). That work is distinctive for its focus on the connections between scientific management and the early development of marketing management ideas.

Schools of marketing thought have attracted increasing attention from marketing historians. Discussions of the so-called traditional schools – institutional (Hollander, 1980), functional (Hunt and Goolsby, 1988) and commodity (Zinn and Johnson, 1990) – have been complemented by studies of more contemporary schools of thought, including consumer behaviour (Kassarjian, 1994; Mittelstaedt, 1990; Sheth and Gross, 1988), macromarketing (Layton and Grossbart, 2006; Savitt, 1990) and others (Shaw and Jones, 2005; Sheth et al., 1988). In *Marketing Theory: Evolution and Evaluation* (1988), Sheth et al. identified, classified and evaluated 12 schools of marketing thought comprising commodity, functional, regional, institutional, functionalist, managerial, buyer behaviour, activist, macro-marketing, organizational dynamics, systems, and social exchange schools. The classification and meta-theoretical 'evaluation' by Sheth et al. could easily be debated, but are not essential to the historical theme which provides the bulk of the presentation. Using the Sheth et al.'s work as a point of departure, Shaw and Jones (2005) identified and chronicled 10 schools of marketing thought, beginning with the traditional functional, commodities, and institutional schools; adding the interregional school; and followed by more modern schools of marketing management, marketing systems, consumer behaviour, macromarketing, exchange, and even marketing history. The theme that emerges from this work is a lament over the growing loss of identity, vagueness of subject matter and lack of disciplinary boundaries in marketing. Much of that theme overlaps with Wilkie and Moore's (2003) study which divided the development of the marketing discipline into four eras: (1) founding the field of marketing (1900–1920); (2) formalizing the field (1920–1950); (3) a paradigm shift to more managerial and scientific perspectives (1950–1980); and (4) fragmentation of the mainstream into specialized interest areas (1980–present).

If the Sheth et al. (1988) book replaced Bartels' (1962, 1976, 1988) classic as the staple reading material for doctoral courses during the late 1980s and into the early 1990s, it too was eventually replaced by a two-volume set of readings by Hollander and Rassuli (1993). Hollander was an outspoken critic of Bartels' work on the history of marketing thought and for the doctoral course Hollander taught at Michigan State University (Jones and Keep, 2009) he developed a comprehensive set of readings on both marketing history and the history of marketing thought (Hollander and Rassuli, 1993), a collection that in several ways suggested a new approach to teaching the history of marketing thought to graduate students of marketing. Hollander believed that one could not understand the history of marketing thought without a parallel understanding of marketing history, and included both fields in this two-volume collection. The readings also included discussions of a wide range of macromarketing issues, marketing research and consumer behaviour, in addition to the more obvious material about the history of various aspects of marketing strategy. The collection also included several selections about historical methods in marketing.

Fourteen important readings about the history of marketing thought are included in Baker's (2001) multi-volume collection on critical perspectives in marketing. The historical work there includes some older, seminal works that are difficult to access. Another distinctive feature of this collection is the inclusion of European authors, for example Gilbert and Bailey (1990) and Vink (1992), whose work is often overlooked.

A more recent, three-volume collection of readings, edited by Tadajewski and Jones (2008) is respectfully entitled *The History of Marketing Thought*. (That was the same title used by Bartels for his seminal work in this area.) Like the Hollander and Rassuli collection of readings, this more recent offering takes a much broader approach than that by Bartels and earlier historians. At the same time, the Tadajewski and Jones (2008) collection is more focused than the Hollander and Rassuli collection or the Baker collection, including only articles on the history of marketing thought, and has more depth in that area, blending vintage historical scholarship with much of the more recent contemporary work.

The Tadajewski and Jones collection begins by examining historical research about pre-twentieth-century marketing thought, segues into several key readings about the early development of the marketing discipline, and includes considerable coverage of the schools of marketing thought. The collection features 35 biographical sketches of marketing pioneers, including recent work on Robert Bartels, Stanley Hollander and Sidney Levy. This extensive collection of biographical sketches provides details about the intellectual backgrounds and political context of key marketing thinkers and in that way is intended to connect theoretical debates in marketing with wider socio-political changes. A final section of the readings in this collection continues that ideal by focusing on more macro, contextualizing influences on marketing thought.

The emerging discipline: today and tomorrow

History adds perspective, richness, and context to the study of marketing. More practically speaking, history provides a framework for building and integrating knowledge. We must know where we've been in order to understand where we are, to know what questions have already been answered and which ones still need further study. The history of marketing and marketing ideas has not always been a popular or rewarding field of study. That has clearly changed. Yet, ironically, there was also a time when the study of the history of marketing thought was required in many, if not most, doctoral programmes in marketing. Sadly, that no longer seems to be the case. So while more scholars are doing more and better historical research in marketing, fewer marketing students are being educated about marketing history and the history of marketing thought.

Historical research in marketing has developed over time, naturally enough, from recording the facts about the founding of the discipline, to studies of marketing practices and the ideas about those practices, to schools of thought and eras of study. Over time marketing historians have extended the scope of history beyond the turn of the twentieth century, beyond the core elements of marketing strategy, and have broadened their tool kit of historical methods of research. We have used history to situate the current status of the marketing discipline and have critically evaluated conventional wisdom about how and when key marketing practices and concepts emerged. There has long been a place for marketing history as a component in the work done by business historians, but more business historians are specializing in marketing history, especially in advertising history, retailing history, and the history of consumption. That is also broadening the study of marketing history in some valuable ways.

Over the past 30 years there has been a dramatic growth of interest and activity in marketing history and the history of marketing thought. Specialized academic associations have been formed that sponsor conferences on historical research in marketing. Historical research is now explicitly included in statements of scope and content for several marketing periodicals and we can celebrate the launch of a new academic quarterly dedicated to publishing historical research in marketing. There is a bounded body of knowledge about marketing history and the history of marketing thought and a critical mass of academics that self-identify as marketing historians. In some ways, marketing history (more broadly defined) might qualify as a discipline according to the criteria used by Richardson in his recent study of the development of accounting history (Richardson, 2008; Witkowski and Jones, 2008).

What are some of the priorities for future historical research in marketing? There needs to be greater synthesis and contextualization of marketing history and the history of marketing thought. Too many studies have focused on marketing practices or marketing ideas in isolation without considering the social, economic, and political conditions of the time period being studied. Further, in that connection, we need to acknowledge that practice is not entirely thoughtless and that thought, especially in a discipline that has relied so much on inductive reasoning, is driven by practice. In other words, marketing history and the history of marketing thought must be integrated. This was the foundation of Stanley Hollander's thinking about historical research in marketing (1989). However, as a 'discipline', marketing history still has not made much progress in that direction.

Most of the historical research about marketing and marketing thought is done by marketing scholars trained in social science research methods and can be, therefore, naive about even the most basic historiographic issues, such as the differences between primary and secondary source material. There is a need for more discussion of the broad range of historical research methods, illustrated with examples from historical research in marketing. Finally, marketing historians need to make their work more relevant to marketing education. Marketing history and the history of marketing thought must be integrated into graduate, certainly, and even undergraduate curricula. As Richardson (2008) notes in his history of accounting history, 'the ultimate test of an academic discipline is its ability to offer courses in its own area' (2008: 268). I hope the student text you are reading now will help in that connection.

Recommended further reading

Journal of Historical Research in Marketing

Marketing history

Blaszczyk, Regina (2009) *American Consumer Society, 1865–2005*, Wheeling: Harlan Davidson Inc.

Laird, Pamela Walker (1998) *Advertising Progress: American Business and the Rise of Consumer Marketing*, Baltimore: Johns Hopkins Press.

Strasser, Susan (1989) *Satisfaction Guaranteed: The Making of the American Mass Market*, New York: Random House.

Tedlow, Richard (1990) *New and Improved: The Story of Mass Marketing in America*, New York: Basic Books.

History of marketing thought

Baker, Michael (ed.) (2001) *Marketing: Critical Perspectives in Business and Management*, London: Routledge.
See especially Volume 2, Part 1.
Bartels, Robert (1988) *The History of Marketing Thought*, 3rd edn, Columbus, Ohio: Publishing Horizons Inc.
Hollander, Stanley C. and Rassuli, Kathleen (eds) (1993) *Marketing, 2 volumes*, Brookfield: Edward Elgar Publishing.
Tadajewski, Mark and Jones, D.G. Brian (eds) (2008) *The History of Marketing Thought*, 3 volumes, London: Sage Publishing.
Wooliscroft, Ben, Tamilia, Robert and Shapiro, Stanley J. (eds) (2006) *A Twenty-First Century Guide to Aldersonian Marketing Thought*, Boston: Kluwer Academic Publishers.

Historical research method in marketing

Brown, Stephen, Hirschman, Elizabeth and Maclaran, Pauline (2001) 'Always historicize! Researching marketing history in a post-historical epoch', *Marketing Theory* 1(1): 48–89.
Golder, Peter (2000) 'Historical method in marketing research with new evidence on long-term market share stability', *Journal of Marketing Research* 37, May: 156–72.
Witkowski, Terrence and Jones, D.G. Brian (2006) 'Qualitative historical research in marketing', in Russell W. Belk (ed.) *Handbook of Qualitative Research Methods in Marketing*, Cheltenham, Edward Elgar Publishing, pp. 131–57.

Other reviews of historical research in marketing

Jones, D.G. Brian and Shaw, Eric (2006) 'Historical research in the *Journal of Macromarketing*: 1981–2005', *Journal of Macromarketing* December: 178–92.
Jones, D.G. Brian, Shaw, Eric and Goldring, Deborah (2009) 'Stanley C. Hollander and the Conferences on Historical Analysis & Research in Marketing', *Journal of Historical Research in Marketing* March: 55–73.

References

Agnew, Hugh E. (1941) 'The history of the American Marketing Association', *Journal of Marketing* 5(4): 374–9.
Applebaum, W. (1947) 'The *Journal of Marketing*: the first ten years', *Journal of Marketing* 11(4): 355–63.

Applebaum, W. (1952) 'The *Journal of Marketing*: post war', *Journal of Marketing* 16(3): 294–300.

Babin, Barry, Boles, James and Babin, Laurie (1994) 'The development of spatial theory in retailing and its contribution to marketing thought and marketing science', in Jagdish Sheth and Ronald A. Fullerton (eds), *Research in Marketing: Explorations in the History of Marketing*, Greenwich, CT: JAI Press, pp. 103–16.

Baker, Michael J. (ed.) (2001) *Marketing: Critical Perspectives in Business and Management*, Volume II, Part 1, London: Routledge.

Bakker, Gerben (2001) 'Stars and stories: how films became branded products', *Enterprise & Society, The International Journal of Business History* 2, September: 461–502.

Barger, Harold (1955) *Distribution's Place in the American Economy Since 1869*, Princeton: Princeton University Press.

Bartels, Robert (1941) 'Marketing Literature: Development and Appraisal', unpublished doctoral dissertation, The Ohio State University, Columbus, OH.

Bartels, Robert (1951) 'Influences on the development of marketing thought, 1900–1923', *Journal of Marketing* 16, July: 1–17.

Bartels, Robert (1962) *The Development of Marketing Thought*, Homewood, IL: Irwin.

Bartels, Robert (1976) *The History of Marketing Thought*, 2nd edn, Columbus, OH: Grid.

Bartels, Robert (1988) *The History of Marketing Thought*, 3rd edn, Columbus, OH: Publishing Horizons Inc.

Beard, Fred (2005) 'One hundred years of humor in American advertising', *Journal of Macromarketing* 25 (1): 54–65.

Beard, Fred and Klyueva, Anna (2010) 'George Washington Hill and the "Reach for a Lucky ..." campaign', *Journal of Historical Research in Marketing*. 2(2)

Belk, Russell W. (1992) 'Moving possessions: an analysis based on personal documents from the 1847–1869 Mormon migration', *Journal of Consumer Research* 19, December: 339–61.

Belk, Russell W. and Pollay, Richard W. (1985) 'Images of ourselves: the good life in twentieth century advertising', *Journal of Consumer Research* 11, March: 887–97.

Benson, Susan Porter (1986) *Counter Cultures: Saleswomen, Managers, and Customers in American Department Stores, 1890–1940*, Urbana, IL: University of Illinois Press.

Berkman, Harold W. (1992) 'Twenty years of the journal', *Journal of the Academy of Marketing Science* 20(4): 299–300.

Bevan, J. (2001) *The Rise and Fall of Marks and Spencer*, London: Profile Books.

Blaszczyk, Regina (2009) *American Consumer Society 1865–2005: From Hearth to HDTV*, Wheeling, IL: Harlan Davidson Inc.

Bourassa, Maureen, Cunningham, Peggy and Handelman, Jay (2007) 'How Philip Kotler has helped to shape the field of marketing', *European Business Review* 19(2): 174–92.

Branchik, Blaine (2007) 'Pansies to parents: gay male images in American print advertising', *Journal of Macromarketing* 27, March: 38–50.

Breen, John (1959) 'History of the marketing management concept', in L. Stockman (ed.) *Advancing Marketing Efficiency*, Chicago: American Marketing Association, pp. 458–61.

Brown, George H. (1951) 'What economists should know about marketing', *Journal of Marketing* 16(1): 60–6.

Brown, Stephen (1994) 'Reilly's Law of Retail Gravitation: What Goes Around, Comes Around', in Ronald Fullerton (ed.) Research Marketing; Explorations in the History of Marketing, Greenwich, CT: JAI Press, pp. 117–50.

Brown, Stephen (2004) 'Theodore Levitt: the ultimate writing machine', *Marketing Theory* 4(3): 209–38.

Brown, Stephen (2009) 'A litotes of what you fancy: some thoughts on Stanley Hollander's writing style', *Journal of Historical Research in Marketing* 1, March: 74–92.

Brown, Stephen, Hirschman, Elizabeth and Maclaran, Pauline (2001) 'Always historicize! researching marketing history in a post-historical epoch', *Marketing Theory* 1(1): 49–89.

Bussiere, D. (2000) 'Evidence of a marketing periodic literature within the American Economic Association: 1895–1936', *Journal of Macromarketing* 20(2): 137–43.

Carlos, Ann M. and Lewis, Frank D. (2002) 'Marketing in the land of Hudson Bay: Indian consumers and the Hudson's Bay Company, 1670–1770', *Enterprise & Society, the International Journal of Business History* 3, June: 285–317.

Cassels, J.M. (1936) 'The significance of early economic thought on marketing', *Journal of Marketing* 1, October: 129–33.

Church, Roy (1999) 'New perspectives on the history of products, firms, marketing, and consumers in Britain and the United States since the mid-nineteenth century', *Economic History Review* 52(3): 405–35.

Church, Roy and Clark, Christine (2001) 'Product development of branded, packaged household goods in Britain, 1870–1914: Colman's, Reckitt's, and Lever Brothers', *Enterprise & Society, The International Journal of Business History* 2, September: 503–42.

Cohen, Lizabeth (2003) *A Consumers' Republic: The Politics of Mass Consumption in Postwar America*, New York: Vintage Books.

Collingwood, R.G. (1974) 'Human Nature and Human History', in Patrick Gardiner (ed.) *The Philosophy of History*, London: Oxford University Press, pp. 17–40.

Converse, Paul D. (1933) 'The first decade of marketing literature', *NATMA Bulletin Supplement*, November: 1–4.

Converse, Paul D. (1945) 'The development of the science of marketing – an exploratory survey', *Journal of Marketing* 10, July: 14–23.

Converse, Paul D. (1959a) *Fifty Years of Marketing in Retrospect*, Texas: Bureau of Business Research, The University of Texas.

Converse, Paul D. (1959b) *The Beginnings of Marketing Thought in the United States*, Texas: Bureau of Business Research, University of Texas.

Coolsen, Frank (1947) 'Pioneers in the development of advertising', *Journal of Marketing* 12, July: 80–6.

Coolsen, Frank (1960) *Marketing Thought in the United States in the Late Nineteenth Century*. Texas: Texas Technical Press.

Corley, T.A.B. (1987) 'Consumer marketing in Britain, 1914–1960', *Business History* 29, October: 65–83.

Cross, Gary (2000) *An All-Consuming Century: Why Commercialism Won in Modern America*, New York: Columbia University Press.

Davis, Judy Foster (2007) '"Aunt Jemima is Alive and Cookin?" An advertiser's dilemma of competing collective memories', *Journal of Macromarketing* 27 (March): 25–37.

De Iulio, Simona and Vinti, Carlo (2009) 'The Americanization of Italian advertising during the 1950s and 1960s: mediations, conflicts, and appropriations', *Journal of Historical Research in Marketing* 1, July: 230–40.

Dixon, Donald F. (1978) 'The origins of macro-marketing thought', in George Fisk and Robert W. Nason (eds) *Macromarketing: New Steps on the Learning Curve*, Boulder: University of Colorado, Business Research Division, pp. 9–28.

Dixon, Donald F. (1979) 'Medieval macromarketing thought', in George Fisk and Phillip White (eds) *Macromarketing: Evolution of Thought*, Boulder: University of Colorado, Business Research Division, pp. 59–69.

Dixon, Donald F. (1981) 'The role of marketing in early theories of economic development', *Journal of Macromarketing* 1, Fall: 19–27.

Dixon, Donald F. (1990) 'Marketing as production: the development of a concept', *Journal of the Academy of Marketing Science* 18, Fall: 337–44.

Dixon, Donald F. (1991) 'Marketing structure and the theory of economic interdependence: early analytical developments', *Journal of Macromarketing*, 11, Fall: 5–18.

Dixon, Donald F. (1994) 'A day's shopping in thirteenth-century Paris', in Jagdish Sheth and Ronald A. Fullerton (eds) *Research in Marketing: Explorations in the History of Marketing*, Greenwich, CT: JAI Press, pp. 13–24.

Donohue, K.G. (2003) Freedom From Want: American Liberalism and the Idea of the Consumer, Baltimore: Johns Hopkins University Press.

Duguid, Paul (2003) 'Developing the brand: the case of alcohol, 1800–1880', *Enterprise & Society, The International Journal of Business History* 4, September: 405–41.

Emmet, Boris and Jeuck, John E. (1950) *Catalogues and Counters: A History of Sears, Roebuck and Company*, Chicago: University of Chicago Press.

Ferrier, R.W. (1986) 'Petroleum advertising in the twenties and thirties: the case of the British Petroleum Company', *European Journal of Marketing* 20(5): 29–51.

Fisk, George (1988) 'Interactive systems frameworks for analyzing spacetime changes in marketing organization and processes', in Terence Nevett and Ronald Fullerton (eds) *Historical Perspectives in Marketing: Essays in Honor of Stanley C. Hollander*, Lexington: Lexington Books, pp. 55–70.

Fox, Richard and Jackson Lears, T.J. (1983) *The Culture of Consumption: Critical Essays in American History, 1880–1980*, New York: Pantheon Books.

Fox, Stephen (1984) *The Mirror Makers: A History of American Advertising and its Creators*, New York: William Morrow & Company.

Friedman, H.H. (1985) 'Ancient marketing practices: the view from Talmudic times', *Journal of Public Policy and Marketing* 3: 194–204.

Friedman, Walter A. (2004) *Birth of a Salesman: The Transformation of Selling in America*, Cambridge, MA: Harvard University Press.

Fullerton, Ronald A. (1985) 'Segmentation strategies and practices in the 19th-century German book trade: a case study in the development of a major marketing technique', in C.T. Tan and Jagdish N. Sheth (eds) *Historical Perspective in Consumer Research: National and International Perspectives*, pp. 135–9.

Fullerton, Ronald A. (1987) 'The poverty of ahistorical analysis: present weakness and future cure in U.S. marketing thought', in A. Fuat Firat, Nikhilesh Dholakia and Richard P. Bagozzi (eds) *Philosophical and Radical Thought in Marketing*, Lexington: Lexington Books, pp. 97–116.

Fullerton, Ronald A. (1988a) 'How modern is modern marketing? Marketing's evolution and the myth of the production era', *Journal of Marketing* 52, January: 108–25.

Fullerton, Ronald A. (1988b) 'Modern Western marketing as a historical phenomenon: theory and illustration', in Terence Nevett and Ronald Fullerton (eds) *Historical Perspectives in Marketing: Essays in Honor of Stanley C. Hollander*, Lexington: Lexington Books, pp. 71–89.

Fullerton, Ronald A. (1990) 'The art of marketing research: selections from Paul F. Lazarsfeld's "Shoe Buying in Zurich" (1933)', *Journal of the Academy of Marketing Science* 18(4): 319–27.

Fullerton, Ronald A. and Nevett, Terence R. (1986) 'Advertising and society: a comparative analysis of the roots of distrust in Germany and Great Britain', *International Journal of Marketing* 5: 225–41.

Germain, Richard (1994) 'The adoption of statistical methods in market research: the early twentieth century', in Jagdish Sheth and Ronald A. Fullerton (eds) *Research in Marketing: Explorations in the History of Marketing*, Greenwich, CT: JAI Press, pp. 87–102.

Gilbert, David and Bailey, Nick (1990) 'The development of marketing – a compendium of approaches', *Quarterly Review of Marketing* 15(2): 6–13.

Godley, Andrew (2006) 'Selling the sewing machine around the world: Singer's international marketing strategies, 1850–1920', *Enterprise & Society, The International Journal of Business History* 7, June: 266–314.

Golder, Peter (2000) 'Historical method in marketing research with new evidence on long-term market share stability', *Journal of Marketing Research* 37, May: 156–72.

Gordon, Robert A. and Howell, James E. (1959) *Higher Education for Business*, New York: Columbia University Press.

Grant, W.T. (1954) *Woolworth's First 75 Years: The Story of Everybody's Store*, New York.

Green, P.E. (2001) 'The vagaries of becoming (and remaining) a marketing research methodologist', *Journal of Marketing* 65(3): 104–8.

Grether, E.T. (1976) 'The first forty years', *Journal of Marketing* 40, July: 63–9.

Greyser, Stephen (ed.) (1963) *Toward Scientific Marketing*, American Marketing Association Proceedings Series, Chicago: American Marketing Association.

Gross, Barbara L. and Sheth, Jagdish N. (1989) 'Time oriented advertising: a content analysis of United States magazine advertising, 1890–1988', *Journal of Marketing* 53(4): 76–83.

Hagerty, J.E. (1936) 'Experiences of an early marketing teacher', *Journal of Marketing* 1(1): 20–7.

Hardy, Harold (1954) 'Collegiate marketing education since 1930', *Journal of Marketing* 19(2): 325–30.

Harris, Garth (2007) 'Sidney Levy: challenging the philosophical assumptions of marketing', *Journal of Macromarketing* 27(1): 7–14.

Hawkins, Richard A. (2009) 'Advertising and the Hawaiian Pineapple Canning Industry, 1929–39', *Journal of Macromarketing* 29, June: 172–92.

Hempel, Carl G. (1959) 'The function of general laws in history', in Patrick Gardiner (ed.) *Theories of History*, Glencoe, IL: The Free Press, pp. 344–55.

Hollander, Stanley C. (1960) 'The wheel of retailing', *Journal of Marketing* 25, July: 37–42.

Hollander, Stanley C. (1963a) 'A note on fashion leadership', *Business History Review* Winter: 448–51.

Hollander, Stanley C. (1963b) 'Anti-salesman ordinances of the mid-nineteenth century', in Stephen Greyser (ed.) *Toward Scientific Marketing*, Chicago: American Marketing Association, pp. 344–51.

Hollander, Stanley C. (1964) 'Nineteenth century anti-drummer legislation in the United States', *Business History Review* 38, Winter: 479–500.

Hollander, Stanley C. (1966) 'Notes on the retail accordion', *Journal of Retailing* 42, Summer: 29–40.

Hollander, Stanley C. (1980) 'Some notes on the difficulty of identifying the marketing thought contributions of the early institutionalists', in C.W. Lamb and P.M. Dunn (eds) *Theoretical Developments in Marketing*, Chicago: American Marketing Association, pp. 45–6.

Hollander, Stanley C. (1984) 'Herbert Hoover, Professor Levitt, simplification and the marketing concept', in Paul Anderson and Michael Ryan (eds) *Scientific Method in Marketing*, Chicago: American Marketing Association, pp. 260–3.

Hollander, Stanley C. (1986) 'The marketing concept: a deja-vu', in George Fisk (ed.) *Marketing Management Technology as a Social Process*, New York: Praeger, pp. 3–28.

Hollander, Stanley C. (1989) 'Introduction', in Terry Nevett, Kathleen Whitney and Stanley Hollander (eds) *Marketing History: The Emerging Discipline*, Lansing, MI: Michigan State University, pp. xix–xx.

Hollander, Stanley C. (2009) 'My life on Mt Olympus', *Journal of Historical Research in Marketing* 1, March: 10–33.

Hollander, Stanley C. and Germain, Richard (1992) *Was There a Pepsi Generation Before Pepsi Discovered It?*, Lincolnwood, IL: NCT Business Books.

Hollander, Stanley C. and Kathleen Rassuli (1993) *Marketing*, 2 volumes, Brookfield, VT: Edward Elgar Publishing.

Hollander, Stanley C. Jones, D.G. Brian Rassuli, Kathleen and Dix, Laura (2005) 'Periodization in marketing history, *Journal of Macromarketing*, Spring: 32–41.

Hotchkiss, George B. (1938) *Milestones of Marketing*, New York: MacMillan Publishing.

Howard, Vicki (2008) '"The biggest small-town store in America": independent retailers and the rise of consumer culture', *Enterprise & Society, The International Journal of Business History* 9, September: 457–86.

Hower, Ralph M. (1946) *History of Macy's of New York, 1858–1919*, Cambridge: Harvard University Press.

Hull, Bradley (2008) 'Frankincense, myrrh, and spices: the oldest global supply chain?', *Journal of Macromarketing* 28, September: 275–88.

Hunt, Shelby D. and Goolsby, Jerry (1988) 'The rise and fall of the functional approach to marketing: a paradigm displacement perspective', in Terence Nevett and Ronald Fullerton (eds) *Historical Perspectives in Marketing: Essays in Honor of Stanley C. Hollander*, Lexington: Lexington Books, pp. 35–52.

Ingebrigtsen, Stig (ed.) (1981) *Reflections on Danish Theory of Marketing*, Copenhagen: Nyt Nordisk Forlag Arnold Busck.

Johnston, Russell (2001) *Selling Themselves: The Emergence of Canadian Advertising*, Toronto: University of Toronto Press.

Jones, D.G. Brian (1992) 'Early development of marketing thought in Canada', *Canadian Journal of Administrative Science* 9(2): 126–33.

Jones, D.G Brian (1993) 'Historiographic paradigms in marketing', in Stanley Hollander and Kathleen Rassuli (eds) *Marketing*, Volume 1, Brookfield, VT: Edward Elgar Publishing.

Jones, D.G. Brian (1994) 'Biography and the history of marketing thought: Henry Charles Taylor and Edward David Jones', in Ronald Fullerton (ed.) *Research in Marketing: Explorations in the History of Marketing*, Greenwich, CT: JAI Press, pp. 67–85.

Jones, D.G. Brian (1998) 'Biography as a methodology for studying the history of marketing ideas', *Psychology & Marketing* 15, March: 161–74.

Jones, D.G. Brian (2004) 'Simon Litman (1873–1965): pioneer marketing scholar', *Marketing Theory* 4, December: 343–61.

Jones, D.G. Brian (2007) 'Theodore N. Beckman (1895–1973): external manifestations of the man', *European Business Review* March: 129–41.

Jones, D.G. Brian and Keep, William (2009) 'Hollander's doctoral seminar in the history of marketing thought', *Journal of Historical Research in Marketing* 1, March: 151–64.

Jones, D.G. Brian and Monieson, David D. (1990) 'Early development of the philosophy of marketing thought', *Journal of Marketing* 54(1): 102–13.

Jones, D.G. Brian and Richardson, Alan (2007) 'The myth of the marketing revolution', *Journal of Macromarketing* 27 March: 15–24.

Jones, D. G. Brian Richardson, Alan and Shearer, Terri (2000) 'Truth and the evolution of the professions: a comparative study of "truth in advertising" and "true and fair" financial statements in North America during the progressive era', *Journal of Macromarketing* June: 23–35.

Jones, D.G. Brian and Shaw, Eric (2002) 'A history of marketing thought', in Robin Wensley and Barton Weitz (eds) *Handbook of Marketing*, London: Sage Publications, pp. 39–65.

Jones, D.G. Brian and Shaw, Eric (2006) 'Historical research in the *Journal of Macromarketing*: 1981–2005', *Journal of Macromarketing* December: 178–92.

Jones, D.G. Brian Shaw, Eric and Goldring, Deborah (2009) 'Stanley C. Hollander and the Conferences on Historical Analysis & Research in Marketing', *Journal of Historical Research in Marketing* 1, March: 55–73.

Jones, Fred (1936) 'Retail stores in the United States, 1800–1860', *Journal of Marketing* 1, October: 135–40.

Jonsson, Pernilla (2009) 'Marketing innovations and the Swedish consumer cooperative movement, 1904–1930', in Richard Hawkins (ed.) *Marketing History: Strengthening, Straightening, and Extending: Proceedings of the 14th Biennial Conference on Historical Analysis & Research in Marketing (CHARM)*, Leicester: University of Leicester, pp. 130–43.

Kassarjian, Harold H. (1994) 'Scholarly traditions and European roots of American consumer research', in G. Laurent, G. Lillien and B. Pras (eds) *Research Traditions in Marketing*, Boston: Kluwer Academic Publishers, pp. 265–79.

Kaufman, Carol J. (1987) 'The evaluation of marketing in a society: the Han Dynasty of ancient China', *Journal of Macromarketing* 7(2): 52–64.

Keehn, Richard H. (1994) 'Jockey International: a brief history of marketing innovation', in Jagdish Sheth and Ronald A. Fullerton (eds) *Research in Marketing: Explorations in the History of Marketing*, Greenwich, CT: JAI Press, pp. 183–204.

Keep, William, Hollander, Stanley C. and Dickinson, Roger (1998) 'Forces impinging on long-term business-to-business relationships in the United States: an historical perspective', *Journal of Marketing* 62, April: 31–45.

Keith, Robert J. (1960) 'The Marketing Revolution', *Journal of Marketing* 4, January: 35–8.

Kelley, William T. (1956) 'The development of early thought in marketing and promotion', *Journal of Marketing* 21, July: 62–76.

Kerin, Roger (1996) 'In pursuit of an ideal: the editorial and literary history of the *Journal of Marketing*', *Journal of Marketing* 60, January: 1–13.

Kirkwood, R.C. (1960) *The Woolworth Story at Home and Abroad*, New York: Newcomen Society.

Kitchell, Susan (1992) 'Foundation of the Japanese distribution system: historical determinants in the Tokugawa period (1603–1868)', in Carole Duhaime (ed.) *Marketing Proceedings*, Administrative Sciences Association of Canada Conference, pp. 108–16.

Kleindle, Brad (2007) 'Marketing practices used by the emerging American public library system from inception to 1930', *Journal of Macromarketing* 27, March: 65–73.

Koehn, Nancy F. (2001) *Brand New: How Entrepreneurs Earned Consumers' Trust from Wedgwood to Dell*, Boston, MA: Harvard Business School Press.

Kopp, Steven W. and Charles R. Taylor (1994) 'Games, contests, sweepstakes, and lotteries: prize promotion and public policy', in Jagdish Sheth and Ronald A. Fullerton (eds) *Research in Marketing: Explorations in the History of Marketing*, Greenwich, CT: JAI Press, pp. 151–66.

Kose, Yavuz (2007) 'Nestlé: a brief history of the marketing strategies of the first multinational company in the Ottoman Empire', *Journal of Macromarketing* 27, March: 74–85.

Kreshel, Peggy J. (1990), 'John B. Watson at J. Walter Thompson: the legitimation of "science" in advertising', *Journal of Advertising* 19(2): 49–59.

Kumcu, Erdogan (1987) 'Historical method: toward a relevant analysis of marketing systems', in A. Fuat Firat, Nikhilesh Dholakia and Richard P. Bagozzi (eds) *Philosophical and Radical Thought in Marketing*, Lexington: Lexington Books, pp. 117–33.

Laird, Pamela Walker (1998) *Advertising Progress: American Business and the Rise of Consumer Marketing*, Baltimore: Johns Hopkins University Press.

La Londe, Bernard J. and Morrison, Edward J. (1967) 'Marketing management concepts, yesterday and today', *Journal of Marketing* 31(1): 9–13.

Layton, Roger and Grossbart, Sanford (2006) 'Macromarketing: past, present, and possible future', *Journal of Macromarketing* 26, December: 193–213.

Lazer, William (1965) 'Marketing theory and the marketing literature', in Michael Halburt (ed.) *The Meaning and Sources of Marketing Theory*, New York: McGraw-Hill, pp. 58–94.

Lazer, William and Shaw, Eric (1988) 'The development of collegiate business and marketing education in America: historical perspectives', in Stanley Shapiro and A.H. Walle (eds) *Marketing: A Return to the Broader Dimensions*, Proceedings of the Winter Educators' Conference, Chicago: American Marketing Association, pp. 147–52.

Lears, Jackson (1994) *Fables of Abundance: A Cultural History of Advertising in America*, New York: Basic Books.

Leigh, Faith (1986) 'Half a century of professional bodies in sales promotions', *European Journal of Marketing* 20(9): 27–40.

Litman, Simon (1950) 'The beginnings of teaching marketing in American universities', *Journal of Marketing* 15, October: 220–23.

Low, George S. and Fullerton, Ronald A. (1994) 'Brands, brand management, and the brand management system: a critical-historical evaluation', *Journal of Marketing Research* 31, May: 173–90.

Marburg, Theodore (1951) 'Domestic trade and marketing', in H.F. Williamson (ed.) *The Growth of the American Economy* 551–3.

Marchand, Roland (1985) *Advertising the American Dream: Making Way for Modernity, 1920–1940*, Berkeley, CA: University of California Press.

Marx, Thomas G. (1985) 'The development of the franchise distributive system in the United States auto industry', *British History Review* 59, August: 465–74.

Maynard, H.H. (1941) 'Marketing courses prior to 1910', *Journal of Marketing* 5, April: 382–4.

Maynard, H.H. (1951) 'Developments of science in selling and sales management', in Hugh G. Wales (ed.) *Changing Perspectives in Marketing*, Urbana: University of Illinois Press, pp. 169–84.

McCracken, Grant (1987) 'The history of consumption: a literature review and consumer guide', *Journal of Consumer Policy* 10, June: 139–66.

McCarthy, E. Jerome (1988) 'Marketing orientedness and economic development', in Terence Nevett and Ronald Fullerton (eds) *Historical Perspectives in Marketing: Essays in Honor of Stanley C. Hollander*, Lexington: Lexington Books, pp. 133–46.

McGarry, E.D. (1953) 'Some new viewpoints in marketing', *Journal of Marketing* 18(1): 33–40.

McKendrick, N. (1960) 'Josiah Wedgwood: an eighteenth century entrepreneur in salesmanship and marketing techniques', *Economic History Review* 12: 408–31.

McKendrick, Neil, Brewer, John and Plumb, J.H. (1982) *The Birth of a Consumer Society: The Commercialization of Eighteenth-Century England*, Bloomington, IN: Indiana University Press.

McLeod, Amanda (2009) 'Pseudo-scientific hokus pokus: motivational research's australian application', *Journal of Historical Research in Marketing* 1, July: 211–20.

Meyer, Timothy P. (1994) 'Tobacco advertising on trial: an assessment of recent attempts to reconstruct the past and an agenda to improve the quality of evidence presented', in Jagdish Sheth and Ronald A. Fullerton (eds) *Research in Marketing: Explorations in the History of Marketing*, Greenwich, CT: JAI Press, pp. 205–20.

Miracle, Gordon E. and Nevett, Terence (1988) 'A comparative history of advertising self-regulation in the United Kingdom and the United States', *European Journal of Marketing* 22(4): 7–23.

Mishra, Karen (2009) 'J. Walter Thompson: building trust in troubled times', *Journal of Historical Research in Marketing* 1, July: 221–30.

Mittelstaedt, Robert (1990) 'Economics, psychology, and the literature of the subdiscipline of consumer behavior', *Journal of the Academy of Marketing Science* 18, Fall: 303–12.

Monod, David (1996) *Store Wars: Shopkeepers and the Culture of Mass Marketing, 1890–1939*, Toronto: University of Toronto Press.

Muncy, James A. (1991) 'The *Journal of Advertising*: A twenty year appraisal', *Journal of Advertising*, 20, December: 1–12.

Myers, K. and Smalley, D. (1959) 'Marketing history and economic development', *Business History Review* 33, Autumn: 387–401.

Nason, Robert (2009) 'An uncommon scholar', *Journal of Historical Research in Marketing* 1, March: 34–54.

Nevett, Terence (1982) *Advertising in Britain: A History*, London: Heinemann.

Nevett, Terence (1985) 'The ethics of advertising, F.P. Bishop Reconsidered', *International Journal of Advertising* 4(4): 297–304.

Nevett, Terence (1988a) 'American influences in British advertising before 1920', in Terence Nevett and Ronald Fullerton (eds) *Historical Perspectives in Marketing: Essays in Honor of Stanley C. Hollander*, Lexington: Lexington Books, pp. 223–40.

Nevett, Terence (1988b) 'Reform in Great Britain – the Scapa Society', in Stanley Shapiro and A.H. Walle (eds) *Marketing: A Return to the Broader Dimensions*, Chicago: American Marketing Association, pp. 120–4.

Nevett, Terence (1988c) 'The early development of marketing thought: some contributions from British advertising', in Stanley Shapiro and A.H. Walle (eds) *Marketing: A Return to the Broader Dimensions*, Chicago: American Marketing Association, pp. 137–41.

Nevett, Terence (1988d) 'Thomas Barratt and the Development of British Advertising', *International Journal of Advertising* 7: 267–76.

Nevett, Terence (1989) 'The uses of history in marketing education', *Journal of Marketing Education* Summer: 48–53.

Nevett. Terence (1991) 'Historical investigation and the practice of marketing', *Journal of Marketing* 55, July: 13–23.

Nystrom, Paul H. (1915) *The Economics of Retailing*, New York: Ronald Press.

Nystrom, Paul H. (1951) 'Retailing in Retrospect and Prospect', in Hugh G. Wales (ed.) *Changing Perspectives in Marketing*, Urbana: University of Illinois Press, pp. 117–38.

Norris, James D. (1990) *Advertising and the Transformation of American Society, 1865–1920*, New York: Greenwood Press.

Phillips, C.F. (1935) 'A history of the F.W. Woolworth Company', *Harvard Business Review* 13: 225–36.

Pirog, Stephen F. (1991) 'Changes in U.S. distribution output, 1947–1977: the effects of changes in structure and final demand', *Journal of Macromarketing* 11, Fall: 29–41.

Pollay, Richard W. (1977) 'The importance, and the problems of writing the history of advertising', *Journal of Advertising History* 1(1): 3–5.

Pollay, Richard W. (1978) 'Maintaining Archives for the History of Advertising', *Special Libraries* 69 (4): 145–154.

Pollay, Richard W. (1979) *Information Sources in Advertising History*, Riverside, Connecticut: Greenwood Press.

Pollay, Richard W. (1984a) 'The Identification and Distribution of Values Manifest in Print Advertising 1900–1980', in E. Pitts Jr. and Arch Woodside (eds) *Personal Values and Consumer Behavior*, Lexington: Lexington Press, 111–135.

Pollay, Richard W. (1984b) 'Twentieth Century Magazine Advertising: Determinants of Informativeness', *Written Comunication* 1(1): 56–77.

Pollay, Richard W. (1985) 'The Subsiding Sizzle: A Descriptive History of Print Advertising, 1900–1980', *Journal of Marketing* 49 (Summer): 24–37.

Pollay, Richard W. (1988a) 'Current events that are making advertising history', in Terence Nevett and Ronald Fullerton (eds) *Historical Perspectives in Marketing: Essays in Honor of Stanley C. Hollander*, Lexington: Lexington Books, 195–222.

Pollay, Richard W. (1988b) 'Keeping advertising from going down in history – Unfairly', *Journal of Advertising History* 1, Autumn: 21–32.

Pollay, Richard W. (1994) 'Thank the editors for the buy-ological urge! American magazines, advertising, and the promotion of the consumer culture, 1920–1980', in Jagdish Sheth and Ronald A. Fullerton (eds) *Research in Marketing: Explorations in the History of Marketing*, Greenwich, CT: JAI Press, pp. 221–36.

Pollay, Richard W. and Lysonski, Steven (1990) 'Advertising sexism is forgiven, but not forgotten: historical, cross cultural and individual differences in criticism and purchase boycott intentions', *International Journal of Advertising* 9(4): 319–31.

Pope, Daniel (1983) *The Making of Modern Advertising*, New York: Basic Books.

Porter, Glenn and Livesay, Harold (1971) *Merchants and Manufacturers: Studies in the Changing Structure of Nineteenth-Century Marketing*, Baltimore: Johns Hopkins Press.

Rassuli, Kathleen M. (1988) 'Evidence of marketing strategy in the early printed book trade: an application of Hollander's historical approach', in Terence Nevett and Ronald Fullerton (eds) *Historical Perspectives in Marketing: Essays in Honor of Stanley C. Hollander*, Lexington: Lexington Books, pp. 91–108.

Rassuli, Kathleen M. and Hollander, Stanley C. (1986) 'Comparative history as a research tool in consumer behaviour', in Melanie Wallendorf and Paul Anderson (eds) *Advances in Consumer Research*, Association for Consumer Research, 14: 442–6.

Richardson, Alan (2008) 'Strategies in the development of accounting history as an academic discipline', *Accounting History* 13(3): 247–80.

Robinson, Daniel (2004) 'Marketing gum, making meanings: Wrigley in North America, 1890–1930', *Enterprise & Society, The International Journal of Business History* 5, March: 4–44.

Ross, Billy and Richards, Jef (2008) *A Century of Advertising Education*, American Academy of Advertising.

Savitt, Ronald (1980) 'Historical research in marketing', *Journal of Marketing* 44, Fall: 52–8.

Savitt, Ronald (1982) 'A historical approach to comparative retailing', *Management Decision* 20(4): 16–23.

Savitt, Ronald (1988) 'A personal view of historical explanation in marketing and economic development', in Terence Nevett and Ronald Fullerton (eds) *Historical Perspectives in Marketing: Essays in Honor of Stanley C. Hollander*, Lexington: Lexington Books, pp. 113–32.

Savitt, Ronald (1990) 'Pre-Aldersonian antecedents to macromarketing: insights from the textual literature', *Journal of the Academy of Marketing Science* 18, Fall: 293–302.

Savitt, Ronald (2009) 'Teaching and studying marketing history: a personal journey', *Journal of Historical Research in Marketing* 1, July: 189–99.

Schudson, Michael (1984) *Advertising, the Uneasy Persuasion: Its Dubious Impact on American Society*, New York: Basic Books.

Schultz, Quentin J. (1982) 'An honourable place: the quest for professional advertising education 1900–1917', *Business History Review* 56(1): 16–32.

Schwartz, George (1963) *Development of Marketing Theory*, Cincinnati, OH: South-Western Publishing.

Seaton, A.V. (1986) 'Cope's and the promotion of tobacco in Victorian England', *European Journal of Marketing* 20(9): 5–26.

Shapiro, Stanley and Doody, Alton F. (1968) *Readings in the History of American Marketing: Settlement to Civil War*, Homewood, IL: Irwin.

Shaw, Arch W. (1915) *Some Problems in Market Distribution*, Cambridge, MA: Harvard University Press.

Shaw, Eric (1987) 'Marketing efficiency and performance: an historical analysis', in Terence Nevett and Stanley Hollander (eds) *Marketing in Three Eras*, Lansing: Michigan State University, pp. 181–200.

Shaw, Eric (1990) 'A review of empirical studies of aggregate marketing costs and productivity in the United States', *Journal of the Academy of Marketing Science* 18, Fall: 285–92.

Shaw, Eric H. (1994) 'The Utility of the Fair Utilities Concept, in Ronald Fullerton (ed.) *Research in Marketing: Explorations in the History of Marketing*, Greenwich, CT: JAI Press, pp. 47–66.

Shaw, Eric (2007) 'A Twenty-First Century Guide to Aldersonian Marketing Thought', *Journal of Macromarketing* 27, June: 193–6.

Shaw, Eric and Jones, D.G. Brian (2005) 'A history of schools of marketing thought', *Marketing Theory* September: 239–82.

Shaw, Eric and Tamilia, Robert (2001) 'Robert Bartels and the history of marketing thought', *Journal of Macromarketing* 21(2): 156–63.

Sheth, Jagdish and Gross, Barbara L. (1988) 'Parallel development of marketing and consumer behaviour: a historical perspective', in Terence Nevett and Ronald Fullerton (eds) *Historical Perspectives in Marketing: Essays in Honor of Stanley C. Hollander*, Lexington: Lexington Books, pp. 9–34.

Sheth, Jagdish N., Gardner, D.M. and Garrett, D. (1988) *Marketing Theory: Evolution and Evaluation*, New York: Wiley and Sons.

Silk, A. and Stern, Louis (1963) 'The changing nature of innovation in marketing: a study of selected business leaders, 1852–1958', *Business History Review* 37: 182–99.

Sivulka, Julian (1998) *Soap, Sex, and Cigarettes: A Cultural History of American Advertising*, Belmont, CA: Wadsworth Publishing.

Smith, George L. (ed.) (1964) *Reflections on Progress in Marketing*, Proceedings Series, Chicago: American Marketing Association.

Smith, Ruth Ann, and Lux, David S. (1993) 'Historical method in consumer research: developing causal explanations of change', *Journal of Consumer Research* 19, March: 595–610.

Speece, Mark (1990) 'Evolution of ethnodominated marketing channels: evidence from Oman and Sudan', *Journal of Macromarketing* 10, Fall: 78–93.

Stanger, Howard (2008) 'The Larkin Clubs of Ten: consumer buying clubs and mail-order commerce, 1890–1940', *Enterprise & Society, The International Journal of Business History* 9, March: 125–64.

Stern, Barbara B. (1988) 'Medieval allegory: roots of advertising strategy for the mass market', *Journal of Marketing* 52, July: 84–94.

Stern, Barbara B. (1990) 'Literary criticism and the history of marketing thought: a new perspective on "reading" marketing theory', *Journal of the Academy of Marketing Science* 18, Fall: 329–36.

Strasser, Susan (1989) *Satisfaction Guaranteed: The Making of the American Mass Market*, Washington: Smithsonian Books.

Tadajewski, Mark (2006) 'Remembering motivation research: toward an alternative genealogy of interpretive consumer research', *Marketing Theory* 6(4): 429–66.

Tadajewski, Mark (2008) 'Relationship marketing at Wanamaker's in the 19th and early 20th Centuries', *Journal of Macromarketing* 28(2): 169–82.

Tadajewski, Mark (2009a) 'The foundations of relationship marketing: reciprocity and trade relations', *Marketing Theory* 9(1): 11–40.

Tadajewski, Mark (2009b) 'Eventalizing the marketing concept', *Journal of Marketing Management* 25(1): 191–217.

Tadajewski, Mark (2009c) 'Competition, cooperation and open price associations: relationship marketing and Arthur Jerome Eddy (1859–1920)', *Journal of Historical Research in Marketing* 1(1): 122–43.

Tadajewski, Mark (2009d) 'Quaker travels, fellow traveler? Wroe Alderson's visit to Russia during the Cold War', *Journal of Macromarketing* 29(3): 303–24.

Tadajewski, Mark (forthcoming) 'Reading "The Marketing Revolution" through the prism of the FBI', *Journal of Marketing Management*.

Tadajewski, Mark and Jones, D.G. Brian (eds) (2008) *The History of Marketing Thought*, 3 vols, London: Sage Publishing.

Tadajewski, Mark and Saren, M. (2008) 'The past is a foreign country: amnesia and marketing theory', *Marketing Theory* 8(4): 323–38.

Tadajewski, Mark and Saren, M. (2009) 'Rethinking relationship marketing', *Journal of Macromarketing* 29(2): 193–206.

Tedlow, Richard (1990) *New and Improved: The Story of Mass Marketing in America*, New York: Basic Books.

Tedlow, Richard and Jones, Geoffrey (eds) (1993) *The Rise and Fall of Mass Marketing*, London: Routledge.

Usui, Kazuo (2000) 'The interpretation of Arch Wilkinson Shaw's thought by Japanese scholars', *Journal of Macromarketing* 20(2): 128–36.

Usui, Kazuo (2008) *The Development of Marketing Management: The Case of the USA c. 1910–1940*, Farnham, UK: Ashgate Publishing.

Vargo, S. and Lusch, R. (2004) 'Evolving to a new dominant logic for marketing', *Journal of Marketing* 68(1): 1–17.

Vargo, S.L. and Morgan, F.W. (2005) 'Services in Society and Academic Thought: An Historical Analysis', Journal of Macromarketing 25(1): 42–53.

Vink, Nico (1992) 'Historical perspective in marketing management, explicating experience', *Journal of Marketing Management* 8: 219–37.

Wales, Hugh (ed.) (1951) *Changing Perspectives in Marketing*, Urbana, IL: University of Illinois Press.

Ward, Douglas (2009) 'Capitalism, market research, and the creation of the American consumer', *Journal of Historical Research in Marketing* 1, July: 200–10.

Weld, L.D.H. (1941) 'Early experience in teaching courses in marketing', *Journal of Marketing* 5, April: 380–1.

Wilcox, Gary B. (1991) 'Cigarette brand advertising and consumption in the United States: 1949–1985', *Journal of Advertising Research* August/September: 61–7.

Wilkie, William L. and Moore, Elizabeth (2003) 'Scholarly research in marketing: exploring the "4 eras" of thought development', *Journal of Public Policy & Marketing* 22, Fall: 116–46.

Wilkinson, Ian (2001) 'A history of network and channels thinking in marketing in the 20th century', *Australasian Marketing Journal* 9(2): 23–52.

Witkowski, Terrence H. (1989a) 'History's place in the marketing curriculum', *Journal of Marketing Education* Summer: 54–7.

Witkowski, Terrence (1989b) 'Colonial consumers in revolt: buyer values and behavior during the nonimportation movement, 1764–1776', *Journal of Consumer Research* 16, September: 216–26.

Witkowski, Terrence (1994) 'Data sources for American consumption history: an introduction, analysis, and application', in Jagdish Sheth and Ronald A. Fullerton (eds) *Research in Marketing: Explorations in the History of Marketing*, Greenwich, CT: JAI Press, pp. 167–82.

Witkowski, Terrence (1998) 'The early American style: a history of marketing and consumer values', *Pyschology & Marketing* 15, March: 125–43.

Witkowski, Terrence (2003) 'World War II poster campaigns: preaching frugality to American consumers', *Journal of Advertising* 32, Spring: 69–82.

Witkowski, Terrence (2004) 'Re-gendering consumer agency in mid-nineteenth-century America: a visual understanding', *Consumption, Markets, and Culture* 7, September: 261–83.

Witkowski, Terrence (2007) 'The *American Marketing Journal*, the *National Marketing Review*, and the intellectual origins of the *Journal of Marketing*', paper presented at the 13th Biennial Conference on Historical Analysis & Research in Marketing (CHARM), Durham, NC, May.

Witkowski, Terrence (2009) 'General Book Store in Chicago, 1938–1947: linking neighborhood to nation', *Journal of Historical Research in Marketing* 1, March: 93–121.

Witkowski, Terrence and Jones, D.G. Brian (2006) 'Qualitative historical research in marketing', in Russell W. Belk (ed.) *Handbook of Qualitative Research Methods in Marketing*, Cheltenham, Edward Elgar Publishing, 131–57.

Witkowski, Terrence and Jones, D.G. Brian (2008) 'Historiography in marketing: its growth, structure of inquiry, and disciplinary status', *Business and Economic History On-Line* 6, June: 1–18.

Wittink, D.R. (2004) 'An accidental venture into academics', *Journal of Marketing* 68(3): 124–32.

Wooliscroft, Ben, Tamilia, Robert and Shapiro, Stanley (eds) (2006) *A Twenty-First Century Guide to Aldersonian Marketing Thought*, Boston: Kluwer Academic Publishers.

Wright, John S. (1989) 'Return biography to the *Journal of Marketing*: a polemic', in Terence Nevett, Kathleen Whitney and Stanley C. Hollander (eds) *Marketing History: The Emerging Discipline*, Lansing: Michigan State University, pp. 132–48.

Wright, John S. and Dimsdale, Parks B. (1974) *Pioneers in Marketing*, Atlanta, GA: Georgia State University.

Zinn, W. and Johnson, S.D. (1990) 'The commodity approach in marketing research: is it really obsolete?', *Journal of the Academy of Marketing Science*, 18: 345–54.

4
Marketing ethics
Patrick E. Murphy

Chapter Topics

Introduction

The field of marketing ethics has matured in recent years. If one were to apply the product life-cycle concept to it, the introductory stage would be the 1960s and 1970s, while the growth period occurred during the 1980s and 1990s (as will be noted later, the most articles on this topic were published in the 1990s), and the time since the turn of the century could be labelled as the maturity stage. The earliest work appeared in the 1960s and was mostly published in the *Journal of Marketing*. The 1970s and 1980s saw marketing ethics topics beginning to be published with some regularity in other academic journals. According to Murphy (2002: 166), 'marketing ethics came of age in the 1990s. At that time, substantial attention was devoted to it in the academic and business press. Marketing ethics, then, moved from being called an 'oxymoron' to a subject of academic legitimacy. Since the turn of the century, more scholarship has been devoted to this topic but most of it is now being published in specialty journals rather than ones that most marketing academics would consider as top tier.

At the outset, it is important to characterize the field of marketing ethics and its theoretical underpinnings. The definition that will be used here is: 'Marketing ethics is the systematic study of how moral standards are applied to marketing decisions, behaviors and institutions' (Laczniak and Murphy, 1993: x). Many observers view marketing ethics as a subfield within business ethics, much like ethics in finance, accounting, human resources and quantitative analysis. Business ethics is also considered to be an 'applied' area similar to legal or medical ethics. The theoretical foundation is often viewed as coming primarily from moral philosophy, but other disciplines associated with ethics are law, psychology and theology.

One barometer that a field is maturing and gaining a substantial literature base is the publication of review articles on the topic. During approximately the last 30 years, a number of such articles have been written on marketing ethics. The first was Murphy and Laczniak's review piece (1981) where they characterized this area at that time as being mostly comprised of philosophical essays. Another review article focusing on marketing ethics was published in the *Journal of Business Ethics* a few years later (Tsalkis and Fritzsche, 1989). Since 2000, three such efforts have been undertaken, with Whysall (2000) focusing primarily on work undertaken in Europe, and Nill and Schibrowsky (2007) emphasizing some of the more recent work in the field. An extensive literature review that traces marketing ethics back to its roots in the 1960s has just been published (Schlegelmich and Oberseder, 2009). They categorize almost 550 articles on marketing ethics according to 18 areas and draw several conclusions about the state of the field.

Another indicator that any subfield has standing within the overall discipline is articles appearing in major research anthologies on a topic. In recent years, marketing ethics, societal marketing and corporate social responsibility have chapters devoted to them in several important handbooks including Bloom and Gundlach (2001), Gundlach et al. (2007) and Kotabe and Helsen (2009). This chapter's inclusion in the second edition of *Marketing Theory* is another testament to the fact that marketing ethics is seen to be a legitimate subfield in marketing.

Still another factor is the publication of textbooks on a particular subject. Six texts (excluding anthologies or casebooks) have been published to date on marketing ethics. The first two appeared in 1993 (Laczniak and Murphy; Smith and Quelch). Two followed in that decade (Chonko, 1995; Schlegelmilch, 1998). (For a brief description of these four books, see Murphy (2002).) Since 2000, only two new books have been published. Murphy et al. (2005) introduced an updated version of the Laczniak and Murphy book and changed the title to *Ethical Marketing* to reflect a more positive approach to the subject. Most recently, Brenkert (2008) wrote a new text on marketing ethics from a more philosophical perspective. The fact that most of the books have not been revised is a signal that few courses on marketing ethics are offered in business curricula throughout North America and Europe.

Although 58 journals (Schlegelmilch and Oberseder, 2009) have been identified as publishing articles in marketing ethics, the vast majority of the work in this area appears in a handful of them. The dominant outlet is the *Journal of Business Ethics* which has featured nearly 30 per cent of all articles over the years and has a dedicated section editor for marketing ethics. Marketing ethics has been the focus of several special issues of *JBE* (for a synopsis, see Murphy (2002)). Other academic journals that have published several marketing ethics articles in the last two decades include *European Journal of Marketing, International Marketing Review, Journal of the Academy of Marketing Science, Journal of Advertising, Journal of Public Policy & Marketing* and *Marketing Education Review.* Two other major business ethics journals, *Business Ethics Quarterly* and *Business Ethics: A European Review,* have only included marketing ethics articles on a sporadic basis.

Theoretical focus in marketing ethics

As noted above, the theoretical foundation of all ethics is moral philosophy and several other disciplines. Marketing ethics too draws from these areas. However, substantial efforts have been made by a number of scholars to build a theoretical basis for the field that extends its social science roots. Table 4.1 summarizes 19 different articles that have contributed to the growing theoretical basis for marketing ethics. In this section several of them will be discussed in detail.

The first article that could be considered a major theoretical contribution was Laczniak (1983) on frameworks for normative ethics in marketing which he presented as a series of questions based on nonteleological works by leading twentieth-century philosophers. Ferrell and Gresham's (1985) *Journal of Marketing* article

Table 4.1   Frameworks for ethical decisions-making in marketing

Article approach(es)	Level/focus	Orientation	Normative approach(es)	Use of detailed examples
Abela and Murphy (2008)	Individual and corporate managers	Normative	Service-dominant logic and the separation thesis	Multiple success metrics and cash flow
Dunfee, Smith and Ross (1999)	Individual marketers and society	Normative	Integrative social contracts	Bribery
Enderle and Murphy (2009)	International marketers	Normative	Rawls, human rights, Golden Rule	American Marketing Association norms & values
Ferrell and Gresham (1985)	Individual marketers	Descriptive (framework)	Dependent on decision maker	None
Hunt and Vitell (1986)	Individual marketers	Descriptive (model of decision-making)	Deontological/ teleological	Two short scenarios (gifts, auto safety)
Laczniak (1983)	Marketing decision makers	Normative	Nonteleological (Ross, Rawls and Garrett)	Six short scenarios
Laczniak (1999)	Individual and corporate managers	Normative	Catholic social thought	Vulnerable consumers
Laczniak and Murphy (2006)	Individual, corporate and societal responsibility of managers	Normative	Duty- and virtue-based ethics	American Marketing Association norms & values
Laczniak and Murphy (2008)	Marketing managers	Normative	Rawls	Vulnerable consumers

(Cont'd)

Table 4.1

Article approach(es)	Level/focus	Orientation	Normative approach(es)	Use of detailed examples
Mascarenhas (1995)	Marketing decision makers	Instrumental/ diagnostic	Pluralistic	Breast implants, consumer use profiles
Murphy, Laczniak and Wood (2007)	Individual and corporate marketers	Normative	Virtue ethics	Lego, UPS, Harley Davidson
Nantel and Weeks (1996)	Individual marketers	Normative	Deontology	None
Nill (2003)	Individual marketers	Normative	Communicative ethics	AIDS drugs, WTO
Nill and Shultz (1997)	Individual marketers	Normative	Dialogic ethics	None
Robin and Reidenbach (1987)	Multilevel (societal/ organizational/ individual)	Normative	Descriptive (contextual, bounded relativism)	None
Santos and Laczniak (2009)	Multinational Marketing managers	Normative	Integrative justice model	Marketing to the poor
Smith (2001)	Individual marketer	Normative		
Thompson (1995)	Individual marketer	Instrumental/ normative	Ethics of care/ ethical relativism	None
Williams and Murphy (1990)	Multilevel (individual, organization)	Normative	Ethics of virtue	Johnson & Johnson, Nestlé

Source: Partially adapted from Dunfee et al., 1999: 15.

was the second contribution of this type to appear in the literature. They examined a contingency framework for ethical decision-making in marketing and drew from several different literatures in developing their model. While they did not explicitly apply the usual background theories in the article, they stated: 'marketers develop guidelines and rules for ethical behavior based on moral philosophy' (1985: 88). Probably the most widely cited and applied theory in marketing ethics was published a year later by Hunt and Vitell (1986). They called theirs a 'general theory' of marketing ethics and, as indicated in Table 4.1, both deontological and teleological arguments were used to ground their theory. As will be noted in the next section, many articles have subsequently appeared testing aspects of this model. Robin and Reidenbach (1987) posited a framework for integrating social responsibility and ethics into the strategic marketing planning process.

As shown in Table 4.1, the decade of the 1990s was a fruitful time for the scholarly efforts on ethical theory in marketing. It seems noteworthy that the authors of these works are all different with one exception from those discussed above. A conclusion that can be drawn was that theory development in marketing ethics was not at this time the province of just a few marketing scholars. Williams and Murphy (1990) introduced the ethics of virtue into the discussion as a foundation for marketing ethics and this article was partially in response to Robin and Reidenbach (1987) who did not utilize this theory in their analysis. Three articles appeared in 1995 and all were published in different journals. Smith (1995) formulated a test of consumer sovereignty that requires marketers to establish that consumers can exercise informed choice. Mascarenhas (1995) proposed a diagnostic framework for assessing the individual responsibilities of marketing executives for the consequences of their unethical actions. Thompson (1995) used a contextualist, rather than a normative, approach to conceptualizing and studying marketing ethics. Nantel and Weeks (1996) argued for the superiority of duty-based thinking over utilitarian guidelines for making ethical marketing decisions. Drawing on the European tradition of dialogic idealism, Nill and Schultz (1997) contend that solving ethical issues in marketing is related not so much to opportunity as will. Dunfee et al. (1999) proposed that integrative social contracts theory (ISCT) was a useful theory to apply to ethical questions in marketing. They advanced the ISCT decision process (1999: 21) which is predicated on multiple communities and multiple competing norms. Laczniak (1999) introduced the notion of Catholic social thought as another important foundation for marketing ethics. He noted that principles such as the dignity of the person, stewardship and the importance of treating vulnerable markets fairly can be applied to many issues facing marketing ethics.

Table 4.1 depicts a different picture for the early years of the twenty-first century. Most of the theoretical work that has been undertaken in marketing ethics during this decade can be attributed to Laczniak and Murphy and their co-authors. Seven articles have appeared since 2000 and they have been involved in all but two of them. Smith (2001) proposed that normative ideas are central to the development and application of marketing ethics in a response to an article that called into question the field of marketing ethics (Gaski, 1999). The Abela and Murphy (2008) article shows how marketing ethics and integrity are integral to the application of the service-dominant logic paradigm. They identify seven tensions that exist between current marketing theory and ethics. In their groundbreaking work on a new dominant logic for marketing, Vargo and Lusch (2004) have challenged the marketing profession to look at marketing as having services, not tangible goods, as the central organizing framework for the field. These services are co-created by the marketer and consumer. Enderle and Murphy (2009) explored the relevance of ethics and corporate responsibility for marketing in the global marketplace. Several theoretical underpinnings for ethics and corporate social responsibility (CSR) in marketing were advanced: an overlapping consensus from John Rawls (1996); the Golden Rule; human rights; and human capabilities (Enderle and Murphy, 2009: 515–17). Nill (2003) examined normative concepts in international marketing ethics and proposed that a dialogic approach was superior to other conceptualizations.

Laczniak and Murphy (2008), in an introduction to a special issue of the *Journal of Macromarketing*, stated that one of the overarching issues with regard to assessing distributive justice in marketing are the questions: what is fair? Or, whose conception of fairness should be used to settle competing marketing claims? They too invoked Rawls' (1999) notion of fairness and his powerful notions of the original position, veil of ignorance and difference principle (Laczniak and Murphy, 2008: 8). In their most recent work Santos and Laczniak (2009) develop a new normative framework for marketing to the poor. It is called the 'integrative justice model' and is built on seven important elements. This marketing to impoverished segments integrated several concepts that are widely used in the ethics and CSR literature: a stakeholder perspective; the triple bottom line approach; socially responsible investing; and the sustainability perspective (Santos and Laczniak, 2009: 10–11).

The final two articles discussed here have both been recognized with 'best paper' awards from the journals that published them and have had an impact on marketing scholarship since these works were selected from a competitive set that included articles on many other marketing topics. The Laczniak and Murphy (2006) article was entitled: 'Normative perspectives for ethical and socially responsible marketing'. Thus, the focus was decidedly normative and seven 'Basic Perspectives' (BPs) were advanced. Figure 4.1 shows the seven essential BPs and how they fit together. Each builds on the next and BP1 notes that ethical marketing puts people (e.g. customers, employees, managers, etc.) first or at the centre, as is shown in Figure 4.1. BP2 focuses on legal and ethical questions and basically says that ethics creates a higher standard for managers than the law does. There are three central elements (intent, means and ends) to BP3, and four types of managers (i.e. egoist, legalist, moral strivers and principled) in BP4. There are five points related to BP5, six stakeholders are identified in BP6 and a seven-step model for making ethical decisions in BP7. In addition to extensive discussion of each of the seven BPs, Laczniak and Murphy draw ethical lessons from this set and provide implications for researchers, managers and educators. The authors conclude with the following synopsis:

> This article presents a comprehensive, normative examination of ethical marketing practice. Our approach is firmly grounded in the centrality of exchange to marketing and the inherent role of societal outcomes attributable to the marketing system. Seven BPs are advanced, and each builds on the preceding ones. Furthermore, the sophistication of ethical analysis that is required by the marketing manager escalates as one internalizes these perspectives *because they are integrative*. (Laczniak and Murphy, 2006: 173, emphasis in original)

The Murphy et al. (2007) article appeared in the *European Journal of Marketing*. It presented a normative approach to relationship marketing. The ethical theory that served as the foundation for this work was virtue ethics. Figure 4.2 shows the model that was formulated in the paper. The middle of the diagram depicts the three stages of relationship marketing: establishing, sustaining and reinforcing. Paired with these three stages are three central virtues that should be associated with the stages. In other words, trust is essential if one is to establish a relationship with another person or organization. Commitment is necessary if one wants to maintain such a

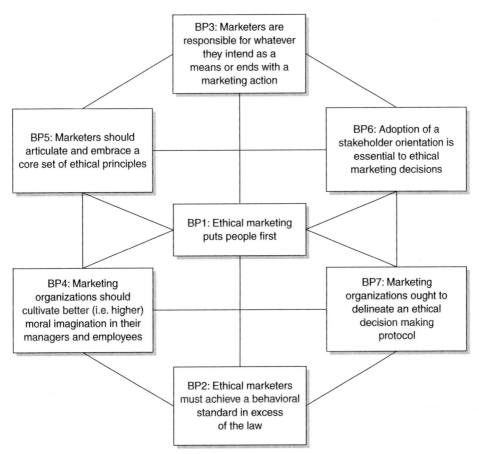

Figure 4.1   A summary of the essential basic perspectives (BPS) for evaluation and improving marketing ethics (Laczniak and Murphy, 2006: 157)

relationship. Finally, diligence is needed if the relationship is to be maintained or reinforced. Surrounding these stages are four facilitating or supporting virtues. Integrity is a hallmark virtue of all professions, including marketing. It has been labelled a 'supervirtue' by the late Robert Solomon (1992). The second critical virtue to enhancing relationship marketing is fairness. This notion of fairness ties in with the recent work of Santos and Laczniak (2009). Respect is another virtue that is increasingly important in the multi-cultural world of this century. It has been recognized that one can 'respectfully disagree' with the point of others in a marketing context (Murphy, 1999). Empathy is the final facilitating variable and has resonance with the Golden Rule and the ethic of care. Marketers who are successful in a relationship setting seem to know the importance of and practice this virtue. Transparency surrounds the other virtues and is needed in communication and action. This writer spent a year in Ireland in the early 1990s and found that transparency was a regularly used word, especially in business settings. Since the Enron and

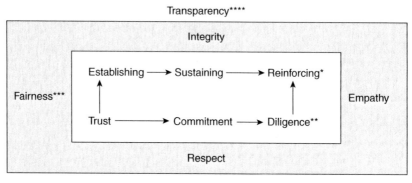

Figure 4.2   Ethical bases of relationship marketing (Murphy et al., 2007: 44).

Andersen debacle a few years ago, transparency is invoked on a much more frequent basis by both executives and business critics in the United States.

Empirical research in marketing ethics theory

In addition to the substantial theoretical literature in marketing ethics examined above, a number of empirical studies have been conducted which are theory based. While the list is long, only those projects which have been undertaken as tests of theories are reviewed here. Goolsby and Hunt (1992) undertook a study of cognitive moral development in marketing and found this theory helps to explain the ethical views of consumers. Another of Hunt's graduate students, John Sparks (Sparks and Hunt, 1998), examined the concept of ethical sensitivity in the context of the marketing research profession and found that awareness of norms is an influence on ethical sensitivity. Smith and Cooper-Martin (1997) also undertook an empirical study and developed a typology based on product harm and consumer vulnerability.

As noted above, the most extensive theory testing has occurred with the Hunt-Vitell theory of marketing ethics. Scott Vitell, Anusorn Singhapakdi and various coauthors have undertaken numerous tests of some aspects of the Hunt-Vitell model. Some of the applications have focused on sales professionals (Singhapakdi and Vitell, 1991), marketing managers (Singhapakdi et al., 1996), international managers (Singhapakdi et al., 1994) and organizational culture (Vitell et al., 1993). Furthermore, Vitell has also used the Hunt-Vitell theory to evaluate the ethics of consumers (Vitell and Muncy, 1992). The topic of consumer ethics is receiving more attention, especially by European scholars (see Brunk, 2010). A more extensive discussion of the empirical work in marketing ethics is contained in Schlegelmilch and Oberseder (2009).

Future research directions

Marketing ethics is not a static field. The conception of ethical marketing practice has taken on greater meaning in the wake of the global financial meltdown. Subprime mortgages, which were at least partially responsible for the collapse of financial institutions throughout the globe, have long been understood in the context of marketing ethics as unfair to many consumers and irresponsibly utilized by some financial institutions. This issue was folded into the indictment of finance but it is very much a marketing ethics problem since over-selling and marketing contributed to this dire situation.

It is hard to predict which issues within marketing will be hot topics in the future. (This writer identified several areas in an earlier work (Murphy, 2002) and they will not be repeated here.) It seems safe to say that sustainable marketing, health and safety issues and base of the pyramid topics are ones that will be investigated using marketing theories for the foreseeable future.

Sustainable marketing

Environmental issues in marketing were studied in some depth during the 1970s and 1980s. However, until the last few years, the attention devoted to these issues has been minimal. Although the Bruntland Commission (1987) developed the most commonly used definition of sustainability – meeting the needs of the present without compromising the ability of future generations to meet their own needs – some time ago, efforts to examine sustainable marketing did not 'take off' until some time this decade. Terms such as green marketing and environmental marketing have been supplanted with the new terminology of sustainability.

Global issues such as climate change, energy use, and water shortages have brought renewed attention to this area. In response, marketing scholars have redoubled their efforts in focusing on overall environmental issues (Belz and Peattie, 2009; Grant, 2007), as well as specific ones like energy (Press and Arnould, 2009). One more general evaluation of sustainable marketing (Murphy, 2005) proposed several ethical bases for sustainable marketing including the precautionary principle, ethic of the mean/balance, power and responsibility equilibrium, the environment as a stakeholder and planetary ethics. In addition to these, the notion of stewardship proposed earlier by Laczniak (1999) provides some needed theoretical foundation for future work in this area.

Health and safety issues

The recent selling of toys tainted with lead-based paint was a major blemish on toy makers, retailers and, of course, the Chinese production facilities that produced them. This incident has caused all members of the supply chain for these products to be more vigilant. While not reaching international proportions, problems with tainted meat, produce that causes illness and sometimes death, have also focused attention on food marketing in a new way. Marketing ethics scholarship is needed to 'sort out' some of these emerging safety issues and get beyond the rhetoric in the media and blogs on these topics. Both conceptual and empirical work is necessary to gain a more complete understanding of how product safety is understood by consumers and marketers in the twenty-first century.

A major health issue that has also emerged in recent years is obesity, both of the population in general and in children especially. More academic study of this topic has occurred and is serving as one input to regulatory bodies in their assessment of how best to move forward in mitigating these serious health issues. Unfortunately, obesity leads to a host of medical maladies that plague some consumers throughout their lives.

In an introduction to a special issue of the *Journal of Public Policy & Marketing,* Moore (2007) detailed the magnitude of the problem by stating that childhood obesity has become an increasingly serious health problem in the United States, and around the world. Obesity among pre-school and school-aged children in the US has increased almost three-fold since the late 1970s, with 14 per cent of 2–5 year-olds and 19 per cent of 6–11 year-olds now characterized as overweight. The role of marketing in contributing to this issue is receiving attention. Serious questions are being asked about the impacts of food marketing in both public and private sectors. Two comprehensive research reviews have been published, one by the Food Standards Agency in the UK (Hastings et al., 2003) and the other in response to a Congressional Directive by the Institute of Medicine (2006). Moore concludes her essay by stating that childhood obesity has become an epidemic in our nation and around the world (World Health Organization, 2003); the associated risks to children's health and well-being are substantial. Marketing's role as both a contributor to the problem and as a force in its alleviation is a complex one; many significant questions are yet to be addressed. This appears to be the challenge for researchers in the future.

_____ Base of the pyramid _____

A topic that is likely to receive more attention in the coming decades is the ethical treatment of consumers at the 'base of the pyramid' – those individuals at the lowest socio-economic level of the financial pyramid (Prahalad, 2005). As noted above, Santos and Laczniak (2009) have outlined a new conceptual approach to dealing with the impoverished market. Vachani and Smith (2008) have identified several precepts that should exist in 'socially responsible distribution' by studying an innovative company, an education-based NGO and the government-run postal service in India. The lessons they identify focus both on improving the financial and educational position of those at the base of the pyramid as well as the ways socially responsible distribution can enhance the workings of the market.

In Prahalad's (2005) influential book, he identifies a number of organizations that he sees as succeeding in serving this market. One firm profiled is Casas Bahia, based in Brazil. It is a large retailer selling mostly clothing and household and durable goods to the middle and lower classes, usually on an extended payment plan.

Although Prahalad shows the impressive growth the company has experienced, he does not discuss the fact that the firm forces consumers to make their payment in the store and they tend to buy other products (sometimes unneeded ones) on these trips to the store. This situation was explained in an article in the *Wall Street Journal* (Jordan, 2002) and was reprinted in a marketing ethics casebook (Murphy and Laczniak, 2006). The point in raising this example is that academics in marketing ethics should be alert to seemingly successful strategies aimed at this vulnerable market and discuss them with students and colleagues to raise awareness of the quality of the products they are offered, the level of fairness in pricing these products, and the most viable distribution channels that need to exist in these emerging markets.

The Santos and Laczniak (2009) article helps marketers better understand impoverished markets. If companies are going to be successful in marketing in an ethical manner to these underserved markets, much more intensive investigation needs to be undertaken. To that end, Santos (2009) has also completed the most thorough analysis of this area to date and the title of his dissertation shows the way for future research in this emerging field: 'Marketing to the impoverished: developing a model for markets that justly and fairly serve the poor'. It is up to other researchers to help further illuminate this challenging issue.

Suggestions for conducting research on marketing ethics

In examining this significant literature base in marketing ethics theory, several suggestions come to mind on how best to undertake research in this field. Before moving to the positive developments, a number of trends that this writer has identified earlier (Murphy, 2002) as being 'not so positive' should be addressed. One troubling trend in empirical research on marketing ethics is the continued and even growing use of student samples. Ethical decisions are made in companies and in the transaction situation (whether online or in the store). Thus, use of inexperienced students as surrogate consumers or managers seems misguided. The only exception is executive MBA students who are usually practising managers during the time of their programme. A related area is cross-cultural research where the same instrument is given to respondents in multiple countries. Unless there is a theoretical reason for the selection of the samples, such exercises seem too often to confirm obvious cultural differences. Of course, the situation is compounded if student samples are used in multiple countries. Some ethics-based research uses short scenarios. The criticism here is not with the technique, but that the scenarios are too many (one study had 20 scenarios) or too few (one or two) or too old (scenarios developed 10 or 20 years ago). If the researcher uses scenarios in an experimental fashion, valuable and generalizable information can be gained. Such experimentation might study recent ethical issues like, online selling, privacy on the web and online surveys. A final area of concern is the testing of narrow theoretical propositions. In the 1990s, much empirical research was undertaken to test various aspects of the Hunt and Vitell

(1986) model. Some of this research seemed to focus too narrowly on one aspect of that or other models. The assessment made several years ago bears repeating here:

> While it is quite difficult to operationalize generalized theories and models, some marketing scholars have been content to investigate such narrow propositions and theories that the outcome of their work is marginalized. The field of marketing ethics seems increasingly to be using the same narrow lens that has characterized much of the consumer behavior research over a prolonged period ... The work of marketing ethics can impact the practice of marketing if researchers keep in mind that they are not engaged in just a narrow academic exercise. (Murphy, 2002: 171)

The quote above leads to the type of research that this individual believes is most effective. First, the impressive list of articles shown in Table 4.1 confirms that it is possible to publish important theoretical and conceptual articles on marketing ethics. Future researchers are encouraged to not be intimidated by this somewhat daunting task of contributing to the theoretical base of this field. Second, theory testing is needed especially for the new more global theories of marketing ethics depicted in Figures 4.1 and 4.2. As noted in the quote above, the task of operational-izing the BPs or virtues will likely take a significant investment in scale construction and validation. Furthermore, a sample of managers would most likely need to be studied in order to draw conclusions about which aspects of these models are most applicable to marketing practice. Third, depth interviews of managers are one (but certainly not the only) method to study marketing practitioners. Some of the insights gained by the consumer culture theory (CCT) researchers may be valuable for those interested in studying marketer behaviour. This writer has been involved with two projects in marketing ethics where depth interviews were conducted (Drumwright and Murphy, 2004, 2009) and though the process of interviewing executives is arduous, the insights gained are very valuable. Fourth, a thrust of current ethics research, especially in Europe, appears to be on consumer ethics and responsible consumption (Brinkmann, 2004; Ozcaglar-Toulouse, 2007). Several of the caveats mentioned above regarding avoiding student samples and narrow cross cultural studies should be heeded here as well. The notion of responsible consumption is important from a marketing, sustainability and societal perspective, but the projects that will make the most contribution will likely be those that are the hardest to carry out. Another fruitful area is to examine marketing ethics from the standpoint of another foundational discipline. The highly cited Gundlach and Murphy (1993) article is an illustration of this type of endeavour. Certainly, dissertations are not meant to be a life work, but slicing the project 'too thin' means that the future impact of the work will be affected.

Conclusion

This chapter has provided an historical discussion of theoretical research in marketing ethics. A brief analysis of some of the empirical work in this field was also covered. The emerging areas for future research in marketing ethics, of sustainable marketing, health and safety issues and base of the pyramid, were proposed as potential areas for future research. A number of challenges and opportunities for conducting research on marketing ethics were outlined. It is hoped that at least some future scholars build on this substantial body of knowledge in marketing ethics.

Recommended reading

Dunfee, Thomas, Smith, N. Craig and Ross, William (1999) 'Social contracts and marketing ethics', *Journal of Marketing*, 63(2): 14–32.

Goolsby, Jerry R. and Hunt, Shelby D. (1992) 'Cognitive moral development and marketing', *Journal of Marketing* 56(1): 55–68.

Gundlach, Gregory T. and Murphy, Patrick E. (1993) 'Ethical and legal foundations of relational marketing exchanges', *Journal of Marketing* 57(4): 35–46.

Hunt, Shelby and Vitell, Scott (1986) 'A general theory of marketing ethics', *Journal of Macromarketing* 6(1): 6–15.

Laczniak, Gene R. (1983) 'Frameworks for analyzing marketing ethics', *Journal of Macromarketing* 3(1): 7–18.

Laczniak, Gene R. and Murphy, Patrick E. (2006) 'Normative perspectives for ethical and socially responsible marketing', *Journal of Macromarketing* 26(2): 154–177.

Murphy, Patrick E., Laczniak, Gene R. and Wood, Graham (2007) 'An ethical basis for relationship marketing: a virtue ethics perspective', *European Journal of Marketing* 41(1 & 2): 37–57.

Nill, Alexander (2003) 'Global marketing ethics: a communicative approach,' *Journal of Macromarketing* 23(2), 90–104.

Smith, N. Craig (2001) 'Ethical guidelines for marketing practice: a reply to Gaski and some observations on the role of normative marketing ethics', *Journal of Business Ethics* 32: 3–18.

Williams, Oliver F. and Murphy, Patrick E. (1990) 'The ethics of virtue: a moral theory for marketing', *Journal of Macromarketing*, 10(1): 19–29.

References

Abela, Andrew V. and Murphy, Patrick E. (2008) 'Marketing with integrity: ethics and the service-dominant logic for marketing', *Journal of the Academy of Marketing Science* 36: 39–53.

Belz, Frank-Martin and Peattie, Ken (2009) *Sustainability Marketing: A Global Perspective*. London: John Wiley.

Bloom, Paul N. and Gundlach, Gregory T. (eds) (2001) *Handbook of Marketing and Society*. Thousand Oaks, CA: Sage.

Brenkert, George (2008) *Marketing Ethics*. Cambridge, MA: Blackwell.

Brinkmann, Johannes (2004) 'Looking at consumer behavior in a moral perspective', *Journal of Business Ethics* 51: 129–41.

Brunk, Katja H. (2010) 'Exploring origins of ethical company/brand perceptions – A consumer perspective of corporate ethics', *Journal of Business Research* 63(3): 255–62.

Chonko, Lawrence B. (1995) *Ethical Decision Making in Marketing*. Thousand Oaks, CA: Sage.

Drumwright, Minette E. and Murphy, Patrick E. (2004) 'How advertising practitioners view ethics: moral muteness, moral myopia and moral imagination', *Journal of Advertising* 33(2): 7–24.

Drumwright, Minette E. and Murphy, Patrick E. (2009) 'The current state of advertising ethics: industry and academic perspectives', *Journal of Advertising* 38(1): 83–107.

Dunfee, Thomas, Smith, N. Craig and Ross, William (1999) 'Social contracts and marketing ethics', *Journal of Marketing* 63(2): 14–32.

Enderle, Georges and Murphy, Patrick E. (2009) 'Ethics and corporate social responsibility for marketing in the global marketplace', in Masaaki Kotabe and Kristiaan Helsen (eds) *The Sage Handbook of International Marketing*. London: Sage, pp. 502–29.

Ferrell, O.C. and Gresham, Lawrence (1985) 'A contingency framework for understanding ethical decision making in marketing', *Journal of Marketing*, 49(3): 87–96.

Gaski, John F. (1999) 'Does marketing ethics really have anything to say?–a critical commentary of the literature', *Journal of Business Ethics* 18, February: 315–34.

Goolsby, Jerry R. and Hunt, Shelby D. (1992) 'Cognitive moral development and marketing', *Journal of Marketing* 56(1): 55–68.

Grant, John (2007) *The Green Marketing Manifesto*. West Sussex, UK: John Wiley.

Gundlach, Gregory T. and Murphy, Patrick E. (1993) 'Ethical and legal foundations of relational marketing exchanges', *Journal of Marketing* 57(4): 35–46.

Gundlach, Gregory T., Block, L. and Wilkie, William L. (eds) (2007) *Explorations of Marketing and Society*. Cincinnati, OH: Thomson Southwestern.

Hastings, Gerard et al. (2003) *Review of Research on the Effects of Food Promotion to Children*, Report to the Food Standards Agency, Glasgow, UK: Centre for Social Marketing, University of Strathclyde.

Hunt, Shelby and Vitell, Scott (1986) 'A general theory of marketing ethics', *Journal of Macromarketing* 6(1): 6–15.

Institute of Medicine (2006) *Food Marketing to Children and Youth: Threat or Opportunity?* Washington, DC: National Academies Press.

Jordan, Miriane (2002) 'A retailer in Brazil has become rich by courting poor', *The Wall Street Journal*, June 11, 14.

Kotabe, Masaaki and Helsen, Kristiaan (2009) *The Sage Handbook of International Marketing*. London: Sage.

Laczniak, Gene R. (1983) 'Frameworks for analyzing marketing ethics', *Journal of Macromarketing* 3(1): 7–18.

Laczniak, Gene R. (1999) 'Distributive justice, catholic social teaching, and the moral responsibility of marketing', *Journal of Public Policy & Marketing* 18(1): 125–29.

Laczniak, Gene R. and Murphy, Patrick E. (1993) *Ethical Marketing Decisions: The Higher Road*. Needham Heights, MA: Allyn & Bacon.

Laczniak, Gene R. and Murphy, Patrick E. (2006) 'Normative perspectives for ethical and socially responsible marketing', *Journal of Macromarketing* 26(2): 154–77.

Laczniak, Gene R. and Murphy, Patrick E. (2008) 'Distributive justice: pressing questions, emerging directions and the promise of a Rawlsian analysis', *Journal of Macromarketing* 18, March: 5–11.

Mascarenhas, Oswald A.J. (1995) 'Exonerating unethical marketing behaviors: a diagnostic framework', *Journal of Marketing* 59(2): 43–57.

Moore, Elizabeth (2007) 'Perspectives on food marketing and childhood obesity: introduction to the special section', *Journal of Public Policy & Marketing* 26(2): 157–61.

Murphy, Patrick E. (1999) 'Character and virtue ethics in international marketing: an agenda for managers, educators, and researchers', *Journal of Business Ethics* 18: 107–24.

Murphy, Patrick E. (2002) 'Marketing ethics at the millennium: review, reflections, and recommendations', in Norman E. Bowie (ed.) *The Blackwell Guide to Business Ethics*, Cambridge, MA: Blackwell, pp. 165–85.

Murphy, Patrick E. (2005) 'Sustainable marketing', *Business & Professional Ethics Journal*, 24(1 & 2): 171–98.

Murphy, Patrick E. and Laczniak, Gene R. (1981) in Ben M. Enis and Kenneth J. Roering (eds) *Review of Marketing*. Chicago, IL: American Marketing Association, pp. 107–24.

Murphy, Patrick E., Laczniak, Gene R., Bowie, Norman E. and Klein, Thomas (2005) *Ethical Marketing*. Upper Saddle River, NJ: Pearson Education.

Murphy, Patrick E. and Laczniak, Gene R. (2006) *Marketing Ethics: Cases and Readings*. Upper Saddle River, NJ: Pearson Prentice-Hall.

Murphy, Patrick E., Laczniak, Gene R. and Wood, Graham (2007) 'An ethical basis for relationship marketing: a virtue ethics perspective', *European Journal of Marketing* 41(1/2): 37–57.

Nantel, James and Weeks, Willliam (1996) 'Marketing ethics: is there more to it than the utilitarian approach?' *European Journal of Marketing* 30(5): 9–19.

Nill, Alexander (2003) 'Global marketing ethics: a communicative approach,' *Journal of Macromarketing* 23(2) 90–104.

Nill, Alexander and Schibrowsky, John A. (2007) 'Research on marketing ethics: a systematic review of the literature', *Journal of Macromarketing* 27(3): 256–73.

Nill, Alexander and Shultz, Clifford (1997) 'Cross cultural marketing ethics and the emergence of dialogic idealism as a decision making model', *Journal of Macromarketing* 17(1): 4–19.

Ozcaglar-Toulouse, Nil (2007) 'Living for "ethics": responsible consumption in everyday life', in Russell W. Belk and John F. Sherry, Jr. (eds) *Consumer Culture Theory: Research in Consumer Behavior*, Vol. 11, pp. 421–36.

Prahalad, C.K. (2005) *The Fortune at the Bottom of the Pyramid*. Upper Saddle River, NJ: Wharton School Publishing.

Press, Melea and Arnould, Eric J. (2009) 'Constraints on sustainable energy consumption: market system and public policy challenges and opportunities', *Journal of Public Policy & Marketing* 28(1): 102–13.

Rawls, John (1996) *Political Liberalism*. New York: Columbia University Press.

Rawls, John (1999) *A Theory of Justice*, revised edn. Cambridge, MA: Harvard University Press.

Robin, Donald P. and Reidenbach, Eric R. (1987) 'Social responsibility, ethics and marketing strategy: closing the gap between concept and application', *Journal of Marketing* 51(1): 44–58.

Santos, Nicholas J.C. (2009) 'Marketing to the impoverished: developing a model for markets that justly and fairly serve the poor', unpublished dissertation, Marquette University.

Santos, Nicholas J.C. and Laczniak, Gene R. (2009) 'Marketing to the poor: an integrative justice model for engaging impoverished market segments', *Journal of Public Policy & Marketing* 28(1): 3–15.

Schlegelmilch, Bodo (1998) *Marketing Ethics: An International Perspective*. London: International Thomson Business Press.

Schlegelmich, Bodo and Oberseder, Magdalena (2009) 'Half a century of marketing ethics: shifting perspectives and emerging trends', *Journal of Business Ethics*.

Singhapakdi, Anusorn, and Vitell, Scott (1991) 'Analysing the ethical decision making of sales professionals', *Journal of Personal Selling & Sales Management* 11: 1–12.

Singhapakdi, Anusorn, Vitell, Scott and Leelakulthanit, C. (1994) 'A cross cultural study of moral philosophies, ethical perceptions and judgements: a comparison of American and Thai marketers,' *International Marketing Review* 21(4): 65–78.

Singhapakdi, Anusorn, Vitell, Scott and Kraft, K. (1996) 'Moral intensity and ethical decision making of marketing professionals', *Journal of Business Research* 36: 245–55.

Smith, N. Craig (1995) 'Marketing strategies for the ethics era', *Sloan Management Review* 36, Summer: 85–97.

Smith, N. Craig (2001) 'Ethical guidelines for marketing practice: a reply to Gaski and some observations on the role of normative marketing ethics', *Journal of Business Ethics* 32: 3–18.

Smith, N. Craig and Cooper-Martin, Elizabeth (1997) 'Ethics and target marketing: the role of product harm and consumer vulnerability', *Journal of Marketing* 35, July: 3–12.

Smith, N. Craig and Quelch, John A. (1993) *Ethics in Marketing*. Homewood, IL: Irwin.

Solomon, Robert C. (1992) *Ethics and Excellence: Cooperation and Integrity in Business*. New York: Oxford University Press.

Sparks, John R. and Hunt, Shelby D. (1998) 'Marketing researcher ethical sensitivity: conceptualisation, measurement, and exploratory investigation', *Journal of Marketing* 62(April): 92–109.

Thompson, Craig T. (1995) 'A contextualist proposal for the conceptualization and study of marketing ethics', *Journal of Public Policy & Marketing* 14(1): 177–91.

Tsalikis, John and Fritzsche, David J. (1989) 'Business ethics: a literature review with a focus on marketing ethics', *Journal of Business Ethics* 8(9): 695–743.

Vachani, Sushil and Smith, N. Craig (2008) 'Socially responsible distribution: distribution strategies for reaching the bottom of the pyramid', *California Management Review* 50(2): 52–84.

Vargo, Stephen L. and Lusch, Robert F. (2004) 'Evolving a new dominant logic for marketing', *Journal of Marketing* 68, Spring: 1–17.

Vitell, Scott and Muncy, James (1992) 'Consumer ethics: an empirical investigaton of the factors influencing ethical judgements of the final consumer', *Journal of Business Ethics* 11(8): 585–97.

Vitell, Scott, Rallapalli, K. and Singhapakdi, Anusorn (1993) 'Marketing norms: the influences of personal moral philosophies and organizational ethical culture', *Journal of the Academy of Marketing Science* 21(4): 331–7.

Whysall, Paul (2000) 'Marketing ethics – an overview', *Marketing Review* 1(2): 175–95.

Williams, Oliver F. and Murphy, Patrick E. (1990) 'The ethics of virtue: a moral theory for marketing', *Journal of Macromarketing* 10(1): 19–29.

World Health Organization (2003) 'Obesity and overweight' Global Strategy on Diet, Physical Activity and Health, available at: www.who.int/dietphysicalactivity/publications/facts/obesity/en/ (accessed 12 July 2007).

Section B

Disciplinary Underpinnings of
Marketing Theory

5

The economics basis of marketing*
Richard J. Varey

Chapter Topics

Forethoughts

In beginning a discussion of the economic thinking that has become common marketing thinking, it is important to distinguish that part of the marketing field concerned with managerial control of markets and that which is a science of markets. Marketing thus sits in a commercial exchange economy between producers and consumers, as well as between economics and managerial practices. If we understand how 'the market' operates as an alternative to state authority, then we can see what marketing is supposed to do before focusing down on how to do marketing. To do this it is better to investigate economics from beyond the confines of the typical marketing or introductory economics textbook.

Marketing, when seen at the macro level, is a process for maximizing society's overall satisfaction – of economic enrichment – from the consumption of scarce resources. When seen at the micro level it appears much more like a process for inter-firm competition that manipulates consumer preferences. Marketing operates in and on the *market*. Since the eighteenth century, this has meant the society-wide space (institution) in which prices communicate preferences to producers of goods

---

* The author gratefully acknowledges the generously extensive recommendations for fruitful readings that Associate Professor Peter E. Earle provided, and recognizes the substantial influence this collegial attitude has had on the writing of this chapter.

and services – so, not any longer the public meeting-place of earlier times, but, in the neoclassical tradition, an abstract supra-individual equilibrium mechanism, which stands as the bold alternative to tradition and central planning.

The notion of a competitive market is attractive to liberal sensibilities, since it implies shared meanings and fairness, social interdependence, and equal human dignity in transactions, contracts and promises, as well as the sanctity of contractual obligations. It aligns with conservative thought in offering a self-regulating alternative to state authority. Yet, the marketplace is recognizably fraught with opportunities for fraudulent behaviour, as rational human beings compete independently of each other in society.

The philosophic origins of marketing are largely founded on the liberal neoclassical economic thinking that has dominated the academic economics profession since the middle of the twentieth century – Hayek and Friedman are notable representatives. J.K. Galbraith calls this the 'central tradition' (Galbraith, 1970). This modern liberal tradition has been concerned with tempering the neoclassical economic analysis and advocating government intervention to correct market imperfections and failures. There are reservations about laissez-faire policies, and the power of large corporations is recognized as working against the perfect market competition assumption. The social desirability and consumption of some commodities is recognized as part of society's general well-being, even though private capitalists would not make a profit from their production. Externalities are recognized as the cause of divergent private costs and social costs. The solution for all of these market imperfections is government intervention in the economy, rather than any extreme or perfect laissez-faire.

Some economists don't take marketing very seriously, and consider the research and theory development to be facile. We will see that this is an interesting stance to take, given the status of economics. Those who study market efficiency within the structure-conduct-performance (SCP) paradigm see little significance in the practice of marketing. Others are looking to marketing to provide explanations of real market behaviour. For example, a major role of marketing is to present buyers with rules for making choices[1] and connections between products, vendors and lifestyles, and with cases for adopting these rules in their consumption decisions.

The purpose of this chapter is not to make economics experts out of marketing students, but rather to highlight the key origins, understandings and assumptions upon which marketing thought is apparently supported. We will explore the important consumer theory and producer theory concepts that we think we are familiar with from our marketing principles textbooks and lectures. The historical perspective, well beyond the current crop of introductory textbooks, reveals some intriguing insights and quite a few issues. It may be that many marketing students – and their lecturers – are not at all clear about the diversity of approaches to explaining market behaviour. An understanding of classical, neoclassical, behavioural and institutional perspectives can raise insights that are not evident when a single perspective is (perhaps unwittingly) taken. It is widely believed that economics began with one of Adam Smith's books published in 1776. Economics then progressed with the

---

[1] A choice requires the relinquishment of desirable alternatives.

work of Jevons and Menger in 1871, adding marginal utility in the founding of the Austrian School of thinking. For others, modern economics came about in Hicks' 1937 formalization of the modelling approach (the neoclassical synthesis). A rather more diligent inquiry reveals important developments dating from 1570 and 1660, and an historical exploration of ideas, people and circumstances, is both intriguing and revealing. 'History of economics' texts are plentiful and rewarding reading (Canterbery, 1987; Guillet De Monthoux, 1993; Hunt, 2002; Roll, 1992; Routh, 1989). In the context of marketing, we consider what are the important concepts, interpretations, issues, and what misconceptions and vagueness in use are evident, as well as what is the essential nature of marketing when seen from the economics point of view?

Why have certain central concepts (exchange, value, etc.) become so prominent in everyday talk? Why did 'consumer behaviour' develop as a parallel field of study along with managerial marketing? We look below the surface appearances to understand the consequences and implications of adopting certain ideas and assumptions as the basis for the logic of marketing. In doing so, we are concerned that there seems to be an over-dependence on a misguiding, even incomplete, orthodoxy in our undergraduate (and much of our postgraduate) marketing education. We can summarize this by observing that for most students of marketing, the subject of economics is synonymous with neoclassical (general equilibrium) thinking, and with the central assumption that growth is good (more is better). The mantra of 'marketing principles' is (almost entirely without reflection), 'wealth creation though competition and choice'.

As we will see, there is so much strong criticism and opposition to neoclassical economic thinking, that it seems prudent to disregard it as a satisfactory basis for understanding twenty-first-century marketing. Whereas Adam Smith is held up as the hero and founder of economics, and thus as a guide to the market and market control (marketing), that version of economics might be best disregarded. How can this be?

Economics

This discussion is about economy, and the field that studies human activity in the dynamic (changing) markets of economies is economics. Although 'the market' is rarely studied by marketing specialists, it is the *raison d'être* of the practices of marketing, and of the logic of economics, or rather marketing is the managerial technology for ensuring that the 'perfect' market isn't allowed to operate. The proactive form of managed marketing distorts the market for its own interests. Pretty much all of the economic theory that underlies orthodox marketing theory (Jones and Monieson, 1990) is of a neoclassical market model[2] that is widely adopted as a guide to practice. This is a problem because the model is largely a rhetorical tool. It purports to be descriptive, but only of an abstract theoretical institution, and

[2] For the typical economist, a 'model' is a small system of equations to describe some or all of an entire economy in terms of a few aggregative variables, often without recourse to actual data.

presents difficulties when applied to practical business problems, and, worse, it is also used prescriptively on that basis. Further, it doesn't represent actual market behaviour very well at all (Carrier, 1997)! The model is a simplification of a complex whole, yet it is common for people to simplistically invoke the 'laws of the market' in planning to persuade people to think and act in certain ways. The neoclassical economics framework is useful within limits, given its extreme assumptions about human behaviour, social structure and the nature of the biosphere (Ekins and Max-Neef, 1992; Stokes, 1992), yet is used well beyond situations for which the assumptions can be held valid.

In Western/Northern states, societies are market-directed as the primary basis for economic choices. That is the most convenient way of organizing economic aspects of life, especially when markets are not dominated by a few large corporations. The market logic has become firmly embedded in the modern mind, in both the private and public spheres, although most of us are peripherally aware that centrally planned (authoritative) and tradition-directed (historically determined) economies have existed and do operate, even as the market mechanism predominates. Citizens of democratic societies tend to equate market choice with freedom (or liberty, both narrowly defined) and the right to be individuals.

The dominant capitalist *provisioning system* (taking Applbaum's (2004) extension beyond mere exchange and sales) is the shared, sometimes co-operative, process in which producers and consumers act to satisfy needs through the production and distribution of objects and the enactment of services. In this, the market, and therefore marketing, are central ideas. This capitalism, as we now understand it, has certain institutional and behavioural arrangements (Hunt, 2002): market-oriented commodity production; privately owned means of production; a majority of the population earning buying power by selling labour in the employment market; and ruggedly individualistic, acquisitive, utility-maximizing private enterprise behaviour by most individuals. The products have physical features that make them useable – they have use value. Further, they are valued because they can be sold for money in the market – they have exchange value. There is no direct connection between a person's productive capacity (to work) and their consumption, so exchange in the market mediates. Further, a person has no direct relationship with the producers of what they consume. Again, the market is a mediator since there is physical and psychological distance of producers from consumers.

> In a social economy, where the maker of economic goods does not use them and the provider of economic services does not benefit from them, there is a real separation between producers and consumers. But while they are separated, they are also necessarily related. Hence, the separation is accompanied by an interdependence which is very real ... There is a natural, necessary attraction between the parties. Another name for this real, interdependent relationship between producer and consumer is a market. The market is the gap which separates producer and consumer. As the separation of producer and consumer grows greater under an expanding division of labor and increasingly differentiated consumer wants, the relationship becomes no less real but only more complex. (McInnes, 1964: 56)

Economics can be thought of as a 'derived' normative 'social science' that deals with what ought to be done to organize for economic tasks that maximize accomplished objectives (ends) with the allocation of scarce resources (means) through decision-making processes. Although economists have long strived to claim economics as a science, it is not now, and never has been, value-free. Robert Clower recalled that Swedish economist Johan Wicksell once said that it should not be the job of economists to make the commonsense difficult (Colander and Coats, 1989: 26).

Economics is limited (inexact) as a science because it is simplified and abstracted. Salient properties are selected from the multitude of variables that bear on the complex real-world economy, in intellectual experiments in the laboratory of the imagination, for the purpose of problem solving. It is thus an endeavour for understanding problems, as well as providing a basic language, and a common metaphor in 'the market'. It has provided concepts (tenets) for the marketing discipline, so we trace the sources of the foundational economic theories. In so doing, we get a picture of the current status, and a look towards the future of marketing. The dominant paradigm that persists was established in the seventeenth century during the Scientific Revolution and prior to the Industrial Revolution. Marketing's quest for scientific status is rather shakily, in the minds of many, built on the presumption that economics is an established science, although this is seemingly wrong!

The basic concepts of economics are a price economy, household and individual decision-making units, competitive business firms, a system of competitive pricing, and economic power to interfere with (manipulate) the supply-demand-price adjustment process. The market system produces order out of the decentralized decision making of buyers and consumers, reconciling many conflicting interests, and solving the problems of economic choice. The complex social and economic relationships of the market appears to each person as just so many impersonal relationships among things, and each person depends on the impersonal forces of buying (demand) and selling (supply) for the satisfaction of their needs.

Fundamental to the idea of the market, modern social conventions and pervading attitudes see the market as the source of satisfaction of subjectively recognized needs and of happiness, if only one can buy more things. This 'more is better' thinking is right to a point, yet extensive research shows that once a threshold of wealth is achieved, then diminishing returns set in and the more one gets the more needy one feels (see, e.g. various discussions of consumerism (De Graaf et al., 2002; Hamilton and Denniss, 2005; James, 2006, 2007; Lane, 2000, 1991)). Economic growth isn't necessarily creating high levels of life satisfaction, genuine well-being and true happiness for society (Myers, 2000; Speth, 2008).

We can think of economics as the social 'science' that analyses decisions about the allocation of scarce resources among alternative uses by individuals, companies and states to satisfy wants – what to produce, how to produce, and how to distribute to society, and the consumption of exchangeable personal property ('goods[3] and services'). This is mostly about how markets are organized, participants and

[3] What is the origin of referring to exchangeable objects as 'goods', given that this sounds like a generally applicable positive evaluation?

their behaviour, and the effects of patterns of behaviour on social welfare. Marketers are interested in the (assumed) rationality of buying behaviour, which is the behaviour of individuals in markets when faced with a choice. The challenge is to understand why people behave as they do in economic situations. If marketing is the answer, what (from an economics point of view) are the questions? How does the market operate? How do decision-making units behave in and out of the market?

Whereas micro-analysis deals with how individual buyers interact through the market with sellers in terms of prices, income, preferences, and so on, macro-analysis attends to the economy as a whole. Micro-economics has a role in relation to management that is akin to the role that macro-economics plays in politics (Kay, 1996). Importantly, we should note the distinction between thinking of a society as an economy and thinking of a society as having an economy, and understand economy as an autonomous sphere of trading activity that impresses rules on everything else. Increasingly, society is governed by the rules of the market as the commercial ethos takes root (see for example, *In Praise of Commercial Culture* (Cowen, 1998)). 'The whole society is in one sense part of the economy, in that all of its units, individual and collective, participate in the economy. Thus households, universities, hospitals, units of government, churches etc. are in the economy. But no concrete unit is "purely economic"' (Parsons and Smelser, 1956: 14).

Knowledge of marketing in a range of fields attempts to understand human organization and behaviour and modification for human ends. In this multitude of perspectives, economics seems to be the natural integrative discipline of management science. Significantly, it explains, but also influences market behaviour.

All societies produce, distribute and consume things. It is only in modern societies that such 'goods' and their prices, and the conditions of ownership and work, are determined by 'laws' of economic efficiency (note, not equality) in pursuit of material wealth accumulation (Sachs, 1992).

Sociology examines the internal structure of marketing groups and their interaction, whilst *political science* considers legislation, regulation, and the judiciary that determine market structure and behaviour. *Psychology* studies manifestations of personal behaviour in market activity, examining unobservable attitudes, learning, motivation and personality to explain the observable behaviour. *Social psychology*, on the other hand, examines marketing activities as the behaviour of socialized individuals. *Anthropology* is concerned with physical, social and cultural origins of market relationships. Importantly, these perspectives deal with understanding relations of meaning rather than explaining cause and effect relations. The *ecology* perspective seeks to understand the relationship of market participants and their environment.

Although marketing is usually learned as a managerial technology, it has considerable scope beyond. Indeed 12 schools of thought covering economic and non-economic purposes, and interactive and non-interactive forms, of which managerial marketing is just one possibility, can be discerned (Sheth et al., 1988).

Economics is the study of market organization and the behaviour and interaction of producers and consumers, and the effects on resource use and allocation. The subject is people contemplating the money they earn and the money they need for consumption (Galbraith and Salinger, 1978). This perspective presupposes the dominance of an economic enrichment motive, and the natural environment as a set of resources for this purpose.

The economic, social and ethical are inextricably intertwined – any 'pure' economics is simplified and abstracted from reality and is of limited use. The world cannot be represented completely from a single point of view, nor intelligibly if represented with all! The non-economic – moral, social and political – are important aspects of our lives, so it is better to view from many points of view sequentially, thus being aware of particular prejudices of specific views.

In considering the economics basis for marketing, we are interested in appreciating what we need to understand in economics in order to understand marketing's purpose and practices, so it is easy to think of marketing as just applied economics. Partly this involves the mastering of the language of economists, who are concerned with explaining and predicting the satisfaction of wants through the supply of industrial and consumer goods and services and the achievement of economic exchange relationships played out in the buying and selling activities in which assets are exchanged by two parties, each motivated by the desire for gain.

Economics emerged at the end of the nineteenth century out of the political economy[4] of Adam Smith and later early thinkers, just as the discipline of marketing was also emerging formally. This narrowed the field of inquiry, assuming that government was outside the market in which producers and consumers came together. All important needs would be supplied by the market, the all-powerful regulatory force in society. Galbraith observes that economics was political economy 'cleansed of politics' (Galbraith and Salinger, 1978: 5). As we will see later in this discussion, some economists these days are arguing for a return to political economy.

Marketing is an economic activity, for sure, but it is important to recognize that economic tools can be used to accomplish economic as well as other objectives. Further, knowledge beyond economics may be required for the effective use of economic resources. This highlights the social nature of marketing (Douglas, 1975). Indeed, well before the emergence of relationship marketing, the scope of marketing was recognized. Bartels proposed two ways to understand marketing, as a managerial technology, and as a social process. As a technology of things, marketing is an impersonal act for the achievement of self-determined corporate goals, drawing on economic concepts, space–time, processes, intangibles, objects. Alternatively, marketing is a process of social interaction, a system of role relationships, and a type of management responsibility. In this view, the process of marketing is social, in which society fulfils personal and institutional needs for goods and services, in the action and interaction of *people*. Thus, marketing is understood as the sets of relationships which arise in the performance of the process of economic want-satisfaction, and is behaviour in relationships (Bartels, 1970). This highlights the co-ordinating function of the discipline of marketing, as a social system for organizing.

---

[4] This name was current before it became fashionable to treat economics as a science, then for the purpose of gaining respectability. Clearly it is not, since the economist's subject 'is flooded by the human powers of discovery and imagination' (Shackle, 1973: 122). In other words, the market, in this view, is not a 'mechanism', since individual action is subjective.

The evolution of economics and the adoption of neoclassical thought

Economics provides analytical tools for the interpretation of recorded history. Facts never tell their own story, so theorizing is necessary in applying the humanities and sciences in the political economy of life. Logical reasoning is fundamental in making all economics useful in describing, analysing and explaining, and at the higher levels of economic theory, mathematics is also necessary for modelling and correlation in a systematic pattern. So what did the emerging field of economics assume about the individual and their fate in a commercial society?

Economics has its Western foundations in the thinking of a number of important figures who have contributed to the discipline leading up to and during the eighteenth-century Scottish Enlightenment, in the outpouring of the assertion of reason above authority, and the 'science of man'. Most of these people were British (and men). Then, during the birth of the discipline of marketing at the beginning of the twentieth century, the men who established the first university departments in the United States of America had mostly studied in the Austrian School.[5] Their perspective emphasizes the spontaneous organizing power of the price mechanism, holds that the complexity of subjective human choices makes mathematical modelling of the evolving market extremely difficult (or impossible) and therefore advocates a laissez-faire approach to the economy – focusing on the entrepreneur as the matcher of capabilities and wants. They are the founding figures who influenced early foundational marketing thinking. Economists' ideas cannot be dissociated from their personal situations and the prevailing social conditions of their time, and so a historical perspective is important. The early economists mostly had little influence during their lifetimes and not until several generations later did their thinking impact on ideas about social betterment, now deeply embedded in the institutions we live by, including our notions of social justice. These people made the history – they shaped our modern minds on what we still regard as the idea of market economy.

Critique of mainstream 'neoclassical marketing': the economic functions of markets and marketing

Economics is the study of how people and society end up choosing, with or without the use of money, to employ scarce productive resources that could have alternative uses, to produce various commodities and distribute them for consumption, now or in the future, among various persons and groups in society. It analyzes the costs and benefits of improving patterns of resource allocation. (Samuelson, 1976: 3)

---

[5] The Austrian School emphasizes the market as a discovery process, naturally and spontaneously evolving out of human interdependence and interaction. (see, e.g. Hayek, 1978).

There is a rich tradition around the birth of formalized marketing in the early 1900s. Some would argue that marketing emerged as a sub-discipline of economics, whilst others would suggest that marketing is a branch of applied economics, with its origins in economics as a foundation, plus a strong emphasis on the seller's viewpoint. Marketing has evolved considerably, taking in non-economic explanations of seller and buyer behaviour, and increasingly emphasizing the viewpoint of the buyer (Sheth et al., 1988). Marketing has had a highly focused, but rather narrow, explanation of marketplace behaviour, assuming economic values as drivers of actor behaviour. The purpose of the marketing system is seen as the fulfilment of individual consumer needs, seeking efficiency in their actions to maximize profits. Critical economic variables are production and distribution efficiency, prices and outputs, and consumer income levels. The underlying condition is the use of finite incomes to satisfy unlimited wants. Non-economic factors would be the domain of the psychologist, sociologist and anthropologist, and would increasingly come into marketing thinking in the twentieth century. The economic perspective applies certain values, orientation, and 'basic' philosophies to the problem of market operation.

Orthodox economists see the market automatically adjusting supply and demand. Heterodox economists (e.g. Williamson, 1985) and sociologists (e.g. Herbert Simon) see managerial practices shaping the market, and see choice objectives other than utility maximization. Thus, in this view, marketing *performs* the market, it doesn't just react to it. Interestingly, it can be observed that whilst economics has been the inspiring discipline for marketing, it has not directly provided useful frameworks (Cochoy, 1998).

Political economy, or the classical school, originated in moral philosophy and came to be the study of production and buying and selling, in relation to custom, law and government. This field flourished from about 1700 to almost the end of the nineteenth century, just prior to the establishment of the institution of marketing in the early twentieth century. Reference to the *Oxford English Dictionary*, however, shows that a system of provisioning had been developing since the sixteenth century, long before a marketing discipline was formalized (in theory or in practice).

By about 1870, the term 'economics' had been adopted for the neoclassical school of thought, following Alfred Marshall. Whereas the classical school studied factors of long-run growth and change in the then emerging capitalist economy, the neoclassical focus was on the way that resources are allocated to meet the wants of the population of the state. The market was seen as the mechanism that could harmoniously reconcile the differing interests of producer and consumer and of employees and employers. A market model and theory of individual choice were developed to explain individual decision making towards profit maximization by the firm, and utility (happiness) maximization by each individual consumer. Economics became the study of market actor behaviour and material decisions.

It is vital to realize that the market is not what people do and think, and how they interact when they buy and sell, give and take. It is a conception of an idealized form of buying and selling – a culturally-determined construct, an idea of a sphere of life. The evolving marketing logic largely adopted the early economists' constructions of market system and market actors.

The market model is a representation of a mechanism for generating personal sustenance and prosperity (looking to the future). It was considered natural (as evolving) – what people would do spontaneously if not constrained. Economies exist because people trade, and not the other way around. Thus, wealth was created because of the division of labour through the increased efficiency of specialization and consequent technical progress. This mechanism was capable of producing greater utility and satisfaction than by other means, through efficiency in resource allocation. Thus a rational motor for growth was identified that could provide the greatest net human welfare.

In adopting neoclassical thinking, a number of significant *assumptions* are made about people and their conditions, with departures from the ideal having been considered sinful or negligent or incompetent, such has been the power of this rationality. These theories to which undergraduates are subjected instil misconceptions, and it is helpful to recognize that the orthodox market model is too unrealistic to be generally acceptable, yet, this is just how it is passed on, as established 'common knowledge'. We will now reflect on some key assumptions that make the model unlike anything real.

Firstly, choice is taken, axiomatically, to be the *essence* of the economy. In 'economic choice-making' it is most rational to maximize utility, but the model did not account for individual behaviour but rather the average behaviour of a system of the economy. In this view, we live in an atomistic world of individuals, each with an individual identity and autonomy. Market actors are and must be autonomous, so the market is a means of communication between consumers and producers. This plays out secular, acquisitive individualism. The basic goal of the individual is to satisfy their own materialistic wants, in pursuit of self-centred, hedonistic tastes ordered in a pattern of desire, a pre-existing and unchanging set of preferences. In this economic (instrumental) rationality of marginality, we always want more for less. Because ends are infinite, in the rational calculating spirit of capitalism individuals choose the best action according to stable preference functions and the constraints facing them. This is a world of asocial buyers and sellers focused on self-interest in interaction, wielding dispassionate judgement in their calculation of gain, dealing with each other from a distance, in conflict because each wants more for less. There is displayed in this thinking a belief that the exchange process monitors individual values ('laws of the market' and 'the invisible hand of the market'). This equates market prices and social values. In earlier thinking, a civilizing and pacifying influence and moralizing agency was ascribed to the market in the eighteenth century, in which exchange would create prosperity by dealing to mutual interests, thus inhibiting aggression.

Hirschman examines the notion of 'interest' and the rather narrow meaning that is adopted in marketing as the drive for material economic advantage. This motivation for rational instrumental action was assumed in the eighteenth century and is still regarded by some as a 'law' of human motivation, obviously preferable to 'destructive passions'. Hirschman elaborates this view well, that interest is 'the construct of the self-interested, isolated individual who chooses freely and rationally between alternative courses of action after computing their prospective costs and benefits to him or herself, that is while ignoring costs and benefits to other people and to society at large' (Hirschman, 1986: 36). This is a person who is self-centred in 'minding their own business'. Since Adam Smith (1776), who saw growth as an inherent characteristic of capitalism, there has been a belief that the pursuit of private gain indirectly serves the public interest. The Scottish satirical writer, essayist, historian and social commentator, Thomas Carlyle (1795–1881), observed this shift from medieval values of glory and chivalry to the calculation of 'a profit and loss philosophy'. Some argue that commerce produces civilized society, whilst others see civilized society as the basis for commerce.

This world view further presumes that buyer choice is a moral good, entailing competition among sellers,[6] who will thus innovate, extending choice and increasing efficiency. The producing firm is a 'black box', and people are selfish individuals who will act deviously if the price is right in one-off encounters around price. Enlightened self-interest is a sense of the necessity to 'give up something to not lose everything'.

All moral rights are taken to lie in the individual, who is the legitimate decision maker. Thus, 'consumer sovereignty' implies and accepts that attempts to modify tastes are inappropriate. The market comprises many price-taking anonymous buyers and many sellers supplied with perfect information to support the most efficient decisions. This perfect competition is the regulator impersonally setting prices, and beyond the power of any individual. At the point of equilibrium, when supply and demand naturally balance, there appears to actors to be no other price deal that would improve their allocation of resource. This is a natural mechanism, and as such requires little government intervention to ensure 'free trade'.

The abstract modelling positivistic science of neoclassical economics provides a convenient simplified explanation of the world which is purely competitive, with perfect information, moving towards general equilibrium of supply and demand, in which buyers are indifferent to rival suppliers of identical product characteristics. Real-world ambiguities are assumed away in explaining society as a 'price system'. This was to be expected in the emergent modernism, which emphasizes the institutions of science (mechanistic causality), state (bureaucratic rationality) and market (law of supply and demand). This is, of course, a limited culture-specific logic, not generally applicable as it appears.

The neoclassical synthesis approach as we now know it was developed in the 1930s (Hicks, 1946; Hicks and Allen, 1934). It is *deductive*, in that axioms are assembled to build rigorous models of consumer behaviour, each with its own simplifying assumptions: well-defined preferences and constraints, equilibrium states, constrained optimization. In this paradigm, it is presumed that we 'know' that demand, supply and price are co-determined and tend to equilibrium. It is assumed that all that is necessary to be known is known. This global rationality comes about because of the bounded rationality of the neoclassical economist. For past decades, economists have had a predilection for deductive reasoning, rather than empirical investigation (Eichner, 1983).

---

[6] Adam Smith observed many small firms in increasingly intense competition as the Industrial Revolution emerged in England, following the Scientific Revolution in Europe. Much of his thinking is still applied today, even though we experience quite different circumstances, and his assumptions, drawn from his religious beliefs and naive natural science, no longer fit.

In Routh's view, the standard economics textbooks (especially those of Samuelson and Lipsey) are 'powerful instruments of disorientation; for confusing the mind and preparing it for the acceptance of myths of growing complexity and unreality' (Routh, 1989: 339). Notable exceptions are Robinson and Eatwell (1973), Koutsoyiannis (1975) and Heilbroner and Thurow (1982).

The 'economistic fallacy' identifies the abstract model with reality, thus considering real behaviour only to the extent that it corresponds to the model, and moving to policy conclusions from a highly abstract basis. It universalizes the nature of the economic activity of a particular place and time, and assumes that as the essence of economic activity at all times and places (it is radically ethnocentric). The economics focus is economizing behaviour that pursues optimal resource allocation. Alternative 'heterodox' approaches, however, study the ways in which different societies provide for their material needs, and the various ways in which they solve their economic problem. The *institutionalist* approach, thus, is concerned with social rather than market values (Stanfield, 1983).

Heterodox analysis does not assume full rationality – psychological factors are accounted for. By the 1950s, a more *inductive* approach was developing, in which actual decision making problems were examined to generate generally applicable theory (Simon, 1957, 1959). In this view, choice is an ongoing problem-solving process during which consumer viewpoints, aspirations, habits, beliefs and wants evolve through a decision cycle. A burgeoning consumer behaviour field has been developed on this basis (Blackwell et al. 1969, 2005). Herbert Simon argued that all decisions are made within bounded rationality: 'The capacity of the human mind for formulating and solving complex problems is very small compared to the size of the problems whose solution is required for objectively rational behavior in the real world' (1957: 198). The market model simply was too simple! *Behavioural* economics integrates insights from neoclassical economics and psychology to take account of cognitive and emotional factors in better understanding economic decisions, thus challenging assumptions of rational behaviour. Importantly, Adam Smith (1776) had described psychological aspects of individual behaviour, and Jeremy Bentham's work on utility (1793) considered psychological factors extensively. Gary Becker's economic *theory of crime* (1968) is considered a seminal work on psychological elements of economic decision making.

By the 1980s, marketers and economists had differing perspectives! Whereas the neoclassical perspective saw selling costs as wasteful and pernicious, and product differentiation as no more than trickery, marketers had qualifying assumptions within the emerging thinking about the firm's competitive strategies (Earle, 1995).

The operation of the economy and behaviour of its actors can best be understood as part of the wider reality. The simplified modelling removes the extensive richness of non-equilibrium conditions. For example, much of the controversy over perfect and imperfect competition analysis of pricing behaviour and supply and demand theory seems to have passed by the world of the marketing student and their lecturers. As early as the 1950s, imperfect competition became the normal assumption (Chamberlin, 1933; Robinson, 1933, 1953). It is also revealing to note that, among others, Nicholas Kaldor, a market equilibrium fan in 1934, then thought it irrelevant by 1972 (Kaldor, 1934, 1972). Also, notable is Hicks' 1979 comment: 'As economics pushes on beyond "statics", it becomes less like science and more like history' (Hicks, 1979: xi). Other critics have seen that a static equilibrium never can, and never should, exist, and regarded the continuing belief in this idea as a 'major ill' in (especially American) economics. The mechanistic view cannot deal adequately with the dynamic, interactive complexity of society.

Given the assumptions outlined earlier, it remains to be asked whether the market mechanism as the basis for society produces social integration (Durkheim, 1964 [1893]; Simmel, 1955 [1922]) or corrosive atomism (Horkheimer, 1974; Schumpeter, 1954)? The assumption of autonomous individuals each with a freely-chosen different identity denies sociality, morality and cultural values. Bagozzi has recently propounded a corrective (Bagozzi, 2005), because the neoclassical *homo economicus* does not account for altruism, commitment to ethical values, concern for the group and the public interest, and a variety of non-instrumental behaviour.

Heterogeneity of interests is assumed away, and reasons for desires are considered irrelevant in that world of 'if you want it, you can have it all – if you can pay for it'. Rationality assumes that each individual can foresee the consequences of their actions and the actions of others, as well as everyone's abilities and intentions. Yet, in practice there are highly significant information imperfections. There is ignorance and incomplete information on both the supply side and among buyers (actual and potential customers).

In theory, of the neoclassical kind, sovereign consumers influence what should be produced through continuing marginal adjustments. But this is not how consumers really behave. The information needed to construct a market demand curve, which purports to show what demand would be at various prices, is never known before the fact of actual market outcomes. Such a simple analysis also assumes that expectations are realized. This raises another issue with the role of utility. This is an abstract concept denoting subjective pleasure, usefulness, or derived satisfaction. But in market activity, consumers may also be disappointed in their expectations. They may also be cheated, misled, or otherwise suffer, resulting in remorse instead of enjoyment of utility.

Nor does the market model very accurately represent the actual behaviour of firms – it is common that firms that deal with each other over an extended period seek stability in the face of uncertainty (the future and the behaviour of others), and establish relatively durable relations with a clear moral aspect. These marketing relationships are regulated by criteria of fairness and strong expectations of trust and abstention from opportunism. These firms abandon autonomy and competition for the possibility of certainty. There is a considerable recent literature on marketing relationships and so-called 'contracting' (see Block, 1990; Dore, 1983; Foxall, 1999; Granovetter, 1985; Macauley, 1963).

Nor is competition perfect in that the reality is an oligopoly. There is a concentration of market power (to set prices and other terms) when there are a few large corporations (20 per cent of marketers win 80 per cent of the business), then the market model mechanism will not operate as an impersonal competitive market. Each powerful actor has market power to set prices for itself. Even without this problem, there are logical difficulties with the notion of a supply curve – who sets the price if all producers are price-takers? (Arrow, 1959).

Other issues that make the market model untenable include: the prevalence of non-price aspects of competition; the interdependence of cost and revenue functions; the dynamic changing nature of the market; innovation and new product launch ('creative destruction') in which buyer and seller both learn (Schumpeter, 1991); competitors who respond to market devices (dynamic competition); uneven distribution of power among sellers and buyers; and identical product offerings that do not lead to pro-rata market share. Because the 'no information problem' assumption is invalid, and consumers do not choose randomly among identical offers, increased goodwill leads to increased market share, and word-of-mouth effects and trust-based relationships are effective.

Nor does the model account for moral commitments. It is easily observed that our normative and affective values and emotions heavily influence our choices. Social groups and communities are often the context for decisions, and normative rules apply for commitment to fairness in competition and trust that this is the commitment of others. Social bonds reflect the reality that competition thrives in social communities where they are strong enough to sustain 'natural' trust and low transaction costs, but not so strong as to suppress exchange. This is not so in impersonal calculative systems of independent actors unbounded by social relations. It is important to understand that firms exist to modify market relationships by introducing mutuality, thereby turning them into marketing relationships (Foxall, 1999). The neoclassical paradigm under-emphasizes the significance of ethical judgements in accounting for market behaviour and policy making.

For example, economist Gary Becker appears to treat children as 'durable consumer goods' that can be traded-off for other goods (a new car, for example) (Becker, 1976). This calculative mentality debases moral values, secularizing cost–benefit calculations in the otherwise sacred, for example legitimizing the selling of rights to pollute.

Finally, the term 'free market' imputes a pejorative feel to the notion of government intervention, yet there are no examples of workable intervention-free economies.

It is peculiar that only one view of economics is adopted, especially since that is invariably neoclassical economics with its limited practical application! This way of thinking is ill-suited to framing business and public-policy problems. Perhaps this is all that textbook authors were taught in business school. This approach circumscribes the possibilities of recognizing the implications of this particular way of thinking.

Then again, why should we expect a way of thinking that was crafted before the dawn of large corporations and our age of affluence, that we now take for granted – especially the Generation X – to remain eternally relevant and helpful? We still expect the economic basis of marketing to be the neoclassical (equilibrium market) logic, but it should by now be behavioural (consumer choice) and institutional (firms) economics to which we turn for analytical support of our problem-solving – to understand people in pursuit of profit for a purpose. 'Betterment' was the term used by Adam Smith in the language of the eighteenth century, but see also Kenneth Boulding on *welfare* economics more recently (Boulding, 1984).

So what form of economic analysis is more useful for understanding and shaping the form and purpose of marketing? The 'invisible hand' of the market is a far too well entrenched idea, and even economists doubt its usefulness: 'Is it true that the pursuit of private interests produces not chaos but coherence, and if so, how is it done?' (Hahn, 1970: 1).

There has been extensive *reformation* of the market model. The *institutional* view extends the traditional view, by asking questions the neoclassical approach claimed not to address. For example, social institutions are considered as existing prior to, and thus conditioning, individual behaviour. Markets are considered to be the result of the complex interactions of a range of institutions with diverging interests. Key figures include Thorstein Veblen, John R. Commons (Commons, 1924, 1934), Adolf Berle (1895–1971) and John Kenneth Galbraith. Institutional analysis defines the economy differently, adopts a different method of inquiry, and applies alternative values in constructing meaning from its inquiry.

Transaction cost economics deals with the reality of a lack of knowledge and less than perfectly rational decision making (Williamson, 1975, 1985). However, it is important to realize that Williamson adheres to the neoclassical assumption that people are selfish individuals who will act deviously if the price is right – he considers only the opportunism scenario. Information economics deals with the lack of information, often asymmetric, and thus the inevitability of information costs, divergence of interests, and the firm as the nexus of contracts in various forms.

Markets are seen as partly mechanisms that facilitate contractual agreements and the exchange of property rights by supporting consensus on prices and communicating information about products, prices, quantities, potential buyers and potential sellers. Thus, the market can be defined as 'a set of social institutions in which a large number of commodity exchanges of a specific type regularly take place, and to some extent are facilitated and structured by those institutions' (Hodgson, 1988: 174).

Economic sociology focuses on how market exchange arises from social relations, shifting attention from exchange as events in pre-existing markets, to understanding markets as social institutions. It is argued that marketing brings about markets – marketing is a market-making activity (Araujo, 2007; Callon, 1998; Callon et al., 2007).

Reflections

We should be careful to not ask what economics is, but rather what is has been, how it got to be what it is now, and what it can be? It is a developing discipline, which corrects its mistakes and omissions. The value of a knowledge of economics to a prospective marketing executive is in understanding the market metaphor and thus the purpose of marketing. But there is a social responsibility to not limit understanding to 'market' and 'exchange' in the pursuit merely of how to do better marketing. It raises the possibility of answering what can marketing be and for what purpose?

Economics has always been focused on human action, with the goal of predicting and explaining the behaviour of people in social groups, as distinct from that of the individual. Yet, studies of 'rational economic man' are blind to social organization. As one of the humanities, economics inquiry can provide understanding, which in turn drives the very social system it studies. 'Modern' economists have formulated economic 'laws' as if they are immutable 'laws of nature', yet economics must deal with people.

It has to deal with the social and political if it is to be truly helpful outside the academic discipline (Canterbery, 1987). Too much modern economics supposes that people behave like inanimate particles in a clock-like mechanism. Microeconomic analysis explained decision making by individual buyers, who maximized satisfaction by choosing among assortments of goods and services, and individual sellers, whose manipulation of marketing variables contributed to social welfare. However, market behaviour could not be studied in isolation if the market is understood as a social institution. Macroeconomic thinking was necessary to an understanding of the interactions between the market and other social institutions (Dixon, 2002).

The study of marketing can be for the accumulation of market intelligence, but also for understanding the possibilities for social betterment. In this regard, we can ask whether scholars of marketing need to treat consumers like fish in the way that fishermen study them, or in the way that marine biologists study them? (Tuck, 1976).

It is hard to separate attitude to market form and function from political views. The market seems attractive from the marketing point of view. However, the market, according to the economist, controls income as well as spending power since most consumers are also earners. So, for the individual, the market is a discipline that many would prefer to escape. In returning to the political economy of the moral philosophers, it would seem that rehumanizing our provisioning needs is a reorientation to a greater focus on people and a lesser emphasis on things. A balance of natural, economic and social systems for sufficiency in a resource-light economy focuses on whether less emphasis on economic expansion can enhance the quality of civilization by asking 'how much is enough?' (Diener and Seligman, 2004; Durning, 1992).

The blindness of the market to any claim on society's output except wealth and income creates very serious problems (Heilbroner and Thurow, 1982). In redefining wealth we might observe that the 'faster, further, more' mentality may be counterproductive. Even as wants (ends) seem infinite and mostly unmet, creating a sense of scarcity of means, there is a simultaneous assumption of abundance of sources and sinks for the production and waste of material output that is to supply satisfactions, and thus presumed to be the source of wealth and well-being. This presumption, since the nineteenth century, of continuously expanding wants, of course renders any and all means insufficient. Well-being has been understood as 'well-having', that welfare depends on material output. Production growth has been taken for granted, so the solution to resource limits has been to improve efficiency of means.

In conditions of abundance, product utility is taken for granted, so experiences and identity, that is, the symbolic value of goods and services, becomes paramount. By labelling nature as 'resource', as useful inputs to industry, we have removed limits on exploitation. In industrial society's consumption of nature – by producers, and thus consumers – we have become 'cheerful enemies of nature' (Sachs, 1999) in our ever-expanding commodification.

The problem facing economics today is not the efficient allocation of resources, but how society should live, or what, how much and in what way it should produce and consume – this focuses on values and institutional patterns (qualities) rather than energy-material processes (quantities). Indeed, lower levels of production may enhance well-being. Opportunities abound in the search for a society that is able to not want what it would be capable of providing. Self-restraint and intermediate performance, within forms of prosperity that don't require permanent growth, will require a suitable form of marketing: 'the productivity of a sustainable society will be measured not by the eco-efficiency of an ever expanding number of technologies, but by the quality of the civilization it creates out of limited means' (Sachs, 1999: 182).

So, my final thought is what if the economics basis of marketing was less tautological, more empirical, and non-axiomatic and non-atomistic? Typical teaching does not recognize the effects of the loss of historical connections in the field of economics. The problem addressed in the neoclassical foundation, especially in the basic maximizing model, is not of the real world of actual buyers and sellers interacting, but of the abstracted models in the mental operations of theorists. Much of the work is the outcrop of a mere fascination with the problems of optimal resource allocation, and many of the key propositions cannot be empirically demonstrated. The 'introductory principles of economics' are useful as a beginner's tool kit, but are grossly over-extended when applied to real management problems. Neoclassical economics, especially of the mathematical formalist, aims to explain all of reality without even looking at it (Mini, 1974). There is little real relevance to everyday life!

In accepting, even seeking, an economic basis for marketing, we need to also deal with the problems of adopting, uncritically, the orthodoxy. There remain serious concerns about assuming a stable, stationary equilibrium as the foundation for marketing principles. The resulting convenient analyses are practically meaningless, and worse, misleading. What of a marketing that has a more realistic basis? This is already the case, well beyond the 'useful myth' of the 'self-regulating' market mechanism.

Recommended further reading

Applbaum, Kalman (2004) *The Marketing Era: From Professional Practice to Global Provisioning*, London: Routledge.

Bakan, Joel (2004) *The Corporation: The Pathological Pursuit of Profit and Power*, New York: The Free Press.

Dixon, Donald F. (1999) 'Some late nineteenth-century antecedents of marketing theory', *Journal of Macromarketing* 19(2): 115–25.

Dixon, Donald F. (2002) 'Emerging macromarketing concepts: from Socrates to Alfred Marshall', *Journal of Business Research* 55: 737–45.

Earle, Peter E. (1995) *Microeconomics for Business and Marketing*, Aldershot: Edward Elgar Publishing.

Galbraith, John Kenneth (1970) *The Affluent Society*, 2nd revised edn, London: Pelican Books.

Guillet De Monthoux, Pierre (1993) *The Moral Philosophy of Management: From Quesnay to Keynes*, Armonk, NY: M.E. Sharpe.

Heilbroner, Robert L. (1961) *The Worldly Philosophers: The Lives, Times, and Ideas of the Great Economic Thinkers*, revised edn, New York: Time Inc. Book Division.

Hirschman, Albert O. (1970) *Exit, Voice and Loyalty: Responses to Decline in Firms, Organizations, and States*. Cambridge, MA: Harvard University Press.

Jones, D.G. Brian and Shaw, Eric H. (2006) 'A history of marketing thought', in Barton Weitz and Robin Wensley (eds) *Handbook of Marketing*, London: Sage Publications, pp. 39–65.

Lindblom, Charles E. (2001) *The Market System: What It Is, How It Works, and What to Make of It*, New Haven, CT: Yale University Press.

Marshall, Alfred (1890) *Principles of Economics*, 1st edn, London: Macmillan. Any edition will prove illuminating.

Muller, Jerry Z. (2002) *The Mind and the Market: Capitalism in Modern European Thought.* New York: Alfred A Knopf.

Wilkie, William L. and Moore, Elizabeth S. (2003) 'Scholarly research in marketing: exploring the "4 eras" of thought development', *Journal of Public Policy & Marketing* 22(2): 116–46.

─────── **References** ───────

Applbaum, Kalman (2004) *The Marketing Era: From Professional Practice to Global Provisioning,* London: Routledge.

Araujo, Luis (2007) 'Markets, market-making and marketing', *Marketing Theory* 7(3): 211–26.

Arrow, Kenneth J. (1959) 'Towards a theory of price adjustment', in Moses Abramowitz et al. (eds) *The Allocation of Economic Resources: Essays in Honor of Bernard Francis Haley,* Stanford, CA: Stanford University Press.

Bagozzi, Richard P. (2005) 'Socializing marketing', *Marketing – Journal of Research and Management* 2: 101–10.

Bartels, Robert (1970) *Marketing Theory and Metatheory,* Homewood, IL: R.D. Irwin.

Becker, G. (1968) 'Crime and Punishment: An Economic Approach'. *The Journal of Political Economy* 76: pp. 169–217.

Becker, G.S. (1976) *The Economic Approach to Human Behavior,* Chicago, IL: University of Chicago Press.

Bentham, J. (1793) Manual of Political Economy.

Blackwell, R.D., Engel, J.F. and Kollat, D.J. (1969) *Cases in Consumer Behavior,* Fort Worth, TX: The Dryden Press.

Blackwell, Roger D., Miniard, Paul W. and Engel, James F. (2005) *Consumer Behavior* (10th edn), Florence, KY: South-Western College Publishing.

Block, Fred (1990) *Postindustrial Possibilities: A Critique of Economic Discourse,* Berkeley, CA: University of California Press.

Boulding, Kenneth E. (ed.) (1984) *The Economics of Human Betterment,* Albany, NY: State University of New York Press.

Callon, Michel (ed.) (1998) *The Laws of the Market,* Oxford: Blackwell Publishers.

Callon, Michel, Millo, Yuval and Muniesa, Fabian (eds) (2007) *Market Devices,* London: Wiley-Blackwell.

Canterbery, E. Ray (1987) *The Making of Economics,* 3rd edn, Belmont, CA: Wadsworth Publishing Co.

Carrier, James G. (ed.) (1997) *Meanings of the Market: The Free Market in Western Culture,* Oxford: Berg.

Chamberlin, Edward H. (1933) *The Theory of Monopolistic Competition,* Cambridge, MA: Harvard University Press.

Cochoy, Franck (1998) 'Another discipline for the market economy: marketing as a performative knowledge and know-how for capitalism', in M. Callon (ed.) *The Laws of the Markets,* Oxford: Blackwell Publishers.

Colander, David C. and Coats, A.W. (eds) (1989) *The Spread of Economic Ideas,* Cambridge: Cambridge University Press.

Commons, John R. (1924) *The Legal Foundations of Capitalism,* Clifton, NJ: Augustus M. Kelley.

Commons, John R. (1934) *Institutional Economics,* New York: Macmillan.

Cowen, Tyler (1998) *In Praise of Commercial Culture,* Cambridge, MA: Harvard University Press.

De Graaf, John., Wann, David and Naylor, Thomas H. (2002) *Affluenza: The All-Consuming Epidemic,* San Francisco, CA: Berrett-Koehler Publishers.

Diener, Ed and Seligman, Martin (2004) 'Beyond money: toward an economy of well-being', *Psychological Science in the Public Interest* 5(1): 1–31.

Dixon, Donald F. (2002) 'Emerging macromarketing concepts: from Socrates to Alfred Marshall', *Journal of Business Research* 55: 737–45.

Dore, Ronald (1983) 'Goodwill and the spirit of market capitalism', *British Journal of Sociology* 34: 459–82.

Douglas, Edna (1975) *Economics of Marketing*, New York: Harper & Row.

Durkheim, Emile (1964 [1893]) *The Division of Labor in Society* (trans. G. Simpson), New York: The Free Press.

Durning, Alan Thein (1992) *How Much is Enough? The Consumer Society and the Future of the Earth*, New York: W.W. Norton/WorldWatch Institute.

Earle, Peter E. (1995) *Microeconomics for Business and Marketing: Lectures, Cases and Worked Essays*, Aldershot: Edward Elgar Publishing.

Eichner, Alfred S. (ed.) (1983) *Why Economics is Not Yet a Science*, London: Macmillan Press.

Ekins, Paul and Max-Neef, Manfred (eds) (1992) *Real-Life Economics: Understanding Wealth Creation*, London: Routledge.

Foxall, Gordon R. (1999) 'The marketing firm', *Journal of Economic Psychology* 20: 207–34.

Galbraith, John Kenneth (1970) *The Affluent Society*, 2nd revised edn, London: Pelican Books.

Galbraith, J.K. and Salinger, Nicole (1978) *Almost Everyone's Guide to Economics*. London: Andre Deutsch Ltd.

Granovetter, Mark (1985) 'Economic action and social structure: the problem of embeddedness', *American Journal of Sociology* 91: 481–510.

Guillet De Monthoux, Pierre (1993) *The Moral Philosophy of Management: From Quesnay to Keynes*, Armonk, NY: M.E. Sharpe.

Hahn, Frank H. (1970) 'Some adjustment problems', *Econometrica* 38: 1–17.

Hamilton, Clive and Denniss, Richard (2005) *Affluenza: When Too Much is Never Enough*, Sydney: Allen & Unwin.

Hayek, F.A. (1978) *New Studies in Philosophy, Politics, Economics and the History of Ideas*, London: Routledge and Kegan Paul.

Heilbroner, Robert L. and Thurow, Lester (1982) *Economics Explained*, Englewood Cliffs, NJ: Prentice Hall.

Hicks, John R. (1946) *Value and Capital*, 2nd edn, London: Macmillan.

Hicks, J.R. (1937) 'Mr Keynes and the "classics": a suggested interpretation', *Econometrica* 5(2): 147–59.

Hicks, J.R. (1979) *Causality in Economics*, Oxford: Basil Blackwell.

Hicks, John R. and Allen, R.G.D. (1934) 'A reconsideration of the theory of value: Parts I and II', *Economica* 1: 52–76.

Hirschman, Albert O. (1986) *Rival Views of Market Society and Other Recent Essays*, New York: Harvard University Press.

Hodgson, Geoffrey M. (1988) *Economics and Institutions: A Manifesto for a Modern Institutional Economics*, Cambridge: Polity Press.

Horkheimer, Max (1974) *Critique of Instrumental Reason*, New York: Seabury.

Hunt, E.K. (2002) *History of Economic Thought: A Critical Perspective*, 2nd edn, Armonk, NY: M.E. Sharpe.

James, Oliver (2006) *Affluenza*, London: Vermillion/Random House.

James, Oliver (2007) *The Selfish Capitalist: The Origins of Affluenza*, London: Vermilion.

Jones, D.G. Brian and Monieson, David D. (1990) 'Early development of the philosophy of marketing thought', *Journal of Marketing* 54: 102–13.

Kaldor, Nicholas (1934) 'The equilibrium of the firm', *Economic Journal* 44: 60–76.

Kaldor, Nicholas (1972) 'The irrelevance of equilibrium economics', *Economic Journal* 82: 1237–55.

Kay, John (1996) *The Business of Economics*, Oxford: Oxford University Press.

Koutsoyiannis, Anna (1975) *Modern Microeconomics*, London: Macmillan.

Lane, Robert E. (1991) *The Market Experience*, New York: Cambridge University Press.

Lane, Robert E. (2000) *The Loss of Happiness in Market Democracies*, New Haven, CT: Yale University Press.

Macauley, Stewart (1963) 'Non-contractual relations in business: a preliminary study', *American Sociological Review* 28(1): 55–67.

McInnes, William (1964) 'A conceptual approach to marketing', in Reavis Cox, Wroe Alderson and Stanley J. Shapiro (eds) *Theory in Marketing*, Homewood, IL: Richard D. Irwin.

Menger, C. (1950) *Principles of Economics*, Glencoe, IL: The Free Press.

Mini, Piero V. (1974) *Philosophy and Economics*, Gainesville, FL: University Presses of Florida.

Myers, David G. (2000) *The American Paradox: Spiritual Hunger in an Age of Plenty*, New Haven, CT: Yale University Press.

Parsons, Talcott and Smelser, Neil, J. (1956) *Economy and Society: A Study in the Integration of Economic and Social Theory*, London: Routledge & Kegan Paul.

Robinson, Joan V. (1933) *The Economics of Imperfect Competition*, London: Macmillan Press.

Robinson, Joan V. (1953) 'Imperfect competition revisited', *Economic Journal* 63: 579–93.

Robinson, Joan V. and Eatwell, John L. (1973) *An Introduction to Modern Economics*, Maidenhead UK: McGraw-Hill.

Roll, Eric (1992) *A History of Economic Thought*, 5th edn, London: Faber & Faber.

Routh, Guy (1989) *The Origin of Economic Ideas*, 2nd edn, London: Macmillan.

Sachs, Wolfgang (1992) 'The economist's prejudice', in Paul Ekins and Manfred Max-Neef (eds) *Real-Life Economics: Understanding Wealth Creation*, London: Routledge.

Sachs, Wolfgang (1999) *Planet Dialectics: Explorations in Environment and Development*, London: Zed Books.

Samuelson, Paul A. (1976) *Economics*, 10th edn, New York: McGraw-Hill.

Schumpeter, Joseph A. (1954) *History of Economic Analysis*, New York: Oxford University Press.

Schumpeter, J.A. (1991) *The Economics and Sociology of Capitalism*, Princeton, NJ: Princeton University Press.

Shackle, G.L.S. (1973) *An Economic Querist*, Cambridge: Cambridge University Press.

Sheth, J.N., Gardner, D.M. and Garrett, D.E. (1988) *Marketing Theory: Evolution and Evaluation*, Chichester: John Wiley & Sons.

Simmel, Georg (1955 [1922]) *Conflict and the Web of Group Affiliations* (trans. Kurt, H. Wolff), Glencoe, IL: The Free Press.

Simon, Herbert A. (1957) *Models of Man*, New York: John Wiley & Sons.

Simon, Herbert A. (1959) 'Theories of decision-making in economics and behavioral sciences', *The American Economic Review* 49: 253–83.

Smith, A. (1776) An Inquiry into the Nature and Causes of the Wealth of Nations, London: Strahan and Cadell.

Speth, James Gustave (2008) *The Bridge at the Edge of the World: Capitalism, the Environment, and Crossing from Crisis to Sustainability*, New Haven, CT: Yale University Press.

Stanfield, J. Ron (1983) 'Institutional analysis: toward progress in economic science', in Alfred S. Eichner (ed.) *Why Economics is Not Yet a Science*, London: Macmillan Press.

Stanley Jevons W. (1871) *The Theory of Political Economy*, London: Macmillan Press.

Stokes, Kenneth M. (1992) *Man and the Biosphere: Toward a Coevolutionary Political Economy*, Armonk, NY: M.E. Sharpe.

Tuck, M. (1976) *How Do We Choose?*, London: Methuen & Co.

Williamson, O.E. (1975) *Markets and Hierarchies: Analysis and Antitrust Implications. A Study in the Economics of Internal Organization*, New York: The Free Press.

Williamson, O.E. (1985) *The Economic Institutions of Capitalism: Firms, Markets, and History*, Cambridge: Cambridge University Press.

W. Stanley Jevons (1871) The Theory of Political Economy, Carl Menger (1871) Principles of Economics.

6

The psychological basis of marketing

Allan J. Kimmel

Introduction

Whether one considers marketing as a managerial process or as a formalized field of inquiry, it is clear that it is interdisciplinary in nature, spanning a variety of academic fields, including the behavioural and social sciences, communications and economics. These disciplinary links serve to enrich the marketing enterprise, providing it with empirically-grounded theories and concepts that lie at the heart of the pluralistic perspective typically employed by marketers to ply their trade. The purpose of this chapter is to focus on the psychological foundations of marketing – a daunting task in light of the breadth of contributions of psychology to the marketing discipline, but one that nonetheless is essential to carry out in order to gain a fuller understanding of what marketing is and how the marketing process functions. Psychology's contributions to marketing are perhaps most evident in the study of consumer behaviour, which serves as the focus of Chapter 12; however, a broader perspective reveals psychology's relevance to each of marketing's various activities, including product design, promotion, pricing, and the like.

Psychology as a discipline

Psychology encompasses the scientific study of behaviour and mental processes. Like marketing, the discipline of psychology has strong connections to other fields of inquiry, including philosophy, biology, evolution, and the social sciences. It also

Table 6.1   Psychological Constructs and Some Associated Marketing Areas

Construct	Marketing areas
Learning	Brand recall, loyalty
Motivation	Consumer needs, choice conflicts
Perception	Product packaging, advertising content
Decision making	Brand selection, consumer involvement, post-purchase evaluation
Attitudes	Customer satisfaction, trust, ad influence
Personality	Consumer segmentation, materialism, addictions

similarly is comprised of numerous sub-fields, such as: experimental psychology (e.g. the rules governing how people perceive, learn and remember); cognitive psychology (e.g. the mental mechanisms that underlie how people make judgements and decisions); personality psychology (e.g. the measurement, origins and influence of personality differences); social psychology (e.g. how individuals' attitudes, thoughts, emotions, and behaviours affect and are affected by other people and the social environment); industrial-organizational psychology (e.g. the factors that influence job motivation and satisfaction); clinical, counselling and community psychology (e.g. how behaviour and mental processes become disordered, and how they can be treated or prevented); and developmental psychology (e.g. changes in thinking, social skills and personality that occur throughout the lifespan). This is but a small sampling of psychology's sub-fields and their corresponding topical areas and issues; in fact, the American Psychological Association formally recognizes 54 specific divisions of the discipline. These areas are dominated by a core set of psychological constructs (see Table 6.1); that is, explanatory concepts that conceptualize intangible elements of the domain studied within a particular science.

Psychological constructs are essential to fields like psychology because they help explain how and why people think and behave the way they do within their physical and social contexts. For example, learning is a construct that helps explain observable changes in behaviour that come about from experience, as when a consumer develops a loyalty to a particular brand that has proven to have high quality across previous usage situations. The utility of psychological constructs is not limited to the discipline of psychology; as will become evident in this chapter, they are essential to understanding the marketing process. Nonetheless, for a construct to be of any value, it first must meet certain criteria: it must be precisely and unambiguously defined, including specification of its domain and clarification as to its distinctiveness relative to similar other constructs, and it must be capable of being measured (Churchill, 1979). Marketers have adopted many of the measurement and observation techniques developed and honed over the years by psychologists, including a wide range of self-report measurement tools (such as opinion surveys, attitude scales, personality scales), projective techniques (such as the interpretation of ambiguous illustrations), and interview approaches (such as in-depth interviews and personal journals or diaries). Consider, for example, the need for cognition, which falls within the domain of the psychological construct of personality. This trait, which reflects the chronic tendency to engage in purposive thinking and to enjoy problem-solving, is measured by a series of statements (e.g. 'I really enjoy a task that involves coming up with solutions to problems') that comprise the need for cognition scale (Cacioppo and Petty, 1982). When employed in advertising research, the scale revealed interesting differences between high and low need for cognition consumers. Compared with low scorers, high need for cognition consumers processed advertising information more thoroughly, had superior recall for brands and brand claims, and relied more heavily on print sources than television for news information. Consistent with elaboration likelihood theory (see 'Persuasion' below), high need for cognition consumers are apt to base their attitudes on message arguments and brand features, whereas lows use peripheral cues, such as music and emotional elements to guide their attitudes (Haugtvedt et al., 1992). The insight provided by such measurement approaches can prove invaluable to advertisers in the design of message content and the selection of channels of message delivery.

The application of knowledge derived from systematic research in psychology and other disciplines is crucial to the ongoing evolution of the hybrid field of marketing. For example, psychologist George Katona pioneered the use of survey methodologies in order to assess consumer expectations and attitudes. His work resulted in effective predictors of purchasing behaviour which ultimately were incorporated into the index of consumer sentiment, a leading economic indicator (Friestad, 2001). The applied tradition in psychology also in part can be traced back to the work of social psychologist Kurt Lewin who, in his often quoted comment that 'there is nothing as practical as a good theory', implied that once we have obtained scientific understanding of some aspect of behaviour, it should be possible to put that knowledge to practical use. During the Second World War, in a series of experiments, Lewin set out to determine the most effective persuasive techniques for convincing women to contribute to the war effort by changing their families' dietary habits. The goal was to influence the women to change their meat consumption patterns to less desirable, but cheaper and still nutritious meats, to buy more milk in order to protect the health of family members, and to safeguard the well-being of their babies by feeding them cod-liver oil and orange juice. Lewin compared the effectiveness of two kinds of persuasive appeals by randomly assigning housewives to an experimental condition involving either a lecture or group discussion on the recommended changes. The results of the research revealed that actively discussing ways to achieve good nutrition resulted in greater changes towards healthier eating habits than passively listening to lectures. Lewin explained the findings by suggesting that group processes had come into play to reinforce the desired normative behaviour for those individuals who had participated in the discussions. To some extent, contemporary support groups, such as Alcoholics Anonymous and Weight Watchers, can be seen as part of the legacy of Lewin's wartime research (Brehm and Kassin, 1993).

A survey of the psychological foundations of marketing

It has been suggested that one way of defining marketing is to consider it as psychology applied to business. Although an overly simplistic definition given the evolving complexity and breadth of the marketing discipline, the definition fits perfectly with the key objective of this chapter, which is to describe the various ways that the discipline of marketing is psychological in nature. To satisfy that objective, the remainder of this chapter surveys five essential topical areas that exemplify the ways that psychology provides insight into customer behaviour and can be incorporated within formulations for marketing actions and marketing management decision making. In turn, the following areas are covered: (1) motivation; (2) perception; (3) decision making; (4) attitudes; and (5) persuasion.

Motivation

A good starting point for surveying the psychological underpinnings of marketing is by considering some basic notions related to motivation. Indeed, the essence of marketing, as clarified by the well-known marketing concept, is firmly rooted within the context of motivational needs. The marketing concept presumes that the various aspirations and objectives of marketing practitioners are oriented to beneficial outcomes for all of the stakeholders involved in a marketing exchange. Primarily, marketing is held to play a useful role in helping consumers satisfy their needs and thereby enables the smooth operation of the exchange relationship between consumers and organizations. This is done through the development of needed products and services that are priced so as to give good value to buyers, while providing profit to the product producer, service provider, and other intermediaries. Thus, marketers are beholden to identify the physiological and psychological needs that motivate consumers and the means through which those needs can be satisfied through the development and provision of appropriate marketplace offerings.

Derived from the Latin term *movere* ('to move'), motivation is a psychological construct that encompasses a range of processes that energize, direct and sustain goal-directed behaviour. It is widely understood that consumer behaviour typically is stimulated by an internal deficiency that results in an imbalance or disequilibrium attributed to a discrepancy between the present condition and some ideal state. The resulting state of tension tied to the unfilled need gives rise to a drive – an internal psychological force that impels a person to engage in an action designed to satisfy the need. Such behaviour is goal-directed, that is, it is not randomly selected, but chosen on the basis of learning (e.g. the outcomes of previous experiences) and cognitive processes (e.g. expectations of future outcomes). Motivated behaviour is directed towards certain end states or outcomes (typically referred to as 'goal objects' or 'incentives') that the individual anticipates will satisfy extant needs, reduce the inner state of tension, and thereby restore the system to a state of balance.

Consumers play an active role in selecting their goals, and products and services represent means by which they can satisfy their various needs. Goal objects that attract the behaviour of consumers (so-called 'positively-valent' objects) reflect consumer wants or desires and, in that sense, represent external manifestations of consumer needs. By contrast, undesired goal objects (so-called 'negatively-valent' objects) repel behaviour, as would be the case when a consumer avoids a brand of soap that is thought to cause drying of the skin. A person's needs are strongly interrelated, and, as a result, needs can operate simultaneously on behaviour. An expensive fur coat can satisfy certain practical or utilitarian needs (e.g. to be warm during the winter) as well as more emotional or experiential needs (e.g. the excitement associated with wearing the coat in public) and status needs (e.g. the personal satisfaction that comes from being envied by others). Divergent forces can place consumers in a state of motivation conflict, as when the attracting forces of the expensive fur coat are opposed by the need to maintain one's budget or the desire to protect the rights of endangered animals. In such cases, marketers can assist consumers in overcoming such 'approach-avoidance' conflicts by designing appeals that emphasize the desirable aspects of the product and downplay the negative (e.g. by offering a suitable financing arrangement for the purchase). Many marketing messages are designed specifically to make consumers aware of the needs that can be satisfied through the purchase or use of certain products or services. Thus, an Ericsson advertisement heralded the GH388 cellphone as the one 'made to match the needs of the international traveller' and a Barney's of New York advertisement claimed that the shopper 'will have no difficulty finding anything you need' at the retail clothing store.

It is important to note that both physiological needs (e.g. hunger, thirst, pain avoidance, security, maintenance of body temperature) and psychogenic needs (e.g. achievement, affiliation, status, approval, power) motivate consumer behaviour. For example, conspicuous consumption, a concept that can be traced back to the work of economist Thorstein Veblen (1899) to explain 'the waste of money and/or resources by people to display a higher status than others' is clearly linked to the psychological ego-related needs for status, approval and self-confidence, although it may be influenced in part by extrinsic factors, such as social norms and cultural values. The lavish expenditure of money that is primarily guided by a desire to display one's wealth and success can be seen in the purchase of luxury brand products (e.g. a 20,000 euro Patek Philippe watch). This motive can operate at an unconscious level, such that consumers may not be consciously aware of the actual forces that have guided their purchasing behaviour. Projective research techniques are often utilized by marketing researchers to gain insight into the unconscious motives that explain the root causes of unconsciously-motivated behaviour (Kassarjian, 1974; Rook, 2006).

Certain needs may become more or less compelling for the consumer as circumstances change. A consumer predilection towards conspicuous consumption is likely to be offset when the satisfaction of certain basic needs is threatened. This was evidenced during the global financial crisis which began in 2008, a period during which consumers grew increasingly responsive to marketers' sales promotions, such as money-off offers. During the fourth quarter of 2008, coupon distribution in the US rose 7.5 per cent and redemptions rose 15 per cent relative to the preceding year, and online searches reflected consumers' concerns about their economic well-being. Searches of value-related words such as 'coupons' rose 161 per cent to 19.9 million compared with 2007 and 'discount' rose 26 per cent to 7.9 million (Howard, 2009). This shift from higher- to lower-order needs is consistent with early conceptualizations of human motivation, such as Maslow's (1943) hierarchy of needs and Herzberg's (1959) motivation-hygiene theory. The fact that the economic recession also reportedly spawned a significant increase in the volume of candy consumed

(Haughney, 2009) suggests that transformational needs, as expressed by a desire for sensory gratification, may also influence consumers at the same time they strive to overcome problems or satisfy basic needs (Rossiter et al., 1991).

A good example of how psychological principles of motivation conceptually clarify the effectiveness of promotional marketing messages is illustrated by Rogers' (1983) protection motivation theory, which illuminates the circumstances by which fear appeals have persuasive effects on audiences. In this view, the effectiveness of messages that demonstrate the negative aspects or physical dangers associated with a particular behaviour (e.g. smoking cigarettes, drug abuse, spousal abuse) or improper product usage (e.g. drinking and driving) is less a matter of the degree of fear the messages induce, but rather the extent to which they motivate people to protect themselves from the negative consequences and take steps to deal with the danger. Accordingly, a fear appeal must contain four components if it is to succeed in changing attitudes or behaviour; it must: (1) clearly specify how unpleasant the consequences will be if the recommended actions are not followed; (2) communicate the likelihood or probability of those negative consequences; (3) indicate how the negative consequences can be avoided if the recommendations are followed; and (4) explain that the targeted individuals are capable of performing the recommended action. According to their ordered protection motivation model, Arthur and Quester (2004) propose that the first two components, severity of threat and probability of occurrence, comprise a threat appraisal dimension (i.e. they arouse fear), whereas the last two components, response-efficacy and self-efficacy, comprise a coping appraisal dimension (i.e. they compel a person to behaviour). Evidence suggests that both dimensions must be considered when creating fear appeals (e.g. Eppright et al., 1994).

Other recent marketing applications of motivational concepts can be seen in research on consumer self-control (Vohs and Faber, 2007), response to marketing scams (Langenderfer and Shimp, 2001), dietary behaviours (Bock et al., 1998), and product usage and abandonment (Wansink et al., 2000).

Perception

Perception refers to a set of psychological processes that enable individuals to experience and make sense of their surrounding environment through the active cognitive processes of selection, organization and interpretation. Unprocessed sensory information received via the sensory systems that enable vision, hearing, taste and touch is rendered meaningful on the basis of innate human abilities, prior learning and past experiences. For example, seeing a red can on the table might be perceived as a Coca-Cola soft drink, without any apparent indication of the brand name. Marketers must be attentive to perceptual principles because it is the consumer's subjective experience or personal construction of objective reality that determines his or her reactions to marketing phenomena. Many difficult lessons have been learned when marketing decisions have been made without a concern for consumer perception, including new product launches, promotional campaigns, and pricing considerations. For example, Starbucks was forced to pull from stores its 'Collapse into Cool' promotional posters for the popular coffee chain's new Tazo citrus drinks when consumers complained that the poster's imagery (flying insects surrounding two tall iced beverages) was too reminiscent of the September 11 attacks on New York's Twin Towers. Although the ad had nothing to do with the event, the combination of the term 'collapse' and the unfortunate choice of illustration was perceived by some consumers as insensitive on the part of the company and a malicious attempt to capitalize on the misfortunes of others (Roeper, 2002).

The perceptual process can be understood as comprised of a chain of events that begins with sensorial input (i.e. the immediate response of our sensory receptors to basic stimuli like light, sound and texture) and ends with the conscious recognition (i.e. a meaningful perception) of an external event (e.g. 'Aha, there's a Coke on the table'). In other words, perception is not a single, discrete experience, but rather the conscious determination of a sequence of non-conscious processes. This point helps us understand why certain stimuli may not be noticed by individuals even after exposure to the stimulus has occurred (e.g. 'I didn't even see the can on the table because I was concentrating on the song that was playing in the background'). As the initial stage of the perceptual process, exposure tends to be influenced by stimulus factors (colour, size, position, novelty, contrast) and personal factors (past experience, expectations, motives, needs, mood). Thus, some stimuli are more likely to capture our attention (e.g. those that are unexpected, unique, or in direct contrast from their surroundings) than are others (non-changing, repetitive, and similar to background stimuli), because the former are more utile in overcoming the tendency for *sensory adaptation*, the process whereby responsiveness to an unchanging stimulus decreases over time. Perceptual vigilance describes the tendency for people to have a heightened sensitivity to stimuli that are capable of satisfying their motives (e.g. 'I noticed that Coke right away because I was so thirsty'), whereas perceptual defence pertains to the tendency for people to screen out stimuli that are too threatening, even though exposure may have occurred (e.g. 'I probably didn't see the soft drink because I'm trying to stick to my diet').

The relevance of these perceptual notions to marketing should be apparent. Marketers and advertisers clearly want consumers to perceive their offerings and messages (i.e. to select them), but must counter consumers' tendency to screen out marketing-related stimuli, whether it be an advertisement in a magazine, a package on a store shelf, an email that announces a promotion, and so on. The problem of capturing consumer attention has increased in recent decades as the number of offerings and marketing communications to promote those offerings have steadily proliferated. Indeed, the excessive bombardment of promotional messages has led to *advertising clutter*, the 'proliferation of advertising that produces excessive competition for viewer attention, to the point that individual messages lose impact and viewers abandon the ads (via fast-forwarding, changing channels, quitting viewing, etc.)' (Lowrey et al., 2005: 121). Beyond the most obvious case of television advertising, the problem of clutter also characterizes consumers' rising aversion to other marketing formats, including outdoor signage, email spamming, internet pop-up messages, and SMS messaging. Clutter is likely to impede message recall, especially when one considers that a majority of consumers engage in multi-tasking, such as using their PC or mobile phone while watching television (Greenspan, 2004).

The ability for any one promotional message to break through marketing clutter in order to capture attention, arouse interest, and have its intended effects has become exceedingly difficult. Marketing research must be carried out to determine the appropriate strategies for capturing attention and enhancing recall; for example, by developing messages that are at odds with commonly-held beliefs, including a lot of white space or vivid colours in print ads, incorporating humour or allusions to sexuality in the message content, presenting incomplete stimuli that stimulate audience involvement in the message, and so on. In retail settings, where the number of stock-keeping units (SKUs) continues to rise – the average number of products carried by a typical supermarket has more than tripled since 1980, from 15,000 to 50,000 (Nestle, 2002) – effective product packaging and display are required in order to be noticed and selected by shoppers. As a result, many consumer goods companies now view product packages not only as containers for shipping and storing products, but as three-dimensional ads for grabbing shopper attention (Story, 2007). This is seen in Pepsi's striking bottle designs for its Mountain Dew soft drink, Evian's luxurious glass container for a line of bottled water, rounded Kleenex packages bearing artistic imagery, and NXT's men's products bearing light-emitting diodes that light up the product every 15 seconds to illuminate air bubbles suspended in the clear gel.

Beyond considerations related to stimulus exposure and attention, psychological principles of perception also explain how stimuli are organized and interpreted. The ground-breaking work on perceptual organization was carried out by a group of German psychologists during the early twentieth century who suggested that people tend to organize their perceptions according to certain innate tendencies, such as closure (the tendency to derive meaning from incomplete stimuli by forming a complete perception), figure/ground (the tendency to designate part of the perceptual field as a figure and the rest as background), and grouping (the tendency to group stimuli automatically according to proximity, similarity, or continuity so they form a unified and meaningful impression) (Sternberg, 2008). These principles help explain how the overall unity of perception or 'Gestalt' (i.e. organized form or total configuration) is greater than or fundamentally different from the sum of its individual sensations. Applications of Gestalt principles are apparent in a variety of marketing activities, such as the development of promotional messages (e.g. advertisements that are purposely left incomplete or interrupted before their expected finish in order to involve the perceiver more actively in the message itself and enhance recall), the presentation of goods in the retail setting (e.g. private label brands packaged to look like market leaders and shelved next to them in order to appear to have comparable quality), and pricing (e.g. partitioning the base price and the surcharge so that consumers perceive the total price as cheaper than if the all-inclusive price had been given).

Another basic notion of perception that underlies marketing practice has to do with the fact that there are limits in human sensory reception. The point at which individuals are incapable of detecting weak stimulation is referred to as the absolute threshold, whereas the differential threshold demarcates the point below which people are incapable of noticing changes in a stimulus or differences between similar stimuli (the so-called 'just noticeable difference' or JND). Research has shown that the JND for two stimuli is not equal to an absolute amount, but an amount that is relative to the intensity of the initial stimulus, a proportionate relationship that is described by Weber's law. Briefly, Weber's law suggests that the greater the initial intensity of a stimulus, the more the stimulus must be changed in order to be detected by the perceiver. This relationship is utilized by marketers in determination of changes that are not intended to exceed the JND and be noticed (e.g. decreases in product size or reductions in product quality attributed to the rising costs of ingredients) or changes that are intended to exceed the JND while keeping costs to a necessary minimum (e.g. product improvements, price reductions).

Other recent applications of perception in marketing are apparent in ongoing research on eating behaviour. In addition to identifying the motivational forces that spark a rise in obesity levels, marketing researchers are actively engaged in studies intended to illuminate how diet is influenced by perceptual factors. Research has shown that low-fat labels increase snack-food consumption for normal-weight and overweight consumers who are apt to misperceive 'low-fat' foods as lower in calories and to overestimate appropriate serving size (Wansink and Chandon, 2006). Consumers also tend to underestimate the caloric content of main dishes, leading them to choose higher calorie side dishes, drinks or desserts (Chandon and Wansink, 2007).

For a discussion of the critical role of perceptions in the marketing of brands, see Batey (2008).

_____ Decision making _____

A fundamental focus of psychological research and theory is that of human decision making; specifically, the cognitive processes by which people make judgements. These processes provide significant insight into our understanding of human consumption, which can be conceptualized as a sequence of decision-making stages, ranging from the decision to consume (whether to spend or save, timing of the consumption, amount of goods to consume), product category spending (the category of goods or services to consume), brand selection (choice of benefits, role of reputation and status, loyalty and preference, brand image and positioning), buying behaviour (how and where to shop and pay, whether to comparison shop, frequency of shopping and product acquisition), and product usage and disposition (nature of product usage, how to dispose of products, environmental concerns).

Decision making typically begins with problem recognition; that is, the individual perceives a discrepancy between a current state of his or her condition and a desired state. As suggested by motivation theory, the imbalance arouses tension that in turn provokes behaviour. This initial decision-making stage may be attributed to changes in one's actual condition (e.g. depletion of stock, dissatisfaction with current products, changes in one's finances) or ideal state (e.g. new need or want circumstances, recent purchases that create a need for other product add-ons, new product opportunities). In most cases, the imbalance between these states will be perceived as a problem that must be eliminated (such as the depletion of breakfast cereal that requires replenishment), although in other cases, a perceived opportunity will stimulate action (as when an increase in one's finances motivates one to spend).

Problem recognition is likely to be followed by information search, such that one considers the various alternatives available for solving or eliminating the problem. Information search may be comprised of two steps, an internal search, which involves scanning one's memory for previous experiences that recall the current situation, and an external search, which involves the search for relevant information from a variety of alternative sources, including social relations (e.g. friends, family members), public sources (e.g. news channels, independent product-rating organizations, online forums), and marketing-dominated sources (e.g. advertising, company websites, salespersons). The degree to which such searches are carried out by the individual will depend upon that person's involvement in the problem or the focal concern of the problem. Psychologists conceptualize *involvement* as a construct related to self-relevance; specifically, the term has been defined as 'a motivational state induced by an association between an activated attitude and some aspect of the self-concept' (Johnson and Eagly, 1989: 283). Depending upon the psychological theory, this definition has varying interpretations, suggesting three types of involvement (Verplanken and Svenson, 1997). *Ego-relevant involvement*, derived from social judgement theory (e.g. Sherif and Hovland, 1961), refers to the psychological state resulting from the activation of enduring attitudes (i.e. evaluative reactions to some stimulus or situation; see 'Attitudes' below) that define a person. According to this perspective, attitudes are comprised of so-called 'latitudes of acceptance' (a range of positions one finds acceptable), 'latitudes of rejection' (a range of positions one finds unacceptable) and 'non-commitment' (positions towards which one is indifferent). Because high ego involvement attitudes are less easily influenced, high ego involvement tends to enhance latitudes of rejection (i.e. the range of positions one finds unacceptable), thereby inhibiting persuasion (Johnson and Eagly, 1989).

Impression-relevant involvement, a concept which stems from dissonance theory, refers to self-presentation motives that are activated in situations in which someone expresses an attitude. This type of involvement pertains to the concern one has with defending a position, and thus increases when an individual believes that the expression of an attitude will have an impact on the impression others form of him or her (Leippe and Elkin, 1987; Zimbardo, 1960). Finally, *outcome-relevant involvement*, which stems from dual-process persuasion theory (Chaiken, 1987; Petty and Cacioppo, 1986), has to do with the degree to which situations or issues are linked to the attainment of desirable outcomes. This type of involvement is assumed to be associated with message-relevant thinking, such that high involvement in a message is likely to result in careful scrutiny of the merits of the arguments that comprise a persuasive message. By contrast, argument strength is less likely to influence the attitudes of persons with low involvement in the message (see 'Persuasion' below).

Aspects of each of these psychological conceptualizations of involvement are reflected in marketing applications of the involvement construct and its role in the information search and evaluation of alternative stages of consumer decision making (Andrews et al., 1990). From a marketing perspective, *consumer involvement* has been defined as the motivation to process product-related information

(Solomon, 2008). Implicit in this definition is the understanding that involvement relates to the importance or relevance of a product/service or its purchase and the perceived risks involved in the purchase, elements that maintain the self-relevance notion rooted in the psychological conceptualizations.

During the information search stage of the decision-making process, consumers are likely to be motivated to engage in an extensive external search to the extent that a purchase is high in relevance and perceived risks (i.e. perceived negative consequences, which may be functional, financial, social or personal in nature). Products that evoke high-involvement processes tend to elicit high levels of perceived risk, given that they are infrequently purchased, higher in cost, complex, personally relevant and publicly visible to others (e.g. a new car, home, computer, expensive suit). The high involvement decision-making process involves extensive problem solving; that is, considerable time and effort are devoted to an external search for information and the subsequent evaluation of alternatives. The abundant information, gathered from a wide array of external sources, is likely to be applied to an evaluation of alternatives through a compensatory approach, which implies that an offer or brand will be selected through a determination of the preponderance of desired product attributes (i.e. characteristics or features that come to mind when considering a product category), weighted according to personal preference (the so-called 'weighted-additive rule'). Because the decision is based on a careful, rational scrutiny and comparison of all the facts, an alternative may be selected even though it has certain weaknesses or drawbacks, so long as they are compensated by important, personally-relevant strengths. For example, after careful evaluation, a new car buyer may opt for the Toyota Camry, despite its high cost (a key drawback), because its higher ratings on specific features (e.g. performance, safety, comfort) result in an overall evaluation that surpasses that of the considered alternatives. Further, preferences are likely to be shaped during the analysis of alternatives, such that a favourable attitude towards one alternative will precede its selection (i.e. preference precedes trial).

By contrast, products that evoke low-involvement processes are associated with low levels of perceived risks – they are frequently purchased, inexpensive, and low in personal relevance (e.g. household cleaning products, soft drinks, candy). Such purchase situations are unlikely to motivate the consumer to devote much time or effort to the information search; rather, the problem-solving approach utilized is often limited to a minimal external search or internal search of stored memories pertaining to the various alternatives. For example, when choosing from among the soft drink beverages in a supermarket, a consumer may select Pepsi Max as a result of a point of purchase display that stimulates recall of the slogan, 'Max your Life', which had been stored in memory during exposure to ads associated with the launch of the brand. Because the consumer lacks the motivation to engage in extensive information search for such a low involvement product, a distinct preference is unlikely to be developed until after the choice is made and the product is consumed.

Consumers are apt to apply non-compensatory decision-making rules or other heuristics when evaluating low-involvement alternatives; in essence, these are approaches that provide shortcuts for a relatively effortless and speedy decision. One example of a non-compensatory strategy, 'satisficing', involves the selection of the first adequate option, without the consumer exploring or giving consideration to the entire set of options. A similar strategy is to apply the lexicographic rule, which consists of selecting an alternative among those to be considered that receives the highest evaluation on the most important or salient attribute; in the case that a choice is not clear, the remaining brands are compared on the second most important attribute, and so on until one alternative remains. With such approaches, alternatives that excel on other features will not be selected; that is, a trade-off of the benefits of some attributes against the deficits of others will not occur. Satisficing and the lexicographic rule represent examples of *heuristics*, which are simple rules of thumb, educated guesses, or intuitive judgements that simplify the decision-making process, leading to outcomes that often lead to satisfactory, albeit sub-optimal, outcomes. In the marketing context, consumers may approach complex choices by simply concluding that the most expensive brand has the highest quality, or simply select a brand which offers the most extra features because it is thought that one will probably wish to have those features later. The nature of heuristics and their potential pitfalls (see Table 6.2) have been experimentally studied and elaborated on by cognitive psychologists Daniel Kahneman and Amos Tversky (Kahneman and Tversky, 2000; Kahneman et al., 1982).

Although beyond the scope of the present chapter, it should be noted that psychologists have identified a number of additional factors that are likely to influence decision making, including personality (e.g. some consumers are more likely

Table 6.2   Examples of Heuristic Biases and Marketing Examples

Bias	Description	Marketing example
Affect heuristic	Hastily judging objects or people by an immediate feeling of 'goodness' or 'badness'	Overly trusting a friendly seller; exaggerating the performance quality of a product due to its external appeal (e.g. a freshly painted used car)
Availability heuristic	Salient memories override normative reasoning	A consumer rejects all Sony products because of an early bad experience with one cheap Sony product
Confirmation bias	The tendency to seek out opinions and facts that support one's own beliefs and hypotheses	Tendency to take into account product reviews that laud an item you want to purchase, while ignoring negative reviews
False consensus effect	Inclination to assume that one's beliefs are more widely held than they actually are	Assuming that others will be satisfied with the same brands and service providers that you prefer
Gambler's fallacy	Pervasive false beliefs about the nature of random sequences	Lottery players who play the same numbers every time, assuming the number is 'due' to win

Table 6.2   *(Cont'd)*

Bias	Description	Marketing example
Planning fallacy	People consistently underestimate the amount of time and effort it will take for them to accomplish a given task	A consumer waits until the last minute to shop for presents; people underestimating the time and effort required to assemble a newly purchased item
Representativeness heuristic	The tendency to blindly classify objects based on surface similarity; 'like goes with like'	Assuming that the quality of a cheaper brand is equal to that of a brand leader due to similar packaging

Source: Adapted from Anissimov, 2004. Reprinted with kind permission.

to seek variety than others, or are more receptive to new and innovative options), lifestyles and values (e.g. consumption decisions are influenced by one's personal priorities and characteristic way of living), learning (e.g. consumers are likely to be influenced by previous decisions and experiences), social influences (e.g. word-of-mouth recommendations from friends can have a significant influence on a person's choices), and situational forces (e.g. store atmospherics can enhance the shopping experience and influence choices). Finally, psychological insight into the decision-making process has been applied by marketers in the design of advertising and other types of promotions (see Mehta, 1994; Rossiter et al., 1991).

_____ Attitudes_____

The topic of attitudes has been the focus of an enormous amount of research attention in psychology, although interest in the construct dates back to the turn of the twentieth century (Kraus, 1995; Rajecki, 1990). One reason for the intense scrutiny of attitudes has to do with their pervasiveness in everyday life. Any time people make evaluations of something in their social world, or react positively or negatively to the things they encounter, in essence, they are revealing their attitudes. Thus, whenever marketers or consumer researchers ask consumers what they think or how they feel about something in the marketplace – a product, brand, price, service, store, advertisement, and so on – their effort is oriented towards the assessment of attitudes. A common assumption is that attitudes influence how people react in a behavioural sense, that is, that attitudes precede and influence behaviour. Although once the subject of contentious debate, the causal link between attitudes and behaviour in certain specified circumstances (assuming appropriate measurement approaches are utilized) is indisputable (Kraus, 1995). These points help us understand why the attitudes of the various stakeholders in the marketing process are so compelling to marketers, and why the measurement of attitudes is considered so important to researchers. If accurate measures of consumer attitudes can be obtained, then it should be possible to predict behaviour with a certain degree of accuracy.

A common view of the attitude construct is that it represents a person's tendency to respond favourably or unfavourably to the object of the attitude, which may be a concrete entity (such as a product), something more abstract (such as quality of service), other persons, or ideas. According to Eagly and Chaiken (1998: 269), *attitude* is defined as 'a psychological tendency that is expressed by evaluating an entity with a certain degree of favor or disfavor.' One view of the attitude construct conceptualizes it as a relatively enduring organization of three interrelated psychological dimensions: (1) cognitive, which is comprised of beliefs about the attitude object; (2) affective, which consists of feelings towards the object; and (3) conative, which refers to intentions leading to behaving in a certain way towards the object. This so-called tricomponent theory emphasizes the ABC of attitudes (affect, behaviour, and cognition) (Rajecki, 1990).

It has long been held that attitudes are capable of serving four useful functions for the individual, including: (1) utilitarian (i.e. attitudes guide behaviour in order to maximize rewards and minimize punishments administered by others; (2) ego-defensive (i.e. attitudes serve as a defence mechanism that can protect the individual from personally threatening realities); (3) knowledge (i.e. attitudes provide order and structure to one's social world); and (4) value-expressive (i.e. attitudes assist the individual in expressing his or her values to others) (Katz, 1960; McGuire, 1969). Each of these functions can readily be applied to understand various aspects of consumer behaviour, including brand preferences, customer loyalty, and reactions to promotional efforts (Solomon, 2008). For example, a straightforward example of the utilitarian function is evident in situations in which consumers develop positive attitudes towards products that bring pleasure and negative attitudes towards products that make them feel bad. Advertisements are often designed to express the utilitarian benefits that can be accrued from the consumption of a product or brand (e.g. Diet Coke, 'Just for the taste of it').

The power of attitudes in the marketing sphere is especially apparent in the context of customer loyalty to a brand. Brand loyalty is conceptualized as a pattern of repeat product purchasing, accompanied by an underlying positive attitude towards the brand. This suggests that there are two key components that comprise loyalty, one of which is behavioural (the purchasing support that comes from buying a particular brand repeatedly) and the other of which is attitudinal (brand commitment attributed to a strong positive attitude or liking for the brand). In what Knox and Walker (2001) deem the 'brand loyalty matrix', considering both of these components together as either high or low suggests different kinds of brand consumers (see Figure 6.1). When both commitment and purchasing support are low for a brand, consumers fall into the 'switchers' category; that is, they show no loyalty towards any one brand but rather switch from brand to brand, assuming they are all essentially alike and the one selected should be that which offers the most savings. 'Habituals' are high on purchasing support, but low on commitment. Such consumers regularly purchase the same brand repeatedly, not out of any true loyalty towards the brand, but more out of habit (or so-called *inertia*, i.e. they lack the motivation to put forth

	Brand Commitment	
	High	Low
High	**LOYALS** – active decision making, based on product features and quality – high perceived risk in changing – small portfolios	**HABITUALS** – passive decision making, based on simplification – will readily change if first brand is unavailable – small portfolios
Brand Support		
Low	**VARIETY SEEKERS** – multi-brand buying – active search based on quality – large portfolios – seek variety for own sake or alternative use occasions	**SWITCHERS** – sensitive to price and promotion – large and varied portfolios – low perceived risk in changing

Figure 6.1   Brand loyalty matrix and characteristics of loyalty types (Knox and Walker, 2001)

Source: Knox, S. and Walker, D. (2001) 'Managing and measuring brand loyalty', *Journal of Strategic Marketing* 9: 111–28. Reprinted by permission of the publisher (Taylor & Francis Groups, http://www.informaworld.com).

the effort to evaluate and compare specific brands). 'Variety seekers' tend to have a strong brand preference (i.e. high commitment), but like to play the field and thus show low purchasing support. Such consumers are apt to try out alternative brands, even though they have a preferred brand that they ultimately will return to, because they like to experiment, especially for different use situations (e.g. buying an imported brand to share with guests during a party).

'Loyals' are those consumers who score high on both purchasing support and commitment. These are persons who are truly committed to a brand, take pride in using it, recommend it to others, and view the brand as important to their self-concept. The commitment to the brand is likely to be reflective of an underlying attitude that serves the utilitarian function (i.e. the consumer has a strong liking for the brand because it is viewed as highest in quality and therefore is rewarding) as well as the value-expressive function (i.e. true brand loyals define themselves, in part, through their commitment to the brand and can project this sense of self to others through an association with the brand). Personality psychologists suggest that the *self-concept*, defined as one's perceptions of or feelings about oneself, can be extended or modified by the possessions that one owns and uses. In essence, consumers can create themselves and allow themselves to be created by the products, services and experiences they consume, and this is especially likely to be the case for brand loyals, some of whom have such admiration for a brand that they will tattoo themselves with the brand logo. Thus, some persons may define their rebellious and free-spirited self-concept by owning a Harley-Davidson motorcycle, others exhibit their conscientious and caring nature by purchasing Body Shop products, and others demonstrate their environmental sensitivities by driving a Toyota Prius (Maynard, 2007).

Consistent with the increasing difficulties in reaching consumers through traditional media channels and the growing trend towards consumer-to-consumer influence via social networking, blogging, brand communities, and other forms of social connectedness, marketing strategists have begun to seek out new approaches for engaging customers and converting their loyalty into advocacy. Brand advocates are consumers who appreciate a product or brand so much that they are willing to serve as ambassadors for the offering, enthusiastically recommending it to others. One approach is simply to offer consumers a monetary incentive for each brand referral that leads to a purchase (Ryu and Feick, 2007), a strategy that was utilized by Procter & Gamble during the successful launch of Whitestrips, a leading brand of teeth whitening strips. Another approach is the icecard process, which enables brand adorers (i.e. current buyers especially satisfied with the brand and who have a strong connection and loyalty to it) to order free sets of branded contact cards ('icecards') featuring brand artwork on one side and their own personal details on the other. Hugely popular among young brand loyals, research has revealed that a majority of cards (78 per cent) are distributed to friends and acquaintances, and in 65 per cent of the cases, distribution triggers a brand conversation (Rusticus, 2006). Such approaches can be seen as a form of push marketing in which companies encourage customers with favourable attitudes towards certain offerings to spread the word to others; that is, in each case, the goal is to convert attitudes into behaviours above and beyond a purchase.

Efforts to convert brand loyals into advocates inevitably leads us back to a consideration of the extent to which behaviours can be accurately predicted from measurements of attitudes. In efforts to assess the causal link between attitudes and behaviour, consumer researchers have utilized the self-report research approach pioneered by such psychologists as Louis Thurstone (1928) and Rensis Likert (1932). Measures are obtained by having people describe their own behaviour or state of mind through the use of direct interviews, questionnaires, diaries, and the like. Researchers have found that attitudes are good predictors of behaviour when the following conditions are met: (a) there is a correspondence between the attitude and behavioural measures (i.e. specific attitudes predict specific behaviours); (b) a correspondence exists between attitudinal and behavioural objects, such that the attitude target (i.e. the object of the attitude) matches the behavioural target (i.e. the object towards which behaviour is directed) and the attitude action (i.e. what one would like to do with the object) matches the behavioural action (i.e. the activity that comprises the behaviour); (c) measures of attitudes and behaviours are obtained from the same people; and (d) other factors that influence the attitude–behaviour relationship are considered (e.g. situational variables, other competing attitudes, attitude strength and attitude accessibility) (see Fazio, 1986; Kraus, 1995).

Several of these insights into the attitude–behaviour relationship were taken into account in the development of the behavioural intentions model by social psychologists Fishbein and Ajzen (Ajzen and Fishbein, 1980; Fishbein and Ajzen, 1975). Consistent with their theory of reasoned action (now revised as the theory of planned behaviour), they contend that behaviour can most accurately be predicted from a consideration of an individual's *intention* to perform or not perform the

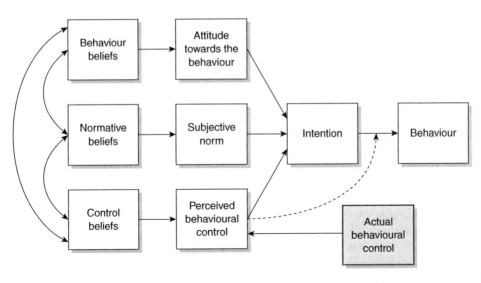

Figure 6.2   Behavioural intentions model based on theory of planned behaviour/reasoned action (Ajzen, 1991)

Source: Reprinted from Ajzen, I. (1991) 'The theory of planned behavior', *Organizational Behavior and Human Decision Processes* 50: 179–211. Copyright 1991, with permission from Elsevier.

behaviour, where intention is defined as the subjective estimate of the probability that one will behave in a certain way towards an attitude object. According to Ajzen's revised model (see Figure 6.2), intention is shaped by one's attitude towards the behaviour (i.e. beliefs about the anticipated consequences of the behaviour under consideration and one's evaluations of those consequences) and by subjective norms (i.e. the extent to which one's behaviour is influenced by beliefs about what others prefer and one's motivation to comply with their wishes). The relative importance of these two sets of intention-influencing factors will determine the nature of a person's intention, assuming the person holds a sufficient degree of perceived control over performing the behaviour, and intention should serve as an efficient guide as to how likely a person is to perform or not perform the behaviour.

As an example applied to the marketing context, consider the case of a young student who has been saving to purchase her first car. If we wanted to predict the likelihood of her purchasing a sports car that aroused her interest at a local dealership, we might first try to gauge her attitude towards purchasing it. Through appropriate questioning – Fishbein and Ajzen utilized written questionnaires with closed-ended rating scales for this purpose – we might learn that, for the most part, she believes the purchase will have positive consequences (e.g. the car will impress others, she will feel good about herself by driving such a cool car, parking will be easier with a small car, the car will require few repairs), albeit with a couple of potential negative outcomes as well (e.g. she may have to borrow a small sum of money from her parents to make the purchase, car parts may be difficult to locate). Overall, however, the preponderance of positive outcomes is likely to result in a strong positive attitude toward purchasing the sports car. In terms of subjective norms, the story might be quite different. When considering the student's perceptions about the beliefs of important others, we may learn that, overall, the people she cares about do not think the purchase is a good idea (e.g. her parents think the sports car is too extravagant and unsafe, her boyfriend thinks the car is too expensive and he would be a bit jealous). On the other hand, she believes the dealer thinks the sports car was 'made for her' and that she would be unwise to forego such a great deal. Because the seller's reactions are less important to the student than those of her parents and boyfriend, it is likely that a strong negative subjective norm will be working against her intention to purchase the sports car. Finally, our prediction must take into account the students' beliefs about the presence of factors that may facilitate or impede her purchase (e.g. a friend knows the dealer and may be able to encourage him to offer an attractive financing arrangement). If the balance of these three sets of forces (attitude towards the behaviour, subjective norms, and perceived control) results in a relatively high intention to buy the car, it is likely that we will be correct in predicting that she will buy it, assuming the measures are obtained within a reasonably close temporal proximity to when the behaviour is likely to occur.

The behavioural intentions model is an example of a psychological framework that has been borrowed and applied by researchers and practitioners in a variety of other disciplines, and marketing is no exception. The model has successfully predicted purchases for a wide variety of product and service categories (e.g. toothpastes, automobiles, laundry detergents, clothing, medical therapies, weight control drugs) and other consumption activities (e.g. dieting, exercising, use of money-saving coupons, donating blood) (see Ajzen, 2008; Sheppard et al., 1988).

 Persuasion

Another reason that researchers and practitioners have devoted such formidable attention to the attitude construct has to do with the interest in attitude change, commonly referred to as 'persuasion'. Attitude change is related to the assumption that attitudes and behaviour are causally linked; in short, if attitudes influence behaviour, then it should be possible to have an impact on behaviour by first changing the attitudes that give rise to the behaviour. The ability to change or somehow influence consumer preferences, their likes and dislikes, and their loyalties to companies or brands is of fundamental interest to marketers. For example, if a competitor's brand is preferred over that offered by another company, resulting in higher market share for the former, then the latter company could attempt to modify how customers feel about the respective brands in order to have an impact on their buying behaviour. The means by which such attitude change can be accomplished have been the focus of an enormous amount of research over the years by social psychologists and communication researchers (Gilbert et al., 1998; Hovland et al., 1953). One of the pioneers in persuasion research, social psychologist Carl I. Hovland, borrowed as the guiding focus for this research the didactic statement attributed to communication theorist Harold Laswell, 'who says what to whom with what effect'. Each element of the statement has served as the focus of research programmes since the Second World War, the results of which have been utilized by marketers in the design of marketing messages (e.g. one-sided vs. two-sided messages; order of arguments), determination of message source (e.g. celebrity endorsements; salesperson characteristics), audience variables (e.g. utilized in segmentation and targeting considerations), development of social marketing programmes (e.g. safe driving campaigns), among a broad array of other applications.

In one widely applied approach for understanding and implementing persuasive interventions, social psychologists Petty and Cacioppo (1986) incorporated notions related to involvement theory in the development of their elaboration likelihood model (ELM). In their view, there are two possible paths or 'routes' to persuasion, a central route and a peripheral route. The route taken depends on one's motivation and ability to process information presented in the message; that is, to think about and carefully scrutinize arguments in the persuasive communication. When the central route is followed, the receiver is thought to be very active and involved, as in situations where persuasive messages deal with issues that are important and personally relevant. In contrast, the peripheral path is likely to be taken when messages deal with issues that are uninvolving or unimportant for the recipient.

In order to better distinguish between the two explanations for how attitude change can be effected, imagine the case in which you are actively shopping for a new car. Because a new car purchase is something very important to you – that is, it is high in risk, an expensive purchase, and a choice that entails complex consideration – your head will be spinning with questions as you contemplate the arguments being presented to you by a salesperson who is attempting to convince you to purchase a car that you had expressed interest in. Are you better off with an earlier offer? Will you be able to keep up with the payments? Is this really the right car for you? In other words, when confronted with a personally significant message, we do more than simply listen for the sake of acquiring information, we think about the message, its arguments and their implications. This process is what Petty and Cacioppo refer to as 'high elaboration', which consists of evaluating the strength or rationality of a persuasive message, considering whether the message contents agree or disagree with one's current belief system, and weighing the personal implications of the message points and arguments.

Now imagine that you are not interested at all in buying a car. However, while in the cinema awaiting the start of a movie, a 30-second advertisement for a new Chevrolet car model is shown that captures your attention. It begins by showing the popular singer Bruce Springsteen and his band performing the song 'Born in the USA'. The music continues as the Chevrolet appears, transporting an attractive young couple through the idyllic landscape of the American West. Copy text describing various features of the car are eventually superimposed on this scene, and the advertisement ends with the car eventually disappearing over the horizon. Chances are, because of your lack of involvement in a car purchase and your lack of interest in cars in general, you paid little attention to the message arguments (i.e. the car's features), and no doubt would be unable to recall them even immediately after the ad was aired. Because your motivation was low to process the brief message, message elaboration did not occur; rather, your attention was placed on so-called 'peripheral (or persuasion) cues', – features of the communication that were incidental to message content, such as characteristics of the message source (Bruce

Springsteen) and the style or form of the message (the music and compelling images, the attractive couple inside the car).

Attitude change might be accomplished in both of the scenarios described above, but in different ways. At the car dealership, the quality and strength of the message arguments presented by the salesperson would determine the ability of his or her communication to influence your attitudes towards the car being considered. This is because when people are motivated to consider a message carefully, their reaction to it depends on its content. If the arguments are strong and they stimulate favourable evaluation, the message will be persuasive. In the second case, you may leave the cinema with a more favourable attitude towards the Chevrolet depicted in the ad, but for reasons unrelated to message arguments. When you think of the car, it might remind you of Bruce Springsteen, or the song, or of images of the American West, and those thoughts may enhance your feelings about the product.

The ELM model helps to clarify some of the research findings accrued through experimental research on persuasion. For example, it has been found that strong arguments result in more post-communication attitude change than weak arguments, but mostly for research participants who are highly involved in the communication. On the other hand, a message delivered by an expert source (e.g. an endorsement of a new medication by a noted doctor) results in more post-communication attitude change, but mostly for research participants who are not very involved in the message. In the first case, message strength had an impact on highly involved persons who followed the central route to persuasion, whereas in the second case, a characteristic of the source (degree of expertise) had an impact on low-involved persons who followed a peripheral course to persuasion (White and Harkins, 1994).

The implications of the ELM model for marketing strategy are relatively straightforward: strategy should be based on the level of cognitive processing the target audience is expected to engage in and the route they are likely to follow to attitude change. If the processing level is low, due to low motivation and involvement, the peripheral route should dominate, and emphasis will need to be placed on the way messages are executed and on the emotions of the target audience. If the central route is anticipated, then the content of the messages should be dominant – messages will need to be informative and the executional aspects need only be adequate (to maintain attention) (see Mehta, 1994; Petty and Wegener, 1998).

Conclusion

This chapter has provided an overview of the psychological basis of marketing through a focus on five topical areas of the behavioural sciences. Other areas that were only briefly alluded to here due to space constraints, but which have significant implications for marketers, include learning, personality, social behaviour, and developmental psychology (see Chapter 12). Because the marketing enterprise is comprised of exchange activities that involve people, it is not an exaggeration to suggest that psychological principles and concepts permeate every marketing action in one sense or another. As the examples presented in this chapter attest, much can be gained when marketing activities are planned and implemented with an eye towards psychology's role in the process.

The future holds great promise for further applications of psychology in marketing as our understanding of human behaviour and mental processes continues to evolve. For example, new technologies are making it possible to track what happens in buyers' brains as they consider difficult choices. In one recent study (Hedgcock and Rao, 2009), volunteers' brains were scanned as they pondered a choice between sets of equally appealing options. When the choice set also included a third, less attractive option, the choice between the preferred options became easier and relatively more pleasurable, as indicated by decreased activity in an area of the brain associated with negative emotions. By contrast, the brain scans for persons choosing between only two equally preferred options revealed irritation attributed to the difficulty of the choice process. Apparently, the participants were using heuristics when evaluating three-item choice sets rather than a more complex evaluation process.

It is important to add that although this chapter concerns the impact of psychology on marketing, the discipline of psychology in turn has drawn from the marketing process. For example, marketing tactics are utilized by psychologists to seek coveted research funds for scientific and therapeutic programmes, as well as for influencing public policy and obtaining government support for public interventions (e.g. in efforts to control obesity and other eating disorders and programmes to control domestic abuse and other forms of violence). Mutual sharing and exchange between the disciplines is likely to continue through the twenty-first century, resulting in further benefits for both marketing and psychology.

References

Ajzen, I. (1991) 'The theory of planned behavior', *Organizational Behavior and Human Decision Processes* 50, 179–211.

Ajzen, I. (2008) 'Consumer attitudes and behaviour', in C.P. Haugtvedt, P.M. Herr and F.R. Cardes (eds) *Handbook of Consumer Psychology*, New York: Lawrence Erlbaum Associates, pp. 525–48.

Ajzen, I. and Fishbein, M. (1980) *Understanding Attitudes and Predicting Social Behavior*, Englewood Cliffs, NJ: Prentice Hall.

Andrews, J.C., Durvasula, S. and Akhter, S.H. (1990) 'A framework for conceptualizing and measuring the involvement construct in advertising research', *Journal of Advertising* 19: 17–40.

Anissimov, M. (2004) 'A concise introduction to heuristics and biases', June, available at: www.acceleratingfuture.com

Arthur, D. and Quester, P. (2004) 'Who's afraid of that ad? Applying segmentation to the protection motivation model', *Psychology and Marketing*, 21: 671–96.

Batey, M. (2008) *Brand Meaning*, New York: Routledge.

Bock, B.C., Marcus, B.H., Rossi, J.S. and Redding, C.A. (1998) 'Motivational readiness for change: diet, exercise, and smoking', *American Journal of Health Behavior* 22: 248–58.

Brehm, S.S. and Kassin, S.M. (1993) *Social Psychology*, 2nd edn, Boston: Houghton Mifflin.

Cacioppo, J.T. and Petty, R.E. (1982) 'The need for cognition', *Journal of Personality and Social Psychology* 42: 116–31.

Chaiken, S. (1987) 'The heuristic model of persuasion', in M.P. Zanna, J.M. Olson and C.P. Herman (eds) *Social Influence: The Ontario Symposium, Vol. 5*. Hillsdale, NJ: Erlbaum, pp. 3–39.

Chandon, P. and Wansink, B. (2007) 'The biasing health halos of fast-food restaurant health claims: lower calorie estimates and higher side-dish consumption intentions', *Journal of Consumer Research* 34: 301–14.

Churchill, G.A., Jr. (1979) 'A paradigm for developing better measures of marketing constructs', *Journal of Marketing Research* 16: 64–73.

Eagly, A.H. and Chaiken, S. (1998) 'Attitude structure and function', in D.T. Gilbert and S.T. Fiske (eds) *The Handbook of Social Psychology*, Boston, MA: McGraw-Hill, pp. 269–322.

Eppright, D.R., Tanner, J. and Hunt, J.B. (1994) 'Knowledge and the ordered protection motivation model: tools for preventing AIDS', *Journal of Business Research* 30: 13–24.

Fazio, R.H. (1986) 'How do attitudes guide behavior?', in R.M. Sorrentino and E.T. Higgins (eds) *Handbook of Motivation and Cognition*, New York: Guilford Press, pp. 204–43.

Fishbein, M. and Ajzen, I. (1975) Belief, Attitude, Intention, and Behaviour: An Introduction to Theory and Research, Reading, MA: Addison-Wesley.

Friestad, M. (2001) 'What is consumer psychology?' *Eye on Psi Chi* 6: 28–9.

Gilbert, D.T., Fiske, S.T. and Lindzey, G. (1998) *The Handbook of Social Psychology*, New York: Oxford University Press.

Greenspan, R. (2004) 'Media multitaskers may miss messages', 2 April, available at: www.clickz.com

Haughney, C. (2009) 'When economy sours Tootsie Rolls soothe souls', *The New York Times*, 23 March, available at: www.nytimes.com

Haugtvedt, C.P., Petty, R.E. and Cacioppo, J.T. (1992) 'Need for cognition and advertising: Understanding the role of personality variables in consumer behaviour', *Journal of Consumer Psychology* 1: 239–60.

Hedgcock, W. and Rao, A.R. (2009) 'Trade-off aversion as an explanation for the attraction effect: A functional magnetic resonance imaging study', *Journal of Marketing Research* 46: 1–13.

Herzberg, F. (1959) *The Motivation to Work*, New York: John Wiley and Sons.

Hovland, C.I., Janis, I.L. and Kelley, H.H. (1953) *Communication and Persuasion*, New Haven, CT: Yale University Press.

Howard, T. (2009) 'Coupon search clicks: sweet sound for web marketers', *USA Today*, 10 March, available at: www.usatoday.com

Johnson, B.T. and Eagly, A.H. (1989) 'Effects of involvement on persuasion: a meta-analysis', *Psychological Bulletin* 106: 290–314.

Kahneman, D. and Tversky, A. (eds) (2000) *Choices, Values and Frames*, Cambridge, UK: Cambridge University Press.

Kahneman, D., Slovic, P. and Tversky, A. (eds) (1982) *Judgement under Uncertainty: Heuristics and Biases*. Cambridge, UK: Cambridge University Press.

Kassarjian, H.H. (1974) 'Projective methods', in R. Ferber (ed.) *Handbook of Marketing Research*, New York: McGraw-Hill, pp. 2–87.

Katz, D. (1960) The functional approach to the study of attitudes. Public Opinion Quarterly 24: 163–204.

Knox, S. and Walker, D. (2001) Managing and measuring brand loyalty. *Journal of Strategic Marketing* 9: 111–28.

Kraus, S.J. (1995) 'Attitudes and the prediction of behaviour: A meta-analysis of the empirical literature', *Personality and Social Psychology Bulletin* 21: 58–75.

Langenderfer, J. and Shimp, T.A. (2001) 'Consumer vulnerability to scams, swindles, and fraud: a new theory of visceral influences on persuasion', *Psychology & Marketing* 18: 763–84.

Leippe, M.R. and Elkin, R.A. (1987) 'When motives clash: issue involvement and response involvement as determinants of persuasion', *Journal of Personality and Social Psychology* 52: 269–78.

Likert, R. (1932) 'A technique for the measurement of attitudes', *Archives of Psychology* 140: 44–53.

Lowrey, T.M., Shrum, L.J. and McCarty, J.A. (2005) 'The future of television advertising', in A.J. Kimmel (ed.) *Marketing Communication: New Approaches, Technologies, and Styles*, Oxford, UK: Oxford University Press, pp. 113–32.

McGuire, W.J. (1969) The nature of attitudes and attitude change (pp. 136–314). In G. Lindzey & E. Aronson (eds) *The handbook of social psychology* (2nd ed., Vol.3) Reading, MA: Addison Wesley.

Maslow, A.H. (1943) 'A theory of human motivation', *Psychological Review* 50: 370–96.

Maynard, M. (2007) 'Toyota hybrid makes a statement, and that sells', 4 July, *The New York Times*, available at: http://query.nytimes.com

Mehta, A. (1994) 'How advertising response modeling (ARM) can increase ad effectiveness', *Journal of Advertising Research* 34: 62–74.

Nestle, M. (2002, September) 'The soft sell: how the food industry shapes our diets', *Nutrition Action Healthletter*, September.

Petty, R.E. and Cacioppo, J.T. (1986) *Communication and Persuasion: Central and Peripheral Routes to Attitude Change*, New York: Springer-Verlag.

Petty, R.E. and Wegener, D.T. (1998) 'Attitude change', in D. Gilbert, S.T. Fiske and G. Lindzey (eds) *The Handbook of Social Psychology*, 4th edn, New York: Oxford University Press.

Rajecki, D.W. (1990) *Attitudes*, 2nd edn, Sunderland, MA: Sinauer Associates.

Rogers, R.W. (1983) 'Cognitive and physiological processes in fear appeals and attitude change: A revised theory of protection motivation', in J. Cacioppo and R. Petty (eds) *Social Psychophysiology*, New York: Guilford Press.

Roeper, R. (2002) 'Starbucks buckles under to 9/11 hypersensitivity', *Chicago Sun-Times*, 10 July.

Rook, D.W. (2006) 'Let's pretend: projective methods reconsidered', in R. Belk (ed.) *Handbook of Qualitative Research Methods in Marketing*, Cheltenham, UK: Edward Elgar, pp. 143–55.

Rossiter, J.R., Percy, L. and Donovan, R.J. (1991) 'A better advertising planning grid', *Journal of Advertising Research* 31: 11–21.

Rusticus, S. (2006) 'Creating brand advocates', in J. Kirby and P. Marsden (eds) *Connected Marketing: The Viral, Buzz and Word of Mouth Revolution*, Oxford, UK: Butterworth-Heinemann, pp. 47–58.

Ryu, G. and Feick, L. (2007) 'A penny for your thoughts: referral reward programs and referral likelihood', *Journal of Marketing* 71: 84–94.

Sheppard, B.H., Hartwick, J. and Warshaw, P.R. (1988) 'The theory of reasoned action: a meta-analysis of past research with recommendations for modifications and future research', *Journal of Consumer Research* 15: 325–43.

Sherif, M. and Hovland, C.I. (1961) *Social Judgement: Assimilation and Contrast Effects in Communication and Attitude Change*, New Haven, CT: Yale University Press.

Solomon, M.R. (2008) *Consumer Behavior: Buying, Having, Being*, 8th edn, Englewood Cliffs, NJ: Prentice-Hall.

Sternberg, R.J. (2008) *Cognitive Psychology*, 5th edn, Belmont, CA: Wadsworth.

Story, L. (2007) 'Product packages now shout to get your attention', *The New York Times*, 10 August, available at: www.nytimes.com

Thurstone, L. (1928) 'Attitudes can be measured', *American Journal of Psychology* 33: 529–54.

Veblen, T. (1899) *Theory of the Leisure Class: An Economic Study in the Evolution of Institutions*. New York: Macmillan.

Verplanken, B. & Svenson, O. (1997) 'Personal involvement in human decision making: conceptualisations and effects on decision processes', in W.R. Crozier, R. Ranyard and O. Svenson (eds) *Decision Making: Cognitive Models and Explanations*, London: Routledge, pp. 40–57.

Vohs, K.D. and Faber, R.J. (2007) 'Spent resources: self-regulatory resource availability affects impulse buying', *Journal of Consumer Research* 33: 537–47.

Wansink, B. and Chandon, P. (2006) 'Can "low-fat" nutrition labels lead to obesity?', *Journal of Marketing Research* 43: 605–17.

Wansink, B., Brasel, S.A. and Amjad, S. (2000) 'The mystery of the cabinet castaway: why we buy products we never use', *Journal of Family and Consumer Science* 92: 104–8.

White, P.H. and Harkins, S.G. (1994) 'Race of source effects in the elaboration likelihood model', *Journal of Personality and Social Psychology* 67: 790–808.

Zimbardo, P.O. (1960) 'Involvement and communication discrepancy as determinants of opinion conformity', *Journal of Abnormal and Social Psychology* 60: 86–94.

7

The sociological basis of marketing
Kjell Grønhaug and Ingeborg Astrid Kleppe

Chapter Topics

Overview

This chapter claims that marketing is a basic social activity, and shows how the discipline of marketing has borrowed from and been influenced by sociology. Also, the sociological influence on marketing has probably been more profound in Europe than in the US.

The similarities between the basic characteristics of marketing and sociology are illustrated and it is demonstrated that marketing is essentially a societal activity which has borrowed significantly from sociological thinking. Marketing demands that consumers are considered not only as individuals, but also in terms of the groups in which they exist – for example families, social classes, and indeed the wider society around them – taking into account their status, lifestyle, culture and so on. Then marketing must look at relationships within these groups: networking, conflict and power all have a bearing on the marketing approach to be adopted. Furthermore, sociology can be drawn upon to enlighten the marketer on socialization and learned behaviour. Consideration is also given to how a sociological approach might influence the marketing of the future.

Introduction

Marketing has long been recognized as a 'borrowing' discipline, in particular from the social sciences (Cox, 1964), and is itself claimed to be a social science discipline (Hunt, 1991). The historical roots of marketing are embedded in classical economics. Citation analysis to determine the influences of other disciplines on marketing also shows extensive borrowing from (among others) sociology (Goldman, 1979). An interesting observation is that there has been a considerable mutual influence between economics and sociology as reflected in the sub-discipline of economic sociology (for excellent overviews, see Smelser (1963) and Granovetter and Swedberg (1992)). However, so far marketing has only had a modest influence on sociology. The borrowing consists of concepts, theories and models, and methods and techniques for doing research. Particularly important is the conceptual borrowing. Concepts are the building blocks of any theory, model or hypothesis. The concepts and how they are used (and related) guide and direct. They give focus and largely determine what is captured.

As will be demonstrated in the following, the borrowing from sociology has had – and still has – a considerable influence on marketing thinking. The emphasis here is primarily on the concepts (and perspectives) borrowed from sociology and how they have influenced marketing thinking as reflected in major marketing textbooks. The main reason for using marketing textbooks as a mirror of the sociological influences is that textbooks reflect what is taught and disseminated, and thus capture important aspects of the sociological impact on marketing thinking (and practice). Marketing – as other disciplines – has changed and developed over the years. This is also reflected in changes in the borrowing from other disciplines (e.g. sociology) over time.

The chapter proceeds as follows: first, characteristics of marketing and the discipline of sociology are emphasized. In this section it is also demonstrated that marketing is a societal activity. Similarities in marketing and sociological reasoning are also discussed. Then the dominant focus in marketing thinking and practice, and how this has influenced conceptual borrowing and use is discussed. Next, specific concepts and ideas borrowed from sociology are emphasized. A distinction is made between concepts and ideas primarily used to characterize individuals, groups and the larger society, and contributions taking relationships between social actors directly into account, as well as contributions focusing on change. Finally, characteristics of the borrowing from and influences of sociology on marketing are summarized and future influences from this discipline (sociology) on marketing are indicated.

Marketing and sociology

Marketing activities have a long history. Through thousands of years man has transacted goods to satisfy needs and enhance standards of living. As a scientific discipline, however, marketing is young with its origins at the turn of the twentieth century.

Marketing as exchange

Marketing takes place in a societal context. The core of marketing as a scientific discipline relates to exchange between social actors, e.g. individuals, groups or organizations, or as claimed by Hunt (1983: 129): 'marketing (science) is the behavioural science which seeks to explain exchange relationships'.

(Social) exchange requires

- the presence of (at least) two parties

- that each party has something to offer that might be of value to the other party

- each party is capable of communicating and delivering

- each party is free to accept or reject an offer

- each party believes it is appropriate or desirable to deal with the other party (Kotler, 1984: 8).

Exchange as phenomenon is, however, a huge area of inquiry, and has been extensively dealt with in sociology and other disciplines. Exchange theory consists not just of one, but several theories. A distinction is often made between individualistic and collective approaches to the study of exchange. Different modes of exchange have been identified as well, such as the market mode (i.e. exchange through markets), the reciprocal exchange mode (which can be thought of as gift exchange between members of a network with reciprocal obligations), and the redistributive mode of exchange, (i.e. exchange based on some principle of sharing, e.g. blood donations, (Polanyi, 1944)). More lately there has been an emphasis on value creation (see e.g. the definition of marketing by American Marketing Association from 2004). However, exchange between actors is seen as a prerequisite for value creation.

For a long time, marketing has primarily been associated with the market mode of exchange, where the market is often thought of, in a neoclassical sense, as a large number of exchange partners, and where market prices yield the necessary information and incentives. The idealized market mode of exchange is considered impersonal (as reflected in neoclassical economics), or, as emphasized by Polanyi, 'it is important to emphasize the abstract and impersonal nature of market exchange' (Polanyi, 1944: 5). In modern societies, reciprocal and redistributive exchanges are also taking place. Forty years ago Codere even claimed that the proportion of market exchanges to all exchanges taking place is declining (Codere, 1968: 57).

Marketers have devoted substantial effort to studying and understanding exchanges. One of the first marketing scholars to recognize the limitations of 'faceless' transactions (i.e. exchange outcomes) in understanding markets and marketing was Wroe Alderson, recognized for his influential contributions on marketing thinking. He introduced the notion of the 'organized behavior system' (Alderson, 1950) to capture the fact that the various actors operating in the market are more or less connected (as reflected in the recent emphasis on 'relationship' marketing). Alderson thus recognized the benefit of sociology, and claimed: 'The initial plunge into sociology is only the beginning since the marketing man must go considerably further in examining the functions and structures of organized behaviour systems' (Alderson, 1957:12).

_____ Sociology _____

Sociology is one of the major social sciences. The term 'sociology' was invented by Auguste Comte, and first published in the fourth volume of his *Cours de philosophie positive* in 1838, even though the ancient roots of the discipline can be traced back, to among others, Plato and Aristotle. The term (sociology) has two stems, the Latin *socius* (companion) and the Greek *logos* (study of), and literally means the study of the processes of companionship. The term 'sociology' can be (and has been) defined in various ways, for example as proposed by Giddens, 'sociology is the study of human life, groups and societies' (Giddens, 1993).

A key point in the sociological perspective is that man does not operate in a vacuum, but is embedded in the surrounding social context. The individual forms and holds expectations about others, and because he or she is assumed to behave purposefully, expectations about others are taken into account. This basic point of departure has a distinct parallel in marketing. Marketing activities take place in a societal context. Exchange requires the presence of and access to others. Since man started transacting goods and services thousands of years ago, the importance of 'others' has been recognized. Sellers have tried to identify potential buyers, their needs and how they make evaluations. Buyers learn about sellers and their product offerings. Through word of mouth, their own experiences and other sources of information, buyers' expectations towards sellers are shaped and influence their behaviour as well.

The individual-in-context is a human being interacting with her or his social environment. The sociological perspective tries to encompass the acting person and the acting group. The acting person is a specific human being who pursues goals, interprets experiences, responds to opportunities and confronts difficulties. As an individual-in-action he or she does not necessarily stay within neat boundaries of specialized activity, nor does he or she always conform to conventional expectations. For example, the seller may cheat, the buyer shoplift, and the marketing entrepreneur may 'break the rules', change the 'social game' – and become successful.

_____ Social organization _____

To capture the social influences in a society, sociologists study how it is organized. In doing so they often make use of the general term, *social system*, emphasizing the interdependencies and interactions among social actors. The same underlying idea can easily be traced in marketing, e.g. as reflected in 'distribution systems', 'system sales', 'relationships' and 'networks'.

In their study of social organizations sociologists also distinguish between different levels, for example micro-level (individual and group) and macro-level or social order. Concepts used and phenomena focused on vary across levels (Collins, 1981). There are, however, interactions and interdependencies between the various levels. Changes at the macro-level may influence expectations and behaviour at the micro-level and vice versa. For example, the automobile has dramatically changed the mobility of the individual (consumer), which has influenced shopping behaviour – and the structure of the distribution system, as reflected in the dramatic changes in the retail trade. A drop in individual fertility, for example influenced by a pessimistic outlook for the future, may add up to dramatic changes in demand for specific goods or services. Such demographic changes are (among others) studied by sociologists – and experienced by marketers. Markets have also been an arena for sociological inquiry, generating substantial insights which in turn have also been of importance for the marketing discipline (for an overview, see Lie, 1997).

Our examples so far show that there are close parallels between sociology and marketing unrecognized in most contemporary marketing textbooks. In what follows the focus will be on the main concepts borrowed from sociology, how they are used and why they are used that way.

Marketing focus and scientific borrowing

The present writers view the borrowing from other disciplines as purposeful behaviour, that is the borrowing is done to obtain something, for example to understand the functioning of markets and/or to improve marketing practices. On the other hand what is borrowed, and how the borrowings are used are heavily influenced by the dominant focus of the borrowing discipline, in this case marketing.

The term 'marketing' has been used with at least three different meanings (Arndt, 1980):

1. marketing as a management orientation or discipline

2. marketing as a science

3. marketing as an ideology.

According to the stated purpose, that is to capture the influence of sociology on marketing thinking, as reflected in major textbooks, primarily the first meaning of the term (marketing) will be emphasized.

As a management orientation or discipline marketing can be – and has been until now – primarily considered a *business* discipline. In spite of efforts to apply marketing thinking to the public sector, and in non-business and non-profit settings, there is little doubt that most marketing thinking and activities relate to business firms.

Any business firm specializes and offers a more or less limited set of products (services). The firm is dependent on its surrounding environments, in particular on its market(s), that is on actual and potential customers. For the firm to survive and prosper a sufficient number of customers must be willing to buy its products

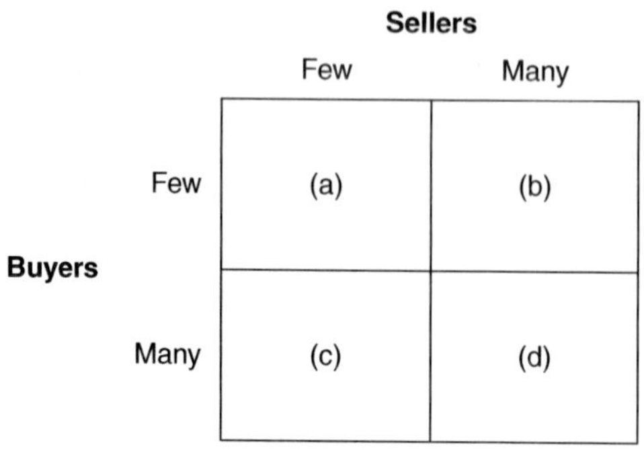

Sellers

	Few	Many
Few	(a)	(b)
Many	(c)	(d)

*(left axis label: **Buyers**, with rows Few and Many)*

Figure 7.1   Number of sellers and buyers

(services) at prices which at least cover costs. Even though a business firm can survive some losses, in the long run costs must be covered in order to stay in business. Surplus profit which will create optimism, attract admiration and allow for investments, and so on, is – of course – considered advantageous.

The number of buyers and sellers varies across markets, and the products and services offered are multiple. Modern marketing as reflected in the majority of (American) textbooks primarily deals with *mass-marketing*. Most textbooks are influenced by the underlying (but implicit) perspective that the market frequently exhibits a situation where a few firms sell their products and services to many customers (primarily individuals and households as reflected in cell (c)) in Figure 7.1.

In such markets with a great many customers, there is little room to pay attention to the individual buyer. This is particularly so for low-priced items, where the contribution from the individual buyer is lowest and allows for modest individual attention only. In such cases the market is often considered an 'aggregate' of individual customers to which the firm tries to offer its products (or services). Deighton (1996), however, shows how advances in modern information technologies allow for the individualization of mass markets and thus adjust to and serve what Alderson once labelled the heterogeneous market, that is the consumers held different preferences (in contrast to homogeneous preferences as assumed in neoclassical economics). Marketing situations as reflected in the other cells are also taking place. An important point, however, is that the situation as depicted in cell (c) reflected – until now – the dominant perspective on marketing thinking and influenced the borrowing from other disciplines.

Cell (a) in Figure 7.1 reflects the prototypical 'small numbers' market. In such markets the numbers of sellers and buyers are few. The actors are highly visible, and each customer really counts. The growing emphasis on relationships and networks primarily relates to small numbers and industrial markets, even though such approaches are highly relevant in consumer markets. When the focus is on relationships and networks the presence of others is also directly brought into account, and thus the social aspect of marketing. The growing emphasis on relationships and networks has also contributed to a growing emphasis on sociological aspects by marketers.

Marketing is – as noted above – primarily a business discipline. Business firms are headed by managers. In the marketing literature managers are conceived as active individuals (or groups) who, it is assumed, make wise decisions to reach the goals and influence the destiny of the firms they manage.

Due to the firm's dependence on its market(s) it is of crucial importance for the marketing manager to identify and understand actual and potential customers as the basis for designing and implementing successful marketing strategies. This need to identify, understand, and thus in mass markets, to 'profile' customers in order to become effective can be traced in marketing's borrowing from sociology as reflected in most marketing (and consumer behaviour) textbooks.

Concepts and ideas

This section focuses on the main concepts and ideas borrowed from sociology. The section is organized as follows. First, concepts and ideas to capture the characteristics of individuals, groups and larger social segments are described. Contributions focusing respectively on relationships between actors, and contributions directed towards change are then discussed.

Individuals, groups and the larger society

Role

An important sociological concept is (social) 'role', which can be conceived as 'the bundles of socially defined attributes and expectations associated with social positions' (Abercombie et al., 1988). For example, the role of 'mother' carries with it certain expected behaviours irrespective of the woman's feeling at any one time. Therefore it is possible to generalize about role behaviour regardless of the individual characteristics of the people who occupy these roles. The concept of role is sociologically important because it reflects how individual activity is socially influenced and thus follows regular patterns. It should also be noted that sociologists employ roles as 'building blocks' to study various social institutions, for example families and organizations (to be discussed later on).

In social life an individual may occupy several roles, for example the role of mother or father, university professor or marketing manager. The number of roles occupied may vary considerably between people. The number of roles occupied by an individual need not be static, as the individual may acquire new roles (and leave others). An individual may also perceive two or more roles to be in conflict. For example, the role of employee, perhaps requiring frequent and lengthy travel, can come in conflict with the parental role of father, associated with expectations of spending time with his child(ren).

The concept of role is a true sociological concept as it implies social relationships. For example, the role of 'husband' is primarily relevant in a household setting, in the presence of a 'wife'. The role concept has been used and has influenced marketing in various ways. The prototypical expectations associated with various roles, for example 'mother', and 'working woman', have been used to identify and profile target groups as the basis for designing appropriate marketing approaches. The frequently quoted roles of 'influencer', 'decider', 'user' and 'gatekeeper' in the organizational (industrial) buying literature have been used in a similar way as the basis for who (and how) to target, as has the focus on 'husband' and 'wife' in the study of family (households). This is a somewhat 'one-eyed' perspective on how the concept of role has been translated into marketing as relationships between actors (e.g. between sellers and buyers) which are crucial in marketing. Some researchers have, however, looked outside the narrow role of the individual as buyer and consumer and addressed consumers as 'real people' who must balance simultaneously multiple role demands, which has contributed to a deeper understanding of consumption in everyday life. However, as noted by Wallendorf (1978), so far only a fraction of the potential of role theory has been exploited in a marketing context.

Status

In any social system (e.g. group, organization or society) one may distinguish between different social positions (compare the discussion of social roles). Such positions can also be rank-ordered, implying that positions may be lower, higher or equal in status. Sociologists have long studied how status is achieved. Often a distinction is made between ascribed (e.g. by heritage) and achieved attributes as a basis for status (e.g. education or sports performance). The concept of status has directly (and indirectly) influenced marketing thinking. For example, the observation that things (and behaviours) may symbolize status has been extensively used to develop, introduce and communicate products. In other words, marketers have exploited sociological insights by relating status to consumption alternatives, as reflected in Levy's seminal article, 'Symbols for sale' (1959), as well as designing strategies to get access to new markets.

Norm

The term 'norm' refers to social expectations about correct or proper behaviour. Thus norms imply the presence of legitimacy, consent and prescription. When norms are *internalized* they are learnt and accepted as binding the social values and guidelines of conduct relevant to the individual, or her or his group, or wider society. Internalized norms are central for social order. Deviations from norms are punished by sanctions.

The sources of norms can be found in established values, law, expectations and accepted behaviours. Often (in most cases) norms are not written, but are learnt through socialization. Norms may also be more or less specific. For example, specific norms may prevail with regard to specific role behaviours.

For marketers it is important to know the norms in the marketplace in order to behave appropriately. In marketing the concept and knowledge of norms are extensively used as input in market research to get adequate information about target groups. For example, prevailing norms may be barriers to the acceptance of new products. By knowing the norms the marketer may adjust to, or even contribute to, a change of norms. Mason Haire's well known 'shopping list' study is an example.

When instant coffee was introduced several decades ago, the acceptance rate of the new product was modest. The shopping list study exposed a sample of housewives to one of two shopping lists. The shopping lists were identical, but for one item, coffee. One list contained 'instant coffee', while the other contained the brand name of a well-known regular coffee. The respondents were asked to describe the shopping person. Housewives (who were in the majority at that time) tended to describe the shopper behind the list containing instant coffee as 'lazy', 'not a good housewife', while women working outside the home described the shopping person as 'smart', 'modern', 'effective', and so on. Apparently the new product was conceived to be in conflict with existing norms of being a good housewife. This knowledge was successfully used in designing marketing strategies to alter this aspect of the prevailing 'housewife norm'. As norms may vary across societies (and social segments), an understanding of prevailing norms represents a true challenge when expanding internationally. More recently marketers have also studied how norms may influence the governance of seller–buyer relationships.

Groups

Social groups are collectives of individuals who interact and form social relationships. A distinction is often made between *primary* and *secondary* groups. The former are small groups, defined by face-to-face interaction. The household (nuclear family) and the clique may serve as examples. Secondary groups are usually larger in number, and each member does not necessarily directly interact with every other member. Examples are unions and associations where the members (at best) interact only with a subset of other members, and where most of the communication is formalized, for example through newsletters. Sociological insights regarding groups have influenced marketing thinking. For example, the family (household) can be conceived as a primary group, and plays an important role in marketing thinking, primarily as a buying and consuming unit. A common observation is that firms' (organizations') buying is usually made by a group, rather than a single individual. This has led to the notion of 'the buying group' or 'buying centre', heavily influenced by sociological group insights. The focus among marketers has been on the role (position) of the buying group, identification (or prediction) of who is included, their tasks and activities, and on their relative influence in purchasing situations, as a basis for designing effective marketing strategies.

A third form of groups is *reference groups*. In forming their attitudes and beliefs, and in performing their actions, people will compare or identify themselves with other people, or other groups of people (reference groups). People can make references both to membership and non-membership groups. Reference group knowledge has influenced marketing thinking. In particular these insights have been applied to relate products or brands to groups to whom it is assumed they will appear attractive. Research findings have demonstrated that reference group influence can be made both at the product category level (particularly for expensive goods) as well as at the brand level. For example, brands of perfume, clothes and equipment are often associated with (distant) attractive reference groups (e.g. movie stars or sports idols). Specific information about the actual reference group(s) of the target group is needed when designing marketing strategies.

Family (household)

The notion of family (household) is extensively used by marketers. In most cases marketers use the notions of 'family' and 'household' interchangably, indicating the Western perspective that family of a kind (i.e. the nuclear family) often coincides with households (i.e. the unit of dwelling). The family (household) is often considered as an important primary group. The family (household) can also be considered as an important social *institution*. The term (social institutions) refers to established patterns of behaviour, or as defined by Nicosia and Mayer, 'a set of specific activities performed by specific people in specific places through time' (1976: 67). Sociological insights regarding families (households) have in particular been used by marketers to study the relative influence of spouses (and also children) in buying decisions, but also as a basis for studying buying decision processes and how households (families) allocate their scarce economic resources and time.

Family life-cycle

The sociological term 'life-cycle' is used primarily to describe the development of a person through childhood, adolescence, mid-life, old age and death. The concept does not refer to purely biological processes of maturation, but to the transition of an individual through socially constructed categories of age and to the variations in social experiences of ageing. Even though life-cycle is a dynamic concept, the main focus in marketing has been to classify people according to *stages* in the life-cycle, and – in particular – to characterize buying and consumption at the various stages. Such insights have been used to profile target groups and predict future market developments.

Community

Communities or communes come in many forms, for example villages, sections of cities or other groups with something in common (e.g. the domestic lifestyle in the kibbutz). Traditionally communities are located in a discrete geographical area. However, more recently, since the internet has grown in importance, marketing has borrowed the concept (idea) of community and transferred it to a space where actors interact electronically. Examples are online consumer and brand communities. A brand community is 'a specialized, non-geographically bound community, based on a set of structural social relations among addressees of a brand' (Muniz and O'Guinn, 2001: 415). Thus a brand community shares characteristics with traditional communalities, that is consciousness of kind (shared identity), shared traditions and rituals, and moral responsibility.

Social class and lifestyle

In most (all?) societies individuals are ranked hierarchically along some dimension, for example, wealth, education, prestige, age, or some other characteristics (see discussion of status above). Such rank-ordering is the basis of social class, referring to strata of that rank-ordering, for example, the 'upper', 'upper-middle', 'lower-middle' classes and so on. In Western societies wealth, education and prestige (among other things) are important characteristics to determine social class membership. In particular Bourdieu's work related to social class and lifestyle has had an impact on marketing thinking (Bourdieu, 1984). Extensive research has shown that members of the various strata or social classes tend to have common characteristics, for example similar consumption patterns and values. For instance, research findings demonstrate that the middle classes spend more on housing and the home, they save more, spend substantially more on education, books and the arts than do the lower classes. (For a detailed description of findings regarding class differences, see Berelson and Steiner (1964). Marketers have primarily used such insights to characterize consumption patterns across social classes in order to identify and characterize target groups and segment markets.

The way people live, their consumption patterns and values vary across social strata (and groups). Such differences in lifestyle are *visible* indicators of class position. In sociological research the lifestyle concept has been related to broad classes, for example to distinguish between rural and urban, and urban and suburban forms of social life, as well as age segments and specific interest groups. In marketing, the lifestyle concept has a more psychological orientation, with an emphasis on identifying specific lifestyles based on detailed mapping of consumption activities, media habits, attitudes and opinions.

Culture

Culture has for long been intensively studied by anthropologists and sociologists. Culture is a multidimensional and complex phenomenon, and for decades there has been an ongoing debate about what is meant by the concept; for example, in 1952 Kroeber and Kluckhon reviewed 164 definitions of culture. It is commonly assumed that culture includes patterns of behaviours and values, that culture is learned and shared with other people, and influences not only how one behaves, but also how one expects others to behave. How culture can be best understood and how to explain the functioning of culture, have, however, changed over the years. For example, many anthropologists now prefer the term 'enacted' (instead of learned), which recognizes that people don't just passively accept culture, they actively create it. Swidler (1986) in her penetrating analysis sees culture as shaping a repertoire, creating a 'tool kit' of habits, skills and styles from which people construct 'strategies of action' (1986: 273). The acquisition of a repertoire of skills, habits and styles reflects that how to behave in a deliberately rational (goal-directed) fashion can be learned and that this knowledge is context bound, with the cultural context influencing what is conceived as relevant.

Marketing has for long recognized the importance of culture and has extensively borrowed research findings from anthropology and sociology. For example, culture can be characterized according to its *context of communication*, often dichotomized as 'high' versus 'low' (Hall, 1976). Many foreign cultures are characterized as 'high cultural contexts', exhibiting a dependence on non-verbal, 'hidden' insights of communication in contrast to low cultural contexts, relying more on explicit verbal communications and symbols. Such insights have been used to explain market failures and to prepare the marketer when crossing borders. Another finding from cultural research is that the cultural *distance* may vary considerably in importance for marketers when considering new markets to enter. Other aspects from cultural research adopted and used by marketers are differences in media-structure and use, the importance of language and symbols, and variations in specific cultural values and the culture associated with consumption. Cultural knowledge has been used to characterize and choose markets, design adequate marketing strategies, and to understand and improve international negotiations. Also, the culture of consumers related to the consumption of market-made commodities and marketing activities has attracted substantial interest in the last decades (Arnould and Thompson, 2005). (The following chapter contains an extended discussion of these ideas.)

Sub-culture

This term refers to a system of values, attitudes, behaviours and lifestyles of a social group which is distinct from, but related to, the dominant culture of a society. In sociology the concept has been of most use in the study of youth and deviancy. In marketing the concept has primarily been adopted and used to study the buying and consumption activities and lifestyles of specific social groups, for example, teenagers. Such insights have primarily been used as the basis for target group descriptions and thus to improve marketing activities and performance.

The idea of sub-culture has also been applied to understanding consumption, defined as a distinct sub-group of society that self-selects on the basis of a shared commitment to a particular product class, brand, or form of consumption. An example is the study of the specific culture among owners of Harley-Davidson motorcycles by Shouten and Alexander (1995). In such a study the unit of analysis is changed from the individual acting unit to the relationship between actors.

As noted above, many sociological concepts (and elements of theories) have been borrowed, primarily as tools to identify and characterize target groups in the effort to improve marketing performance. Thus – even though the concepts are borrowed from a discipline concerned with social relationships – the unit of analysis in the marketing use of these concepts has been the individual acting unit (Zaltman and Wallendorf, 1977).

Marketing has also borrowed and applied sociological concepts which in a true sense capture aspects of social relationships. This has in particular been the case in situations other than mass-marketing, for example in industrial markets where the numbers of buyers are often limited (cf. cells (a) and (b) in Figure 7.1).

_____ Relationships, power and conflict _____

Relationships

A relationship takes place between (at least) two actors, and the _dyad_ is frequently used as the unit of analysis. To be a relationship it has to last (at least for some minimum time). A purposeful relationship assumes some flow of activities. The relationships can be of various kinds and focus on exchange of goods, information, money, and so on.

The importance of relationships has for long been recognized in disciplines like sociology and anthropology and business, but has until recently received scant attention in the marketing literature. A shift in focus is now apparently taking place, as reflected in the growing focus on and interest in 'relationship marketing' (Webster, 1992). An interesting observation is the rather late interest in relationships and networks in American marketing thinking in spite of the fact that such ideas have been dealt with by European marketing scholars for more than four decades.

A common observation in industrial marketing is that buyers and sellers tend to enter into rather long-term relationships, that is they tend to transact not only once, but perform re-occurring transactions. There are several reasons for doing so. For example, it takes time, skill and economic resources to identify, negotiate with and adjust to exchange partners. Such efforts can be conceived as (partly) transaction specific investments easing future transactions. Relationships between exchange partners ease interaction and flow of information, thereby reducing transaction costs and thus explaining why they (relationships) last. Relationships may, in addition to economics, convey and be influenced by social values and concerns, as reflected in the notion of 'embeddedness' (Granovetter, 1985). More recently the role and functioning of relationships have escalated in marketing.

Any transaction or relationship is guided by a *contract*, either explicitly or implicitly. There is a vast literature on contracts by researchers from several disciplines. Sociologists have primarily been preoccupied with the importance 'social contracts', which can deviate from legal contracts. Marketers now focus to an increasing degree on various types of contracts, in particular with the purpose of structuring and monitoring relationships (Macneil, 1980).

Relationships vary in strength. Strong relationships are valuable and give access to various resources, for example support. However, weak relationships more easily allow for new information of importance for innovations (Granovetter, 1973).

Network

The notion of 'network', often used to describe systems of relationships between actors, has a long tradition in sociology and anthropology. More recently there has been an increasing use of the network approach to understand the functioning of markets, and how – through their networking activities – firms may acquire resources, competence, gain access to technologies, and achieve competitive advantages. The influential role of modern information and communication technologies (ICT) – in particular the internet – has influenced network thinking, especially electronic networks and types of such networks, for example what has been termed 'electronic tribes', their functioning and how they can be studied. It is claimed that the internet is a new social room where 'weak ties' of importance for diffusion of ideas, opinion and meanings are established. Marketing, to an increasing degree, adopts sociological concepts to capture the new reality created through the internet, which also influences marketing practices.

Relationships and networks imply reciprocity, that is the implicit norm to do things for each other. A central premise is that relationships and networks may be valuable, as reflected in the term '*social capital*'. Coleman (1988) in his penetrating analysis has shown the use of social capital, that is that the value embedded in relationships and networks may give rise to human capital. The idea of social capital has been borrowed and exploited by marketers and applied to activities that enhance the success rate in new product development.

Conflict and cooperation

When social actors exhibit purposeful behaviour, for example to gain market share or to make money, the interests of social actors may come into conflict. For example, competition can be seen as conflict over the resources or advantages desired by others. Insights regarding the causes of conflicts, and factors and mechanisms influencing conflict development and solution are important for marketers and have been applied in several ways, for example to understand and solve conflicts between marketing and other functions, and conflicts between members of the distribution channel (for an interesting discussion, see Levy and Zaltman, 1975).

Conflict is closely related to *competition* addressed both in sociology and marketing. However, both sociology and marketing address *co-operation*, implying that potentially conflicting interests are turned into mutual ones. The potential benefits from cooperation have been studied intensively. In marketing, cooperation has been related to cooperation in new product development, brand alliances, new market entrance and more. A related phenomenon *co-optition*, that is how actors simultaneously handle conflicting and mutual interests, has for long been addressed in sociology. The idea of co-optition has more recently been adopted by marketers, in particular how actors can simultaneously do business and be friends.

Power

The study of power has a long tradition in sociology. There are several distinct perspectives of power, and the concept has been defined in many ways, for example, 'the probability that a person in a social relationship will be able to carry out his or her own will in the pursuit of goals of action, regardless of resistance' (Weber, 1946: 180).

The above definition implies that power is exercised by social actors, and involves agency and choice. Power is exercised over others and may involve resistance and conflict. Insights from sociological studies of power (and conflict) have, for example, been applied to understanding and improving the functioning of distribution systems. An interesting phenomenon is how modern ICT allows multiple consumers to interact, exchange experiences and meanings and form joint opinions. This has allowed the many formerly independent consumers in a weak position to change their power vis-à-vis producers, as reflected in the report 'Power at last. How the internet means the consumer really is king' (*Economist*, 2005). Thus, modern ICT allows consumers to interact and become a countervailing power, which may be indicated as a change in market situation from cell (c) to cell (a); (see Figure 7.1).

―――――――――― Learning and change ――――――――――

Socialization

This term is used to describe the process whereby people learn to conform to social norms, a process that makes possible an enduring society and the transmission of its culture between generations. Socialization has been extensively focused on in sociological research. In marketing – so far – the focus has primarily been on how children are socialized as consumers. However, the recent focus on phenomena such as consumer communities and brand communities has directed the attention to socializing activities.

Social change

Sociologists have extensively studied how social systems (e.g. societies) change. This has important implications for marketing. The introduction of marketing thinking and practices to newly developing countries is, for example, assumed to enhance standards of living. A successful introduction of marketing thinking and practice will probably also imply dramatic social changes. Societal characteristics may hamper and/or alter the intended changes as well.

Even though marketing activities are conducted to bring about changes in a societal context, relatively few marketing studies have addressed the problem of social change (Levy and Zaltman, 1975). This is, however, changing. Marketers now to an increasing extent address how attitudes towards stigmatized groups may be altered, how marketing can be applied to change unhealthy behaviour (e.g. smoking) and to change eating habits to fight obesity, and more.

Diffusion of innovations relates to how innovations (e.g. new ideas, practices or products) are spread within social systems. This subject has been intensively studied by researchers from many disciplines, with a great impact from sociology (see Rogers (2003) for an overview). The diffusion of innovation literature has had a profound impact on marketing thinking, and researchers from the (marketing) discipline have contributed to this field as well. When studying diffusion of innovations, the innovation (e.g. a new product) represents something new to the potential adopter, but need not be a novelty in an absolute sense. For example, studies have demonstrated that some technologies take decades to be adopted. Diffusion of innovation is a true social phenomenon as it takes the social context directly into account. This becomes clear when looking at the elements in a diffusion process, that is: (1) the innovation, and (2) its communication (3) from one individual (social actor) to another, (4) within a social system (e.g. a society) (5) over time.

More than 30,000 studies related to diffusion of innovations have been conducted (Rogers, 2003). Research findings show that characteristics of the innovation influence both the extent to which and how fast an innovation is diffused. For example, the perceived relative advantage has been demonstrated to have a profound effect on the propensity to adopt an innovation. This very robust finding is, of course, of prime interest for marketers, and gives direction for marketing activities, for example, new product development.

A large number of studies demonstrates that the number of adopters over time follow an S-shaped curve. The time dimension for the total adoption process may, however, vary tremendously across innovations. Based on this observed pattern, adopters can be grouped according to when they adopt an innovation. Those adopting at an early point in time, 'innovators' (or 'pioneers'), and 'early adopters' have been found to differ in characteristics and use of information sources compared to later adopters. For example, those adopting at an early stage tend to be more interested in and know more about the actual innovation, and tend to be more willing to try something new compared to later adopters and non-adopters. Such findings are of prime importance for marketers when defining target groups and designing effective marketing strategies. An important finding from diffusion of innovation research is that later adopters tend to seek earlier adopters' advice, and that mass-media information is diffused into the society via personal communication. Those adopting early and/or those who play a key role in personal communication of mass-media information are frequently termed *opinion-leaders*.

Findings from research on diffusion of innovation have influenced marketing in many ways, for example in marketers' search for, development and evaluation of new products, marketing research and the profiling of target groups, design of marketing communication strategies, positioning of products and the 'stretching' of the products' life-cycles.

Summary and future outlook

Marketing has borrowed extensively from sociology. A large proportion of this borrowing has been done in a mass-marketing context with the prime purpose of profiling target groups as a basis for designing more effective (mass-)marketing. Marketing (as other disciplines) changes. More recently the borrowing has changed to encompass the relationships between social actors.

An interesting observation is the rather modest borrowing from sociology to study change. This is surprising as marketing is primarily a dynamic phenomenon taking place in ever-changing social contexts; in fact a prime purpose of marketing is to bring about changes.

An additional observation is that the marketing discipline has primarily been preoccupied with transactions and exchanges falling within socially accepted norms, or even more restrictive, visible, socially accepted market transactions (Grønhaug and Dholokia, 1987). In most societies many (legal) exchanges are taken out of the visible, legal market, for example an exchange of services between neighbours. In addition, illegal exchanges occur. In several countries the 'black economy' booms and is estimated to constitute something in the range of 20–40 per cent of the gross national product. The distribution and marketing of illegal drugs, and the selling of stolen goods, are examples of deviant behaviours, but so far – in spite of their importance – they have received only scant attention from marketers. As noted by Zaltman and Wallendorf (1977) there are reasons to believe that the study of illegal exchanges can improve our understanding of marketing and its potential influence within legal and accepted social settings.

To summarize:

- Much of the borrowing from sociology has been used as a basis for characterizing and profiling consumers and target groups, that is the use of the concepts has been 'one-sided', overlooking their social relational intentions as reflected in the mother discipline. (This 'individualistic' perspective can probably also explain the predominant influence from individual psychology as reflected in any major textbook on consumer behaviour.)

- The borrowing from sociology has primarily been applied to legal, visible exchanges, that is only a subset of all marketing exchanges taking place. The extensive work in sociology on deviant behaviour has so far been almost neglected.

- The borrowed concepts and ideas have mainly been used as static descriptors and only to a modest extent utilized to capture the dynamics of and understand societal changes. This is also seen in scholarly empirical marketing research. In spite of the dynamic character of marketing – which involves time – the majority of empirical research is still based on cross-sectional research designs, or on experiments which capture only a limited time period between pre- and post-tests.

- However, to capture, adjust to and benefit from the 'new social reality' created by modern ICT – in particular the internet – marketing applies sociological concepts and thinking. Also, an interesting and important aspect is that ICT and access to a multitude of relationships and networks primarily relates to weak relationships or ties which ease access to novel information.

Recent developments and changes in marketing perspectives indicate that more focus will be placed on social aspects, emphasizing relationships between social actors. This trend is probably only in an early stage, and is likely to continue. The influence of sociology on marketing thinking will very likely increase in the years to come, and probably be manifested in the following ways:

- Previously borrowed concepts, for example, 'role', 'status' and 'group' will be applied to capture social dimensions as they were created to do, that is to capture aspects of relationships.

- The borrowing of concepts and ideas to understand relationships and networks, their initiation, changes, duration and termination, will increase dramatically in the years to come.

- The importance of the social context, and how it influences relationships and exchanges, will be more emphasized in future marketing thinking and research.

It is also believed that dynamics and change as emphasized in much of sociology will have a greater impact on thinking and research in marketing in the years to come.

_____ Recommended further reading _____

Arnould, E.J. and Thompson, C.J. (2005) 'Consumer culture theory (CCT): twenty years of research', *Journal of Consumer Research* 31, March: 868–82.
Blau, P.M. (1964) *Exchange and Power in Social Life*, New York: Wiley.
This book represents a penetrating analysis of various forms of social exchanges and offers important insights into marketing phenomena.

Coleman, J.S. (1988) 'Social capital in the creation of human capital', *American Journal of Sociology* 94: S95–S120.

A penetrating analysis of how relationships between social actors as such represent value and function.

Dulsrud, A. and Grønhaug, K. (2007) Is friendship consistent with competitive market exchange', *Acta Sociologica* 50(1): 7–18.

Emerson, R.M. (1962) 'Power-dependence relations', *American Sociological Review* 27: 31–41.

An important and very influential article, often quoted by marketers, which deserves to be read.

Granovetter, M. (1985) 'Economic action and social structure: the problem of embeddedness', *American Journal of Sociology* 91: 481–570.

An important contribution to understanding the importance and disciplining effect of the social context on relationships and transactions.

Grayson, K. (2007) 'Friendship versus business in marketing relationships', *Journal of Marketing* 71(4): 121–39.

Haire, M. (1950) 'Projective Techniques in Marketing Research', *Journal of marketing*, 14, (April): 649–56.

Heide, J. and John, G. (1992) 'Do norms matter in marketing relationships?', *Journal of Marketing* 56: 32–44.

One of the few empirical marketing contributions on the importance of norms relationship.

Katz, E. and Lazarsfeld, P. (1955) *Personal Influence*, New York: Free Press.

An important study which shows the importance of social networks and of personal interactions. An important contribution to the 'two-step-flow of information' hypothesis.

Kozinets, R.V. (2002) 'The field behind the screen: using netnography for marketing research in online communities, *Journal of Marketing Research* 39(1): 61–72.

Levy, S.J. and Zaltman, G. (1975) *Marketing Society and Conflict*, New Jersey: Prentice Hall, Inc.

Considers marketing from a social system perspective, and focuses in a useful way on marketing as a cause of consequences of change, and inherent conflict.

Lie, J. (1997) 'Sociology of markets', *Annual Review of Sociology* 23: 341–60.

An interesting contribution capturing multiple aspects of markets.

Nicosia, F.M. and Mayer, R.N. (1976) 'Toward a sociology of consumption', *Journal of Consumer Research* 3: 65–75.

A useful contribution to understanding the importance of consumption and how it is shaped by social forces.

Rauch, J.E. and Castella, A. (eds) (2001) *Networks and Markets*, New York: Russell Sage Foundation.

Rothschild, M.L. (1999) Carrots, sticks, and promises: a conceptual framework for the management of public health and social issue behaviors, *Journal of Marketing* 63, October: 24–37.

Swidler, A. (1986) 'Culture in action: symbols and strategies', *American Sociological Review* 51: 273–86.

This is a very thought-provoking book on the functioning of culture and its importance for marketers.

Thompson, C.J. (1996) 'Caring consumers: gendered consumption meanings and the juggling lifestyle', *Journal of Consumer Research* 22, March: 388–407.

Wallendorf, M. (1978) 'Social roles in marketing contexts', *American Behavioral Scientist* 21: 571–81.

A useful contribution regarding the potential of applying the role concept to marketing problems.

Watts, D.J. and Dodds, P.S. (2007) 'Influentials, networks, and public opinion formation', *Journal of Consumer Research* 34, December: 441–58.

Zaltman, G. and Wallendorf, M. (1977) 'Sociology: The missing chunk or how we've missed the boat', in B.A. Greenberg and D.N. Bellimger (eds) *Contemporary Marketing Thought 1977: Educators' Proceedings*, Chicago, IL: American Marketing Association, pp. 235–8. This paper identifies important topics neglected by marketers, and discusses how sociology can be useful.)

References

Abercombie, N., Hill, S. and Turner, B.S. (eds) (1988) *Dictionary of Sociology*, 2nd edn, London: Penguin Books.

Alderson, W. (1950) 'The analytical framework for marketing', in D.J. Duncan (ed.) *Proceedings: Conference of Marketing Teachers from the West*, Berkeley, CA: School of Business Administration, University of California.

Alderson, W. (1957) *Marketing Behavior and Executive Action. A Functionalist Approach to Marketing Theory*, Homewood, Illinois: R.D. Irwin Inc.

American Marketing Association (2004) www.marketingpower.com/Pages/default.aspx

Arndt, J. (1980) 'Perspectives for a theory of marketing', *Journal of Business Research* 8: 389–402.

Arnould, E.J. and Thompson, C.J. (2005) 'Consumer culture theory (CCT): Twenty years of research', *Journal of Consumer Research*, 31, March: 868–82.

Berelson, B. and Steiner, G.A. (1964) *Human Behavior: An Inventory of Scientific Findings*, New York: Harcourt, Brace and World, Inc.

Bourdieu, P. (1984) *Distinction: A Social Critique of the Judgement of Taste*, Cambridge MA: Harvard University Press.

Codere, H. (1968) 'Social exchange', in D.H. Sills (ed.) *International Encyclopedia of the Social Sciences*, Vol. 5, New York: The Macmillan Company and the Free Press, pp. 238–344.

Coleman, J.S. (1988) 'Social capital in the creation of human capital', *American Journal of Sociology* 94: S95–S120.

Collins, R. (1981) 'On the microfoundations of macrosociology', *American Journal of Sociology* 86: 984–1014.

Cox, R. (1964) 'Introduction', in R. Cox, W. Anderson and S.J. Shapiro (eds) *Theory in Marketing*, Homewood, IL: Irwin.

Deighton, J. (1996) 'The future of interactive marketing', *Harvard Business Review*, November–December: 151–62.

Economist, The (2005) Crowned at last. A survey of consumer power, *Economist* 2 April.

Giddens, A. (1993) *Sociology*, 2nd edn, London: Polity Press.

Goldman, A. (1979) 'Publishing activity in marketing as an indicator of its structure and disciplinary boundaries', *Journal of Marketing Research* 16: 485–94.

Granovetter, M. (1973) 'The strength of weak ties', *American Journal of Sociology* 78: 1360–80.

Granovetter, M. (1985) 'Economic action and social structure: the problem of embeddedness', *American Journal of Sociology* 91: 481–570.

Granovetter, M. and Swedberg, R. (eds) (1992) *The Sociology of Economic Life*, Boulder, CO: Westview Press.

Grønhaug, K. and Dholokia, N. (1987) 'Consumer, markets and supply systems: a perspective on marketization and its effects', in A.F. Firat, N. Dholokia and R.P. Bagozzi (eds) *Philosophical and Radical Thoughts in Marketing*, Lexington, MA: Lexington Books.

Hall, E.T. (1976) *Beyond Culture*, Garden City, NY: Anchor Press/Doubleday.

Hunt, S.D. (1983) 'General theories and the fundamental explanda of marketing', *Journal of Marketing* 47: 9–17.

Hunt, S.D. (1991) *Modern Marketing Theory. Critical Issues in the Philosophy of Marketing Science*, Cincinatti, OH: South-Western Publishing Co.

Kotler, P. (1984) *Marketing Management, Analysis, Planning and Control*, 4th edn, New Jersey: Prentice Hall, Inc.

Kroeber, A.L. and Kluckhon, C. (1952) 'Culture: A critical review of concepts and definitions', *Papers of Peabody Museum* 47: No. 1A.

Levy, S.J. (1959) 'Symbols for sale', *Harvard Business Review* 37: 117–24.

Levy, S.J. and Zaltman, G. (1975) Marketing, Society, and Conflict, Prentice-Wall Inc, Englewood Cliffs, New Jersey.

Lie, J. (1997) 'Sociology of markets', *Annual Review of Sociology* 23: 341–60.

Macneil, I.R. (1980) *The New Social Contract: An Inquiry into Modern Contractual Relations*, New Haven, CT: Yale University Press.

Muniz, A.M. and O'Guinn, T.C. (2001) 'Brand community', *Journal of Consumer Research* 27: 412–32.

Nicosia, F.M. and Mayer, R.N. (1976) 'Toward a sociology of consumption', *Journal of Consumer Research* 3: 65–75.

Polanyi, K. (1944) *The Great Transformation*, Boston: Beacon Press.

Rogers, E.M. (2003) *Diffusion of Innovations*, 5th edn, New York: The Free Press.

Shouten, J.W. and Alexander, J.H. (1995) 'Subcultures of consumption: an ethnography of bikers', *Journal of Consumer Research* 20, June: 43–61.

Smelser, N.J. (1963) *The Sociology of Economic Life*, New Jersey: Prentice Hall, Inc.

Swidler, A. (1986) 'Culture in action: symbols and strategies', *American Sociological Review* 51: 273–86.

Wallendorf, M. (1978) 'Social roles in marketing contexts', *American Behavioral Scientist* 21: 571–82.

Weber, M. (1946) 'Class, status, party', in H.H. Gerth and C. Wright Mills (eds) *From Max Weber: Essays in Sociology*, New York: Oxford University Press.

Webster, F.E. (1992) 'The changing role of marketing in the corporation', *Journal of Marketing* 56: 1–17.

Zaltman, G. and Wallendorf, M. (1977) 'Sociology: the missing chunk or how we've missed the boat', in B.A. Greenberg and D.N. Bellinger (eds) *Contemporary Marketing Thought 1977: Educators' Proceedings*, Chicago, IL: American Marketing Association, pp. 235–8.

8

Cultural aspects of marketing

Kam-hon Lee and Cass Shum

Overview

According to Hatch (1989), culture is:

the way of life of people. It consists of conventional patterns of thought and behavior, including values, beliefs, rules of conduct, political organization, economic activity, and the like, which are passed on from one generation to the next by learning – and not by biological inheritance. (1989: pp. 178–179)

Also, culture is 'governed by its own principles and not by the raw intellect, and the differences among people do not reflect differences in levels of intelligence' (ibid.) As such, there are many cultures in the world. In a way, there can be many cultures in a nation (Swanson, 1989). It is widely recognized that theories in management and marketing are culture bound (Hofstede, 1993; Tse et al., 1988). Marketing in one culture can be very different from marketing in a number of other cultures. A marketing campaign created in developed countries may or may not be transferable to developing countries. International marketers may need to modify the marketing activities generated in one culture and to consider cultural factors when launching marketing activities in another culture. It becomes important to understand various issues related to launching marketing activities in a different culture.

The heart of the matter in marketing is to form a market and strike a business deal, which will bring benefits to all parties involved in the transaction. 'The marketing concept', the fundamental concept in marketing, refers to a philosophical conviction that customer satisfaction is the key to achieving organizational goals. Whether the customer is an individual or an organization, and whether the customer is nearby or in a foreign country, the challenge to the marketer is the same. Thus, the mission of marketing is to facilitate exchange and form a win–win relationship with other parties. This is no easy task when the marketer and the other parties share the same culture. It becomes even more difficult to accomplish when the marketer and the other parties do not share the same culture. What makes things even worse is that within the same nation or ethnicity, people are culturally differentiated. One good example is the Hispanic market in the United States. There is cultural difference between Hispanics and non-Hispanics. There are also cultural variances among all segments of the Hispanic market. For example, while Mexicans and most Central and South Americans are soccer fans, Cubans and Caribbean Hispanics enjoy baseball. Using only one sport in advertisements would result in only partial success in the Hispanic market. An AT&T advertisement was a failure when portraying a wife asking her husband to call a friend to say that they would be late. Although AT&T employed Puerto Rican actors, AT&T failed to notice that in Latin America, it is a norm to be half an hour late and no one phones to warn their friends about this. Also, no Latin American wives dare order their husbands around (Herbig, 1998: p. 117).

People in different cultures do not just speak different languages. With different values and norms, they have different needs and different attitudes towards advertisements and brands. Customers would not be satisfied if marketers failed to notice the cultural differences both within the same culture and between different cultures.

This chapter will specifically examine three related issues on marketing in a different culture. First, can a marketing success in one culture be reproduced in another culture? If not, why not? If so, what are the conditions of success? Second, should a marketing success in one culture be reproduced in another culture? This is a more basic question than the first one. It examines the ethical foundation of marketing activities. Last, but not least, will cultures eventually converge? This is even more fundamental than the first two questions. When there is only one culture in the whole world, there is no need to study the cultural aspects of marketing.

Culture can pose marketing problems

First, can a marketing success be reproduced in another culture? Marketing people are supposed to be very sensitive to the changing needs of customers. Marketers know that they have to study customers' needs carefully, and deliver products which can meet those needs. When customers have different needs, marketers have to come up with different product offerings. Since customers in different cultures have minds which are programmed quite differently, it becomes important to differentiate their needs and to try to meet those needs differentially. However, other cultural moderating factors are not so obvious. Even world-class marketers may not be sensitive enough to detect the differences in different cultures all the time.

Procter & Gamble (P&G) is an American giant, a company widely known to practice the marketing concept. Procter & Gamble meets basic consumer needs with a strong research commitment to create products that are demonstrably better than the competition when compared in blind tests. They use brand and category management systems and value market research highly, believing that it can enable the company to identify a new trend early on and take the lead in it.

Based on new liquid detergent technology and after extensive blind tests and market tests, P&G launched a new clothing detergent brand named Vizir in the early 1980s in Germany and Europe. Vizir was positioned as a complete main wash product, having superior performance in removing tough, greasy stains even in low temperature washing (Bartlett, 1983).

Vizir got off a good start all over Europe, and quickly became number one in the heavy-duty detergent category. However, in 1983, business began to weaken and the Vizir brand eventually lost about 15 per cent of its sales volume that year. In 1984, there was an additional 15 per cent sales decline. What P&G had failed to take into account was that European washing machines were at that time equipped to accept powder detergents but not liquids. When liquid detergent was added to a powder dispenser, as much as 20 per cent of the liquid was lost to a collecting point at the bottom of the machine. Thus, the product was not meeting customers' performance expectation.

Procter & Gamble changed the packaging to explain better to consumers how to use Vizir, but research showed that this would not work. Subsequently, P&G managed to convince washing machine manufacturers in Europe to design liquid dispensers, but this had little impact on a market where, on average, a washing machine was replaced only once every 15 years. The next P&G attempt was to develop a retrofit system – a plastic device that fitted into existing powder dispensers and kept the liquid from leaking, while dispensing it at the same time. Procter & Gamble would mail the device to consumers, free of charge, immediately after housewives told them the model number of their washing machines. However, most European machines were bolted to the wall, and the housewives were unable to see the model number; they did not know and they could not tell.

Finally, one technician in a French P&G product development laboratory invented a unique solution – a 'dosing ball' that P&G called a Vizirette. The consumer could fill the porous Vizirette 'dosing ball', place it in the washdrum on top of the clothes, and start the machine. The Vizirette would gradually dispense the detergent, with no waste. Vizir and Vizirette were subsequently introduced as a system (The Editors of *Advertising Age*, 1989).

Customers in different cultures may have different needs. This, in turn, determines whether a marketing success can or cannot be reproduced in another culture. Marketers, at all times, should be sensitive to the changing needs of their customers. This is especially important for international marketers when they launch marketing activities in a different culture. They should understand that when customers' needs change, marketing activities should change accordingly to meet these different needs.

Furthermore, as the world becomes more globalized, there will be more international business negotiations. However, the cultural differences remain and intercultural negotiations exhibit extra sources of tension on negotiators. America has been the engine for world economic growth. China is the most important emerging economy. Let us review the negotiation challenge between American and Chinese business executives. For the Chinese, greater levels of tension led to an increased likelihood of agreement, but also led to lower levels of interpersonal attraction and in turn lower trust for their American counterparts. For the Americans, greater levels of tension decreased the likelihood of an agreement, did not affect interpersonal attraction, but did have a direct negative effect on trust (Lee et al., 2006). We can see that culture not only affects marketing activities like product design and promotion, but also pre-marketing activities like negotiations.

Marketing efforts can overcome cultural problems

Procter & Gamble entered the Japanese market first in 1972–73. The consumer mind-set in Japan was quite unique. The primary buyer of packaged goods was the housewife. In Japan at least half the adult women were employed, but almost no Japanese mothers worked outside the home. Child-rearing was the first priority for a Japanese woman. The average family home was 50 square metres. Lack of storage necessitated several shopping trips per week and affected the structure of the distribution outlets, the market information the housewife commanded, and the relationship between shopkeeper and housewife. Thus, the market structure was quite indirect and long. Specialty and small retail stores constituted the bulk of retail outlets, commanding 72.3 per cent in 1982. There was also a close interpersonal relationship between the neighbourhood shopkeeper and the housewife. The typical Japanese customer for branded packaged goods was highly uncompromising, demanding superior quality and defining value more in terms of product performance, quality and reliability, rather than price. This attitude was even more pronounced in the area of personal hygiene. Thus, in Japan virtually all companies manufactured products to a standard of zero defects.

Procter & Gamble entered Japan through a joint venture with Nippon Sunhome. They picked Cheer laundry detergent powder as a wedge to open the Japanese market for other major brands to follow. Procter & Gamble followed their 'successful' formula in the USA to position and advertise 'Cheer' as an all-temperature laundry detergent powder in 1973, featuring price promotions to support the advertising campaign, and went directly to the major retail chains to promote and distribute it. Cheer gained a substantial market share and managed to capture up to 12.6 per cent in the laundry detergents market in 1979. However, Cheer did not bring in profits. Also, when the featured pricing stopped in 1979 Cheer kept losing market share to different competitive brands (Kao's Wonderful, New Beads, Zab Total and Lion's Top Powder). Upon closer examination, it became clear that the three-temperature washing concept was not relevant to Japanese laundry habits. Women typically washed clothes in tap-water and occasionally the recycled family bath-water in the winter. The aggressive pricing practice only forced all players in the industry to incur substantial losses together. For example, P&G's all-temperature Cheer had been selling at 555 yens for two boxes against a suggested retail price of 800 to 850 yens for one box. Kao's New Beads large box had been selling at 400 yens against a previous retail price of 700 to 750 yens. This aggressive pricing practice antagonized all the competitors. In addition, the distribution policy through the major retail chains alienated the wholesalers and the small retailers, who were the gatekeepers of mass distribution in Japan.

Practically all other P&G brands either failed in the test market or were preempted by competition due to a competitor's national launch of a copycat brand prior to the conclusion of P&G's 24-month test market period. The only exception was Pampers, which was launched in 1981 and immediately captured 85 per cent of the disposable diaper market. However, even Pampers was not completely successful. Unicharm, a relatively unknown company in Japan, introduced Moony in 1982, which was sold at a 40 per cent price premium to Pampers and managed to capture 40 per cent of the market share in 1983. In the meantime, Pampers dropped from its 1981 high of 90 per cent to its 1985 low of 6 per cent. It was quite clear that P&G could afford no more illusions. They had underestimated the sophistication level of Japanese consumers. They had also underestimated the competitive strength of the Japanese companies. The operation in Japan was a total disaster (Yoshino and Stoneham, 1990a).

It became clear to P&G in 1983 that what was best in the USA might not be good enough in Japan. This was at least true in the consumer packaged goods industry. Procter & Gamble could join other well-respected packaged goods companies such as General Foods, General Mills and Colgate, who had all failed in Japan and retreated. However, P&G was convinced that Japan was a leading-edge country in the consumer goods industry, and the world leader had to be successful there. There was no other choice. If P&G could not compete with the Japanese companies in Japan, they would eventually have to compete with them in the USA. This conviction led to P&G's subsequent success in Japan, which managed to show that marketing efforts could overcome cultural problems (Yoshino and Stoneham, 1990b).

The changing mentality at P&G started with the changing belief in research and development. By that time P&G believed that while American and European trends were helpful, the worldwide centre of innovation should be focused on Japan and Japanese competition. Thus, the R&D team in Japan was trying to develop products that would meet the needs of Japanese consumers. While there were only 60 people in the P&G R&D group in Osaka, in comparision with Kao's 2000 in Japan, P&G could depend on the unreserved support from the R&D group in Cincinnati. The race in R&D in the diaper product industry was instructive. Procter & Gamble, Kao and Unicharm took turns to leapfrog one another in product upgrades, rendering the latest generation of diapers obsolete within six months. Eventually P&G's R&D groups in Osaka and Cincinnati jointly developed the world's thinnest and most absorbent diaper, which became a clear winner over both Unicharm's Moony and Kao's Merries.

The biggest marketing challenge for P&G was to determine what advertising would work. It became clear to P&G that there was a virtual absence of side-by-side comparisons in Japanese advertising because of the indirectness of communication and the importance of harmony in Japanese culture. The tone of advertising was always friendly and never aggressive. Commercials often used background music and well-known celebrities. The author (Lee) reviewed the P&G commercials used in Japan in the late 1970s and those of the early 1990s. The improvement was obvious. For example, previously Pampers commercials featured an unhappy baby in an unhappy situation, while later commercials featured happy babies in happy situations. To promote Cheer originally, P&G had merely applied the American copy to Japan, although Japanese housewives had no problems with water temperature. Later commercials focused on the primary product benefits of dirt and odour removal.

There were commensurate changes in the distribution, manufacturing and organization areas. The whole package of changes showed that P&G was willing to take the other culture seriously, and make a commitment to investing resources to meet customers' needs. While noticing cultural differences is important, it is even more important to develop culture-specific marketing activities to meet local customers' needs. Where there is a will, there is a way, and marketing efforts can overcome cultural problems.

Procter & Gamble invested US$10 million in China in 1998 and set up an R&D centre in Beijing. The centre, located next to Tsinghua University, had a twofold mission. It enabled P&G to adapt products to local conditions and it also enabled P&G to take advantage of local ideas in improving products around the world (Walsh, 2001). One can see in China the shadow of the earlier hard won successful experience in Japan.

Marketing power should respect culture

The examination of the ethical foundation of marketing in a different culture is equally if not more important. Should a marketing success be reproduced in another culture? Although marketing power is formidable, there should also be a limit. The limitation need not come from customers' resistance, which in fact is important in the marketplace to differentiate the capable from the less capable marketers. Such limitation is part of the reality in marketing interaction. However, there is another kind of limitation. It comes from company efforts to restrain the marketing power when it is necessary for the company to do so. When customers are able to choose what would be best for themselves, consumer sovereignty can be assumed, and companies are free to exercise their marketing power to overcome the resistance and eventually manage to meet the customers' needs and conclude the deals. On the other hand, when customers are not able to choose what would be best for themselves, consumer sovereignty does not exist and it becomes the responsibility of the company to restrain the marketing power for the sake of the public. One notable example is the case of infant formula selling in the Third World (Lee, 1987).

Infant formula was developed by leading food giants in developed countries. The product was initially sold in developed countries as a substitute for breast milk. The case for infant formula is that it is available when breast milk is not (a less than 10 per cent chance), and when properly used it is an excellent alternative among all existing alternatives. In the developed and rich countries like the USA, mothers can usually afford to buy infant formula and know how to use it in hygienic conditions. Their education level is high and consumer sovereignty can be assumed. It would be enough to promote breast milk as the best choice while providing mothers a choice of settling with the 'second best' – the infant formula.

However, while infant formula is not defective in itself, it is demanding. When risk conditions are present, it can be harmful to users. This became a serious issue in 1970 when the infant formula manufacturers adopted aggressive marketing efforts in developing nations (Post, 1986). The problem became obvious when infant formula manufacturers promoted heavily in a much less developed and poor country like Zambia. There are two real dangers. First, through poverty, compounded by ignorance, mothers tend drastically to dilute the infant formula in order to make it last. As a result, infants starve and die. Second, poor hygiene causes serious troubles. Nestlé and other companies in the industry repeatedly claimed that they had no desire or intention to see unqualified consumers using their formula products. However, in 1978 at the US Senate hearings, when representatives from these companies were asked whether they had conducted any post-marketing research studies to determine who actually used their products, all representatives answered that their companies did no such research and did not know who actually used the products.

It becomes clear that the companies should be responsible for their marketing efforts. In order to guarantee that the users of infant formula products have proper information on their safe use and can make intelligent consumer choices, the companies may want to withdraw the marketing efforts or even the products from those countries. Mass marketing would certainly not be appropriate in view of the consumers' culture in such countries. If the product supply is meant to be helpful, it may be wise to do the promotion through the medical and health care system. Professionals there can exercise their judgement and make recommendations to mothers. Nestlé's infant formula should not be regarded as an isolated case. Rather it should be seen as an illustrative case for all kinds of First-World products being sold in the Third World. There should be a similar level of sensitivity in reviewing the situation. It is important for marketing power to respect culture.

Another example illustrating that marketing power should respect culture is the sustainable development of ecotourism. If managed properly, ecotourism can benefit both tourists and the local community. Tourists can learn more about the local cultures and environment. Through education programmes, tourists can also understand the importance of preserving the local culture and environment. Their spending provides extra sources of funding for environmental protection projects. The local community can enjoy increased income and better quality of life. However, when the marketing activities and development is out of control, the local community, the environment, and the customers will all suffer. The case of Zhangjiajie is a good example of this.

Zhangjiajie National Forest Park is the first national park in mainland China. Also, it is the main component of the Wulinyuan Scenic Area, a UNESCO world natural heritage site. The government noticed its potential as a world-class ecotourism site in 1982 and began to promote and develop the destination heavily. Due to its rich cultural resources and beautiful scenery, Zhangjiajie became very popular in a few years. The annual average arrivals increased from around 88,000 visitors in the early 1980s to more than 720,000 visitors in the early 1990s. However, as the marketing campaigns and site development were not managed properly, tourism development impacted on the quality of the park. Tourism activities reduced the biodiversity in the area. As some tourists damaged the trees and threw rubbish in the park, air and water became heavily polluted. The environment suffered seriously. In 1998, experts from the UNESCO committee visited Zhangjiajie and warned that the Zhangjiajie area had been largely transformed. If Zhangjiajie continued to be mismanaged, it would be placed on the UNESCO World Heritage in Danger List. Furthermore, in order to develop the area, some local residents had been relocated. At the same time, more immigrants migrated to the area for better jobs. The local cultural traditions cannot be easily retained under these circumstances. Tourists' experiences were negatively influenced by the environmental and socio-cultural changes. In the visitor survey by Zhong, Deng and Xiang (2008), over 85 per cent of respondents reported that they did not feel a strong ethnic ambience during their stay in the park. Local residents' friendliness towards tourists also faded over time. The area became very commercialized and disappointed tourists (Deng et al., 2003; Zhong et al., 2008).

Marketing campaigns can utilize cultural features

The above discussion may leave readers with the impression that marketing is the conqueror and culture is always trying to defend itself. This need not be the case. As a matter of fact, marketing campaigns can make use of the unique cultural features of the customers and the company to make a lasting impact. When a marketing programme is deeply rooted in a particular culture, the marketing programme can easily enjoy sustainable competitive advantages. In some situations, a company may 'discover' such a 'different' and perfectly compatible culture at home. The turnaround of Harley-Davidson in the American motorcycle industry is one of the most celebrated examples.

Before 1960 the motorcycle market in the USA had been mainly served by the American Harley-Davidson; BSA, Triumph and Norton of the US; and Moto-Guzzi of Italy. Harley-Davidson was the market leader in 1959. However, in that year Honda and Yamaha entered the American market. The Japanese motocycle industry had expanded rapidly after the Second World War to meet the need for cheap transportation in Japan, and in 1959 the major Japanese producers, Honda, Yamaha, Suzuki and Kawasaki, together produced some 450,000 motorcycles, which was 10 times more than retail sales in the USA. Honda was already the world's largest motorcycle producer. These Japanese producers approached the American market in a systematic way. They started by penetrating the low end, lightweight market niche. They all placed an emphasis on market share and sales volume. To realize their growth goals, the Japanese producers constantly updated or redesigned products to meet the needs of American customers; set prices at levels designed to achieve market share goals; reduced prices further when necessary; appointed full-time dealers to set up an effective distribution and mainte- nance network; and launched well-planned and heavy advertising campaigns. Because of scale economy and long-term strategic planning, by 1966 Honda, Yamaha and Suzuki together had 85 per cent of the US market. By 1974 Harley- Davidson was virtually the only non-Japanese company left in the market, keeping a mere 6 per cent market share (Buzzell and Purkayastha, 1978).

The only option left for Harley-Davidson was to adopt niche marketing in a matured market. Harley-Davidson just concentrated on the super-heavyweight motorcycle market. However, because of the aggressive Japanese marketing efforts, their market share in that niche had fallen from 75 per cent in 1973 to less than 25 per cent in 1980. At that time the parent company AMF was losing interest in Harley-Davidson. Early in 1981 Vaughn Beals and 12 other Harley executives wanted to take over the company through a leveraged buyout arrangement. They thought that they could do a better job and rescue the company. Subsequently, Harley-Davidson made several strategic moves that eventually led to the celebrated turnaround. In April 1983, President Reagan approved a recommenda- tion by the International Trade Commission (ITC), raising the tariff on 'heavy- weight' motorcycles (with engine displacements over 700 cc) from 4.4 per cent to 49.4 per cent for four years. The ITC's recommendation was to protect the domes- tic industry, and essentially the Harley-Davidson operation. Harley-Davidson made tremendous efforts to renovate the production process. They learned just-in- time manufacturing systems from the Japanese companies and adopted measures to encourage employee involvement. Production cost and product reliability were significantly improved. However, the major change and the secret of their success was on the marketing side.

Harley-Davidson formed the Harley Owners' Group in 1983. The acronym HOG is the affectionate name given by Harley riders to their motorcycles. Since motorcycles are often an impulse purchase, one of Harley's biggest challenges is to hold its new customers after they have bought a bike. The Harley Owners' Group gives the new rider instant companionship through organized rides, rallies and charity runs. In 1991, with more than 155,000 members in 700 chapters world- wide, HOG had become the motorcycle industry's largest company-sponsored enthusiast organization. Club members enjoy such features as a bi-monthly newsletter (HOG Tales), an automobile-club-type travel centre and reimbursement for motorcycle safety courses. The major attraction has been that at state, regional, national and international rallies, thousands of HOG members unite with company employees for a weekend of fun, entertainment, motorcycle demo rides and camaraderie in an atmosphere that clearly defines the 'Harley-Davidson lifestyle experience'. The rallies also give Harley executives a chance to find out what is on customers' minds.

When management celebrated Harley's 85th birthday in 1988, they arranged a party which reflected their unique way of getting close to customers. Motorcyclists were invited to participate in the event. All they had to do was to contribute US$10 to Harley-Davidson's favourite philanthropic organization, the Muscular Dystrophy Association. Starting from as far away as San Francisco and Orlando, Florida, groups of cyclists headed for Milwaukee. Each group was led by a Harley-Davidson executive, including the board chairman Vaughn Beals, and chief executive officer Rich Teerlink. Thousands of Harleys, many flying American flags, rumbled into Milwaukee on 18 June, shaking the air with the sound of their engines. Some riders had dogs, others their children. Riders wore different kinds of clothing, and they were all ages. The celebrants spent the day participating in such activities as slow races. Beals and Teerlink, among other executives, submitted themselves to the celebrity dunk tank, where they were dumped into a tank of water by on-target baseball throwers. Music resounded all the time. At the final ceremonies, 24,000 bikers watched videotapes of their ride to Milwaukee projected onto two giant screens. As riders saw their own groups, they would shout. Thousands of Harley owners rose to their feet and burst into an unrivalled demonstration of product loyalty.

In 1989 Harley-Davidson had managed to capture close to 60 per cent of the super-heavyweight motorcycle market in the USA (Rose, 1990). The momentum has continued since and Harley-Davidson has become an exemplar of the 'marketing community' concept. The charity events and public-spirited programmes such as company reimbursement for Harley owners who took rider education classes, helped a great deal in promoting the company image. The HOG and cross-country motorcycle treks come from the roots of American culture. Only Harley-Davidson can utilize these cultural features and promote nationalism in a natural way. Honda tried to form a similar group to HOG, which quite expectedly soon faded away (*Fortune*, 1989). The case of Harley-Davidson demonstrates that utilizing cultural features can make a marketing campaign more effective.

Brand community has become a powerful concept to advocate brand loyalty (McAlexander et al., 2002; Muniz and O'Guinn, 2001; Thompson and Sinha, 2008). Harley-Davidson and HOG became an exemplar of understanding the concept of brand community (Bagozzi and Utpal, 2006; McAlexander, et al., 2002). A brand community rooted in culture is a brand built on a rock.

Culture and the globalization of markets

It would not be appropriate to discuss the cultural aspects of marketing without mentioning Levitt's widely cited article on the globalization of markets (1983). In this powerful article, Levitt asserted that well-managed companies had moved from an emphasis on customizing items to offering globally standardized products that are advanced, functional, reliable and low priced. Will cultures eventually converge? If so, it will no longer be necessary to examine the cultural aspects of marketing. Levitt's thesis was derived from his observation of a powerful force – technology – which was driving the world towards a converging commonality. High-tech products were standardized. High-touch products like Coca-Cola, Levi jeans and Revlon cosmetics would be the same. According to Levitt, 'everywhere everything gets more and more like everything else as the world's preference structure is relentlessly homogenized' (1983: 93). Levitt predicted that the global corporation will know everything about one great thing. The corporation will know about the absolute need to be competitive on a worldwide basis as well as nationally and seek constantly to drive down prices by standardizing what it sells and how is operates. Its mission is modernity and its mode, price competition, even when the corporation sells top-of-the-line, high-end products. What all markets have in common is an overwhelming desire for dependable, world-standard modernity in all things, at aggressively low prices. Later, in 1988, in one of the editorials he wrote for the *Harvard Business Review*, Levitt created a concept called 'the pluralization of consumption' to supplement his theory of global homogenization. According to his prediction, the whole world is made up of one market segment, which consists of people with plural preferences – the new world of the heteroconsumer.

While we enjoy reading all Levitt's writings and accept the points he made in most of his articles, we must challenge this contention by Levitt. If world-class marketers like P&G encountered clear cultural problems in Europe and Japan, it is quite obvious that the market is not homogenized even among the most developed countries. The case of Nestlé's infant formula is even more convincing. The economic gap between the North (those who have) and the South (those who have not) is highly conspicuous. It is not possible to assume that people in the Third World should be approached in the same way as people in the First World. If this is still not enough, the case of Harley-Davidson shows us clearly that even in the most developed marketplace in the world, the USA, culture and its consequences play a key role in marketing. Harley-Davidson depends on cultural features to guard its market niche. No Japanese company can reproduce the same cultural impact on American consumers. The foundation of Hofstede's (1984) seminal studies on culture is the nation. As long as national boundaries exist, and as long as there are reasons for nations to reinforce the differences between nations, the impact of culture will be here to stay.

Coca-Cola is probably the best known brand name in the world. If there is a universal standard product in the world, Coca-Cola is very likely to be one of the best, if not the best, contender. However, when the Coca-Cola company began to sell their products aggressively in China, it was clear that the reception there was atypical. Contrary to expectation, Sprite (the number two brand from the Coca-Cola company) was selling much better than Coca-Cola (the flagship in China). Also, it was quite clear that the universal advertising copy was not at all well received in China. This led to a special advertising production for China. The company gave local managers in mainland China control over advertisement operation. In the new advertising commercial that was launched in 1992, one could see the favourite

Chinese images such as family ties, wedding ceremonies, Chinese New Year and the great earth. These cultural themes were clearly unique to China and the Chinese. A pop singer from Taiwan, who was well received on the mainland, was commissioned to compose and sing the theme song for that advertising commercial. In addition to localized advertisement operation, Coca-Cola changed its usual distribution strategies when they operated in China. When Coca-Cola first started its operation in China, its direct-to-retail distribution strategy, which was successful in developed countries like the United States, only accounted for a minority of the company's unit sales. In mainland China, around 75 per cent of Coke products went through independent wholesalers. These independent wholesalers might be large state-owned enterprises, private companies, or most often, family business. To handle distribution and sales to these wholesalers, Coca-Cola operated at least one sales centre, which also served as warehouses, in most Chinese cities with a population above one million. Coca-Cola also provided training and management assistance to these independent wholesalers through a programme called 'Partnership 101'. This unique distribution strategy allowed Coca-Cola to reach more customers through its giant distribution network, with about 215,000 active retail outlets in 2001. Coca-Cola's 'think local, act local' approach made Coca-Cola the most recognized soft drink brand in mainland China for six consecutive years from 1995 to 2001 (Clifford and Harris, 1996; Weisert, 2001). This is clear evidence that consumers are not homogenized. The impact of culture is here to stay.

Balance between localization and standardization strategy

The above discussion may leave readers with the impression that marketing in different cultures should adopt the local culture or fail. However, the choice between standardization and localization is not an either–or decision. Instead, marketers should balance the two approaches so that they can maximize the benefit from their marketing campaigns. While localization allows marketers to develop marketing campaigns relevant to the local customers' needs, standardization allows marketers to enjoy economies of scale and deliver a consistent branding message (Ferle et al., 2008).

Operating in more than 100 countries, McDonald's is probably the most iconic fast-food chain in the world. For years, McDonald's has used the famous Golden Arches as its logo with red and yellow as the major colour tone. It operates everywhere with the same principle of providing customers with efficient fast food in a clean environment. However, since the 1990s, McDonald's marketing message has fallen flat. In 2002, the world's largest restaurant chain's stock price dropped to a seven-year low due to decreasing earnings (ElBoghdady, 2002). It was clear that its attempts in creating an emotional connection with its customers were not working and its advertisements were notorious for lacking focus and being out of touch with the culture (Arndorfer, 2005). Even though advertisements were made by local agents, they were given small budgets and worked on similar projects, focusing on price reduction and product attributes (Fowler, 2005). Standardization did not help McDonald's stand out from its rivals. Moreover, selling the Big Mac, the brand-famous product, is not possible in many countries like India where no pork or beef are allowed in the diet. In Israel, the chain has to sell 100 per cent Kosher beef, processed in accordance with Jewish rites. They cannot sell any dairy product nor operate on the Sabbath nor on any religious holidays. A total standardization is impossible.

In 2003, McDonald's executives were convinced that the traditional one-size-fits-all approach could not cater to the different needs of customers in different cultures. They understood that no one message could tell the whole brand story. However, they also saw a totally localized approach as being too risky and creating confusion. In order to address both local relevance and message consistency, they adopted a new approach – 'brand journalism' which recognized the multidimensional nature of a brand. In the 'brand journalism' approach, McDonald's marketers reach its customers in different cultures with different relevant concepts under the same theme. In other words, creative themes are developed on a global basis. However, local marketers may tailor the theme in locally relevant ways (Cardona, 2004). Accordingly, they launched a series of marketing campaigns all around the world under a unified theme called 'I'm lovin' it'. The theme connected McDonald's with its customers in a highly relevant and culturally significant way. Local marketers were allowed to use locally relevant advertising channels, tailor-make advertising context and develop new products to suit the needs of local customers. At the same time, through its promotions, media planning, new product developments, merchandising and internal marketing, a single brand message was sent to employees and customers in over 100 countries expressing the 'Forever Young' positioning. It provided message consistency while capturing the spirit, music and flavour of each local country (PR Newswire, 2003). This approach allowed McDonald's to sell one facet of the brand in a culturally relevant way and resulted in 86 per cent advertising awareness in its top 10 markets. Sales increased. At the same time, customers and employees were excited about the 'new' brand (Cardona, 2004).

In different cultures, advertisements under the McDonald's 'I'm lovin' it' theme told different real stories about what their customers like, and how McDonald's relates to them. McDonald's experiences in Asia demonstrate how successful the new strategy is. Like other countries, McDonald's Asian advertisements were made under the 'I'm lovin' it' theme. The 2009 Hong Kong Chinese New Year prosperity campaign was not an exception. However, it was tailored to suit local customers' needs. In terms of product, they developed the Mala Grilled Pork Burger, the Mala Grilled Chicken Burger and Mala McNuggets. As local customers preferred pork and chicken to beef, these Sichuan style products were relevant to local tastes. In terms of the advertisement, it featured Hong Kong slang, pandas and Chinese traditional lanterns. It also employed SoftHard, a local band popular among the youth, as actors. Furthermore, customers could purchase SoftHard Rangers, a set of 12 Chinese animal zodiac dolls. More importantly, the whole marketing campaigns sent consistent brand messages to its customers under the 'I'm lovin' it' theme. The marketing success was reflected in its 10.2 per cent monthly sales increase in the Asia Pacific,

Middle East and Africa region (PR Newswire, 2009). McDonald's demonstrated how marketers can balance standardization and localization and become successful.

Learning from different cultures

When operating in a global environment, it becomes important to understand and learn from different cultures. Executives from a 'strong' business culture should always be sensitive to the opportunity to learn from executives from a seemingly 'weak' business culture. One good example comes from the experience of Sino-US business. After 1993, many more American multinational companies took business in China seriously. There was a renewed interest in studying the Chinese business negotiating style (e.g. Fang, 1997), trying to re-examine what was known in the early days (e.g. Pye, 1982). While this whole research area is still quite unclear, American executives have already discovered that they have at least one important lesson to learn from Chinese executives in negotiating more effectively (Intercultural Training Resources, Inc., 1995). American executives usually arrange negotiation items one by one and prioritize the issues. They would try to negotiate and settle first the most important issue, and then move on to the next one. If there is no settlement for the first issue, they would hesitate to move on. At the same time, once the first issue is settled, they would hesitate to open up the discussion again when they have already moved on and discussed the second issue (sequential approach). Chinese executives are just the opposite. If they cannot come to an agreement on the most important issue, they are willing to put that aside for the time being and move on to discuss the next issue. In addition, even if they have already reached an agreement on the first issue, they are willing to open up the discussion again on the first issue when they are discussing the second issue (holistic approach). Theoretically, the Chinese holistic approach would enhance significantly the chances for both parties to create more value from the business deal.

Dynamic culture and dynamic marketplace

While it is unlikely and undesirable that cultures will converge and form one world culture in the foreseeable future, this does not mean that cultures are stagnant. The impact of culture is here to stay, but culture itself is dynamic and changing. When the culture of a particular economy is changing, more often than not there should be commensurate changes of marketing efforts in order to enable the company and the brand to ride together with the tide. The case of Hong Kong should be instructive since it has gone through significant changes in the past several decades.

Hong Kong had been a British colony for more than 90 years. Culturally, Hong Kong has always been a Chinese society. When the Communist Party was about to take power in mainland China, many Chinese industrialists in the textile industry came to Hong Kong. They brought with them their best technicians and operators, together with money and their best equipment. In the 1950s and the 1960s Hong Kong became a rapidly growing manufacturing centre with a firm base in textiles and clothing. The typical work ethic at that time was diligent and frugal, carried over from the previous agricultural society. Because of continued growth and prosperity, Hong Kong became quite affluent in the 1970s and well into the 1980s. In the meantime, Hong Kong people began to work more shrewdly rather than harder. They no longer felt that they were poor and even if they actually were they felt that they can become rich if they do it right tomorrow. The issue of the end of colonization in 1997 was much felt in Hong Kong, beginning in late 1982, and remains a part of daily news. Hong Kong people have been forced to reflect on their own identities. Before the issue of 1997 became real, Hong Kong people had refused to think about it, and regarded themselves as Chinese. When the changes in 1997 became a reality, Hong Kong people began to see that there is a difference between the identity of a Hong Kong person and the identity of a Chinese person. Although Hong Kong people are also Chinese, they are not Chinese in the same way as those from the mainland or Taiwan. This development is gradual but real and carries implications for marketing campaigns. It may be instructive to review the development of advertising themes for a popular soft drink in Hong Kong, since the soft drink industry may best reflect the preference of the mass society. It is about the story of Vitasoy, a soya bean milk developed in Hong Kong (Lai, 1991).

The Vitasoy story began with a big idea and a little bean. Vitasoy was a milk substitute made from soya beans ground with water and sugar. It was launched as 'the poor people's milk' in the 1940s. Its major principle was to deliver adequate nutrition at low cost. The company promised that people would become taller, stronger and healthier. Vitasoy had always been sold at about two-thirds of the price level of leading soft drinks such as Coca-Cola. Vitasoy met two kinds of needs. People took Vitasoy because it was thirst quenching and at the same time good for body strength. It also appealed to people who were poor and frugal. This product position continued to function well in the 1950s and 1960s. However, in the 1970s this advertising theme became ineffective. Hong Kong people no longer thought of themselves as poor and malnourished. In 1974 Vitasoy decided to make a drastic change and reposition the product. They used Tetra Brik Asceptic packaging to present a new image and to make the product available in supermarkets, which had started to become a more important retail outlet than grocery stores. They raised the product price level to the ordinary price level for prestigious soft drinks, since price was no longer a concern among customers. The incremental margin would enable the company to put up more aggressive marketing campaigns. The advertising theme was changed to 'more than a simple soft drink'. The new theme created a 'Fun' image and at the same time preserved the 'nutritious/ healthy' image, which was still helpful to differentiate Vitasoy from other soft drinks. This advertising theme went well for more than a decade, and then ran out of steam. In 1988 they adopted another new theme, 'you must have been a beautiful baby'. This theme reinforced the Hong Kong identity and also enabled Vitasoy to differentiate itself from all other soft drinks which were from different countries. Since Hong Kong people at that time had begun to have confidence in their own identity, this advertising theme was timely and effective. In the 2000s,

Hong Kong people were able to identify the dual identity of Hong Kong people in relation to China (Brewer, 1999). The new Vitasoy's advertising theme was 'One small step, one leap forward'. It featured a son gaining support from his traditional father by showing a childhood drawing of Vitasoy. This advertisement made use of the father–son relationship to portray the relationship between Hong Kong and mainland China. It became quite effective. Vitasoy has been continuously successful and the advertising themes adopted over the years have kept pace with the changing culture in Hong Kong. This is strong evidence that culture and marketing go together in a dynamic fashion. There will be no effective marketing if full attention is not paid to its cultural aspects.

Conclusion

Marketing theories are culture bound. Marketing success is also culture bound. When a company has developed a successful marketing formula in one culture, it is justified to try to enjoy the benefits of scale economy and apply it in another culture. However, it is important to take heed and make sure that the conditions exist there to reproduce the same marketing success. Otherwise, the marketing failure can be very costly. The story of the P&G launch of Vizir is very instructive. On the other hand, the eventual success of P&G in Japan is reassuring. McDonald's 'I'm lovin' it' marketing campaign further demonstrates how to balance the decision between localization and standardization. Good marketing efforts, even in a different culture, will pay off.

Marketing is not just profit making. When a company launches a marketing programme in a different culture, the first question that should be asked is whether the company respects the host culture. In some special situations, as demonstrated in Nestlé's infant formula case and in the Third World and Zhangjiajie ecotourism development, it may even be appropriate to adopt various demarketing measures at the expense of 'marketing success'. When a company learns to respect culture, the efforts will pay off. When the marketing programme and the culture are joined together, sustainable competitive advantages are guaranteed. The rebirth of Harley-Davidson celebrates this truth.

Although there are merits in Levitt's vision of a convergent world culture (1983, 1988), it is unlikely that that vision will become a reality in the foreseeable future. Coca-Cola's 'think local, act local' marketing activities and the differentiated cultural effects on tension felt during negotiation demonstrated that. In view of the fact that people can learn even from a seemingly 'weak' culture, it becomes desirable to preserve cultural diversity so that marketers can learn more effectively. Thus, it will continue to be important to examine the cultural aspects of marketing, Levitt's thesis, in a way, reinforces the conviction that culture is developing and changing. It becomes important for the marketer to continue to study the cultural aspects of marketing, even when the company is operating in the same place as before. Since culture is constantly developing and changing, even the home culture can become very different in the course of time. It becomes imperative to examine the cultural aspects of marketing whether one is operating at home or abroad.

References

Arndorfer, James B. (2005) 'McDonald's lovin' its new model', *TelevisionWeek* 24: 17.

Bagozzi, Richard P. and Dholakia, Utpal M. (2006) 'Antecedents and purchase consequences of customer participation in small group brand communities', *International Journal of Research in Marketing* 23(1): 45–61.

Bartlett, Christopher A. (1983) *Procter & Gamble Europe: Vizir Launch*, Boston, MA: Harvard Business School.

Brewer, Marilynn B. (1999) 'Multiple identities and identity transition: implications for Hong Kong', *International Journal of Intercultural Relations* 23: 187–97.

Buzzell, Robert D. and Purkayastha, Dev (1978) *Note on the Motorcycle Industry – 1975*, Boston, MA: Harvard Business School.

Cardona, Mercedes M. (2004) 'Mass marketing meets its maker', *Advertising Age* 75: 1–2.

Clifford, Mark L. and Harris, Nicole (1996) 'Coke pours into Asia', *Business Week* 3499: 72.

Deng, Jinyang, Qiang, Shi, Walker, Gordon J. and Zhang, Yaoqi (2003) 'Assessment on and perception of visitors' environmental impacts of nature tourism: a case study of Zhangjiajie National Forest Park, China', *Journal of Sustainable Tourism* 11: 529–48.

The Editors of *Advertising Age* (1989) *Procter & Gamble, How P&G became America's Leading Marketer*, Lincolnwood, IL: NTC Business Books.

ElBoghdady, Dina (2002) 'At McDonald's, supersize problems', *The Washington Post* 18 September.

Fang, Tony (1997) *Chinese Business Negotiating Style*, Linkoping, Sweden: Linkoping University.

Ferle, Carrie La, Edwards, Steven M. and Lee, Wei-Na (2008) 'Culture, attitudes, and media patterns in China, Taiwan, and the U.S.: balancing standardization and localization decisions', *Journal of Global Marketing* 21: 191–205.

Fortune (1989) 'How Harley beat back the Japanese', *Fortune* 25: 93–6.

Fowler, Geoffrey A. (2005) 'McDonald's Asian marketing takes on a regional approach', *Wall Street Journal* 26 January.

Hatch, Elvin (1989) 'Culture', in Adam Kuper and Jessica Kuper (eds) *The Social Science Encyclopedia*, London: Routledge.

Herbig, Paul A. (1998) *Handbook of Cross-Cultural Marketing*, Binghamton, NY: The International Business Press. P. 117.

Hofstede, Geert (1984) *Culture's Consequences, International Differences in Work-Related Values*, Beverly Hills, CA: Sage Publications.

Hofstede, Geert (1993) 'Cultural constraints in management theories', *Academy of Management Executive* 7: 81–94.

Intercultural Training Resources, Inc. (1995) *Working with China Series*, San Francisco, CA: Intercultural Training Resources, Inc.

Lai, Linda (1991) 'Fortune built on a bean', *Hong Kong, Inc.* 18: 26–47.

Lee, Kam-hon (1987) 'The informative and persuasive functions of advertising: a moral appraisal – a further comment', *Journal of Business Ethics* 6: 55–7.

Lee, Kam-hon, Yang, Guang and Graham, John L. (2006) 'Tension and trust in international business negotiations: American executives negotiating with Chinese executives', *Journal of International Business Studies* 31: 623–41.

Levitt, Theodore (1983) 'The globalization of markets', *Harvard Business Review* 61: 92–102.

Levitt, Theodore (1988) 'The pluralization of consumption', *Harvard Business Review* 66: 7–8.

McAlexander, James H., Schouten, John W. and Koenig, Harold F. (2002) 'Building brand community', *Journal of Marketing* 66: 38–54.

Muniz, Albert M. Jr. and O'Guinn, Thomes C. (2001) 'Brand community', *Journal of Consumer Research* 27: 412–32.

Post, James E. (1986) 'Ethical dilemmas of multinational enterprises: an analysis of Nestlé's traumatic experience with the infant formula controversy', in W. Michael Hoffman, Ann E. Lange and David A. Fedo (eds) *Ethics and the Multinational Enterprise*, Lanham, MD: University Press of America, Inc.

PR Newswire (2003) 'McDonald's® unveils 'I'm lovin' it™' worldwide brand campaign', *PR Newswire* 2 September.

PR Newswire (2009) 'McDonald's reports global comparable sales up 7.1% in January', *PR Newswire* 9 February.

Pye, Lucian W. (1982) *Chinese Commercial Negotiating Style*, Cambridge, UK: Oelgeschlager, Gunn & Hain.

Rose, Robert L. (1990) 'Harley regains lead in big bike market', *Asian Wall Street Journal* 7–8 September.

Swanson, Lauren A. (1989) 'The twelve "nations" of China', *Journal of International Consumer Marketing* 2: 83–105.

Thompson, Scott A. and Sinha, Rejiv K. (2008) 'Brand communities and new product adoption: the influence and limits of oppositional loyalty', *Journal of Marketing* 72: 65–80.

Tse, David K., Lee, Kam-hon, Vertinsky, Ilan and Wehrung, David A. (1988) 'Does culture matter? A cross-cultural study of executives' choice, decisiveness, and risk adjustment in international marketing', *Journal of Marketing* 52: 81–95.

Walsh, Daniel (2001) 'P&G China lab has global role', *Research Technology Management* 44: 4–5.

Weisert, Drake (2001) 'Coca-Cola in China: quenching the thirst of a billion', *The China Business Review* 28: 52–5.

Yoshino, Michael and Stoneham, Paul H. (1990a) *Procter & Gamble Japan (A)*, Boston, MA: Harvard Business School.

Yoshino, Michael and Stoneham, Paul H. (1990b) *Procter & Gamble Japan (C)*, Boston, MA: Harvard Business School.

Zhong, Linsheng, Deng, Jinyang and Xiang, Baohui (2008) 'Tourism development and the tourism area life-cycle model: A case study of Zhangjiajie National Forest Park, China', *Tourism Management* 29: 841–56.

Section C

Theories of Marketing Management and Organization

9

The marketing mix – a helicopter view

Walter van Waterschoot and Thomas Foscht

Marketing mix origin and background

The marketing mix concept follows directly from the very nature of marketing. The concept is inherent to any marketing situation without any exception, irrespective of its peculiarities – even if this is more obvious in some situations than others. In other words, the mix concept is quintessential to marketing (van Waterschoot and De Haes, 2008: 42). Logically, therefore, the origin and traces of the concept are intertwined with those of the marketing discipline. The antecedents of marketing practice go a long way back into the histories of many economies, even if their individual histories show different time patterns (Fullerton, 1988). History study reveals that managerial marketing practice and corresponding conceptual thinking as a distinct discipline (Bartels, 1962) resulted from dramatically changing market circumstances in the Western world, predominantly taking place around the end of the nineteenth and during the first half of the twentieth centuries. An increasing divide between production and consumption contributed to the structural presence of substantial supply and demand potential in diverse product and service areas. Over the years both supply and demand potential tended to become increasingly substantial as well as heterogeneous,

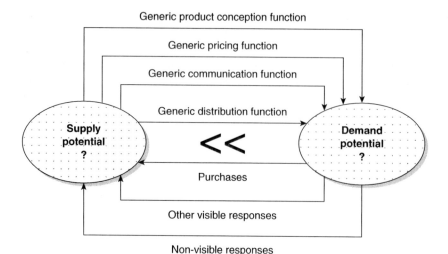

Figure 9.1   The new exchange model (van Waterschoot et al., 2006)

and as a result became also more or less non-transparent. Importantly also, even if potential demand typically increased, for example as a consequence of rising incomes, potential supply was or became typically even larger in relative terms, for example as a result of innovations. The rise of these buyers' markets forced or allowed marketers to carry through all sorts of marketing efforts to attract the attention, interest and preference of potential customers (van Waterschoot and De Haes, 2008).

The outcome of the previous developments was the rise of a basically new exchange model fundamentally different from the one traditionally assumed by economists (see Figure 9.1). The new model generically synthesizes the essential forces and properties of any marketing situation as opposed to other types of exchange situations. As such it summarizes the basics of both marketing theory and practice. Their subject matter concentrates on particular types of exchanges, the core conditions of which were generically defined by Philip Kotler (1972). For marketing exchanges to occur, the following conditions are necessary:

> **(1) [the presence of] two or more parties believing that it is appropriate or desirable to deal with one another; (2) a scarcity of goods [in the generic sense of the latter term]; (3) concept of private property which allows to make, accept or reject an offer; (4) each of the parties must possess something that might be of value to the other; (5) the 'wanting' party must be able to offer some kind of payment for it; and (6) the 'owning' party must be willing to forego the object or service for the payment. (Kotler, 1972: 47)**

On top of these structural exchange conditions there are some typical properties explaining the distinct character of the new exchange model: heterogeneity and non-transparency of demand and supply as well as the prevalence of buyers' markets (represented in Figure 9.1 by dots, question marks and inequality signs respectively) (van Waterschoot and De Haes, 2008). A major distinctive idea of the new model as opposed to the traditional microeconomic model is the implied type(s) of buyer response(s). The outcomes of the new model are far more differentiated than the sole key question in the traditional economic models, which is 'to buy or not to buy'. Additional types of visible responses become important like, for example, store visits or active information gathering. On the other hand also non-visible reactions are considered like, for example, brand learning, as well as delayed reactions like, for example, possibly consumer satisfaction. Consequently, the new exchange model allows the integration of subjective and even of non-rational behaviour (Bagozzi, 1975).

This new exchange model structurally implies four unavoidable and therefore generic marketing exchange functions. These are in spectacular contrast with the absence of those functions in the traditional models of microeconomics during the birth era of the new marketing discipline, which were focusing mainly on pure, transparent markets ruled by rationality (van Waterschoot, 2000; van Waterschoot and De Haes, 2008; van Waterschoot and Van den Bulte, 1992; van Waterschoot et al., 2006). In Figure 9.1 these four generic marketing exchange functions are represented by arrows originating from the marketer(s) towards the market(s). In 'reciprocal marketing' they go both ways (van Waterschoot and De Haes, 2008).

1. *A generic product conception function* – in the era of the emergence of the new exchange model products and services are increasingly becoming heterogeneous implying a passive or active product conception by marketers. This is in sharp contrast with homogeneous markets, which do not pose any significant strategic choice in terms of product composition. Now a choice needs to be made anyway – actively or passively – between the many imaginable alternative product concepts, to determine which specific product composition(s) would be marketed. So, a first vital, unavoidable exchange function consists of configuring something that would be valued by the prospective exchange party.

2. *A generic pricing function* – market participants enjoy more or less price freedom compared to the harsh reality of solely having to take or leave a market price. Now they have the opportunity to – again actively or passively – follow a pricing strategy. In fact in many cases marketers are even forced to. So, a second unavoidable exchange function consists of determining the compensation and sacrifices to be brought by the prospective exchange parties.

3. *A generic communication function* – the previous two functions would not allow any exchange if no communication could take place. In the described setting, communication with an eye on information and persuasion has become inevitable as well. The respective parties need to be informed about one another's existence, intentions and requirements and perhaps be persuaded about the attractiveness of the other party's offering, or even about entering into such an exchange relationship at all. This third fundamental exchange function therefore consists of bringing the offer to the attention of the prospective exchange party and influencing its feelings and preferences about it.

4. *A generic distribution function* – in the described setting, production and consumption are separated by different types of gaps – geographic, choice, time and amount (Bucklin, 1966, 1972) – which market participants have to bridge in order to make their products or services available for acquisition. No exchange would come about, if the respective parties were actually unable to deliver the object or service that is exchanged for some higher valued object or service. Here arises a fourth fundamental exchange function of placing the offer at the disposal of the prospective exchange party.

The marketing discipline considers these four functions as generic, in the sense that they have to be fulfilled anyhow, for exchange to come about. This necessity follows from the marketing discipline's realistic market assumptions, which would be called impure by economists because of the supposed lack of instantaneous transactions and perfect knowledge (Houston and Gassenheimer, 1987: 15). Consequently, poor execution of any of these functions would bring about poor exchange results or worse results than those that could potentially have taken place. However, if any of these generic functions were not carried out, no exchange could take place, no demand could be created, fulfilled or maintained (van Waterschoot and Van den Bulte, 1992).

The nature and scope of the marketing mix metaphor and concept

In view of the properties of the new exchange model the four generic exchange functions are unavoidably needed to influence demand to a greater or lesser extent. Those functions, however, cannot possibly be instrumental in themselves. In fact they materialize via actual choices in terms of demand impinging instruments, namely controllable elements affecting demand like, for example, all sorts of product and/or service attributes, product and/or service ranges, price schemes, all sorts of communication messages, personal and non-personal communication, communication vehicles and schedules, distribution networks, compensation schemes for intermediaries, exclusiveness arrangements, merchandising schemes, etc. These demand impinging instruments can theoretically be spread out over time as well as targeted in numerous ways and combined in a myriad of ways. The underlying concept is that of a controllable mixture of demand impinging elements – instruments – with divergent potential results depending on the timing and composition of the mixture. This idea received the suggestive and figurative label of 'marketing mix' (concept). It is indissolubly inherent to marketing activity. The reality of a large number and variety of demand impinging instruments that had to be combined was indeed structurally implied by the new exchange model from its very beginnings. That said, this idea was not clearly identified and described for a long period. It was not only a hardly identified concept; for a long time it remained a kind of implicit concept without a name (van Waterschoot and De Haes, 2008). The term 'marketing mix' was only coined in 1953 by Neil Borden in his presidential address to the American Marketing Association. He had been inspired by James Culliton (1948) who in the preceding decade had pictured the marketing executive as somebody combining different ingredients (van Waterschoot and Van den Bulte, 1992). The term 'marketing mix' from that point on referred not only to a picture or metaphor of pursuing certain market responses by using mixtures of instruments, but also to the corresponding concept (Borden, 1964) as well as to the included instruments.

The mix metaphor not only suggested the availability of a wide range of possible ingredients, as well as the numerous ways in which these elements could be combined. It also indicated the fact that different amalgamations might produce different results, with some more preferable than others. The marketing mix expression reminds one of many other types of combination with similar characteristics. Not every mixed grill is as delicious as any other and not every drink can be combined successfully with any other. The metaphor also suggests that the 'mixer' has control over a number of elements which he can self-reliantly mix as he likes. This is applicable only to some extent since marketing reality is always subject to some constraints. The mix metaphor contains even some more suggestions which cannot be taken literally in all instances like, for example, the suggestion of a one-time operation versus the reality of interactive operations and a longer term orientation (van Waterschoot and De Haes, 2008).

Formally defined, the concept of the marketing mix refers to the set of 'controllable demand-impinging elements (instruments) that can be combined into a marketing programme used by a firm (or any other organization) to achieve a certain level and type of response from its target market' (van Waterschoot and Van den Bulte, 1992: 88). By definition instruments are concerned that they more or less directly influence demand to a greater or lesser extent, like the price of a product or the way in which it is advertised.

However, not all marketing instruments are also marketing mix instruments. For example, marketing research – if carried out properly and if its information value exceeds its costs – is often a useful marketing instrument, without belonging to the marketing mix. The reason is that marketing research, normally speaking – unless the 'research' project is intended as a communications campaign in the first place – does not directly influence demand in any way or to any extent. Customers will not start buying more of a brand for the mere reason that its producer or distributor increases his marketing research budget, employs more competent research, personnel, hires a more skilled research agency, or starts using more appropriate research techniques. Adequate marketing research will normally only influence demand indirectly, for example by helping to (re-) specify product characteristics to better match customer needs and desires (van Waterschoot, 2000).

Next to exerting a more or less direct effect of a variable magnitude sooner or later, the demand impinging element should also be controllable to be a marketing mix instrument. Fine weather fosters coastal tourism, but is not a marketing mix instrument. However, the distinction between controllable and non-controllable elements, is not always obvious and lack of control does not necessarily imply lack of influence. Controlling over a variable means being able to establish its value. Influence over a variable means having some but not complete control of it (Ackoff, 1981: 174). A country's birth rate, for example, is an important but uncontrollable demand impinging element for a manufacturer of baby clothes. If, however, government measures such as birth premiums can significantly raise demand and if government measures are highly dependent on company lobbying, then the birth rate can be called susceptible to influence. As the example suggests, controllable (marketing mix) variables may be used to influence crucial, but uncontrollable environmental elements (van Waterschoot and Van den Bulte, 1992).

Marketing arguably applies without any exception to any voluntary exchange situation matching the properties of the new exchange model. Consequently, not just business organizations and their dealings with client publics may be concerned, but possibly also other organizations like, for example, non-profit organizations and possibly also other sorts of publics like, for example, employees or donators. At least, to the extent that and as long as the properties of the new exchange model prevail. This observation fully matches the conclusions of the broadening controversy amongst academics in the early 1970s and the corresponding, generic definition of marketing by Philip Kotler (1972).

All the applications or situations embraced by Kotler's (1972) generic marketing definition imply the mutual prevalence and use of the earlier mentioned four generic exchange functions, because otherwise exchanges simply cannot be realized. Partial applications in terms of generic exchange functions being used can consequently only be borderline cases. An example of the latter would be when the police try to convince the general public that they are their friend, thereby relying basically on communication only. But in any of those cases – full-fledged or partial – marketing mix instruments are inherently and indissolubly needed. The generic exchange functions are structurally present in any marketing situation, but can at the same time not materialize without the use of concrete demand impinging instruments. In other words, by definition the mix concept applies to any marketing situation without any exception: consumer marketing, B2B marketing, non-profit marketing, service marketing, retail marketing, etc. The mix concept even applies by definition also to less traditional sub-fields such as e-marketing (Möller, 2006) and relationship marketing.

Self-evidently, the inevitable, logical conclusion that the mix concept applies to any marketing situation without exception, does not counter-argue the fact that major differences would exist between those different groups of applications and corresponding schools of thought. Just like there exist lots of differences within those groups, for example as a consequence of different strategic and/or tactical options. Relationship marketing is a case in point. In many instances, relationships (in terms of reciprocal personal knowledge, social contacts, emotional ties, etc.) naturally develop between marketers and their customers (or any other relevant public). Naturally also, marketers capitalize on cultivating those relationships as this is an expedient towards gaining control over the exchange process, or, in other words, a means of increasing the likelihood of positive responses from the market. As long as relationships do not completely rule the game – that is, as long as the desired responses of the market are not structurally guaranteed – there is still a marketing situation at stake. Otherwise, other exchange mechanisms (e.g. social, emotional, financial, ownership, contractual systems, etc.) take over and the situation can no longer be considered as possessing a marketing character. The point therefore is, that as long as the upper limits of the relationship have not been reached in terms of magnitude and strength, and as long there is still a marketing exchange framework at hand, the generic exchange functions still largely and unavoidably determine the outcome of the exchange process. These exchange functions in turn cannot do else but materialize by means of demand impinging instruments under some or other form. Consequently, demand needs to be managed under some form or other. So, also under relationship marketing prices are charged, product concepts are being conceived, developed, delivered and communicated. The specific mix approach will probably be affected and characterized by the relationship context, resulting, for example, in a relatively great deal of personal and ongoing communication, pricing schemes based on loyalty, etc. The prevalence of these peculiarities, however, does not counter-argue the basic presence of a marketing mix. So, for logical reasons, we fully agree with those authors who are keen on underscoring the peculiarities of their sub-field, as far as they point at genuine differences (Grönroos, 1994). However, also for logical reasons, we do not agree with those who would go as far as denying the undeniable, namely the common generic roots of their sub-field with the overall marketing field, including the marketing mix.

Marketing mix functions, instruments and effects

The generic exchange functions materialize by means of the marketing mix, implying that those functions also represent the generic functions of the marketing mix itself. The most general marketing mix effects are those following from the simultaneous pursuit or execution of all exchange functions by means of the overall mixture of instruments. This will be discussed in the first subsection. The second subsection explores the horizon of possible effects of the mix still further as well as that of of individual instruments. The third subsection distinguishes between strategic and tactical effects and instruments, also with an eye on the discussion of mix classifications further on.

Primary vs. secondary functions, instruments and effects

In practice, numerous marketing mix instruments exist. Out of an endless theoretical list of mix instruments a specific actual combination or combinations have to be chosen, targeted and timed, taking into consideration their expected effects. A fundamental observation is the fact that any instrument out of that mixture, in itself, predominantly serves one of the four generic functions mentioned previously, but that at the same time it also contributes – albeit to a lesser extent – to the fulfilment of the three other functions.

It should be underscored that all possible individual marketing mix instruments do have primary as well as secondary effects, when looked at from a functional point of view. This distinction follows from the vital observation that any marketing mix instrument serves any generic marketing mix or exchange function. However, any marketing mix instrument actually serves primarily one of the four generic functions (at the same time it may also primarily serve the so-called 'promotional' function – see pp. 200–3). The corresponding effects on demand are the instrument's primary effects. At the same time it is crucial to observe that any marketing mix instrument also contributes, to a lesser extent, to the other generic functions (van Waterschoot, 2000: 189). The corresponding effects on demand are the instrument's secondary effects. The idea is summarized in Table 9.1.

Advertising is a classical communication instrument within the marketing mix, meaning that its primary function (and corresponding effect) is one of bringing the offer to the attention of the prospective exchange party and influencing their feelings and preferences about it (van Waterschoot, 2000; van Waterschoot and Van den Bulte, 1992). At the same time, however, advertising may add extra need fulfilment to the product – for instance, by providing prestige or the suggestion or belief of power or excellence. This is typically the case, for example, with Nike or Adidas advertisements. Conversely, advertising may imply a cost and hence influence the pricing function of the marketing mix. Such could be the case if a highly distinguished, favourite brand of wristwatch were featured in a notorious magazine like – supposedly – *Playboy*. Advertising also contributes to the availability function of the marketing mix – for instance by informing the public about the available points of sale. Finally, advertising contributes to the promotion function (see pp. 200–3) of the marketing mix, even if theme advertising is concerned, which by definition tries to build a long-term image and to prepare for long-term sales. Coca-Cola theme advertisements, for instance, next to establishing and maintaining this picture of young, smart and joyful people who at crucial moments of their lives never fail to think of Coca-Cola, will also make some people under some circumstances aware of their current thirst, or at least make them search almost on the spot for their favourite thirst-quencher.

Each individual marketing mix instrument may in itself foster, or hamper, any marketing mix function from several points of view. The use of tetra bricks, for example, fosters large-scale distribution of fruit juice, whereas the use of fragile fantasy bottles would rather hamper that sort of distribution. When the instruments are being mixed it is logical, that any positive or negative primary instrumental and also any secondary effect may – or even will – interact positively or negatively with any other instrument's primary and secondary effects. Tetra bricks would suit sales via hypermarkets and discount establishments, but might sustain less well a quality brand image. The latter would probably be more sustained if the beverage were packed in elegant bottles and sold via upmarket establishments. If the interaction amongst instruments is harmonious, this will contribute to positive synergy creation within the marketing mix. If the interaction amongst instruments is negative though, dis-synergy will follow. The possible mix interactions are manifold

Table 9.1 The multi-functional effects of marketing mix instruments

	Marketing mix instruments				
	Product instruments	Price instruments	Communication instruments	Distribution instruments	Promotion instruments
Generic functions					
Need-fulfilment function					
Configuration of something valued by the prospective exchange party	xxxxx	x	x	x	x or xxxxx
Pricing function					
Determination of the compensation and sacrifices to be brought by the prospective exchange party	x	xxxxx	x	x	x or xxxxx
Communication function					
Bringing the offer to the attention of the prospective exchange party and influencing its feelings and preferences about it	x	x	xxxxx	x	x or xxxxx
Distribution function					
Placing the offer at the disposal of the prospective exchange party	x	x	x	xxxxx	x or xxxxx
Promotional function					
Inducing immediate, overt behaviour by strengthening the generic functions during relatively short periods of time	x or xxxxx	x or xxxxx	x or xxxxx	x or xxxxx	xxxxx

Notes: xxxxx = primary effects/x = secondary effects

Source: van Waterschoot and Van den Bulte, 1992: 89

and not necessarily easily identifiable and predictable at the level of primary effects. At the level of secondary effects, they are typically even still much less obvious and less easy to predict – a phenomenon adding to the impression of creative genius required to find the magic mix formula.

So, any specific marketing mix instrument affects all four generic marketing mix functions anyhow, but predominantly typically only one of them. On the other hand, any generic marketing mix function is served by any specific marketing mix instrument or hampered by it. Since in actual applications several specific instruments contribute to the fulfilment of all four generic functions, coordination becomes of the utmost importance. The instrumental choices should be made in such a way that the different elements do not only reinforce one another's positive effects and neutralize one another's negative effects with regard to one single generic function, but also with regard to all four such functions simultaneously. Moreover, each generic function actually consists of a set of specific sub-functions that require specific instrumental goals. Communication, for example, presumes amongst other things the creation of awareness, knowledge, preference and conviction.

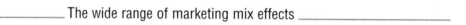

The wide range of marketing mix effects

The range of marketing mix effects is particularly wide and can be looked at from several points of views. Marketing mix effects can be looked at from the point of view of functions, from the stance of the overall mixture, from the stance of specific instruments, or from the perspective of interactions amongst instruments at primary or secondary functional level, etc. Each of those viewpoints though can still be differentiated further by looking into, for example, the magnitude and timing of the effect, its desirability, and so forth. The effects of marketing mix instruments may, for example, be greater or smaller, may take place sooner or later, and may lead to general demand changes for the whole product category and/or for particular offerings. This section briefly explores some of the most important distinctions (van Waterschoot, 2000: 183–94).

A first distinction to be made is between behavioural versus mental responses. Marketing mixes may lead to actual purchases or else to other forms of visible behaviour like, for example, the visiting of trade shows or word-of-mouth-communication. They may also lead to non-visible behaviour in the form of mental responses like increased brand awareness, certain brand associations, increased knowledge of product or service features, strengthening of attitudes, etc. Ultimately, most marketing programmes aim at making people act in a specific way favoured by the marketer. In an economic setting this is mostly buying. This does not conflict, however, with the fact that other sorts of reactions may also be favoured and somehow fit a marketing programme. The type of response provoked by marketing mix instruments may therefore range all the way from mental changes to visible behaviour. Depending on the case, these changes may (be intended to) take place in a shorter or longer time period. The building of a brand image or preference may take a long time. Conversely, when a supermarket chain announces a significant price reduction on a popular brand of soft-drink during one week, its goal is to create store traffic within the course of that particular week. Marketing mix instruments typically provoke both direct and indirect effects or responses. A direct reaction is one that follows from the use of mix instruments without any intermediate reaction. The opposite is the case for indirect effects. The famous Michelin guides, for example, were originally introduced with the intention of encouraging French drivers to travel further and thus to use more tyres. They did this by informing car owners of the location of attractive towns, hotels, restaurants, etc. Marketing mix effects can range all the way from constructive to destructive ones. For example, as a result of charging a discount price for a prestige brand, massive sales may accrue, but the brand image may become damaged. Marketing mix effects can be desirable versus undesirable. For example, a low price strategy may bring about an aspired market share gain, but also cause the undesirable organization of a 'grey' parallel distribution channel supplying neighbouring countries (Cespedes et al., 1988). The use of marketing mix instruments may lead to major versus minor effects. An advertising campaign, for example by a government organization, may cause an extremely small effect only, probably in spectacular contrast to what had been expected beforehand. Immediate effects may be caused versus delayed effects. The immediate effect of a price penetration strategy may be relatively modest in the short run for example, but have as a consequence that the corresponding brand can position itself as a mainstream brand in the future.

Last but not least it should be remarked, that most typically marketing mix instruments are used to increase demand. Because of possible differences between desirable and undesirable demand though, other possibilities also prevail. It could be advisable, for example, to limit demand temporarily and/or selectively and/or to synchronize demand to bring it into harmony with the organization's production capacity (Kotler and Levy, 1971).

Strategic vs. tactical marketing mix instruments and effects

With an eye on the discussion of marketing mix classifications in the next sections, some of the distinctions discussed in the previous paragraphs can best be combined already at this point into the crucial distinction between strategic and tactical marketing mix effects and instruments. Strategic instruments are the ones that have their effects essentially spread out over time. They do not have their main effect taking place immediately, but largely in the medium and relatively longer term. Strategic instruments are also the ones of which the effects are not necessarily visible, in the sense of not necessarily leading to overt (visible) behaviour. Tactical instruments on the other hand are instruments that predominantly lead to visible, short-term effects.

This distinction results from the fact that the strategic use of the four generic exchange functions does not always suffice to bring about exchanges. There are four typical reasons for this: physical inertia, psychological inertia, typical forms of risks and finally also competitive inertia (Beem and Shaffer, 1981: 16, 18). Direct inducement or provocation is in some situations a necessary condition for the exchange to take place. As a result, an additional 'situational' or 'promotional exchange function' may be needed at times to overcome these forms of inertia or to take extra advantage of favourable market developments, next to the four generic exchange functions. Direct inducement or provocation is indeed in some situations a necessary condition for exchange to take place, or else is called for to boost demand to a still more favourable level. Hence, promotion represents a 'situational' or 'complementary' marketing function (van Waterschoot and Van den Bulte, 1992: 88). This non-generic, but oppositely situational marketing mix function, specifically provokes immediate, visible reactions.

The instruments which specifically execute this promotional function are tactical or sales promotion (mix) instruments as opposed to strategic marketing mix instruments. Examples are direct-effect-advertisements as opposed to indirect-effect-advertisements. The latter can be found often when companies try to maintain their image in advertisements with more or less general statements. Direct-effect-advertisements in many cases focus on price elements and more paticularly on temporary price reductions. Therefore this type of advertisement typically provokes short-term demand reactions and thus is a promotional instrument. The promotional mix/instruments can more generally be positively defined as follows:

> **The subset of demand-impinging instruments that have no power of themselves but can, during relatively short periods of time, complement and sustain the basic instruments of the marketing mix (namely product, price, distribution, and communication) for the purpose of stimulating prospective exchange partners (commonly referred to as target market(s)) to a significant degree of desirable forms of immediate, overt behaviour. (van Waterschoot and Van den Bulte, 1992: 89)**

In summary, promotional instruments possess the following properties:

(a) Their primary effect is visible (overt) behaviour, e.g. purchase or trial use.

(b) The instruments are used on a temporary basis, because if they were used for a longer time they would lose their potential effectiveness.

(c) They are supplementary instruments.

(d) They supplement *any* sort of basic category (see functional marketing mix classification, p. 201).

(e) They cannot possibly exist on their own.

(f) They are used as tactical instruments, depending on the circumstances.

(g) Their secondary effect(s) are often not visible (at least not immediately).

It should be emphasized that the multifunctionality of instruments, including the distinction between primary and secondary functionality, also extends to promotional instruments. Promotion or sales promotion instruments (e.g. temporary price discounts) by definition primarily contribute to the promotion function next to their primary generic function (e.g. the pricing function) (van Waterschoot, 2000). Yet, these instruments also affect the (strategic aspects of the) other generic functions, sometimes in a negative way. Temporary price reductions, for instance, by their very nature primarily influence the pricing function next to the promotion function. They could more specifically limit the bracket of pricing possibilities for the future. If customers' price expectations were reshaped by massive price reductions, it may indeed turn out to be difficult to charge a higher price again afterwards. Promotion instruments may, however, also play a secondary, even undeniable, role outside their own strict field of operations. Consumer price discounts may result in, say, retailers spotting massive sales opportunities and therefore granting much more shelf space to the brand than they would have done otherwise. As a result, not only the availability function, but the communication function may also be influenced. More seriously, the impression might be created that a very ordinary brand would be involved, available everywhere, with no distinct features except its price. If for that reason, the exclusiveness of the product would be(come) endangered, this loss of exclusiveness touches upon the need fulfilment function of the marketing mix.

Pragmatic, mnemonic and pedagogical mix classifications

In the development of a new body of thought, such as marketing throughout the twentieth century, the making of listings and taxonomies is one of the primary tasks actually carried through. Not surprisingly therefore, early taxonomies were not developed in a deductive way on strictly logical grounds as a derivation from existing theory (Hunt, 1991). Rather they were made in an inductive way. Known elements, supposedly belonging to the investigated population, were inventoried and grouped into more or less crude, somewhat judgemental or even intuitive classes on the basis of their similarity. In this way early writers on the marketing mix tried to itemize the large number of controllable demand impinging instruments. Frey (1956) and Borden (1964) adopted a checklist approach. Other authors developed more succinct and convenient classifications that could be easily memorized (Frey, 1956; Howard, 1957; Lazer and Kelly, 1962; McCarthy, 1960). Of the many developed schemata, only McCarthy's has survived and has even become the 'dominant design' or 'received view', or at least the most popular view.

The McCarthy typology has become known as the 'Four P classification' of the marketing mix, since it distinguishes four classes of items under four headings beginning with the letter P: Product, Price, Place and Promotion. Although McCarthy only named these classes without defining them, three of them correspond more or less roughly to the previously mentioned generic marketing mix functions.

The first class contains Product-related instruments such as product variety, product quality, design, features, brand name, packaging, sizes, services, warranties and return. The second class comprises Price-related instruments like the list price of products, discounts, allowances, the payment period and credit terms. The third class holds Place-related instruments like the choice of distribution channels, the coverage of existing outlets or the location of outlets. The fourth class of instruments in the McCarthy typology is a hybrid one. Whereas the three previous classes do roughly correspond to three of the generic exchange functions of the new exchange model, McCarthy's fourth P does not even roughly correspond to the fourth generic function. Indeed this fourth P is typically subdivided into four sub-classes, of which only the first three exclusively encompass instruments that mainly aim to bring the offer to the attention of the prospective exchange party and to influence feelings and preferences about it. These three sub-classes are: mass communication; personal communication and publicity. The fourth P of the McCarthy typology, however, also encompasses a large, residual fourth sub-category, which serves as a catch-all to host all marketing mix instruments that do not find a place in any other category. In contrast with the three previously mentioned typical communication sub-classes, only the fourth sub-category of McCarthy' s fourth P consists of actual promotion instruments in the strict sense of the word, whereas the other three are basically strategic communication instruments. A traditional description representative of this (sales) promotion category of McCarthy's popular split-up is the following: 'Those marketing activities, other than personal selling, advertising and publicity, that stimulate consumer purchasing and dealer effectiveness, such as displays, shows and exhibitions, demonstrations, and various nonrecurring selling efforts not in the ordinary routine' (Alexander, 1960).

In terms of appeal and popularity the McCarthy typology has been and still is amazingly popular, presumably as a result of the P-mnemonic. From a classificatory point of view though, the classification fails to meet most of the basic quality criteria as put forward by Hunt (1991). It has no clearly defined classification dimensions, no positive definition of its classes, it suffers in terms of mutual exclusiveness and implies a major catch-all category.

Since the 1960s, the use and interpretation of the concept of the marketing mix has evolved and developed, not least through the classification of the four Ps by McCarthy (1960) in spite of its classificatory shortcomings. This classification, although it quickly became a standard, has not remained static. Later researchers have indeed sought to expand the classification; whereas others still have sought to criticize it.

Throughout the years a number of alternative marketing mix classifications have been formulated, often to reflect the peculiarities of a specific field of application. Remarkably, in most instances this adaptation was realized by adding one or more Ps to McCarthy's mnemonic four Ps list. In instances where an explication of a sub-category of instruments is concerned, such an addition – although conceptually not strictly necessary – is defensible on pedagogical grounds. In instances where an extension outside the boundaries of the marketing mix is concerned, no conceptual justification exists. Despite the indisputable relevance of the managerial issues behind the added Ps, the extension of the mnemonic list mainly serves as a sometimes disputable eye catcher. In further instances, the proposed names of the new categories are indeed not appropriate as a result of the obligatory P. The subsequent paragraphs summarize the main examples of such explications and extensions.

Occasionally, a separate fifth P is added to denote People, Personnel or Personal selling. In this way a collective noun is provided to stress the importance of all types of selling and servicing efforts which are being carried out by any person within the organization. In applications where sales efforts are of a typically high strategic value – as, for example, in the case of service marketing – no fundamental objection can be made to/against this explication, although there is no conceptual necessity since the provision of services belongs to the P of the (service) Product, and sales efforts form part of the 'P' of 'Communication'. In retail marketing, as well as the supplementary P of People a further P is often added to denote the Presentation of merchandise as well as the store layout. Again an explication is involved that is defensible on pedagogical grounds, but which is not necessary from a conceptual or classificatory point of view, since the generically rooted four Ps also hold these elements.

In service marketing Ps have also been added to represent Participants, Physical evidence and Process (Booms and Bitner, 1981). The Participants in a service marketing situation can significantly improve or harm the quality of the execution of service. However, the activities of the personnel carrying out the service conceptually belong to the first P of Product, encompassing all instruments which aim primarily at want fulfilment. In so far as the clients are meant by Participants, the addition becomes conceptually incorrect, since the marketing mix groups demand impinging elements and not the actual demand constituting elements. The Physical environment where the service is provided, together with tangible elements which are used to support the service, obviously influences demand. Where these elements are under the control of the marketer, they form part of the Product or Place instruments. If these elements cannot be controlled by the manager, they are by definition not marketing mix variables. The same remark also holds for the procedural elements of servicing, meaning that a separate P for Process is not really necessary.

With regard to the persuasion of the public outside the most typical target groups, Kotler (1986) has introduced the concept of 'megamarketing', denoting the art of supplying benefits to parties other than target consumers and intermediaries like agents, distributors and dealers – parties such as governments, labour unions and other interest groups that can block profitable entry into a market. Specific instruments in this context are Public Relations and Power. Public relations try to influence public opinion, mainly by means of mass-communication techniques. Power on the other hand addresses itself to 'influential industry officials, legislators, and government bureaucrats to enter and operate in the target market, using sophisticated lobbying and negotiating skills in order to achieve the desired response from the other party without giving away the house' (Kotler, 1986: 120). The term power is not at all appropriate though in this instance. Power refers to the ability of the marketer to get some other party (consumer, distributor, government, etc.) to do what they would otherwise not have done (buy, search for information, give a permit) (Coughlan et al., 2006: 197). Marketing mix instruments of whatever kind – if properly combined – are capable of developing a certain (smaller or larger) amount of power. Calling one instrument category, applied in a specific context, Power, implies both a linguistic and conceptual distortion to make the instrument fit a mnemonic row.

Pragmatic classifications, and especially those expressed in particular mnemonics – like a number of P's – may well be meritorious during the infant stage of a discipline. Intuitive categorizations under the form of mnemonics, rightly help in summarizing and memorizing crude key essentials of a new field during its pioneering stage. Over time, however, the drawbacks of this sort of infant classification become more disturbing as the discipline matures and becomes – or should become – more sophisticated. The divisions of the intuitive typologies are not clear cut but arbitrary, and the 'all other' categories become larger and larger, thereby causing increasing confusion (van Waterschoot and De Haes, 2008). The mnemonic form of the early typologies paradoxically risks becoming obligatory, leading to mnemonic extensions which further risk distorting or prohibiting logical reasoning. Those disturbing phenomena are very typical of the most well known of those pragmatic classifications namely the overly popular four Ps classification of McCarthy (1960).

So, in conclusion, sticking to pragmatic mnemonics in a mature discipline is unjustified both from a conceptual and consequently also from a managerial point of view. It prohibits the development of logical reasoning as well as the process of scientific fact finding and the formulating of managerial recommendations. Extending mnemonics for eye-catching reasons is tempting, but risky from the point of view of conceptual and terminological distortion.

Table 9.2   The essence of a functional marketing mix classification

		Dominant generic marketing mix function			
		Primary instruments of the generic product conception function	Primary instruments of the generic pricing function	Primary instruments of the generic communication function	Primary instruments of the generic distribution function
Situational marketing mix function dominant or not?	Primary strategic instruments				
	Primary tactical instruments				

Source: Based on van Waterschoot and Van den Bulte, 1992.

A functional classification of the marketing mix

In view of the fact that marketing mix instruments make up the central weaponry for influencing demand, common sense suffices for understanding that it is more than advisable to possess a reliable classification of those instruments. This could be compared with the literal weaponry of an army, where it would matter for instance to know what sorts of guns make up part of the arsenal in terms of impact, range, etc. A good classification is one that can host any element of the corresponding – well defined – population, and leaves no room for any outlier. It uses explicit classification criteria clearly informing users about the grounds of the split-ups used. The classification criteria should be independent of each other. Moreover the resultant classes should be capable of capturing any element belonging to the population, and any element should fit not more than one class at the same time.

This section provides a functional classification of the marketing mix, thereby using two main, explicit criteria (van Waterschoot and Van den Bulte, 1992). As a first criterion we will look at the primary generic function of the instruments within the context under study. This enables straightforward classification, since any marketing mix instrument is linked to any exchange function in a secondary fashion. However, the primary link is unique, provided the setting. In traditional retailing, for example, packaging could be seen as part of the product concept in the first place. In the self-service atmosphere of a hypermarket on the contrary, packaging may in the first place be a communication device.

The second classification criterion is based on the distinction between strategic marketing mix functions versus the tactical, situational or promotional function. In fact, each marketing mix instrument has both strategic and tactical effects. Some marketing mix instruments are primarily strategic instruments though. Some mix instruments on the other hand are primarily tactical (see earlier discussion). The combination of those two explicit classification criteria leads to the fundamental categorization of marketing mix instruments as represented in Table 9.2. The more detailed definitions of the different categories are available in Tables 9.3a and 9.3b.

The columns of Table 9.3 (a and b) represent a classification of the marketing mix instruments on the basis of the generic function they primarily fulfil. Vertically, the marketing mix variables are subdivided according to the criterion of whether the instruments are basic to the consummation of an offer (Table 9.3a) or whether those instruments are more complementary (Table 9.3b). This supplementary mix actually contains the elements fulfilling the previously mentioned 'situational' function that is by definition found in the promotion mix.

Criticism on the marketing mix metaphor and concept

In spite of the immediate and widespread acceptance of the marketing mix concept, it – or sometimes much more the metaphor – has been criticized in several respects.

Table 9.3a   The details of a functional marketing mix classification

Marketing mix	Product mix	Price mix	Communication mix		Publicity mix	Distribution mix
			Mass communication promotion mix	Personal communication mix		
Basic mix	Basic product mix	Basic price mix	Basic mass communication mix	Basic personal communication mix	Basic publicity mix	Basic distribution mix
	Instruments that mainly conceive the way and extent in which the prospective exchange party's needs are satisfied.	Instruments that mainly fix the size and the way of payment exchanged for the goods or services.	Non-personal communication efforts that mainly aim at announcing the offer or maintaining the awareness and knowledge about it; evoking or maintaining favourable feelings and removing barriers to wanting.	Personal communication efforts that mainly aim at announcing the offer or maintaining awareness and knowledge about it; evoking or maintaining favourable feelings and removing barriers to wanting.	Efforts that aim at inciting a third party (persons and authorities) to favourable communication about the offer.	Instruments that mainly determine the intensity and manner of how the goods or services will be made available.
	e.g. product characteristics options, assortment, brand name, packaging, quantity, factory guarantee	e.g. list price, usual terms of payment, usual discounts, terms of credit, long-term savings campaigns	e.g. theme advertising in various media, permanent exhibitions, certain forms of sponsorship	e.g. amount and type of selling, personal remunerations	e.g. press bulletins, press conferences, tours by journalists	e.g. different types of distribution channels, density of the distribution system, trade relation mix (policy of margins, terms of delivery, etc.) merchandising advice

Source: van Waterschoot and Van den Bulte, 1992: 90

Table 9.3b   The details of a functional marketing mix classification

Marketing mix	Product mix	Price mix	Communication mix		Publicity mix	Distribution mix
			Mass communication mix	Personal communication mix		
Promotion mix	Product promotion mix	Price promotion mix	Mass communication promotion mix	Personal communication promotion mix	Publicity promotion mix	Distribution promotion mix
	Supplementary group of instruments that mainly aim at inducing immediate overt behaviour by strengthening the basic product mix during relatively short periods of time.	Supplementary group of instruments that mainly aim at inducing immediate overt behaviour by strengthening the basic price mix during relatively short periods of time.	Supplementary group of instruments that mainly aim at inducing immediate overt behaviour strengthening the basic mass communications mix during relatively short periods of time.	Supplementary group of instruments that mainly aim at inducing immediate overt behaviour strengthening the basic personal communications mix during relatively short periods of time.	Supplementary group of instruments that mainly aim at inducing immediate overt behaviour strengthening the basic publicity communications mix during relatively short periods of time.	Supplementary group of instruments that mainly aim at inducing immediate overt behaviour strengthening the basic distribution mix during relatively short periods of time.
	e.g. economy packs, 3-for-the-price-of-2 deals; temporary luxury options on a car at the price of its standard model	e.g. exceptionally favourable price, end-of-season sales, exceptionally favourable terms of payment and credit, short-term savings campaigns, temporary discounts, coupons	e.g. action advertising, contests, sweepstakes, samples, premiums, trade shows or exhibitions	e.g. temporary demonstrations, salesforce promotions such as salesforce contests	e.g. all measurements to simulate positive publicity about a sales promotion action	e.g. extra point of purchase material, trade promotions such as buying allowances, contests; temporary increase of the number of distribution outlets

Source: van Waterschoot and Van den Bulte, 1992: 90

Van den Bulte (1991) summarized these criticisms under nine headings. The following reflects Van den Bulte's inventory, together with our personal assessment.

The marketing mix concept is accused of applying to micro issues only, because it takes the stance of only one exchange party, namely the seller or the 'cake mixer' or the 'channel captain' rather than the consumer or society at large. Indeed, the channel captain perspective typifies the marketing discipline as a whole, except for those fields where social goals dominate from the outset, as in the case of true charity marketing. The marketing mix concept cannot be criticized in this respect, since the usefulness of a known and classified set of demand impinging instruments – even if suggested by the specific metaphoric expression – is not by its own nature limited to channel captain applications, but can apply to any exchange situation.

A second criticism concerns the concept's limited managerial use in an organizational context, because of its attributed 'lack of attention to the internal tasks of the marketing function, like disseminating information to all people involved in or affected by marketing activities, human resources management, and developing incentive and control systems' (Van den Bulte, 1991: 11). Also, this point of criticism results from unrealistic expectations about a fundamental and powerful but at the same time limited concept. The marketing mix concept has not been developed to encompass guidelines for internal organization and communication. On the other hand, a clearly defined and classified set of demand impinging instruments contributes to a sound demand management. The existence of the mix concept and a sound corresponding classification should be seen as a necessary, but at the same time insufficient, condition for theoretical and practical development.

Valuable research has been conducted regarding interactions and interdependencies between mix variables. The mix concept is criticized because the hypotheses cannot be derived from the metaphor itself. This criticism can again be countered quite easily. The mere inventory of a set of instruments cannot be supposed to encompass a theory about the interactions amongst them. The classification of these instruments, however, to some extent, can. Empirical investigation and theory building rely heavily on the way such instruments are classified. The classification itself, however, cannot be anything more than a solid tool for theory building and empirical investigation, which it cannot replace.

A fourth point of criticism accuses the marketing mix concept of a mechanistic view on markets. The market is often described in terms of response curves, depending on a certain 'parameter' or 'marketing decision variable' or on the entire mix. In this way the optimization problem upon which the concept of the marketing mix focuses is solved. Modelling the relationship between demand impinging instruments and market responses serves analytical and forecasting purposes. Forgetting the limitations and assumptions of the model or technique represents an undeniable risk, which cannot be attributed to the marketing mix as a concept though. Models – whether they are of a stimulus-response or of an interactive type – suppose a sound marketing mix concept and classification, but the characteristics of the former should not be attributed to the latter and vice versa.

A fifth point of criticism comes very close to the previous one. The concept is accused of having a one-way (stimulus-response) character, which would impede marketing from shifting its focus from exchange as an isolated act towards the richer concept of exchange relationships. The marketing mix concept conflicts in no way with an idea of interaction. Indeed, its instruments and their categorization perfectly fit such approaches, as they also fit the idea of an exchange relationship. An exchange relationship supposes, for example, a more pronounced quality and service accent than would a mere one-time exchange.

The concept's poor market orientation also follows from the suggested view of the customer as someone to whom something is done – by the cake mixer – and not as someone for whom something is done. The stimulus-response approach that is attributed to the marketing mix is at the same time criticized for proposing to lump individuals into a market of homogeneous respondents. Presence or absence, as well as degree of market orientation, depends on factors like market structure, power balance between parties, organizational structures and procedures, personal attitudes, and corporate culture, mission and goals. However, to blame the mix concept for causing a lack of market orientation is intellectually incorrect. This basic, but by its very nature limited, concept is a factual device in any market approach.

The mix concept is also criticized for implying a view of the firm (or any exchange-seeking party in general) – perhaps suggested to some people by the picture of the independent cake mixer – as being a rather self-sufficient social unit having access to a considerable resource base. Except for manufacturer-distributor links, the concept would remove resource dependency between social units. As a result the different bridging strategies – such as, for example, bargaining contracting, cooption, joint programmes, licensing, integration, trade associations and government action – are issues that would not be taken into consideration. Once again this is an example of unjustified criticism, resulting from unrealistic expectations. Also, here the argument can be turned round. Inter-organizational 'bridges' will influence the specific marketing mix choice. As such an argument is given not against but in favour of a clear concept and classification.

A further point of criticism concerns the concept's supposed reactive attitude towards the environment.

> **Traditionally, marketing mix proponents have myopically considered the transactional environment to be composed of customers and dealers only, putting all other social units into the category 'contextual', hence lumping them together into faceless environmental forces. Thus blinding themselves, they have not taken into consideration the fact that the links with some transaction-environmental units and the activities these deploy can be changed through lobbying, legal action, public relations, issue advertising, strategic partnering and so on. Finding a way to control or influence variables that were previously considered to be beyond discretion, is often the cornerstone of great marketing creativity and the gateway to superior profitability. (Van den Bulte, 1991: 18)**

This citation contains a major and well-expressed lesson in marketing management. Marketing practice and marketing theory have been putting too much emphasis on their traditional public, but there is no logic in blaming the mix concept for it.

Finally, critics accuse the mix concept of possessing a mechanistic and rational-economic neoclassical view of markets and firms, and stripping out the institutional and social supports to market processes such as attraction, trust, friendship, power and interdependency. As a result, the marketing mix would be 'rendered impotent before many strategic management problems' (Van den Bulte, 1991: 20). In this case the criticism also concerns actual marketing practice as well as the conceptual development that has taken place at an instrumental, tactical and strategic level; the criticism does not hit the mix concept itself though.

Conclusion

The mix concept is quintessential for marketing, as it links generic exchange functions to demand management. Even if unavoidably implied by the new exchange model, it was formulated – more especially under the form of a metaphor – only several decades after the new discipline's name 'marketing' was mentioned for the first time in 1902 as a course title (Bartels, 1962). Even if the marketing discipline, together with the underlying new exchange model and the implied mix concept originated from the consumer goods field, they generically stretch out to any exchange matching the underlying assumptions, including, for example, B2B marketing, service marketing, e-marketing and relationship marketing. That said, the peculiarities of those sub-fields are well worth being studied and also emphasized. Not to the extent, however, that the undeniably universal mix concept would be denied.

The mix metaphor has gained usage spectacularly quickly as a result of its expressiveness, liveliness, compactness and therefore memorability. Equally imaginative has been McCarthy's pragmatic grouping of the instruments. His four Ps classification also received acceptance speedily and easily, presumably as a result of its strong mnemonic appeal. The four Ps have even become synonymous with the marketing mix. They are so closely twinned that they could be considered 'Siamese' twin metaphors (van Waterschoot and De Haes, 2008). The mnemonic row, however, has too often been used as a means of explication of submixes (e.g. in the case of service marketing) or in order to draw attention to marketing aspects that were not always mix issues. Over the years the limitations of the original mnemonic approach have become apparent, amongst other things as a result of the increased importance of promotion instruments in marketing practice. Consequently, the four Ps classification, with its mixing up of strategic and tactical instruments and inherent negatively defined Promotion category within the communication family, has been contested by many authors. Its adaptation, based on modern insight into promotion, significantly improves the original scheme.

The marketing mix concept itself is as elementary, powerful, and at the same time limited in marketing thinking as the alphabet is in the use and development of language. It is therefore unjustifiable to blame the mix concept for the peculiarities of the overall discipline. In the same way the concept cannot be blamed for the limitations of the metaphor, which contributed so significantly to its popularity and understanding during the infancy of the discipline.

The marketing mix concept forms a fundamental building block in theory and practice. A clearly defined, named and classified concept is a necessary, but at the same time insufficient, condition for successful theory building and practical implementation. Marketing theory should concentrate its attention on measuring, explaining and predicting the isolated as well as the combined effects of the mix instruments, as a solid basis for actual practice in diverse fields and circumstances.

Recommended further reading

Allenby, G.M., Arora, N. and Ginter, J.L. (1998) 'On the heterogeneity of demand', *Journal of Marketing Research* 62: 384–89.

Mason, J.B., Mayer, M.L. and Wilkinson, J.B. (1993) *Modern Retailing: Theory and Practice*, 6th edn, Homewood, IL: Richard D. Irwin, Inc.

Payne, A. (1993) *The Essence of Services Marketing*, London: Prentice Hall International.

O'Malley, L., Patterson, M. and Kelly-Holmes, H. (2008) 'Death of a metaphor: reviewing the "marketing as relationships" frame', *Marketing Theory* 8: 167–87.

Shaw, E.H. and Jones, D.G.B. (2005) 'A history of schools of marketing thought', *Marketing Theory* 5: 239–81.

References

Ackoff, R.L. (1981) *Creating the Corporate Future: Plan or Be Planned For*, New York: John Wiley.

Alexander, R.S. (1960) *Marketing Definitions: A Glossary of Marketing Terms*, Chicago: American Marketing Association.

Allenby, G.M., Arora, N. and Ginter, J.L. (1998) 'On the heterogeneity of demand', *Journal of Marketing Research* 62: 384–89.

Bagozzi, R.P. (1975) 'Marketing as exchange', *Journal of Marketing* 39: 32–9.

Bartels, R. (1962) *The Development of Marketing Thought*, Homewood, IL: R.D. Irwin.

Beem, E.R. and Shaffer, H.J. (1981) *Triggers to Action – Some Elements in a Theory of Promotional Inducement* (Report 81–106), Cambridge, MA: Marketing Science Institute.

Booms, B.H. and Bitner, M.J. (1981) 'Marketing strategies and organization structures for service firms', in J.H. Donnelly and W.R. George (eds) *Marketing of Services*, Chicago: American Marketing Association proceedings.

Borden, N. (1964) 'The concept of the marketing mix', *Journal of Advertising Research* 4: 2–7.

Bucklin, L.P. (1966) *A Theory of Distribution Channel Structure*, Berkely, CA: IBER Special Publications.

Bucklin, L.P. (1972) *Competition and Evolution in the Distributive Trades*, Englewood Cliffs, NJ: Prentice Hall.

Cespedes, F.V., Corey, E.R. and Rangan, V.K. (1988) 'Gray markets: causes and results', *Harvard Business Review* 66: 75–82.

Coughlan, A.T., Anderson, E., Stern, L.W. and El-Ansary, A. (2006) *Marketing Channels*, 7th edn, Upper Saddle River, NJ: Pearson Prentice Hall.

Culliton, J.W. (1948) *The Management of Marketing Costs*, Boston, MA: Division of Research, Graduate School of Business Administration, Harvard University.

Frey, A.W. (1956) *The Effective Marketing Mix: Programming for Optimum Results*, Hanover, NH: The Amos Tuck School of Business Administration, Dartmouth College.

Fullerton, R.A. (1988) 'How modern is modern marketing? Marketing's evolution and the myth of the "production era"', *Journal of Marketing* 52: 108–25.

Grönroos, C. (1994) 'From marketing mix to relationship marketing', *Management Decision* 2: 4–20.

Houston, F.S. and Gassenheimer, J.B. (1987) 'Marketing and exchange', *Journal of Marketing* 51: 3–18.

Howard, J.A. (1957) *Marketing Management: Analysis and Decisions*, Homewood, IL: Richard D. Irwin, Inc.

Hunt, S.D. (1991) *Modern Marketing Theory: Critical Issues in the Philosophy of Marketing Science*, Cincinnati, OH: South-Western Publishing Company.

Kotler, P. (1972) 'A generic concept of marketing', *Journal of Marketing* 36: 46–54.

Kotler, P. (1986) 'Megamarketing', *Harvard Business Review* 64: 117–24.

Kotler, P. and Levy, S.L. (1971) 'Demarketing, yes, demarketing', *Harvard Business Review* 49: 71–80.

Lazer, W. and Kelly, E.J. (1962) *Managerial Marketing: Perspectives and Viewpoints*, revised edn, Homewood, IL: Richard D. Irwin, Inc.

McCarthy, E.J. (1960) *Basic Marketing: A Managerial Approach*, Homewood, IL: Richard D. Irwin, Inc.

Möller, K. (2006) 'Comment on: The marketing mix revisited: Towards the 21st Century Marketing by E. Constantinides', *Journal of Marketing Management* 22: 439–50.

Van den Bulte, C. (1991) *The Concept of the Marketing Mix Revisited: A Case Analysis of Metaphor in Marketing Theory and Management*, Ghent, Belgium: The Vlerick School of Management, University of Ghent.

van Waterschoot, W. (2000) 'The marketing mix as a creator of differentiation', in K. Blois (ed.) *The Oxford Textbook of Marketing*, Oxford: Oxford University Press, pp. 183–211.

van Waterschoot, W. and De Haes, J. (2008) 'Marketing mix metaphorosis: the heavy toll of too much popularity', in P.J. Kitchen (ed.) *Marketing Metaphors and Metamorphosis*, Basingstoke: Palgrave Macmillan, pp. 42–61.

van Waterschoot, W. and Van den Bulte, C. (1992) 'The 4P classification of the marketing mix revisited', *Journal of Marketing* 56: 83–93.

van Waterschoot, W., Lagasse, L. and Bilsen, R. (2006) *Marketing Beleid: Theorie en Praktijk*, 11th revised edn, Antwerpen: De Boeck.

10

Marketing strategy

Robin Wensley

Introduction

Marketing strategy sometimes claims to provide an answer to one of the most difficult questions in our understanding of competitive markets: how to recognize and achieve an economic advantage which endures. In attempting to do so, marketing strategy, as with the field of strategy itself, has had to address the continual balance between strategy formulation and strategic implementation. At the same time, it has also had to address a perhaps more fundamental question: how far, at least from a demand or market perspective, can we ever develop general rules for achieving enduring economic advantage.

_____ Strategy: from formulation to implementation _____

From the late 1960s to the mid-1980s at least, management strategy seemed to be inevitably linked to issues of product-market selection and hence to marketing strategy. Perhaps ironically this was not primarily or even mainly as a result of the contribution of marketing scholars or indeed practitioners. The most significant initial contributors, such as Bruce Henderson and Michael Porter, both to be found at or closely linked to the Harvard Business School, were neither located within Marketing. However in various institutions the marketing academics were not slow to recognize what was going on and also to see that the centrality of product-market choice linked well with the importance attached to marketing. This expansion of the teaching domain had a much less significant impact on the research agenda and activity within marketing itself, where the focus continued to underplay the emerging importance of the competitive dimension (Day and Wensley, 1983). Hence the relatively atheoretical development continued into the process of codification of this new area, most obviously in the first key text by Abell and Hammond (1979), which was based on a, by then, well established second year MBA option at Harvard.

In retrospect, this period was the high point for the uncontested impact of competitive market related analysis on strategic management practice. With the advantage of hindsight, it is clear that a serious alternative perspective was also developing, most obviously signalled by Peters and Waterman (1982), which was to have a very substantial impact on the what was taught in strategic management courses and what was marketed by consultancies.

As the decade progressed, it was inevitable that at least to some degree each side recognized the other as a key protagonist. Perhaps one of the most noteworthy cases is that in which Waterman (1988) challenged the value of a Porter-based analysis of competition. Equally, the economists did not take such attacks lying down: Kay (1993) attempted to wrest back the intellectual dominance in matters of corporate strategy and Porter (1990) extended his domain to the nation-state itself. In terms of the disciplinary debate, what was originally broadly a debate between economists and sociologists, now also involved psychologists, social anthropologists, and, if they are a distinct discipline, systems theorists.

However, the key change in emphasis can be summarized as from analysis to process, from formulation to implementation. Perhaps the single most important contributor to this change has been Henry Mintzberg, who has developed over the period an extensive critique of, what he calls the 'Design School' in strategic management, culminating in his 1994 book. Since then, he has extended his critique to the domain of management teaching, particularly MBAs, rather than just strategic planning (Mintzberg, 2004). Overall, whilst his approach and indeed critique of strategy analysis is itself rather polemical and overstated, there is little doubt that the general emphasis in strategic management has shifted significantly towards implementation and away from formulation and planning.

The nature of the competitive market environment

As our analysis of marketing strategy has developed over the last 35 years, so our representation of the marketing context has also changed. In particular there was much less recognition of competitors and distribution was clearly seen as a solely logistical function in the 1970s. On top of this, customers were often very much represented as 'at a distance', with intermediaries such as advertising agencies and market research companies. More recently, marketing has recognized much more explicitly a further range of issues including the key role of competition and the importance of a longer term so-called relationship perspective, particularly in the context of customers. On top of this, various entities in the distribution chain are now clearly seen as very active intermediaries rather than just passive logistics agents.

However, the development of this more complex dynamic representation of the competitive market, which can be represented broadly in the marketing strategy triangle of the 3Cs: customers, competitors and channels, also implies a more fluid and complex environment within which to understand the nature of competitive advantage.

Customers, competitors and channels

The early more static model of the nature of the competitive market, which informed many of the still current tools of analysis was both positional and non-interactive. It was assumed that the market backcloth, often referred to as the product-market space, remained relatively stable and static so that at least in terms of first order effects, strategies could be defined in positional terms. Similarly, the general perspective, was that actions by the firm would generally not create equivalent reactions from the relatively passive 'consumers'.

With the adoption of the more interactive and dynamic perspective implied in the 3Cs approach the nature of market-based strategy becomes much more complex. We must be wary of the temptation to continue to apply the old tools and concepts without considering critically whether they are appropriate in new situations. They represent in general a special or limiting case which quite often distorts the nature of the environment that we are attempting to characterize. How far is this distortion, as our legal colleagues would say, material, is another but frequently unresolved matter. This notion of materiality is really linked to impact on actions rather than just understanding and the degree to which in practice particular forms of marketing strategy analysis encourage actions which are inappropriate.

This chapter is mainly written around the assumption that we need to recognize in using these simplifying approaches, that: (i) the degree to which they actually explain the competitive performance outcomes of interest will be limited; and (ii) the underlying assumptions can cause unintentional biases.

The evolution of analysis, interpretation and modelling in marketing strategy from customers to competitors to channels

Given that the underlying representation of the competitive market environment has changed, so, not surprisingly, have our processes of analysis, interpretation and modelling. Initially the key focus was on customer-based positioning studies in particular product-market space. Such work remains a key component in the analysis of much market research data, but from the marketing strategy perspective we need to recognise that the dimensionality of the analytical space has often been rather low, indeed in some situations little more than a single price dimension which has been seen as highly correlated with an equivalent quality dimension.

The increased emphasis on the analysis of competitors has also required us to make certain compromises. One, of course, relates to the balance between three forms termed public information, legitimate inference and private information. The other to the fact that our colleagues in business strategy now give emphasis to two rather different perspectives on the nature of competitive firms, one essentially based on similarities (strategic groups: McGee and Thomas, 1986) and the other on differences (resource based view (RBV): Wernerfeld, 1984, 1995). Sound competitor analysis should at least enable us to avoid making inconsistent assumptions, particularly in the context of public data, like, for instance, assuming that we will be able to exploit an opportunity which is known to all, without a significant amount of competitive reaction.

Finally there is the question of channels or, in more general terms, supply chains. The issue of retailers in particular as independent and significant economic intermediaries rather than just logistical channels to the final consumer has been an important consideration in consumer marketing at least since the 1970s. Similarly in industrial markets the issue of the supply chain and the central importance of some form of organization and coordination of the various independent entities within the chain has been seen as an increasingly important strategic issue. Both these developments have meant that any strategic marketing analysis needs to find ways to evaluate the likely impact of such independent strategies pursued by intermediaries, although in many cases our tools and techniques for doing this remain rather limited and often rely on no more than an attempt to speculate on what might be their preferred strategic action.

Beyond this there has been a broader attempt to introduce what has become known as relationship marketing. It is outside the remit of this chapter to provide a full overview but from a strategic viewpoint there are two important issues that need to be emphasized. The first is that a recognition of the relatively stable pattern of transaction relationship within, particularly, most industrial markets, often described as the 'markets as networks' perspective is not necessarily the same as a more prescriptive notion of the need to manage such relationships. The second is that whilst the relationship perspective rightly moves our attention away from individual transactions towards patterns of interaction over longer time periods it often seems to assume that the motivations of each party are symmetric. In both consumer (Fournier et al., 1998) and industrial markets (Faria and Wensley, 2002) this may prove to be a very problematic assumption.

The codification of marketing strategy analysis in terms of three strategies, four boxes and five forces

What can now be regarded as 'traditional' marketing strategy analysis was developed primarily in the 1970s. It was codified in various ways, including the strategic triangle as developed by Ohmae (1982), based on customers, competitors and the corporation. The most significant elements in such analysis can defined in terms of the three generic strategies, the four boxes (or perhaps more appropriately strategic contexts), and the five forces.

These particular frameworks also represent the substantial debt that marketing strategy owes to economic analysis; the three strategies and the five forces are directly taken from Michael Porter's influential work, which derived from his earlier work in Industrial Organization (IO) Economics. The four contexts was initially popularized by the Boston Consulting Group under Bruce Henderson, again strongly influenced by microeconomic analysis. Whilst each of these approaches became a significant component in much marketing strategy teaching (see Morrison and Wensley, 1991), we also need to recognize some of the key considerations and critical assumptions hold in any application.

The three strategies

Porter really reintroduced the standard economic notion of scale to the distinction between cost and differentiation to arrive at the three generic strategies of focus, cost and differentiation. Indeed, in his later formulation of the three strategies they really became four in that he suggested, rightly, that the choice between an emphasis on competition via cost or differentiation can be made at various scales of operation.

With further consideration it is clear that both of these dimensions are themselves not only continuous but also likely to be the aggregate of a number of relatively independent elements or dimensions. Hence scale is in many contexts not just a single measure of volume of finished output but also of relative volumes of sub-assemblies and activities which may well be shared. This is even truer in the case of 'differentiation', where we can expect that there are various different ways in which any supplier attempts to differentiate their offerings. On top of this, a number of other commentators, most particularly John Kay (1993), have noted that not only might the cost-differentiation scale be continuous rather than dichotomous but it also might not be seen as a real dimension at all. At some point this could become a semantic squabble but there clearly is an important point that many successful strategies are built around a notion of good value for money rather than a pure emphasis on cost or differentiation at any price. Michael Porter (1980) might describe this as a 'middle' strategy but he has consistently claimed that there is a severe danger of getting 'caught in the middle'. In fact it might be reasonable to assume that in many cases being in the middle is the best place to be: after all, Porter never presented significant and substantial systematic evidence to support his own assertion (cf. Wensley, 1994) .

_____ The four contexts _____

The four boxes (contexts) relates to the market share/market growth matrix originally developed by the Boston Consulting Group (BCG) under Bruce Henderson. Although inevitably a whole range of different matrix frameworks has emerged since the early days the BCG, one remains an outstanding exemplar not only because of its widespread popularity and impact, nowadays even University vice-chancellors have been heard to use terms such as 'cash cow', but because there was an underlying basic economic logic in its development. Many other similar frameworks just adopted the rather tautologous proposition that one should invest in domains which were both attractive and where one had comparative advantage!

The market growth/market share matrix however still involved a set of key assumptions which were certainly contestable. In particular, alongside the relatively uncontroversial one that in general over time the growth rate in markets tends to decline, there were the assumptions that it was in some sense both easier to gain market share in higher growth rate markets, and also that the returns to such gains were likely to be of longer duration. However, it could be that early investment in market share is inherently more risky so yields, on average, better returns and that there are other ways of dealing with such risks. Yet companies can benefit from a focus on market share position when it encourages them to place greater emphasis on the marketing fundamentals for a particular business.

More generally, the matrix as an analytical device suffers from some of the problems which we illustrated for the three strategies approach: an analysis which is essentially based on extreme points when in practice many of the portfolio choices are actually around the centre of the matrix. This implies that any discrimination between business units needs to be on the basis of much more specific analysis rather than broad general characteristics.

_____ Five forces _____

The five forces analysis was originally introduced by Michael Porter to emphasize the extent to which the overall basis of competition was much wider than just the rivalries between established competitors in a particular market. Whilst not exactly novel as an insight, particularly in suggesting that firms also face competition from new entrants and substitutes, it was presented in a very effective manner and served to emphasize not only the specific and increasing importance of competition, as we discussed, but also the extent to which competition should be seen as a much wider activity within the value chain as Porter termed it.

Porter used the term value chain when in essence he was concentrating more on the chain of actual costs. Whilst ex post from an economic point of view, there is no difference between value and cost, it is indeed the process of both competition and collaboration between various firms and intermediaries which finally results in the attribution of value throughout the relevant network. In this sense, as others have recognized, a supply chain is an intermediate organization form where there is a higher degree of cooperation between the firms within the chain and a greater degree of competition between the firms within different chains. In this context Porter's analysis has tended to focus much more clearly on the issue of competition rather than cooperation. Indeed, at least in its representational form, it has tended to go further than this and focus attention on the nature of the competitive pressures on the firm itself rather than on the interaction between the firm and other organizations in the marketplace.

The search for generic rules
for success amidst diversity

As we have suggested above, the codification of marketing strategy was based on three essential schema. This schemata, whilst it was based on some valid theoretical concepts, did not really provide a systematic approach to the central question, that is, the nature of sustained economic performance in the competitive market place. Whilst such an objective was clearly recognized in the so-called search for Sustainable Competitive Advantage (Day and Wensley, 1988), there remained concerns as to whether such a notion was realistic given the dynamic and uncertain nature of the competitive marketplace (Dickinson, 1992).

Indeed not only is it dynamic and uncertain but it is also diverse: firms are heterogeneous and so is the nature of demand. A useful way of looking at demand side heterogeneity is from the user perspective directly. Arguably from its relatively early origins, marketing or at least the more functional focused study of marketing management, has been concerned with managerially effective ways of responding to this heterogeneity, particularly in terms of market segmentation. Whilst there remains a substantial debate about the degree to which this market-based heterogeneity is indeed 'manageable' from a marketing perspective (cf. Saunders, 1995; Wensley, 1995), our concern at the moment is to consider the degree to which such diversity on both the supply and demand side facilitates or negates the possibility of developing robust 'rules for success'.

To address this question, we need to consider the most useful way of characterizing the competitive market process. Let us consider the field of ecology where we observe wide diversity in terms of both species and habitat as well as high interactivity. There are two critical aspects which must inform any attempt to transfer this analogy into the field of strategy. The first is the interactive relationship between any species and its habitat, nicely encapsulated in the title of the book by Levins and Leowontin (1985): *The Dialectical Biologist*. Particularly in the context of strategy, it is important to recognize that the habitat (for which read market domain) evolves and develops at least as fast as the species (for which, rather more problematically, read the individual firm).

The second aspect addresses directly our question of 'rules for success'. How far can we identify, particularly through the historical record, whether there are any reliable rules for success for particular species characteristics? Of course, it is very difficult to address this question without being strongly influenced by hindsight and most observations are seen as contentious.

It would seem that we should at least be very cautious in any search for rules for success amidst a world of interactive diversity. Hence we should hardly be surprised that marketing strategy analysis does not provide for consistent and sustainable individual success in the competitive marketplace. However, we do have a set of theoretical frameworks and practical tools which at least allow us to represent some of the key dynamics of both customer and competitive behaviour in a way which ensures we avoid errors of inconsistency or simple naivety.

As we have discussed above, most analysis in marketing strategy is informed by what are essentially economic frameworks and so tend to focus attention on situations in which both the competitive structure of the market and the nature of consumer preferences are relatively well established. As we move our attention to more novel situations these structures tend to be at best indeterminate and therefore the analytical frameworks less appropriate. We encounter the first of many ironies in the nature of marketing strategy analysis. It is often least applicable in the very situations in which there is a real opportunity for a new source of economic advantage based on a restructuring of either or both the competitive environment and consumer preferences.

Models of competition: game theory versus evolutionary ecology

To develop a formal approach to the modelling of competitive behaviour we need to define:

1. The nature of the arena in which the competitive activity takes place

2. The structure or rules which govern the behaviour of the participants

3. The options available in terms of competitor behaviour (when these consist of a sequence of actions through time, or over a number of 'plays', then they are often referred to in game theory as strategies).

In this section, however, we particularly wish to contrast game theory approaches which in many ways link directly to the economic analysis to which we have already referred and look in more detail at analogies from evolutionary biology which raise difficult questions about the inherent feasibility of any systematic model building at the level of the individual firm.

Game theory models of competition

A game theory model is characterized by a set of rules which describe: (1) the number of firms competing against each other; (2) the set of actions that each firm can take at each point in time; (3) the profits that each firm will realize for each set of competitive actions; (4) the time pattern of actions – whether they occur simultaneously or one firm moves first? and (5) the nature of information about competitive activity – who knows what, when? The notion of rationality also plays a particularly important role in models of competitive behaviour. Rationality implies a link between actions and intentions but not common intentions between competitors. Models describing competitive activity are designed to understand the behaviour of 'free' economic agents. Thus, these models start with an assumption of 'weak' rationality – the agents will take actions that are consistent with their longer-term objectives. The models also assume a stronger form of rationality – the intentions of the agents can be expressed in terms of a number of economic measures of outcome states such as profit, sales, growth, or market share objectives.

Do the results of game theory models indicate how firms should act in competitive situations? Do the models describe the evolution of competitive interactions in the real world? These questions have spawned a lively debate among management scientists concerning the usefulness of game theory models. Kadane and Larkey (1982) suggested that game theory models are conditionally normative and conditionally descriptive. The results do indicate how firms should behave given a set of assumptions about the alternatives, the payoffs, and the properties of an 'optimal' solution (the equilibrium). Similarly, game theory results describe the evolution of competitive strategy but only given a very specific set of assumptions.

The seemingly unrealistic and simplistic nature of the competitive reactions incorporated in game theory models and the nature of the equilibrium concept led some marketers to question the managerial relevance of these models (Dolan, 1981). However, all models involve simplifying assumptions, and game theory models, whilst often highly structured, underpin most attempts to apply economic analysis to issues of competition among a limited number of firms. Indeed, as Goeree and Holt (2001) observe: 'Game theory has finally gained the central role ... in some areas of economics (e.g. industrial organization) virtually all recent developments are applications of game theory' (2001: 1402).

Evolutionary Ecological Analogies

Evolutionary ecology has also emerged as a popular analogy for understanding the types of market-based strategies pursued by companies (Coyle, 1986; Lambkin and Day, 1989). These analogies have been previously used to describe both the nature of the competitive process itself (Henderson, 1983) as well as the notion of 'niche' strategy (Hofer and Schendel, 1977).

Organizational theorists and sociologists have adopted an ecological model, describing the growth of a specie in an ecology, to describe the types of firms in an environment. Environments are described by two dimensions: variability and frequency of environmental change. In a highly variable environment, changes are dramatic, and fundamentally different strategic responses are required for survival. In contrast, strategic alterations are not required to cope with an environment of low variability. A specialist strategy in which high performance occurs in a narrow portion of the environment is surprisingly more appropriate when environmental changes are dramatic and frequent. Under these conditions, it is unlikely that a generalist would have sufficient flexibility to cope with the wide range of environmental conditions it would face, whilst the specialist can at least out-perform it in a specific environment. A generalist strategist is most appropriate in an environment characterized by infrequent, minor changes because this environment allows the generalist to exploit its large-scale efficiencies.

_____ Comparing the key elements in different models of competition ____

The strategic groups and mobility barriers in the Industrial Organization economics approach recognize the critical asymmetries between competing firms. It identifies three methods by which firms can isolate themselves from competition: (1) differentiation; (2) cost efficiency; and (3) collusion, although the third approach has tended to be ignored. The developments within the IO paradigm have therefore tended to usefully focus on the nature and significance of various mechanisms for isolating the firm from its competition. The evolutionary ecological analogy, on the other hand, focuses on the notion of scope with the general distinction between specialists and generalists. The ecological approach also raises interesting questions about the form, level and type of 'organization' that we are considering. In particular we need to recognize most markets as forms of organization in their own right, as those who have argued the 'markets as networks' approach have done, and question how far we can justify an exclusive focus on the firm as the key organization unit. Finally, the analogy raises more directly the concern about the interaction between various different units (species) and their evolving habitat. The marketplace, like the habitat, can become relatively unstable and so both affect and be affected by the strategies of individual firms.

As we have suggested, any analogy is far from perfect, as we would expect. The limitations are as critical as the issues that are raised because they give us some sense of the bounds within which the analogy itself is likely to be useful. Extending it outside these bounds is likely to be counter-productive and misleading.

The IO approach in practice tends to neglect the interaction between cost and quality. We have already suggested that while the notion of 'focus' within this analogy is an attempt to recognize this problem; it is only partially successful because it subsumes a characteristic of any successful competitive strategy into one generic category. We must further consider the extent to which we can reasonably reliably distinguish between the various forms of mixed strategies over time and the extent to which the strategic groups themselves remain stable.

The limitations of analogies from evolutionary ecology are more in terms of the questions that are not answered than those where the answers are misleading. The nature of 'competition' is both unclear and complex, there is confusion as to the level and appropriate unit of analysis, and the notion of 'niche', which has become so current in much strategy writing, overlooks the fact that by definition every species has one anyway.

Characterizing marketing strategy in terms of evolving differentiation in time and space

Central to any notion of competition from a marketing strategy viewpoint is the issue of differentiation in time and space. In a 'real' market: (i) demand is heterogeneous; (ii) suppliers are differentiated; and (iii) there are processes of feedback and change through time. Clearly these three elements interact significantly, yet in most cases we find that to reduce the overall complexity in our analysis and understanding we treat each item relatively independently. For instance, in most current treatments of these issues in marketing strategy we would use some form of *market segmentation* schema to map heterogeneous demand, some notion of the *resource-based view* of the firm to reflect the differentiation amongst suppliers and some model of market evolution such as the *product life-cycle* to reflect the nature of the time dynamic.

Such an approach has two major limitations which may act to remove any benefit from the undoubted reduction of analytical complexity by looking at three sub-systems rather than the whole system. First it assumes implicitly that this decomposition is reasonably first order correct: that the impact of the individual elements is more important than their interaction effects. To examine this assumption critically we need some alternative form of analysis and representation such as modelling the phenomena of interest as the co-evolution of firms and customers in a dynamic phase space, which allows for the fact that time and space interact. Second, it assumes that the ways of representing the individual elements that we use – in particular market segmentation and product life-cycle concepts – are in fact robust representations of the underlying phenomena. In terms of the adequacy of each element in its own terms, we need to look more closely at the ways in which individual improvements may be achieved and finally we might wish to consider whether it would be better to model partial interactions, say between two elements only rather than the complete system.

Differentiation in space: issues of market segmentation

The analysis of spatial competition has of course a long history, stretching back at least to the classical Hotelling model of linear competition such as that faced by the two ice cream sellers on the sea-front. In marketing, the competitive space is generally characterized in terms of market segmentation. There is by now a very large body of empirical work in the general field of market segmentation but even so there remain some critical problems. In particular:

1. We have evidence that the cross-elasticities with respect to different marketing mix elements are likely to be not only of different orders but actually imply different structures of relationship between individual product offerings.

2. Competitive behaviour patterns, which, after all, in a strict sense determine the nature of the experiment from which the elasticities can be derived, seem to be, to use a term coined by Leeflang and Wittick (1993), 'out of balance' with the cross-elasticity data itself.

For the purposes of this chapter we wish to concentrate on the specific question as to how far segmentation provides us with an appropriate definition of the space within which competition evolves. In this sense the key questions are, as we discussed above, about the dimensionality of the space concerned, the stability of the demand function and the degree of mobility for individual firms (or more correctly individual offerings) in terms of repositioning.

These are in practice very difficult questions to deal with for two critical reasons:

(i) The nature of the choice process is such that for many offerings, individual consumers choose from a portfolio of items rather than merely make exclusive choices, and, hence, in principle it is difficult to isolate the impact of one offering from the others in the portfolio.

(ii) The dimensions of the choice space are often inferred from the responses to current offerings and therefore it is difficult to distinguish between the effects of current offerings and some notion of an underlying set of preference structures.

Segmentation and positioning

In principle we can describe the nature of spatial competition in a market either in demand terms or in supply terms. Market segmentation represents the demand perspective on structure whilst competitive positioning represents the supply perspective. Market segmentation takes as its starting point assumptions about the differing requirements that individual customers have with respect to bundles of benefits in particular use situations. Most obviously in this context it is an 'ideal' approach in that it is effectively assumed that each customer can/does specify their own ideal benefit bundle and their purchase choice in the relevant use situation is based on proximity to this ideal point. In consumer psychology this is equivalent to an assumption that individuals have strong and stable preferences.

The competitive positioning approach uses consumer judgements, normally on an aggregate basis to the similarities and differences between specific competitive offerings. In principle this provides an analytical output roughly equivalent to the spatial distribution in the Hotelling model. Such an analysis can also be used to provide an estimate of the dimensionality of the discriminant space, but in many situations for ease of presentation the results are presented in a constrained 2D format. Equally benefit segmentation studies can be used along with techniques such as factor analysis to try and arrive at an estimate of the dimensionality of the demand side.

We can be reasonably certain that the attitude space for customers in any particular market is generally, say, $N>3$: factor analytical studies might suggest at least four or five in general and that of competitive offerings is of at least a similar order. Indeed in the last case if we considered the resource-based view (RBV) of the firm very seriously we might go for a dimensionality as high as the number of competitors.

Of more interest from a strategy point of view is how we represent what happens in terms of actual purchase behaviour in a competitive market through time. There have been a number of attempts to apply segmentation analysis to behavioural data with much less information as to attitudes or intention. In one of the more detailed of such studies, Chintagunta (1994) focused on the degree to which the data analysis reveals interesting differences in terms of brand position as shown by individual purchase patterns through time. He suggested that the dimensionality of the revealed competitive space was two-dimensional but even this might be really an over-estimate. It would appear that we can rather surprisingly reduce the effective competitive space to a single dimension with the possibility of only some second order anomalies (Wensley, 1996).

A simple model of spatial competition might therefore be one in which a considerable amount of competition can be seen as aligned along a single dimension, in circumstances in which multiple offerings are possible, and where there is no reason to believe a priori that individual offerings will be grouped either by common brand or specification, with a fixed entry cost for each item and a distribution of demand which is multi-modal. To this extent it may actually be true that the very simplifications that many criticize in the Porter 'three generic strategies' approach may be reasonably appropriate in building a first order model of competitive market evolution (see Campbell-Hunt, 2000). In the short-run, following the notion of 'clout' and 'vulnerability' (Cooper and Nakanishi, 1988), we might also expect that changes in position in this competitive dimension could be a function of a whole range of what might often be seen as tactical as well as strategic marketing actions.

We must now consider, however, particularly in the context of understanding the time-based nature of market strategies, how we might incorporate in more detail a longer term time dimension with a stronger customer focus.

Differentiation in time: beyond the PLC. Characterizing the nature of competitive market evolution

Few management concepts have been so widely accepted or thoroughly criticised as the product life cycle (Lambkin and Day, 1989: 4)

The product life-cycle has the advantage that it does represent the most simple form of path development for any product (introduction, growth, maturity, decline) but as has been widely recognized, this remains a highly stylized representation of the product sales pattern for most products during their lifetime. Whilst it is reasonably clear that it is difficult, if not impossible, to propose a better single generic time pattern, any such pattern is subject to considerable distortion as a result of interactions with changes in technology as well as both customer and competitor behaviour.

Lambkin and Day (1989) suggested that an understanding of the process of product-market evolution required a more explicit distinction between issues of the demand system, the supply system and the resource environment. However, they chose to emphasize the nature of the demand evolution primarily in terms of diffusion processes. This approach tends to underestimate the extent to which demand side evolution is as much about the way(s) in which the structure of the demand space is changing as the issue of aggregate demand itself.

Later work on the process of market evolution, partly building on some the ideas developed by Lambkin and Day (1989), has attempted to incorporate some insights from, amongst other areas, evolutionary ecology. In particular, work on the extensive

Disk-drive database, which gives quarterly data on all disk drive manufacturers allowed Christensen (1997) to look at the ways in which at the early stages in the market development, the existence of competitive offerings seems to encourage market growth whereas at later stages the likelihood of firm exit increases with firm density. Other computer-related industries have also provided the opportunity for empirical work on some of the issues relating to both the impact of standardization and modularization and the nature of generation effects (Sanchez, 1995), although in the latter case it must be admitted that the effects themselves can sometimes be seen as a result of marketing actions in their own right.

The nature of research in marketing strategy: fallacies of free lunches and the nature of answerable research questions. Distinguishing between information about means, variances and outliers

As we indicated at the start of this chapter, much research in marketing strategy has attempted to address what is in some senses an impossible question: what is the basic and general nature of a successful competitive marketing strategy. This presumes the equivalent of a free lunch. Before we explore this issue further we need to establish a few basic principles. The competitive process is such that:

1. Average performance can only produce average results which in the general nature of a competitive system means that success is related to above average and sometimes even outlier levels of performance.

2. We can expect our competitors to be able on average to interpret any public data to reveal profitable opportunities as well as we can. In more direct terms it means that on average competitors are as clever or as stupid as we are. The route to success cannot lie in simply exploiting public information in an effective manner, although such a strategy may enable a firm to improve its own performance.

3. As we have discussed above, the basis of individual firm or unit performance is a complex mix of both firm, competitor and market factors. We therefore can expect that any attempt to explain performance will be subject to considerable error given that it is difficult, if not impossible, to identify an adequate range of variables which cover both the specifics of the firm's own situation and the details of the market and competitor behaviour.

For these reasons empirical research in marketing strategy, as in the strategy field as a whole, has almost always tended to be in one of the two categories:

(i) database, quantitative analysis which has relied on statistical and econometric approaches to produce results which indicate certain independent variables which on average correlate with performance. As McCloskey and Ziliak (1996) indicated more generally in econometric work, there is a danger that we often confuse statistical significance with what they term economic significance. This notion of economic significance can be decomposed into two elements: firstly the extent to which the relationship identified actually relates to a significant proportion of the variation in the dependent variable, and second the extent to which, even if it does, this regularity actually enables one to produce a clear prescription for managerial action.

(ii) case-study based research on selected firms, often around outliers such as those that perform particularly well. Here the problems are the extent to which the story which is told about the particular nature of the success concerned can be used to guide action in other organizations. In practice this often results in managerial prescriptions that are at best rather tautological and at worst meaningless.

We will now consider examples of both types of this research.

Market share and ROI: the 10 per cent rule in practice

One of the most famous results from the PIMS database was that first reported by Bob Buzzell, Brad Gale and Ralph Sultan in the *Harvard Business Review* in 1975 under the title 'Market share: a key to profitability'. They reported on the relationship between ROI and market share on a cross-sectional basis within the then current PIMS database. Although over the years estimates of the R^2 of this relationship have varied, it generally shows a value of only around 10 per cent up to a maximum of 15 per cent. In their original article Buzzell, Gale and Sultan 'removed' much of the variation by calculating cohort means.

The cohort mean approach, although now not commonly used in empirical research of this sort, normally shows some deviations from the straight line trend but as samples get even larger the deviations get, on average, even smaller: indeed some textbook representations of the results go as far as merely illustrating the trend with no deviations at all. Hence in the process of producing a clearer message from the data we have eliminated nearly nine-tenths of the variability in our performance variable.

What does it mean and what about the 'unexplained' 90 per cent?

In developing our understanding of what such a result actually means, the first set of problems relate to the nature of the data itself and the way in the which the axes are measured. In most analysis of this sort, and in the PIMS data as we discussed above, the data is essentially cross-sectional and averaged out over a fixed period. It therefore excludes any lead or lag effects and also compensates for particular one-off effects only to the extent that they are already discounted from the input data which is normally based on management accounts. The nature of the axes in a standard market share/ROI analysis is also a problem in that they are both ratios. There are very considerable advantages that accrue from using ratios in this situation: most obviously the fact that it is possible to plot on the same graph units of very different absolute sizes, but we do then have the problem of measurement errors in both the numerator and denominator for both axes.

Finally, the basic data is also inevitably limited in the extent to which it can measure the specifics of any particular business unit situation. Using basic financial and accounting data we cannot take into account issues such as managerial effectiveness as well as the degree of integration to achieve scale economies and efficiencies in terms of marketing and other functional activities.

However, we must also put this overall critique of 'market share/return' analysis in context. We should not underestimate the original impact of the 'market share' discovery. Even if it only 'explains' around 10 per cent of financial performance, this is still a considerable achievement. The problem is that, as we have seen, even at this level we face difficult interpretation problems. In the end, one perhaps concludes that its greatest impact was merely that it legitimized debate and discussion about key competitive market assumptions in any strategy dialogue.

Getting to management action: the additional problem of economics

Even if we can identify the source of a particular success or indeed the cause of a particular failure it is a big jump to assuming that suitable action can be taken at no cost or even at a cost which is justified by the subsequent benefits.

We therefore need to overlay our notion of practical significance with one of economic significance: a factor or set of factors which explain a significant proportion of success can also be used as a decision rule for subsequent successful management action. This is a big jump. To return to the market share/ROI relationship even if we conclude that there is a significant correlation between market share and profitability we have to make two further assumptions to justify an economic rule of 'investing' in market share. First we have to move from the more general notion of 'correlation' or 'explanation' to the much more specific one of 'causation' and, second, we have to assume that whatever its benefits market share is somehow under-priced. If our first assumption is correct then broadly it can only be under-priced if either our competitors, both current and potential, have a different view, or, for some unspecified reason, happen to value the asset (market share) significantly lower then we do. In fact in specific situations this latter assumption could hold: our competitors will value the benefits given their differing portfolio of assets and market positions but it all depends on the specifics and the details of the individual situation rather than the general picture.

In the end, it is likely that the continued search for general rules for strategic success via statistical analysis and large databases will prove illusory. This does not make the research effort worthless, we merely have to be realistic about what can and cannot be achieved. After all, the in-depth case study narrative approach, which we will consider shortly, often results in another type of economic rule: the truth which is virtually impossible to apply in general. Perhaps the best example is to be found in Peters and Waterman's original work. Amongst many memorable criteria for success to be found in *In Search of Excellence* (1982) was that undeniable one: the achievement of simultaneous 'loose–tight' linkages. To those who thought that this might seem contradictory Peters and Waterman provided the helpful observation that: 'These are the apparent contradictions that turn out in practice not to be contradictions at all' (1982: 320).

_____ The Honda case: interpreting success _____

One of the best known examples of a case history which has been interpreted to generate a number of marketing strategy lessons is the case of Honda and their entry into the American motorcycle market.

In summary, the original consultancy study conducted for the UK government by the Boston Consulting Group interpreted the success that Honda enjoyed in the USA, particularly at the expense of UK imports, as the result of substantial economies of scale for their small bikes based on the Cub model along with a market entry strategy to identify and exploit a new segment and set of customers. Richard Pascale, on the other hand, interviewed a number of the key executives who had worked for American Honda at the time and they told a story which suggested the whole operation was very much working on a shoestring and the final success was down to a number of lucky breaks including a buyer from Sears persuading them to let him sell their small model bikes when they were really trying, and failing, to break into the big bike market.

In the later debate, Goold who worked for BCG at the time, focused attention on the 10 per cent that can be explained analytically whilst Mintzberg argued that a realization of specific causes of success can be achieved more effectively through processes such as learning (Goold, 1996; Mintzberg, 1996a, 1996b). This is in practice a strong assertion about the efficacy of learning processes in organizations that others might dispute.

Hence the same story can be interpreted in very different ways. One of the underlying dilemmas for Honda, as indeed for any new market entrant, was that if they took the existing market structure as fixed and given then the possibilities for them were remote; on the other hand market knowledge could only really hint at possibilities for new market structures.

The recourse to processes, people and purpose in _____ marketing as well as strategy as a whole _____

More recently in marketing strategy, as in strategy as a whole, there has been a move away from analysis based on real substantive recommendations for management action towards a concern more for processes, people and purposes rather than structure, strategies and systems. This change in emphasis was particularly introduced by Bartlett and Ghoshal (1995) in their influential *Harvard Business Review* article.

Whilst this shift can be seen as a reasonable response to our lack of substantive and generalizable knowledge about the nature of successful marketing strategies in a competitive marketplace, as we have discussed above, it should also be seen as one which itself has rather limited evidence to support it. In marketing strategy in particular, two areas can be identified where this trend has been very evident and we will look critically at both of these: the shift towards a focus on networks and relationship marketing and the increased emphasis on marketing processes within the firm.

———————— Markets as networks ————————————

It is clear, as Easton (1990) has indicated, that actual firm relationships must be seen on a spectrum between outright competition at one end and collusion at the other. At the very least, such a self evident observation raises the issue of the firm (or business unit) as the basic, and often only, unit of analysis: in certain circumstances we might more appropriately consider an informal coalition of such firms as the key unit.

However, the recognition that there is a network of relationships is merely the first step. Approaches need to be developed for the analysis of the network. Hakansson (1987) has, for instance, suggested that the key elements of any network are actors, activities and resources. He also suggests that the overall network is bound together by a number of forces including functional interdependence, as well as power, knowledge and time-related structure.

There is a danger in confusing a detailed descriptive model with a simple but robust predictive one, let alone one which aids the diagnostic process. The basic microeconomic framework which underlies the 'competitive advantage' approach, central to much marketing strategy analysis, should not be seen as an adequate description of the analytical and processual complexities in specific situations. It is a framework for predicting the key impacts of a series of market mediated trans-actions: at the very least outcomes are the joint effect of decisions themselves and the selection process. In this sense the more valid criticisms of the application of such a model is that either the needs of the situation are not met by the inherent nature of the model or that the model fails to perform within its own terms.

———————— Relationship marketing ————————————

Equally we may wonder to what extent the new found concern for relationship marketing is indeed new at all. The recognition that customers faced switching costs and that therefore the retention of existing customers was clearly an effective economic strategy is certainly not new.

Mattsson (1997) has considered much more critically the relationship between the underlying approaches in the 'markets as networks' and relationship market-ing perspectives. He rightly observed that much of the problem lies in the various different approaches claiming to represent relationship marketing.

More recently, Vargo and Lusch (2004), developed the argument further on the assumption of a dominant trend from the marketing of goods to the provision of services. They argued that, inter alia, all economies are service economies, that the customer is always a co-producer and that the enterprise can only make value propositions. In a sense, however, to describe, as they do, the trend as being from goods-dominant to service-dominant perspectives over a period of around 100 years is to describe a genuine shift in managerial perspective but a less clear shift in the underlying realities.

The whole development might remind one rather more of M. Jourdain in Moliere's *Le Bourgeois Gentilhomme* who discovers he has been effortlessly speaking prose all his life. The proposed move towards a more relational and service-based perspective reflects more a changing view of the nature of the customer, from consumer to co-producer, than the fact that those who used be characterized as consumers are now in some objective way more co-producers. We would do well to remember that memorable expression of Ivan Illich (1981) 'shadow work' to describe real work which we do not see because of the nature of our measurement or value systems. Arnould (2006) notes the clear potential link between the approach advocated by Vargo and Lusch and consumer culture theory but also notes that this aspect is less well developed in their initial presentation. Moreover, Schembri (2006) suggests that the approach adopted still remains somewhat rooted in the more traditional goods centred logic and needs to engage more with approaches focused around the nature of the customer experience.

It may well be that the relationship marketing movement will in the end have a rather similar impact on marketing as the market share one did in the 1970s and early 1980s. As such the renewed emphasis on the nature of the customer relationship, which is self evidently important in industrial markets, will encourage retail marketers to take their customers more seriously – even to regard them as intelligent and rational agents. To do so, however, would also mean recognizing severe scepticism about the underlying reality of various developments in relationship marketing such as 'loyalty' cards and one-to-one targeting.

However, it may also be true that the relationship and network perspective will in the longer run change our perception of the critical strategic questions faced by firms as they and their 'markets' evolve and develop. Easton et al. (1993), for instance, suggest that the notion of competition and markets is really only appropriate at specific stages in the life-cycle of the firm or business unit. Indeed, their approach could be taken further to suggest that at a time when there is significant indeterminacy in terms of competitor and customer choice, this way of characterizing strategic choice is, of itself, of limited theoretical or practical value. Almost by definition the product technology and market structure needs to be relatively stable for such strategic choices to be formulated, yet by this stage the feasible choice set itself may be very restricted.

Emergent or enacted environments

The notion of emergent phenomena has itself emerged as a key concept in organizational strategy. Much of the credit for this must go to Mintzberg (1994) but ironically his analysis of the concept itself has been perhaps rather more limited than it could have been. Indeed in his more recent work, he has tended to define the nature of emergent phenomena in a rather idiosyncratic manner. He implies that emergent phenomena are such that they can ex post be related to the intentions or actions, through time, of the individual actors. However, a more common use of the term emergence incorporates some notion of interpretation at different levels of aggregation. After all, for instance, as a number of authors have previously commented, markets themselves are emergent phenomena. It was originally Adam Smith's insight that each actor in a market following their own interest could, under certain conditions, create an overall situation of welfare maximization: in this sense the invisible hand was much more effective than any attempts at local or even global optimization.

Others have paid much greater attention to the nature of emergent properties, but we also need to recognize a further distinction between what have been termed emergent and enacted environments. In a number of relevant areas, such as information systems, there is no overall agreement on the nature of the differences (see Mingers, 1995) but in the absolute an emergent environment is one in which there are a set of rules but they are generally undetermining of the outcome states – or at least the only way in which an outcome state can be predicted is by a process of simulation, whereas an enacted environment is one in which the nature of the environment is itself defined by the cognitive patterns of the constituents.

This distinction is particularly important when we consider the possibility of 'markets-as-networks' as a perspective to understand the nature of competitive market phenomena. If we recognize the nature of the phenomena we are trying to understand as essentially emergent then there remains considerable value in attempting to model the relevant structure of rules or relationships that characterize the environment. If, on the other hand, we are more inclined to an enactive view of the relationship between organizations and their environment, we need to consider the degree to which the structure of the network is not more than a surface phenomenon resulting itself from other deeper processes. We need to consider the phenomenon that Giddens (1979) identifies in terms of 'structuration', whereby agents and organizations are simultaneously both creators of structures but also have their actions constrained by these structures.

However, even if we are willing to give a relatively privileged ontological status to the detailed network structure in a particular context, we may still face insurmountable problems in developing high-level regularities from a more and more detailed analysis. Cohen and Stewart (1995) warn convincingly about the dangers of drowning in the detail of low-level rules but they give only limited useful advice as to the practical nature of the alternatives.

Despite the fact that some of these general notions have been seen in the mainstream of strategic management thought for some considerable time (see Stacey, 1995), we should remain cautious. Horgan (1997) suggested that we should be wary of the likely advances to be made in the field that he has dubbed 'chaoplexity':

> **So far, chaoplexologists have created some potent metaphors, the butterfly effect, fractals, artificial life, the edge of chaos, self-organised criticality. But they have not told us anything about the world that is both concrete and truly surprising, either in a negative, or in a positive sense. They have slightly extended the borders of our knowledge in certain areas, and they have more sharply delineated the boundaries of knowledge elsewhere. (1997: 226)**

Marketing processes

Not surprisingly, the 1990s saw a renewed interest in the marketing process and particularly in the nature of the processes which support the development of a marketing orientation. This approach was encouraged by the renewed attempts to model the nature of marketing orientation of both Narver and Slater (1990) and Kohli and Jaworski (1990). In essence the shift is one that Herb Simon (1979) recognized in his original distinction between substantive and procedural rationality. He suggested that it was an appropriate response to the problem of bounded rationality to focus attention more on the process for arriving at a particular choice rather than developing a general analytical approach to make that choice in any particular situation.

Much empirical research, particularly based on key informant surveys has been undertaken to establish the extent to which various operational measures of marketing orientation are correlated with commercial success. On top of this there has been work to establish some of the possible antecedents for such orientation including measures related to the accumulation and organizational dispersion of market research data. The results remain somewhat contradictory but it seems likely that some level of association will finally emerge, although whether it will achieve the minimum 10 per cent target which we considered earlier is rather another question.

It is also important to note that the two approaches to measuring market orientation focused on substantially different approaches; one essentially related to a more organizational 'cultural' or attitude measure and the other related to an information processing perspective around market-based data. Hult et al. (2005) reported on a study, still based primarily on survey data, which not only incorporated both of these measures but also attempted to overcome one of the common criticisms of much of the other empirical work in that they used independent and leading performance measures.

On top of this, we need to address more fundamental questions about the underlying logic of procedural rationality in this context. As we have suggested above, it is reasonable to argue that some consideration in any marketing context of each element in the 3Cs (customers, competitors and channels) must surely be seen as sensible. How far such a process should be routinized within a particular planning or decision-making schema is another matter. Much of the writing in the area of marketing orientation suggests that the appropriate mechanisms and procedures are unproblematic yet everyday experience in organizations suggests that achieving effective response to the market is difficult and indeed may not be susceptible to programmed responses.

The new analytics: resource advantage, co-evolution and agent-based modelling

Earlier on in this chapter we identified a number of key characteristics of a competitive market which determine the effectiveness of any specific strategic analysis, in particular: the heterogeneity of demand; the interaction between customer choices and producer offerings; and the degree to which both producers and customers are active agents in this process. More recently various new analytical approaches have given us new and different ways to address these central issues.

First, Hunt (2000a) has argued that the more traditional resource-based view of the firm is so dominated by a supply-side perspective that a more comprehensive theoretical approach, which he labels 'Resource Advantage' is required.

There are some concerns, however, as to whether Hunt's framework actually provides the most effective way of incorporating heterogeneity of demand (Wensley, 2002), particularly in the context of the evolution of marketing structure. For instance, one of the most established issues in the nature of a market structure is what Wroe Alderson referred to as the sequential processes of 'sorting' between supplier offerings in order to 'match' specific portfolios of customer demands, yet

Hunt himself observes that so far he is unclear how this might be incorporated within his framework (Hunt, 2000b).

At best therefore it remains an open question as to how far the developments proposed by Hunt will help us to further understand not only a static view of market demand but even more a dynamic and evolving one, although they do provide a very useful perspective on the nature of strategic choices for the individual firm or business unit.

An alternative approach, which resonates with developments in the field of strategic management, is to focus more on the ability of firms to adapt to an evolving and changing market through what are termed 'dynamic capabilities' (Helfat et al., 2007; Teece et al., 1997; Winter, 2003). Whilst previously Day (1994) has suggested that an analogous approach to understanding the nature of market-based firms can prove useful, the overall study of such dynamic capabilities has so far proved to be 'riddled with inconsistencies, overlapping definitions, and outright contradictions' (Zahra et al., 2006: p. 917).

Second, there have also been interesting developments in empirical studies of co-evolution, but unfortunately most of these so far have focused solely on the competitive and cooperative processes between organizations (Lewin and Volberda, 1999). From a market strategy perspective, however, it is noteworthy that even those few studies which attempt to model the nature of market evolution specifically, rather than treat it more as a backcloth upon which other sociological and economic processes take place, tend to represent the actual process in very limited ways. Only in the resource partitioning approach (Carroll et al. (2002)) do we perhaps see the direct opportunities for a more complex model of market development which represents both its continuity, in the sense that one can reasonably expect cycles of competitive imitation followed by the emergence of new forms and market positions for competition, and its indeterminacy, in that various new 'realized niches' could emerge. Even here, however, the implicit emphasis is on the individual firms as the motivating force rather than the collective of customers in the various markets.

Third, advances in agent-based modelling promise new ways of simulating more complex interactive processes of spatial competition (Ishibuchi et al., 2001; Tesfatsion, 2001). Agent-based modelling essentially depends on allowing a simulation to evolve with individual 'agents' making choices within an undetermining but defined rule structure. It may well provide us with a better understanding of the patterns of market-based evolution and the nature of some of the key contingencies. However, again it is proving difficult to adequately reflect the evolving behaviour of customers in the marketplace. Chang and Harrington (2003) did include a process of consumer search in their model but their focus remained on the potential advantages of centralization for what were, in effect, multi-unit retailers.

Conclusions: the limits of relevance and the problems of application

The study and application of marketing strategy therefore reflects a basic dilemma. The key demand in terms of application is to address the causes of individual firm or unit success in the competitive marketplace, yet we can be reasonably confident from a theoretical perspective that such knowledge is not systematically available because of the nature of the competitive process itself. In this way the academic study of marketing strategy remains open to the challenge that it is not relevant to marketing practice. Yet to represent the problem solely in this way is to privilege one particular notion of the nature and use of academic research in marketing as well as the relationship between research and practice. Recognizing the limits to our knowledge in marketing strategy may also help in a constructive way to define what can and cannot be achieved by more investigation and research.

There are a number of areas in which we can both improve our level of knowledge and provide some guidance and assistance in the development of strategy. First, we can identify some of the generic patterns in the process of market evolution which give some guidance as to how we might think about and frame appropriate questions to be asked in the development of marketing strategy. Such questions would be added to those we are used to using in any marketing management context, such as the nature of the (economic) value added to the customer based on market research evidence and analysis. More recently it has been suggested in strategy that such additional questions are most usefully framed around questions of imitation and sustainability, but, as Dickinson (1992) argues, this really assumes sustainability is a serious option. It may be more appropriate to frame such additional questions around the more general patterns of market evolution – standardization, maturity of technology and stability of current networks – rather than attempt to address the unanswerable question of sustainability directly.

When it comes to the generics of success, we face an even greater problem. By definition, any approach which really depends on analysis of means or averages leaves us with a further dilemma: not only does any relative 'usable' explanation only provide us with a very partial picture where outcomes are more unexplained than explained, but also the very notion of a publicly available set of 'rules for success' in a competitive market is itself contradictory, except in the context of a possible temporary advantage. We can try and resolve the problem by looking at the behaviour of what might be called successful outliers but here we face a severe issue of interpretation. As we have seen, the sources of such success are themselves ambiguous and often tautological: we often end up really asserting either that to be successful one needs to be successful or that the route to success is some ill-defined combination of innovation, effectiveness and good organization.

It may well be that the best we can do with such analysis is to map the ways in which the variances of performance change in different market contexts: just like our finance colleagues we can do little more than identify the conditions under which variances in performance are likely to be greater and therefore, through economic logic, that the average performance will increase to compensate for the higher risks.

Finally, we may need to recognize that the comfortable distinction between marketing management, which has often been framed in terms of the more tactical side of marketing, and marketing strategy is not really sustainable. At one level all marketing actions are strategic: we have little knowledge as to how specific brand choices at the detailed level impact or not on the broad development of a particular market, so we are hardly in a position to label some choices as strategic in this sense and others as not. On the other hand, the knowledge that we already have and are likely to develop in the context of the longer term evolutionary patterns for competitive markets is unlikely to enable us to engage directly with marketing managerial action choices at the level of the firm: the units of both analysis and description are likely to be different. In our search for a middle way which can inform individual practice it may well be that some of the thinking tools and analogies that we have already developed will prove useful, but very much as means to an end rather than solutions in their own right.

Recommended further reading

Bettis, R.A. and Prahald, C.K. (1995) 'The dominant logic: retrospective and extension', *Strategic Management Journal* 16: 5–14.

Bogner, W. and Thomas, H. (1994) 'Core competence and competitive advantage: a model and illustrative evidence from the pharmaceutical industry', in G. Hamel and A. Heene (eds) *Competence Based Competition*, Wiley: Chichester.

Caves, R.E. and Porter, M.E. (1977) 'From entry barriers to mobility barriers: conjectural decisions and contrived deterrence to new competition', *Quarterly Journal of Economics* 91, May: 241–62.

Cooke, P. (2002) *Knowledge Economics: Clusters, Learning and Co-Operative Advantage*, London: Routledge.

Ehrenberg, A.S.C. (1972) Repeat Buying: Theory and Applications, Amsterdam and New York: North-Holland Publishing Co.

Ehrenberg, A.S.C. and Uncles, M. (1995) 'Dirichlet-type markets: a review', working Paper, November.

Hannan, M.T. and Freeman, J. (1977) 'The population ecology of organizations', *American Journal of Sociology* 82(5): 929–63.

Harland, C. and Wensley, R. (1997) 'Strategising networks or playing with power: understanding interdependence in both industrial and academic networks', working paper presented at Lancaster/Warwick Conference on 'New Forms of Organization', Warwick, April.

Henderson, B. (1980) 'Strategic and natural competition', *BCG Perspectives*, 231.

Henderson, J.M. and Quant, R.E. (1958) *Microeconomic Theory: A Mathematical Approach*, New York: McGraw Hill.

Hunt, M.S. (1972) 'Competition in the major home appliance industry, 1960–1970', unpublished doctoral dissertation, Harvard University.

Jones, H.J. (1926) *The Economics of Private Enterprise*, London: Pitman and Sons.

Kaufmann, S. (1995) *At Home in the Universe*, New York: Oxford University Press.

Kotler, P. (1991) 'Philip Kotler explores the new marketing paradigm', *Marketing Science Institute Review*, Spring: 1–5.

Moorthy, J.S. (1985) 'Using game theory to model competition', *Journal of Marketing Research* 22, August: 262–82.

Morrison, A. and Wensley, R. (1991) 'A short history of the growth/share matrix: boxed up or boxed in?', *Journal of Marketing Management* 7(2): 105–29.

Muth, J.F. (1961) 'Rational expectations and the theory of price movements', *Econometrica* 29(3): 315–35.

Peterson, H. (1965) 'The wizard who oversimplified: a fable', *The Quarterly Journal of Economics* 79(2): 209–11.

Porter, M.E. (1979) 'The structure within industries and companies performance', *Review of Economics & Statistics* 61, May: 214–27.

Porter, M.E. (1985) *Competitive Advantage*, New York: Free Press.

Prahalad, C.K. and Bettis, R.A. (1989) 'The dominant logic: A new linkage between diversity and performance', *Strategic Management Journal* 10(6): 523–52.

Rumelt, R.P (1996) 'The many faces of Honda', *Californian Management Review* 38(4): 103–11.

Roberts, K. (1997) 'Explaining success – hard work not illusion', *Business Strategy Review* 8(2): 75–7.

Wernerfeld, B. (1995) 'A rational reconstruction of the compromise effect', *Journal of Consumer Research* 21, March: 627–33.

References

Abell, D. and Hammond, J. (1979) *Strategic Marketing Planning: Problems and Analytical Approaches*, Englewood Cliffs, NJ: Prentice Hall.

Arnould, E.J. (2006) 'Service-dominant logic and consumer culture theory: natural allies in an emerging paradigm', *Marketing Theory* 6: 293–7.

Bartlett, C.A. and Ghoshal, S. (1995) 'Changing the role of top management: beyond systems to people', *Harvard Business Review* 73(3): 132–42.

Buzzell, R.D., Gale, B.T. and Sultan, R.G.M. (1975) 'Market share – a key to profitability', *Harvard Business Review* 53: 97–106.

Campbell-Hunt, C. (2000) 'What have we learned about generic competitive strategy: a meta-analysis', *Strategic Management Journal* 21(2), February: 127–54.

Carroll, G.R., Dobrev, S.D. and Swaminathan, A. (2002) Organizational processes of resource partitioning. *Research in Organizational Behavior*, 24: 1–40.

Chang, M.-H., Harrington, J.E. Jr. (2003) 'Multi-market competition, consumer search, and the organizational structure of multi-unit firms', *Management Science* 49: 541–52.

Chintagunta, P. (1994) 'Heterogeneous logit model implications for brand positioning', *Journal of Marketing Research* XXX1, May: 304–11.

Christensen, C.M. (1997) *The Innovator's Dilemma*, Boston, MA: Harvard Business School Press.

Cohen, J. and Stewart, I. (1995) *The Collapse of Chaos*, New York: Penguin Books.

Cooke, P. (2002) *Knowledge Economics: Clusters, Learning and Co-Operative Advantage*, London: Routledge.

Cooper, L. and Nakanishi, M. (1988) *Market Share Analysis: Evaluating Competitive Marketing Effectiveness*, Boston: Kluwer Academic Press.

Coyle, M.L. (1986) 'Competition in developing markets: the impact of order of entry', the Faculty of Management Studies Paper, University of Toronto, June.

Day, G.S. (1994) 'The capabilities of market-driven organizations', *Journal of Marketing* 58(4): 37–52.

Day, G.S. and Wensley, R. (1983) 'Marketing theory with a strategic orientation', *Journal of Marketing*, Fall: 79–89.

Day, G.S. and Wensley, R. (1988) 'Assessing advantage: a framework for diagnosing competitive superiority', *Journal of Marketing* 52, April: 1–20.

Dickinson, P.R. (1992) 'Toward a general theory of competitive rationality', *Journal of Marketing* 56(1): 68–83.

Dolan, R.J. (1981) 'Models of competition: a review of theory and empirical findings', in B.M. Enis and K.J. Roering (eds) *Review of Marketing*, Chicago: American Marketing Association. pp. 224–34.

Easton, G. (1990) 'Relationship between competitors', in G.S. Day, B.Weitz and R. Wensley (eds) *The Interface of Marketing and Strategy*, Conneticut: JAI Press.

Easton, G., Burell G., Rothschild, R. and Shearman, C. (1993) *Managers and Competition*, Oxford: Blackwell.

Faria, A. and Wensley, R. (2002) 'In search of "interfirm management" in supply chains: recognizing contradictions of language and power by listening', *Journal of Business Research* 55(7): 603–10.

Fournier, S., Dobscha, S. and Mick, D.G. (1998) 'Preventing the premature death of relationship marketing', *Harvard Business Review* January-February: 42–50.

Giddens, A. (1979) Central Problems in Social Theory: Action, Structure and Contradiction in Social Analysis, London: Macmillan.

Goeree, J.K. and Holt, C.A. (2001) 'Ten little treasures of game theory and ten intuitive contradictions', *The American Economic Review*, 91(5): 1402–22.

Goold, M. (1996) 'Learning, planning and strategy: extra time', *California Management Review* 38(4): 100–2.

Hakansson, H. (1987) *Industrial Technological Development: A Network Approach*, Croom Helm: London.

Helfat, C.E., Finkelstein, S., Mitchell, W., Peteraf, M., Singh, H., Teece, D. and Winter, S.G. (2007) *Dynamic Capabilities: Understanding Strategic Change in Organizations*, Oxford: Blackwell.

Henderson, B.D. (1983) 'The anatomy of competition', *Journal of Marketing* 47(2): 7–11.

Hofer, C.W. and Schendel, D. (1977) *Strategy Formulation: Analytical Concepts*, St Paul, MN: West Publishing.

Horgan, J. (1997) *The End of Science*, New York: Broadway Books.

Hult, G.T.M., Ketchen, D.R. Jr. and Slater, S.F. (2005) 'Market orientation and performance: an integration of disparate approaches', *Strategic Management Journal* 26: 1173–81.

Hunt, M.S. (1972) 'Competition in the major home appliance industry, 1960–1970', unpublished doctoral dissertation, Harvard University.

Hunt Shelby, D. (2000a) A General Theory of Competition: Resources, Competences, Productivity and Economic Growth, Thousand Oaks, CA: Sage Publishing.

Hunt Shelby, D. (2000b) 'A general theory of competition: Too eclectic or not eclectic enough? Too Incremental or not incremental enough? Too neoclassical or not neoclassical enough?' *Journal of Macromarketing* 20(1), June: 77–81.

Illich, I. (1981) *Shadow Work*, London: Marion Boyars.

Ishibuchi Hisao, Ryoji Sakamoto, and Tomoharu Nakashima (2001) 'Evolution of Unplanned Coordination in a Market Selection Game,' *IEEE Transactions on Evolutionary Computation*, 5, 5.

Kadane, J.B. and Larkey, P.D. (1982) 'Subjective probability and the theory of games', *Management Science* 28(2): 113–20.

Kay, J. (1993) *Foundations of Corporate Success*, Oxford: Oxford University Press.

Kohli, A.K. and Jaworski, B.J. (1990) 'Market orientation: the construct, research propositions and managerial implications', *Journal of Marketing* 54(2): 1–18.

Lambkin, M. and Day, G. (1989) 'Evolutionary processes in competitive markets: beyond the product life cycle', *Journal of Marketing* 53(3): 4–20.

Leeflang, P.S.H. and Wittick, D. (1993) 'Diagnosing competition: developments and findings', in G. Laurent, G.L. Lillien and B. Pras (eds) *Research Traditions in Marketing*, Norwell, MA: Kluwer Academic.

Levins, R. and Leowontin, R. (1985) *The Dialectical Biologist*, Cambridge, MA: Harvard University Press.

Lewin, Arie Y. and Henk W. Volberda (1999) 'Prolegomena on Coevolution: A Framework for Research on Strategy and New Organizational Forms', *Organizational Science*, 10, 5, Sep-Oct, 519–34.

Mattsson, L.-G. (1997) '"Relationship marketing" and the "markets-as-networks Approach" – a comparative analysis of two evolving streams of research', *Journal of Marketing Management* 13: 447–61.

McCloskey, D.N. and Ziliak, S.T. (1996) 'The standard error of regressions', *Journal of Economic Literature* XXXIV, March: 97–114.

McGee, J. and Thomas, H. (1986) 'Strategic groups: theory, research and taxonomy', *Strategic Management Journal* 7: 141–60.

Mingers, J. (1995) *Self-Producing Systems*, New York: Plenum Press.

Mintzberg, H. (1994) *The Rise and Fall of Strategic Planning*, Harlow: Prentice Hall.

Mintzberg (1996a) 'Reply to Michael Goold', *California Management Review* 38(4): 96–9.

Mintzberg (1996b) 'CMR forum: the Honda effect revisited', *California Management Review* 38(4): 78–9.

Mintzberg, H. (2004) *Managers Not MBAs: A Hard Look at the Soft Practice of Managing and Management Development*, Berrett-Koehler Publishers, Inc: San Fransisco CA.

Morrison, A. and Wensley, R. (1991) 'A short history of the growth/share matrix: boxed up or boxed in?', *Journal of Marketing Management* 7(2): 105–29.

Narver, J.C. and Slater, S.F. (1990) 'The effect of market orientation on business profitability', *Journal of Marketing* 54(4): 20–35.

Ohmae, K. (1982) *The Mind of the Strategist*, London: McGraw Hill.

Peters, T.J. and Waterman, R.H. (1982) *In Search of Excellence*, New York: Harper and Row.

Porter, M.E. (1980) *Competitive Strategy*, New York: Free Press.

Porter, M.E. (1985) *Competitive Advantage*, New York: Free Press.

Porter, M.E. (1990) *The Competitive Advantage of Nations*, New York: Free Press.

Sanchez, R. (1995) 'Strategic flexibility in product competition', *Strategic Management Journal* (special issue), 16: 135–59.

Saunders, J. (1995) 'Invited response to Wensley', *British Journal of Management* (special issue), 6.

Schembri, S. (2006) 'Rationalizing service logic, or understanding services as experience?', *Marketing Theory* 6: 381–92.

Simon, H.A. (1979) 'Rational decision making in business organizations', *American Economic Review*, September.

Stacey, R.D. (1995) 'The science of complexity: an alternative perspective for strategic change processes', *Strategic Management Journal* 16(6): 477–95.

Teece, D.J., Pisano, G. and Shuen, A. (1997) 'Dynamic capabilities and strategic management', *Strategic Management Journal* 18(7): 509–33.

Tesfatsion, L. (2001) 'Guest Editorial: Agent-Based Modelling of Evolutionary Economic Systems' *IEEE Transactions on Evolutionary Computation*, 5, 5.

Vargo S.L. and Lusch, R.F. (2004) 'Evolving to a new dominant logic for marketing', *Journal of Marketing* 68(1): 1–17.

Waterman, R.H. (1988) *The Renewal Factor*, London: Bantam Books.

Wensley, R. (1994) 'Strategic marketing: a review', in M. Baker (ed.), *The Marketing Book*, London: Heinemann Butterworth, pp. 33–53.

Wensley, R. (1995) 'A critical review of research in marketing', *British Journal of Management* (special issue), 6: S63–S82.

Wensley, R. (1996) 'Forms of Segmentation: Definitions and Empirical Evidence', MEG Conference Proceedings (CD Version) Session G Track 8, Department of Marketing, University of Strathclyde July 9–12, 1–11.

Wensley, R. (1997a) 'Explaining success: the rule of ten percent and the example of market share', *Business Strategy Review* 8(1): 63–70.

Wensley (1997b) 'Rejoinder to "Hard work, not Illusions"', *Business Strategy Review* 8(2): 77.

Wensley (1997c) 'Two marketing cultures in search of the chimera of relevance', keynote address at joint AMA and AM seminar 'Marketing Without Borders', Manchester, July 7.

Wensley, R. (2002) 'Marketing for the New Century'. *Journal of Marketing Management*, Vol. 18 Issue 1, February: 2002, 229–38.

Wernerfeld, B. (1984) 'A resource-based view of the firm', *Strategic Management Journal* 5(2): 171–80.

Wernerfeld, B. (1995) 'The resource-based view of the firm: ten years after', *Strategic Management Journal* 16: 171–4.

Wernerfeld, B. (1995) 'A rational reconstruction of the compromise effect', *Journal of Consumer Research* 21, March: 627–33.

Winter, S.G. (2003) 'Understanding dynamic capabilities', *Strategic Management Journal* 24(10): 991–95.

Zahra, S.A., Sapienza, H.J. and Davidsson, P. (2006) 'Entrepreneurship and dynamic capabilities: a review, model and research agenda', *Journal of Management Studies* 43(4): 917–55.

|11|
Target segment strategy
Sally Dibb and Lyndon Simkin

Introduction

Market segmentation principles are well established in marketing theory and a recognized component of marketing strategy (Weinstein, 2004). As customer needs become increasingly diverse, market segmentation offers organizations the means to handle this complexity. This is achieved by grouping into segments customers who are homogenous in terms of their needs and buying behaviour (McDonald and Dunbar, 2004). For organizations the benefits include more efficient resource allocation, marketing programmes which are a better fit with customer needs, and improved competitiveness (Beane and Ennis, 1987; Wind, 1978). Despite these attractions, organizations which implement a segmentation approach have many decisions to make about the methods they will use and how they will interpret and implement the outcomes (Dibb and Simkin, 2008).

This chapter provides an overview of the market segmentation process and explores what is involved in target segment selection. The chapter begins by outlining the reasons for carrying out segmentation and the associated benefits. Various methods for developing segments are then described, illustrated with topical examples from the mobile phone and energy markets. The criteria for judging the quality of the resulting segments are highlighted, followed by a discussion of targeting decisions and segment choice approaches. The chapter concludes with a series of warnings for segmentation users, designed to minimize the most commonly encountered impediments to the process and to the implementation of its outputs.

Managing diverse customer needs

Most markets are characterized by the diverse nature of customers, whose characteristics, needs, expectations, and buying behaviour vary. Organizations are faced with the problem of managing this diversity and considering the extent to which it is feasible to develop tailored product and service propositions. While it may be possible in some business markets to develop bespoke offerings for certain key accounts, this is not the case for most markets. Furthermore, organizations rarely have the required resources to pursue all potential customers, so difficult trade-offs are often needed. Market segmentation offers a route to making these decisions, helping to address the practical resource constraints facing leadership teams in all types of organizations.

Organizations of all sizes and from all sectors use market segmentation to tackle a variety of market challenges. Perhaps the market has become mature and is suffering from a proliferation of competitors; maybe the organization is seeking to reduce costs and to maximize marketing or business development returns; or marketers maybe identifying how best to launch a new product or brand. In all of these cases, a market segmentation approach could help, resulting in smarter target marketing and more effective utilization of resources. The UK's Chartered Institute of Marketing recently identified that shrewder use of segmentation is deemed to be one of the most important priorities for marketers striving to tackle the current economic downturn.

Segmentation has recently enjoyed a resurgence (Dibb and Simkin, 2009b; Yankelovich and Meer, 2006), led partly by technology advances which have improved the capacity of organizations to capture and manage customer data and partly by the importance of shrewd targeting in times of recession. Scarce marketing resources must be used more prudently during periods of difficult trading, so ensuring an excellent fit between company capabilities and customer needs is more important than ever. New uses of segmentation and targeting have also played a role. For example, social marketers are increasingly drawing on segmentation and targeting ideas to ensure the effective positioning and communication of anti-smoking, healthy eating, and good cause messages.

Segmentation involves organizations in considering how best to group their customers; which of these customers to serve; making effective resource allocation decisions; developing persuasive propositions for targeted customers; and helping to ensure that an organization 'goes to market' with clearly differentiated propositions and positioning. This chapter explores the nature of market segmentation, segment creation and target segment selection. Other chapters in this book consider the development of a compelling basis for competing and brand positioning.

Most textbooks describe segmentation as the process of grouping a heterogeneous customer base into smaller, more similar or homogeneous groups (segments).

In other words, market segmentation is the grouping of like-minded and similarly behaving consumers or business customers together for the purposes of developing products/services, targeting sales and marketing activities, managing customer service and determining internal resourcing. A market segment is defined as a group of individual consumers (in B2C markets) or business customers (in B2B markets) sharing one or more similar characteristics that cause them to have relatively similar product needs and buying behaviour. All customers allocated to a particular market segment should respond to the same marketing strategy and marketing programme in a similar fashion. In lay-person's terms, segmentation is understanding what customers want and how they buy, grouping similar or like-minded ones together, choosing with which groups to do business, and then tailoring a proposition accordingly.

Market segments

Referring to an example helps to illustrate what we mean by segments and how segmentation leads to the identification of like-minded groups of similarly behaving customers. One mobile phone company's recently launched segmentation scheme included eight main customer segments, three of which are:

- *Gaming Youths* – 'The game-oriented, mobile world addict', rarely using the phone for conversations, but focused instead on games, music and texts. The desired proposition is youth-oriented, modern, innovative and games-led.

- *Sophisticated Careerists* – 'Be successful with mobile technology'. These are career-oriented individualists, with lots of contacts, needing a mobile phone to organize every aspect of their lives: address book, diary, communications, networking, work and socializing. They are interested in the internet, network reliability and talk-led tariffs, but not TV downloads, games or music.

- Laggards – 'Torn between conservative values and the modern world'. These 'late mass' consumers simply do not see the relevance of this technology or how it fits into their lifestyles. Many have a mobile phone but rarely use it.

You will, no doubt, recognize people that you know who fit these profiles. Clearly, the games, music and text packages offered to the *Gaming Youths* will have little relevance to either the *Sophisticated Careerists* or the *Laggards*, while the approaches designed to entice greater usage from the *Laggards* are unlikely to appeal to *Gaming Youths* or *Sophisticated Careerists*. Were the mobile phone company to develop only one marketing strategy and marketing mix with which to target all mobile phone users, it would fail to address the needs and behaviours of each of these consumer groups. The role of segmentation is to identify such differences between customer groups and make use of them for marketing purposes. Case study 11.1 below explains in more detail the approach followed by this mobile phone company.

Case Study 11.1   Teleco segmentation

Background

As the mobile phone market matures and becomes saturated, service operators are seeking new ways to target and serve their customers in order to generate revenue. This particular telecommunications company operates throughout much of northern and eastern Europe, regions which are known for their advanced mobile phone usage. Faced with growing competition, the organization sought a more sophisticated customer segmentation approach for four countries in its Eurasian markets. Previously, the company divided its market only into corporate and private users, with a further split between customers on pay-as-you-go and monthly contracts. Until recent years, this kind of approach to splitting up the mobile phone market was not uncommon.

A German marketing research organization was retained by the telecommunications company to conduct the required data collection and segmentation analysis. Initially the focus was to develop a consumer segmentation scheme, quickly followed by a review of the needs, usage and behaviour of corporate users. There were five main phases to the segmentation project (see also Figure 11.1).

Phase 1: Preparation
- Internal scoping workshop
- Selection of project partners
- Detailed brief/contract
- Qualitative exploratory research (focus groups)
- Preparation of questionnaire for quantitative phase

Phase 2: Quantitative Study
- Four countries
- N = 2,500 interviews per country (including rejecters)
- N = 1,000 current/potential users
- Coverage of many issues: needs, benefits, usage, attitudes, lifestyles, etc.

Phase 5: Implementation
- Present segments
- Internal marketing of emerging strategy
- Agree targeting criteria and select target priorities
- Deep-dive focus group research into targeted segments
- Creation and roll-out of marketing programmes for targeted segments
- Ongoing tracking studies

Phase 4: Reporting
- Management presentation of segments
- Management report
- Tailored report for each country
- Tables/cross-tables
- Special analyses:
    Trends, competitors, revenues, etc

Phase 3: Segmentation Analysis
- Customized solution
- Conjoint trade-offs
- Factor and cluster analyses
- Workshops for debate and evaluation of emerging solutions

Implementation planning was built-in from the outset.

This project lasted 18 months.

Figure 11.1   The five phases of the segmentation project (Anette Bendzko GfK, Germany)

Phase 1: A preparatory phase exploring the current market structure, involving the organization's senior leadership team, external experts and the research organization. This phase also involved exploratory focus groups, so as to examine consumers' mobile usage and buying behaviour.

Phase 2: 10,000 consumer interviews were conducted (2,500 in four countries: 40 per cent were current users) to allow for quantitative analysis of consumers' needs, required benefits, usage, lifestyles and attitudes towards mobile phones. A further 2,000 interviews addressed corporate subscribers in the four countries, examining similar issues, plus buying centre dynamics and decision-making, and tariff considerations.

Phase 3: Multivariate techniques, including conjoint, factor, cluster analyses and structural equation modelling, were used to generate customer segments. These were then refined through input from managers and from 'deep-dive' customer focus groups.

Phase 4: The segments were presented throughout the organization, with careful tailoring to each of the specific country markets of the operating brands.

Phase 5: The final stage involved implementing the segmentation. Follow-up qualitative marketing research tested consumer and business customer views of the marketing propositions and competitive standing within each of the targeted segments.

Identifying the market segments

The segmentation solution was developed using a clustering approach. Input variables generated from the earlier interviews included: peer group orientation, trend/fashion influences, tradition/family values, communication needs/usage, emotional aspects of usage, technology affinity, demographics/lifestage/lifestyles, media usage, tariff requirements, purchasing policies, factors influencing buying, and buying centre dynamics. A statistically sound and intuitively robust eight cluster solution was generated, which was also intuitively appealing to managers. The emerging segments reflected the overall set of behaviours in evidence: some were consumer-focused, others were business user-orientated. The segments were profiled using behavioural and aspirational variables (see Table 11.1). The chosen segment labels closely reflected the allocation of customers to segments using easily remembered language. The clarity aided internal communication, convincing managers that customers could be readily allocated to segments. Existing subscribers were then analysed and allocated to one of the segments.

Table 11.1   Cluster analysis input variables

- Peer group orientation
- Trend/fashion influences
- Tradition/family values
- Communication needs and usage
- Fun and emotional aspects from mobile usage
- Mobile and e-world immersion
- Technology affinity
- Interest in teleco applications and services
- Demographics/lifestage/lifestyles
- Media usage
- Tariff plans and requirements
- Purchasing policies
- Buying centre dynamics
- Influencing factors

Cluster analysis produced a statistically sound 14 cluster solution. As the organization had previously operated with just two customer groups (business users and consumers on 'pay as you go' tariffs), managers felt that progressing from two to 14 customer groups was too major a transition to handle. The focus shifted instead to the next cut-off point in the clustering, the eight cluster solution. Tests of the statistical robustness of these eight segments proved satisfactory. Initial reviews suggested the groupings were intuitively robust, with managers readily able to visualize the customers contained within them. The different segments were also mutually exclusive, with each consumer or business user clearly allocated to one of the segments. The segments were then profiled in terms of the behavioural and aspirational variables considered in the analysis and descriptive labels identified (see Table 11.2).

Table 11.2　The eight segment profiles

Talk 'n' Texters – 'I just have a mobile phone because it is practical.'

- The conservative customer, not immersed in technology but with a few practical needs that can be fulfilled by technical appliances. S/he relies on mobile phones for practical reasons only.
- Interested in basic functions, especially SMS, but not attracted at all by more sophisticated or fun services, be it via mobile phone or the internet.

Talkative Trendies - 'Talk around the clock.'

- The modern, fun- and fashion-oriented socializer. This customer needs a mobile phone to keep in constant touch with the social scene and fulfil a strong need for communication.
- Interested in all applications and services.

Aspiring to be Accepted – 'Would like to have it but is not really up to it.'

- Wants to be part of the in-crowd, but is not there yet, and possibly never will be! These customers have a mobile phone because they just want to have it (show off) and seek to have trendy handsets they believe are adopted by peer sets they aspire to join.
- Show a special affinity towards photo, video and MP3 applications.

Laggards – 'Torn between conservative values and the modern world.'

- Traditionalist views with low communication needs and basic technical usage.
- The Luddites or those late into the market!
- S/he holds specific aversions to mobile phones (SMS) but also views them as a practical-only device (e.g. for emergency calls only).

Gaming Youths – 'Game oriented mobile world addict.'

- Young and very technology-oriented people, belonging to the mobile generation, who need a mobile phone in order to maintain a fast-living fun life.
- Games, games, games! And music.
- These customers search for images and brands that help them keep track of the modern world.

Sophisticated Careerists – 'Be successful with mobile technology.'

- Career-oriented individualists with lots of contacts. Highly immersed in technology and very mobile.
- Demanding on value for money. Customer care and respect are very important to these customers.
- They need a mobile phone to organize their life and business, but they are not emotionally attached.
- Self-choosers for work mobiles are included here.

Organization Paid – 'No choice – the corporation decides.'

- Demanding on value for money and customer care.
- Network coverage, reliability and volume discounts are the focus.
- Users have little influence in selection, so not particularly fashion or technology-led.

Table 11.2   *(Cont'd)*

International Business Users – 'Frequent connected business travellers.'

- Easy quad-band roaming and smooth data transfer.
- Some similarities with *Sophisticated Careerists* but with much greater emphasis on functionality and flexibility of at-destination services.
- Influenced by corporate choice of network and tariff plans.

The first five are consumer segments. The last two are business user segments. The *Sophisticated Careerists* are mainly business users who self-select mobile network, handset and tariff options and behave as consumers. These segments have been disguised.

The chosen segment labels were felt to closely reflect the allocation of customers to segments using easy to remember language. The clarity aided internal communication and meant managers were optimistic about the ease with which customers could be allocated to the segments. As part of the project, all of the corporation's existing subscribers in the data warehouse were analysed and allocated to one of these segments.

Quality checking the segments

Having statistically and qualitatively identified the segments, the marketing research company applied an agreed set of evaluation criteria to test the quality of the segments. This process took place *prior* to the selection of segments to target with marketing resources. The criteria used were a mix of statistical and qualitative measures, routinely applied by this organization as part of the segmentation projects it undertakes for clients. The rationale is that statistical tests are used to verify the robustness of the segment identification process and its outcomes. The qualitative criteria enable the intuitive managerial logic of the recommendation to be judged. This stage is deemed crucial to the satisfactory implementation of any segment solution.

Outcomes

In all four countries, the adopted segmentation strategy resulted in market share and income gains, and significant improvements to brand awareness and customer satisfaction in the targeted segments. At that time, the mobile phone company's rivals were not adopting such a focused approach to target marketing or campaign development. In situations where the organization was market leader, challengers' shares were eroded. Where the organization was the challenger brand, there were impressive gains in market share. In all four countries, there were market share gains within targeted segments and aggressive competitors were pre-empted from making any further inroads. Revenues per subscriber in priority segments increased and the more focused marketing programmes improved the company's reputation with targeted consumers and corporate users. These segments have been disguised.

This case is adapted from material in Dibb and Simkin 'Judging the Quality of Customer Segments: Segmentation Effectiveness', *Journal of Strategic Marketing*.

Case Study

Figure 11.2   The role of target market selection in the strategic marketing process

Why market segmentation is important

Market segmentation is pivotal to the strategic marketing process (see Figure 11.2), and one of the most important activities which marketers undertake. Segmentation results in a better developed understanding of customers' behaviours, differences and similarities, and so directs the development of marketing propositions and programmes. In order to make informed decisions about which segments to target, managers need to understand key marketing environment trends and drivers, competitors' capabilities and plans, internal resources and capabilities, and likely fit with corporate strategy. The process of undertaking market segmentation, therefore, acts as a catalyst to achieving such insights. The resulting decisions about resource allocation and marketing programmes are likely to be much better directed as a consequence of the segmentation study.

_____ The accepted benefits _____

The benefits of segmentation are perhaps best articulated by practitioners who use the approach on a day-to-day basis. The CEO of one of the world's largest IT corporations recently commented that, 'Segmentation-based marketing is the essence of sound business strategy and value creation'. A multinational energy company's strategy director builds on this theme, saying that, 'Segmentation is about recognizing some customers are not worth targeting. Sure, you'll sell to them if they come calling, but you won't invest in chasing them'. For one of the largest bankers, 'Segmentation makes handling smaller accounts profitable'. Meanwhile a leading global construction equipment manufacturer's CEO suggests that, 'Segmentation is just common sense good practice – it gets you closer to the right customers and encourages you to look after them properly'. Although none of these executives is a marketer, they still value the important role of segmentation to their organizations' strategies and operations.

The key benefits associated with carrying out segmentation include:

- *Improved customer insights*: in order to create segments an organization must have up-to-date intelligence, so the process forces a re-think about customers and their current issues. Segmentation focuses on customers' needs, expectations, aspirations and share of wallet, building stronger relationships with customers.

- *More focused product and service propositions, differentiated from rivals' propositions*: there is every chance that competitive advantage will result from a well executed segmentation strategy, possibly building barriers to competitors' moves.

- *Enhanced awareness of external market trends and competition*: an organization cannot decide which segments to target without examining these issues.

- *Focused resource allocation and marketing spend on the most worthwhile opportunities*: segmentation reveals who *not* to target and which customer groups will be the best recipients of resources.

- *Internal clarity*: segmentation invariably aligns the efforts of sales, business development, marketing, proposition development and campaign execution. This is arguably one of the most significant benefits. Segmentation establishes commitment and single-mindedness within the organization: one vision, one voice, harmonized messages.

- *Increased revenues from targeted customers*: the resulting benefit from the points above should be enhanced performance in the selected target segments.

Many organizations recognize the value of this realignment and the resulting improvements in the allocation of resources associated with carrying out segmentation. Greater clarity around which customers to pursue is also a significant benefit, particularly in multi-product, multi-segment, multi-territory organizations. Enhanced customer insight and better direction for how best to attract and engage with these customers are strong drivers for pursuing this practice.

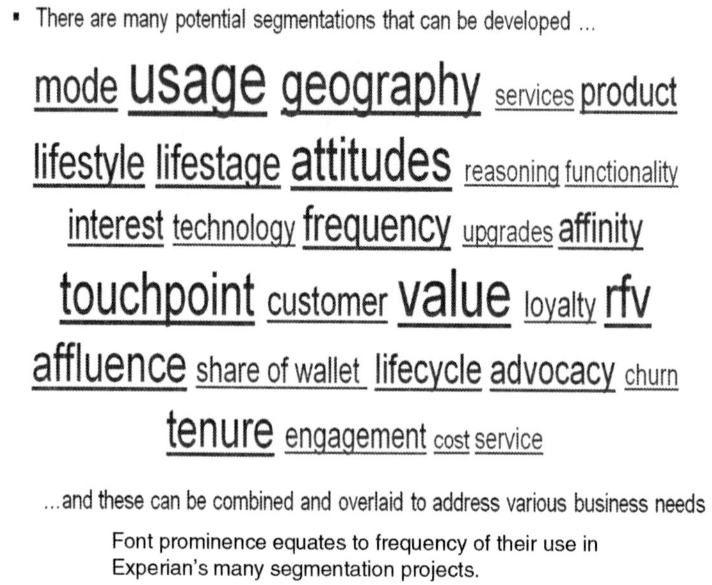

- There are many potential segmentations that can be developed ...

mode usage geography services product

lifestyle lifestage attitudes reasoning functionality

interest technology frequency upgrades affinity

touchpoint customer value loyalty rfv

affluence share of wallet lifecycle advocacy churn

tenure engagement cost service

...and these can be combined and overlaid to address various business needs

Font prominence equates to frequency of their use in
Experian's many segmentation projects.

Figure 11.3   The popularity of segmentation bases (Gareth Mitchell-Jones, Experion; presented at the Chartered Institute of Marketing's Annual Conference, Birmingham, November 11 2008)

Segmentation approaches

While the reasons for undertaking segmentation are compelling, there is no 'magic bullet' or standardized off-the-shelf approach. There is, however, a growing body of opinion that the selected approach needs to reflect an organization's goals and reasons for embarking on segmentation (Dibb and Simkin, 2008; Yankelovich and Meer, 2006).

Figure 11.3 summarizes the many different bases which can be used in pursuit of market segments, as developed by Experian's analytics team for clients seeking to develop segmentation strategies. In days gone by, demographics, socio-economics, lifestyles, benefits, usage and attitudes were all 'in vogue' at various times as *the* trendy platform for segmentation. Today, great strides in information technology have radically enhanced organizations' ability to capture and manage customer data. Most have access to a wealth of customer insights, including their characteristics, needs, buying behaviour, the influences upon their decisions, perceptions, motives, attitudes, usage and purchasing activity. As the mobile phone example illustrates, these insights can be modelled and data from different sources mined to identify segments of similarly behaving and like-minded customers. The more an organization knows about customers in a particular market, the stronger the likely insight in the resulting segmentation solution.

There are many different approaches to developing market segments; some are more technical, while others follow a more pragmatic route. Perhaps the most common include (Dibb and Simkin, 2008):

(a) The 'traditional' survey-based approach, as advocated in many marketing textbooks and frequently described in the research literature, is illustrated by the case of the mobile phone company featured above. In its approach, this began with qualitative research (depth interviews/focus groups), followed by a quantitative survey of 10,000 consumers, and finally a confirmatory qualitative research phase. The survey findings were statistically analysed and modelled, to produce the eight segment solution, described in Case study 11.1. The solution was not predetermined and no consideration was taken of the existing segmentation approach.

(b) An alternative scenario involves segments which emerge almost by accident, perhaps when an organization is carrying out customer research for other purposes. For example, when creating a new brand strategy, one leading manufacturer of ready meals conducted qualitative research into consumers' buying behaviour and views of the leading brands. These focus groups identified different clusters of consumer behaviour, and five segments were developed as a result. Such an outcome is not uncommon when marketers are researching their customer base. Even though the resulting customer groups (segments) may not be statistically validated, they may be intuitively appealing to managers who are keen to embrace them as part of the target market strategy.

(c) In business-to-business and service markets, the macro-micro approach has achieved popularity, not least because it deals pragmatically with existing market structures. Sometimes this is precipitated by managerial brainstorming about client types, behaviours, attitudes, their needs and the influences impacting on their choices of brand or service provider. The brainstorming starts by examining the buying behaviour characteristics of the organization's existing customer groupings, first seeking to disaggregate these into more homogeneous groups, and then re-aggregating across the original customer typology to create market segments. This approach was adopted by the energy business described in Case study 11.2 below.

Case Study 11.2 Segmenting the energy market: the macro-micro approach

Background

When electricity supplies first spread throughout the UK they were provided by a plethora of local private companies, all using different specifications and power outputs, seeking to capitalize on the surge in demand for this then 'alternative' energy. In order to maximize uptake, harmonize operating standards and ensure the public's safety, government regulation eventually led to state-controlled regional monopolies. Commercial and household customers in a geographic region such as the Midlands or the South East had no choice but to receive both infrastructure and energy from the region's designated regional electricity company (REC). Price and service levels were fixed by regulation and the REC, with customers only able to buy from one supplier. During the 1980s, the UK government privatized or deregulated

Case Study

nearly all remaining state-run enterprises, such as the large airports (BAA), state airline (BA), logistics company (NFC/Excel), defence supply (BAe), car producers (Jaguar, Land Rover and Rover) and telecoms (BT). By the 1990s it was the turn of the remaining utilities, including gas (British Gas/Transco), and the regional water and electricity companies. For the first time in living memory, consumers and business customers had a choice of electricity supplier.

The newly deregulated market was attractive for other organizations to enter, with many well-known brands such as Tesco, Virgin and Sainsbury's deciding to retail the electricity generated by the major producers. The RECs became acquisition targets, mainly for larger energy businesses in France, Germany and the USA. Over the next decade, mergers and acquisitions led to the situation where just six energy firms dominated the supply of electricity and gas in the UK: British Gas, French-based EDF Energy, Npower (owned by Germany's RWE), Scottish and Southern, Scottish Power (owned by Spain's Iberdrola) and Germany's E.on after its purchase of PowerGen.

Initially, consumers were slower to consider switching suppliers than business customers, but now – over a decade since deregulation – many consumers have been enticed to switch electricity supplier by the lure of lower prices or a guarantee of no price inflation for a fixed period. The current recession has motivated increasing numbers of consumers to seek better deals, facilitated by online comparison websites and hype in the media. The market has become increasingly price sensitive and few customers exhibit much brand loyalty.

In an increasingly price-led and competitive environment, several of the larger energy suppliers have sought to differentiate themselves on other dimensions, including their green credentials, tariff innovations and customer service capability. As often happens in maturing and highly competitive markets, these companies have also turned to market segmentation in order to identify the most attractive groups of commercial and private customers on which to focus their marketing resources. For example, E.on identified segments based on the lifetime value for the account, to ensure the resources required to capture a new customer will be recouped before the customer switches to a rival supplier.

One of the main providers of generating capacity, infrastructure and energy distribution decided to adopt the principles of market segmentation in order to energize the efforts of its sales and key account managers, and to help identify the sub-groups of customers on whom the business should focus its sales, marketing and customer support developments. Amongst this company's leadership team were several MBA graduates familiar with market segmentation benefits and two directors who had successfully deployed market segmentation when working in other sectors.

Project objectives and the adopted segmentation process

Despite understanding what market segmentation could offer, this energy business felt that there would be resistance within the company to the changes which might result. This would be for a variety of reasons, not least inertia and a dislike of changing working remits. The Strategy Director preferred to engender internal support and to foster buy-in by involving senior management, line managers and key account management personnel throughout the segmentation process. It was decreed that the resulting segments must be sizeable enough to warrant serving, markedly unique in their composition and characteristics, easy to populate by sales managers, prioritized in terms of profitability and costs to serve, and based on the characteristics and purchasing behaviour of the customers. A rigorous process was needed that would stand up to external scrutiny and be compliant with regulations governing this sector.

The energy business wanted to:

1. Identify sub-groupings of customers based on a mix of characteristics, including purchasing behaviour and spend, rather than profitability measures alone.
2. Generate enthusiasm through the process amongst those managers engaging directly with customers.
3. Develop a transparent segmentation solution, so that staff knew instinctively in which segment a particular customer should be located.
4. Seek market leadership in an attractive set of market segments in a differentiated, competitively effective and regulatory-compliant way.
5. Facilitate marketing propositions tailored to targeted customer requirements using innovative sales and marketing programmes.
6. Update its insights into customers, competitors, market trends and associated organizational capabilities.

The energy company began by running an externally facilitated workshop to orientate senior personnel and line managers responsible for sales, marketing, marketing research, key account management and customer service. This workshop established the requirements for the ongoing segmentation process in terms of actions, resources, personnel, timeframes and reporting structures. A cross-functional sub-group of these executives became the core project team. A new marketing manager was recruited to administer the segmentation project. This team and the marketing manager had the support of external experts.

There are numerous approaches to carrying out market segmentation. Many textbooks promote the quantitative survey-based approach, ignoring the company's existing classifications of customer groups and instead analysing the usage and attitude, buying behaviour and characteristics of customers in a quantitative survey. Multivariate analysis then identifies the emerging market segments. So long as internal structures and personnel can be expediently realigned to address these market segments, such an approach can work well. In practice, many organizations struggle to realign their operations to fit redefined customer groups and target market priorities. Many business marketers prefer the easier to use macro-micro approach. This approach starts with the company's existing customer groupings and then uses its knowledge of these customers to identify new groupings from within these. For cost and time reasons, and also to ensure the full involvement of the organization's personnel, this energy business decided to use the macro-micro approach.

In accordance with best practice, a template was produced which captured the characteristics of customers, buying centre dynamics, energy usage and consumption data, customer needs and expectations, the buying decision-making process and factors which influence it. This template was applied to each of the company's existing customer groupings. Cross-functional teams knowledgeable of these customer groupings were assembled for a series of workshops which over a three-week period, examined all of the company's customer types. Each team comprised senior and line managers, sales, marketing, key account and customer service personnel, and the marketing manager as facilitator.

In practice, these teams found it impossible to generalize customer insights for the different customer groups because each contained a mix of dissimilar consumers. It became clear that customers had previously been allocated to groups as a result of various factors, including industry 'norms', operational convenience, and regulatory compliance. In general, understanding of customers' behaviour was poor. As a result, those involved in the workshops went through a process of splitting each customer group into sub-groups of like-minded and similarly behaving consumers. Typically between five and 12 groups (or separate templates) emerged out of each initial customer group. During subsequent meetings, the project team was able to use the many templates generated by the workshops to develop new market segments by merging sub-groups which exhibited similar characteristics and behaviours. Many of these new segments contained sub-groups from a number of the original customer groups.

In parallel to identifying the market segments, the marketing team was updating its competitor intelligence and awareness of market trends. These activities were designed to aid the target segment selection stage. The project team, in conjunction with the company's leadership team, decided to use a portfolio planning tool to assist these targeting decisions. The chosen tool was the directional policy matrix, the use of which involved agreeing a set of market attractiveness criteria which would subsequently be weighted and used to rank the attractiveness and capability fit of the emerging segments.

The resulting segmentation solution

Two segmentation schemes emerged: one for consumers (private households) and one for commercial customers (public and private sectors). Although full details cannot be divulged for reasons of corporate confidentiality, there were 10 consumer segments and 14 business segments. The directional policy matrix identified three consumer and two business segments to grow, several to harvest and hold, and also several segments to de-prioritize or ignore. Some of the emerging business segments are described in Table 11.3.

Table 11.3   Examples of the segment profiles

In the business market, segments included two in the public sector:

- *The Professionals.* Professional purchasing managers – focused on seeking value for the tax payer and good service levels, while becoming increasingly concerned about carbon footprint and green issues, often with in-house energy specialists.
- *No Change Traditionalists.* More risk-averse public sector traditionalists, committee-led decision making, very influenced by their own networks and similar organizations.

There were several commercial small business segments, including:

- *Independents.* Price-conscious owners of small enterprises such as shops, business services or restaurants, very much focused on reducing operating costs to support profitability and influenced by media views.
- *Ego-stroked Proprietors.* Deal-seeking localized chains/SMEs, in which the entrepreneur's ego must be massaged.
- *The Buyers.* Energy-aware light manufacturing and small industrial firms with energy managers and facilities managers, who want simplified buying and a good deal.

Organizations operating across numerous sites fell into five segments, including:

- *Energy Savvy.* Large multi-site energy aware businesses, with an in-house knowledgeable energy team seeking significant cost savings and reliable multi-site billing.

Table 11.3   *(Cont'd)*

- *Low Awareness Purchasers*. Multi-site customers requiring cost savings, but not energy savvy or really focused on energy trends.
- *Site Churners*. Multi-site operators with quickly changing site portfolios; price is important but not as much as service levels.
- *Frequent Switchers*. Multi-site frequent switchers, fully deal-led and quick to change supplier, with no loyalty.

(This case is adapted and extended from material in Dibb and Simkin (2009c).)

There are advantages and disadvantages in the different segmentation approaches:

(a) The survey-based quantitative approach, adopted by the mobile phone company, can be effective in creating segments, but is expensive and takes time (18 months in this case), requires expert marketing research that is well specified, in this case for brand development, and its adoption frequently involves considerable disruption to the organization.

(b) The qualitative-only 'accidental' approach, as in the ready meals food example (p. 247), is certainly quick and easy. However, it is vulnerable to poor scoping and misinterpretation, and is only ever as good as the thinking behind the qualitative marketing research that is specified. In practice, it must be followed with a quanti-tative confirmatory study, to avoid companies committing to segments which are based on the opinions of a very few.

(c) The macro-micro approach 'evolves' segments out of the company's existing understanding of customers. It involves many organizational members, engender-ing ownership amongst those involved in the process. It also takes into considera-tion the existing status quo, so can be less disruptive than some other approaches. However, this approach also requires some subsequent validation and is princi-pally a B2B option (Simkin, 2008).

Segment quality

Having created a segmentation scheme, it is necessary to 'sanity-check' the quality of the segments. Segment quality criteria are a set of desirable segment characteristics which can be used in both consumer and business-to-business contexts. The original version developed by Kotler (1967) refers to: segment *measurability*, enabling segment size and potential to be judged; *accessibility*, in order that a segment can be reached and served; *substantiality*, ensuring that a segment is of sufficient size and profit potential; and *actionability*, so that a segment can be reached effectively with a marketing programme. These criteria have been endorsed by other authors (e.g. Bonoma et al., 1983; Wind, 1978), some of whom developed their own check-lists for assessing the quality of segmentation output. These criteria are distinct from those variables used when assessing segment attractiveness during targeting (cf. Goller et al., 2002), as discussed in the next section of this chapter.

This distinction is clarified by Hlavacek and Reddy's (1986) view of segmentation, comprising: (i) segment identification; (ii) segment qualification; and (iii) segment attractiveness. Under this scheme, segment identification relates to the design of the segments, while the qualification phase concerns the extent to which emerging customer groups can be operationalized. Segment attractiveness relates to targeting decisions, resource allocation and segment prioritization. This approach establishes the role of qualifying criteria which appraise the quality of segments, rather than those which are used to judge targeting attractiveness.

Segmentation theory is based on assumptions of market heterogeneity (Beane and Ennis, 1987; Wedel and Kamakura, 2002; Wind, 1978). Once this assumption is met, segment qualification criteria can help to assess whether a segment has distinct user characteristics and needs, if the scale of the opportunity is worthwhile, the extent to which these features are measurable/stable over time, whether the competitors can be readily identified, and if a marketing programme can effectively target it. Kotler's (1967) criteria of measurability, accessibility, substantiality and actionability are central to many of the other proposed schemes. Reviewing the literature reveals the following *segment quality* themes are recognized.

1. *Segments are homogeneous.* Each segment being distinctive in terms of its customer profile and needs. This will impact upon the extent to which the segments are accessible.

2. *Segment size and potential profitability.* This involves two sub-themes: the first is that the size of the segment is sufficient so that resource allocation can be justified and future profitability judged adequate. This fits with Kotler's notion of substantiality, yet more specifically expresses the underlying components. The second sub-theme concerns the ability to predict size and profitability, closely fitting with Kotler's measurability criterion.

3. *Segment stability.* Although not directly included by Kotler, given that profitability could rely upon it, this is implied by the substantiality criterion.

4. *Segment accessibility.* This theme mirrors one of those originally expressed by Kotler, concerning whether suitable and distinctive marketing programmes can be developed for emerging segments.

5. *Segment compatibility.* Perhaps the most complex theme, this concerns the extent to which the segment output fits the organizational context. This includes: synergy with corporate and/or marketing strategy; match to resources and capabilities; and fit with organizational factors such as culture, structure and operational considerations. Although this theme is not the same as Kotler's notion of actionability, it highlights issues which affect whether a segment can be served.

6. *Segment actionability.* This theme is consistent with Kotler's original interpretation of the term, referring to whether the organization has the resources and capabilities to serve the emerging segments.

(Adapted from material in Dibb and Simkin (2009a).)

Targeting approaches

No organization has the resources or capabilities to adequately serve all segments in its market with segment-specific sales and marketing programmes. Some tough choices are needed about where to concentrate resources and marketing programmes. Even the largest corporations, such as GM, P&G, IBM, Marriott, Tesco or HSBC, prioritize certain target markets ahead of others, and do not offer all consumers or business customers a proposition. This section considers the available options for selecting target segments. Only by targeting the 'right' segments will an organization enjoy the benefits of adopting the market segmentation concept and enable the costs of identifying segments to be repaid.

A few organizations adopt a single-segment targeting strategy and, in effect, become niche specialists. Most organizations opt for targeting several segments, sometimes called a multi-segment strategy. By pursuing such strategies, organizations are spreading their risks by trading in several different segments and seeking increased sales volumes and revenues. The costs of a multi-segment strategy can be considerable: developing a variety of product offerings and marketing programmes requires substantial resources. Nonetheless, a multi-segment strategy is the more commonly adopted approach in the vast majority of organizations. For these organizations, the challenge is to ensure that the selection of segments is carefully managed, so that resources are allocated to the 'best' mix of segments.

The literature examining the targeting stage of the market segmentation process has identified various factors that impact upon an organization's assessment of target market attractiveness, including:

- The organization's existing *market share* and *market homogeneity* – a company's knowledge of an existing market will influence its view as to the relative attractiveness of this market vis-à-vis others.

- Existing *product expertise* – in related applications or adjacent markets on which the organization can build.

- The likelihood of *production and marketing scale economies* – although each segment targeted will require a bespoke marketing programme, there may be certain savings in product development, brand building activity, customer service, logistics, or marcomms (marketing communications) between two or more segments, which are not available if the organization chooses to prioritize a different set of segments.

- The nature of the *competitive environment* – one segment may be particularly well served by one or two very strong competitors, whereas there may be the opportunity to establish a competitive advantage in a separate segment.

- The forces of the *marketing environment* and *market trend*s – these external developments will present opportunities and threats.

- Capability and ease of matching *customer needs* – the behaviour and expertise of the organization may synergize more strongly with one segment than with the consumers or business customers in another segment.

- Segment attractiveness in terms of *size, structure and growth* – some organizations may deem a segment to be too small or low in spending to be attractive or there may be volatility and instability.

- Available *corporate resources* – no organization has the time, money, people or skills available to address all segments in a market: some segments will be resourced ahead of others.

- Anticipated *profitability and market share* – ultimately an organization must satisfy its owners, shareholders and investors, who generally equate profitability and ROI with successful business strategies. In certain organizations, notably in the Asia-Pacific region, there is a sensible goal to increase market share, which may be possible in only certain segments.

Best practice suggests that 'a basket' of variables should be considered by managers appraising the attractiveness of segments, including short-term and long-term measures; and internal factors such as financial rewards, budgeting costs, operational requirements; along with external factors, including customer satisfaction considerations, competitive intensity, marketing environment factors, and so forth. Not all of the factors which are considered will be equally important in determining whether or not a particular segment is attractive to the organization. Some variables will be more important than others, so there needs to be a process for weighting the selected attractiveness criteria. The importance of variables will also vary for separate organizations. Various portfolio planning models – such as the Directional Policy Matrix or Segment Evaluation Matrix (cf: Dibb, 1995) – have been developed to assist managers in choosing which segments to target. For more information on these approaches see Dibb and Simkin (2008). For the purposes of this chapter, the focus will be on one of these methods, the Directional Policy Matrix (DPM), which is now widely used to identify which segments to prioritize.

The market attractiveness/business strength model or Directional Policy Matrix (DPM) employs multiple measurements and observations. Although originally created to examine product and brand portfolios, the tool works well in directing target segment selection. The *market attractiveness* dimension includes all aspects that relate to the market, such as expected profitability or ROI, seasonality, economies of scale, competitive intensity, ability to develop a competitive advantage, industry sales, the overall cost and feasibility of entering the market, or whatever is deemed appropriate for a particular sector and organization in judging the relative merits of segments. By using a set of variables (rather than a single financial indicator) the technique forces managers to consider attractiveness more broadly than in relation to short-term profitability. The *business strength* dimension is also a composite of factors, perhaps including relative market share, research and development expertise, price competitiveness, product quality and technical performance, market knowledge, customer handling/service, production and logistical competencies, financial resources, managerial expertise, and so forth. Such strengths or capabilities are internal issues unique to the organization in question and are generally benchmarked against the strongest and most successful competitor. Each organization using the tool selects its own market attractiveness and business strength criteria, but should apply the same ones over time so that comparisons can be made and changes monitored. The DPM grid-clearly portrays the attractiveness of segments, providing a numerical value of their relative attractiveness, as depicted in Figure 11.4. The use of the DPM in directing target segment selection is described in Case Study 11.3.

Case Study 11.3   Targeting decisions and outcomes in the mobile phone segmentation case

Following segment quality checks, managers from the four countries considered their targeting options and reviewed the allocation of resources to the emerging segments. Although all eight segments were found in each of the four countries studied, the size and relative attractiveness of each varied for the countries and separate operating companies. Using a jointly agreed set of attractiveness variables (see Table 11.4 below) within a Directional Policy Matrix (DPM) analysis, the management teams in each country decided which segments should be prioritized. The managers were helped in their task by having a full range of information about each of the segments and the customers contained within them. This included detailed breakdowns of the customers' technology affinity, communication and mobility, mobile phone attitudes and usage behaviour, spending and price sensitivity, internet and mobile office usage, brand awareness, preferences for operator/service providers, current network satisfaction, demographics/lifestage, and lifestyle/leisure activities.

Each national team had particular market and competitive conditions in which to operate, so each made its own decisions about which segments to target. For one country, marketing resources were focused primarily on three of the consumer segments. One of these had particularly strong growth prospects, while in the others a challenger brand had been stealing market share. A second national team opted to address five of the eight segments. None of the countries

Table 11.4   Illustrative target market attractiveness criteria

Attractiveness variables

- Disposable income in the segment
- Willingness to spend on mobiles in the segment
- Interest in value-added services (mobiles) in the segment
- ARPU/revenue/profitability (the financial worth of the segment)
- Share in prospects in the segment
- Loyalty level in the segment
- Size of the segment
- Competitive intensity (degree of competition in the segment)
- Potential growth of the segment
- Existing market share in the segment

These criteria were the variables that managers chose to use in the Directional Policy Matrix (DPM) which they deployed to aid the selection of segments to target.

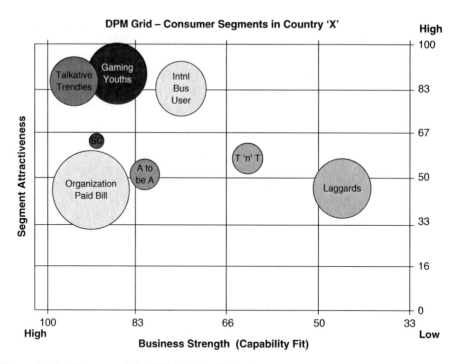

Figure 11.4   The use of the DPM in identifying segments to target

focused on all eight segments and no two national teams shared exactly the same selection of target marketing priorities. Figure 11.4 presents an example of one country's DPM.

Once the targeting had been finalized, each country's management team developed a bespoke marketing plan, focusing on each of the chosen target segments. These plans were designed to reflect the needs of targeted customers, the competitive and regulatory context, and distribution channel characteristics in each country. The detailed consumer insights obtained from the marketing research were invaluable to this process.

Using the directional policy matrix is just one of a number of ways in which managers can make decisions about segment priorities (Dibb and Simkin, 2008, provides a more comprehensive review). Whatever method is used, it is important to recognize that decisions about targeting are likely to dictate the success or otherwise of the entire segmentation strategy. Consequently, this stage inevitably requires further analyses and input from colleagues armed with financial performance data and details of operational costs. Before any final decisions are made, it is often necessary to allocate some or all of the organization's existing customers to the newly created segments, so that a fuller assessment of likely revenue streams and profitability levels can be made. This form of data mining can be extremely costly and demanding in terms of the required time and skills.

Overcoming operational problems

Whichever segmentation approach is adopted, there is much more to segmentation than merely identifying segments. Once segments have been identified, managers must decide which of these segments to target or prioritize. For those segments which are deemed to be priorities, an appropriate and compelling brand positioning must be developed. Then a suitable go-to-market plan is needed, creating appropriate marketing programmes and suitable methods of engagements with these customers. This is likely to involve re-thinking existing marketing programmes and approaches to handling the organization's customers.

Segmentation inevitably requires a reallocation of staff and resources, often resulting in disquiet and disruption within the organization. Operationalizing the segments is likely to involve the realignment of reporting systems and performance measurement to reflect the new target segment strategy. There are likely to be significant data mining demands, as managers explore the current customer base and attempt to allocate these customers to the newly created segments. This will require appropriate skills, time and expense. It is important not to underestimate the likely required changes and to ensure that they are carefully managed.

The implementation literature reveals a range of potential problems that can strike before the segmentation project even gets underway. Typically these relate to skill gaps, data deficiencies, internal behaviours, leadership and the extent to which there are realistic expectations about the nature of the journey. With segmentation under-way, there are resource, skill and behavioural impediments likely to jeopardize progress. Once segments have been identified, the problems do not cease. The nature of these well-observed problems together with some of the remedies are summarized in Table 11.5 (see also Dibb and Simkin, 2009c). Some of these difficulties can be pre-empted by beginning the segmentation programme with a systematic period of auditing. This often takes the form of a review of available financial, data and other resources matched to the project requirements. Early identification of a suitable project team is also important, particularly in ensuring clear allocation of project responsibilities. This team should involve managers from a variety of functional areas. Outside experts can also have a role to play in filling internal skills gaps and bringing greater objectivity to the programme. Involving such expertise from the outset is important where shortages of personnel or of particular skills are identified.

Devices such as workshops and briefings can play a crucial role in involving organizational members in the segmentation programme. These events help managers to set aside the people and time needed for the project. Using external facilitators helps smooth political sensibilities around the project. Off-site events can be especially valuable as a mechanism to begin the process; to carry out some of the required analysis; or to negotiate implementation changes. Cross-functional events are particularly important in breaking down internal barriers to the project. Establishing a system of personal mentoring can also be invaluable, particularly for projects with far-reaching strategic and operational implications. Managing anxiety among staff through periods of uncertainty reduces the likelihood that personal interests might threaten the project outcomes.

Table 11.5   Diagnosing and treating Key Segmentation Barriers

	Infrastructure	Segmentation process	Implementation
DIAGNOSIS	Problems include data gaps or lack of an MIS; shortfalls in other required resources; low level of marketing or segmentation expertise; lack of customer focus; weak inter/intra-functional communication; organizational resistance to change; insufficient commitment from senior management.	Barriers include a shortfall in required data for identifying segments; insufficient budget; lack of suitably skilled personnel; weak understanding of the segmentation process; poor sharing of data and ideas; inadequate inter-functional buy-in; poor appreciation of the fit with corporate strategic planning.	Problems include inadequate financial resourcing for implementation; insufficient time or suitably skilled employees committed to the segment roll-out; poor internal/external communication of the segment solution and lack of senior management involvement; unclear demarcation of implementation responsibilities; poor fit between tactical marketing programmes and the segment solution; organizational resistance to required changes and/or inflexibility in the distribution system.
TREATMENT	Prior to undertaking segmentation: • Conduct a review of available marketing intelligence. • Identify relevant skills and personnel. • Ensure there is senior management participation. • Plan and facilitate channels of communication. • Earmark required resources. • Instigate internal orientation of segmentation principles and of the programme.	During the segmentation process: • Specify sequential steps for the segmentation process. • Identify skills gaps. Seek external advice and training. • Prioritize information gaps. Collect data. Create/update the MIS. • Instigate regular internal debriefs of data and ideas. • Review the on-going fit with corporate strategy.	Facilitate implementation: • Identify key internal and external audiences. • Prepare an internal champion-led marketing programme to communicate the segment solution to audiences. • Facilitate necessary changes to organizational culture/structure/distribution. • Re-allocate personnel and resources to fit the segmentation solution. • Specify a schedule and responsibilities to roll-out segment solutions. • Instigate a mechanism for monitoring segment and associated marketing plan roll-out.

Source: Adapted from Dibb and Simkin, 2001.

No matter how well planned, segmentation projects seem inevitably to incur problems. These do not cease with the creation of the segments or after targeting decisions have been made. Problems are also likely during the implementation of the target segments and with the execution of newly created marketing plans/ programmes. Expecting there to be problems is an important step towards overcoming them, increasing the likelihood that the segmentation will be effective.

Summary

Market segmentation focuses on customers' needs, buying behaviour, expectations, aspirations and share of wallet, assisting in building improved and stronger relationships with customers in targeted segments. The approach assists organizations in identifying the most attractive customer groups and in deciding where to focus marketing programmes and resources. Barriers to competition are created and better focused product and service propositions can result, which are differentiated from rivals' propositions. Increased revenues from targeted segments are the desired outcome. Within the organization, there are important 'wins' associated with segmentation. These include determining which customers *not* to pursue, instead focusing resources and marketing spend on the most worthwhile opportunities. Above all, undertaking segmentation establishes commitment and single-mindedness within the organization – one vision, one voice, and harmonized messages. As the *Gaming Youths, Sophisticated Careerists, Laggards* illustration from the mobile phone example shows, segments exist in all markets.

Different approaches can be used to create market segments. Sometimes new segments emerge almost accidentally, as a result of marketing research insights attained by an organization for other purposes. The macro-micro model, which was illustrated using the energy company example, is also popular, particularly in business-to-business markets. However, many organizations still opt for a more 'traditional' survey-led quantitative approach, as in the mobile phone illustration. Each of these approaches has advantages and disadvantages, which organizations must consider when deciding how to proceed. In general, as access to data and the technological capacity to manage them improve, organizations are using a broader mix of customer insights to generate segments.

Emerging segments should be assessed for their quality along several key dimensions, including segment size and potential profitability, segment stability, segment accessibility, segment compatibility, and segment actionability. Once deemed robust, organizations must make trade-off choices in selecting which segments to pursue. Most organizations opt to target only some of the emerging segments. Bespoke tools such as the Segment Evaluation Matrix can help in this selection process, or more general portfolio planning approaches such as the Directional Policy Matrix can help in prioritizing target segment selection. When such approaches are used, it is important to ensure that a balanced and broad set of criteria is used to judge segment attractiveness. Detailed marketing plans and compelling brand positionings must then be produced for each of the segments selected as the priorities for an organization's marketing programmes and resources.

Marketers need to be realistic about the difficulties which are associated with undertaking segmentation and operationalizing a new segment strategy. These impediments can be encountered *before* the segmentation commences, *during* the segmentation process, and *after* segments have been identified and the new targeting is being implemented. Understanding the scope and scale of these problems is critical if their impact is to be minimized and damage avoided. Although market segmentation is rarely problem-free, by taking a proactive stance on these issues, organizations are more likely to reap its rewards.

References

Beane T.P. and Ennis, D.M. (1987) 'Market segmentation: a review', *European Journal of Marketing* 21, October: 20–42.

Bonoma, T.V., Benson, I. and Shapiro, B.P. (1983) *Segmenting Industrial Markets*, New York: Lexington Books.

Dibb, S. (1995) 'Developing a decision tool for identifying operational and attractive segments', *Journal of Strategic Marketing* 3: 189–203.

Dibb, S. and Simkin, L. (2001) 'Market segmentation: diagnosing and overcoming the segmentation barriers', *Industrial Marketing Management* 30: 609–25.

Dibb, S. and Simkin, L. (2008) *Market Segmentation Success: Making it Happen!*, New York: Routledge/The Haworth Press.

Dibb, S. and Simkin, L. (2009a) 'Judging the quality of customer segments: segmentation effectiveness', *Journal of Strategic Marketing* 18(2).

Dibb, S. and Simkin, L. (2009b) 'Bridging the segmentation theory/practice divide', guest editorial, *Journal of Marketing Management* (special issue) 25(3/4): 219–25.

Dibb, S. and Simkin, L. (2009c) 'Implementation rules to bridge the theory/practice divide in market segmentation', *Journal of Marketing Management* 25(3/4): 375–96.

Goller, S., Hogg, A. and Kalafatis, S. (2002) 'A new research agenda for business segmentation', *European Journal of Marketing* 36(1/2): 252–71.

Hlavacek, J.D. and Reddy, N.M. (1986) 'Identifying and qualifying industrial market segments', *European Journal of Marketing* 20 (2): 8–21.

Kotler, P. (1967) *Marketing Management*, Englewood Cliffs, NJ: Prentice Hall.

McDonald, M. and Dunbar, I. (2004) *Market Segmentation*, Basingstoke: Macmillan Press.

Simkin, L. (2008) 'Achieving market segmentation from B2B sectorisation', *Journal of Business & Industrial Marketing* 23(7): 464–74.

Wedel, M. and Kamakura, W.A. (2002) *Market Segmentation: Conceptual and Methodological Foundations*, Boston: Kluwer.

Weinstein, A. (2004) *Handbook of Market Segmentation*, New York: Routledge/The Haworth Press.

Wind, Y. (1978) 'Issues and advances in segmentation research', *Journal of Marketing Research* 15, August: 317–37.

Yankelovich, D. and Meer, D. (2006) 'Rediscovering market segmentation', *Harvard Business Review* 84(6): 141–5.

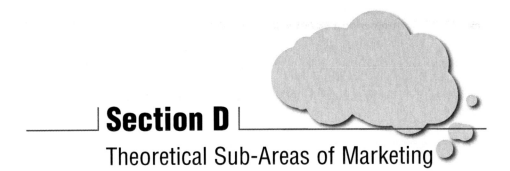

Section D

Theoretical Sub-Areas of Marketing

12

Consumer behaviour

Rob Lawson

Chapter Topics

Introduction

In reflecting on a 30-year career researching and teaching in marketing it seems that the academics who are interested in consumer behaviour often deliberately distinguish themselves as not working in managerial topics. Consumer behaviour research represents an extremely large body of work but one that does not always appear well integrated into other research in marketing. In the last 35 years consumer researchers have generated their own set of specialist journals such as the journals of *Consumer Research*, *Consumer Behaviour*, *Consumer Psychology*, *Customer Behaviour*, *Consumer Affairs*, *Consumer Policy*, *Advances in Consumer Research*, *Psychology and Marketing* and more recently *Consumption, Markets and Culture*. There are even examples of well established, but very specialized, publications such as the *Journal of Satisfaction, Dissatisfaction and Complaining Behavior*, which has now celebrated over 20 years of publishing. The potential separation of consumer research from other areas of marketing is difficult to understand in terms of the history of research on the topic since my reflections would suggest that historically the stimuli for much research in consumer behaviour were exactly the same as those that brought about the rich growth and development of managerial marketing thought that originated in the 1950s. One possible difference though is that research in consumer behaviour quickly differentiated itself from the economics frameworks that were used for much managerial marketing by turning to other behavioural disciplines. An understanding of theory in consumer behaviour cannot be grasped without some comprehension of the wider roles of psychology, sociology and anthropology in marketing. These are covered elsewhere in this book and many marketing academics who have researched and published on consumer behaviour received their initial training in one of these behavioural sciences. As we shall see, the dominant discipline of them all in consumer research is psychology, where ideas from cognitive and social psychology have been used extensively in the search to explain aspects of purchasing and consumption.

In the chapter on consumer behaviour in the first edition of *Marketing Theory* three main periods were identified where research on consumer behaviour had highlighted different marketing and consumption issues. Starting in the 1950s there was a 20-year period where research on segmentation was prolific. As noted above, this directly parallels the emergence of the managerial school of thought as identified by Sheth, Gardner and Garrett (1988), and buyer behaviour theory was a logical accompaniment to the development of ideas relating to the different aspects of the marketing mix. This period saw classical papers published on the family life-cycle, personality, social class, lifestyles and psychographics, all testing the efficacy of these constructs for segmentation.

Developing rapidly in the 1960s, and overlapping with the previous research theme, we have a corresponding interest in consumer decision making with key early contributions from authors such as John Howard (1963) and Everett Rogers (1959; 1963). The 1960s saw attempts to develop comprehensive models of consumer decision making by Nicosia (1966), Engel and Blackwell and Howard and Sheth (1969) and the rapid adoption of developments in attitude theory from psychology, especially the idea of multi-attribute approaches following the work of people such as Rosenberg and Fishbein. Working with Ajzen, Fishbein's early work was developed into more general models of human behaviour which are still used extensively by consumer researchers, especially it seems those working in social marketing areas. A summary of the most recent material in this area is offered later in the chapter.

The early 1980s, I suggest, saw something of a switch in consumer behaviour research. It saw the abandonment of attempts to develop comprehensive decision-making models and a diversification of interests. There was more research on affect and emotions as opposed to a concentration on the cognitive dimensions of consumer decision making and, at the same time, a fresh look at actual consumption as opposed to purchasing. Studies in consumption started to use more interpretative methods to examine possessions and their meanings.

A good example of this transition can be seen in the research around the ideas of self concept. Work in the 1970s culminating in Sirgy's 1982 review paper in the *Journal of Consumer Research* (JCR) was linked into traditional psychological frameworks around ideas of actual and ideal selves. This approach has continued in mainstream psychology with similar conceptualizations of the self being cited consistently over the past 20 years but it has received almost no attention in the marketing journals. In contrast, in consumer behaviour, Belk and others took work on the self in a different direction and in particular linked it to symbolic communication as they sought to explain how possessions formed part of a person's identity and were used to communicate meaning to others. In this respect we can see that authors like Belk and Hirschman were perhaps ahead of influential European sociologists like Giddens (1991) and Chaney (1996) who later focused on identity and possessions as key indicators of delivering status in a postmodern society. Perhaps the key idea here is that in a modern society people are less constrained by traditional elements that define social class. Constructing an identity through consumption patterns in order to display a particular lifestyle becomes the key method of acquiring status and position within society.

This view of the evolution of theory in consumer research is of course a very simplified big picture. Shortly we will look in more detail at the type of work published in the last 30 years but before discussing that in detail it is worth reflecting a little more about the early origins of consumer research in marketing. While the emergence of a distinctive body of research on consumers clearly becomes evident in the 1950s, a focus on understanding the consumer can also be seen in some of the earliest publications in marketing which sought to provide working classifications of goods that could be used as a basis for marketing strategies and actions. Of those classifications clearly the most famous and enduring has been Copeland's 1923 *Harvard Business Review* paper suggesting one could classify all products into either convenience, shopping or speciality goods. While these papers are seen to be motivated by the need to provide necessary typologies for an emerging discipline they are clearly based on an analysis of factors in consumer behaviour, such as the extent of information search and levels of perceived risk. Later Aspinwall's (1958) classification of red, orange and yellow goods includes other consumer behaviour factors such as replacement rates, or repeat purchase, replacement. However, a closer comparison with later theory developed in consumer behaviour relating to involvement shows how authors such as Copeland were predicting differences not just in high and low involvement but also in different types of involvement. While convenience goods clearly relate to low involvement situations, the difference between shopping and speciality goods in Copeland's classification primarily relates to changing the focus of involvement from the purchase itself to involvement with the product or brand. Sometimes this is termed the difference between situational involvement around the purchasing decision to enduring involvement with the product and its use.

As mentioned above, there are many specialist journals that deal with consumer behaviour theory and applications. The first of these, established in 1974, and still regarded as the leading specialist journal in the subject, is *the Journal of Consumer Research* (JCR). In 2004 the journal produced a 30-year cumulative index of their articles including a classification by subject. Using this classification as the starting point, the following sections attempt to give a more contemporary overview of the subject. Closely related categories such as affect and emotion have been collapsed and information from keywords and abstracts from 1974 through to 2008 have been coded against the categories below. The results are not claimed as a comprehensive content analysis of the whole subject of consumer research but they are intended to give a feel for the scope of the subject as it has been published upon in the leading specialist journal. Moreover, the information presented is perhaps best viewed as a description of how researchers in consumer behaviour actually describe their work in the search terms and abstracts they use to promote their papers. For example, it is clear that most, if not all, papers mention key theoretical constructs or problem areas but many fewer advertise any area of application to any industry sector or particular population.

Table 12.1   Behavioural research

Consumer behaviours	Number of studies
Acquisition patterns	6
Charity/gift giving	27
Deviant behaviours	12
Possessions	6
Shopping behaviour	10
Situational influences	75
Symbolic consumption	74
Time	12
Variety seeking	52

Theoretical focus

The three tables in this section categorize research papers into broad areas according to whether they mainly deal with actual behaviours, psychological processes or wider sociological issues. In Table 12.1 there are a range of studies that report some aspect of *actual* or *intended* behaviour as a focus for the study. Aspects of symbolic consumption are the most comprehensively discussed behavioural topic. These papers reflect both the kinds of meaning that people communicate through consumption and also the behavioural processes that underlie symbolic consumption. The other two major categories in this area are research which deals with time and situational influences. Both these categories are actually quite diverse and they also cover research that crosses into the psychological area. For example, they may deal with other factors and behaviours impacting on decision making. Even with time and situational factors both classified in this group it is surprising that the total number of studies that identify themselves as dealing with some aspect of behaviour or usage is not larger.

Two areas in particular would seem very general and central to the subject – acquisition patterns and shopping behaviour. One would expect that, since most decisions and purchases we make as consumers are clearly not independent of other purchases, acquisition patterns and understanding these inter-relationships might have received more attention. Perhaps it is timely to remember Alderson's (1954) idea regarding 'potency of assortment' which makes it quite clear that the utility or value associated with any particular marketplace exchange is dependent upon its contribution to some total mix, or holding, by the consumer. Furthermore, it is interesting to note that all the papers that identify themselves as dealing with acquisition patterns were published between 1979 and 1987. It is not at all clear why this should be the case but it could be seen as at least consistent with the start of the third general research phase identified in the introduction.

In contrast, all the papers that reference or use the term shopping behaviour have been published since 2000. It is possible that this reflects a change in the use of keywords and referencing within the subject since there are earlier papers that reference retailing but this term is not used after the 1990s.

Table 12.2 presents a summary of the types of essentially psychological constructs that have been identified in articles in JCR. The most obvious feature displayed in

Table 12.2   Psychological research

Consumer psychology	Number of studies
Aesthetics and hedonics	16
Affect, emotion and mood	73
Attention and perception	101
Attitudes and preferences	248
Choice and choice models	106
Cognitive processing	110
Consumer socialization	28
Decision theory and processes	205
Expertise and knowledge	57
Inference	35
Information processing	402
Learning	38
Memory	66
Motivation and involvement	130
Perceived risk	30
Personality	55
Satisfaction and dissatisfaction	46
Self concept and image	68
Values	17

Table 12.2 is the sheer number of papers that deal with these issues compared to those that deal directly with the behavioural aspects of consumption, or indeed the more macro level and societal issues that are presented in Table 12.3. This imbalance is completely consistent with William Wells' critical appraisal of the state of consumer research published in the *Journal of Consumer Research* in 1993. Wells argued how research had been dominated by a concentration of work investigating the pre-purchase aspects of mainly brand choices and how it had largely ignored both post-purchase issues and also 'higher level' consumer decisions that substantially affect life directions. Examples of the latter would be decisions about further education, housing or careers. In other words, research had concentrated on the simpler choices between more equivalent options rather than dealing with the complex situations where choices often have to be made between non-comparable alternatives with abstract attributes. The frequencies certainly endorse Wells' claim about a concentration on the pre-purchase stages of the buying process. Within the list the dominant topics are those that relate to information processing and evaluation in some way. Search and acquisition of information is a significant part of the information processing group and articles on these topics have appeared consistently throughout the history of the journal.

The second major group relates to attitude and preference studies which, as noted above, became popular about the time of the founding of the journal. Similarly publications on decisions process and structures have been constant since the inception of the journal. Other topics, however, do show periods of popularity with more intensive research and much less activity at other times. Satisfaction and dissatisfaction is one example of this with most work in the 1980s and 1990s. Similarly, with the exception of a couple of papers in the early part of this century, all the papers on values were published in the late 1980s and early 1990s, while papers on learning were not classified until the late 1980s but since that date they have appeared at consistent intervals. One recent topic to emerge is that of cognitive processes and processing which have all been published in the last 10 years. As in the parent discipline of psychology, it would seem that the prevailing ethos in consumer behaviour has moved away from social psychology to cognitive psychology and, if the subject in marketing is to continue to follow the parent discipline, it would seem that this trend will only accelerate. Indeed it is interesting to speculate whether marketing research will perhaps follow the move towards neurological approaches to the analysis of the brain to understand consumer behaviour. The first tentative steps in this direction have already been made with so called neuromarketing which focuses on activation levels in the brain when exposed to stimuli such as products, brands and advertising. In recent mainstream psychology it would seem that memory research for example is now dominated by more clinical studies analysing chemical changes in the brain. As a 'synthetic subject' (Baker, 2000) marketing has always drawn appropriately from other disciplines so it is interesting to speculate whether marketing curricula will have to involve biochemistry and clinical psychology as basic requirements in the future.

The absolute dominance of psychological perspectives on consumer behaviour in the *Journal of Consumer Research* becomes very evident when looking at the sociological and macro studies that have been reported in the journal (See Table 12.3). In making this observation one must be careful to recall we are only dealing here with research published in one long-established journal, and that specialist journals such as the *Journal of Consumer Affairs* and the *Journal of Consumer Policy* exist to deal specifically with consumerism issues, while more recently *Culture, Markets and Consumption* has established itself to deal with work involving cultural theory. On the other hand, two other well established journals – *Psychology and Marketing* and the *Journal of Consumer Psychology* – also exist to concentrate on this discipline base.

While not being very extensively researched and published upon in the journal, it is also worth noting that some topics, including lifestyles, social class and the family have received very little attention in recent years. Indeed four of the papers on social class were published in the first three years of the journal's life while the bulk of the lifestyles papers appeared from 1988 to 1993. The family has received virtually no attention at all in the last 10 years. Of all these

Table 12.3   Societal issues in consumer research

Macro/sociological issues	Number of studies
Consumer ethics	2
Culture	18
Family	62
Lifestyles	17
Social and reference groups	66
Social class	12
Welfare/well-being	8
Women in the workforce	22

Table 12.4   Perspectives in consumer research

Theory/philosophy perspectives	Number of studies
Critical theory	13
Economic analysis	78
Feminism	3
Literary theory	5
Marxism	1
Naturalistic inquiry	2
Phenomenology	6
Philosophy of science	35
Positivism	3
Postmodernism and post-structuralism	10
Post-positivism	40
Sociological analysis	73

macro and sociological topics, the one that is clearly receiving most current attention is culture with the bulk of the papers published since the year 2000.

Research paradigms and methods

By no means all papers make reference to the paradigm within which they are based or even explicitly describe aspects of the method within keywords and abstracts. Those papers counted in Table 12.4 that mention a particular philosophy of science, such as naturalistic inquiry or literary theory, tend to be discursive papers on that topic in consumer research. Those articles that make reference to the more general terms of economic and sociological analysis cover many different methods but include the description of the overall orientation of the research paper or the context in which it was set. For example, the term sociological analysis is often used in the early years in the journal in articles that studied aspects of family decision making or reference group influence. It would seem that the need to describe this overall orientation is less common now than in the earlier years of the journal. In both the general categories of economic and sociological analysis about two-thirds of the papers were published in the first 10 years of the journal's history.

The range of research methods mentioned in the review is very extensive but, as with the more general theoretical and philosophical perspectives, it is only a fairly small proportion of papers that explicitly mention methods in their abstracts and keywords. Methods such as causal modelling and choice modelling are referred to consistently throughout the history of the journal while the most referred to method, experimental design, has become more common since the 1980s. Other methods with smaller occurrence levels such as discourse, grounded theory and hermeneutics have also emerged during this same period. This seems to reflect the increasing diversity of research work in consumer theory but the dominant perspective that is also reflected here would still seem to be based very much in cognitive psychology. A significant surprise is the small number of

Table 12.5   Research methods in consumer research

Research methods and issues	Number of studies
Bayesian approaches	4
Causal modelling	29
Choice modelling	27
Content analysis	12
Depth interviews	12
Discourse and literary analysis	4
Econometrics	2
Ethnography	18
Experimental design	55
Grounded theory	2
Hermeneutics	2
Historical methods	5
Interpretative methods	5
Mathematical models	3
Measurement and psychometrics	26
Meta-analysis	6
Multi-method approaches	3
Multivariate methods	7
Network analysis	4
Observation	1
Panel data analysis	3
Physiological research	17
Questionnaire design	2
Sampling	3
Semiotics	8
Simulation	3
Structural analysis	1
Survey methods	10
Validity and reliability	78

published research papers that make reference to common techniques employed in the commercial research on consumers. For example, observation panel data and survey methods are all widely applied in commercial market research but they play little part in the make-up of the methodologies employed by academic researchers of consumer behaviour.

The largest single grouping in the methods and issues table (Table 12.5) are those papers identifying themselves as concerned with either or both of validity and reliability. Studies referencing these issues became popular in the 1980s and continue to the present. It is probable that a similar examination of publications in other areas of marketing would reveal a similar growth in research papers referencing these topics. Although there is some recent revision of thinking regarding measurement in marketing with interest in alternative approaches such as formative measures, COARSE procedures (Rossiter (2002)) (Ewing, Salzkerger and Sinclovics (2000)) and Rasch methods, it is hard to underestimate the influence of Churchill's 1979 paper on measurement in marketing. This was a paper that raised awareness of these problems and provided a template for aspects of the research process which is still followed. A check on GoogleScholar on 20 March 2009 revealed 3,425 citations for Churchill's paper. As a comparison, this is approximately three times the citations received by Levitt's classic paper on 'Marketing myopia'. While the early attitude scaling theorists like Guttman and Thurstone have always been acknowledged in marketing, what Churchill did was to tie much research in marketing, especially in consumer behaviour, to those particular reflective psychological scaling methods as the standard way of approaching the development of theory and knowledge.

Study populations of interest

There are relatively few research papers in JCR that mention a particular demographic as the focal point of their research and most that do concentrate on a particular age group, with more research on children and adolescents than on older people. This is slightly surprising given both the increasing proportion of elderly people within most Western populations and also the concentration of discretionary expenditure that resides in that part of the population. In terms of changes over time, studies on children and adolescents appear to be more common in the earlier years of the journal than in later decades, while the reverse is true for cross-cultural studies. Only five cross-cultural studies appear in the first 10 years of the journal and since 1985 they occur regularly at a rate of about two a year.

One other feature remains hidden in the reported study populations that are summarized in Table 12.6. This is the quantity of research in consumer behaviour that uses student samples. It would be a mistake to assume that all, or even the majority of the remaining papers published in the journal were research studies that investigated consumer behaviour and purchasing amongst the general population. As noted in the table on research methods (Table 12.5) experimental formats are the most frequently reported method. A more detailed sampling of one randomly chosen issue from each of the past five years shows that approximately three-quarters of the papers in those issues were experimental studies using student samples. For example, the February 2009 edition of the journal has 12 full papers. Nine of these are experimental studies, primarily around some aspect of information processing using student samples. The

Table 12.6 Target population

Sample/population of interest	Number of studies
Adolescents and children	55
Older consumers	20
Sex and sex roles	25
Cross-cultural comparisons	51

remaining three papers include a qualitative study with a population of 30 gamblers, a participant observation study on illicit pleasure and, very unusually for consumer research, a meta-analysis on consumer knowledge. It is arguable whether any of the studies using student samples actually investigated a topic specifically and only relevant to that cohort of the population. Hence, while new relationships are tested and useful insights are contained in all the papers, only the meta-analysis has any real pretence at producing conclusions that have any generalizability. It would seem that consumer research has really continued to emphasize internal validity, at the expense of external validity, and once more Wells' (1993) conclusion about the imbalance in consumer research, in at least its leading journal, is supported. Findings from experimental work, using student samples on the pre-purchase aspects of decision making dominate what we know about consumer behaviour.

Marketing applications of consumer research

Table 12.7 describes the areas of marketing applications that are referred to in JCR papers. The frequencies in this table related to advertising and communication research support the previous conclusion about the overwhelming dominance of enquiries on pre-purchase behaviour. These two areas, together with research on product and brand choice have dominated throughout the 35-year history of JCR. Amongst the other categories, it is interesting to note that the branding literature is more recent, with most papers being published since the mid-1990s, while most of the segmentation work was carried out during the 1980s. The lack of work on market segmentation is somewhat surprising considering the importance of the concept in marketing and the need to understand heterogeneity amongst consumers. However, since segmentation work normally requires larger scale survey work with samples drawn from the general population it is clearly not regarded as a priority by consumer researchers where the major conversations take place around developing and testing theory for different aspects of information processing.

Table 12.7   Marketing applications of consumer research

Marketing application	Number of studies
Advertising and advertising effects	222
Bargaining and negotiation	24
Branding	17
Communication and persuasion	180
Innovation and diffusion	36
New products	25
Pricing	71
Product/brand choice	144
Segmentation	23

Table 12.8   Area of economic activity

Industry or economic sector	Number of studies
Alcohol and drugs	17
Consumer credit	9
Consumer education and information	25
E-consumption	10
Energy	31
Health care and related issues	30
Industrial and organizational buying	8
Leisure and recreation	19
Public and not-for profit	13
Retailing	22
Services	11
Voting behaviour	7

The other interesting facet of Table 12.7 is the lack of research that deals with the distribution element of the marketing mix. While some research relating to this element is perhaps described in Table 12.8 in the few studies that relate to retailing or services, there are no mentions at all of research that deals with issues such as after-sales service, guarantees, dissatisfaction or complaint behaviour. Clearly, research has been conducted on all these topics but it is not promoted in an obvious way in the main consumer research journal. Actual purchasing and the continued involvement of consumers in market relationships have generated very little research in consumer behaviour in contrast to organizational and business relationships. While it is now much more common for papers in the *Journal of Consumer Research* to contain the results of several related studies in order to give depth and reliability to the conclusions, there are very few studies that involve investigation over consumer problems over time. Nearly all knowledge on consumer behaviour is based upon cross-sectional studies which are necessarily limited in the kinds of problems that they can address.

Some research is motivated by particular problems that occur within particular industries or sectors. Table 12.8 provides a summary of where this research is located. The spread of contexts covered in the table is quite broad but the overall number of papers specifying an industry area is quite small. It is not surprising to see areas such as alcohol, drugs and health listed since they present particular problems to groups of consumers. Similarly, energy and credit became major issues even before global warming and the current recession made them items of general news. Indeed since credit is such an integral part of many major consumption decisions it is amazing how little investigation has taken place on this topic in the last 30 years.

In Table 12.1 it was noted how few studies in consumer behaviour actually referred to shopping. In a similar way it is surprising how few consumer research papers actually specify any relevance to retailing or retail services, and considering the pervasiveness of the internet there are also very few that deal with e-consumption.

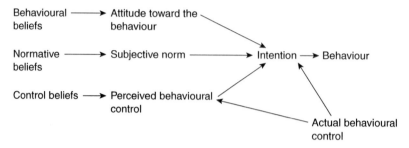

Figure 12.1   The Theory of Planned Behavior (Ajzen, 2009)

Source: Ajzen I. Theory of Planned Behavior home page (2006). Available at: http://www.people.unless.edu/ajzen/tpb.html. Accessed 21 March 2009.

Developing an integrated approach to consumer behaviour

Drawing together the information presented in the previous tables I am reminded of a recent description of marketing by Cova (2005: 205) 'that it is an increasingly dispersed sum of constituent parts'. While there is a clear dominant paradigm that has dominated consumer behaviour research over the last 30 years there have been very few attempts to produce any integrative models that provide any general theories equivalent to those guiding the earlier development of the subject, such as the Theory of Reasoned Action as it was developed in the 1970s and later extended to the Theory of Planned Behavior (Ajzen, 1991). Interestingly, while the Theory of Planned Behavior is now infrequently referenced in marketing journals it does remain a popular framework in consumer research published in areas like health, physical activity and leisure. The theory is based on three central components as predictors of intentions, as shown in Figure 12.1. The principles are straightforward and suggest that our behaviour as consumers is goal orientated and determined by three fundamental forces:

1. Our attitude towards the activity or object. This measures the appeal of the item or behaviour under investigation.

2. Our view of social norms around the consumer behaviour under consideration and our desire to comply with those social norms.

3. Our ability to be able to control the situation and act in the way we wish. Ability to control may be conditioned by outside factors such as prices or internal aspects such as addiction if we were trying to model a behaviour such as cessation of smoking or drinking.

Together these drivers are seen to determine our intentions, which allowing for situational factors, for example a stockout at the store, predict our final behaviour. Ajzen clearly argues that with appropriate and precise specification of the behaviour, the

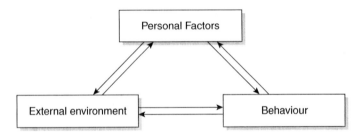

Figure 12.2   A social cognitive model of behaviour (Bandura, 1986)

Planned Behavior model will give useful predictions. Examples where it is less successful and greater discrepancies arise between attitudes and behaviours are usually in cases where there is less precision or more abstraction in the definition of the behaviour. Thus, it may not be a good predictor of how many alcoholic drinks you are likely to have in the next week or month, but will be more successful in explaining how much wine you are likely to drink at your birthday dinner.

Also widely used in the social marketing arena is an alternative comprehensive approach to considering consumer behaviour known as social cognitive theory. This approach was developed primarily by Bandura in the 1980s building on earlier ideas of social learning theory. Social learning theory emphasized humans learning by imitation and stresses how we learn to cope with our environment by watching others cope with similar situations. Bandura developed this idea by introducing personal characteristics, especially motivation and self-efficacy as mediating effects. As a construct self-efficacy refers to the belief that one can master a particular behaviour and adopt it as a regular practice, so it has a close association with Ajzen's idea regarding perceived behavioural control. Bandura shows the three elements of the person, the environment and the behaviour interacting in a reciprocal triangle as shown in Figure 12.2.

Social cognitive theory has many elements that are similar to Planned Behavior. For example, there are roles for social norms and support, sets of beliefs about the outcomes of the behaviour (e.g. improved health from eating your daily quota of fruit and vegetables), tastes and preferences, and perceptions of the environment which can include factors such as price which determine accessibility. However, there is a fundamental difference in approach between the two models. While Planned Behavior sees behaviour as more goal orientated and moderated by the environment, social cognitive theory tends to emphasize 'environmental' influences but then allows for them to be mediated by an individual's level of motivation and self-efficacy. In this model the emphasis for encouraging behavioural change lies as much, or more, on changing the environment in order to encourage the desired response, as it does on persuasive advertising or education in order to try to raise levels of individual motivation.

Although they are not linked in the literature, it seems that the principles of social cognitive theory accord well with the work of Bettman, Luce and Payne (1998) who have tried to provide an integrated framework for understanding decision-making. They present a complex view of decision-making processes and strategies that are heavily influenced by the environment. In essence they argue that consumers construct the decision framework they use, including the choice of the appropriate heuristic according to the particular context. Hence environmental factors, such as the number and type of both attributes and alternatives under consideration and the amount of time available, structure how the decision is made as well as the individual's own goals and abilities.

In some respects then, social cognitive theory can be seen as a step towards the behaviourist tradition in psychology which was not mentioned at all in the earlier discussion of the contents of the *Journal of Consumer Research*. This is surprising since although cognitive psychology clearly holds the ascendency, there have been some strong advocates of this approach, including Gordon Foxall, who has arguably been the UK's leading consumer behaviour theorist for the last 30 years (Foxall, 1990). Evidence to support basic behaviourist theories as potentially important in explaining consumer behaviour can also be garnered from the work of Andrew Ehrenberg and his colleagues. For over 30 years Ehrenberg has been primarily looking at aggregate forms of consumer behaviour with panel data and showing consistent patterns of consumer responses to matters such as repeat purchasing and loyalty irrespective of the precise particulars of the market. For example, his work on double jeopardy (Ehrenberg et al., 1990) shows quite clearly that market share is closely linked to behavioural measures of loyalty, so that the idea of specialist niche products controlling a small but secure part of the market and protected by high levels of loyalty is potentially misleading. The implications of this type of finding in Ehrenberg's work for consumer behaviour are quite simple. It suggests that, as an aggregate body, consumers usually respond quite consistently to simple cues that they receive in the marketplace. If they are more familiar with a market leader, which probably has more shelf space and more promotional support, consumers are also likely to buy it more often than the alternatives. It also suggests that in most situations consumers are essentially satisficers as opposed to utility maximizers, and that our behaviour as consumers is not likely to be overcomplicated and too goal orientated.

Overall, the 'mixed' approach suggested by social cognitive theory is appealing. It has the advantage of not reducing humans, who are clearly capable of forethought and planning, to the same level of decision making as their pets, but at the same time it does not turn every decision and behaviour into a complex goal-directed extensive problem. Furthermore, the bi-directional aspects of Bandura's relationships in his social cognitive approach also seem to fit with recent ideas in marketing such as co-creation. They allow causality to flow back from the individual to the environment in any situation and confirm that the marketing manager may influence, but is never in control in a way that the purely behaviourist approaches might suggest could be the case.

Outside the dominant cognitive and social psychology research the other main stream of research published in JCR has been the interpretative material focusing on actual consumption and possessions. In this area there has been at least one explicit recent attempt, by Arnould and Thompson in 2005, to generate an integrative framework to bring together much of this research under the banner of consumer culture theory (CCT). Even so, Arnould and Thompson are absolutely explicit in saying that they are not trying to create any sort of general theory in the area but are rather providing an evaluation and classification of the research in this area. They draw together a large number of articles into a fourfold classification as follows:

1. Research that develops theory around consumer identity

2. Studies of marketplace culture where the important role of consumption configures cultural blueprints

3. Investigations into socio-historic patterns of consumption, involving the institutional and social structures that influence consumption

4. The examination of mass-mediated marketplace ideologies.

It is accepted that classifications such as this are often the first step towards substantial theory development since they provide both a basis for future integration and assist with the generation of future research questions and propositions so we may expect strong theoretical developments in the area in the future.

Missed opportunities in consumer behaviour theory

In 1991 Wind, Rao and Green identified a series of seven shifts in consumer research that they felt pointed to the future at that time. Briefly these were:

1. A change in the unit of analysis from the individual to more realistic assessments of households and groups

2. Consideration of assortments of products and sets of behaviours as opposed to single instances

3. Examination of situation-specific behaviours in order to increase the validity of consumer research

4. A move from deterministic to stochastic modelling of consumer behaviour

5. A lessening of the US focus in consumer research

6. A shift from a 'low tech' to a 'high tech' consumer environment with consequent changes for consumer research and methodologies

7. The use of integrated sets of research methods rather than single approaches.

All of these seemed reasonable predictions at the time since they were based on known needs at the end of the 1980s and observable trends and developments in research methods. However, nearly two decades later virtually none of these have come to pass. The main unit for research is still the individual, with most research using experimental formats with individuals (often students as noted earlier). While some research has been conducted on product and brand constellations in an effort to understand the inter-relationship between sets of items, this is still very much the exception. The JCR index which clarifies research on situational aspects of consumer behaviour shows no observable increase in this work over time and the researchers following in the Ehrenberg tradition with stochastic modelling are still very much in the minority. The US focus in the research is still very much apparent despite the policies of some recent editors to internationalize their publications. There has been a shift for many consumers to a 'high tech' environment but this has not been followed by researchers using the kind of methods and materials envisaged by Wind, Rao and Green. Panel scanner data and internet data, for example, may be common in marketing science publications but not elsewhere in the consumer behaviour literature. Finally, while there does seem to have been a change in one respect regarding research in consumer behaviour at least, it is not towards the use of integrated sets of research methods but rather towards integrated studies using similar methods. Looking through articles in the last few years in JCR, for example, it is much more common to see repeated studies with a programme of research reported, as opposed to seeing single snapshot studies.

One other call for consumer research was made in 1991 by Hirschman, who made a strong plea for more research into a range of social problems associated with consumption. She argued that many such problems were the result of 'consumption gone wrong' and that some of these issues would inevitably rebound as consequences for marketing managers. While there is clearly some evidence of research related to health, addiction and gambling in the consumer journals, they are still a very small proportion of the work carried out. As with Wind, Rao and Green's list of opportunities from the same time, Hirschman's call looks like another missed opportunity by marketing scholars. Journals in areas such as energy and health are now replete with studies of consumer behaviour arising from the need to deal with issues such as increasing energy efficiency and combating global warming, through to managing the Western obesity crisis. While social marketing studies have increased in number they have not become part of the mainstream material in consumer research. One difference, as alluded to earlier, is that studies in these areas, usually conducted by people outside business schools, have tended to stay with integrated approaches to analysing consumer behaviour such as the Theory of Planned Behavior of Social Cognitive Theory. Another construct that they have adopted widely but which is now hardly referred to in the consumer behaviour literature is that of lifestyles. Largely abandoned in marketing and consumer behaviour after being criticized as both atheoretic and also impractical, they are widely referred to in the health literature. A search on the term in GoogleScholar in March 2009 revealed that of the first 100 articles (mainly written in the last 10 years), 78 were health references with most of the rest arising from sociology, geography or planning. When lifestlyes were first introduced into marketing in the 1960s as a meso-systemic approach for understanding consumer behaviour, it was well in advance of scholars from those areas in realizing the potential use of the construct for understanding an integrated pattern of resources, attitudes and behaviours that could usefully describe the heterogeneity found in the marketplace.

Summarizing on what are some missed opportunities, I believe consumer research has probably become too fragmented and over-concerned with internal as opposed to external validity. As such it has lost touch with important issues facing the marketing system. For example, while some acknowledgement of aspects of sustainability can be found, particularly related to environmental issues, some of the problems associated with the current credit crisis were no surprise to those who had followed credit card or savings behaviours. Similarly, the idea of 'peak oil' has been known for decades, the same with global warming and the need to reduce carbon emissions. These important consumer behaviour issues, together with their consequences for businesses and all the other actors in the marketing system, simply do not figure as issues in building theory and knowledge on consumer behaviour in marketing. I believe that consumer behaviour must strive to regain its relevance both for marketing managers and for policymakers.

References

Ajzen, I. (1991) 'The theory of planned behavior', *Organizational Behavior and Decision Processes* 50: 179–211 (also see http://people.umass.edu/aizen/tpb).

Alderson, W. (1954) Problem Solving and Marketing Science, The Charles Coolidge Memorial Lecture, accessed from marketing.whorton.upenn.edu/.../Alderson/problem_solving_and_marketing_science.pdf-

Aspinwall, L. (1958) The Characteristics of Goods and Parallel Systems Theories. In: J. Sheth and D. Garrett, Editors, *Marketing Theory: Classic and Contemporary Readings*, South-Western Pub Co., Cincinnati, OH (1958), pp. 252–70.

Arnould, E.J. and Thompson, C.G. (2005) 'Consumer culture theory (CCT): twenty years of research', *Journal of Consumer Research* 31, March: 868–81.

Baker, M.J. (2000) *Marketing Theory*, London, Thomson Learning (Preface page v).

Bandura, A. (1986) *Social Foundations of Thought and Action.* Englewood Cliffs, NJ: Prentice Hall.

Bettman, J.R., Luce, M.J. and Payne, J.W. (1998) 'Constructive consumer choice processes', *Journal of Consumer Research* 25, December: 187–217.

Chaney, D. (1996) *Lifestyles*, London: Routledge.

Churchill, G.A. (1979) 'A paradigm for developing better measures of marketing constructs', *Journal of Marketing Research* 42, February: 64–73.

Copeland, M.T. (1923) 'Relation of consumer buying habits to marketing methods', *Harvard Business Review* 1(3): 282–9.

Cova, B. (2005) 'Thinking of marketing in Meridian terms', *Marketing Theory* 5(2): 205–14.

Ehrenberg, A.S.C., Goodhardt, G.J. and Barwise, T.P. (1990) 'Double jeopardy revisited', *Journal of Marketing* 54(2): 82–91.

Engel, J.F., Kollat, D.T. and Blackwell, R.D. (1968) *Consumer Behavior*, New York: Holt Rinehart and Winston.

Ewing, M.T. Salzberger, T. and Sinkovics, R.R. (2005) An Alternate Approach to Assess Cross-Cultural Measurement Equivalence in Advertising Research. Journal of Advertising, 34(1): 17–36.

Foxall, G.R. (1990) *Consumer Psychology in Behavioural Perspective*, London: Routledge.

Giddens, A. (1991) *Modernity and Self-Identity. Self and Society in the Last Modern Age.* Cambridge: Polity.

Hirschman, E.C. (1991) 'Secular mortality and the dark side of consumer behavior: or how semiotics saved my life', in R.H. Holman and M.R. Solomon (eds) *Advances in Consumer Research*, Vol. 18, Provo, UT: Association for Consumer Research.

Howard, J.A. (1963) *Marketing Management: Analysis and Planning*, Homewood IL, Richard D. Irwin.

Howard, J.A. and Sheth, J.N. (1969) *The Theory of Buyer Behavior*, New York: John Wiley and sons.

Nicosia, F. (1966) *Consumer Decision Processes: Marketing and Advertising Implications*, Engelwood Cliffs, NJ: Prentice Hall.

Rogers, E., (1959) *The Adoption of New Products: Process and Influence*. Ann Arbor, MI: Foundation for Research on Human Behavior.

Rogers, E., (1963) *Diffusion of Innovations*, New York: Free Press.

Rossiter, J.R. (2002) The C-OAR-SE Procedure for Scale Development in Market Research *International Journal of Research in Marketing*, 14(4): 305–35.

Sheth, J.N., Gardner, D.M. and Garrett, D. (1988) *Marketing Theory: Evolution and Evaluation*, New York: Wiley and Sons.

Sirgy, J.M. (1982) 'Self concept in consumer behavior: a critical review', *Journal of Consumer Research* 9, December: 287–92.

Wells, W.D. (1993) 'Discovery-oriented consumer research', *Journal of Consumer Research* 19(4): 489–504.

Wind, J., Rao, V.R. and Green, P.E. (1991) 'Behavioral methods', in T.S. Robertson and H.H. Kassarjian (eds) *Handbook of Consumer Behavior*, Englewood Cliffs, NJ: Prentice Hall.

|13|

Innovation and new product development

Susan Hart

Chapter Topics

Chapter objectives

This chapter is concerned with how innovation and new product development (NPD) can be conceptualized as a developing body of knowledge. Drawing on literature spanning some 30 years, this chapter reveals NPD as a fundamentally cross-disciplinary field of study that has markets and customers as twin focal points around which theoretical and practical perspectives of management are examined. The primary objectives of the chapter are:

1. To present the multi-disciplinary nature of new product development

2. To identify the centrality of the process in NPD and distinguish other factors leading to the successful development of new products, including organizational structures, people and information

3. To describe the core activities (models) commonly used to guide new product success

4. To calibrate the utility of process models for theory and practice managerial guidance.

─────────── Learning outcomes ───────────────────────────

On completion of this chapter you will:

1. Appreciate the multiplicity of perspectives in models of new product development

2. Understand NPD model utility and shortcomings as tools of management

3. Be able to integrate contemporary ideas impacting the models in NPD, including organization, people management and information.

─────────── **Introduction** ───────────────────────────

The chapter attempts to synthesize the major issues involved in developing successful new products. Traditionally, the term 'new products' was quite specific, largely confined to physical products, and, in much of the early writing on NPD, implicitly denoting *consumer* physical products. Alternative terminology, reflected in the major organ of dissemination of NPD research (the *Journal of Product Innovation Management*) is the term 'product innovation'. In recent years, wider attention given to the dominance of service as the focus of exchange has resulted in more attention being given to new service development – also known as service innovation. Even so, a recent comparison of 16 years of NPD research, noted that only 52 out of 815 articles included data from service organizations and that only 21 articles actually focused on the specifics of new service development (Page and Schirr, 2008). In this chapter, therefore, the terms new product development and product innovation are coloured by the context of physical products, since the theory is based on research whose predominant subject is, at least implicitly, concerned with physical products. The author, however, having conducting studies specifically focusing on service innovation, would contend that many of the ideas relating to product innovation are equally applicable to service innovation (Hart et al., 2008).

One of the enduring features of new product development theory is that it is developed in many different disciplines and sub-fields of business studies. A recent analysis of highly-cited articles on NPD showed that three broad journal domains accounted for a majority of high-impact research during the period 1989–2004: management, marketing and research and development, accounting for 16 per cent, 14 per cent and 23 per cent of all articles respectively. (The remaining 58 per cent, the single biggest 'domain', was accounted for by the multi-disciplinary *Journal of Product Innovation Management* (Page and Schirr, 2008)). In addition, this analysis traced the leading knowledge domains in NPD research, noting the following as important: management and strategy, marketing, organizational behaviour, finance, psychology and technology management. Two further 'domains' were identified – NPD and exploratory/theoretic approaches. In addition to these conclusions regarding the disciplinary roots of developing

NPD schema, other research domains which feature studies of NPD include operations research, design management, engineering and creativity/aesthetic studies. These bases give rise to a wide array of 'topics of study'.

Forty-two streams of research were identified, including supply chain considerations, networking, organizational learning, entrepreneurship, organization for innovation, process development technology and international considerations. Given the thematic diversity of NPD research and theory emanating from relatively few, mostly US journals, any attempt to produce 'new product development theory' in the confines of one chapter would be misleading. Central to the ideas of developing new products, however, are a number of themes forming the foundations of the development of knowledge in NPD. These are:

- The basic activities required to develop new products
- The knowledge of what separates success and failure in NPD
- The necessary considerations for NPD activities to be managed effectively.

This chapter, therefore, is split into three sections. The first gives an overview of various models of NPD in order to identify the tasks required to bring new products and services to market; next, a summary of research into the factors associated with success and failure in NPD is given; and the final section presents methods for developing the models with insights from studies of success and failure, including considerations of organizational structure, and people and information management.

New product development models

New product development (NPD) process models attempt to distill the essence of the activities needed to complete a project; they are therefore general in their orientation and often criticized for not being applicable to individual contexts. For instance, does the development of new services require different stages in the models? Will hi-tech product development follow the same steps as fast-moving consumer goods? In a recent reflection on de-bunking the myths of his Stage-Gate model, Cooper (2008) points out that models take numerous forms and have evolved in their level of prescription over the years. Early representations of new product development models were confining, often describing the NPD process by focusing on the departments or functions that were presumed to carry out various tasks. Through the last three decades these early representations evolved, becoming increasingly based on activities, which were recognized to be fluid, overlapping, open systems, which retain a reference process, widely-known examples being those of Booz Allen Hamilton, and Cooper's Stage-Gate™ shown in Figures 13.1 and 13.2 respectively.

These commonly comprise periods of development activity, followed by points of evaluation (gates), where the decision to continue (or not) with the development

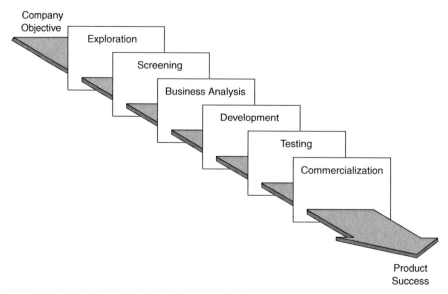

Figure 13.1   The Booz Allen Hamilton model of new product development

Source: Baker, M. and Hart, S. (2007) *Product Strategy and Management*, 2nd edn. Electronically reproduced by permission of Pearson Education, Inc., Upper Saddle River, New Jersey.

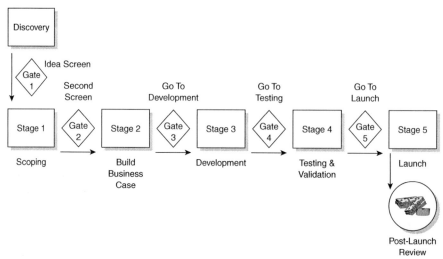

Figure 13. 2   Cooper's Stage-Gate™ model

Source: Baker, M.J. and Hart, S.J. (2007) *Product Strategy and Management*, 2nd edn. Harlow: Pearson Education. Reproduced with permission.

is made . Both the existence and importance of feedback loops are explicit, where each stage is viewed in terms of its potential output into the next stage of the development, as shown in the further refinement of the process in Figure 13.3.

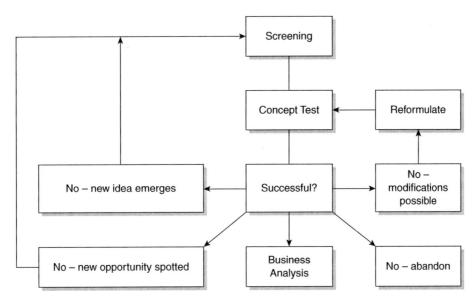

Figure 13. 3   Evaluative gates in NPD

The key stages are briefly summarized below.

_____ Idea generation_____

In many instances, the term idea *generation* might be inappropriate because
although ideas abound and do not have to be 'generated', they must be managed.
The outputs of this stage in the process is the production of ideas that fall within
the mission of the organization and what it seeks to achieve with its NPD efforts.
New product idea sources exist in and outside the firm. Internal sources include
technical areas such as R&D, design, engineering; all of which work on translating
applications and technologies into new product ideas. Customer-facing functions
such as sales and marketing can provide ideas and many company employees may
have actionable ideas. Outside the company, distributors, inventors and universities, as well as competitors and customers, provide rich sources of information
from which new product ideas may flow, if organized in such a way as to extract
ideas. Much of the theory in NPD deals explicitly with how fertile repositories of
information might be activated, using a battery of techniques, including simple
brainstorming or one of its many derivatives such as morphological analysis, or
perceptual mapping and scenario planning. The output from this stage is a pool of
ideas which can be further evaluated for their suitability as future products or
services of a company.

Screening

An initial assessment of the extent of demand for the ideas generated and of the capability the company has to make the product is at the core of this second stage in the NPD process. It is, therefore, the first of a number of stages of evaluation and, as such, only a rough estimation of an idea can be made as the latter is not yet fully expounded in terms of design, materials, features or price. The primary locus for the initial judgement of the viability of ideas will be internal company opinion from R&D, sales, marketing, finance and production, against criteria such as whether the idea would fit a market demand and could be produced by existing plant, and the estimated payback period. The output of this stage in the process is typically a bank of ideas which are suitable for further development. Much research has served to produce tool kits and checklists designed to guide this early appraisal of ideas.

Concept development and evaluation

The initial screening of ideas allows the development team to turn fewer, high-potential propositions into more clearly specified concepts and testing them for fit with company capability and customer expectations may commence. The task of transforming a new product idea into a fully elaborated new product concept is more than semantic labelling. As Montoya-Weiss and O'Driscoll (2000) explain:

> **an idea is defined as the initial, most embryonic form of new product or service idea – typically a one-line description accompanied by a high-level technical diagram. A concept, on the other hand, is defined as a form, technology plus a clear statement of customer benefit. (2000: 145)**

Essentially, there are two sub-phases concerned, the first requires that the idea be more fully elaborated, to include drafting of product or service features, levels of specification, materials, design, aesthetic values and so on. This in turn allows for a more careful presentation of the concept to potential customers, to allow assessment of market fit, done through direct customer research. In addition, the development team needs to assess which configurations are most compatible with current production plant, which require plant acquisition and which require new supplies. Together with idea generation and screening, concept development is worth spending time and effort on, collecting sufficient data to provide adequate information upon which the full business analysis will be made. These activities make up what is often referred to as the 'fuzzy front end', proficiency in which is often associated with superior NPD outcomes (Cooper et al., 2004). The outcome of this step in the process is the information required to carry out the analysis of the full business case.

Business analysis

A pivotal stage, it is at this juncture that the major 'go vs. kill' decision will be made. There needs to be conviction at this point in time, that the venture is potentially viable, because once physical development resource has been committed, expenditure will increase exponentially after this stage. The analysis of the business case, therefore, has to be thorough and comprises:

1. Estimation of potential total market, market share within specific time span, evaluation of competing products, likely price bracket, break-even volume, identification of early adopters and specific market segments

2. Specification of technical aspects: production methods and implications, supplier identification and management, any further R&D required, or investment in plant, equipment or other know-how

3. Justification of the project's fit with corporate strategy.

The sources of information for this stage are both internal and external, incorporating any market or technical research carried out thus far. Where the result of the business analysis is the decision to 'go' with the development, a further stage output will be the development plan with budget and an initial marketing plan.

Product development and testing

In the case of physical products, at this stage prototypes are physically made, involving several tasks. First, the prototype will be tested for its level of functional performance, sometimes called 'alpha testing'. Until this point, the product has only taken theoretical form – a description, drawing or model. Now that component parts are brought together in a functioning product, the viability of the theoretical product can be established. Second, although manufacturing considerations have entered into previous deliberations, only when the prototype is developed, can adjustments to the design or to manufacturing specifications be drafted and implemented. Third, potential customers now have the opportunity to assess their reactions to the product in its real, rather than depicted form. Some kinds of product are more easily tested by customers than others. Services and capital equipment are difficult to 'test', the former due to inseparability, and the latter due to logistics and cost implications. In the case of the latter, however, in-situ testing of new equipment, called 'Beta-testing', is practised widely. In consumer markets, numerous market research techniques are commonly used to test new products.

Product testing has been much aided by the use of the internet for a number of reasons. The cost of 'building' and 'testing' prototypes virtually is small compared to that required by physical prototypes. Consequently, market research costs are lower, and more concepts can be tested by potential customers than is the case with physical products, resulting in a final design which is more attuned to the voice of the customer. In addition, more end customers can be sampled more efficiently via the internet, although the risk of population deterioration is increased as is the likelihood of bias, since not all potential customers selected will be willing to 'test' the product virtually. Research by Dahan and Srinivasan (2000) reported that 'virtual parallel prototyping and testing on the Internet provides a close match to the results generated in person using costlier physical prototypes … ' (2000: 108). The output of this stage in the process is the final specification of the product which will then be produced for the whole market, including the segment or geographical variations.

Test marketing

Test marketing consists of small-scale tests with customers. Until now, the idea, the concept, and even the product have been 'tested' or 'evaluated' in contexts other than a 'real' purchase situation. Other elements of the marketing mix have not been tested, nor has the likely marketing reaction by competitors, nor the attractiveness of the product once offered alongside competing products. For test marketing, the total product appeal is evaluated among the mix of activities comprising the market launch: salesmanship, advertising, sales promotion, distributor incentives and public relations.

As an expensive stage, developers must decide whether the costs of test marketing can be justified by the additional information that will be gathered. Moreover, some new offerings are unsuitable for a small-scale test launch: cars have market testing complete before the launch, while services such as personal insurance cannot be withdrawn once launched on a small scale. The delay caused by a test market to the 'real' launch of the new product to market may benefit competitors who, appraised of a new product launch in the offing, can use the delay to be 'first-to-market'. Alternatively, competitors may profit from the results of a test market as input to their own launch. Further, for some new services, a direct market entry (perhaps on a limited scale) is a viable strategy because new product launch has fewer tangible elements in which to invest, so costs (and therefore risks) are lower.

Test-market simulations use basic models of consumer buying as inputs. Elements such as consumer awareness, trial and repeat purchases, collected via limited surveys or store data, are used to predict adoption of the new product. The output of this stage in the process is the final marketing mix and plan for the market launch.

Commercialization or launch

The last stage of the NPD process comprises decisions such as when to launch the product, where to launch it, how and to whom to launch and is very costly. These decisions are based on information collected throughout the development process and will be moderated by the resources available. Launch strategy includes advertising and necessary trade promotions, together with the production of materials both for the launch proper and for the pre-sales into the distribution pipeline. Sales force and service personnel training may also need to be planned pre-launch to sell and deliver the new product/service effectively.

Attention is focused on reaching the likely early 'innovators' or 'early adopters' of innovation and on targeting communications to them. In industrial markets, early adopters are often innovators in their own markets. These categories are described under the theory of the adoption and diffusion of innovation (Rogers, 1962).

A critique of the NPD process model

The usefulness of the staged process models is attributable to the indication they provide of the magnitude of the project required to develop and launch a new product. Cooper, Edgett and Kleinschmidt (2004) have shown that using a model or 'roadmap' for product development was not a majority practice in US businesses, but was more commonly used by the best NPD performers (38 per cent using) than the worst performers (19 per cent using).

Despite this endorsement, models have been criticized on a number of counts. First, a general view that no two firms will seek to develop products in the same way using the same steps calls the validity of NPD process models into question. The sequence and shape of any step-by-step representation of new product activities will depend on the type of new product being developed and its relationship with the firm's current activities. Moreover, in real situations there is no clear beginning, middle and end to the NPD process. One idea, for example, may spawn several product concept variants, each of which might lead the development process in directions different from those originally intended, challenging the view of linearity in the process model. Equally challenging is the notion of iteration in NPD, resulting from the fact that after each evaluative episode (gate), numerous outputs might be produced, implicating both previous development work and future development progress. Uncritical following of the linear view gives little, if any, guidance of what to do if, for example, a new product concept fails the concept test. Figure 13.4 shows alternative courses of action, after the screening stage, further described below.

It is possible that although the original concept is faulty, a better one is found through the concept tests; it would then re-enter the development process at the screening stage. Alternatively, a new customer may be identified through the concept testing stage, since the objective of concept testing is to be alert to customer needs when formulating a new product. These and other possibilities are shown in Figure 13.4, underlining that process models viewed simply as linear or sequential, are inadequate, particularly regarding up-front activities, which have been shown to be critical to the success of NPD outcomes.

As noted above, the topic of NPD is multi-disciplinary, mirroring the multi-functional tasks required to identify and develop a new product that is fit for purpose in the market. The single-strand linear representation ignores these multi-functional inputs, which include marketing, technical (design) and production tasks or decisions that occur as the process unwinds. Each of these strands of development creates both problems and opportunities within the other two. For example, if, at the product development stage, production has difficulties, costs may increase affecting market potential through increased pricing and rendering the product less attractive to potential buyers. In this case, the new information requires reworking of the market and technical assumptions. New courses of action might include a

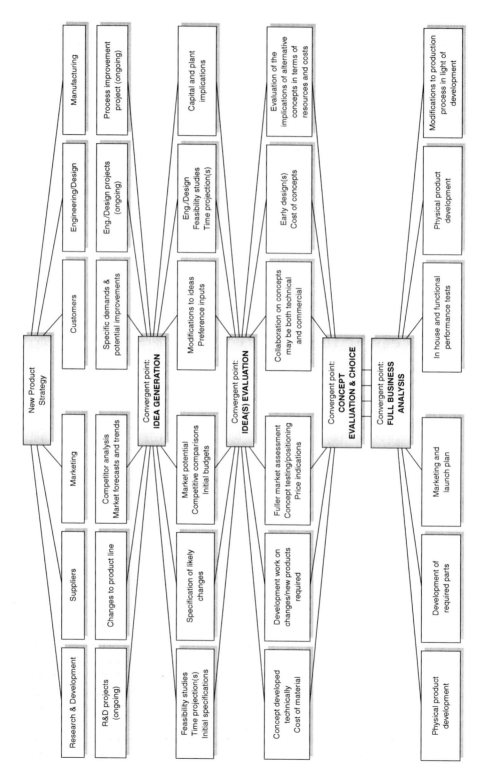

Figure 13.4   Horizontal and vertical iteration in the NPD process (Baker and Hart, 2007: 185)

new design, alternative distribution, acceptance of longer payback horizons, none of which are represented by the single-strand view of NPD. Whatever the nature of the final solution, it has to be based on the interplay of technical, marketing and manufacturing development issues, meaning that product development activity is iterative, not only between stages, but also within stages.

This shortcoming has resulted in the advancement of a number of 'new style' process models, including Nexgen (Cooper, 2008). These amended activity-decision models acknowledge the iterations between and within stages, include principles from related disciplines and functions, such as 'lean and rapid' product development, are recommended for bespoke tailoring to the demands of specific industries and market conditions and have become scalable to match different levels of risk and complexity. They are particularly designed to emphasize multi-disciplinary integration, embracing technical and commercial functions, as well as external parties, since these too are seen as crucial to the outcome of new products. In short, the development of the process theory acknowledges that the manage-ment of the NPD process goes beyond the number and sequencing of its constituent tasks. An example of one of these newer processes is the Multiple Convergent Process™ by Baker and Hart (2007), shown in Figure 13.5.

The next section looks at the wider body of literature which informs theory by identifying factors beyond the process activities which have an impact on new product success and failure.

Factors affecting success and failure of new product development

The recent overview by Page and Schirr (2008) suggested that the proportion of published articles analysing factors which differentiate successful and unsuccessful NPD is somewhat low (at about 4 per cent of the total the authors consulted), whilst Guo (2008) estimated that 16 per cent of the articles published in the *Journal of Product Innovation Management* between 1984 and 2005 were concerned with NPD performance measures and drivers. Whatever the precise figures, it is fair to say that the 'performance' studies have had a large and enduring impact on theory development in the field. Also, many of these studies' influence is derived from being supported directly by the Product Development Management Association, under the auspices of 'Best Practices' research. In the PDMA best practices research, for example, 59 per cent of products in development made it to market and, of these, 60 per cent were commercially successful. For decades, success (or failure) rates for new product development, reported in aggregate, tended to give varying results. Cooper (2001) gave a market success rate of 15 per cent, whilst Hultink, Hart, Robben and Griffin (2000) reported an average 60 per cent successful launch rate in the US, the UK and the Netherlands, and in 2004, Cooper, Edgett and Kleinschmidt reported success rates of 60 per cent on average. Despite this variation, it is clear that a sizeable proportion of new product devel-opment effort goes to waste, encouraging researchers to continue to research

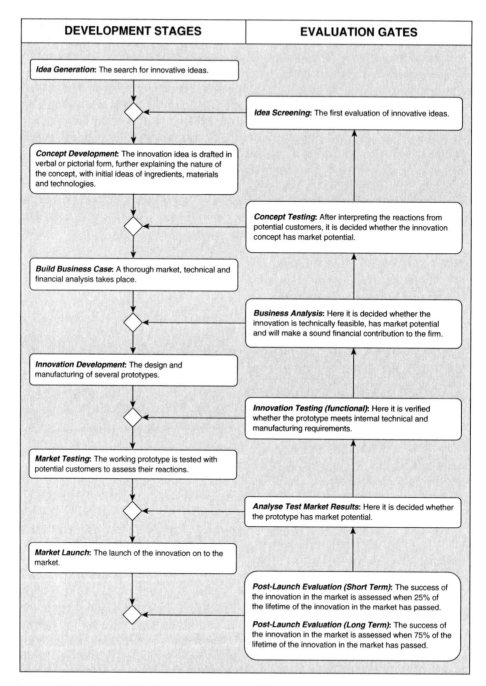

Figure 13.5   The Multiple Convergent Process™ (Baker and Hart, 2007)

factors that make a difference in bringing new products to market successfully. The results of these studies are summarized in the next section.

Previous reviews of the literature (Craig and Hart, 1992; Henard and Szymanski, 2001; Montoya-Weiss and Calantone, 1994) have identified key themes in the NPD literature as being crucial to the success of NPD activities.

The themes can be grouped at two levels: strategic and operational. The former is comprised of those factors that describe how an organization is managed as a whole, its strategic orientation, strategy for NPD, or top managers' styles. These have a vital contribution in setting the scene for new product development and can and do have a profound effect on the outcomes of development programmes. The latter refers to a number of task-specific factors, which although influenced by the strategic issues, exert their own influence on the outcome of *a particular* NPD project. This brief review, therefore, summarizes findings on success and failure across these two levels.

Strategic level success factors

Innovation strategy

The strategy of a company contextualizes its internal operation as well as its interfaces with the outside world. To be successful, theory advocates that NPD should be derived from the corporate strategy of the company, that in turn sets clearly defined objectives for its NPD endeavours. The Beerens et al. (2004) report for Booz Allen Hamilton found that most companies have difficulty in controlling their product development activities. Symptoms included ignorance of the NPD roles and responsibilities, frequent reprioritizing of projects and the discovery of projects by top management previously unknown to them, as well as lack of robustness in the process and its management. In other words, a lack of a strategic focus on product innovation. Setting a clear strategy for new product development, on the other hand, not only provides guidelines for resource allocation, but also sets up the key criteria against which all projects can be managed through to the market launch. The approach Komatsu took to compete with Caterpillar throughout the 1970s and 1980s consisted of numerous strategies, amongst which feature the frequent launch of new products developed to extend the product lines, future new products based on envisioning programmes and a period of matching increased product variety with efficiency gains. The NPD benchmarking study by Cooper, Edgett and Kleinschmidt (2004) found that more of the best performing companies defined the strategic arena for NPD, clearly identified NPD goals, took a long term view of NPD and strategically allocated resources to portfolios of NPD projects. While it is often argued that new product development should be guided by a new product strategy, the strategy should not be so prescriptive as to restrict, or stifle, the creativity necessary for NPD. The history of Canon's success is described by Hamel and Prahalad (2005) as one where their strategic intent ('beat Xerox') was broken down into a series of product (and market) development tasks, including competitive study and technology licensing to gain experience, developing technology in-house and selective market entry to exploit the weakness of competition, before going on to develop completely new technological solutions in the form of disposable cartridges.

The way in which the strategic focus or intent of product development is formed can be seen as a function of four, inter-related aspects: technology and marketing inputs, product differentiation, synergy and risk acceptance.

Technology and marketing. The emphasis on a balance between the technological and the marketing orientations in the literature reflects an overall trend away from arguing the benefits of one orientation above the other, towards an acceptance that there should be a *fusion* between technology-led and market-led innovations at the strategic level. The examples of Komatsu and Canon show how both market and technology orientations have played their part.

Product differentiation. Many of the success–failure studies refer to new product strategies pursuing differential advantage, through the product itself, comprising: technical superiority, product quality, product uniqueness and novelty, product attractiveness and high performance to cost ratio (Hultink and Hart, 1998).

Synergy. The relationship between the NPD and existing activities describes the extent of synergy, high levels of which are seen to be less risky, because a company will have more experience and expertise. In their 2001 meta-analysis, Henard and Szymanski called for more research into both product advantage and marketing synergy as these had a strong predictive power with success rates.

Risk acceptance. Successful new product strategies account for the creation of an internal orientation or climate which accepts risk. Although synergy might help avoid risk associated with lack of knowledge, the pursuit of product differentiation and advantage must entail acceptance that some projects will fail. An atmosphere that refuses to recognize this tends to stifle activity and the willingness to pursue something new.

Top management influence

Early research into success and failure examined the role of top management in the eventual success of NPD. The classic Stanford Innovation Project (Maidique and Zirger, 1984) found new product successes underpinned by a high level of top management support, as did the work of Hart and Service (1988), whilst Cooper and Kleinschmidt (1987) found less proof of top management influence, discovering that new product failures often do have the support of top management.

Top management plays a crucial role in setting the climate for innovation by signalling the nature of the corporate innovation culture (Goltz, 1986; Gupta and Wilemon, 1988 Gupta, Raj and Wilemon, 1986; McDonough, 1986). In some cases it is necessary for the firm to change its philosophy on NPD, in turn causing a change in the whole culture. Nike's NPD process changed dramatically during the 1990s, from a belief that every new product started in the lab to the view that it is the consumer who leads innovation. Research by Wei and Morgan (2004) in China has shown that the relationship between organizational climate and new product performance is in fact increased as climate affects market orientation. In other words, the climate of the firm affects how those responsible for NPD respond to the changing market conditions, which in turn affects the performance of NPD. Although a theoretical focus on top management's influence on NPD has become less fashionable as a topic in recent years, again, the meta-analytic study of research-based correlates of NPD success found that amongst the strategic factors predicting success, market orientation was a significant variable (Henard and Szymanski, 2001). In addition, a recent study by Gumusluoglu and Ilsev (2009) found strong positive associations between transformational leadership and the level of innovation in SMEs.

Operational level success factors

The previous paragraphs have reviewed the major *strategic* themes of theory development in NPD. Much of the research and theory base of product innovation, however, has been derived from examination of the way in which *specific* processes are executed, the people involved and the role of information being instrumental in its outcome.

NPD process activities

Over the past 30 years, much research has examined what steps comprise the efficient and effective execution of the development process, an example of which was described earlier in this chapter. Companies including ExxonMobil, Bausch and Lomb, and Air Products and Chemicals have specific processes guiding the development of new products in the belief that the payback from following these guidelines has improved their success rates (Cooper et al., 2004).

Although a fulsome completion of the NPD process may be desirable, each additional activity extends the overall development time and may lead to late market introduction, for which there can be penalties in terms of competitive advantage. Therefore a trade-off has to be made between completing all the suggested activities in the NPD process and the time which these activities take.

Cooper, Edgett and Kleinschmidt's (2004) benchmarking report highlights that in general, marketing tasks were more poorly carried out than the technical activities and that, in particular, many firms do not have adequate go-no-go decision points. A study of the Korean telecommunications market also highlights that in new service development, factors such as 'poor demand forecasting' and 'ineffective marketing strategies' are often associated with failure (Ahn et al., 2005). The importance of the market research activities in the NPD process has been highlighted often yet there is still a valid argument to suggest that any notion of formal market research may well be redundant, particularly if the customers' technical knowledge is inferior to that of the developer. That said, a study by Varela and Benito (2005) found that both marketing and technical activities were ranked as more important to new product projects where there was a high degree of novelty. In addition, there has been much attention given to the need for increasing proficiency in the early stages of the NPD process, often called 'the fuzzy front end', because uncertainties loom larger at the early stages of the process.

Given that uncertainty is a defining feature of developing new products, it is unsurprising that information and theories relating to its management feature in successful new product development.

Information management

Central to efficient NPD *processes* and achievement of *functional co-ordination* is information management. Since the NPD process is often viewed as one in which uncertainties are inherent (Souder and Moenart, 1992) information is central to the diminution of uncertainty and progress in the process. At the beginning of the NPD process uncertainties regarding the optimal technological solution to a particular problem abound, as does uncertainty about which of the technological solutions will be adopted by the market. As the NPD process proceeds, these uncertainties may be reduced, although new kinds of uncertainties arise, such as those related to manufacturing, delivery and specifics of the marketing mix. Research by Tzokas, Hart and Saren (2001) identified seven types of uncertainty:

- Customer-need uncertainty

    o How stable is the need in the long run?
    o How strongly is it felt by customers?

- Market-based uncertainty

    o Is the market big enough?
    o Do we have access to distribution?
    o Do we have experience in this market?

- Technological uncertainty

    o Can the chosen technology deliver the benefit?
    o Will the chosen technology become the standard?
    o Do our people have good knowledge of the chosen technology?
    o Which OEMs and/or suppliers should we collaborate with?

- Competitive uncertainty

    o What will be the reaction of our immediate competitors?
    o What would be the new competitive products?
    o What is the threat of other technologies from other industries?

- Resource-based uncertainty

    o Do we have the resources to complete the project on time?
    o Do we have the resources to support the product in the market?

- Product strategy uncertainties

    o What would be the effect on other products in the firm?
    o What would be the effect on resources for other NPD projects?

- Organizational uncertainties

    o Do we have the support of top management?
    o Are there any interdepartmental conflicts?

A further thread of research relating to information impact in NPD success is that of knowledge management and organizational learning in NPD. Specifically, the role of learning from past projects by reviewing and using information that is stored in the organization's memory is yet another seam of NPD research (Lynn et al., 2000; Sherman et al., 2000). More recently, Sherman, Berkowitz and Souder (2005) found that 'effective recording of information from past projects and the efficient retrieval of that information, coupled with effective cross-functional integration, result in improved prototype development and product launch proficiency.

Accommodation of third parties and networks

Several studies have shown the importance of involving users in the NPD process to increase success rates (Hillebrand and Biemans, 2004; Thomke and von Hippel, 2002; von Hippel, 1988). Equally, there is growing interest in the need for greater supplier involvement, in order to benefit from the advantages of supplier innovation and just-in-time (JIT) policies. For example, Dell has shifted much of its component design work – laptop screens, optical drives – to supplier partners (Dolan, 2005). Recent research has emphasized the benefits of leveraging networks through the NPD process (Story et al., 2008), again requiring a flexible approach to modelling NPD processes.

This brief review of research into the correlates of success and failure in NPD does not claim to be exhaustive, but it does give a flavour of the variety of issues and disciplines central to furthering our understanding of the processes of product and service. Nearly all contributions to the literature on NPD, irrespective of the 'base discipline' of the author, will touch on aspects of either the process of development, or the people responsible for carrying out the process. The inter-relationships between the two, however, are rarely given explicit attention, yet the development of theory requires acknowledgement of their interdependence and how they might be integrated from a theoretical perspective. The next section reviews these interdependencies and concludes with recent trends in thinking about how to manage the process and structure the people involved in the process.

Inter-relationships in process, people and management of NPD

The processes involved in developing new products and the people who carry them out are related to three of the most commonly cited critical success factors in NPD.

- *The need for interdisciplinary inputs.* In order to combine technical and marketing expertise, a number of company functions have to be involved: R&D, manufacturing, engineering, marketing and sales. As the development of a new product may be the only purpose for which these people meet professionally, it is important that the NPD process adopted ensures that they work well and effectively together. One of Samsung's practices is to have designers and engineers visit labs around the world to gauge views from the potential consumers (Edwards et al., 2005). Linked to this is also the need for the voice of the suppliers, where changes to supply may be required or advantageous.

- *The need to develop product advantage.* Technical and market information – the building blocks of NPD – have to be both accurate and timely, and must be constantly reworked in the light of changing circumstances during the course of the development to ensure that the product under development does have competitive advantage in the eyes of the customer. Therefore the *people* must deliver the appropriate expert information to inform the *process.*

- *The need for speed in the process.* The NPD process has to be managed in such a way as to be quick enough to capitalize on the new product opportunity before competitors do. The extent to which *people* work together enhances the speed of the *process.* Flextronics, the worldwide electronics design, fabrication, assembly and test company, shrank its mobile phone development time from between 12 and 18 months two years ago to three months currently, by linking all steps of the NPD process (which were previously independent), from initial artists' renderings to producing the mould, through software which encourages far more interaction among the players (Dolan, 2005).

Much of the knowledge regarding NPD, based on empirical research, underlines the importance of processes, information and people – all of which require management in circumstances of high risk and uncertainty. It follows, then, that it is critically important for firms to have structures which allow not only for professional specialism and expertise, but also for sharing information across disciplinary boundaries to ensure the development is fulfilling both sides of the success mandate: technological competence and market relevance. The structures discussed in the body of literature refer to the need for 'coordination' and 'integration' of the perspectives of different disciplines and are discussed below.

Research has covered a variety of aspects, for example, the R&D–Marketing interface (Gupta and Wilemon, 1988), the Marketing–Design interface (see the *Journal of Product Innovation Management* Volume 22 (1& 2) (2005) for several articles in this area) and the Marketing–Engineering interface (Michalek et al., 2005). Whatever the precise focus of the integration, companies need to institute processes and design structures which promote integration and coordination, at the same time as preserving the efficiencies and, importantly, the expertise within functional speciality. Many alternatives have been described over the years, from bureaucratic control mechanisms to more organic and participative structures, where the structural complexity of the mechanisms increases. Generally accepted principles agree that the more organic and participative approaches are more likely to share information across functional boundaries and to undertake interdependent tasks concurrently rather than sequentially (Olson et al., 1995), echoing the classic theoretical contribution of Burns and Stalker (1961). Relatively organic mechanisms such as 'design teams' or 'new venture groups' have some important potential advantages for coordinating product development. Such participative structures can also create an atmosphere where innovative ideas are proposed, criticized and refined with a minimum of financial and social risk whilst the participative decision making, consensual conflict resolution and open communication processes of such a structure can help reduce barriers between individuals and functional groups.

Fewer functional barriers also help ensure that unanticipated problems appearing during the development can be tackled directly by the people concerned, reducing the chances of vital information being delayed, lost or altered.

More participative structures also carry potential disadvantages, especially in terms of costs and temporal efficiency. Creating and supporting several development teams can lead to overabundance in staff and facilities. The main reason for this is that employees have less relevant experience when developing innovative product concepts and then depend more heavily on other functional specialists for the expertise, information and other resources needed to achieve a creative and successful product. Thus, there is potential for stagnation in the process if the focus of control is unclear. O'Reilly and Tushman (2004) describe what they call 'the ambidextrous organisation', to describe the challenges facing many organizations where they have to be able to exploit current products at the same time as exploring the future. Looking at the example of Ciba Vision, a Unit of the Swiss pharmaceutical company Ciba-Geigy (now Novartis), their article describes how Ciba Vision's management realized that radical new products were required to grow the company (and even to fend off decline) at the same time as continuing to make money from its more conventional portfolio of contact lens and eye care products. The decision was taken to launch six formal development projects aiming at revolutionary change, two in manufacturing processes and four in new products. Many smaller R&D projects, aimed at on-going product improvement were cancelled to release cash for the more ambitious R&D imperatives. Traditional business sections were still able to pursue incremental innovations of their own, but the R&D budget was dedicated to the development of real breakthroughs. These were freed from the structures of the old organization and instead autonomous units for the new projects were developed, each with its own R&D, finance and marketing functions.

There is, however, a final set of issues which impact upon the management of product and service innovation projects, namely, the extent to which this now takes place in networks that cross firms' traditional boundaries.

Managing networks for NPD

Although there has been an implicit within-firm perspective on much of the research into NPD and innovation, attention in specific quarters – for example, radical innovation and 'open' innovation, the importance of 'inter-organisational collaboration' and 'innovation networks' – has also been highlighted (Powell et al., 2005; Pyka, 2002). The fortunes of companies such as Wal-Mart and Microsoft have been attributed to their system of networks (Ianitsi and Levien, 2004). Due to the emphasis on speed in the NPD process, together with the fact that it is a resource-hungry activity, firms will have to be engaged in learning races, requiring the capacity to work with specialized companies in their networks so that all participants get better and faster (Hagell and Seely Brown, 2005; Powell, 1998). In addition, due to the many different technologies involved in new product development, networks will be needed to leverage the functional integration required for success. (Håkansson et al, 1999; Owen-Smith and Powell, 2004).

Powell (1998) argues that in order to reduce the inherent uncertainties associated with new products or markets, inter-organizational learning in firm's networks plays a crucial role in creating a firm's competitive advantages. Eisenhardt and Martin (2000) define 'dynamic capability' as 'the firm's processes that use resources to integrate, reconfigure, gain and release resources – to match and even create market change ... by which firms achieve new resource configurations ...' (2000: 1107). Dynamic capabilities consist of processes such as alliancing – product development by which managers combine varied skills and functional backgrounds through inter-firm collaboration. Moreover, 'dynamic capabilities', by achieving new resource configurations, turns the inter-organizational relationships in new product development networks into another important topic: 'the changing dynamics of competition and cooperation' (Wind and Mahajan, 1997).

More recently, Dittrich and Duysters (2007) have examined how innovation networks can be used to deal with a changing technological environment, concluding that innovation networks offer flexibility and speed in innovation together with the ability to adjust more smoothly to changing market conditions. Although there are some adjacent topics such as knowledge creation and transferring in studying inter-firm learning in new product development networks, it is far from developed enough to be able to propose normative theory in this context. Of course, the wider topic of relationship marketing has not been widely studied in relation to innovation and product development, but as relationships are conceptualized as the means by which companies cope with their increasing interdependence, and build themselves into a network of interactions that are linked by economic, technical and social dimensions, this is a promising field for future theory development in NPD. In particular, the theoretical perspectives of transaction cost economics (Williamson, 1985), resource dependency theory (Pfeffer and Salancik, 1978), relational exchange theory (Dwyer et al., 1987) and models of business networks (Håkansson and Snehota, 1995) present fertile furrows for the NPD researcher to plough.

Conclusion

This chapter has presented an overview of some of the key themes in the development of NPD theory. Essentially a cross-disciplinary field, NPD researchers come from general management, organizational behaviour, economics, technology, operations, design, engineering and marketing management. Most, however, recognize some form of skeletal process at the core of NPD, bringing different perspectives and inflections to bear on the steps and procedures that make up their view of the core. Three such models are shown in this chapter and a brief discussion of some generic stages is offered. An influential sub-field of NPD research has been the long tradition of deciphering what factors distinguish success from failure and this is summarized in this chapter, concluding with the implications of the success–failure studies for the development of themes and theories in NPD.

Recommended further reading

Dyer, B., Gupta, A.K. and Wilemon, D. (1999) 'What first-to-market companies do differently?' *Research Technology Management* 42(2): 15–21.

Eisenhardt, K. and Martin, J. (2000) 'Dynamic capabilities: what are they?', *Strategic Management Journal* 21: 1105–121.

Soulsby, D. (2004) 'Products launched with consumer research', *Marketing* 2 September: 40.

Von Hippel, E. (1978) 'Successful industrial products from customer ideas – presentation of a new customer-active paradigm with evidence and implications', *Journal of Marketing* January: 39–49.

References

Baker, M.J. and Hart, S.J. (2007) *Product Strategy and Management*, 2nd edn, Harlow: Pearson Education.

Beerens, J., Van Boetzelaer, A. et al. (2004) 'The road towards more effective product/service development', New York: Booz Allen Hamilton.

Burns, T. and Stalker, G.M. (1961) *The Management of Innovation*, London, UK: Tavistock Publications.

Cooper R.G. (2001) 'Introducing successful new industrial products', *European Journal of Marketing* 10(6): 300–29.

Cooper, R.G. (2008) 'The Stage-Gate® idea-to-launch-process – update. What's new and NexGen systems', *Journal of Product Innovation Management* 25(3): 213–32.

Cooper, R.G. and Kleinschmidt, E.J. (1987) 'New products: what separates winners from losers?' *Journal of Product Innovation Management* 4(3): 169–84.

Cooper, R.G., Edgett, S. and Kleinschmidt, E. (2004) 'Benchmarking best NPD practices – I', *Research Technology Management* 47(1): 31–43.

Craig, A. and Hart, S. (1992) 'Where to now in new product development research?', *European Journal of Marketing* 26(11): 3–49.

Dahan, E. and Srinivasan, V. (2000) 'The predictive power of internet-based concept testing using visual depiction and animation', *Journal of Product Innovation Management* 17(2): 99–109.

Dittrich, K. and Duysters, G. (2007) 'Networking as a means to strategy change: the case of open innovation in mobile telephony', *The Journal of Product Innovation Management* 26(6): 510–21.

Dolan, K. (2005) 'Speed, the new X factor', *Forbes* 176(13): 74.

Dwyer, F.R., Schurr, P.H. and Oh, S. (1987) 'Developing buyer-seller relationships', *Journal of Marketing* 51(2): 11–28.

Dyer, B., Gupta, A.K. and Wilemon, D. (1999) 'What first-to-market companies do differently?' *Research Technology Management* 42(2): 15–21.

Edwards, C., Lowry, T. et al. (2005) 'The lessons for Sony at Samsung', *Business Week* (3954): 37.

Eisenhardt, K.M. and Behnam, N.T. (1995) 'Accelerating adaptive processes: product innovation in the global computer industry', *Administrative Science Quarterly* 40: 84–110.

Eisenhardt, K. and Martin, J. (2000) 'Dynamic capabilities: what are they?', *Strategic Management Journal* 21: 1105–1121.

Goltz, G.E. (1986) 'A guide to development', *R&D Management* 16: 243–9.

Gumusluoglu, L. and Ilsev, A. (2009) 'Transformational leadership and organizational innovation: the rules of internal and external support for innovation', *The Journal of Product Innovation Management* 26 (3): 255–77.

Guo, L (2008) 'An analysis of 22 years of research in *JPIM*', *Journal of Product Innovation Management* 25(3): 233–48.

Gupta, A.K., Raj, S.P. and Wilemon, D. (1986) 'A model for studying R&D/marketing interface in the product innovation process', *Journal of Marketing* April: 7–17.

Gupta A.K. and Wilemon D. (1988) 'The credibility/co-operation connection at the R&D/marketing interface', *Journal of Product Innovation Management* 5(1): 20–31.

Hagell J. III, and Seely Brown, J. (2005) 'The shifting industrial landscape', *Optimize*, 4(4): 30–8.

Håkansson, H. and Snehota, I. (1995) '*Developing Relationship in Business Networks*', London: Routledge.

Håkansson, H. Havila, V. and Pedersen, A. (1999) 'Learning in networks', *Journal of Marketing Management* 28(5): 443–52.

Hamel, G. and Prahalad, C.K. (2005) 'Strategic intent', *Harvard Business Review*, July–August 2005: 148–61.

Hart, S.J. and Service, L.M. (1988) 'The effects of managerial attitudes to design on company performance', *Journal of Marketing Management* 4(2): 217–29.

Hart, S.J., Ozdemir, S. and Tagg, S. (2008) 'NSD vs NPD? An analysis of similarities and differences between the anatomy of innovation in services and products: processes, stages and evaluation gates', paper presented to the Annual Conference of the Product Development Management Association, Florida.

Henard, D.H. and Szymanski, D.M. (2001) 'Why some new products are more successful than others', *Journal of Marketing Research* 38(3): 362–75.

Hillebrand, B. and Biemans, W.G. (2004) 'Links between internal and external cooperation in product development: an exploratory study', *Journal of Product Innovation Management* 21(1): 110–22.

Hultink, E. and Hart, S. (1998) 'The world's path to the better mousetrap: myth or reality? An empirical investigation into the launch strategies of high and low advantage new product's, *European Journal of Innovation Management* 1(3): 106.

Hultink, E. and Hart, S.J., Robben, H.S.J. and Griffin, A. (2000) 'Launch decisions and new product success: an empirical comparison of consumer and industrial products', *Journal of Product Innovation Management* 17(1): 5.

Lynn, G., Reilly, R. and Akgun, A.E. (2000) 'Knowledge management in new product teams: practices and outcomes', *IEEE Transactions on Engineering Management* 47(2): 221–31.

McDonough, E.F. III (1986) 'Matching management control systems to product strategies', *R&D Management*, 16(2): 114–19.

Maidique, M.A. and Zirger, B.J. (1984) 'A study of success and failure in product innovation: the case of the US electronics industry', *IEEE Transactions on Engineering Management* 31: 192–203.

Michalek, J., Feinberg, F. and Papalambros, P. (2005) 'Linking marketing and engineering product design decisions via analytical target cascading', *Journal of Product Innovation Management* 22(1): 42.

Montoya-Weiss, M.M. and Calantone, R. (1994) 'Determinants of new product performance: A review and meta-analysis', *Journal of Product Innovation Management* 11(5): 397–417.

Montoya-Weiss, M. and O'Driscoll, T. (2000) 'Applying performance support technology in the fuzzy front end', *Journal of Product Innovation Management* 17(2): 143–61.

Olson, E.M. Walker, O.C. Jr. and Ruekert, R.W. (1995) 'Organizing for effective new product development: the moderating role of product innovativeness', *Journal of Marketing* 59: 48–62.

O'Reilly, C.A. III and Tushman, M.L. (2004) 'The ambidextrous organization', *Harvard Business Review* April: 74–81.

Owen-Smith, J. and Powell, W. (2004) 'Knowledge networks as channel and conduits: the effects of spillovers in the Boston biotechnology community', *Organization Science* 15(1): 5–21.

Page, A.L. and Schirr, G.R (2008) 'Growth and development of a body of knowledge: 16 years of new product development research, 1989–2004', *Journal of Innovation Management* 25(3): 233–48.

Pfeffer, J. and Salancik, G.R. (1978) *The External Control of Organizations: A Resource Dependence Perspective*, New York, NY: Harper & Row Publishers.

Powell, W. (1998) 'Learning from collaboration: knowledge and networks in the biotechnology and pharmaceutical industries', *California Management Review* 40(3): 228–40.

Powell, W.W., White, D.R., Koput, K.W. and Owen-Smith, J. (2005) 'Network dynamics and field evolution: the growth of interorganizational collaboration in the life sciences', *The American Journal of Sociology* 110(4): 1132–205.

Pyka, A. (2002) 'Innovation networks in economics: from the incentive-based to the knowledge-based approaches', *European Journal of Innovation Management* 5(3): 152–63.

Rogers, E.M. (1962) *Diffusion of Innovations*, New York: Free Press.

Sherman, J.D., Berkowitz, D. and Souder, W.E. (2005) 'New product development performance and the interaction of cross-functional integration and knowledge management', *Journal of Product Innovation Management* 22(5): 399–411.

Sherman, J.D., Souder, W. and Jenssen, S. (2000) 'Differential effects of the primary forms of cross functional integration on product development cycle time', *Journal of Product Innovation Management* 17(4): 257–67.

Souder W.E. and Moenaert R.K. (1992) 'Integrating marketing and R&D project personnel within innovation projects: an information uncertainty model', *Journal of Management Studies* 29(4): 485–511.

Soulsby, D. (2004) 'Products launched with consumer research', *Marketing* 2 September: 40.

Story, V., O'Malley, L., Hart, S.J. and Saker, J. (2008) 'The development of relationships and networks', 8: 187–200.

Thomke, S. and von Hippel, E. (2002) 'Customers as innovators: a new way to create value', *Harvard Business Review* 80(4): 74–81.

Tzokas, N., Hart, S. and Saren, M. (2001) 'Critical information and the quest for customer relevant NPD processes', Unpublished report for the EU, University of Strathclyde.

Varela, J. and Benito, L. (2005) 'New product development process in Spanish firms: typology, antecedents and technical/marketing activities', *Technovation* 25: 395–405.

Von Hippel, E. (1978) 'Successful industrial products from customer ideas – presentation of a new customer-active paradigm with evidence and implications', *Journal of Marketing* January: 39–49.

Von Hippel, E. (1988) *The Sources of Innovation*, New York: Oxford University Press.

Wei, Y. and Morgan, N. (2004) 'Supportiveness of organizational climate, market orientation, and new product performance in chinese firms', *Journal of Product Innovation Management* 21(6): 375–88.

Williamson, O.E. (1985) *The Economic Institutions of Capitalism*, New York: The Free Press.

Wind, J. and Mahajan, V. (1997) 'Issues and opportunities in new product development: an introduction to the special issue', *Journal of Marketing Research* 34(1): 1–12.

14

Relationships and networks*

Kristian Möller

Introduction

This chapter takes a fresh look at relationship marketing (RM) and business or industrial networks (BN) as sub-fields of the marketing discipline. Some scholars, including Gummesson and Grönroos, see these as nested and use relationship marketing as a generic term to cover the research on both consumer and business relationships and on inter-organizational networks. However, several authors have emphasized the dispersed origin of relationship marketing and suggested a need to explore the differences between business-to-business marketing relationships and consumer marketing (Egan, 2008; Eiriz and Wilson, 2006; Pels, 1999). Möller and Halinen (2000) claim that relationship marketing consists of two theoretically different and distinctive approaches: market-based RM (MRM) and network-based RM (NRM). This view is supported by Mattsson (1997) who makes a clear distinction between the theoretical assumptions that provide the foundation for relationship marketing research and network research.

---

* This work, although independent, draws on Möller and Halinen (2000) and Möller, Pels and Saren (2009). The author wishes to thank all the colleagues involved in these publications. The work goes on. The work is related to the ValueNet Project which is part of the Liike2 Programme of the Academy of Finland.

In fact, both of these domains can be seen as relatively broad and fragmented research traditions in which the founding researchers, by utilizing concepts and theories from a variety of social science disciplines, have tried to cover and synthesize phenomena. These range from the behaviours of marketers and customers and the processes that constitute relationships, to business networks, their structures and their dynamics. In addressing this complexity and diversity, this chapter seeks to:

- Examine and articulate the origins of the different views underlying current relationship marketing thought and the business networks approach

- Provide a theoretical comparison of the disciplinary foundation of RM and BN

- Articulate two distinctive theoretical views covering the marketing phenomena captured by the RM and BN terms: the market-based relationship marketing (MRM) and the network-based relationship marketing (NRM)

- Provide a 'theory map' of the research streams constituting the current RM and BN

- Discuss the theoretical consequences of the proposed 'multi-theory' approach.

The outlined conceptual analysis, which also describes the structure of this chapter, is helpful in revealing the differences and similarities in the key approaches to the RM and BN, and this is indispensable for any marketing scholar. Without a proper understanding of the fundamental disciplinary approaches, it is difficult to navigate through the assortment of research and literature that constitutes the widespread relationship marketing and business networks domains. Thus, in order to utilize different traditions efficiently or to challenge them, it is essential to understand their theoretical positions and core assumptions. By providing an articulated theory map, this chapter contributes not only to current marketing knowledge but to its future development as well.

Relationship marketing and business networks research

Extant research suggests that the emergence of business networks (BN) and relationship marketing (RM) as important schools of marketing thought was influenced by several intertwined research streams ongoing in marketing since 1970 (Egan, 2008; Eiriz and Wilson, 2006; Möller and Halinen, 2000; Möller, 1994; Pels et al., 2009). These include services research, customer–supplier relationships and interaction in business marketing and in international business, research concerning marketing channel relationships, and more pragmatic knowledge concerning the emerging practices of database and direct marketing (labelled later as interactive marketing). The industrial network approach, arriving on the stage in the late 1980s, represents the last piece in the relationship marketing puzzle. The role of these streams in understanding RM is crucial. They are not

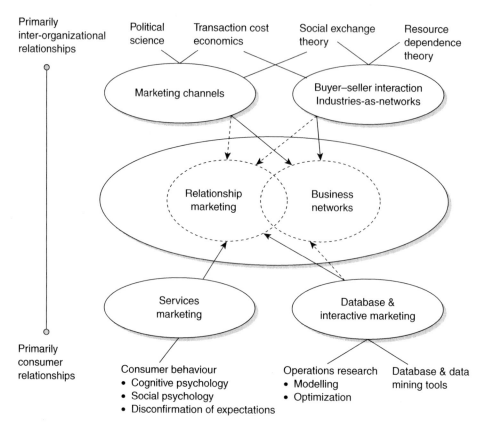

Figure 14.1   Sources and constituents of relationship marketing and business networks

only the roots or sources of current relationship marketing but actually the streams of research that constitute RM and BN. What makes matters even more complicated is that these research streams are not monoliths. Their researchers draw from a variety disciplines and theories ranging from economics and organizational sciences to political science and social psychology. This disciplinary multiplicity is described in Figure 14.1 and builds on the work of Möller and Halinen and Eiriz and Wilson. Next, these streams are discussed, and their disciplinary backgrounds and key aspects are summarized in Table 14.1.

_____ Primary constituents of relationship marketing _____

Services marketing

The emphasis on marketing relationships and the consequent relationship marketing tradition has several origins. By the late 1970s, researchers interested in services were beginning to question the marketing management school. Their main concern was that the school did not provide conceptualizations for describing and managing the service

Table 14.1 Research approaches constituting relationship marketing and business networks domains – a comparison matrix

Research tradition characteristics	Database & interactive marketing	Services marketing	Channel research	Interaction & networks
Basic goals	Managerial goal: enhance marketing efficiency through better targeting of marketing activities, especially marketing communications. Strong managerial emphasis, integrated marketing communications (IMC) an important agenda. Customer retention, share of a customer database as a device for managing direct communications, integrated use of channels.	To explain and understand services management and services marketing relationships. To understand the organization of service production. Managerial goal: how to enhance the efficiency of managing customer encounters and relationships through managing the perceived quality of the service offer and relationship.	Theoretical goal: explain governance structures and dyadic channel member behaviour in the channel context. Normative goal: determine efficient relational forms between channel members.	Three interrelated sets of goals: (i) understand and explain inter-organizational exchange behaviour and relationship development at a dyadic level in a network context; (ii) understand how nets of relationships between actors evolve; and (iii) understand how markets function and evolve from a network perspective. Managerial goal: gain a more valid view of reality through network theory for management in a network context.
Key research questions	How to provide value for the customer, how to develop loyal customers, how to adapt marketing activities along the customer's life-cycle, how to retain customers?	How to create and manage customer relationships, how to co-create value with customers, how to organize service production and create a service-driven organization.	What forms of governance are efficient for what types of channel relationships? How is use of power related to the relationship efficiency? How does trust evolve and facilitate relationship development and commitment? In what way is the dyadic relationship contingent on the larger channel context?	How are relationships created and managed; how do nets of relationships evolve, how can an actor manage these relationships and create a position in a net? How to describe markets as networks; network structures and the processes driving network emergence and change.

(Cont'd)

Table 14.1 (cont'd)

Research tradition characteristics	Database & interactive marketing	Services marketing	Channel research	Interaction & networks
View of relationships	Pragmatic – no explicit assumptions; implicitly assumes competitive markets of customers; stimulus response view with feedback. Organization-personal customer relationships, generally comprising discrete transactions over time, handled through media enabling customized interactive communication.	Personal customer relationships attended by service personnel and influenced through other marketing activities. Earlier a strong focus on the service encounter, later expanded to include the life-cycle of relationships.	Dyadic, multidimensional interorganizational relationships, which are interactive and dynamic. Both parties can be active.	Relationships exist between different types of actors: firms, government and research agencies, individual actors; not only goods but all kinds of resources are exchanged through relationships. Relationships are seen as vehicles to access and control resources and to create new resources.
View of context	No explicit theory of context; working consumer markets implicitly assumed. Also customer database as a 'context' for customer classification and competition for preferences and retention.	Primarily the management perspective; dyadic interactive relationship but customers often seen as objects. Interdependence between the seller and the customer varies from weak to relatively strong. The basic service is often relatively substitutable, but the service relationship can be differentiated and individualized.	Well developed theory on 'environment' in the political-economy approach. Structurization perspective: the dyadic behaviour and efficient forms of governance are influenced by the channel context and dyadic behaviour influences the channel context.	Environment is seen as networks of actor relationships. Actor behaviour is highly embedded, i.e. specific actions cannot be understood out of their historical context. Firms learn and construct their environment through enactment, i.e. the environment is not transparent; the actor–environment relationship is reciprocal.

Table 14.1 (Cont'd)

Research tradition characteristics	Database & interactive marketing	Services marketing	Channel research	Interaction & networks
Disciplinary background	No clear disciplinary background; driven by information technology, marketing communication applications, data processing techniques and modelling. Marketing decision making and optimization perspectives important.	No clear disciplinary background: early phase a response to 'traditional marketing management', later consumer behaviour applications, operations and human resource perspective and general management outlook. Both empirically and theory driven with heavy managerial orientation.	Primarily theory driven, tries to combine the economic and political aspects (power, dependency) of channel relationships. The tradition relies on: (i) transaction cost theory; and (ii) social exchange theory, political economy, power and conflict in organizational sociology. The transaction cost approach provides the economic perspective and the social exchange theory the behavioural perspective.	Both empirically and theory driven; earlier influenced by channels research, organizational buying behaviour, resource dependency theory, social exchange theory, and institutional economics; later by institutional theory, dynamic industrial economics, organizational sociology, and resource-based theory. Eclectic tradition.
Unit(s) of analysis & view of actor(s)	A rational marketer generally looked from a single firm (unit) perspective, a machine-like view of organization. Individual customer(s) defined by preferences and response profiles. Also customer types (segments) as unit of analysis.	Multiple foci of analyses: rational marketer, service provider–client relationship, individual customer, customer group or segment. Generally a machine-like organization, but some interest in organizational culture.	Multiple foci of analysis: firm, dyadic relationship in channel context. Structurization perspective: the dyadic perspective: the dyadic behaviour and efficient forms of governance are influenced by the channel context and dyadic behaviour influences the channel context. Actors generally treated as single units with bounded rationality, they are defined through their goals and roles.	Multiple foci of analysis: an actor can be an organization, person, dyadic relationship, a net or a network. Transactions are episodes in the long-term relationship. Emphasis on the embeddedness of actors in networks. Actors are sensemaking through enactment. Actors defined through resources, roles (goals) and relationships; organizations seen as 'organic' and adaptive.

provider–customer relationship. Consumers' quality experiences and subsequent satisfaction towards the service were argued to be an outcome of an interaction relationship between the personnel and the customer, which was augmented by the traditional marketing communications, institutional image, and service delivery technology (Berry and Parasuraman, 1993, Grönroos, 1990; Zeithaml and Bittner, 1996). Initially, the relational emphasis was on relatively short-term service provider–customer encounters, which was later expanded to include the life-cycle of the customer relationship.

Besides the joint production roles and enduring relationships, the services marketing school (SMS) stresses the organizational aspects apparent in the successful marketing of services. Indeed, the whole organization should be targeted and culturally fine-tuned for the service of target customers. This notion was captured via the internal marketing concept, which was suggested by Grönroos (1981) for achieving organizational awareness and skills. Another prominent construct was that of service quality and its operationalization with the service gap model and the consequent SERVQUAL measurement system. The ultimate goal was better management of customer satisfaction (cf. Parasuraman et al., 1985; Zeithaml et al., 1988).

Services marketing brought to the foreground two principal issues: the interactive and process nature of customer relationships, and the organizational aspects of marketing. These are both important areas about which the marketing management tradition had remained silent. Services scholars also provided some of the early attempts to define relationship marketing. According to Berry et al. 'Relationship marketing is attracting, maintaining and – in multi-service organizations – enhancing customer relationships' (1983: 66).

In spite of the conceptual breakthroughs, services research was relatively shallow in terms of theory development. This is related to the key goals of this school. Much of the services marketing research is driven primarily by empirical and managerial issues. Inductive orientation is especially strong among the Nordic researchers. Instead of developing an in-depth, theory-based understanding, services research seems to aim at broad, managerially oriented frameworks. However, a stronger theoretical base has been constructed for the customer service expectations and behaviour by drawing from the psychological and social psychological foundations in consumer behaviour, especially the disconfirmation theory of expectations (Oliver, 1980). Concerning the service production and interface organizing, the school indeed advanced relevant issues; nevertheless, because these lack relations to organizational theory, it has not developed them to the potential they merit. Another noteworthy aspect is the silence concerning the context or environment of service relationships and encounters. The school seems to implicitly assume a working market context with multiple customers and service providers.

Database and direct marketing – interactive marketing

From the mid-1980s onwards, rapidly developing information technology created a primarily practice-based and consultant-driven literature on managing customer relationships through databases (database marketing) and direct marketing activities (see Jenkinson, 1995; McKenna, 1991; Peppers and Rogers, 1993, 1997; Pine et al., 1995; Rapp and Collins, 1991; Shaw and Stone, 1988; Shepard, 1995). The buzz words 'mass customization' and 'one-to-one marketing' had arrived. This technology-driven approach included a strong emphasis on marketing communications and is often referred to as integrated marketing communications (IMC) (Schultz et al., 1993). Later development, driven by the internet and mobile technology, has further extended marketers' opportunities to customize their offerings and messages per individual customer (Blattberg and Deighton, 1991; Malthouse and Blattberg, 2005). While used predominantly in consumer marketing, the technologies involved in interactive marketing have also had a clear impact on the customer relationship management (CRM) practices in business marketing (Kumar, 2008).

Database and interactive marketing are primarily practice driven. These include a strong managerial emphasis that aims to enhance the efficiency of marketing activities, especially communication targeting, media usage and message personalization. Through the use of optimization tools, interactive marketing targets the maximization of customer lifetime value as well as the customer equity of the firm (Kumar, 2008; Rust et al., 2004). Here, competitive markets are implicitly assumed. The organization–customer relationship perspective is narrow and portrays the image of a relatively loose and distant connection. The focus is on interactive communication, where the seller is the active partner who plans communication and offerings on the basis of customer profile and feedback. Relationships are seen as long-term in nature, evidenced by the customer life-cycle concept, but concrete theoretical and empirical efforts to tackle the dynamism of customer relationships have been limited. The main focus is on how to keep customers loyal and profitable in an efficient manner. Essentially, this is an optimization problem and paradoxically, the 'interactive marketing' actually achieves many of the normative goals of the marketing management tradition (Möller, 2006).

Channels research tradition

In the late 1970s, researchers interested in marketing channels began to develop frameworks and theories that focused on the relationships between business marketers and channel members. Research in the channels research tradition (CRT) examines how actors in a marketing channel behave, and how and why various forms of channels evolve. Here, the basic normative goal is defining efficient relational forms between channel members.

The tradition attempts to combine the economic aspects and the behavioural aspects that influence channels relationships (Stern and Reve, 1980). The economic perspective is strongly influenced by the transaction cost economics, which tries to define the efficient governance structure in dyadic exchange relationships through the use of a set of transaction and market characteristics (Rindfleisch and Heide, 1997; Williamson, 1985). Its core concepts include asset specificity, uncertainty and transaction frequency, and under-specific combinations of these contingency factors, matching governance structures, are postulated.

The behavioural perspective draws from social exchange theory and organizational sociology, and it employs political economy concepts, such as power and dependency and social aspects – expectations, cooperation, trust, commitment, communication and conflict behaviour – in analysing channels relationships

(Anderson and Narus, 1990; Dwyer et al., 1987; Emerson, 1962; Frazier, 1983; Gaski, 1984; Heide, 1994; Scanzoni, 1979).

An essential aspect of channels research is its strong programmatic and systemic nature. In fact, its inherent dualism – polity and economy – and context are its dominant features. Driven by the political economy framework (Stern and Reve, 1980) and utilizing a rich multidisciplinary base, CRT offers three essential points: (1) both economic and political aspects and their interactions must be considered in examining channel behaviour; (2) a focal channel and a dyadic relationship form the recommended unit(s) of analysis; and (3) complex relationships cannot be understood outside their context or environment, as the 'dyadic behaviour' and 'channel' are reciprocally interrelated (Heide, 1994; Möller, 1994; Möller and Halinen, 2000; Rindfleisch and Heide, 1997; Wathne and Heide, 2004).

One should note, however, that the channel context/environment dyadic behaviour linkage, as modelled through the political economy framework, has received relatively little empirical attention (see, however, Wathne and Heide, 2004). Another limitation is the insufficient empirical research on the development processes of channel relationships and channel structures.

Interaction and network approach

The interaction and network approach is associated primarily with the work centred on the Industrial Marketing and Purchasing (IMP) Group (Anderson et al., 1994; Axelsson and Easton, 1992; Ford, 1990; Håkansson and Snehota, 1995; Möller and Halinen, 1999; Möller and Wilson, 1995). Its birth can be traced to the late 1970s and early 1980s when a number of European scholars began to develop a theory of supplier–customer relationships based on an extensive multi-country case study (Håkansson, 1982). The resulting relationships were seen essentially as interactive and dynamic. During the 1980s, the emphasis was on understanding how such relationships are created and managed. Both parties were seen as active and the key constructs in describing relationships included interaction processes, adaptation and investments in relationships, actor bonds, resource ties, activity chains, relationship outcomes, and phases of relationships (see Ford, (1990, 1997, 2002) for compilations of the IMP research).

The interaction approach was influenced by early channels research, resource dependency theory and social exchange theory. As the channels school, it utilizes economic aspects – the investments in relationships – and behavioural aspects – expectations, relationship atmosphere, mutuality – in analysing relationships. There is, however, a clear difference in how the interaction approach emphasizes the processual character of relationships and describes them through resource and social exchange processes and adaptations. This dynamic perspective is enabled empirically through case studies whereas the channels research is dominated by structural equation modelling.

Since the 1990s, the primary focus of the approach has been on understanding business networks and organizational action in the network context. Notably, this development was led by Håkansson (1987, 1989) and Ford (1990) (see also Axelsson and Easton (1992)) and manifested itself in the actors-resources-activities (ARA) framework (Håkansson and Snehota, 1995). Three levels of analysis and related goals can be discerned in the IMP-driven network research.

At the micro level, the question is how individual organizations act in a network context, specifically how they develop, maintain and dissolve network positions and roles. Relationships play a key role in this research, and the relationships that exist between different types of actors are seen as vehicles for accessing and controlling resources, and for creating new resources in the relationships. A key issue is to understand how organizations and personal actors try to achieve their goals through relationships depending on their capabilities or competences. This perspective relates the network view to the resource-based theory of the firm and offers a new viewpoint to strategic thought (Håkansson and Ford, 2002; Mattsson, 1985; Möller and Törrönen, 2003).

The meso level addresses the issue of how focal networks – also known as value nets or strategic nets – evolve, and to what extent, and how these structures can be created and managed (Alajoutsijärvi et al., 1999; Möller and Halinen, 1999). Applications of this view involve an analysis of technological development (Håkansson and Waluszewski, 2002), the nature of the internationalization of firms and international cooperative relationships (Johansson and Mattsson, 1988; Håkansson and Johanson, 1988). Important issues include the goals and structures of specific focal networks (e.g. supply nets, competitive coalitions and R&D, and innovation networks) and their governance (de Man, 2004; Jarillo, 1988).

Finally, the macro-level research addresses the questions of how extensively the network structures evolve and what factors influence these dynamics. This view, sometimes called the 'markets as networks', challenges the industrial organization view of markets (Porter, 1980). It contends that markets – or industries or clusters – are constructed by complex and interdependent, inter-organizational relationships, rather than by independent actors (Håkansson and Snehota, 1995; Thompson et al., 1994). The macro network perspective has been employed primarily to examine how technological networks evolve (Håkansson, 1987; Lundgren, 1995; Möller and Svahn, 2009; Powell et al., 1996).

From the perspective of theoretical assumptions, the network approach contains several departures from mainstream marketing studies. Both relationships and networks form the unit of analysis, and the focus is on their structures and dynamics. More importantly, the worldview of network studies emphasizes contextuality and time. That is, singular events or relationships cannot be understood without knowledge of their context and evolution. This adoption of historical perspective is related to the primary use of qualitative case analysis. Moreover, the environment is not regarded as transparent; actors are seen as perceiving its structure and meanings and learning about them through enactment (Weick, 1985).

The historical explanation view that has been adopted has important consequences for the normative and managerial applications of the network approach. The approach can provide only relatively broad guidelines regarding how to manage in a network environment. More specific normative suggestions require a historical understanding of the particular network situation and must always remain context dependent. Nevertheless, this view is being challenged by the more recent 'strategic net[work]' approach, which is interested in networks as quasi-organizations and especially in the management mechanism of different types of strategic nets (Möller and Rajala, 2007; Möller and Svahn, 2006). These researchers generally adopt a more reductionist ontological view of networks and apply contingency thinking based theoretical frameworks.

World view of relationship marketing and business networks constituents

The description of the research streams constituting relationship marketing and business networks uncovered considerable differences, as summarized in Table 14.1. Related to this, a fundamental question becomes whether RM and BN should be handled as one domain that can be covered adequately by a single, albeit broad and eclectic, theory. Otherwise, are the goals, disciplinary backgrounds and key assumptions – or world views – between the constituting traditions so discrepant that we must treat them as interrelated but distinctive sub-theories of RM and BN? Can some of the root traditions be merged to achieve if not one homogenous theory, then at least a more elegant set of theories to address this important marketing domain?

In order to facilitate a more feasible drawing of conclusions, the following aspects are used to compare the four constituting traditions:

- The views they have on marketing exchange and exchange relationships

- The views they have on the context or embeddedness of marketing exchange behaviour

- The views they have on the actors or units conducting the exchange behaviour

These perspectives are seen to cover the key theoretical aspects of enquiries into marketing (cf. Möller and Halinen, (2000) and Möller et al. (2009) for a discussion of this meta-theoretical analysis).

View of marketing exchange

A close examination of how researchers in each of the four traditions view exchange relationships and the kinds of questions they are asking about them reveals substantial variety in their complexity, particularly regarding the type of dependencies that emerge between buyer and seller. Relational complexity seems to be closely associated with whether the research tradition primarily concerns marketer–consumer relationships or inter-organizational relationships. Since this division seems the most powerful in differentiating the underlying assumptions each tradition makes about exchange characteristics, it is selected as the basis for further analysis. Table 14.2 outlines the assumptions behind consumer-related and organization-related traditions.

Research on consumer relationship-related traditions (primarily services marketing and interactive marketing) has focused on the relationship between the marketer and

Table 14.2   Exchange characteristics in consumer vs. inter-organizational relationship-focused research traditions

Consumer relationships: low relational complexity	Inter-organizational relationships: high relational complexity
• The focus is on marketer–individual customer relationships. • A large number of customers.	• The focus is on: (i) supplier–buyer dyads; and (ii) exchange within focal nets. • A small number of actors ranging from profit/non-profit-organizations to governmental organizations and key persons.
• Low interdependence since resources (relationships, products, information, etc.) are substitutable. • Switching is relatively easy. • The seller is primarily active. • The focus is on few episodes – seldom on long-term relationships. • The emphasis is on managerial, economic, and psychological views of exchange.	• Mutual interdependence through resource ties; resources are relatively heterogeneous making switching difficult. • Any actor can be active. • Transactions are episodes in long-term relationships. • The emphasis is on resource, social, and inter-functional exchange relationships.

the customer. In contrast, inter-organizationally-oriented approaches (channels research and interaction and networks research) have focused on exchanges between suppliers and buyers of various types and even between several actors at a time. In these two perspectives on exchange relationships, the assumption about the level of interdependence between the buyer and the seller is a significant differentiating factor. Consumer relationship approaches assume a large number of potential partners, where both buyers and sellers have several alternatives from which to choose. Here, the resources exchanged and the relationships created are substitutable, since relationships rarely develop into strongly interdependent connections. Alternatively, in the inter-organizational case, there are fewer potential partners and the resources they control tend to be heterogeneous because of specialization and historical development. Therefore, such relationships are characterized by mutual interdependency, which may vary from weak to strong and which may make switching partners much more difficult. Again, unlike inter-organizational approaches, relationships between marketers and consumers are considered to be much looser since the bonds that tie the parties together are weaker and fewer. Social bonds are seen as having great importance (see, e.g. Gwinner et al., 1998; Liljander and Strandvik, 1995), whereas different economic, technological, planning, social, legal and knowledge related bonds coexist and are seen as essential in inter-organizational relationships (see, e.g. Håkansson and Snehota, 1995: 13; Möller and Wilson, 1995).

In line with the managerial emphasis on consumer-oriented relationship research, the seller is generally viewed as the active party and the consumer more as an object, although the interactive character of the relationships is recognized. The long-term view is stressed, but it remains relatively unexploited relative to the conceptual or managerial tools needed to master relationship development and the effects of history on relationships. Thus far, the long-term perspective has been seen in terms of recurring transactions and their successful management rather than the process or other dynamic relationship features.

Table 14.3   Relationship context assumptions in consumer relationship vs. inter-organizational relationship focused research traditions

Consumer relationships: market perspective	Inter-organizational relationships: network/systemic perspective
• There are many potential customers who form a market of potential 'relationships'. • Many customers/marketers and relatively homogeneous resources lead to atomized markets characterized by low interdependence. • The S-O-R view emphasizing customers' response profiles and how they react to marketers' activities. • Customers can be classified based on their response profiles; the ultimate level is individual 'segments'. • The market is generally taken as a given model of competition, which forms the context of exchange relationships. • The market is a resource allocation mechanism. • Competition for relationships provides the market dynamics.	• There is a limited number of potential partners. Interdependence based on resource heterogeneity forces the actors to cooperate; network environments emerge. • Relationships are embedded in networks and the channel system. • Mutuality and history are essential in understanding episodes, relationships, and the network context. • There are several 'levels' in network relationships (supplier, supplier's supplier, buyer, buyer's buyer). • Competition and cooperation are the primary forces that shape relationships and networks. • Relationships are important in coordinating and creating resources, and not only in allocation. • Relationships shape networks, yet the network structure and channel system influence relationships; structurization and network dynamism are relevant.

As a result of the particular emphasis (managerial or theoretical) and the basic difference in relationship focus (individual customer or organization), the contributions of the two approaches to relationship marketing vary. Consumer approaches have been dominated by the managerial, economic and psychological view of exchange and relationships, while inter-organizational approaches have placed greater emphasis on resources and social and inter-functional exchanges within and between relationships.

_____ View of exchange context _____

In addition to examining the characteristics of individual exchange relationships, it is also important to recognize the context in which such exchanges take place, or more precisely, to examine the assumptions different authors and traditions make about this issue. The contextual aspect is relevant as it illuminates further the kinds of mechanisms employed to understand exchange relationships. Table 14.3 contrasts the assumptions of database and interactive marketing and services marketing (both basically assuming a market context) with those of the network approach and channels research, assuming a systemic exchange context. This analysis is indebted to the ideas of Mattsson (1997) and Möller and Halinen (2000).

As can be seen, the underlying assumptions behind the market and network/ channel perspectives on exchange relationships are fundamentally different and represent almost polar views. As such, these contextual assumptions form the critical dividing line between the constituent streams of relationship marketing. The consumer-based approaches clearly stem from the traditional theory of markets as the context of managing customer relationships, where competition is the dominant force. It seems that this linkage is often not explicitly recognized.

Inter-organizationally-oriented traditions assume a complex network of interrelated actors whose actions are shaped by both competition and cooperation. Companies and dyadic relationships between them are embedded in networks of relationships and channel systems. The world is not transparent, and experience and history matter in understanding any particular relationship as well as the nature of existing networks.

Our analysis of the assumptions made in the root disciplines of relationship marketing yields a picture of strongly divided views of the phenomenon. Both the character of exchange and the context in which it takes place have been subject to very different assumptions in consumer-related research traditions and in inter-organizational traditions.

View of the marketing actors

The discussion of the views and assumptions research traditions have about the marketing exchange and its context has obviously also touched on the actors that conduct the exchange. This allows us to make only a few remarks about how the traditions view marketing actors.

Database and interactive marketing sees the marketer as a rational actor (firm) making marketing programme decisions by using analytical tools. The approach assumes, in an implicit fashion, a metaphorical, machine-like organization (Morgan, 1996), which is interested primarily in organizing issues from the perspective of how to combine and utilize databases and marketing activities. Customers are represented through their beliefs, preferences and, especially, actions – media behaviour, responses to marketing messages and purchasing. Implicitly, they are taken to be subjectively rational in their behaviour.

Essentially, services marketing assumes a rational marketer striving to create and manage customer relationships. The marketer is either an organization or a person depending on the level of analysis. The organization has an interest in the services process, which amounts to 'backroom operations' and internal marketing, as well as an interest in examining the cultural aspects of a company engaged in services provision or relationship marketing. The view held by services marketing researchers on organizational culture is mechanistic and instrumental (Alvesson, 2002; Deshpande et al., 1993). Culture is seen as being composed of elements that can be influenced relatively easily by management pursuing a 'targeted organizational culture', which is expected to be instrumental in a particular services business or market.

The channels research is relatively heterogeneous in its theoretical bases. Research that focuses on manufacturer–channel member relationships, particularly on governance, and drawing on the transaction cost approach and social exchange theory (e.g. Heide, 1994; Wathne and Heide, 2004), holds a rational and mechanistic outlook on the actors, which are generally viewed as firms or organizations. Research driven by the political economy framework (Stern and Reve, 1980) also focuses on the channel structure and company (and dyad) interaction and observes, at least implicitly, organizations as adaptive agents being boundedly rational. Organizations remain, however, very much like 'black boxes' being described primarily through their roles (in the channel system) and goals.

The interaction and network approach describes organizations through their network roles, positions and relationships, and through their resource configurations. Roles are constructed by carrying out value activities and actors are seen simultaneously as adapting to their networks and influencing them through their value activities. Actors are clearly learning organizations that make sense of the network environment through enacting relationships.

The analysis of the assumptions made in the root disciplines of relationship marketing and business networks gives a picture of strongly divided views of the phenomenon. Both the character of exchange, the context in which it takes place, and the actors carrying out that exchange have been subject to very different assumptions in consumer-related research traditions on the one hand and in inter-organizational traditions on the other. The next section elaborates the relevance of these findings from a theoretical perspective.

Synthesis – the key research streams of relationship marketing and business networks

A comparative analysis of the root traditions of relationship marketing and business networks revealed that it is misleading to discuss a single 'relationship marketing theory' without any reference to the fundamental distinctions exposed. In fact, there seems to be good reason to distinguish between the two basic types of relationship marketing theories: market-based relationship marketing and network-based relationship marketing. The former deals with fairly simple exchange relationships and assumes a market context, whereas the latter examines complex relationships and presumes a network-like business environment. This proposition was made by Möller and Halinen (2000). It is used here as a platform for developing a less abstract, but also a more complex view of current research schools focused on marketing relationships and business networks.

Market-based relationships and network-based relationships

The idea that the research conducted among the identified root traditions of relationship marketing and business networks (cf. Figure 14.1 and Table 14.1) can cluster to market-based relationship marketing (MBRM) and network-based relationship marketing (NBRM) is related to how these traditions view the exchange

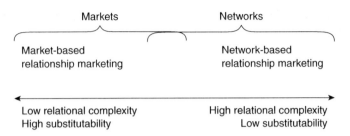

Figure 14.2 Relational complexity and marked-based RM and network-based RM (adapted from Möller and Halinen, 2000)

relationships and the context in which the exchange takes place (Figure 14.2). However, as noted by Möller and Halinen (2000), buyer–seller relationships rarely exist in pure types and they are therefore portrayed more effectively on a continuum of varying degrees of relational complexity. Complexity, as used here, is a multidimensional construct. It refers to the number of actors involved in an exchange, to their interdependence, intensity, and nature of interaction, and to the potential temporal contingencies in the relationship. Complexity is closely related to the kind of task that is exchanged or administered through the relationship, how standardized the task is, and how complex and novel it is. In that respect, it is also related to the relative substitutability of the product or service and its provider.

With this in mind, what is the relationship between relational complexity and the context of exchange? On the basis of the research tradition analysis, it is suggested that complex exchange relationships generally occur in a network context, whereas less complex relationships are characterized by a market-like exchange context, as depicted in Figure 14.2.

There are several reasons for this occurrence. Complex exchange tasks demand a high level of mutual understanding, which is not fostered in market-governed relationships. Through increased mutual learning and relationship-specific investments, actors become interdependent, thus making switching difficult. When these conditions characterize exchange behaviour, the exchange context also tends to become network-like. In contrast, there are several generally acceptable alternatives for customers at the low complexity end of the exchange continuum. This makes switching possible, and leads to less interdependent relationships. These kinds of relationships tend to be more efficiently governed by markets.

Based on this reasoning, Möller and Halinen (2000) made their suggestion of the theoretical usefulness of distinguishing between two relationship marketing theories: market-based relationship marketing and network-based relationship marketing:

> **These theories have unique features and they are efficient in explaining the particular relationship-marketing phenomena that exist in the domains of exchange described. Although these theories are closely related to consumer-directed relationship marketing and interorganizational relationship marketing, their theoretical bases are anchored in exchange characteristics and the exchange context, not in the 'consumer-business' division. (Möller and Halinen, 2000: 44)**

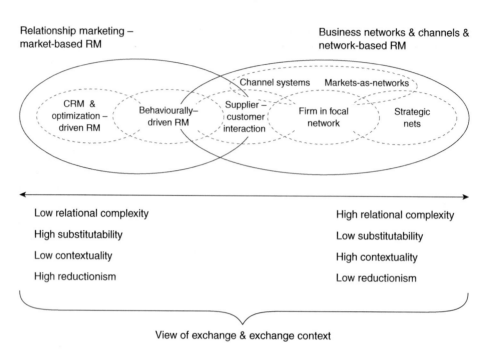

Figure 14.3   Key constituents of relationship marketing and business networks

Although highly valuable, this distinction is also very abstract and conceals many important differences between the examined research traditions that constitute both the RM and BN domains. So, what was just aggregated will next be disaggregated.

Key constituents of relationship marketing and business networks

Drawing on the previous analysis, it is useful to portray the identified key constituent research traditions on a 'theory continuum' as depicted in Figure 14.3. The continuum reflects how the traditions view relational exchange, what kind of role the context plays – or fails to play – in the traditions, and whether the theorizing of the traditions is relatively reductionist or 'embedded'; that is, taking into account the context and history of the focal behaviour.

CRM-driven RM

The market-based relationship marketing domain is seen to be composed of customer relationship management (CRM)-driven relationship marketing and behaviourally driven relationship marketing. The former utilizes the tools and opportunities offered by customer databases and data mining techniques, and aims at optimizing a firm's customer equity and the customer lifetime value through customer relationships and customer portfolio management (Malthouse and Blattberg, 2005). Although the approach aims at increasing customer loyalty by tailoring marketing communications and offerings, it is not deeply interested in the psychological and behavioural aspects of those relationships. The analytical tools within CRM presume relatively reductionist research settings with low contextuality. Its applications cover both consumer and business customer products and services, and these are essentially prominent in the fields of internet and mobile marketing (Kumar, 2008).

Behaviourally-driven RM

Behaviourally-driven RM (BRM) represents much about what is generally regarded as 'relationship marketing'. The key theoretical interest lies in understanding supplier–customer relationships, their elements and development, and the factors influencing them. Besides utilizing the services marketing research, BRM has been influenced substantially by social exchange (SOE) theory and its applications within channels research and business relationships. Since the seminal publications by Håkansson (1982, business relationships and interaction) and Dwyer, Schurr and Oh (1987), key SOE concepts, such as dependence, power, attraction, trust and commitment, have played central roles in examining buyer–seller and consumer–marketer relationships. These also form the key elements of Morgan and Hunt's (1994) 'commitment–trust theory of relationship marketing'.

It is relevant to recognize that the social exchange theory forms an important bridge between the BRM and the supplier–customer research both in the channels research and in the industrial network tradition. Although the BRM offers theory-based tools for rigorous modelling of the relationships, it is relatively weak in its contextuality. That is, it tries primarily to explain the outcomes of relationships (e.g. perceived satisfaction, relationship duration, and performance) by factors related to the actors forming the relationship or to the relationship itself.

Channel systems

In order to provide an in-depth understanding of the research comprising the business networks and channel domains, these are depicted through five interrelated streams. The research into channel systems and markets-as-networks form the upper or macro layer of this domain and are discussed first.

Channel systems refers to studies that examine the channel structures, their characteristics and evolution, and the factors that influence specific structures and change (Robicheaux and Coleman, 1994). This channel system research often addresses issues concerning the influence of the channel system on channel relationships as posed by the political economy approach (Stern and Reve, 1980). (For an illustrative study, cf. Grewal and Dharwadkar (2002).) The channel system research is relatively scarce, which is unfortunate as it addresses fundamental questions, such as why do we have different channels structures, how do they evolve, are there different evolutionary patterns and why? How do the different channel structures influence channel member roles and their interaction and relationship structures?

Markets-as-networks – macro networks

In the business networks domain, the 'markets-as-networks' label is employed to refer to the similar macro-level research as the channel systems in the channels tradition. It addresses questions such as how do networks emerge, why do we have different network structures, what are their key drivers, and through what kinds of processes do networks evolve? This kind of knowledge is also fundamental in understanding the dynamics of more restricted focal networks and dyadic network relationships. Again, we have relatively few macro network studies. In the IMP tradition, Håkansson and Waluszewski (2002) have examined the role of cognition and technology in network dynamics, Lundgren (1995) provides a strong historical analysis of the 'networked' evolution of a new business field, and Möller and Svahn (2009) offer a framework model identifying key patterns in the evolution of new networks. The issue of network structures has also been addressed in economic sociology where the work by Powell and his colleagues (Powell et al., 1996, 2005) address the new field's emergence and structure (biotechnology and life sciences); and in organization science and strategy studies, where Rosenkoph and her colleagues (Rosenkoph and Padula, 2008; Rosenkoph and Schilling, 2007) examine network formation through strategic alliances.

Supplier–customer interaction – channels context

Turning to the dyadic supplier–customer interaction research, it is useful to examine how relationships are studied in the channel context and in the network environment, as well as make a comparison to the behaviourally-driven RM (BRM) research. As previously mentioned, both channel research on relationships and BRM share the conceptualization provided by social exchange (SOE) theory. The major difference is that in the channels tradition the majority of studies combine the behavioural concepts (from the SOE) and the transaction cost framework when they study efficient governance forms for manufacturer–channel member relationships and examine the influence of governance on relational performance. Another theme that is exclusive to channels research is the investigation of how parties develop safeguards against becoming overly dependent on the other. Heide and his colleagues' work provide good exemplars (Heide, 1994; Heide and John, 1988, 1992; Wathne and Heide, 2000). Advanced studies examine also the influence that the channel system exerts on the relationship-level behaviour (Wathne and Heide, 2004).

Actor interaction – network context

Compared to the channel research in business relationships, the network approach is more interested in the issues of through what kind of resource ties, activity links and social and organizational bonds the network actors are connected and through what kind of interactive processes – resource exchange, social exchange and adaptations – the relationships evolve (Håkansson and Snehota, 1995). The economic aspect is included in terms of the investments the parties are making in the relationship (Easton, 1992). Besides the emphasis on relationship processes, the notion that dyadic relationships actually cannot be usefully studied outside their network context forms the major distinction compared to the behaviourally-driven RM. The current actor roles and network positions, being aggregations of actors' network relationships, cannot be understood without some level of knowledge of their evolution (Easton, 1992). In relation to methodology this requires understanding that is mainly offered by historical analysis and case studies. This is another major division to the channels tradition which primarily uses causal modelling frameworks and techniques.

Focal networks and strategic nets

In addition to the macro network research and the network relationship research it is useful to distinguish between studies examining the firm and its relationships in a focal network context and the so-called strategic nets or value nets (see Möller and Halinen (1999), for a discussion on the levels of analysis in network research). The term focal network refers to the view that although networks as such are borderless the cognitive capacity of the actors, as well as their limited resources, constrain their ability to make sense of and utilize these borderless networks. Thus actors are primarily dealing with actors forming their focal network, that is, the actors they are able perceive (Alajoutsijärvi et al., 1999).

The point that networks are not transparent is highly relevant for network management. Because of the non-transparency, actors are assumed to learn about their networks, in depth sense, primarily through enactment (Weick, 1969, 1985). In this respect each actor is assumed to form his or her network view. The formation of the view is seen to be influenced by the accumulated network experience of the actor, on his/her network position and the number and variety of relationships the position enables, and on the learning capacity of the actor (Möller and Svahn, 2009). The resulting view, also called 'network picture or framework', is actually an actor's theory of the network. This network theory influences his/her network perceptions, interpretations and actions (Henneberg et al., 2006; Mouzas et al., 2008). Concerning the focal network, an actor's capacity to make sense of the network forms their network horizon (Dubois, 1998). It should be noted that the network opaqueness and ambiguity, and the resulting emphasis on network cognitions, forms another major distinction to channels systems research and to market-based relationship marketing.

Finally, if focal networks form the network actors' 'playground', what are then the strategic nets or value nets? These terms refer to intentionally planned and mobilized 'network organizations' (Möller et al., 2005). There exist important ontological differences between these 'network organizations' and more generic networks. The studies drawing on economic sociology and the social networks tradition (Powell et al., 1996), as well as the key authors within the industrial network approach, tend to emphasize the historical, evolutionary and embedded character of business networks (Håkansson and Ford, 2002; Håkansson and Snehota, 1995), and view networks as borderless, self-organizing systems that emerge in a bottom-up fashion from local interactions. On the other hand, many scholars representing the strategic management perspective are suggesting that there are also more intentionally created strategic networks or value nets, which contain a specific set of organizations with agreed roles and distributed tasks (see, e.g. Jarillo, 1993; Möller and Svahn, 2003; Parolini, 1999).

This distinction is an essential element in the debate concerning the question of to what extent can networks be managed. While sharing the view that open, borderless networks are not managed, Möller and his colleagues have developed an articulated theory of value nets. Their work explores basic net types and their management requirements (Möller and Rajala, 2007; Möller and Svahn, 2003; Möller et al., 2005). A key suggestion is that the structure and management of specific nets are influenced by the specific value creation logics of the nets. The extent to which this logic can be specified shapes the role of knowledge exploitation and exploration in the value creation (Möller and Svahn, 2006). This is a significant opening as the IMP network theory has been notoriously void of managerially-oriented theory development.

Conclusions

Our analysis shows that the 'relationship marketing' and 'business networks' domains are composed of several research traditions drawing from a variety of disciplines. The 'relationship marketing' domain, especially, resembles a mosaic of partly overlapping and partly distinctive streams of research. This finding, together with the description and comparison of the different traditions constituting this broad domain has several major consequences.

First, it is evident that one cannot meaningfully talk about a single relationship marketing theory. The CRM-driven RM, the behaviourally-driven RM, and the way relationships are conceptualized and studied in channels research and business networks research are all distinctive modes or approaches in marketing relationships.

Second, this mosaic- and medley-like character of relationship marketing research makes it very difficult to derive a comprehensive yet articulated view of the different types of exchange relationships and the theories addressing them. This kind of complex puzzle calls for clarifying tools. It has been proposed that a fundamental division can be drawn between the research approaches assuming a marketing context and the approaches assuming a channel or a network context. Because of its relevance this distinction is briefly discussed.

There are significant differences between the underlying ontological assumptions between the market-based approaches and the networked-based approaches. By assuming a working market context the former approaches consider the exchange relationships as mutually independent. This may be an acceptable assumption in mass type of products and services for both consumer and business customers, but is not satisfactory in the exchange of more complex offerings where the exchange relationships are more directly influenced by their context. In these domains researchers have to develop such theories which inform us about how the context and the exchange relationships are interrelated. The channels research and the business networks approach are good examples. It is also important to note that by 'assuming away' or standardizing the context we voluntarily restrict the seeking for an explanation of the form and dynamics of business relationships to the level of the relationships themselves. The influential commitment-trust theory of relationship marketing by Morgan and Hunt (1994) is a good example of this kind of 'flat modelling'. The relationship outcomes are explained by factors pertaining to the actors and to their views of the relationship.

Third, all the research traditions identified are relatively logical configurations; their research foci and practices follow the goals and the underlying theoretical assumptions. Each tradition has its relative strengths and weaknesses. As such each provides a partial theory or understanding of the complex domain of relational marketing exchange and its embeddedness in our social and economic environment. The key point, however, is that because of their particular theoretical positions and goals they cannot be merged into a comprehensive general theory. Each has a specific role to play in understanding and explaining relationships. However, researchers working within a school do not necessarily recognize the assumptions and their consequences as these have often not been explicitly described.

Fourth, there seem to be important lacunae in the current research approaches. We have very little research and knowledge of such significant questions as what are the principal modes or forms of exchange relationships, how do they vary across different fields or contexts, and why? The point is that such non-contextual approaches as the CRM-driven RM and even the more multidimensional behaviourally-driven RM have severe limitations in addressing these. The oversight of the basic what and why questions is evidently related to the strong normative and managerial character of the market-based RM approaches. Their researchers are predominantly interested in the 'how to manage a relationship question'. Unfortunately, even the channels and business networks research has not been very interested in these questions.

Another limitation, concerning all the examined research approaches except the business networks, is related to the organizing of the marketing relationships. There are some notions of the organizational issues in the service marketing which have partly been adopted in CRM and behaviourally-driven RM. These developments remain limited, however, as the researchers have not established any stronger links with organization theory. In practice, contemporary relationship marketing is not interested in research questions like what kind of marketing organizations exist in different fields and contexts?; or how to explain potential differences; how organizational forms and solutions seems to evolve; what are the performance consequences of different forms and why? Are we leaving these issues to organizational theory or should we bother? It is interesting to compare the situation to the development of consumer behaviour into a new discipline. The most probable reason for this void of research is the narrow focus on influencing customers. We seem to lack both the sociology of marketing organizations and the sociology of exchange relationships.

To conclude, it is hoped that the developed theory map of the relationship marketing and business networks domains will help researchers to become more conscious of the research approaches constituting them. This facilitates both the navigation in these mosaic-like domains and the advancement of theory development. A related point is embracing the theoretical pluralism. We have to accept the fact that there is no single theory of relationship marketing. On the contrary, this broad domain is composed of multiple research streams, partly inter-related but yet distinctive. They all offer only partial understanding of the complex domain. In order to make sense of their knowledge 'offerings' and limitations we have to become theoretically multilingual. It is tough but there is no other way.

Recommended further reading

Dwyer, F.R., Schurr, P.H. and Oh, S. (1987) 'Developing buyer–seller relationships', *Journal of Marketing* 51, April: 11–27.

Grönroos, C. (1994) 'Quo vadis, marketing? Toward a relationship marketing paradigm', *Journal of Marketing Management* 10(5): 347–60.

Håkansson, H. and Snehota, I. (eds) (1995) *Developing Relationships in Business Networks*, London: Routledge.

Heide, J.B. (1994) 'Interorganizational governance in marketing channels', *Journal of Marketing* 58, January: 71–85.

Kumar, V. (2008) *Managing Customers for Profit: Strategies to Increase Profits and Build Loyalty*, Upper Saddle River, NJ: Wharton School Publishing.

Morgan, R.M. and Hunt, S.D. (1994) 'The commitment-trust theory of relationship marketing', *Journal of Marketing* 58, July: 20–38.

Möller, K. and Halinen, A. (1999) 'Business relationships and networks: managerial challenge of a network era', *Industrial Marketing Management* 28(5): 413–27.

Möller, K. and Halinen, A. (2000) 'Relationship marketing theory: its roots and direction', *Journal of Marketing Management* 16(1–3): 29–54.

Möller, K., Rajala, A. and Svahn, S. (2005) 'Strategic business nets – their type and management', *Journal of Business Research* 58: 1274–84.

Stern, L.W. and Reve, T. (1980) 'Distribution channels as political economies: a framework for comparative analysis', *Journal of Marketing* 44, Summer: 52–64.

References

Alajoutsijärvi, K., Möller, K. and Rosenbröijer, C.J. (1999) 'Relevance of focal nets in understanding the dynamics of business relationships', *Journal of Business-to-Business Marketing* 6(3): 3–35.

Alvesson, M. (2002) *Understanding organizational culture*, Thousand Oaks, CA: Sage.

Anderson, J.C. and Narus, J.A. (1990) 'A model of the distributor's perspective of distributor-manufacturer working partnerships', *Journal of marketing* 54: 42–58.

Anderson, J.C., Håkansson, H. and Johanson, J. (1994) 'Dyadic business relationships within a business network context', *Journal of Marketing* 58: 1–15.

Axelsson, B. and Easton, G. (1992) *Industrial Markets: A New View of Reality.*

Berry, L.L. and Parasuraman, A. (1993) 'Building a new academic field – The case of services marketing', *Journal of Retailing* 69(1): 13–60.

Berry, L.L., Shostack, G.L. and Upah, G.D. (eds) (1983) *'Emerging Perceptions on Service Marketing'*, 25–8, Chicago, IL: American Marketing Association.

Blattberg, R. and Deighton, J. (1991) 'Interactive marketing: Exploiting the age of addressability, *Sloan Management Review* 33, Fall: 5–14.

de Man, A.P. (2004) *The Network Economy, Strategy, Structure and Management*, Cheltenham, UK: Edward Elgar.

Deshpande, R.J., Farley U. and Webster, F.E., Jr. (1993) 'Corporate culture, customer orientation, and innovativeness in Japanese firms–a quadrand analysis', *Journal of Marketing* 57(1): 23–27.

Dubois, A. (1998) *Organising industrial activities across firm boundaries*, London: Routledge.

Dwyer, F.R., Schurr, P.H. and Oh, S. (1987) 'Developing buyer seller relationships', *Journal of Marketing* 51, April: 11–27.

Easton, G. (1992) 'Industrial networks: A review', in Axelsson, B. and Easton, G. (eds) *Industrial Networks – A New View of Reality*, 1–27, London: Routledge.

Egan, J. (2008) 'A century of marketing', *The Marketing Review* 8(1): 3–23.

Eiriz, V. and Wilson, D. (2006) 'Research in relationship marketing: Antecedents, traditions and integration', *European Journal of Marketing* 40(3/4): 275–91.

Emerson, R.M. (1962) 'Power dependence relations', *American Sociological Review* 27(2): 31–40.

Ford, D. (ed.) (1990) *Understanding Business Markets: Interaction, Relationships, Networks*, London: Academic Press.

Ford, D. (ed.) (1997) *Understanding Business Markets: Interaction, Relationships and Networks*, 2nd edition, Bridgend: The Dryden Press.

Ford, D. (ed.) (2002) *Understanding Business Markets Purchasing*, 3rd edition, Cornwall: Thomson Learning.

Frazier, G. (1983) 'Interorganizational exchange behavior in marketing channels: A broadened perspective', *Journal of Marketing* 47, Fall: 68–78.

Gaski, J.F. (1984) 'The theory of power and conflict in channels of distribution', *The Journal of Marketing* 48(3): 9–29.

Grewal R. and Dharwadker, R. (2002) 'The role of the institutional environment in marketing channels', *Journal of Marketing* 66, July: 82–97.

Grönroos, C. (1981) 'Internal Marketing – An Integral Part of Marketing Theory', in Donnelly, J.H. and George, W.E. (eds) *Marketing of services* 236–8.

Grönroos, C. (1990) *Service Management and Marketing: Managing the Moments of Truth in Service Competition*, Lexington, Ma: Lexington Books.

Gwinner, K.P., Gremler, D.D. and Bitner, M.J. (1998) 'Relational benefits in services industries: The customer's perspective', *Journal of the Academy of Marketing Science* 26(2): 101–14.

Håkansson, H. (1989) *Corporate Technological Behaviour: Co-operation and Networks*, London: Routledge.

Håkansson, H. and Johanson, J. (1988) 'Formal and Informal Cooperation Strategies in International Industrial Networks', in F.J. Contractor and Lorange, P. (eds) *Cooperative Strategies in International Business*, MA: Lexington Books.

Håkansson, H. and Ford, D. (2002) 'How should companies interact in business networks?' *Journal of Business Research* 55(2):133–9.

Håkansson, H. and Snehota, I. (eds) (1995) 'Developing Relationships in Business Networks', London: Routledge.

Håkansson, H. and Waluszewski, A. (2002) 'Path dependence: Restricting or facilitating technical development?' *Journal of Business Research* 55(7): 561–70.

Håkansson, H. (ed.) (1982) *International Marketing and Purchasing of Industrial Goods: An Interaction Approach*, Chichester: John Wiley & Sons.

Håkansson, H. (ed.) (1987) *Industrial Technological Development. A Network Approach*, London: Croom, Helm.

Heide, J.B. (1994) 'Inter-organizational governance in marketing channels', *Journal of Marketing* 58(1): 71–98.

Heide, J.B. and John, G. (1992) 'Do norms matter in marketing relationships?', *Journal of Marketing* 56, April: 32–44.

Heide, J.B. and John, G. (1988) 'The role of dependence balancing in safeguarding transaction-specific assets in conventional channels', *Journal of Marketing* 52, January: 20–35.

Henneberg, S.C., Mouzas, S. and Naudé, P. (2006) 'Network pictures – Concepts and representations', *European Journal of Marketing* 40(3/4): 408–29.

Jarillo, J.C. (1988) 'On strategic networks', *Strategic Management Journal* 9(1): 31–41.

Jarillo J.C. (1993) *Strategic Networks: Creating the Borderless Organization*, Oxford, UK: Butterworth-Heinemann.

Jenkinson, A. (1995) *Valuing Your Customers: From Quality Information to Quality Relationships Through Database Marketing*, London: McGraw-Hill.

Johanson, J. and Mattsson, L.G. (1988) 'Internationalisation in Industrial Systems. A Network Approach', in Hood, N. and Vahlne, J.E. (eds) *Strategies in Global Competition* 287–314, London: Croom Helm.

Kumar, V. (2008) *Managing Customers for Profit: Strategies to Increase Profits and Build Loyalty*, Wharton School Publishing.

Liljander, V. and Strandvik, T. (1995) The Nature of Customer Relationships in Services, in Swartz, T.A., Bowen, D.E. and Brown, S.W. (eds) '*Advances in Services Marketing and Management: Research and Practice*', Vol. 4, 141–67, Greenwich, Connecticut: JAI Press.

Lundgren, A. (1995) *Technological Innovation and Network Evolution*, London: Routledge.

Malthouse, E. and Blattberg, R. (2005) 'Can we predict customer lifetime value?', *Journal of Interactive Marketing* 19(1): 2–16.

Mattsson, L.G. (1985) 'An Application of Network Approach to Marketing: Defending and Changing Market Positions', in Dholakia, N. and Arndt, J. (eds) *Changing the Course of Marketing: Alternative Paradigms for Widening Marketing Theory*, Greenwich, CT: JAI Press.

Mattsson, L.G. (1997) 'Relationship marketing and the markets-as-networks approach – A comparative analysis of two evolving streams of research', *Journal of Marketing Management* 13(7): 447–62.

McKenna, R. (1991) 'Marketing is everything', *Harvard Business Review* 69(1): 65–79.

Möller, K. and Halinen, A. (1999) 'Business relationships and networks: Managerial challenge of a network era', *Industrial Marketing Management* 28(5): 413–27.

Möller, K. and Halinen, A. (2000) 'Relationship marketing theory: Its roots and directions', *Journal of Marketing Management* 16(1–3): 29–54.

Möller, K. and Rajala, A. (2007) 'Rise of strategic nets – New modes of value creation', *Industrial Marketing Management* 36(7): 895–908.

Möller, K. and Svahn, S. (2003) 'Managing strategic nets: A capability perspective', *Marketing Theory* 3(2): 201–26.

Möller, K. and Svahn, S. (2006) 'Role of knowledge in value creation in business nets', *Journal of Management Studies* 43(5): 985–1007.

Möller, K. and Svahn, S. (2009) 'How to influence the birth of new business fields', *Industrial Marketing Management* 38: 450–58.

Möller, K. and Törrönen, P. (2003) 'Business suppliers value creation potential: A capability-based analysis', *Industrial Marketing Management* 32: 109–18.

Möller, K. and Wilson, D. (eds) (1995) *Business Marketing: An Interaction and Network Perspective*, Boston/Dordrecht/London: Kluwer Academic Publisher.

Möller, K., Pels, J. and Saren, M. (2009) 'The Marketing Theory or Theories into Marketing? Plurality of Research Traditions and Paradigms', Chapter 9 in P. Maclaran et al. (eds) *The Sage Handbook Of Marketing Theory*, London: Sage.

Möller, K., Rajala, A. and Svahn, S. (2005) 'Strategic business nets – Their type and management', *Journal of Business Research* 58: 1274–84.

Möller, K.E. (1994) 'Interorganizational Marketing Exchange: Metatheoretical Analysis of Current Research Approaches', in Laurent, G., Lilien, G. and Pras, B. (eds) *Research Traditions in Marketing*, 348–82, Boston: Kluwer.

Möller, K. (2006) 'Marketing mix discussion – Is the mix misleading us or are we misreading the mix?', Comment on Constantinides, E., The marketing mix revisited: Towards the 21st century marketing? *Journal of Marketing Management* 22: 439–50.

Morgan, R.M. and Hunt, S.D. (1994) 'The commitment-trust theory of relationship marketing', *Journal of Marketing* 58, July: 20–38.

Morgan, G. (1996) *Images of Organization*, London: Sage Publications.

Mouzas, S., Henneberg, S.C. and Naudé, P. (2008) 'Developing network insight', *Industrial Marketing Management* 37(2): 167–80.

Oliver, R.L. (1980) 'A cognitive model of the antecedents and consequences of satisfaction decisions', *Journal of Marketing Research* 17(4): 460–69.

Parasuraman, A., Zeithaml, V.A. and Berry, L.L. (1985) 'A conceptual model of service quality and its implications for future research', *Journal of Marketing* 49, Fall: 41–50.

Parolini, C. (1999) *The Value Net: A Tool for Competitive Strategy*, Chichester, UK: John Wiley & Sons Ltd.

Pels, J., Möller, K.E. and Saren, M. (2009) 'Do we really understand business marketing?' Getting beyond RM-BM matrimony', *Journal of Business and Industrial Marketing* 24(5/6).

Pels, J. (1999) 'Exchange relationships in consumer markets?', *European Journal of Marketing* 33(1/2): 19–37.

Peppers, D. and Rogers, M. (1993) *One-to-One Future: Building Relationships One Customer at a Time*, New York: Currency/Doubleday.

Peppers, D. and Rogers, M. (1997) *Enterprise One to One. Tools for Compering in the Interactive Age*, New York: Currency/Doubleday.

Pine, J.B., Peppers, D. and Rogers, M. (1995) 'Do you want to keep your customers forever?', *Harvard Business Review* 73, March–April: 103–14.

Porter, M.E. (1980) '*Competitive Strategy*', New York: Free Press.

Powell, W.W., Kogut, K. and Smith-Doerr, L. (1996) 'Interorgnizational collaboration and the locus of innovation: Networks of learning in biotechnology', *Administrative Science Quarterly* 41: 116–45.

Powell, W.W., White, D.R., Koput, K.W. and Owen-Smith, J. (2005) 'Network dynamics and field evolution: the growth of interorganizational collaboration in the life sciences', *The American Journal of Sociology* 110(4): 1132–206.

Rapp, S. and Collins, T. (1991) *The Great Marketing Turnaround*, Englewood Cliffs, NJ: Prentice Hall.

Rindfleisch, A. and Heide, J.B. (1997) 'Transaction cost analysis: Past, present and future', *Journal of Marketing* 61(4): 30–54.

Robicheaux, R.A. and Coleman, J. (1994) 'The structure of marketing relationships', *Journal of the Academy of Marketing Science* 22: 38–51.

Rosenkopf, L. and Padula, G. (2008) 'Investigating the microstructure of network evolution: Alliance formation in the mobile communications industry', *Organization Science* 19(5): 1–19.

Rosenkopf, L. and Schilling, M. (2007) 'Comparing alliance network structure across industries: Observations and explanations', *Strategic Entrepreneurship Journal* 1: 191–209.

Rust, R.T., Lemon, K.N. and Zeithaml, V.A. (2004) 'Return on marketing: using customer equity to focus marketing strategy', *Journal of Marketing* 68, January: 109–27.

Scanzoni, J. (1979) 'Social Exchange and Behavioral Interdependence', in R.L. Burgess and T.L. Huston (eds) *Social Exchange in Developing Relationships*, 61–98, New York: Academic Press, Inc.

Schultz, D.E., Tannebaum, S. and Lauterborn, R.E. (1993) *Intergrated Marketing Communications*, Lincolnwood, IL: NTC Business Books.

Shaw, B. and Stone, M. (1988) 'Competitive superiority through data base marketing', *Long Range Planning* 21(5): 24–40.

Shepard, D. (1995) *The New Direct Marketing: How to Implement a Profit-Driven Database Marketing Strategy*, New York: Irwin.

Stern, L.W. and Reve, T. (1980) 'Distribution channels as political economies: A framework for comparative analysis', *Journal of Marketing* 44, Summer: 52–64.

Thompson, G., Frances, J., Levačic, R. and Mitchell, J. (eds) (1994) *Markets, Hierarchies & Networks. The Coordination of Social Life*, SAGE Publications Ltd, Great Britain.

Wathne, K.H. and Heide, J.B. (2000) 'Opportunism in interfirm relationships: Forms, outcomes, and solutions', *Journal of Marketing* 64(4): 36–51.

Wathne, K.H. and Heide, J.B. (2004) 'Relationship governance in a supply chain network', *Journal of Marketing* 68, January: 73–89.

Weick, K.E. (1969) *The Social Psychology of Organizing*, Reading, MA: Addison-Wesley.

Weick, K.E. (1985) '*Sensemaking in Organizations*', Thousand Oaks, CA: Sage Publications.

Williamson, O.E. (1985) *The Economic Institutions of Capitalism*, New York, NY: The Free Press.

Zeithaml, V.A, Berry, L.L. and Parasuraman, A. (1988) 'Communication and control processes in the delivery of service quality', *Journal of Marketing*, 52: 35–48.

Zeithaml, V.A. and Bitner, M.J. (1996) *Service Marketing*, New York: McGraw-Hill Companies Inc.

|15|

Theory in social marketing

Gerard Hastings, Abraham Brown and Thomas Boysen Anker

Chapter Topics

Introduction

At its core, commercial marketing is focused on understanding and influencing consumer behaviour. Marketers want to know what makes people visit retail outlets, listen to persuasive messages, engage with particular brands – and ultimately, buy different products and services. They have devised a range of skills and theories that help them do this, and these are explained elsewhere in this book. Social marketing adopts a slightly different perspective, and focuses not on consumer behaviour, but social and health behaviour. It uses many of the same principles that are used in commerce: understanding the target group, strategic planning and relational thinking, for instance, are all as important in social as commercial marketing. Social marketing also makes use of theory, and its focus draws it particularly towards theories of human behaviour. This chapter will discuss the role of theory in social marketing.

It starts by explaining a little more about social marketing and why its focus on human behaviour is so important. It then goes on to discuss the value of theory – how it distils previous learning and enables us to simplify complex phenomena. This section also draws attention to the need for theory to remain tied to the practical – as Kurt Lewin (1951: 169) said over 50 years ago: there is nothing so practical as a good theory. For social marketers, then, the test of a good theory is whether or not it helps them to do the job more effectively.

The chapter goes on to look at three important theories which help social marketers to think more systematically about the key questions they need to address:

1. How does the target group or population feel about a particular behaviour (stages of change theory);

2. What social and contextual factors influence this positioning (social cognitive theory and social norms)

3. What offerings might encourage them to change their behaviour – or, those in a position to do so, to make the social context more conducive to change (exchange theory).

The intention is not to provide an exhaustive list of all the theories social marketers use, or even to make specific claims for the chosen theories, but instead to illustrate the potential benefits of theory and how social marketers can harness these benefits.

To keep faith with Kurt Lewin's maxim, the chapter refers regularly to practical examples which illustrate the real-world impact of theory. It makes particular use of the case of smoking in the UK, which is a useful example for three reasons. First it represents a very real social problem: one in two smokers who do not quit will die as a result of their habit. Second, smoking is a typically complex human behaviour with many influences and an equal array of possible social marketing responses. Third, real progress is being made in the fight against tobacco: smoking rates have more than halved since Richard Doll first uncovered the health risks back in the 1950s, and highly respected bodies like the Department of Health and the British Medical Association are now predicting a point where smoking in the UK will cease altogether.

Why social marketers care about behaviour change

The commercial marketers' focus on consumer behaviour is self explanatory: if people stop buying products and services they go out of business. The motives of social marketers are less obvious, but stem from an equally compelling truth. Consider for a moment: what do the following have in common: smoking; rape; democracy; vandalism; global warming; teenage pregnancy? They are all pressing social issues. They are of great concern. They have a big impact on our welfare. They can, indeed, become matters of life and death. They have all these similarities. But the most basic trait they share is that each one is a function of human behaviour: of the perpetrators' actions and those of the people who create a social environment that makes them more or less attractive options. Thus teen pregnancy is partly determined by the behaviour of adolescents and partly the result of an over sexualized and hypocritical society which endorses the sale of raunchy dolls, T-shirts and even pole dancing kits to children (see Figure 15.1), but restricts sex education. Similarly, binge drinking is partly due to individuals behaving badly and also to the irresponsible marketing strategies of the alcohol industry.

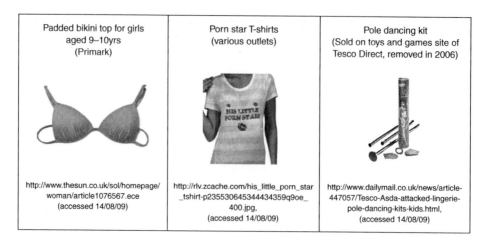

Padded bikini top for girls aged 9–10yrs (Primark)	Porn star T-shirts (various outlets)	Pole dancing kit (Sold on toys and games site of Tesco Direct, removed in 2006)
http://www.thesun.co.uk/sol/homepage/woman/article1076567.ece (accessed 14/08/09)	http://rlv.zcache.com/his_little_porn_star _tshirt-p235530645344434359q9oe_ 400.jpg, (accessed 14/08/09)	http://www.dailymail.co.uk/news/article-447057/Tesco-Asda-attacked-lingerie-pole-dancing-kits-kids.html, (accessed 14/08/09)

Figure 15.1   Marketing sex to children: is it any surprise that the UK has a problem with teen pregnancy?

The vital role of behaviour on human welfare, then, is difficult to overstate. Nearly 20 years ago a study in the *Journal of the American Medical Association* (McGinnis and Foege, 1993) pointed out that more than half the population of developed countries would die prematurely as a direct result of lifestyle choices. In the ensuing two decades a completely new threat to public health – the rise in obesity – has been added to the picture, and the key lifestyle choices of smoking, drinking, poor diet and sedentary living have been vigorously exported to the developing world. Behaviour, then, is a crucial determinate of everyone's longevity and morbidity. Perhaps even more alarmingly, it is also impacting the health of the planet: global warming is driven by our desire for SUVs, overseas holidays and carbon-rich lifestyles.

So, social marketers focus on human behaviour because it matters. Theory helps them to do this more effectively.

_____ **Theory in theory** _____

Theory is a daunting word. It suggests both complexity and abstraction. In reality it should be the reverse of both of these: it should *simplify* and provide *practical* help.

It simplifies in two ways. First it is a means of distilling existing research into a coherent and explanatory perspective on the world which helps us to better understand specific events. Newton illustrated this principle when he explained that he had deduced the theory of gravitation, not through any isolated genius on his own part, but by building on the prodigious efforts of past scientists – or as he elegantly expressed it, by 'standing on the shoulders of giants'. Theory enables us to do the same.

Theory also simplifies by building models of real-life phenomena. So, in the late 1990s when the UK government was trying to decide whether or not a ban on tobacco advertising was justified, it needed to unpack and understand the phenomenon of youth smoking. To do so social scientists had to build models of all the possible influences on the uptake and continuance of smoking among young people and test which were actually having an effect. Theory helped them to identify these possible influences and provide a logical explanation for any observed effect. In other words it helped construct and make sense of the empirical evidence base – the real world. In the case of tobacco advertising some of the theories we will discuss below, especially those concerned with the social construction of meaning, played an important role.

The danger with such model building is that we forget that it is a simplification of reality, and, unless we treat it with circumspection, it can become an over-simplification – and thereby dangerous. This converts into the warning that, when it comes to human behaviour, we need to use theory with subtlety, allowing for the nuances and contradictions in the way we live our lives. Much as with marketing research, theory is not a prescriptive tool but simply an aid to decision making. It suggests likely explanations and plausible connections, but there is still a need for human intuition and intelligent decision making before these can be converted into sensible conclusions and useful actions. Notwithstanding Newton's self effacing acknowledgement of his fellow scientists' efforts, his genius also played a crucial role in the development of gravitational theory.

This also brings us back to Kurt Lewin. Good theory must have practical applicability. The ultimate and overriding test has to be: does it help us to do the job better – or for social marketers, does it improve our chances of successfully changing behaviour in the desired direction. In the case of tobacco promotion, the suggestion from theory that tobacco advertising makes the social context more pro-smoking and thus encourages larger numbers of young people to smoke than would otherwise be the case has stood up to the real-world test. A study in the UK, found that support for smoke-free legislation pre-ban significantly increased perceptions of non-smoking norms post-ban (Brown et al., 2009).

Three theories that interest social marketers

As noted in the introduction, the social marketers' focus on human behaviour can be reduced to three basic questions:

1. How do the target group feel about a particular behaviour

2. What social and contextual factors influence this positioning

3. What offerings might encourage them to change their behaviour – or, those in a position to do so, to make the social context more conducive to change.

Three theories – or groups of theories – have helped to elucidate these questions, and each is now discussed in turn.

1. Stages of change theory

This is also known as the Transtheoretical Model and is the work of two American academics called James Prochaska and Carlo DiClemente (2005). At its heart is a very simple but powerful observation: that when people change complex behaviours they will often do so gradually in a stepwise fashion, rather than in one flip. Thus smokers who decide to quit do not tend to do so spontaneously, without any forethought. Typically they will have given it consideration in the past, and this consideration will initially have been triggered by developing awareness of the downsides of the habit.

Similarly they do not complete the transition to non-smoker instantly – or necessarily even quickly. Many smokers will wrestle with their addiction at least for a short while and some long-term quitters still retain smoking inclinations years later. Indeed, the protracted nature of quitting is officially recognized by cessation experts who do not formally classify a smoker as having successfully quit for at least six, and often 12, months.

Prochaska and DiClemente (2005) noticed this foot dragging phenomenon and began to study it in detail. It occurs not just with smoking but a whole series of addiction-related and other health behaviours including condom use, quitting cocaine, using sunscreen and weight control (Prochaska and Velicer, 1997). They studied the process in detail and concluded that the process of behaviour change can be divided into five stages:

- *Pre-contemplation*: you may be aware of the new behaviour (e.g. quitting smoking or obeying the speed limit) but are not interested in it, at least at this point in your life.

- *Contemplation*: you are consciously evaluating the personal relevance of the new behaviour.

- *Preparation*: you have decided to act and are trying to put in place measures needed to carry out the new behaviour.

- *Action*: you give it a go.

- *Confirmation (or maintenance)*: you are committed to the behaviour and have no desire or intention to regress.

Their initial work hit the classic snag of any theory: it seemed to over-simplify matters. It did not, for instance, allow for the fact that people can move between these stages in both directions, nor that complex behaviour change is often the result of multiple attempts. In the real world there were simply too many exceptions to the rule. However Prochaska, DiClemente and Norcross (1992) responded constructively to the criticisms and developed their thinking further so that the model became circular rather than linear and people's capacity to regress as well as progress was allowed for (see Figure 15.2).

In addition they were able to demonstrate that it is perfectly possible to identify where people are in this process of change. Questionnaires have been developed and validated which can distinguish 'pre-contemplators' from those in 'preparation' and those who are 'maintainers' of an already attempted change.

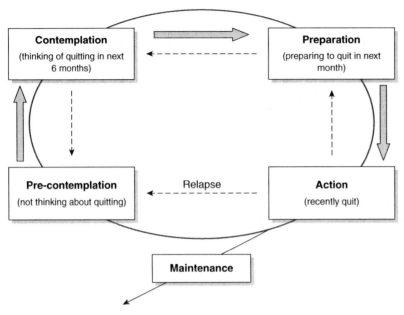

Figure 15.2 Stages of change (mark 2)

Now have a go at Exercise 15.1.

Exercise 15.1

Stages of change in Abbotsford

You are a social marketer faced with developing an intervention to encourage more adults to quit smoking in Abbotsford, a small city in the north of England. How could the stages of change model aid your work? In particular, how would it influence your approach to: (1) determining your target group; and (2) setting objectives?

What does this tell you of the theory's strengths and weaknesses?

You could start by doing primary research, using the sort of questionnaire mentioned above, to establish where the population of Abbotsford is on the stages of change model. Are most of them already trying to give up, for instance, or has the thought never even occurred to them? This in turn would make it possible to devise realistic objectives: moving a population of pre-contemplators right through to ex-smokers would be extremely ambitious, but shifting a proportion of them into contemplation might be doable. It would also make sense to devise different interventions to suit the needs of the various groups – for example pre-contemplators may need information about the harmful effects of smoking and the benefits of quitting, whilst contemplators are more likely to require supportive resources and cessation services.

For the social marketer, then, as Alan Andreasen notes (1994), stages of change has a number of great benefits. For a start, it provides a better understanding of the customer and their proximity to the desired behaviour change. This insight then makes it possible to set realistic and measurable objectives, and helps inform two key elements of the marketing strategy: segmentation and targeting, and the design of the offering.

However, there are also potential pitfalls with stages of change. First it can assume an overly conscious decision making process; that people methodically weigh up the pros and cons of a course of action and always pursue the rational alternative. In this sense it can come to resemble economic thinking which empha-sizes logical reasoning in decision making, rather than marketing thinking which recognizes that we all do things on the basis of emotion as well rationality. In the case of smoking this can leave social marketers languishing in a false reality limited to scientific facts and figures which then struggles to compete with the evocative brands created by tobacco marketing.

The second problem also emerges from an over-zealous application of stages of change. The UK cessation service – one of the best in the world – used the theory as a way of selecting potential clients to the extent that *only* those in the action stage were allowed to use the services – so contemplators and pre-contemplators got ignored. Such precision assumes that the model is spot on (and as has already been noted no model ever is; they are all approximations), and that the measurement procedures are perfect (they never are: research can only reduce uncertainty not produce certainty). As DiClemente himself recently put it, it is a mistake to treat 'the model as a religion and not a heuristic to explore the change process' (DiClemente, 2005, p. 1048). The model simply provides an intelligent way of thinking about how close our clients are to a particular behaviour.

This of course leaves the need to explain how people come to be in this position, and what the social marketer can then do to move them on. Two other theoretical perspectives can help here.

2. Social cognitive theory

As with stages of change the basic idea here is very simple: in this case it is that, as John Donne said, no man (or woman) is an island. All of our decisions and behaviours are a product of both our individual skills and volition, and the social context we live in (see Figure 15.3).

At one level this social dimension to our behaviour is abundantly apparent: a teenager living in London is much more likely to binge drink than his opposite number in Jeddah. The social mores, laws, and availability and promotion of alcohol, together with the behaviours of their respective peers will have an enormous impact on the respective teenagers' choices – probably even more so than any individual inclinations or knowledge they may have.

In other cases the effects are less obvious but still vitally important. In the UK, as in other countries, there is a direct correlation between poverty and health. The social circumstances in which people live have a big impact on the health choices

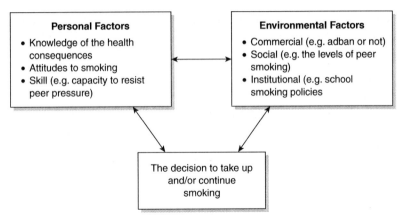

Figure 15.3   Social cognitive theory – personal and environmental determinant of teen smoking

they make – middle-class groups are much less likely to smoke, for instance, than their poorer fellow citizens – and this has a fundamental impact on health outcomes. Thus, a recent WHO study (Gillan, 2006) shows that men living in the underprivileged Calton district of inner-city Glasgow die a full quarter of a century before their affluent peers in the suburbs.

Thinking from *social norms* and *social epistemology* can help social marketers to unpick and respond to this alarming phenomenon.

Social norms

The core tenet of social norms is that people's behaviour is at least partly derived from seeing what most people do or say in similar situations (sometimes referred to as descriptive norms), or by considering what they feel are the accepted or approved behaviours in these situations (injunctive norms). This is based on a natural human tendency to conform with the prevailing and approved behaviours of important others, such as family members, friends, peers and work colleagues. For instance, Cialdini, Kallgren and Reno (1991) argue that this social normative conduct comes from the need to be accepted by important others, as well as systems – whether formal or informal – that ensure that rewards are provided for compliance or sanctions for non-compliance. Furthermore, research has demonstrated that in a setting or environment where a particular behaviour (e.g. anti-littering) is emphasized and therefore becomes normative, people will conform with it.

On the other hand, this can become problematic when undesirable behaviour is encouraged by incorrect perceptions of how other members of the social groups think and act. For example, an individual may overestimate the permissiveness of peer attitudes and behaviours as regards smoking, alcohol, or other drug use, or underestimate the degree to which peers engage in healthy behaviour. Social norms interventions are built on the principle that correcting such misperceptions by providing accurate information is likely to result in decreased problem behaviours and increased healthy behaviours.

These assumptions have been confirmed by extensive research on youth drinking and cigarette smoking and by social norms marketing interventions to reduce binge drinking, smoking initiation, and to promote safe driving. In the United States, for instance, normative campaigns on college campuses that focused on providing accurate information about the prevalence of alcohol and drug use (e.g. most of your peers do not drink) have been largely successful in promoting healthy normative behaviours (Bauer et al., 2000). In most of these colleges, a reduction of 20 per cent or more in high-risk drinking rates occurred within two years of initiating a social norm campaign, and one case resulted in reductions of over 40 per cent after four years.

Social marketers have also promoted healthy behaviour at the societal level by employing public health measures to change social normative behaviours. For example, Hamilton, Biener and Brennan (2008) demonstrated that enacting strong regulations (i.e. clean indoor air regulations and laws prohibiting sales to youths) in Massachusetts significantly affected adults and youths' perceived community norms to be more anti-smoking. Another study in the UK, found that support for smoke-free legislation pre-ban i.e. the smoking ban enacted in Scotland in March 2006, significantly increased perceptions of non-smoking norms post-ban (Brown et al., 2009).

Media campaigns can also address social norms, and these have also been shown to influence behaviour. Thus the tobacco industry has successfully branded their products with images embodied in socially desirable and idealized characteristics. The perceived popularity of 'The Marlboro Man', so familiar in commercials since the 1950s, for instance, has provided an appealing social model for decades. On the other hand, the American Legacy Foundation's counter-marketing 'Truth' social marketing campaign deliberately attacked these erroneous norms by graphically displaying the unscrupulous practices of the tobacco industry (www.thetruth.com). It has resulted in a significant decline in youth smoking in North America.

Now have a go at Exercise 15.2.

Exercise 15.2

Social norms approach to preventing binge drinking

You are employed as a social marketer by a non-governmental organization to design a social marketing campaign to discourage first-year students from binge drinking. Consider how you could use a social norms approach to plan an intervention to decrease binge drinking on campus?

What are the limitations of this approach to your campaign?

As the success of most social norms campaigns is grounded in a sound understanding of the majority attitudes and/or behaviours of the target audience, you could start by doing a survey to gather reliable data about the first-year students. This would need to establish how many students actually drink and to what extent, as well as their perceptions of their peers' drinking habits. Any indicated tendency for students to exaggerate their peers' drinking habits would suggest a need for a campaign correcting these misperceptions. The evidence suggests that repeated exposure to a variety of positive, credible data-based normative messages can correct misperceptions and thereby reduce binge drinking.

Although social norms campaigns hold great promise for behavioural change, some campaigns have failed. In particular there is a problem with target groups questioning, at least initially, the validity of survey data which challenges their (mis)perceptions. However, they will rethink their assumptions if reliable data is presented in an open and engaging manner, and the campaign is sufficiently sustained and deemed to come from a reliable source. This last point is reinforced by social epistemology.

Social epistemology

Social epistemology is the exploration of the social dimensions and conditions of knowledge (Fuller, 1991; Goldman, 1999, 2006). Classic epistemology focuses on how individuals acquire and justify knowledge, whereas social epistemology focuses on how groups of people do so. Though emerging from philosophical theories of knowledge, today social epistemology is an interdisciplinary field of research incorporating contributions from a variety of scientific fields, most notably philosophy, rhetoric, pedagogy, political theory, sociology, economics and information science.

Social epistemology can bridge one of the gaps in social cognitive theory. As has been said, it is crucial for social marketers to be able to understand and explain human behaviour. The main merit of social cognitive theory is that it combines internal, personal factors (knowledge and motivation) as well as external factors from the wider social context (social norms and socio-economic factors) in the explanation of human behaviour. However, the focus on knowledge as a personal, individual thing means that social marketers relying on social cognitive theory are likely not to pay attention to the social aspects of knowledge.

This is problematic because an important aim for most social marketers is to communicate various kinds of information to specific social groups. For example, social marketers involved in campaigns to inform smokers in the pre-contemplation stage about the health consequences of smoking would benefit from having an informed idea about how their target group – as a group – acquires and justifies knowledge. If the informational campaign does not take account of how the target group thinks, reasons and puts emphasis on knowledge, it is unlikely to succeed. Social epistemology comes in handy because it shifts the focus on knowledge from an internal, personal perspective to an external, contextual one.

To get a grasp of the basic difference between focusing on knowledge as an individual rather than a social concept, consider a case where the social marketer draws on social cognitive theory in order to design a campaign that aims at improving the dietary choices in a given target group. Holding up social cognitive theory as a reasonable, rough model of human behaviour, the social marketer would be likely to focus on the individuals' actual knowledge and beliefs about the correlation between food and health. However, the theory would be unlikely to lead the social marketer to an exploration of what kinds of knowledge sources (journalists, doctors, scientists, spiritual leaders, peers, parents, partners) the target group predominantly acquires its knowledge from, and which ones it thinks of as authoritative or reliable. In contrast, social epistemology would do so through its focus on the social conditions of knowledge.

The difference between the two theoretical approaches can be summed up like this: social cognitive theory asks 'what does the client know', whereas social epistemology asks 'how did the client arrive at and justify his or her beliefs'. But is all this talk about knowledge as a social phenomenon of any use?

To answer that question, have a go at Exercise 15.3.

Exercise 15.3

Social epistemology and informational campaigns

You are a social marketer faced with developing an informational campaign to improve the dietary choices of a group of people that: (a) is predominantly vegan; (b) distrusts official public advice on health and relies heavily on 'alternative, non-scientific, spiritual experts'; (c) frequently takes yoga classes; and (d) is subject to malnutrition, because the diet contains too few proteins.

Social epistemology emphasizes how social groups acquire knowledge and whom they trust as reliable sources of information. Why is this perspective important to your campaign?

To design an effective campaign, it is crucial for you as a social marketer to understand how the target group acquires knowledge, and what sources of knowledge it particularly values. If your target group, as in Exercise 15.3, distrusts public experts, an informational campaign that quite clearly originates from a public health department is doomed. To get your message across you will need to tap into a knowledge source, which the target group respects and trusts. In the exercise, a partnership with yoga instructors might be an effective way to support and strengthen your social marketing communications. In this way social epistemology strengthens the marketer's power of persuasion through encouraging an exploration and analysis of the target group's idea of reliable knowledge and harnessing the power of source effect.

In summary, social cognitive theory adds a helpful social perspective to the understanding of behaviour change, and social epistemology and social norms make it easier for social marketers to apply this insight. Specifically, they shed light on why people have a given positioning with regard to a particular behaviour. Why a working-class teenager may be more inclined to smoke than a middle-class one, for example, or why quitting tobacco may be more of a challenge to a resident of inner-city Glasgow than it is to his affluent peer in the suburbs. The theories also begin to identify possible social marketing interventions that might alter this positioning. Exchange theory can also help here.

---

3. Exchange theory

The underlying assumption of exchange theory is that we are all trying to improve our lot in life – to make things better (in whatever way) for ourselves and our nearest and dearest. This acquisitive characteristic is balanced by a recognition that everyone else is also trying to do the same thing, so some sort of exchange or quid pro quo is the best way of achieving our aims. This acceptance of the benefits of 'doing deals' or trading has been traced back to the earliest days of the human race, and arguably is one of the key ways in which we have progressed and developed so effectively compared with other species. (Though the advent of global warming suggests our dealings now need to take on a new level of sophistication if we are not going to develop ourselves out of existence!)

As Philip Kotler points out, (Kotler, 2000) there are alternative approaches to the exchange between the marketer and consumer. We can go it alone and self-produce our own added value; we can resort to force and compel our fellow beings to hand over their added value; or we can sublimate our desires and settle for a simpler existence. All of these options have some currency and are adopted on occasion – but none have proved as adaptable, effective or acceptable as the idea of exchange.

Nonetheless, as Kotler goes on to show, exchange will only happen when five prerequisites are met:

1. There are at least two parties.

2. Each party has something that might be of value to the other party.

3. Each party is capable of communication and delivery.

4. Each party is free to accept or reject the offer.

5. Each party believes it is appropriate or desirable to deal with the other party.

It is easy to see how the idea of exchange and Kotler's five prerequisites apply in a commercial marketing context. There is a very obvious transfer of product for money and the value gained by both parties is easily logged. When I buy a cinema ticket, for instance, the benefits to both me and the seller are readily apparent. In the case of social marketing however, the offering is typically much less tangible: the possible avoidance of an unfamiliar disease sometime in the future, for instance, or an unintended pregnancy. The different types of benefit have been termed 'utilitarian' and 'symbolic', but thinkers in social marketing are adamant that exchange is very much at the core of the field (Bagozzi, 1975). Furthermore commercial marketers can deal in symbolic exchange just as enthusiastically as social marketers: it is, after all, symbolism that underpins the enormous power of branding.

Figure 15.4 illustrates how exchange can operate in social marketing.

There are, however, two remaining concerns about exchange theory in social marketing. The first takes us back to Kotler's third and fourth prerequisites: the capability and freedom to exchange – which reintroduce the vital issues of power and equality. We have already noted the terrible inequalities that persist even in a developed democracy like Britain; the reality is that in many instances people are simply not in a position to engage in mutually beneficial exchange. They may place less value on what middle-class health professionals see as self-evidently desirable offerings, have reduced access to them or little to offer in exchange. Thus men in the Calton district of Glasgow may be less attracted to longer life when

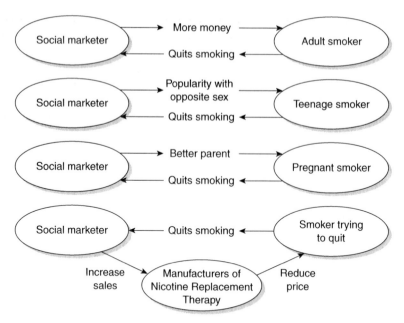

Figure 15.4   Examples of exchange in social marketing smoking cessation

they have no pension to make it comfortable, live in a social context which has little time for cessation services and be a less attractive proposition to health workers bent on meeting onerous quit targets.

This power imbalance does not invalidate exchange for social marketers, but it does underline the need to think carefully about how target groups can be empowered and social marketing offerings made as attractive, available and affordable as possible.

The second concern about exchange theory is addressed in Exercise 15.4.

Exercise 15.4

Altruism or exchange?

Many working in social marketing fields such as health improvement or poverty alleviation take great exception to the idea encapsulated in exchange that the social marketer is seeking to gain from their efforts to help their target groups. Surely, they argue, the whole basis of their work is altruism and doing good without regard to self interest.

How would you argue with this view?

The argument seems plausible initially, but in reality has two basic flaws. First it assumes that the target group has nothing of value to offer; that their view of the world, particular initiatives or what is important in life has no bearing on the work of the health professional or behaviour change specialist. In reality this is both patronizing and foolish. Marketers – whether commercial or social – know that such insights are the lifeblood of their efforts; they offer by far the best way of improving the acceptability of the behaviour change offering.

Second the assumption that behaviour change specialists are all selfless saints belies a world of accountability and targets. Contractual obligations, career development and even remuneration are all built on successful change efforts. The social marketer needs their target group's behaviour change just as much as the target group needs the benefits it will bring.

Conclusion

In this chapter we have looked at the role of theory in social marketing, showing how, far from confusing the process with abstruse complexity, it can clarify and provide tangible help. Specifically we have seen how three theories – stages of change, social cognitive theory (with its sub-theories of social norms and social epistemology) and exchange theory – help social marketers to answer key questions about their customers, and provide them with solutions. In the process we have once again demonstrated the wisdom of Kurt Lewin's words: there really is nothing so practical as a good theory.

References

Andreasen, A.R. (1994) 'Social marketing: its definition and domain', *Journal of Public Policy and Marketing* 13(1): 108–14.

Bagozzi, R.P. (1975) 'Marketing as exchange', *Journal of Marketing*, Vol. 39, pp. 32–39.

Bauer, U.E., Johnson, T.M. and Hopkins, R.S. (2000) 'Changes in youth cigarette use and intentions following implementation of a tobacco control program: findings from the Florida Youth Tobacco Survey', *Journal of the American Medical Association* 284: 723–28.

Brown, A., Moodie, C. and Hastings, G.B. (2009) 'A longitudinal study of policy effect (smoke-free legislation) on smoking norms: ITC Scotland/UK', *Nicotine & Tobacco Research* 11: 924–32.

Cialdini, R.B., Kallgren, C.A. and Reno, R.R. (1991) 'A focus theory of normative conduct: A theoretical refinement and re-evaluation of the role of norms in human behaviour, in L. Berkowtiz (eds) *Advances in Experimental Social Psychology*, Vol. 24, San Diego, CA: Academic Press, pp. 201–34.

DiClemente, C.C. (2005), 'A premature obituary for the transtheoretical model: a response to West (2005)', *Addiction*, Vol. 100, No. 8, pp. 1046–48.

Fuller, S. (1991) *Social Epistemology*, Bloomington: Indiana University Press.

Gillan, A. (2006) 'In Iraq, life expectancy is 67. Minutes from Glasgow city centre, it's 54', *The Guardian* 21 January.

Goldman, A. (1999) *Knowledge in a Social World*, Oxford: Clarendon Press.

Goldman, A. (2006) 'Social epistemology', in E.N. Zalta (ed.) *Stanford Encyclopedia of Philosophy*, available at: http://plato.stanford.edu/entries/epistemology-social/ (accessed 12 August 2009).

Hamilton, W.L., Biener, L., and Brennan, R.L. (2008) 'Do local tobacco regulations influence perceived smoking norms? Evidence from adult and youth surveys in Massachusetts', *Health Education Research* 23: 709–22.

Kotler, P. (2000) 'Marketing management: Analysis, planning, implementation and control', 10th Edition, London: Prentice Hall International.

Lewin, K. (1951) *Field Theory in Social Science: Selected Theoretical Papers* (ed. D. Cartwright). New York: Harper & Row.

McGinnis, J.M. and Foege, W.H. (1993) 'Actual causes of death in the United States', *Journal of the American Medical Association* 270(18): 2207–12.

Prochaska, J.O. and DiClemente, C.C. (2005) 'The transtheoretical approach'. In: Norcross J.C., Goldfried M.R., (Eds.). *Handbook of psychotherapy integration* (pp. 147–171). New York: Oxford University Press.

Prochaska, J.O., DiClemente, C.C. and Norcross J.C. (1992) 'In Search of How People Change', *American Psychologist*, Vol. 47, No. 9, pp. 1102–14.

Prochaska, J.O. and Velicer, W.F. (1997) 'The transtheoretical model of health behavior change', *American Journal of Health Promotion* Vol. 12 No. 1, 38–48.

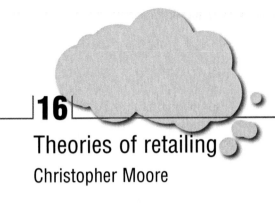

16
Theories of retailing
Christopher Moore

Introduction

It could be argued that retailing theories are much less developed than theories of shopping and they are certainly less diverse. This under-development can be in part attributed to the fact that retailing research has tended to be of secondary importance within many universities and this is principally because retailing has, certainly until the recent past, been perceived to be a marginal, low-skill, low status sector. However, as a result of the perseverance of a cluster of high calibre researchers within the US, the UK and Scandinavia over the past 40 years, a credible, if narrow, theory of retailing has been established.

More recently, the status, scope and pace of research within retailing has improved and this enhancement is clearly linked to improved perceptions of the status of retailing which is due in part to the emergence of retailers such as Wal-Mart, Tesco, Carrefour and Zara, as among the world's largest and most successful companies. As perceptions of retailers have improved, so too have attitudes and orientations towards retailing research.

One area of retail theory dominates the field – that which relates to retail change. Before discussing these aspects of retailing theory in the remainder of this chapter, the next section will consider and locate this area within the wider context of shopping and consumer behaviour.

Shopping for a theory of retail change

Invariably, retailing and shopping are used as interchangeable terms and little or no attempt is made to locate their differences, similarities or functions. Clearly, both are interdependent but distinct: shopping is a consumer act, retailing is a business system. Retailing and shopping are inextricably linked. Shopping is the often repetitive, demonstrable act of acquiring goods and services for personal use by a consumer. Its counterpart in the supply chain is retailing. Retailing is the formalized business system that emerges, establishes and evolves as a means of facilitating, enabling and stimulating the consumer's shopping act.

Arguably, the study of shopping is more theoretically advanced than that of retailing. Drawing contributions from a variety of fields and disciplines (particularly psychology, social anthropology and human geography), the study of shopping is used to provide insights into how products, brands and shopping are adopted by consumers to create, augment and enhance their personal identities, and define their role and status within society, and to explain how individuals find their place within sub-groups and other social forms.

In the past generation, in particular, the case for the study of shopping has advanced as a result of three significant drivers. The first is the emergence of consumer behaviour as a critical component of marketing education. The study of shopping provides an accessible and inclusive platform for researchers to explore and understand a variety of behavioural dimensions, including the dynamics that influence and affect patterns of consumption, the dynamics of group interaction upon brand selection, and the impact of product aesthetics and environmental cues upon product choice within discrete consumption settings.

The emergence of postmodern marketing is an important second driver. While wide in its scope and diverse in its coverage, the postmodern perspective places particular emphasis upon capturing, challenging and reinterpreting the meaning, form and style of the consumption act, particularly in everyday life. The resultant research outputs have provided new interpretations of the purpose and function of the shopping experience and have provided critical commentary for the ceaseless desire among some to acquire pseudo-symbolic, image-laden, brand embossed products. The postmodernist view enables us to view shopping as the new opium of the people and the shopping act as a preoccupation of contemporary living. As such, it really does seem to be the case that *I shop therefore I am*.

The third research driver is practitioner based. Expressed in crude economic terms, shopping is big business, and, by virtue of its significance, the 'professionalization of shopping research' has occurred, whereby consultants – using evidenced-based research – have sought to provide explanations for the process of shopping, from both a retailer and customer perspective. Initially, their research was industry-facing and was used principally to inform the decision making of retail managers and those involved in product and brand management. This research type initially explored how consumers' behaviour and the shopping experience were influenced by particular store layouts, product adjacency, and music and colour systems.

The scope and influence of the professional shopping consultant has in the past decade reached beyond that of the retail sector. Though the development of a new category of books based around the 'science of shopping', the subject has emerged as being of interest to a wider public. Leading this field is the American 'shopping expert' Paco Underhill whose (1999) book, '*Why We Buy: The Science of Shopping*' became an international bestseller. His work brought to the mainstream not only insights into how people shop, but also the various techniques that retailers deploy in order to manipulate consumption behaviour within stores. Non-academic interest in 'shopping science' within the UK was further developed in the 1990s with the Channel 4 series, 'Shop 'til you Drop', while more recently, the 'shopping guru' Mary Portas' BBC series, 'Mary, Queen of Shops' has reignited the public's interest in this area.

While there may be no definitive and/or universal theory of shopping, there does exist an advanced understanding of the characteristics of shopping behaviour, of the impact of shopping within society and its contribution to the creation and maintenance of individual identity.

Retail change theories

Expressed simply, the core theme of retail change theories has been to provide some explanation of the patterns and drivers of change that impact upon the dominant retail formats, the nature of their businesses, their outlets and their trading activities. These theories share a common view that change within retailing is cyclical – and is therefore deterministic and predictable. These theories suggest that retailers follow a sequential pattern of evolvement and development that provides little or no opportunity for deviation. Consequently, the theories infer that retailers have little or no scope for strategic choice. Their advancement is pre-meditated and inevitable.

Brown (1987, 1995) has provided perhaps the most extensive and challenging critique of the various theories of retail change and he questions the extent to which these rigid expectations of retail evolvement reflect an environment that is by its very nature unpredictable, unstable, fragmented and constantly varying. Brown rightly questions their appropriateness in general terms and his reservations will be used to critique the core perspectives of these theories later. However, while mindful of these potential limitations, it is important to note that other researchers see some value in reviewing longitudinal patterns of retail development in order to gain some insight into trends and opportunities within the sector. McGoldrick (2002) noted Hollander's (1986) view that taking a longer term view is advantageous and while history may not repeat itself, it will suggest both questions and useful answers with respect to the nature of retail change.

We will now discuss the three cyclical theories of retail change: the Wheel of Retailing; the Retail Life Cycle; and the Retail Accordion.

—————————— The Wheel of Retailing ——————————

First proposed by Professor Malcolm P. McNair in 1958, the purpose of the Wheel of Retailing was to suggest a cyclical pattern for retail business development. The essence of McNair's hypothesis is that new types of retailers begin life at the lowest end of the retail price, status and margin spectrum. From this low price positioning, they change and become more sophisticated in their activities and complex in their organization and ultimately begin to 'trade-up' in terms of their pricing policy, selling methods and service provision. They achieve this shift upmarket through investments in store environments and by selecting bigger and better locations and through the diverse scrambling of their product and service provision. As a result of these significant investments, these retailers become high operating cost businesses. The final stage of their evolvement (as predicted by the theory) is that these retailers mature to become high-cost, high-price, inefficient businesses. At this stage, these once flexible and efficient businesses become vulnerable to the innovations and cost-efficiencies of newer, more agile low-price entrants.

Brown (1988) provides a clear representation of the Wheel of Retailing as consisting of three distinct phases – Entry, Trading-up, Vulnerability. Further, as Figure 16.1 illustrates, Brown proposes that each phase is characterized by distinct management activities and priorities.

Entry Phase
Innovative retailer
Low status
Low price
Minimal service
Poor facilities
Limited product offerings

Mature Retailer
Top heaviness
Conservatism
Declining ROI

Trading-up Phase
Elaborate facilities
Expected, essential & exotic services
Higher-rent locations
Fashion orientations
Higher prices
Extended product offerings

Figure 16.1   The Wheel of Retailing (Brown, 1988)

In his analysis of McNair's theory, Hollander (1960) acknowledged many examples which conform to this pattern of retailer development. In particular, he noted that department-store merchants, who originally emerged as strong low-price competitors to specialist retailers, themselves became vulnerable to discount houses and supermarket competition. However, as a caveat to the supporting evidence, Hollander also questioned whether the expectation of an increase in operating expenses and a decrease in profitability was indeed inevitable and possible to demonstrate from external evidence. He noted some difficulties associated with the verification methodology – such as the ease by which access could be gained to historical retail expense information due to the scarce and fragmented nature of data sources. Furthermore, such data is usually published on an aggregate basis and as such may mask significant divergent tendencies.

Yet, setting aside the difficulties associated with verifying the theory, Hollander did identify six dimensions which may precipitate the cyclical forms of retail developments as espoused by the Wheel of Retailing. These were as follows:

1. *Retail personalities.* New types of retail businesses are founded by aggressive, highly cost-conscious entrepreneurs who make every penny count and who have no interest in providing unprofitable frills. However, as these entrepreneurs increase in age and wealth, their cost control vigilance deteriorates. Further, their successors may be less competent and they (or their successors) may be less able to manage costs effectively and less dexterous in responding to environmental changes. This change and deterioration in management results in a movement along the wheel.

2. *Misguidance.* Retailers are seduced by the power of supplier advertising and marketing persuasion to install overly elaborate facilities and undertake unnecessary modernizations. This results in a shift towards a higher, more expensive market positioning.

3. *Imperfect competition.* Based upon the premise that most retailers would prefer to avoid direct price competition – principally to avoid damaging retaliation from competitors – they instead seek to compete through service improvements, particularly in terms of selecting better locations. Through, what Hollander described as 'a ratchet process', retailers – across all sectors – appear almost predisposed to provide more elaborate services at increasingly higher margins.

4. *Excess capacity.* Linked to the above, as more retailers enter the market, available demand is spread thinly. As McGoldrick (2002) suggests, in order to avoid suicidal price-cutting, retailers opt instead for non-price competition which typically involves the development of additional service provision.

5. *Secular trend.* As markets become more affluent, opportunities emerge for retailers to trade-up their offer in response to the aspirations of their customers. This results in a shift of the wheel through the provision of additional services and higher-margin goods.

6. *Illusion.* Rather than supporting the premise of the Wheel of Retailing, Hollander suggests that the trend towards the extension of ranges through merchandise scrambling may in fact create an incorrect illusion of trading-up – when the reality is that the margins on the original merchandise may remain unchanged.

A further dimension in support of the 'Wheel Hypothesis' is provided by McGoldrick (2002) who suggested that the personal preferences and tastes of retail owners/senior management may result in their creating enhanced store environments and adding services which they themselves may expect but which are in reality beyond the financial capabilities and interests of their less affluent customers.

Marks and Spencer – a perfect Wheel?

The corporate development of leading British retailer Marks and Spencer, reflects – in broad terms – the various phases included in the Wheel of Retailing. In 1884 Michael Marks, a Russian-born Polish refugee opened a stall in Leeds' Kirkgate Market. All items – ranging from nails and spoons; to soap and luggage labels – were sold for a penny. Within 10 years, the firm had extended to 12 stores and a partner found – Thomas Spencer – who developed the company's skills in organizational structure development and supplier contract management. By 1901 the company had built a stock-holding warehouse to its own specification. After a period of acquisition of other smaller 'Penny Bazaars' before the First World War, the company then began to move up-scale with the launch of their own branded merchandise range, the opening of a flagship store in London's Oxford Street and the establishment of an impressive headquarters in a prime district within central London. Furthermore, throughout the inter-war years, the company extended the scope and complexity of their business to include premium grocery departments, a scientific research lab for garment testing and product development, and went on to provide enhanced customer services in the form of coffee bars and self-service forms of product merchandising.

Internally, from the 1930s onwards, the company became a leading provider of staff welfare programmes, through the development of a generous pension scheme, subsidized canteens, health and dental services, hair dressing and a generous staff clothing allowance.

As the company grew in scale and success in the years after the Second World War, it became more complicated as a business (in 1954 an internal initiative, Operation Simplification removed 26 million paper forms from internal processes), while the products and services offered by the company became more extensive and elaborate. Marks and Spencer was the first UK chain to offer a no quibble refund and exchange policy and the company also pioneered new product categories – such as petite clothing ranges for smaller women – and introduced new food technologies – such as 'boil-in-the-bag' cooking in 1973, followed by sell-by dates marked on all food products and ready-made Chinese and Indian meals in 1975.

Selling space is arguably a retailer's most expensive asset and any attempt to use it for service provision is clearly an indication of business trade-up. In 1979 Marks and Spencer introduced their first fitting rooms – thereby sacrificing valuable selling place to augment and enhance the customer experience.

Buoyed by the successes that emerged as a result of these developments, further trading-up in the form of international store openings, acquisition of premium foreign retailers (such as the American Brooks Brothers and Kings supermarket chains in 1988), premium-priced furniture goods selling and the launch of a financial services company, became an essential element of the firm's trading strategy. By 1997, company pre-tax profits exceeded £1 billion, making Marks and Spencer Europe's most profitable retailer. The following year, pre-tax profits grew a further 6 per cent to £1.17 billion. The Chairman, Sir Richard Greenbury in his statement in their Annual Report for 1998 stated that:

'Our business [Marks and Spencer] has become increasingly complex, both operationally and in terms of product'. Further, he noted that

> there is no longer a typical Marks and Spencer store. Outlets vary enormously in size and each is laid out and merchandised for a specific purpose – from a departmental store of 150,000 square feet serving a wide area such as Newcastle to a sandwich shop in the City of London. The extra space we are acquiring also enables us to create a more comfortable and convenient shopping environment – with improved facilities for elderly people and parents with young children, more and better fitting rooms and toilets and, in larger stores, coffee bars and restaurants. (1998: 5)

The Chairman's final observations were that the company had 'entered a period of bold investment – however, we have always prudently managed our cash resources, and, more important, taken the long-term view when growing your business. I am therefore confident that we will remain as we are today; the most profitable retailer in Europe' (Marks & Spencer Annual Report 1998: 7).

As the old adage goes: pride comes before a fall. This was certainly the case for Marks and Spencer. The next year, 1999, Sir Richard Greenbury, in his last statement as company Chairman, adopted a very different tone. His statement read:

> In the year just ended, the Group suffered a major setback, interrupting our record of consistent and profitable progress over many previous years. Pre-tax profits were £665.7m compared with last year's record breaking figure of £1,114.8m. ... Unfortunately, and notably over the all-important Christmas trading period, clothing sales fell away very badly and significant quantities of fashionable merchandise needed to be reduced in the post Christmas sale. The demand for food was also flat with extremely competitive prices, whilst our Home Furnishings Group suffered from the cyclical downturn in demand for such products. As I forewarned, the ambitious expansion programme in prime selling footage, infrastructure developments, property acquisitions and the Catalogue, has significantly cut into our operating profits. (*Marks & Spencer Annual Report*, 1999: 4–5)

In the 10 years since this fall from grace, the company has suffered significantly from the effects of strong competitors – many of whom, in classic Wheel of Retailing style, operate at the discount/value end of the market. These companies, with their simplified business models, lower operating overheads and agile supply chains have continually outpaced Marks and Spencer in terms of product ranges, value-led pricing and market responsiveness.

Reflecting upon their origins as a 'one penny' market-stall trader, and by tracking the trading-up development of Marks and Spencer to become, at one point, Europe's most profitable retailer, the decade of difficulties that Marks and Spencer has faced fits perfectly with the schema suggested by the Wheel of Retailing.

Non-Conforming retailing formats

While it is possible to find some broad applications for the Wheel of Retailing, many commentators have noted there is a paucity of hard empirical evidence to support its claims. Indeed, there are sufficient examples of retailer formats that do not conform to the Wheel's stages. Three particular formats can be readily identified.

The first is the specialist, luxury retailer. Firms, such as Louis Vuitton, Gucci and Hermes were founded by expert craftsmen who established their businesses in order to serve the needs of affluent customers. The salons that they established were immediately prestigious and impressive – principally to match the expectations and requirements of demanding rich clients. Their service levels were high to match their prices and margins. Consequently, these luxury retailers avoided the low-price, low-service phase as dictated by the linear progression of the Wheel and instead acquired a top positioning from their earliest days.

The advent of e-commerce has provided an opportunity for the internet-only retailer to provide an impressive 'brand experience', complete with a deep and wide merchandise range and an array of relevant and compelling customer service dimensions. Online businesses like Amazon, Net-a-Porter and ASOS have been able to avoid the elementary stages of business development as expected by the Wheel, due to the very nature of their trading medium. Furthermore, these firms have created businesses where none previously existed and have in so doing, secured a dominant market positioning. As such, internet-only retailers are a second non-conforming format.

The third are those retail formats that are created by previously successful entrepreneurs or by established, cash-rich conglomerates that create upscale businesses from scratch from their significant investment capability. These firms are created with a specific target segment in mind and their trading dimensions are precisely defined in order to match the segment's requirements. The American apparel retailer, Abercrombie and Fitch has extended the company's retail format portfolio to include other brands, such as Abercrombie, Holster and Ruehl. Each brand, respectively, is geared towards a progressively older age segment. The product assortment, store environment, pricing strategy and communications plan for each brand is customized to match the aspirations and expectations of their four discrete target groups.

Each of the Abercrombie and Fitch Group brands has been created to be format-precise and ready. None has evolved in the manner predicted by the Wheel of Retailing, since the positioning plan, investment resources and trading support were immediately available from the outset to establish each brand as premium within their respective markets. None entered the market and evolved in the staged and predicted route as suggested by the Retailing Wheel.

Consequently, as Hollander (1960) noted, the number of non-conforming examples clearly indicates that the Wheel of Retailing theory does not universally define the evolvement of all forms of retailing. However, there is sufficient evidence that the Wheel does reflect at least a general pattern of progression for certain retailing forms. Perhaps most importantly, the Wheel of Retailing connects the development of retailing formats with the increasing affluence and prosperity of consumers. As such, this theory of retailing certainly hints that format evolvement is linked to external environmental influences.

_____ The Retail Life Cycle _____

McGoldrick (2002) recognized that the Wheel of Retailing was inadequate in two fundamental areas. Firstly, because of its particular focus upon changes in costs and margins as the sole basis for understanding format evolution, it fails to accommodate the existence of those retailers that enter the market, from the outset, as premium/luxury firms with a high margin position. Nor does it allow for these retailers to retain their high profitable, high cost, high price positioning indefinitely. Secondly, he notes that given the sequential nature of the 'Wheel of Retailing' framework, it is unable to accommodate the speed, diversity and variability of modern retailing developments.

Davidson et al. (1976) proposed in an article in the *Harvard Business Review* an alternative theory of retail development in the form of the Retail Life Cycle. Paralleling the phases and strands of Levitt's (1965) Product Life Cycle, this version for retailing proposes that businesses follow a four-stage pattern of development: Introduction, Growth, Maturity and Decline.

A number of business and trading characteristics are particular to each stage. As retailers enter the introductory stage – motivated by the desire to bring some innovation or novelty in the market – they operate with few competitors. At this first stage, they enjoy a rapid sales growth but gain only low or moderate levels of profitability. The next is the growth stage – where rapid sales increases not only generate uplifts in profitability, they also attract the interest of competitors who likewise will seek to make gains in the new area/sector. The maturity stage follows, and this is when the sector is populated with the largest number of competitors and as a result, price competition increases and profitability levels reach a plateau. Finally, the decline stage sees the emergence of agile, often indirect, competitors in the market – and with the onslaught of such high levels of competitor challenge, the retailer faces the double difficulty of declining sales and reduced profitability.

As McGoldrick (2002) noted, the Retail Life Cycle theory has been applied to both specific retail business and to general retail formats. In terms of the latter, Davidson et al. (1976) provide some interesting observations with respect to the life cycle gestations of a range of retail formats in the USA. Noting the time taken for each format to reach its peak and then to fall into decline, American department stores were found to have reached their maturity stage after 80 years, while variety stores peaked after 45 and discount department stores within 20 years. Other than identifying the gestation of each of the formats, these observations also highlight the fairly rapid contraction in the sustainability and viability of retail formats in recent years.

Looking specifically at examples of the Retail Life Cycle at the retailer level, the decline of Woolworths in the UK provides a clear application of the Retail Life Cycle theory. Established in Liverpool in 1909, as a subsidiary of the American retailer F.W. Woolworth that had been founded 30 years earlier in Pennsylvania, Woolworths entered the UK with an innovative trading, product and pricing formula. With most items costing threepence, and none over sixpence, their product assortment was large and included children's clothes, haberdashery, stationery, toys and of course, pic'n'mix sweets. The business gained a significant cost advantage from the scale economies obtained from its American parent and this enabled Woolworths to sell china and glassware basics at far cheaper price than their British competitors. Significantly, Woolworths were the first variety store retailer to adopt a self-service layout plan. Rather than every product being 'sold' to a customer by an assistant, the Woolworths approach was to allow customers to browse, self-select, purchase and leave.

Woolworths in the UK really accelerated in terms of growth in the mid-1920s – with a new store opening every month across the country. Their British success led the parent company to float a 15 per cent stake in their British subsidiary on the London Stock Exchange in 1931. The floatation was so successful that the company was able to pay 90 cents for every dollar invested as an exceptional dividend to all of its shareholders. The emergence of the post-war baby boomers provided a new consumer category – the teenager – and this brought new and important spending power into the company. With their interest in music, magazines and fashions, the company extended their offer to become the leading entertainment/leisure retailer in the country.

Having been acquired from its American owners in 1982 by Paternoster stores, (a forerunner of the Kingfisher Group), a variety of strategies was deployed in order to resuscitate growth after a sharp decline in the late 1980s. However, by the early 1990s, the company faced formidable competition from specialist firms, such as HMV and Superdrug who offered a more authoritative brand and product offering within Woolworths' core product areas. Further, the rise and expansion of food retailers, particularly Tesco and Asda, into non-food areas meant that Woolworths was further undermined by the huge scale, competitive pricing and convenience offered by these important retailers. New ventures, such as Big W, were launched by the company. This large store format sought to compete head-on with the major food retailers on edge and out-of-town locations. However, without a food offer, these stores failed as destination centres for the more affluent, car-travelling customer and their non-high-street location meant that these stores were inaccessible for the traditionally older and poorer Woolworths customer.

The company was demerged from Kingfisher to become Woolworths Group plc on the London Stock Market in 2001. With an opening (modest) share price of 32p, their shares peaked at 55p in April 2005. However, with relentless price, brand and product competition, company performance withered and their shares fell into constant decline from January 2008. Share dealing was eventually suspended on 26 November 2008. A Woolworth ordinary share was now worth 1.2p. Unable to secure a buyer in December 2008, all 800 stores were closed just short of the company's 100th anniversary of UK trading.

Woolworths provides a competent example of Davidson et al.'s (1976)'s Retail Life Cycle. A once innovative business that pioneered new retail formats, helped create and shape new customer segments and which became part of the very fabric of the British high-street landscape, it eventually fell foul of the twin pressures of the changing consumer and more efficient and enticing competitors.

It is perhaps to oversimplify the history and situation of all failed retailers to explain their demise simply by relying upon the Retail Life Cycle. However, the theory does provide at least some indication of how retailers typically evolve and develop. However, as was identified previously with respect to the Wheel of Retailing, the Retail Life Cycle theory does not accommodate those retailers that are able to sustain demand and increase profitability over protracted periods of time. In particular, luxury retailers, like Louis Vuitton and Cartier, have been able to achieve consistently strong growth and profit performance. Nor does the Life Cycle theory recognize that a retailer may, through brand repositioning and business re-engineering, enhance the long-term sustainability of their business. The theory assumes that retailers are passive victims of the vagaries of market change and competitor action. There are a sufficient number of examples of retailers who have successfully reinvented, repositioned and re-engineered their organizations to significantly grow their businesses to prove that the inevitable decline predicted by the Retail Life Cycle is not necessarily the case.

Perhaps the more significant value of the Retail Life Cycle theory is its application to the evolvement of retail formats in general. Davidson et al. (1976) emphasize the shortening of the life cycle for retailing formats. More recent work by Burns et al. (1997) suggested that earnings for new formats/concepts would be likely to stagnate within a decade after launch. The truncation of retail life cycles has important implications for retailers and McGoldrick (2002) suggested that retailers must carefully consider the implications of long-term investments in expensive, inflexible and confining property assets. Further, the life cycle encourages retailers to adopt a portfolio approach to brand management and so provide for a coherent balance of risk, cost and opportunity. Perhaps, most importantly, contemporary applications of the Retail Life Cycle indicate that in the future retailers must recognize that an acceptable return on investment must be secured within an ever-decreasing timescale.

The Retail Accordion

The third of the three important theories of retail change is the Retail Accordion. Proposed by Hollander (1970) as a means of understanding the oscillations of prominent retailing formats, it proposes that domination by wide-assortment retailers is subsequently followed by domination by narrow-line specialized sellers. McGoldrick (2002) argued that this theory is clearly evident in the evolution of retailing within the USA. He noted that in the early settlements, the general stores offered comprehensive assortments to locals, but as settlements grew in scale and sophistication, more specialist and sophisticated retailers emerged. These specialists subsequently lost ground to department store operators that offered a wide merchandise assortment to a new urbanized customer base. But these wide assortment sellers in turn lost market share to specialised chains who responded better to the particular needs of a more demanding customer. These specialist retailers, in an attempt to retain customer loyalty through the provision of convenience and choice, extended their offering, and so retailers, such as supermarkets and drug store operators, began to sell merchandise categories that were not typically associated with their particular format type. However, as these specialist retailers became more general in their offer, they became susceptible to the impact of other retailers with a particular focus within a product category.

Table 16.1   Tesco's retail formats

Tesco Format Name	Number of Stores
Extra	177
Homeplus	10
Superstore	448
Metro	174
Express	961
One Stop	512

Source: www.Tescoplc.com/plc/media/qf

While the Retail Accordion Theory recognizes the wide-narrow-wide pattern of the dominant retailing forms within a market, it has little or no value for the purposes of predicting or explaining future retailing developments. The theory does not offer any insights as to why one form inevitably gives way to another – nor does it explain why that format should return to dominate at some future point. Instead it serves only to illustrate the predominance of particular formats at specific points in time.

What the model fails to recognize, if applied to the experience of a particular business, is the capability of certain firms to operate wide and narrow formats concurrently. Leading retailers, such as Tesco, Marks and Spencer, The Limited and The Gap have developed a variety of formats and brands which cover a range of different narrow and wide segments. For example, Tesco operates six different formats within the UK market. These range from small local stores – often attached to petrol stations – which trade as One Stop. These outlets, which are, on average, 1,300 square feet, serve to provide essential (often described as distress) products to customers on a 24/7 basis. Tesco Extra stores are typically at least 70 times bigger and cover the majority of consumer goods categories, including foods, clothing, electrical goods, furniture and entertainment.

Tesco has more than 2,200 stores in the UK. Table 16.1 shows the number of stores operated by the company by format as at May 2009.

In an era where retailers have the resources, expertise and management expertise to cover what would appear to be all market eventualities, the usefulness of the Retail Accordion theory to provide any new and relevant insights with respect to retail developments at the macro or the corporate business unit level is at best limited and at worst irrelevant.

—————— Non cyclical theories of retailing change ——————

The cyclical theories of change – while offering some broad insights – are largely inadequate in that their linearity reflects a deterministic, prescriptive and inflexible perspective on the nature of retailer development. These models speculate that businesses are powerless to resist the force of the change cycle and, as such, are predestined to follow a non-negotiable path. Further, as Brown (1991) noted, the models fail to allow for the influence of the economic environment or for the strategic plans and interventions of management. Consequently, he proposed that non-cyclical, environmental theories are more flexible and efficient in providing an explanation for the patterns of change within the sector.

Likewise, McGoldrick (2002) proposed that changes in retail formats are better explained as an outcome of economic and socio-cultural developments within a market. Meloche et al. (1988) identified that the failure of retail businesses and the demise of particular formats was invariably linked to some negative environmental change or market alteration. Failure was not always an inevitable stage in the history of an organization. Nor are retailers passive participants in some grand market lottery. Instead, traders may deploy strategies that either circumnavigate difficult market trends or which exploit opportunities that arise from changed market conditions. Environmental theories therefore provide an alternative explanation for retail change and also provide frameworks which recognize that retailers can proactively respond to market challenges. Corporate fate is not therefore viewed as predestination nor is the survival of a particular trading format destined to be active for a prescribed and finite period as suggested by the cyclical theories.

Environmental change – such as economic downturns – provides some explanation as to why market demand may shift away from premium retailers to those that operate on a value/discount basis. The recent, significant growth in the popularity and profitability of value retailers – such as Aldi, Lidl and Primark – is inextricably linked to the recession that began in 2008 and has affected consumer confidence in the UK and Europe. Survival in periods of change and challenge depends upon a retailer's ability to respond positively to challenging market conditions. Etgar (1984) and McGoldrick (2002) have suggested that the environmental perspective on retail change recognizes that an 'economic ecology' exists within retailing where the principle is that only the fittest survive. It is the level of retailer fitness that determines their continuance and explains their decline.

A second non-cyclical change theory exists. Pioch and Schmidt (2000) noted that conflict theory attributes retail change, not to the impact of environmental challenge, but instead to the trading rivalry that exists between new and established retail businesses. A pattern of conflict emerges which contains three stages: Thesis, Antithesis and Synthesis. When an established retailer is threatened by the differential advantage of a new entrant, it will seek to respond to that challenge by imitating the core features of the competitor's advantage. In response, the new entrant will modify its strategy to regain the momentum. Pioch and Schmidt (2000) predict that the adaptations undertaken by both sides result in their adopting strategies that are largely similar in terms of scope and impact. As such, a position of synthesis is reached and in the end there is much less to differentiate the two businesses that initially appeared to be so different.

Examples exist within both the food and clothing sectors of this form of inter-firm rivalry. The emergence of Asda as the leading innovator and challenger within the British grocery market in the 1970s, prompted Sainsbury's and Tesco, the market leaders, to rapidly adopt the large format, edge and out-of-town locations pioneered by their new up-start competitor. Likewise, through time, Asda adopted many of the trading features of their competitors in such areas as own-brand development, premium food ranges and customer service provision. Within a generation, these initially very disparate operators soon began to merge in terms of their core business and soon there was little to differentiate the top three in terms of their competitive strategies. More recently, in the clothing sector, retailers such as Marks & Spencer and Next have responded to the sharp price challenge of value fashion retailers Primark and New Look by launching their own low price, basic clothing ranges. In turn, both discount challengers have evolved their business models to include bigger, more impressive stores within premium shopping locations. Further, New Look has moved upmarket to include a premium range within their assortment – including a celebrity-range endorsed by pop star Lily Allen and a high fashion range designed by leading designer, Giles Deacon.

Yet, while it is possible to find evidence to support the general principles contained within the conflict theories, Pioch and Schmidt (2000) also recognized that these fail to take into account the importance and impact of environmental drivers related to economic and social change that impact upon a retailer's success. To assume that retail change depends only upon inter-firm rivalries is narrow and incomplete. Therefore, in this regard, the conflict theories are not so different from the limited perspectives contained within the cyclical theories of retail change.

A combination of theories?

While each of the theories of retail change may incorporate dimensions that offer some insight and value in terms of explaining developments within the sector, none provide a comprehensive and complete account of the dynamics of that change. As a means of assimilating all that is good from the theories and models, as well as addressing their areas of weakness, a number of combination models have been proposed. Bringing together dimensions of the cyclical with the environmental and conflict theories, new hybrid-form models have been proposed by researchers, such as Brown (1991) and Sampson and Tigert (1994). These models, which bring together dimensions from all three model formats serve, in particular, to highlight the complexity and diversity of change within the retailing sector. In so doing, they provide a comprehensive system for explaining both the manner and the reasons for change within retailing.

What is perhaps most interesting is the fact that many of the theories of retail change were developed some time ago during a period when retailers were less advanced in their strategic thinking and less efficient in their ability to understand and respond to environmental challenges. As retailers have become more professional, strategic and robust in the planning and execution of their strategies, their capabilities and resources now often exceed the limitations that are implicit in the theories of retail change. As such, the emergence and acceptance of combination models of change – which incorporate more complex systems of influence, is perhaps inevitable and necessary. This reflects the trend towards pluralism of theories and theorizing in the wider marketing domain (Maclaran, et al., 2009) The multidimensionality of these new models better reflect the realities of retailing markets that are both complex and turbulent and which require, by necessity, strategic responses that are complex, agile and robust.

But rather than dismiss these various theories of retailing as inadequate, anachronistic and/or overly simplistic, McGoldrick (2002) reminds us that these do have merit and value – not least in terms of their ability to identify and remind us of the factors and influences that have resulted in the demise and failure of individual firms, or trading formats and/or even whole sectors of retailing. There is value in the recognition that sometimes history does repeat itself – regardless of the why and the how.

References

Brown, S. (1987) 'Institutional change in retailing: a review and synthesis', *European Journal of Marketing* 21(6): 5–36.

Brown, S. (1988) 'The wheel of the wheel of retailing', *International Journal of Retailing* 3(1): 16–37.

Brown, S. (1991) 'Variations on a marketing enigma: the wheel of retailing theory', *Journal of Marketing Management* 7: 131 – 55.

Brown, S. (1995) 'Postmodernism, the wheel of retailing and the will to power', *International Review of Retail, Distribution and Consumer Research* 5(3): 387–414.

Burns, K.B., Enright, H. Hayes, J.F. McLaughlin, K. and Shi, C. (1997) 'The art and science of renewal', *McKinsey Quarterly* 2: 100–13.

Davidson, W.R., Bates, A.D. and Bass, S.J. (1976) 'The retail life cycle', *Harvard Business Review* 54(6): 89–96.

Etgar, M. (1984) 'The retail ecology model: a comprehensive model of retail change', in J. Sheth (ed.) *Research in Marketing*, Vol. 7, Greenwich, CT: JAI Press, pp. 41–62.

Hollander, S.C. (1960) 'The wheel of retailing', *Journal of Marketing* 24(3): 37–42.

Hollander, S.C. (1970) *Multinational Retailing*, East Lansing, MI: Michigan State University Press.

Hollander, S.C. (1986) 'A rear-view mirror might help us drive forward: a call for more historical studies in retailing', *Journal of Retailing* 62(1): 7–10.

Levitt, T. (1965) 'Exploit the product life cycle', *Harvard Business Review* 43: 81–94.

McGoldrick, P. J. (2002) *Retail Marketing*, Berkshire: McGraw-Hill Education.

Maclaran, P., Saren, M., Stevens, L. and Goulding, C. (2009) 'Rethinking theory building and theorizing in marketing', *Proceedings of the 38th European Marketing Academy Conference, 23–26 May*, University of Nantes, France.

McNair, M.P. (1958) 'Significant trends and developments in the post war period', in A.B. Smith (ed.) *Competitive Distribution in a Free High Level Economy and its Implications for the University*, Pittsburgh, PA: University of Pittsburgh Press, pp. 1–25.

Marks & Spencer Annual Report and Accounts (1998, 1999, 2009) London: Marks & Spencer plc.

Meloche, M.S. di Benedetto, C.A. and Yudelson, J.E. (1988) 'A framework for the analysis of the growth and development of retail institutions', in R.L. King (ed.) *Retailing: Its Present and Future*, Charleston, IL: American Collegiate Retailing Association.

Pioch, E.A. and Schmidt, R.A. (2000) 'Consumption and the retail change process: a comparative analysis of top retailing in Italy and France', *International Review of Retail, Distribution and Consumer Research* 10(2): 183–203.

Sampson, S.D. and Tigert, D.J. (1994) 'The impact of warehouse membership clubs: the wheel of retailing turns one more time', *International Review of Retail, Distribution and Consumer Research* 4(1): 33–59.

Underhill, P. (1999) *Why We Buy: the Science of Shopping*, 1st edn, New York: Simon and Shuster.

www.Tescoplc.com/plc.media/gqf

17

An institutional approach to sustainable marketing
William E. Kilbourne

Chapter Topics

In the beginning

Recognition of the relationship between marketing practices and the environment first appeared in the early 1970s. There was, at that time, a flurry of research on various aspects of the relationship as it was then understood. While the intention was to incorporate environmental principles into the marketing process, little was accomplished in making the intention a reality. The focus of these efforts was on identifying environmentally concerned (green) consumers who would be willing to pay a premium for environmentally sensitive products. At the same time, behaviours related to the marketing process were examined as well. The primary focus here was on recycling behaviour that was then suggested to move industrial societies towards environmentally benign behaviour. 'Consume green products and then recycle the waste and the environmental problem will begin to disappear' was the main marketing message in this era. The one notable exception to this mantra was George Fisk's work on socially responsible consumption. His message went unheeded, however.

Moving into the 1980s, the marketing trend began to shift a bit as conservation began to emerge as a necessary consumption behaviour. Here was the first recognition that the quantity of consumption may be a bigger issue than the quality of consumption. Green products are, after all, still products that require resources for their construction, movement, use, and disposal. While each individual product may be say 10 per cent less resource intensive, if consumption is increased by 12 per cent, the incremental environmental consequence is negative. The psychological message consumers seemed to be hearing at the time was, 'If I buy green and recycle, I can buy as much as I want'.

With the resurgence of the market mentality reinforced by both Margaret Thatcher and Ronald Reagan during the 1980s, the message being proffered to consumers was consistent with the message they wanted to hear, 'Buy more, and the environmental problems will disappear.' The environmental problem was redefined within the emergent philosophy now referred to a neoliberalism. That philosophy can be characterized as the belief that free markets can and will solve all problems including those related to environmental degradation. This was a clear indication that marketing practices of the time were well within the constraints of environmental limits. The economic argument was simple and appealing. If the economies of the world continue to grow, increased profits of corporations will result in increasing tax bases for countries. The increased taxes would be used to repair environmental damages caused by economic growth. In the end, we can literally 'eat our cake and have it too'. As a demonstration of this effect, proponents of consumption growth pointed to the US as an example of the positive effects of the neoliberal philosophy. For, indeed, by commonly used measurement tactics, it could be demonstrated that, since the 1950s, deforestation and the accumulation of pollutants had declined in the US. But euphoria has a nasty habit of receding quickly.

The infamous wager

Even before marketers awakened to the plight of the environment and its potential human consequences, biologists had been raising serious doubts about the trajectory of the global environment. Two notable figures appear here. The first is Rachel Carson whose 1962 book, *Silent Spring*, first documented environmental degradation and traced it unequivocally to human industrial activity. This was followed in 1968 by Paul Ehrlich's, *The Population Bomb*, in which world population growth rates were argued to be excessive and would soon lead to both environmental and human population collapse. This Malthusian argument did not resonate well with either citizens or politicians at the time because, as we all knew, Malthus was wrong. But it did raise the question of what might happen if Malthus were not completely wrong. As a result, trouble began brewing in consumer paradise at the same time that marketing was opening up the new world of unrestricted consumption possibilities (so long as we recycle). Outside the fields of marketing and economics, the shroud of doubt was being cast over the cornucopian assumption of limitless growth as both possible and desirable. Thus, at the same time marketers were touting the advantages of green marketing strategies, systems engineers were unknowingly challenging the very core of the marketing philosophy. This challenge was developed around Herman Daly's Impossibility Theorem that said you cannot have infinite growth in a finite system, and, while the earth may be large, it is finite.

But we need not worry yet because the limits to growth hypothesis, as reflected in the highly controversial book, *Limits to Growth* (1972), published by the Club of Rome, was easily deflected by a flurry of criticism from the bastions of the industrial status quo. The acrimonious debate that ensued became the stuff of academic legend and resulted in the infamous wager alluded to in the section heading above. One of the many critics of both the limits to growth and the population bomb was cornu-copian economist Julian Simon who countered with *The Ultimate Resource* in 1981. In this volume, he argued that human intelligence was the ultimate resource, and that the more people there were, the more permutations and combinations of intelligent solutions there would be to solve problems. He essentially argued that there could not be too many people on the earth. He then challenged Ehrlich to a wager in which Ehrlich could pick any 10 resources he wanted and Simon would bet $1,000 each that in 10 years, the price for each resource would have declined. Ehrlich lost all 10 bets because he failed to consider the possibility (now a certainty) that markets 'would not get the prices right'. He essentially assumed that markets were competitive and efficient and that technology was fixed. We now know all of this to be false. In a subsequent proposal, Ehrlich agreed to bet again regarding human welfare measures but under conditions whereby market inefficiencies would not affect the result. Simon refused, which suggests that there were no foolish children in his family.

Now the reader may be asking, 'What does this have to do with sustainable marketing?' The answer is, of course, everything. In the case of marketing practice, our vision has been much too simplistic, and in the case of the wager, much too polemic. First, we must expand our scope within marketing to get at the root causes of environmental degradation and not confuse symptoms of problems with the problems themselves. This is not to suggest that symptoms are not important in their own right, but to understand that alleviating symptoms is a short-term solution that has longer-term consequences. As for the polemical nature of the debate, we must come to a common ground from which to address the structural flaws in modern industrial societies. These are flaws in our behaviour that are caused by flaws in our thinking. This is a critical factor because, as Einstein once said, you cannot solve the problems you have created with the same thinking you used to create them. This turns the sustainability problem back on Western industrial societies whose dominant logic has, for four centuries now, led us into the predicament in which we now find ourselves. As cartoonist Walt Kelly's character, Pogo, informed us on Earth Day 1971, 'We have met the enemy, and he is us'. But we must also not demand perfection out of chaos. There is no utopian ideal to move towards as we are currently witness to the failure of the liberal utopia of the Enlightenment. And as was suggested by Isaiah Berlin through Kant, from the crooked timber of humanity, nothing straight can ever be built (Berlin, 1959).

The sustainable society is the noble goal to which we aspire, but we may not like the path that we must ascend. Sustainable marketing may well look nothing like marketing as it is now practised when we search beneath the assumptions of modern market societies and find them vacuous. The problem is framed well in an old joke about asking questions. A gentleman is driving his convertible a bit too fast on a crooked highway. He fails to navigate a sharp curve and veers off the highway and over a cliff. Half way down to the rocks below he sees and grabs a branch sticking out from the cliff. It saves his life temporarily as the car continues down to the rocks below, crashes and explodes. Hanging from the branch, he looks up to the top of the cliff and realizes he cannot go up and then down to the rocks below which are certain death. Realizing his predicament, he first becomes concerned and then religious. He looks up to the heavens and asks, 'Is there anyone up there?' A voice, sounding not unlike Charlton Heston, comes booming down and says, 'Have faith: let go of the branch'. He looks to the burning car and the rocks below and says, 'What?' The voice repeats, 'Have faith: let go of the branch'. He looks down at the rocks below and then back up to the heavens and asks, 'Is there anyone else up there?' This is the predicament of sustainable marketing. We must now ask questions to which we may not like the answers.

The questions

While it may sound trivial at first glance, we must first ask what sustainability is. The Brundtland Commission (1987) provided the definition most often suggested. To be sustainable is 'to meet the needs of the present without compromising the ability of future generations to meet their own needs'. While this seems clear, closer examination reveals some problems with it. The first relates to the needs of the present. There is no indication of what level of needs we are talking about. This is a marketing problem. The second question relates to the future. How far into the future do we look, and how do we know what their needs will be? This is an ethical question that is referred to as intergenerational justice. Both the marketing and the ethical questions must be delineated much more clearly than the definition of sustainability implies. Because humanity now finds itself 'hanging from the branch' in the story above, we must now ask the questions and be prepared to deal with the answers. The old answers, framed in the idiom of green marketing, no matter how comfortable they make us feel, are facile and insufficient. We must not lose sight of the admonition of Thomas Paine, author of *Common Sense* and contributor to both the American and French revolutions, that the long habit of not thinking a thing wrong creates the superficial impression that it is right. Within the context of sustainability, what is it that we have thought 'not wrong' for so long that we now think it is right?

How did we get here?

Western industrial societies have a long tradition of Enlightenment thinking that has carried them to heights of material abundance that were undreamt of even by the strongest proponents of liberalism during that period. There are two constructs in the previous statement that lead us to the sustainability problem because they form both the antecedents for and the outcome of marketing practices. These are respectively, liberalism and material abundance or, in more common terms, economic growth through free markets. These cannot reasonably be separated from each other. This was the position of Adam Smith in *The Wealth of Nations*, and it remains the underlying philosophy of Western, market-based societies. Stiglitz's controversial book, *Globalization and its Discontents*, argues that it is this philosophy that is being exported in the globalization process because it is still believed within neoclassical economics that liberal principles lead to economic growth and, hence, enhanced societal well-being. It does appear, historically, that material abundance has only been achieved in societies that are imbued with liberal philosophy. So what is this philosophy that pervades Western societies, and why is it believed to be the basis for enhancing the well-being of the world?

Political changes

Political liberalism was legitimized by John Locke in the late seventeenth century. There are three specific aspects of political liberalism that are critical to the sustainability problem and to marketing practice. These are possessive individualism, private property and limited democratic government. Possessive individualism characterizes individuals who are separate from their society and in possession of themselves. While, to the contemporary student of society, this proposition seems self-evident, such was not the case in Locke's time. During the feudal period and before, the concept of an individual separate from the social group was virtually unthinkable. From Locke onward, however, the politically and socially unencumbered individual was the starting point of politics. The possessiveness aspect of the construct is tied to the concept of private property that was also legitimized, though not created, by Locke. He reasoned in the *Second Treatise on Government* that because individuals were in possession of themselves, all they attached their labour to became rightfully theirs. In addition, because the two limitations on accumulation (spoilage and availability) had been resolved in his analysis, the secular limitations on accumulation were removed. Not only was accumulation of property acceptable, it became a virtue (though the church at the time did not agree with this). This has been referred to as the environmentalist's nightmare because it opened the door to the unlimited accumulation of property. Finally, the only legitimate power of the government was to enforce contracts made in the market and to protect property, including property in one's self. Beyond this responsibility, the government was not allowed to go. With these three conditions, atomistic individuals, private property, and unconstrained pursuit of one's interest legitimated, the door was open for the exponential expansion of market society and the full integration of capitalism, though neither would be fully developed for another century or more.

Economic liberalism

With the background conditions in place, it took less than a century for economic liberalism to arrive through Adam Smith. Here, atomistic individuals, each independent of the others, would pursue their personal interests unconstrained by external forces, that is the government, in free-market relationships. The essence of free markets was powerlessness, and this fitted neatly into the political limits legitimated by Locke. The legitimation of markets as the mechanism through which societies' resources would be allocated was completed and the door was now opened for the de-politicization of society. For the classical economists, how this process played itself out regarding wealth and its politically laden distribution was important, but with the development of neoclassical economics still prevalent today, distribution of wealth became a moot issue. This is an example of de-politicization. Rather, the primary issue of economics now is the satisfaction of consumer preferences *as they exist*. It is assumed that such preferences exist within the individual and are not affected by market processes. It is also assumed that all consumer preferences are equally valid requiring no justification by the consumer, and as this market process plays out, society is the beneficiary of individual choices in the market. Thus, it is assumed that the sum of individual choices always results in the common good. This is the function of the invisible hand that guides all exchanges. This should raise immediate questions about what constitutes the common good, but it has not until recently.

The difficulty that must be addressed here is the underlying assumption in marketing practice that all consumer preferences should be satisfied so long as this can be done at a profit and the preferences do not violate laws regarding behaviour. For example, in some societies the sale of addictive drugs, human chattel, and sexual favours is prohibited reflecting the norms of the particular culture. Beyond these few restrictions, market functionaries are charged with the satisfaction of any needs consumers may have. This is the essence of the marketing concept found in the first chapter of virtually all marketing texts, albeit with some restrictions in green marketing texts. Consumers know best what they need, and it is not for the government or marketers to tell them that they should not desire it. This is the market outcome for a political condition known as procedural neutrality that mandates that governments must not favour any particular market outcome over any other. Political policies are developed that allow each individual to pursue 'the good' as he or she sees it. Government cannot proffer or favour any particular version of the good.

Technological rationality

Within this framework of political and economic liberalism, marketing practices have evolved as they now appear. The only remaining background condition is the means by which consumer preferences are satisfied. Here we must address technology as a system of preference satisfactions. In this instance, markets are a technology in that they are a system of organizing and integrating the necessary constituents of the production process. Marketing has been referred to, for example, as a 'provisioning technology'. But we must also examine the promiscuous nature of technology, as it can be used for many purposes with consequences beyond those intended. Science and technology as we now construe them arrived through the Enlightenment beginning most notably with Francis Bacon. What is clear in his work is that science has an overriding purpose and that is liberation from the 'inconveniences of man's estate.' By this he meant making life easier and better and less subject to the vagaries of nature. While we still often hear of science for its own sake, this is a more Aristotelian view. What is virtually indisputable is that technology, united with industry in the modern period, has allowed industrial societies to attain levels of existence in which material needs have been satisfied for the majority of people. This has not been without unintended consequences, however.

Because of the ubiquity of technology in modern society, a new rationality has evolved that has technology as its basis. Every marketing text is a product of this process because they rationalize the marketing activities. This means that the text is deconstructed in a rational way using what is essentially the scientific process in which the marketing function is broken down into its pieces. Each piece of marketing activity (the 4 Ps) is broken out and examined separately and then reconstituted. We have similarly rationalized the consumer and markets. In the early 1970s, Fisk proposed a holistic approach to marketing that was soundly rejected by the market.

This technological rationality privileges means over ends in the pursuit of material progress and redefines the criteria of success within the language of technology: efficiency, objectivity and measurement. While technology has achieved considerable (though not complete) success in the mastery of external nature, its project to master internal nature has failed. As a result, technological advance has been one-dimensional, prompting Thoreau, in *Walden*, to characterize it as 'improved means to unimproved ends' while numerous others in the Romantic tradition lamented the 'disenchantment of nature'. Now, technology mediates both nature and culture. Through economic and technological rationality, nature has been separated from humankind, ethically, intellectually and spiritually. Nature has only instrumental value in the pursuit of material progress through economic growth and development. The inherent value of nature has receded because nature is now characterized scientifically as inert matter in motion. This is represented in the shift from the organic to the mechanical world view begun more than 500 years ago. This resulted in a new view of nature which, in combination with political and economic transformations, became a new paradigm of Western society.

From the standpoint of cultural mediation, technology has resulted in the transmogrification of both individual and social relations. This is because, while technologies are providing solutions to specific problems, they are also creating new 'forms of life' in their wake. In effect, technological change brings with it a social contract, the terms of which are opaque to the participants. They only become evident after they have taken effect. Technology has the potential to free individuals from the hardships of life, but it can also lead to conflicts between what we want in this regard and what we get. To reconcile the conflicts between humans and the conflict between humans and nature, rational reflection is required. This is made more difficult because the market process has framed the conflict in such a way that reflection on the conditions of technology appears to be irrational. Who, within the technological milieu, would challenge the technological progress of the last four centuries? Its benefits are clear and its development came through the market process itself as a series of ostensibly free, independent, efficient and progressive choices. Because the market is itself such a transformational technology of choice, critics are characterized as making a choice against choice, and this is irrational and inconsistent. Technological society is reduced to a 'regime of instrumentality' that carries its own truths within itself as it provides the questions and the answers in its own idiom. This makes it virtually immune to critique.

The combination of economic and political liberalism and technological rationality creates the basis of the paradigm of Western industrial society. While proponents of the sustainable society have called for a new organizing paradigm based on different principles (the New Environmental Paradigm or NEP), the transformation has been slow in coming because of the nature of paradigms themselves. To see why this is and how it relates to sustainable marketing, we must understand what paradigms do and how they work. More importantly, however, we must know how they change.

The new paradigm

While the characteristics of the New Environmental Paradigm (NEP) have been developed and proffered as the solution to the sustainability problem, they are in stark contrast to the characteristics of the dominant social paradigm (DSP) that still prevails in Western societies. It is important that we ask why both the NEP and sustainable marketing practice remain, according to critics, on the distant horizon. One long-time proponent of sustainability, James Speth, captures this idea in the title of his recent (2008) book: *The Bridge at the Edge of the World*. His metaphor is illuminating as it suggests that we are on the precipice staring into the abyss with no way across. His bridge is a new paradigm. Why is this so? Why, after 35 years, do we still not see the true constraints on sustainability? Is the human race a prime candidate for the infamous Darwin Award given to those who contribute most directly to their own extinction? Or are we faced with a problem that is much more complex and intractable than we think? I think the appropriate question is the last one.

Paradigms exert tremendous influence in the daily lives of the cultures they inform. They are the collection of values, attitudes, beliefs and institutions of a society. Each society has a paradigm that is, for it at least, dominant in its influence. It determines what we see in the world when we look, how we see it, and how we evaluate what we see. Thus, the DSP of a society represents its world view.

It is important, however, to understand that the paradigm is not dominant because it was agreed upon by the majority of people. Rather, it is created by the dominant class who use it to justify and legitimize the prevailing institutions in society. Because these are the institutions that support the agenda of the dominant class, the DSP functions as ideology. As described above, the central institutions of the DSP of Western industrial societies are political and economic liberalism and technological rationality. Thus, it is the consequence of Enlightenment thought going back 400 years.

It should be noted that the concept of institutions as used here is much broader than that typically used in marketing. Institutions refer to stable systems of social rules that control social interaction, and as such, they control the way we think, what we think about, and how we make judgements and evaluations, that is what is good and what is not. How we evaluate is a direct function of the criteria by which we evaluate. A criterion can be very general such as whether it is based on the reason for doing something or on the consequence of having done it. Is something evaluated as good because it was done for the right reason or because it achieved the right outcome? If the latter is the case, then the paradigm also provides the criteria by which we evaluate whether the outcome is good or bad. For a particular marketing decision, for example, was the decision good because it resulted in more profit than any other decision or because it benefited more people? Any principles of marketing text will give you the answer to this in the first chapter. The marketing concept tells us that the function of marketing is to satisfy consumer needs (as we find them) at a profit. There is nothing here about benefiting anyone because, as we know, markets readily provide many things that are known to be bad for consumers. But the political dimension of the paradigm says we must remain neutral as to what consumers choose to consume. The economic dimension tells us that these choices should be made in free markets in which no one tell the consumer what they should prefer. Technological rationality tells us consumer preferences should be satisfied by the manipulation of nature in the production process, and this is to be done in the most efficient way. Recall that we take consumer preferences as we find them and cannot resort to second-order preferences in our analysis. That would suggest that consumers should prefer to have better preferences. Rather than choosing Marlboros, for example, the smoking consumer should choose not to smoke. But the dimensions of our paradigm tell us that preferences are sacrosanct. Thus a 'good' marketing outcome efficiently provides individual consumers with what they think they need as they express it in the market.

We can continue this scenario by expanding the economic dimension of the DSP. Each of our individual consumers has a consumer preference function that they bring with them into the marketplace where marketers compete to satisfy them. Those who satisfy them best and most consistently will live to market another day because they will make profits on the exchanges which reputedly satisfy both buyers and sellers. Recall that neither has any interest in benefiting society directly, but they seek to satisfy only their own immediate interests. In doing so, they inadvertently benefit society by producing economic growth (the wealth of nations) that then benefits all equally. Another chapter in the marketing text tells us that all consumers are different, atomistic individuals who can, with proper attention, be accumulated into similar groups called target markets whose needs can be attended to more efficiently. This means we can sell more goods more efficiently thereby increasing sales and profits even more. Here again, we see efficiency at work and the marketing concept being played out. Satisfy consumer needs at a profit!

While marketers never ask who created the rules we are now governed by, we know the answer. It was initially John Locke, Adam Smith and Francis Bacon. From the standpoint of contemporary views of progress, they constitute the pantheon of virtue and the creators of the good life. From a sustainability perspective, they are not held in such high regard. Whether you seek to praise them or bury them, they lead us back to the major issue at hand. That issue is the ideological character of the DSP.

Because ideology is such a loose construct, I will define it specifically as it is used in this essay. There are three possible functions of ideology that are relevant here. The first is to present the specific interests of the dominant class as the general interest. That is, those who occupy a dominant position in society wish to remain dominant, and to do this it is best if all others believe this dominance is justified because it serves their own interest as well. Second, ideology masks contradictions between what people believe should be and how society really is, as the conflicts between interests inevitably arise. Thus, if the game is unfair to certain non-dominant groups, they are led to accept their inferior performance as a personal failing rather than an inevitable consequence of the rules. Sociologists refer to this phenomenon as 'blaming the victim', but economists refer to it as an inequality in initial endowments because it sounds better. The final function of ideology relates to the original propositions developed by the three precursors to modern marketing. Specifically, their ideas have been repeated and reinforced for more than 200 years now, and they still form the foundation within which Western societies function today. In this context, ideology equates the present with the past. What was true decades, or even centuries, ago, is still considered to be true today. What was right then, is right today despite that fact that actual material reality has been significantly transformed. This serves to maintain class dominance across time regardless of the changes that have taken place within society. Resource shortages were, for example, virtually unimaginable a century ago and economic growth universally acclaimed, but this is clearly an issue now as material circumstances have changed. In any or all of these functions of ideology, the idea is to maintain stability of institutional arrangements that are to the advantage of one class over others. This equates to the function of paradigms as well. A paradigm's dimensions are mutually consistent and mutually supporting. When attacked from the outside, the intellectual forces of the paradigm unite to fend off conflicts.

Paradigms are amenable to change from within, however. But change from within is not as nefarious as changes coming from beyond the limits. When conflicts arise within a paradigm, as they often do, they are considered anomalies that must be addressed to bring consistency back to the paradigm. The history of science demonstrates that such anomalies occur with some frequency and do not present a major intellectual challenge. In this case, differences might be considered policy issues or methods issues, but they are not paradigm-level issues. Paradigm issues only arise when anomalies become frequent and persistent. When the intellectual forces of the paradigm cannot force the anomaly back into conformity, then a crisis of knowledge occurs because the constructs within the dominant paradigm cannot solve the problem, but the old constructs are incommensurable with the constructs that are the basis for a new paradigm that might solve the problem. This is when, and only when, paradigms shift. When confronted with incommensurability, the proponents of the old paradigm first refuse to acknowledge the crisis, then they demand that the crisis be resolved from within the existing paradigm, and finally, they acknowledge the superiority of the new paradigm. The superiority of the new paradigm must be acknowledged, in the end, because it solves the problems that the old paradigm could not solve and, in addition, solves the standard problems of the paradigm more parsimoniously or elegantly.

This process plays itself out very slowly in most cases because the proponents of the old paradigm demand that competitors make their claims in the idiom of the old paradigm. This works as a constraint on substantive change because, in most cases, demonstrating the superiority of the new in the framework of the old is virtually impossible, as the different frameworks represent different world views with different constructs and different evaluative criteria. As a result, there is no neutral ground from which to frame the argument. All conflicts initially take the form of a discourse between Tweedledee and Tweedledum with each making seemingly nonsensical claims to the other. Herein lies the intractable path to sustainable marketing. While the path taken here thus far may seem to be a digression, it was necessary for understanding why we have achieved so little despite the efforts of so many.

The profligacy of the West

Thus far, I have tried to demonstrate three points. First, sustainability is a problem to be dealt with either now or later, and thus far we have avoided dealing with it directly. Second, it will not be solved from within the framework of the existing paradigm as the necessary conditions for sustainability are incommensurable with the standard approach to marketing practice that still has its foundations resting on Enlightenment constructs. Finally, Western society will not change to a new sustainability paradigm until it is recognized that the old paradigm is in crisis. This requires explicit recognition that the root causes of the environmental crisis are a consequence of outmoded approaches to contemporary problems. Thus, trying to situate the solution to sustainability within the modern conception of markets and marketing will yield too little, too late. To add to our problems, globalization is exacerbating the situation, not eliminating it as contemporary economics and marketing would have us believe. We see this situation characterized in Lewis Carroll's prescient book, *Alice Through the Looking-Glass*. After racing at great speed, Alice stops to look around and observes, 'Why, we are just where we were when we started'. The Red Queen replies, 'Oh yes. You have to run twice as fast as that to get anywhere else'. This is the situation when one pursues economic growth to solve the problems created by economic growth. No matter how fast you grow, you must grow even faster to keep ahead of the problems created by growth. This is, of course, the ideology of the cancer cell.

As we know from virtually every marketing text, the purpose of marketing is to increase sales and to do it as efficiently as possible. Marketing education has as its prime objective teaching future marketers how to capture the hearts, minds, and wallets of consumers. For consumers, the objective is to consume more and more, being mindful to recycle, while the then President, George Bush, in the US admonishes them to buy even more so the economic problem will go away. Apparently, the environmental problem is on hold until we solve the economic problem, for there appears to be little relationship between the two in the minds of policy makers. But one must ultimately ask, 'To what purpose is all this growth and consumption?' Now, there is a problem! We are not supposed to ask that question because it is the central tenet in the DSP of Western industrial society, and, with no small amount of irony, the former socialist world as well. We may all ask, and are sometimes invited to ask, how to achieve more growth in a more efficient way. That is, we are invited to criticize and improve methods for achieving growth, but never to question the principle of growth itself. The former is within the paradigm, while the latter is against it. So now we must ask the question to which we may not like the answer. Remember the man on the branch?

Why are selling more (marketing practice) and consuming more (consumer behaviour) of such paramount importance that they have become the definition of progress in the Western world? Progress has become defined as material progress in the last century. We are all told repeatedly that 'the rising tide lifts all boats'. As the economy grows, we all share the benefits. Is this fact, or ideology expressing the specific interest of the dominant class as the general interest? If everyone does not gain equally, it is because some work harder or more effectively than others. Is this fact, or ideology masking the contradiction from the first argument. That is, some work very hard and never get ahead. Everyone's material well-being should be continuously improving. Is this fact, or ideology arguing that what used to be true (and still is in the Third World), is still true. In the early part of the twentieth century, peoples' well-being did need improvement, but does it need even more improvement in the twenty-first century? The World Values Survey has consistently demonstrated, for example, that Americans' sense of well-being has not substantially improved for 30 years despite significant increases in material wealth. As can be seen, it does not take much imagination to see the ideological in everyday existence. The DSP is ubiquitous and reinforces our beliefs at every turn, convincing us that material wealth is good and that more is better without end.

Marketing has become the unwitting vehicle through which this agenda is carried out. The process is given many names that have been recently published by critics of the marketing process as used in Western industrial societies. They carry such titles as *Affluenza, The Poverty of Affluence*, and *Is the American Dream Killing You?* and the message is quite clear. Why are we doing this to ourselves? It looks as though we are still trying to get the Darwin Award. The answer, in the context of marketing practice is quite simple, although we continue to walk around the elephant in the living room. Marketers sell more and more because the economic structure of Western industrial societies demands it. Further, we do not globalize marketing as a strategy but as an imperative.

Both growth and globalization are imperatives of capitalism, the DSP of Western industrial societies (with a few minor exceptions). Firms in capitalism, by all accounts, must expand their operations or die. This is an almost self-evident proposition. In order to remain competitive, firms must expand to achieve economies of scale. Expansion requires growth in markets, and growth in markets requires marketing practices that achieve that growth: hence, the marketing concept. When markets become saturated and the marginal cost of growth exceeds the marginal benefits, markets must be found in other places (globalization) or in other forms by bringing social areas not previously subject to the market into the market. This is referred to as economic imperialism or the 'commodification of everything'. In the US for example, we now market education, healthcare and social insurance as consumer products.

When all things are relegated to the market, a new form of life is created in which atomistic individuals are freed of political and ethical constraints on behaviour and seek to satisfy their needs (and greeds) in the marketplace. This is the life of negative freedom in which the individual is freed from constraints traditionally imposed by society, church and government. Freedom becomes redefined as market freedom and political life becomes separated from and inferior to economic life. This de-politicization of society has potentially dire consequences if political institutions are allowed to atrophy because they are no longer necessary. The questions of who we want to be (ideal regarding principles) are reduced to what we want to have (want regarding principles) and all conflicts are adjudicated in the market. We will get what we want to have, but we have little concern for who we become. This is the essence of Erich Fromm's last book, *To Have Or To Be?* (1976) Questions of wealth distribution, for example, no longer exist. Who gets what is decided in the market and is not subject to the reflections of citizens. Every allocation of resources is fair so long as one person does not gain at the expense of another. If one person can be made better off without making anyone worse off, the exchange is efficient. This is referred to as Pareto Optimality, and it is the efficiency criterion of neoclassical economics. Its insidious character is that allocations can be perfectly efficient and, at the same time, be grotesquely unfair and environmentally destructive.

The problem that the Pareto criterion presents relative to sustainability is that the only condition under which it can function as intended (maintaining the maldistribution of wealth and power) is continuous economic growth. With growth, the wealthy can become more wealthy without anyone else being made poorer. And in absolute terms, the poorer elements of society may even get a bit more. Once growth stops, however, then the decision regarding who gets what becomes a political decision that is anathema to those who benefit most from the status quo. What Pareto Optimality justifies, and even promotes, is vast differentials between haves and have nots, or poverty in the midst of wealth. At the same time its logic is destructive of the environment because you cannot have infinite growth in a finite system. This is economic ideology at its very best as it serves to convince the one pulling the plough that he is riding in a golden chariot. Marketing, as it is currently practised, supports this ideology and, because it is consistent with the DSP, moves us farther from sustainability rather than towards it. Every effort at green marketing, even with the best of intentions, plays into the myth of green marketing. That is, in its attempt to move us towards sustainability, it inadvertently provides an intellectual escape from the dystopian shadow of the DSP, reinforcing the belief that, if we consume more and recycle, the naturalness of the DSP will be vindicated.

Marketing and sustainability

What the forgoing suggests is that, as many critics have said before, capitalism contains multiple contradictions. Because marketing in the Western industrial world is played out within a predominantly capitalist framework, it supports, and when successful accelerates, these same contradictions. Only one of these contradictions is immediately relevant in the relationship between marketing and sustainability, and that is the conditions under which production for the market takes place.

This has two dimension, however. These are the biophysical limits to growth and the social limits to growth. Contemporary marketing practice has consistently disregarded these limits because they are contrary to the DSP that projects an image of limitlessness in all activities. Physics tells us that there are biophysical limits resulting from thermodynamic processes that we might express simply as: (1) nothing comes from nothing; and (2) everything goes somewhere. These are the familiar problems of sources and sinks in ecology. To consume, you must produce; to produce, you must use resources – both consuming and producing create waste. The cycle is inevitable but unacknowledged until very recently in history and is still not respected in marketing practice.

There are, in addition to biophysical limits to growth, social limits. While the pernicious effects of materialism are well documented, its relationship to sustainability is discussed less often. Marketing practice has as its fundamental goal, to increase levels of consumption through marketing activities. This is what every marketing text, including green marketing texts, teaches us to do. While it is true that most books have two paragraphs in which they present the societal marketing concept, it is never mentioned again and is certainly never enacted as a constraint on marketing activity. Marketing has a fundamental motivating principle derived directly from the DSP as presented earlier. That principle is that consuming is good and consuming more is better. Under the dimensions of the DSP, this philosophy makes perfect sense. Everyone makes their own choices (political), the market decides which of these choices to satisfy (economic), and advancing technology provides the means to satisfy those choices. And when the garbage gets too deep, technology will emerge to fix it (the 'where there's muck, there's money' mentality). When resources are short, technology will find new ones.

The difficulty here is that this mentality assumes that, what each of us can do individually, all can do collectively. This is infrequently the case in reality. The marketing process, when carried out under visions of limitlessness, encourages each individual to get what they want in the market. As each gets what they want, there is little visible consequence. However, the accumulation of small effects can result in very large effects unintended by any of the individuals. These are called social traps, and they tell us that what each individual may be able to do, all individuals collectively cannot do. The consequences of such social traps are ozone depletion, global warming, pollution, etc. Every individual's contribution is extremely small, but the sum of the effects is potentially disastrous to all. The social limits to growth relate directly back to the biophysical limits to growth, and both working together undermine the conditions of production. Thus, marketing as it is currently practiced will, in the long run undermine the ecological conditions that make it possible. While green marketing seeks to minimize the effect, so long as it operates within the DSP of Western societies, in the long run, it cannot succeed.

It is within this framework of thought that green marketing emerges as a myth. Myth does not suggest that green marketing does not exist. It does exist and it is growing. The myth suggested here is that green marketing is the solution to the paradigm problem and, that it can be incorporated into the paradigm as it exists. This means that the fundamental tenets of the paradigm can remain intact. It characterizes environmental problems, and through them sustainability, as anomalies, not as a crisis of knowledge. Green marketing acts a patch in the framework, suggesting that with only minor amendments, marketers can go about their business of selling more. This is not to discredit green marketing or its proponents. Green marketing is a necessary amendment to traditional marketing practice, but it is not a sufficient transformation. It is a tool in the sustainability tool chest, but it is not the blueprint for survival.

What is needed is not green reform that is framed in the idiom of the DSP (political and economic liberalism and technological optimism). Reformism, as a strategy for change, leaves the fundamental principles of the DSP in place and tries to effect change within the prevailing structure through policy initiatives. If that structure has the form and function of ideology, as was suggested earlier, then reformism will be ineffective in bringing substantive transformation to the marketing process. Rather, it is the underlying principles that must be changed, and then marketing will change to conform to new requirements. Marketing is promiscuous and can be done in many different ways to achieve many different purposes. Contemporary marketing practice takes the form it does because it exists within a set of institutions (the DSP) with which it is compatible. It has evolved within these institutions and is a reflection of their ideology. It is not marketing per se that is leading us away from sustainability but the institutions of the DSP that inform marketing practice. It is here that change must be effected. All the rest will follow. But, as stated earlier, paradigms are highly resilient and protect themselves when confronted with conflicting ideas. They shift only under conditions of crisis and herein lies the real problem. Without acknowledgement of crisis, changes are made only through reform within the paradigm. The unsustainable institutions underlying marketing practice remain intact. This is green marketing.

As mentioned earlier, many critics have called for a new paradigm conducive to sustainability. But we are no closer to that now than we were 30 years ago. This is because people do not intentionally transform paradigms. While it can be shown that paradigms have changed as a result of what one or a few people did, it was never their intention to effect such dramatic changes. It just happened. The power of the reasonable argument is rejected in paradigm conflict. Paradigms change people (and processes) after events leading to crises of knowledge occur. The question is, 'Is the DSP of Western society on the verge of a crisis of knowledge?'

The answer, from all outward appearances, is definitely maybe. Many environmental problems have come and gone because, while they were inconvenient, they were not imperilling life as we know it. We were able to put them out of sight and, thereby, out of mind. All Western countries have done this at one time or another. We were able to think of them as anomalies that could be reconciled within existing frameworks. When global warming enters the picture, however, things change. This phenomenon affects every living thing on the planet and can be escaped by no one. Why it is different is because if the full force of its effects materialize, the profligate lifestyles of the Western industrial societies will have to change. This means that political, economic and technological institutions that exist now will be transformed dramatically. Changes in individual freedom, accumulation of private property, procedural neutrality in government, free markets for allocating resources and technofixes, alongside a variety of other unknown changes, will occur when resource availability diminishes and the satisfaction of basic needs once again becomes problematic. Unfortunately, global warming is not yet recognized as a crisis within the DSP. We have not yet tried to effect or even formulate solutions. There is still hope that reformist measures will be sufficient to remediate the symptom. This suggests that the crisis of knowledge is not yet recognized. It will only be so when all the standard solutions in the arsenal of the DSP have failed. That time is not yet, but it may not be far off. When it comes, the new marketing concept will emerge.

The new marketing concept

One can only imagine what a new concept of marketing will entail, but we can speculate on what some of its features might be. To begin with, we must dismiss the idea that everyone's preferences must be satisfied, and this is particularly true on a global scale. The provisioning technology must provide for the needs of the global population first as suggested in the Brundtland Commission's definition. While we cannot say exactly what that is, we know it is not the level of material existence of Western industrial societies expanded to include the world's population. The new marketing concept will be based on what is enough rather than on how much you want. And more importantly, that enough-ness cannot continue to grow. This was argued more than a century and a half ago by John Stuart Mill, in *Principles of Political Economy*, who theorized about the economics of the steady state. This is a prerequisite to sustainability. In addition, marketing will adopt a systems approach in which the effects of marketing practices will be evaluated by their consequences on both people and the global ecological systems of which they are a part. This will reflect both resource regenerative capacity and the earth's absorption capacity. Technologies must be based on energy flows and throughput assessments that allow humanity to live off nature's income rather than its capital. Successful marketing practice will be based on its contribution to well-being rather than profit. This also requires a redefinition of profit that is multi-dimensional and reflects the true triple bottom line.

Rather than promoting profligacy, sustainable marketing communications must promote a new relationship between humans and their consumption. This is the ethic of enough and the re-signification of the good life that is not based on possessions, but on relationships between humans and between humans and nature. The same tools (marketing is promiscuous!) can be used to foster commonality that were used to produce individuation for the past century. Sustainability, above all, tells us that we are all subject to the same environmental conditions both now and in the future, and that we are all responsible for the earth. Rather than promoting domination as advertising presently does, the ethic of stewardship can become the focal construct creating both a more sustainable life and a better life if the critics of materialism are correct. The options here are limited only by the imagination.

Distribution systems, from production to disposal, will be transformed in the new marketing concept. This is where efficiency remains important in marketing systems. A recent statistic is informative here. If one buys a new Mercedes, the car has more than two million miles on it if you count the distance that each of the parts has travelled in the process of production. I cannot say this is completely accurate, but it gets an important point across. Bio-regionalism is the basis for distribution in the new marketing concept. Whenever possible, all production will take place in the region in which the product will be consumed. Local production for local consumption is compatible with sustainability, but, as the new marketing concept suggests, one cannot have it all. As the London School of Economics' most famous student, Mick Jagger, once wrote, 'You can't always get what you want'. With a systems perspective, however, you can get most of what you need.

Limiting what you want becomes a function of price just as it is now. One of the problems of sustainability is that markets, for a variety of reasons (recall the infamous wager), do not get the prices right. This is because nature's storehouse has been consistently treated as a free good. In the new marketing, the full cost, including the environmental cost, will be in the price of goods. This might be effected in a number of ways through a combination of command and control procedures and market mechanisms. Specifically, carbon taxes can be added to the price of goods based on the 'carbon footprint' of the product. The proceeds of the tax can be used in a number of ways, among which is a refund to consumers who have low carbon footprints in their market choices. Sustainable choices will be subsidized by those who remain profligate in their consumption. This, as only one example, is actually quite easy to effect.

From a product perspective, the range of products will diminish dramatically but need not be reduced to very few with no variation. Planned obsolescence is completely out of the picture and durability is in it. One of the functions of sustainable advertising would be to promote this idea to subvert the DSP's focus on individuation and private property. Products without ownership designed to be shared by multiple consumers represents a novel approach to marketing. This has been done with bicycles in Copenhagen, for example.

These are but a few examples of how sustainable marketing might be different from standard marketing. What is important, however, is that each of these examples contradicts one or more of the tenets of the DSP of Western industrial societies. This is why the transformation in the DSP is necessary and why sustainable marketing is in the future. There are many institutional constraints that inhibit the development of sustainable marketing practices once you get beyond improved technologies to reduce the impact of consumption as it now exists. As suggested earlier, the force of the better argument is of limited use here once one challenges the basic premises of the DSP. Until global warming, or some unknown future problem, assumes a 'crisis of knowledge' status, changes such as those above, as simple as they may be, will not materialize in any substantial way.

Recommended further reading

Daly, H.E. and Townsend, K.N. (eds) (1993) *Valuing the Earth: Economics, Ecology, Ethics*, Cambridge, MA: MIT Press.

Dobson, A. (2007) *Green Political Thought*, London: Routledge Press.

Fromm, E. (1976) *To Have Or To Be?*, New York: Harper and Row.

Heilbroner, R.L. (1985) *The Nature and Logic of Capitalism*, New York: W.W. Norton & Company.

Kilbourne, W., McDonagh, P. and Prothero, A. (1997) 'Sustainable consumption and the quality of life: a macromarketing challenge to the dominant social paradigm', *Journal of Macromarketing*, 17(1): 4–24.

MacPherson, C.B. (1962) *The Political Theory of Possessive Individualism*, Oxford: The Clarendon Press.

Polanyi, K. (1944) *The Great Transformation: The Political and Economic Origins of Our Time*, Boston, MA: Beacon Press.

Prothero, A. and Fichette, J.A. (2000) 'Greening capitalism: opportunities for a green commodity', *Journal of Macromarketing*, 20(1): 46–55.

Smith, T.M. (1999) *The Myth of Green Marketing: Tending Our Goats at the Edge of Apocalypse*, Toronto: University of Toronto Press.

Winner, L. (1986) *The Whale and the Reactor: A Search for Limits in an Age of High Technology*, Chicago, IL: University of Chicago Press.

References

Berlin, Isaiah (1959), *The Crooked Timber of Humanity*. Princeton, NJ: Princeton University Press.

Bruntland Commission (1987), *Our Common Future*. Oxford, UK: Oxford University Press.

Carroll, Lewis (1969[1872]), *Through the Looking Glass (And What Alice Found There)*. London, UK: MacMillan Company.

Carson, Rachel (1962) *Silent Spring*. Harmondsworth: Penguin.

Club of Rome (1972) *Limits to Growth.*

de Graff, John, David Warm, and Thomas H. Naylor (2001) *Affluenza: The All Consuming Epidemic.* San Francisco, CA: Berrett-Koehler Publishers, Inc.

Ehrlich, Paul R. (1968) *The Population Bomb.* New York, NY: Ballantine Books.

Fisk, George (1973) 'Criteria for a theory of responsible consumption', *Journal of Marketing,* 37(1), 24–31.

Fisk, George (1974) *Marketing and the Ecological Crisis.* New York: Harper and Row.

Fromm, E. (1976) *To Have or To Be?* New York: Harper and Row.

Kelly, Walt (1971) *Pogo: We Have Met the Enemy and He Is Us.* New York, NY: Simon and Schuster.

Locke, John (1980[1691]) *Second Treatise of Government.* Cambridge, MA: Hackett Publishing Company, Inc.

Mill, John S. (1872) *Principles of Political Economy: With Some of Their Applications to Social Philosophy.* New York, NY: D. Appleton.

Paine, Thomas (1997[1776]) *Common Sense.* New York, NY: Dover Publications.

Simon, Julian L. (1981) *The Ultimate Resource.* Princeton, NJ: Princeton University Press.

Smith, Adam (1937[1776]) *An Inquiry into the Nature and Causes of the Wealth of Nations.* New York: Random House.

Speth, James Gustave (2008) *The Bridge at the Edge of the World.* New Haven, CT: Yale University Press.

Stiglitz, Joseph E. (2002) *Globalization and Its Discontents.* New York, NY: W. W. Norton & Company.

Thoreau, Henry David (1962) *Walden and Other Writings by Henry David Thoreau.* New York, NY: Bantam Books.

|18|

Brand equity and
the value of marketing assets*
Roderick J. Brodie and Mark S. Glynn

Chapter Topics

Overview

In the last two decades the term 'equity' has been used in marketing to describe the value of brands, customers, channels, and other marketing relationships. We examine the alternative uses of the equity concept and how it links with financial thinking. The chapter then explores issues involved in developing a theory of marketing assets and value that integrates branding, relationship and network thinking with financial thinking.

Introduction

There is a paradox in how senior management views marketing. While a market-focused strategy may be regarded as an essential component in driving strategic success, at the senior management level marketing executives are often not as

---

* This chapter is based on the authors' article 'Towards a theory of marketplace equity: integrating branding and relationship thinking with financial thinking', *Marketing Theory* 2 (1): 5–28, 2002.

strongly represented as executives with a financial background. One reason for this is that marketing's traditional goals such as 'creating value for the customer' and 'winning in the product marketplace' do not clearly link with the financial and strategic issues of business. Hence there is the need for new marketing thinking that links marketing activity more directly with the creation of financial value. This led Srivastava, Shervani and Fahey (1998: 3) to suggest the central focus in marketing should be to 'create and manage market-based assets in order to deliver financial value'. This implies the marketing–finance interface needs to be better coordinated and hence one of the central tasks of marketing is resource integration. Doyle (2000) refers to this new approach to marketing as 'value-based marketing'. More recently, Vargo and Lusch (2004) developed a new service logic that focuses on resource integration and value creation within networks which provides a broader theoretical foundation for this new approach to marketing.

If ideas about financial value are to be integrated into marketing practice there is a need for greater linkages between financial terms and marketing concepts to develop a common lexicon. Such a linkage has occurred in the last decade, where marketing academics and practitioners have used the term 'equity' to describe the financial value of brands and other marketing assets. This term is used in accounting and finance to express the combined value of an organization's financial assets and liabilities. While some marketing academics have used equity in a broader legal and ethical context to indicate fairness, it is the financial use of the term that has been largely adopted.

The concept of brand equity emerged in marketing in the 1980s. Advertising practitioners in the USA used the idea to counter stock market emphasis on short-term results and consequent cuts to brand advertising budgets. In order to convince senior managers of the long-term value of brand advertising and other marketing investments, it was argued that marketing needed financial measures of brand value. Thus the term 'brand equity' was coined to refer to the brand's long-term customer franchise and its financial value.

In measuring that customer franchise, what became apparent was the lack of a clear and consistent conceptual framework for brand equity. While marketing academics had devoted considerable attention to understanding the nature of brand loyalty, little attention had been given to the financial consequences of activities designed to increase brand loyalty. Thus, in the 1990s, the Marketing Science Institute listed brand equity as a priority area for research, which has resulted in an extensive number of brand-related publications in leading international journals.

Aaker (1996: 7) defines brand equity as 'the assets and liabilities linked to a brand, its name and symbol, that add to or subtract from the value provided by a product or service to a firm and/or to that firm's customers'. This asset/liability perspective leads to a broad view about the role of the brand. Aaker groups the brand's assets and liabilities into five categories. The first four are more traditional (i.e. brand loyalty, awareness, perceived quality and brand associations), while the last catch-all category of 'other proprietary assets' can be interpreted as including patents, trademarks, channel relationships, and other stakeholder relationships.

The marketing community has also recently used the term equity to refer to the asset value of other marketing investments. Rust, Zeithaml and Lemon (2000) and

Blattberg, Getz and Thomas (2001) use the term 'customer equity' to focus on the financial value of customers to an organization, while Anderson and Narus (1999) use the term 'marketplace equity' to represent the joint result of investments in brand equity, channel equity, and reseller equity. The importance of understanding the nature of marketplace equity is highlighted vividly when the value of a company's intangible assets as a proportion of market capitalization is examined. For the majority of brand-, technology- and service-driven companies the value of intangible assets as a proportion of market capitalization has been growing in the last decade and it is not unusual for it to exceed 80 per cent.[1]

The chapter proceeds as follows. First the use of the term equity in branding is considered. The next section examines how equity has been used in relation to other marketing assets such as customers, channels and relationships. We then examine how marketing thinking integrates with financial thinking. Finally the issue of developing a theory of brand equity and the value of marketing assets are considered.

Equity concept and branding

Although the exact origins of the term brand equity are unclear, it has been traced back to the mid-1980s. Since then definitions of brand equity abound, as has research on this subject. This research has been based on four different perspectives that are: entity-based; financially-based; process-based; and network-based. Finally we integrate these four different perspectives by suggesting a service-based perspective of brand equity.

Entity-based brand equity

Much of the initial research on brand equity was in response to the advertising industry's need to understand the effects of advertising on building brand image and consumer loyalty. Thus the focus was on mass marketing and the one-way impact of marketing activity (especially advertising) on consumers. This initial research on brand equity was based on concepts from consumer behaviour and marketing communications. It follows the traditional view of marketing where the brand is seen as functioning as an entity and is consistent with the American Marketing Association (2004) definition of the brand (i.e. a name, term, design, symbol, or any other feature that identifies one seller's good or service as distinct from those of other sellers).

Keller (1993) broadens this perspective to include customer behaviour in response to this differentiation. He defines customer-based equity as: 'the differential effect of brand knowledge on consumer response to the marketing of the brand'

---

[1] For discussion of this topic see www.customersandcapital.com/book/brands. Also see the Interbrand website, www.brandchannel.com.

(Keller, 1993 :2) and describes equity in terms of the strength of consumers' attachment to the brand and their associations and beliefs about the brand. A variety of concepts have been used to develop consumer-based measures of brand equity. These include consumer preferences, price premiums, consumer perceptions, price trade-offs, residual intangible value, loyalty, awareness, perceived quality, brand knowledge and consumer learning.

_____ Financially-based brand equity _____

This stream of research uses a more direct financial approach, where the emphasis is less on individual consumers and more on the overall financial value of the brand to the organization. A variety of methods have also been used to develop measures of the financial value of brands to an organization. These methods identify the total asset value of the organization and subtract the tangible assets. The residual value is then used to arrive at a measure of brand equity.

One approach is to take the organization's share market price and subtract the tangible asset value. Another approach is to work directly with the organization. For example, the consulting organization Interbrand undertakes a direct analysis of the organization's financial performance to identify the residual intangible value. An index of brand strength based on seven performance dimensions (leadership, stability of the brand, geographic spread trend, support, protection and market stability) is then developed and used to project future intangible value and to arrive at a measure of the organization's brand equity. These financial methods used by Interbrand typically estimated the brand equity as a proportion of market capitalization for brand-driven companies to be in the order of 50–90 per cent.

_____ Process-based brand equity _____

This third emerging stream of research focuses on the value of relational and experiential aspects of branding. Research in this area was the result of increased interest about the role of branding in other areas such as services, business-to-business and electronic marketing. In these situations customers' interactions and relationships with the organization providing the goods and services play a more important role than simply brand differentiation or identity. In the relational context the organization is the primary determinant of brand equity, in contrast to consumer-packaged goods marketing where the product is the determinant of brand equity. The broader perspective goes beyond brand identity, focusing on the brand functioning as a process. Thus the customers' relationships and experience with the organization are important determinants of brand meaning and brand equity. What is also important is how the reputation and identity of the organization (the corporate brand) are associated with the brand.

Relational and experiential branding can also be important for consumer-packaged goods when the product category is complex and provides considerable choice, and where this choice involves perceived risk and high switching costs between brands.

In contrast to the entity-based branding research, empirical research about brand equity for services, business-to-business, and electronic marketing is more limited and only recently has a process approach been adopted. The implications for building brand equity by taking this process-based perspective is that interactive communications between buyers and sellers and other stakeholders need to be managed. With the development of the electronic commerce environment, Interactive Communication Technology (ICT) plays a central role in facilitating interactivity and in these situations the brand becomes a surrogate for trust about the service provision.

Network-based brand equity

This stream of research builds on the process-based approach and includes co-branding, brand alliances and networks. The network perspective of branding recognizes that the equity of the brand comes not only from the end-customer, but also from a range of relationships within the marketing system. Thus the equity is intrinsically linked with a network of associations with other brands. Some of these associations are based on alliance activities between brands (and the brands' organizations), while other associations are based on less formal arrangements. Formal arrangements include joint promotions, co-branding, alliances, and joint ventures. In addition, sponsorship is playing an increasingly important role in co-branding. Only recently have researchers examined the nature of brand equity in cooperative business relationships (Van Durme et al., 2003).

The additional value or co-brand equity comes also from the network of other stakeholder relationships. Using more than one brand symbolically builds consumer trust and commitment in these relationships. Thus the corporate reputation and identity of the marketing organization play an important role. This brand strategy is referred to as 'umbrella branding' where the umbrella brand augments the equity of the individual brand offerings.

Recently research about brand communities is receiving increased attention. A brand community can be made up of consumers and other stakeholders and the organization marketing the brand (Muniz et al., 2001). Within this network, brand value is co-created by community-based negotiations and symbolic interpretations of brand-related information. Thus the organization marketing the brand no longer has such direct influence over the processes of value creation but becomes a partner in the co-creation of value. Mertz, He, Yi and Vargo (2009) provide a detailed review of the research that has been undertaken within the emerging brand logic that involves brand communities and has a stakeholder focus. 'Stakeholder' brand equity (Jones, 2005) can be considered as a special case of network brand equity.

Service-based brand equity

Recently Brodie, Glynn and Little (2006) developed a theoretical framework of the service brand that integrates the four previous perspectives. The framework

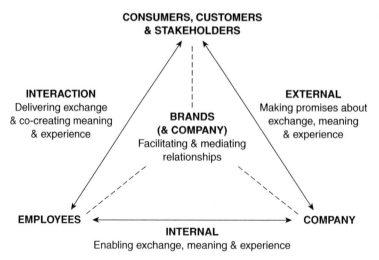

Figure 18.1   The service brand–relationship–value triangle (Brodie et al., 2006)

develops a broader perspective of how the brand functions, drawing on the way service has been defined by Vargo and Lusch (2004: 2), 'where the service-centred dominant logic represents a re-oriented philosophy that is applicable to all marketing offerings, including those that involve tangible output (goods) and the process of service provision'. Hence the concept of the service brand is integrative where 'service' is super-ordinate to the branding of 'goods' and/or 'services'.

Attention is given to integrating the role of the brand in the value-adding processes that create customer experience, dialogue and learning. In this broader theoretical framework the brand is conceptualized as a set of promises. This framework is developed by adapting the framework by Bitner (1995) and Grönroos (1996) about the way service value is delivered. The framework, which is outlined in Figure 18.1, allows for customer, employee and organizational perceptions of the service brand. The three types of marketing that influence these perceptions are:

- *External marketing:* Communication between the organization and its customers and stakeholders *making promises* about the service offer.

- *Interactive marketing:* Interactions between people working within the organization/ network and end-customers that create the service experience associated with *delivering promises* about the service offer.

- *Internal marketing:* The resources and processes *enabling and facilitating promises* about the service offer involving the organization and people working in the organization.

The promises framework extends that a network that explicitly takes into account the perceptions of other stakeholders (e.g. retailers, media, government regulators, etc.). The framework suggests a broader context to examine the impact of brand, because the brand is seen to have meaning not only for end-customers but also for the brand-owning company and its responsibilities to employees and a broader network of stakeholders. The implications for conventional brand management in this wider, more community-orientated conception of brands and socially-constructed notions of meaning are far-reaching.

Within the promises framework Brodie et al. (2006) provide a definition of the service brand where it functions as both an entity and a process:

> **Service brands facilitate and mediate the marketing processes used to realize the experiences that drive co-creation of value. They provide sign systems that symbolize meaning in the marketing network, and hence are a fundamental asset or resource that a marketing organization uses in developing service-based competency and hence competitive advantage. (2006: 373)**

Thus the service brand equity can be defined as 'the differential effect of brand in the co-creation of value between the organization, its customers and network of stakeholders' (ibid.). As noted in the discussion in the previous section, identifying the sources of the differential effect becomes complex because of the multitude of relationships that exist between the organization, its customers and network of stakeholders. This is especially the case for brand communities.

Recent research by Brodie, Whittome and Brush (2009) provides empirical support for the service brand theoretical framework showing the importance of both the 'making of promises' (brand image with company image) with the 'delivery of promises' (employee trust and company trust) in creating customer value and customer loyalty. However further theory development and empirical research is needed to further refine the theory of the service brand.

Equity concept and other marketing assets

In the last decade, the term equity has been used to express the value of other marketing assets, such as channels, resellers and customers.

Channel and reseller equity

While it is recognized that channel members as well as the end-customers have a role in creating equity, there has been a lack of research about how this occurs (Glynn et al., 2007). However, more general research about channels provides sound foundations to develop research in this area.

Anderson and Narus (1999) introduce the concept of marketplace equity as the joint result of brand equity, channel equity, and reseller equity, but provide little further conceptual development. Also, Srivastava et al. (1998) describe channel equity as the outcome of partner relationships between the firm and the members of the channel. This recognizes that channel equity is based on different attributes than those for brand equity. While brand equity is associated directly with consumer demand, channel equity is associated with derived demand and the processes that supply goods in response to consumer demand. Thus aspects of inter-organizational relationships such as experience and knowledge play a central role in conceptualizing channel equity.

Channel relationships have strategic value because strong channel relationships can reduce financial commitment and this relationship dependence has benefits that enhance performance. These long-term inter-firm relationships can increase return on investment, so these relationships are often the firm's most important assets.

Influence of brands on channel equity

Building strong manufacturer's brands has become more difficult due to increased brand competition and the emphasis on retail price promotions. There has also been an increase in the concentration of ownership of retail outlets that has resulted in shifts in power and control within the channels of distribution. Thus the 'trade leverage' provided by manufacturers' brands has been eroded and manufacturers have become more dependent on retailers. Understanding how to influence power and control within channels is thus an important issue.

The equity of the manufacturer's brand can be thought of as a source of non-coercive power within the channel relationship. This power occurs because brands provide channel members with several benefits such as pre-established demand, lower selling costs, image and relationship enhancement of retailers with consumers, higher margins, and better inventory management. However, retailers are also powerful within the channel, and retailer costs such as cooperative advertising and slotting allowances can reduce the marketing funds available for manufacturers to build the brand–consumer relationship.

To ensure that the influence of the brand is maximized, manufacturers' brands have focused on the inter-organizational requirements within the channels of distribution. Aspects of this relationship management approach with resellers include: category management: efficient consumer response; and promotions and pricing management. Conversely, manufacturer actions such as developing other channels and reducing supply chain costs can increase costs for the retailer. Thus the individual actions of both manufacturers and retailers can impact on the supply chain, leading to worsened channel relations and weakened channel equity.

Manufacturers' marketing strategies for a brand usually involve both activities with channel members and direct interactions with the end-customer. Thus, implementing both these strategies means that channel and brand equity are inter-related. Examples of this inter-relationship include the negative effect on brand equity of price reductions, and the favourable effect of store image and distribution intensity on brand equity.

Customer equity

The customer-oriented view has been central in the managerial approach to marketing for a long time. However in the 1980s there was a shift from more general thinking about customer orientation to a focus on the nature and profitability of specific customers. This means issues about relationship building and customer retention have become more important. As a result there has been the development of metrics about the asset value of customers to the organization. The overall asset value of customers has been referred to as 'customer equity'.

Rust et al. (2000: 4) define customer equity as 'the total of the discounted lifetime values over all of the firm's customers' and identify three components:

- *Value equity:* The end-customer's perception of value.

- *Brand equity:* The end-customer's emotional and subjective assessment above the perception of value.

- *Retention equity:* The end-customer's repeat purchase intention and loyalty.

Blattberg et al. (2001) provide a similar framework of customer equity that focuses on the associations between customer preference, image and customer retention and affinity for the brand. These models differ from the process and network models of brand equity because they are restricted to end-customers. Thus they do not explicitly focus on the interactions and relationships between buyers and sellers or the network of interactions between brands.

Recently there has been considerable debate about whether customer equity or brand equity provides a better approach to brand management. For example, Rust, Zeithaml and Lemon (2004a) warn that the brand equity approach places too much emphasis on the company as the brand and detracts from the more important task of growing and managing the company's customer base. However, as discussed above, the co-creation of customer value in most service organizations involves a set of complex interactions between the service organization and its employees, and the channel and other stakeholders, as well as interactions with end-customers. If this broader perspective of co-creation of value is taken, then it becomes far too restricting for brand equity to be viewed as a component of a more all-embracing concept of 'customer equity'. For a further discussion of the links between the two perspectives see Ambler et al. (2002) and Leone et al. (2006).

Integrating with financial thinking

In this section we examine how these perspectives about brands can be integrated with financial concepts. The financial perspective is introduced and then ideas about relationships and governance mechanisms are examined.

A financial asset perspective

The approaches to conceptualizing brand equity reviewed in this chapter provide initial thinking about brands as assets. Srivastava et al. (1998) have advanced this

Table 18.1 Linking marketing activity and performance with cash flow and financial value

Accelerating cash flow	Enhancing cash flow	Reducing volatility and vulnerability of cash flows
Achieving faster response to marketing efforts	Differentiation that leads to price/market share premiums	Enhancing loyalty and raising switching costs
Achieving earlier brand trials	Cross-selling products/services	Differentiation from shifting to services and consumables
Faster time to market acceptance	Developing new uses	Integrating operations to reduce capital requirements
Developing strategic alliances and cross-promotions	Reducing sales service costs	
	Reducing working capital	
	Developing brand extensions	
	Developing co-branding and co-marketing	

Source: Summarized from Srivastava et al. (1998).

thinking by providing a more comprehensive theoretical framework. At a general level the framework views market-based assets as consisting of external relationships such as customer relationships (brands and the installed customer base) and partner relationships (channels, co-branding and the network). To understand how these marketing assets create value the first step is to examine how they influence market performance. Indicators of market performance include faster market penetration, price premiums, share premiums, extensions, reducing sales service costs and increased loyalty and retention.

The next step is to link market performance with financial value. This is achieved by using Rappaport's (1986) financial value planning approach. The approach uses four measures of cash flow that are assumed to determine financial value. These are: increasing cash flows, enhancing cash flows, reducing volatility and vulnerability of cash flows, and enhancing the residual value of cash flows. It is recognized that there is considerable debate about which are the most appropriate financial valuation methods. Other valuation methods include: price/earnings multiples, market-to-book value ratios, economic value added (EVA), or cash flow return.

The specific types of market activities and types of market performance that influence the first three cash flow measures are summarized in Table 18.1. A fourth measure, 'enhancing the residual value of cash flows' is defined as 'the residual value of a business attributable to a business beyond a reasonable forecast period'. This measure is based on expectations about the ability of the organization to increase the size, the loyalty and quality of the customer base.

Srivastava, Shervani and Fahey (1999) extend their framework to include what they consider are the three core business processes that create financial value. These processes are the product development management, supply chain management, and customer relationship management. They then explore how marketing activities are embedded in the three processes. In the case of brands, the dominant interactions and relationships are between the organization that supplies the goods and services and the end-customers. However there are also relationships between the organization and other internal and external stakeholders that need to be considered. These include employees, distributors, retailers, other strategic partners, community groups, and even government agencies.

Srivastava et al.'s framework provides a useful starting point to conceptualize the nature of the relational and network activities that are associated with the core business processes. To extend the framework it is useful to draw on other literatures to help develop a more comprehensive description. These include the IMP[2] research, relationship marketing research, and more general research on marketing strategy and strategic management relating to governance.

_____ Integrating relationship and network thinking _____

The IMP research focuses on the nature of the relationships between buyers and sellers. These are built from interaction processes in which technical, social and economic issues are dealt with. Relationships are developed to cope with increasing heterogeneity in supply and demand, coordinate sophisticated delivery mechanisms and provide innovation. The economic, social and technical interactions between buyers and sellers require trust and mutual commitment beyond legal control mechanisms. Thus markets are seen as institutions for coordination, cooperation and governance. Within these markets the economic content of the relationships is seen as an asset or market investment in a similar way to that by Srivastava et al. (1998). Thus the IMP research provides a richer contextual understanding about the nature of relational assets (Håkansson and Snehota, 2000).

The historical review of the value literature by Payne and Holt (2001) describes how the value chain, customer value and relationship value have been linked to financial value. They conclude that the relationship marketing perspective provides a more comprehensive long-term view of how financial value is created. This is because relationship marketing integrates other aspects of management. However, the division between what is 'relationship marketing' and what is 'relationship management' is somewhat arbitrary. For example, Morgan and Hunt (1994) define relationship marketing as: 'all marketing activities directed towards establishing and maintaining successful relational exchanges' p. 11. Morgan and Hunt's perspective is also important because it integrates the resource-based theory of the firm thus providing a strong theoretical foundation that moves across functional boundaries. As with the IMP perspective it is recognized that it is not only the relationships between sellers and buyers that are important but also a network of other relationships and interactions both within the organization and external to the organization.

Gummesson (2008) develops a more elaborate classification of relationship types. After two decades of studying marketing organizations, he identifies 30 generic types of relationships that he categorizes into five groups. These are: mega relationships (relationships on levels above the market proper, e.g. political

_____

[2] IMP stands for International/Industrial Marketing and Purchasing project and involves a group of international researchers who have undertaken collaborative research into business organizations since the mid-1970s. Håkansson and Snehota (2000) provide a good overview of the nature of its research and its history.

and economic alliances between countries); inter-organizational relationships (such as alliances between companies); mass relationships (such as communications with different segments of a market); individual relationships; and nano ('dwarf') relationships (such as relationships within an organization). In order to understand and manage these relationships, it is important to not focus on simple dyads alone (e.g. buyer and seller interactions), but to understand and manage *all* the networks of relationships and interactions around the dyad. This classification provides a framework to understand how networks of relationships create value for an organization. Similarly, Grönroos (2007) provides detail about how relationship value is created and managed by incorporating the service processes associated with relationships including brand relationships.

Integrating governance thinking

The notion of governance extends the understanding about coordination and cooperation in relationships. Governance refers to the formal and informal rules of exchange and the initiation, maintenance and termination of a relationship between two parties. Heide (1994) outlines a typology of governance forms consisting of market, hierarchical and relational approaches. Market governance is associated with discrete types of exchange. Hierarchical or unilateral governance gives the right of one party to impose conditions on another. Relational or bilateral governance means a more open-ended relationship.

Ghosh and John (1999) extend the traditional transaction cost analysis framework using Heide's (1994) typology of governance mechanisms in channels. Their framework addresses marketing strategy decisions, especially with regard to strategies grounded in cooperative relationships and investments with supply chain partners. End-customers can also make specific investments in the relationship. The investment by the end-customer is important in determining whether an organization decides to adopt an open or closed (proprietary) standard. They suggest that partners in a relationship devise governance forms to safeguard the value of their assets in order to maximize joint value creation. Thus stronger brands are in a better position to use market governance forms to build customer demand for the brand. However, relational governance is better for weaker brands that benefit more from closer relationships with resellers. Many brands, but especially high-priced brands, have product attributes that are not easy to assess, so brand expenditures as well as price premiums act as market governance forms and offer the buyer a safeguard against any potential quality problems.

Towards a theory of brand equity and the value of marketing assets

This chapter has examined how the terms equity and value have been used in the various marketing discourses in order to explore how financial thinking can be integrated with marketing thinking. It has been shown that the term equity has been used extensively in the marketing literature. The initial focus was on entity-based brand equity for packaged consumer goods and the long-term financial value of advertising expenditure. More recently the focus on brand equity has been extended to include all consumer goods, services and business-to-business brands where the brand functions as a process as well as an entity. The term has also been used to express the asset value of investments in channel relationships and other business relationships. In these situations the equity that is generated by marketing activity is much more than the customer's awareness and image of the brand and includes the value generated from customer and organizational relationships. This leads to the concept of the service brand where the brand functions as both as an entity and a process. Service brand equity can be defined as 'the differential effect of brand in the co-creation of value between the organization, its customers and network of stakeholders'.

Value has been used and defined in multiple ways in marketing so it has taken on a number of meanings. In contrast, equity is a more neutral term than value and one that naturally integrates financial thinking with marketing thinking. Equity is a financial term that can be easily understood and is meaningful across organizations and at all levels of management. It is also superior to the term 'goodwill' that has traditionally been used to describe the value of intangible assets and liabilities of a business. Thus it is suggested a theory of marketing assets should be centred on the term equity rather than value.

It is tempting to use brand equity or customer equity as a vehicle to represent the value of everything associated with marketing. However, the review in this chapter indicates that these perspectives are too restricting. Building on the ideas of Anderson and Narus (1999), it is suggested that the term marketplace equity is a more useful concept to represent the value of all market-based assets. The marketplace equity for an organization comes from the broader network of relationships with channels, brands and other marketing entities and can be linked to the core business processes that create financial value. Thus brand equity and customer equity are subsets of marketplace equity.

When defining marketplace equity it is important to distinguish between the roles that marketing and other organizational activities play in the creation of value for an organization. Complications occur when distinguishing between what is relationship marketing and what is relationship management. A further problem occurs in defining market-based assets. For example, Srivastava et al. (1998) distinguish between relational and intellectual market-based assets. They define relational market-based assets as the outcomes of the relationships between the firm and its stakeholders, while intellectual market-based assets are defined as the types of knowledge and intelligence the organization has about its environment. However, the development and evolution of relational and intellectual market-based assets are highly interrelated to the point that they become difficult to separate.

It is suggested that Srivastava et al.'s (1998) market-based assets framework provides a useful starting point to develop a theory of marketplace equity. However, the framework needs to be extended to link relational marketing and network thinking with the three core business processes that Srivastava et al. (1999) suggest are the drivers of financial value. In this framework, networks, relationships and interactions are the building blocks. Hence the IMP, relationship marketing and network literatures provide the necessary background. In addition, the ideas associated with inter-organizational governance provide a useful way to understand how coordination and cooperation occurs within networks and relationships.

Perhaps one of the biggest benefits in developing a theory of marketplace equity is that it focuses on the core business processes that deliver financial value in a way that incorporates the intellectual or knowledge aspects of marketing with other aspects of business. It also leads to the integration of the traditional entity-and consumer-based branding literature with the more recent process-based branding literature.

It is suggested that the theory of marketplace equity should be viewed as a middle-range theory that draws on higher level or more general theories. The idea about the need for middle-range theory in the applied social sciences was first explored by Merton (1967). He defines middle-range theories as, 'theories that lie between the minor but necessary working hypotheses that evolve in an abundance during day-to-day research and all-inclusive systematic efforts to develop a unified theory that will explain all the uniformities of social behaviour, social organisation and social change (Merton, 1967: 39).

Merton further elaborates that middle-range theory should draw on components from higher level general theories, but at the same time should be independent of these theories. It is suggested that Merton's work and the more recent work in organizational science (e.g. Weick, 1989) provides excellent principles to guide the development of a theory of marketplace equity, giving guidance in achieving a balance between relevance and application, and the theoretical insight that comes from higher level theory.

Thus an important consideration is to identify the underlying theories that a theory of marketplace equity should be based on. As shown by Hunt and Morgan (1995) relationship marketing theory is to a large extent derived from the resource-advantage-based view of the firm. Thus it is suggested that the resource-advantage-based view of the firm provides a natural starting point to develop this middle-range theory. However, as discussed in the previous section, there are important links between governance thinking, transaction cost analysis theory and relationship thinking. In addition, consumer-based branding modelling that has closer links to traditional microeconomic and psychological theories needs to be integrated. Thus further research is needed to resolve exactly where the foundations of a theory of marketplace equity lie, and how these theories contribute to this more applied or middle-range theory.

Of particular relevance is how service-dominant logic (SDL), developed by Vargo and Lusch (2004), informs the theory of marketplace equity. The basic tenet of the SDL is *service* (singular) which applies competences for the benefit of another as the basis for all exchange. The SDL focuses on *operant resources* that are intangible, dynamic resources that are capable of creating value. Thus the service brand and other market-based assets can be considered as operant resources. Recently Mertz et al. (2009) explored how the fundamental premises of SDL relate to branding. Of particular relevance are four premises that Vargo and Lusch (2008) suggest are core to developing a general theory of markets. They are:

FP1: Service is the fundamental basis of exchange.

FP6: The customer is always a co-creator of value.

FP9: All economic and social actors are resource integrators.

FP10: Value is always uniquely determined by the beneficiary.

FP1 highlights the need to focus on the application of knowledge and skills, FP6 emphasizes the interactional nature of value creation, FP9 emphasizes the context of value creation within networks, and FP10 recognizes that value is idiosyncratic. These fundamental premises provide a broad foundation to inform a middle-range theory of marketplace equity.

Further consideration also needs to be given to how a theory of marketplace equity links with more general financial theory about assets and market equity. Srivastava et al.'s (1998) framework uses a planning approach and focuses on cash flow as the determinant of shareholder value. However, there is a choice of other valuation methods including price/earnings multiples, market-to-book value ratios, economic value added (EVA), cash flow return on investment (CFROI), and market value added (MVA) that could be used. Thus the choice of valuation method and the more general issue of how a theory of marketplace equity links with general financial theory require further consideration.

The recent studies on marketing metrics and return on marketing provide some important links to financial theory. For example Rust, Zeithaml and Lemon (2004b) present a unified strategic framework that enables competing marketing strategy options to be traded off on the basis of projected financial return, which is opera-tionalized as the change in a firm's customer equity relative to the incremental expenditure necessary to produce the change. Gummesson (2008) also explores the topic of return on marketing paying attention to the non measurable.

Finally, the development of a theory of marketplace equity provides a number of important managerial implications. As Doyle (2000) has emphasized, this 'new' marketing thinking leads to a better understanding about the role marketing plays in value creation in an organization. Rather than just focusing on brand or customer equity, the theory leads to a more comprehensive framework about the core business processes that create financial value. This framework can be used to explore trade-offs in the way marketing resources can be allocated within a marketing system. The theory provides a better way to understand the extent to which an organization's marketing strategy should focus on end-customers versus investments in channels and other business processes. It also leads to better understanding about how to manage alliance activities with other organizations and relationships with key stake-holders within the organization's network. Thus it can provide a managerial 'outside in' perspective to balance the academic 'inside out' perspective.

Recommended further reading

Aaker, D.A. (1996) *Building Strong Brands*, New York: The Free Press.

Brodie, R.J., Glynn, M.S. and Van Durme, J. (2002) 'Towards a theory of marketplace equity: integrating branding and relationship thinking with financial thinking', *Marketing Theory* 2(1): 5–28.

Brodie R.J., Glynn, M.S. and Little, V. (2006) 'The service brand and the service dominant logic: missing fundamental premise or the need for stronger theory', *Marketing Theory* 6(3): 363–79.

Grönroos, C. (2007) *Service Management and Marketing: A Customer Relationship Management Approach*, 3rd edn, Chichester: Wiley.

Gummesson, E. (2008) *Total Relationship Marketing*, 3rd edn, Oxford: Butterworth Heinemann.

Keller, K.L. (1993) 'Conceptualizing, measuring, and managing customer-based brand equity', *Journal of Marketing* 57(1): 1–22.

Mertz, M.A., He, Yi and Vargo, S.L. (2009) 'The evolving brand logic: a service-dominant perspective', *Journal of the Academy of Marketing Science* 37(3): 328–44.

Rust, R.T., Zeithaml, V.A. and Lemon, K.N. (2000) *Driving Customer Equity: How Customer Lifetime Value is Reshaping Corporate Strategy*. New York: The Free Press.

Srivastava, R.K., Shervani, T.A. and Fahey, L. (1998) 'Market-based assets and share-holder value: a framework for analysis', *Journal of Marketing* 62(1): 2–18.

Vargo, S.L. and Lusch, R.F. (2004) 'Evolving to a new dominant logic for marketing', *Journal of Marketing* 68, January: 1–17.

References

Aaker, D.A. (1996) *Building Strong Brands*, New York: The Free Press.

Ambler, T., Bhattacharya, C.B., Edell, J., Keller, K.L., Lemon, K.N. and Mittal, V. (2002) 'Relating branding and customer perspectives on marketing management', *Journal of Service Research* 5(1): 13–25.

American Marketing Association, (2004) Marketing Definitions: A Glossary of Marketing Terms, Chicago, American Marketing Association.

Anderson, J.C. and Narus, J.A. (1999) *Business Market Management: Understanding, Creating and Delivering Value*, Upper Saddle River, NJ: Prentice Hall.

Bitner, M.J. (1995) 'Building service relationships: it's all about promises', *Journal of Academy of Marketing Science* 23(4): 246–51.

Blattberg, R.C., Getz. G. and Thomas, J.S. (2001) *Customer Equity: Building and Managing Relationships as Valuable Assets*, Boston, MA: Harvard Business School Press.

Brodie R.J., Glynn, M.S. and Little, V. (2006) 'The service brand and the service dominant logic: missing fundamental premise or the need for stronger theory', *Marketing Theory* 6(3): 363–79.

Brodie, R.J., Whittome, J.R.M. and Brush, G.J. (2009) 'Investigating the elements of the service brand: a customer value perspective', *Journal of Business Research* 62: 345–55.

Doyle, P. (2000) 'Value-based marketing', *Journal of Strategic Marketing* 8: 299–311.

Ghosh, M. and John, G. (1999) 'Governance value analysis and marketing strategy', *Journal of Marketing* (special issue) 63: 131–45.

Glynn, M.S., Motion, J.M. and Brodie, R.J. (2007) 'Sources of brand benefits in manufacturer-reseller B2B relationships', *Journal of Business & Industrial Marketing* 22(6): 400–9.

Grönroos, C. (1996) 'Relationship marketing logic', *Asia-Australian Marketing Journal* 4(1): 7–18.

Grönroos, C. (2007) *Service Management and Marketing: A Customer Relationship Management Approach*, 3rd edn, Chichester: Wiley.

Gummesson, E. (2008) *Total Relationship Marketing*, 3rd edn, Oxford: Butterworth Heinemann.

Håkansson, H. and Snehota, I.J. (2000) 'The IMP perspective of assets and liabilities of business relationships', in J.N Sheth and A. Parvatiyar (eds) *Handbook of Relationship Marketing*, Thousand Oaks, CA: Sage.

Heide, J.B. (1994) 'Interorganizational governance in marketing channels', *Journal of Marketing* 58, January: 71–85.

Hunt, S.D. and Morgan, R.M. (1995) 'The comparative advantage theory of competition', *Journal of Marketing* 54, April: 1–18.

Jones, R. (2005) 'Finding sources of brand: developing a stakeholder model of brand equity', *Journal of Brand Management*, 13(1): 10–32.

Keller, K.L. (1993) 'Conceptualizing, measuring, and managing customer-based brand equity', *Journal of Marketing* 57(1): 1–22.

Leone, R.P., Rao, V.R., Keller, K.L., Luo, A.M., McAlister, L. and Srivastava, R. (2006) 'Linking brand equity to customer equity', *Journal of Service Research* 9(2): 125–38.

Merton, R.K. (1967) *On Theoretical Sociology: Five Essays, Old and New*. New York: Free Press.

Mertz, M.A., He, Yi and Vargo, S.L. (2009) 'The evolving brand logic: a service-dominant perspective', *Journal of the Academy of Marketing Science* 37(3): 328–44.

Morgan, R.M. and Hunt, S.D. (1994) 'The commitment–trust theory of relationship marketing', *Journal of Marketing* 58(3): 20–38.

Muniz, A.M., Albert M. and O'Guinn, T.C. (2001) 'Brand community', *Journal of Consumer Research* 27, March: 412–32.

Payne, A.F.T. and Holt, S. (2001) 'Diagnosing customer value: integrating the value process and relationship marketing', *British Journal of Management* 12(2): 159–82.

Rappaport, A. (1986) *Creating Shareholder Value*, New York: The Free Press.

Rust, R.T., Zeithaml, V.A. and Lemon, K.N. (2000) *Driving Customer Equity: How Customer Lifetime Value is Reshaping Corporate Strategy*. New York: The Free Press.

Rust, R.T., Zeithaml, V.A. and Lemon, K.N. (2004a) 'Customer-centered brand management', *Harvard Business Review* 84(9): 11–18.

Rust, R.T., Zeithaml, V.A. and Lemon, K.N. (2004b) 'Return on marketing: using customer equity to focus marketing strategy', *Journal of Marketing* 68, January: 108–27.

Srivastava, R.K., Shervani, T.A. and Fahey, L. (1998) 'Market-based assets and share-holder value: a framework for analysis', *Journal of Marketing* 62(1): 2–18.

Srivastava, R.K., Shervani, T.A. and Fahey, L. (1999) 'Marketing, business processes and shareholder value: an organizationally embedded view of marketing activities and the discipline of marketing', *Journal of Marketing* (special issue) 63: 168–79.

Van Durme, J., Brodie, R.J. and Redmore, D. (2003) 'Brand equity in cooperative business relationships: exploring the development of a conceptual model', *Marketing Theory* 3(1): 37–57.

Vargo, S.L. and Lusch, R.F. (2004) 'Evolving to a new dominant logic for marketing', *Journal of Marketing* 68, January: 1–17.

Vargo, S.L. and Lusch, R.F. (2008) 'Service dominant logic: continuing the evolution', *Journal of the Academy of Marketing Science* 36: 1–10.

Weick, K.E. (1989) 'Theory construction as disciplined imagination', *Academy of Management Review* 14(4): 516–31.

Section E

Postscript – a transition phase in marketing thought

19

The new service marketing

Evert Gummesson

Chapter Topics

Overview

A few years ago it would have been much easier to write this chapter. Marketing of services had established itself and become mainstream. It built on differences between goods and services and their consequences for marketing. This was productive for a period and contributed to a deepened understanding of marketing. The problem was that goods and services and other products such as software, information and knowledge – it has never been agreed if these are goods or services or something very different – always appear together. It has now come to a point where goods and services merge and the recognition of the interdependency between the two is a more productive vantage point.

This means that we have entered a transition phase in marketing thought and the student may easily feel lost in contradictions. The transition will take time, some adopting it quickly, with others still attached to the services marketing from the 1980s and 1990s. To facilitate the student's understanding of the differences between mainstream services marketing and the new service marketing, this chapter will explain both and compare them. The chapter therefore starts with a background to the ongoing changes in the perception of service and services and proceeds with a review of the contributions of mainstream services marketing. The second half of the chapter is assigned to the drivers of a new service logic and how this logic enters into the new service marketing. The chapter wraps up with views on the future.

From the marketing of services to the new service marketing

The 1970s was a milestone in marketing. The hegemony of the 1960s marketing management began to crack when conceptualization of services marketing gathered a critical mass of researchers from Europe and the US. It happened in conflict with mainstream marketing management where consumer goods were the focal point of interest. Official statistics had long shown that the service sector, including private and government providers, accounted for the larger part of economic activity. Despite this, services were absent in marketing textbooks. On the other hand, service practitioners had found limited inspiration in marketing theory and advice. Hotels, airlines, consultants and others developed their own practices. Until the 1970s, marketing scholars had failed to note these signs.

Gradually the way was paved for a new tradition in marketing theory, referred to as services marketing or service management and marketing. The latter expression emphasized interfunctional dependency and the avoidance of organizational silos; contributions from human resources, organization, operations management, quality management, and other areas were needed to put services marketing activities in context. This was further supported by recognizing that consumption sometimes (but not always) takes place simultaneously with the customer's active participation in production and delivery.

This observation led to an innovation, *the service encounter*, as a platform for service providers and customers to build interactive relationships. At the same time a school of thought in business-to-business (B2B) marketing began to stress networks between organizational sellers and buyers as the key to efficient marketing, purchasing and resource utilization. Through these contributions *relationships*, *networks* and *interaction* stood out as overriding concepts in marketing. This conclusion has been further reinforced by the internet, e-mail and other information technology (IT) applications.

Inspired by these developments *relationship marketing*, CRM *(customer relationship management)* and *one-to-one marketing* had their breakthrough in the 1990s. With some differences in emphasis all three stress the creation and maintenance of long-term relationships with individual customers. These dimensions of marketing were missing in research and education. Successful practitioners, on the other hand, have always known that relationships with customers and the interaction in networks are fundamental in business. Again, marketing theory and education showed a blind spot.

The new millennium started with a gradual change in our perception of what suppliers deliver and where and when service, value, quality, excellence and customer satisfaction are brought into being. The circle is closed. From an initial focus on goods marketing the focus went to services marketing and now the two have merged on a higher level of understanding, the new service marketing. It prepares the ground for more general, valid and relevant marketing theory.

Above all, three developments are turning the tide. They will be explained later in the chapter but a brief introductory characteristic of them will facilitate the reading. The first, *service-dominant (S-D) logic*, merges goods and services into value propositions and the outcome of economic activity is defined as service and value, no matter if it is based on what is traditionally called services or goods. S-D logic acknowledges the crucial role of the customer in co-creating service. The second is *service science* which aims to develop our ability to design and maintain efficient and innovative service systems. The third, *many-to-many marketing*, is based on the application of network theory to marketing, putting emphasis on the relational, complex and contextual aspects.

In the next sections the characteristics of services marketing as it developed from the 1970s until the 2000s will be reviewed. The vantage point for services marketing was the existence of a service sector of identifiable services. Services were claimed to have certain unique traits that made them different from goods. With the spotlight on differences we learnt new lessons which we should now bring forward to the new service marketing. The marketing of services also established a mythology about goods/services differences that we now carry as a burden. It needs to be weeded out of the minds of researchers, educators, textbook writers and practitioners to form a new era.

The service sector: from garbage can to universal sector

Official statistics report changes in three economic sectors: the manufacturing/industrial sector; the service sector; and the agricultural sector. Once everything was agriculture (including fishing, hunting and forestry). The Industrial Revolution swung the economy towards manufacturing and the industrial sector grew. What was not allocated to these two sectors was labelled miscellaneous, intangibles, invisibles, the tertiary sector and later the service sector. Numerous efforts to define the sector have been made with limited success. Service sector statistics include: trade; hotels and restaurants; transport (including tourism, travel agencies, tour operators); storage and communication; financial services; real estate and dwellings; business services (e.g. accounting, software development, management consultancy, technical consultancy); public administration; defence; education; health services; religious and other community services; legal services; recreation; entertainment; and personal services. What is meant, for example, by 'communication' and 'personal services' and where the internet and the web come in is far from obvious. No wonder that the service sector may seem like a garbage can.

Today official statistics report that the service sector in developed economies is growing while the manufacturing and agricultural sectors are shrinking. Then consider that we:

- never had so many goods and so much product waste

- never had so much food and were never so fat – but at the same time undernourished

- lack basic services such as healthcare for everyone, affordable care for the elderly, good schools, security in the streets, and working legal systems.

The sector definitions are diffuse and arbitrary compromises. For example, a restaurant offers agricultural and manufactured products, and has its own in-house manufacturing plant, the kitchen. Waiters take orders and bring the food and drink to the table. The food cannot be excluded – then it is no restaurant – but the service can be cut down to a minimum. The guests can pick the food themselves at lavish buffets in high-class restaurants or at the counter in cheap fast-food outlets. All the same the restaurant is referred to the service sector.

Scales are presented that range from pure goods to pure services. They may sound compelling but what marketing strategies and action can they inspire? One 'continuum' puts clothing as the pure goods extreme and a visit to the psychiatrist as the pure services extreme. However, retailing offers conveniently located stores which surround clothing with different types of service, from the availability of cheap ready-to-wear and self-service in special fitting-rooms to expensive made-to-measure with assistance in selecting suitable designs. Huge resources are put into clothes brands to fit lifestyle, luxury, romance and sex. The service of the shrink is more often than not a prescription for manufactured pills. It is not possible to 'purify' goods and services.

As the service sector is now defined, 80–90 per cent of all people employed work in services and all new jobs come from services. Keeping in mind how arbitrary the definitions of the economic sectors are and that they do not acknowledge the interdependence between goods, services and other phenomena, the sector division is meaningless for marketers. It has lost its ability to discriminate, which is the meaning of categorization.

The former special case of the service sector has now become the universal case. The way service is being re-conceptualized in the new service marketing – to signify value to customers and complex networks of stakeholders – moves the focus to users without losing sight of suppliers.

What should replace the three economic categories then? Nothing, really, these overriding categories do not serve any purpose. We should talk about healthcare as healthcare and not mix it into a service sector with hamburger restaurants, lawyers and sports events. But even healthcare is so diverse that the category has little meaning. It could be divided into private and government hospitals, physicians' offices, nursing facilities, health insurers and diagnostic labs. It could be divided by type of illness and type of therapy as it is experienced by patients. Performing eye surgery is very different from cosmetic surgery, the treatment of gastric disorders, stopping contagious global epidemics, or offering pain relief. Take another example, the housing sector. It consists of the subsectors and professions of building and construction; building supplies; real estate and mortgage brokers; furniture and appliance manufacturing and distribution; home-supply stores; architects; and interior designers. If we build or repair a house we may need all or part of this. The subsectors and professionals are each operating in their special market contexts requiring different marketing skills and strategies.

A recent addition to the service sector is administrative routines and internal services that have progressively been incorporated to form subsidiaries or are outsourced to independent providers. Examples are computer support, property maintenance, security and cleaning. It means re-registration in the official statistics, augmenting the service sector and reducing the manufacturing sector. The same or similar service is still performed but the hidden services have become visible in the market and are often exposed to competition.

Service sector classifications are concerned with macro level criteria whereas in marketing practice micro level criteria must be considered. Several such efforts were made, for example pinpointing the difference in marketing high versus low contact services, or frequently versus infrequently bought services. It is evident that the diversity within services requires specific marketing solutions for each instance and context. Knowledge of the conditions of a particular service, its provision and markets, is necessary in order to design a proper marketing plan and marketing organization.

Alleged differences between goods and services

In mainstream services marketing literature and education the big issue is differences between goods and services and what effect these may have on marketing strategies and customer behaviour. Unfortunately the 'differences' are seldom well grounded in empirical data and experience. They are generalized far beyond their capacity to discriminate between goods and services, but they may appear together with a plethora of other dimensions in specific marketing situations.

The 'differences' form the introduction to almost every mainstream textbook and chapter on services marketing. They are listed below with examples and their usefulness or inadequacy is exemplified:

- Services are characterized by *intangibility*; goods by *tangibility*. The idea is that services are activities and processes that cannot be touched – for example, the service of getting a meal to your table or an opera performance. A surgeon is in a healthcare service but it seems odd that the service of cutting your belly open, messing around with your physical organs and then suturing your belly together again, could be perceived by either the provider or the patient as intangible. Could it be more tangible? Further, it has often been claimed that services do not need investment in tangible goods to the same degree as manufacturing; services are performed by people and service firms are thus people-intensive while manufacturing is capital-intensive. Then just consider the enormous investment in tangible goods of an airport and an airline in order to make the flying service possible, and the high-tech hardware necessary to make internet and mobile service possible.

- Services are characterized by *heterogeneity, variability* or *non-standardization*; goods by *homogeneity* and *standardization*. This is based on the observation that services are often performed by people and goods are primarily produced by machines. People are individuals who tend to do it their way based on differences in competence, willingness to serve, mood swings and so on. Thanks to IT, service can increasingly be performed in a strictly standardized mode. This is often called 'mass customization', which seems like a paradox. By, for example, withdrawing money from a cash machine, millions of standardized services are performed every day. Although it is standardized mass production, the service is adapted to each customer by considering the sum to be withdrawn, the customer's personal account and its balance, and the time and place for withdrawal. Goods manufacturing can be extremely standardized and even live up to a zero defects strategy.

- Services are characterized by *inseparability* between production, delivery and consumption, also expressed as *simultaneity*; goods by *separability* as goods are produced without the presence of the customer. This service encounter is characterized by interaction between: (1) the supplier's contact personnel (the front line) and the customer; (2) those customers who are present at a specific place and point of time – customer-to-customer (C2C) interaction, for example in a retail store or on a ferry; (3) the customer and the supplier's products and physical environment, the servicescape, which is recognition that physical objects play a role in services marketing; and (4) the customer and the supplier's service system which consists of the logic through which all bits and pieces of a service have been put together to form a coherent network. In many businesses the service encounter constitutes the essence of its marketing but it is not limited to services in the mainstream sense. This will be further explained later in the chapter.

- Services are characterized by *perishability* meaning that they cannot be stored; goods by *non-perishability*. The rationale behind this claim is that a service expires if not used immediately, for example a hair stylist who has no customers at a particular time cannot just style a few heads and store them on a shelf, waiting for buyers to come. On the other hand service can be stored in systems and equipment and a provider's preparedness to perform the service when a customer enters. Although many manufactured goods can be stored, some goods are highly perishable like fresh fish, not to mention oysters. Furthermore, long storage can cause damage; fashion clothes become unfashionable after the season is over and can then only be put on sale at 50 per cent or more discount; and it is costly to store because it ties up capital and physical space. A current 'good' example is the market for passenger cars that went down by 50 per cent in 2008–2009. Where should the cars be stored, what damage will they be exposed to during the storage, what is the cost of storing them, and will they become obsolete?

- An additional dimension that was noted early on but then somehow got lost claims that services are characterized by *non-ownership* and goods by *ownership*. Services are often borrowed or rented, like you pay for a day in a theme park, a night in a hotel room or two hours in a cinema seat. A car can be rented and is then referred to the service sector, while if you buy the car it is a deal with the manufacturing sector. In both cases it is about the same core service, transportation. And how many of the goods we have are owned? A car may be leased or bought with money from a bank loan and most homes are mortgaged. In legal terms they are not owned by the customers although they talk about 'my car' and 'my house'. But again, goods and services are there to provide service in some kind of functional combination, and it is the combination that is marketed and bought.

The first four are the top listed differences between goods and service that built a foundation for mainstream services marketing. Intangibility, heterogeneity and perishability will not be brought forward in the new service marketing except as possible dimensions in contingent marketing situations. Inseparability and the service encounter on the other hand bring out the customer's interactive role in all business and not least in marketing, and are reinforced by IT applications. The ownership issue deserves increased attention in the new service marketing. It is a pricing and financial aspect with a huge impact on customer behaviour. The generosity with which mortgages were granted in the US, the subprime loans, was one of the major triggers of the global financial crisis that broke out in 2008.

Quality, excellent service and value

Quality management and the definition of quality went through a revival in the 1980s. In marketing, quality had been used in a loose sense; it was primarily a technical issue for manufacturing. Service quality had not been dealt with in an organized way and was a constant cause for complaints from customers and citizens.

Defining quality is not so easy as it is multifaceted and related to other phenomena such as satisfaction and value. One distinction is between *quality-in-fact*, which is primarily technical, measurable and objective, and *quality-in-perception*, which is primarily relational, perceptual and subjective. These two are in interaction, though. For example, the delay of a flight can be objectively measured in minutes but the delay is perceived differently if the cabin crew is helpful or indifferent.

In the new service marketing, value has taken over as the key concept. Value is dependent on the circumstances; it is *value-in-context* (Vargo et al., 2008). For a business, value is when customers buy what it sells at a price that leaves a profit. For a consumer value is actualized when you use what you bought.

Services marketing addressed quality by means of the disconfirmation paradigm. It meant that customers have expectations which they compare with their experience of a service and than determine whether their expectations are confirmed or disconfirmed. Ideally there is no gap between the expectations and the experience or the experience exceeds expectations. Marketing can influence customer expectations through, for example, promises in the promotion of the service, and by handling customer relationships well during the service performance. A common problem is the tendency of marketing to overpromise to get an order, leaving the customer dissatisfied and thus jeopardizing long-term relationships.

In earlier publications on the marketing of services I have talked about 'service quality, productivity and profitability' as the triplets, 'separating one from the other makes an unhappy family'. But quality became the pet of services marketing and productivity and profitability were kept at arm's length. However, the disconfirmation paradigm is equally valid for goods.

Today I prefer to call this section 'Quality, excellent service and value'. This is influenced by the new service logic but influences also come from other directions. One is the Malcolm Baldrige National Quality Award which was first handed out in the US in 1988. It approached quality in a holistic way, embracing not only traditional technical dimensions but also such areas as quality of leadership, employee training and marketing, and it put an emphasis on productivity and profitability. It inspired a global upsurge in quality awards but gradually these found difficulties with the broadened quality concept. The Baldrige went over to talking about performance excellence and the European Quality Award changed its name to the EFQM (European Foundation for Quality Management) Excellence Award. Simply put, all these concepts – quality, satisfaction, excellence, value – try to pinpoint whether something is good or bad. They do it from slightly different but overlapping angles. In everyday language we say that the quality of the food in the restaurant was good, so-so, or bad; that we are dissatisfied with our hotel room; that our house has an excellent heating system; and that our new car is good value for money. The list of these everyday expressions is long.

Productivity has little tradition in services but a long tradition in manufacturing. It is defined as the ratio between output and input; the less input of resources (cost) for manufacturing a unit of a product, the higher the productivity. Eventually a business firm has to make a profit to survive and therefore quality and productivity must be linked to *profitability*. In similar vein government operations and NGOs without a profit motive have to make ends meet, which is controlled through budgeting. The linking of quality, productivity and profitability has turned out to be hard work and is not yet successfully managed. For marketing, service quality and productivity affect the price level, margins, sales volume, and competitiveness in general.

In the new service marketing, part of the value co-creation is in interaction within a network of customers, intermediaries, computers, transport companies, factories, and so on. Although mainstream services marketing defined the service encounter and recognized the customer's role, quality and productivity measurements did not include the customer's contribution, thus making them less valid.

For too long services marketing became preoccupied with customer satisfaction measured through statistical surveys and scales. This drew the attention from more intricate and fundamental issues. Among them are the *design and engineering of service systems*, the very topic of service science. Service systems are often launched without proper design and tests of their workability in practical situations. The goods part of a service is usually much better engineered and tested, based on a long tradition in manufacturing. Efforts were made with service flowcharts or blueprints where service activities and customer interaction were defined and analysed for more efficient ways of performing a service. They were excellent contributions but required technical and specific knowledge and hard empirical and analytical work. Such studies became too complex and demanding for academic service researchers and remained in the background.

As service quality was claimed to be different from goods quality, special service quality dimensions were established. The survey technique Servqual first listed 10 'general' dimensions and later reduced them to five. One was 'tangibles', a modest recognition of the goods part of an offering. It always ranked lowest in the surveys, a fact that should make one suspicious. Consider this: is the technical quality of an aircraft – the engine, the seats, leg space and food – low-ranking, even negligible? Of course not.

Service quality focused more on quality-in-perception and treated the technical aspects and quality-in-fact lightly. Among the specific service quality dimensions were reliability, sensitivity, competence, availability, pleasant behaviour, communication, credibility, security, and recovery (compensation for bad service). In contrast, the manufacturing quality tradition listed performance, features, conformance to specification, durability and aesthetics as central. IT quality did not enter the service agenda until the breakthrough of the internet in the 1990s. For services delivered through the web, e-mail and mobile phones quick response, assistance, flexibility, ease of navigation, efficiency, security, clearly stated prices, and adaptation for individual customer use, have been found to be important.

Lists such as these can offer guidance but each company must define those dimensions that are specific to its actual situation; the effect of the combined dimensions is contextual. Caution should be exerted in ranking the dimensions as they are interdependent. They can all contribute to the quality of the total value proposition and appear in a huge variety of combinations.

Several claims about service quality do not stand the test of time. Their departure from courses and textbooks is already long overdue. Among them are the following:

- *Service quality is difficult to determine while goods quality is easy.* This is built on the obsolete idea that goods are manufactured in standardized components by easily controlled machines whereas services are 'handmade' by erratic human beings.

- *Service quality cannot be assessed before consumption while goods quality can.* This builds on the misunderstanding that it is easy to assess the quality of a product 'as it is tangible'. More realistically, consumers understand very little about the technical quality of a car and therefore buy on trust for the brand and under considerable stress and insecurity. Among the few quality properties we can assess are size and colour. Not even the fuel consumption can be checked until the car has been used for some time as it also depends on driving style. In light of the definition of service where the customer is co-creator, the quality of a car is variable and dependent on the way the customer creates value for himself or herself.

- *Better quality costs more.* This taken-for-granted assumption has persisted around quality and may still be around. If true, quality improvements lead to rising prices with a negative effect on sales volume and competitiveness. The good news is that it isn't true. Better quality sometimes costs more, sometimes the same and sometimes less; there are only specific instances. Quality in the form of a bigger hotel room can be more expensive for obvious reasons. A smarter service system reduces the cost of breakdowns, complaints from dissatisfied customers and rework. By improving the technical quality a supplier may save money without lowering the price, which adds to profit.

- *Service productivity does not improve whereas goods productivity keeps improving at a rapid rate.* This is often presented as a shortcoming of the service sector. Productivity indicators have to be adapted to service in the new sense to be meaningful. Productivity is easiest to measure and control when something can be broken down in detail and linked together in one single best sequence. This works well in a factory but is not applicable to the same extent in the less controllable situations of service where the customer is a co-creator. Further, when a manual service like washing was packaged in a machine, the gains were not credited to the service sector.

Marketing mix versus a relational paradigm

In the core of traditional marketing management is the marketing mix, mostly described as a combination of the 4P strategies: *product, price, promotion* and *place*. It was partly taken over by service research and 'product' was made to include services.

The marketing mix has been criticized for being incomplete and manipulative, not properly considering the needs of the customer. *The marketing concept* states that once you know your customers, you can design, price, promote and distribute a product that matches these needs and then become a success in the marketplace. The seller is the active party and the customer is persuaded to buy. The basis of the marketing mix is mass manufacturing and standardized consumer goods. It was never wholly embraced by service firms who found it difficult to apply in practice.

To overcome some of their limitations, the 4Ps were expanded into the 7Ps by adding *participants* (or *people*), *physical evidence* (later referred to as *servicescape*), and *processes*. Although adding Ps has a certain pedagogical appeal it should not form a strategy for theory development; other avenues have to be explored. Such alternatives are found within the relational paradigm which had a breakthrough in the 1990s. As an alternative to the marketing mix, the core of marketing can now be perceived as *relationships, networks* and *interaction*. In the 2000s special attention is given to interaction in S-D logic and to networks in many-to-many marketing.

To some extent the service Ps incorporate relationships and interaction through 'participants' and 'processes' (customers participating in a service process). In addition, relationship marketing emphasizes a long-term interactive relationship between the service provider and the customer and long-term profitability. Relationships need not be restricted to the customer–supplier dyad. Many-to-many marketing adds the more realistic network aspect, recognizing that in today's complex economies we are embedded in networks of stakeholders. In these networks customers are exposed to a bundle of service systems, an issue that is at the core of service science.

The relational paradigm recognizes that both the customer and the seller are active parties. Furthermore, consumers and suppliers should be treated as equal partners, albeit with different objectives. Both should find a relationship rewarding; it should be a win–win relationship. In this spirit, the Ritz-Carlton hotel chain created the now classic but highly relevant catch-phrase: 'We are ladies and gentlemen serving ladies and gentlemen'.

Organizing for service marketing

Mainstream services marketing never offered general guidelines for the services marketing organization nor prescribed in what way it should be different from a goods marketing organization. There is considerable practical knowledge about how to organize, for example, the marketing of hotels, cleaning services or professional services. The difficulty is that it is not possible to give general advice and that the difference is not between goods and services marketing but between other specific properties such as company size, target groups, market conditions and kind of value proposition.

An organization is traditionally built around functions but can also be built around service systems and be perceived as a set of networks. For example, major full service airlines ran into hard competition from small, no-frills airlines with limited service and low fares. Ryanair was one of the first companies to concentrate on their website for information and ticket sales, thus controlling the fares and being able to instantly adjust them according to supply and demand. They organized themselves around this marketing system and the core service of transportation. Big full-service airlines were organized to inform and sell through travel agencies and serve numerous destinations. Ryanair recently surpassed British Airways in number of passengers and long since in profitability; small and agile has become big in a short time.

An organization is a complex network of relationships, systems, processes and functions that gradually transcend into the market and society. The boundary between a company and its environment is diffuse. Three organizational strategies which have developed over a number of years are applicable to the new service marketing and in line with many-to-many marketing:

- *Decentralization and multiplication of a global business concept to local markets.* Large companies are decentralized because of the need for local presence, for example, a retail chain or a firm of accountants. For them growth is a matter of multiplying a well defined business concept to more sites. Franchising, like 7-Eleven and The Body Shop, has proved to be a viable concept as it unites the marketing muscle of a large-scale operation with the agility of small scale and closeness to customers. Direct selling through door-to-door and home parties is a smaller but expanding way of multiplying a business concept with special significance in new economies where entrepreneurship and small business must be encouraged with little financial investment. Even if IT is partially independent of physical presence, it will never make the need for physical proximity between suppliers and customers redundant.

- *Part-time marketers (PTMs) and full-time marketers (FTMs).* The marketing and sales departments, which are populated by FTMs, are unable to handle more than a limited portion of the marketing. They cannot always be in the right place at the right time with the right customer contact. As a consequence of the embeddedness of marketing in the network organization everyone else becomes a PTM, one who is not hired specifically for marketing and sales tasks but in the co-creative processes with customers interacts with them and thus influences their buying behaviour. Although the PTMs were hired for other tasks they have to be aware of their part-time role and be recruited, trained and motivated accordingly, whatever their main job is.

- *Internal marketing.* Services marketing came up with the idea of applying marketing techniques to internal markets, the employees. If a company has 50,000 employees spread in 50 countries it has a huge problem to communicate with the organization. Internal marketing can be used to empower and enable employees. They should understand the company mission, the organization, the service that can be provided, the value it has to customers, and finally, how to interact with customers. They should behave in a way that creates positive rapport with customers and a long-term relationship.

Three drivers of the new service marketing

As was outlined initially, three contributions in particular are the drivers of the reinvention of service and marketing.

S-D logic was first proposed in a 2004 article by Steve Vargo and Bob Lusch in the *Journal of Marketing*. It took the authors five years to get the article accepted for publication but it had an overnight impact on the readers. S-D logic has quickly gained acceptance among marketing scholars and is being continually developed (see Vargo and Lusch, 2008a, 2008b).

While S-D logic emanates from the scholarly world, *Service Science, Management, and Engineering (SSME)*, usually just referred to as *service science*, emanates from a practitioner, IBM. For decades IBM was the world's largest manufacturer of computer hardware. After a crisis it turned to software and consultancy and with its 380,000 employees it is now a global leader in service systems. The service science programme works globally to engage academic researchers and educators in universities and technical institutes to add service to the research agenda and curriculum. The goal is to design, innovate and implement better service systems (see Maglio and Spohrer, 2008).

Many-to-many marketing applies network theory to marketing. Network thinking has long been used in B2B marketing, albeit in a limited way. Now the application of networks embraces all marketing and the new service marketing. It is a further development of relationship marketing, going from the two-party relationship of a single supplier and a single buyer, one-to-one, to the multi-party realism of today's marketing, many-to-many. It's a head-on approach to the complexity, context, systems, relationships and interactions of business and consumption.

These developments have been brewing for decades but the time has not been ripe for them to assume a lead role – until now. They are supportive of each other but emphasize different fundamental facets of service and marketing. They have already been mentioned in the comparison between mainstream services marketing and the new service marketing but will now be further explained and analysed.

Service-dominant (S-D) logic

S-D logic defines itself through 10 foundational premises (Table 19.1). These are the basis for a new philosophy and theory of service and marketing.

According to the first foundational premise (FP1), service is in the core of exchange, not goods as in the hitherto goods-dominant (G-D) logic. Note that it is 'service' and not 'services versus goods'; goods are merely distribution mechanisms for service (FP3). For example, a car is a distribution mechanism for transportation and a carrot for nutrients. Exchange between parties, which once was direct and local, is masked by the complexity of a network of production and distributions processes (FP2). The logistics and the number of parties involved have increased through specialization, outsourcing, globalization, and owner and alliances combinations. It is not just a customer meeting a supplier.

Table 19.1   Foundational premises (FP) of S-D logic.

FP1	Service is the fundamental basis of exchange.
FP2	Indirect exchange masks the fundamental basis of exchange.
FP3	Goods are a distribution mechanism for service provision.
FP4	Operant resources are the fundamental source of competitive advantage.
FP5	All economies are service economies.
FP6	The customer is always a co-creator of value.
FP7	The enterprise cannot deliver value, but only offer value propositions.
FP8	A service-centred view is inherently customer oriented and relational.
FP9	All social and economic actors are resource integrators.
FP10	Value is uniquely and phenomenologically determined by the beneficiary.

Source: Adapted from Vargo and Lusch, 2008a.

Operant resources (FP4) are those which do something to something or somebody. Businesses and customers are operant resources meaning that they both act, using their knowledge and skills. This is contrary to the mainstream marketing idea that suppliers do things to customers who just react as *operand resources*. All economies are *service economies* as their mission is to provide service to someone (FP5). In line with this, the customer is always a *co-creator of value* (FP6). The customers create value themselves and in partial interaction with suppliers as the service encounter indicates. Within this spirit a supplier can only offer *value propositions* on the market (FP7); the value is actualized by users.

As the customer is actively involved in creating and using service in search of value, service has moved from being production centric to become customer centric (FP8). Service is only partially created in the supplier value chain; it is ultimately created in the customer's value network. It follows from the new role allocated to customers that they are social and economic resource integrators in order to evoke the value of service (FP9). The network aspect is implicit through the statement that all social and economic actors are resource integrators – suppliers, customers, intermediaries, governments, the media and others – implying that value creation takes place through interaction in complex networks. Finally, value is defined by those who need the service. Therefore service is individual and contextual (FP10).

The premises may require additional background to be better understood. S-D logic is based on international findings during the heyday of services marketing, the 1980s and the1990s, and even from before that. The fact that goods and services appear together had disturbed many over the years but it was not until conceptualized in the S-D logic that the many scattered thoughts and observations fell into place. For example, efforts had been made to get *product* accepted as a joint term for goods and services and to use *offering, package* or *solution* as all inclusive concepts for what the customer buys. It did not work because there was no framework for goods and services in which to co-exist.

The B2B acronym does not disclose if the first B represents the supplier or the customer. In line with the S-D logic premise of co-creation of value, I would like the acronym for business-to-consumer, B2C, to be expanded to B2C/C2B. Just saying B2C underscores the traditional marketing notion of the seller being the active (operant) resource and the buyer the passive (operand) resource. With co-creation of value in focus, either party can switch from the driver's seat to being a passenger and back again.

In the section about quality it was mentioned that several words are commonly used to define phenomena associated with satisfaction and value. We feel the presence of these phenomena; they are all over but it seems impossible to pinpoint exactly what they *really* are. This may simply be so because they are not exact; they are fuzzy and overlapping by nature. Through S-D logic, the concepts of service and value in particular have caught the attention of marketers. We have already discussed what service is in the new marketing. It now feels urgent to add some more comments about value.

Value means different things to suppliers and customers depending on their different goals and environment; this has already been labelled value-in-context. Value in the terms of the traditional value chain as defined by Michel Porter is the same as cost. When cost is added it is euphemistically called value-added. In similar vein many nations collect sales tax based on cost and it is called value added tax, VAT. For companies there can also be other values than money, such as enjoying a great reputation, being the pride of the owners, being popular among job applicants, and so on. A conflicting force is the trend to allocate all the attention to short-term profit and shareholder value. At the same time owners become increasingly anonymous and therefore owner pride and responsibility are vanishing concepts. An exception is the value of the brand, brand equity, which is gradually entering accounting, and the balanced scorecard is trying to establish the future financial value of customers, employees, and innovation, among other things.

Although the traditional value chain stops when the customer enters we can tie in with a customer value chain (or rather network). B2B buyers buy in order to produce or distribute value for themselves and for consumers and citizens. For consumers and citizens value should match their needs and wants. The financial side – the price and the costs associated with using some products – becomes a substantial part of the consumer's sacrifice in using and enjoying a value proposition and the service it renders. For example, buying a car is officially classified as the outcome of goods marketing, renting a car as the outcome of services marketing. But for each individual, customer value is created in his or her interaction with the car. It is driving the car to a desired destination; driving the car well or badly; taking good care of it or neglecting its maintenance; praising its convenience, or cursing traffic jams, absence of parking space, and rising petrol prices; enjoying music and the privacy of the enclosed space, or getting bored by long, lonely hours on straight highways… The car remains a value proposition whether it is driver owned, owned by your employer, bought with borrowed money, leased, rented or borrowed from your parents.

The next two topics, service science and many-to-many marketing are very much in alignment with S-D logic. To show the compatibility between the three drivers a concluding section deals with them in a joint context.

Service science

Service science and its approach to service systems is best described by IBM's service research programme director Jim Spohrer and his colleague Paul Maglio:

> **Service systems are value-co-creation configurations of people, technology, value propositions connecting internal and external service systems, and shared information (e.g. language, laws, measures, and methods). Service science is the study of service systems, aiming to create a basis for systematic service innovation. Service science combines organization and human understanding with business and technological understanding to categorize and explain the many types of service systems that exist as well as how service systems interact and evolve to co-create value. The goal is to apply scientific understanding to advance our ability to design, improve, and scale service systems. (Maglio and Spohrer, 2008: 18)**

Service science offers a global development programme. It is a call for academia, industry and governments to become more systematic about service performance and innovation. It is a proposed academic discipline and research area that would complement – rather than replace – the many disciplines that contribute to knowledge about service. Service science has adopted S-D logic as its philosophy.

By engaging more than 250 universities and institutes of technology in service science, IBM is using the network strategy of adding resources at very low cost and with little financial commitment. IBM is co-creating value with the academic world.

Service science is needed to master seamless and reliable service systems at a time when systems are becoming increasingly complex and global, making us increasingly vulnerable to systems sluggishness and failure. Service science puts particular emphasis on the dual roles of the traditional supplier and customer; both assume both these roles. Every service system then is a provider *and* a client of service connected by value propositions in value chains, value networks, or value-creating systems.

Service science is a godsend for implementing S-D logic and many-to-many marketing. The road is long though; marketing theory and education have for too long been insensitive to the signals from society and business practice.

Many-to-many marketing

Relationship marketing and CRM focus on the two-party relationship between a customer and a supplier. Many-to-many marketing broadens the context to multi-party relationships. It is defined in the following way: 'Many-to-many marketing describes, analyses and utilizes the network properties of marketing'. (Gummesson, 2008)

For example, in a B2B relationship two companies in a selling and buying negotiating stage are backed by many people and influences. They each represent their own many-headed organization, membership of alliances, commitment to other suppliers and intermediaries, and so on. It is not just one-to-one; it is many meeting many. Shopping consumers, B2C/C2B, can represent a family, buy for their children and dog, and are influenced by advice from friends and the lifestyle groups to which they belong. A consumer network co-creates value with a retailer network.

As marketing and value-creation through service systems is complex, complexity should be an overriding issue for the new service marketing. To handle real world complexity and scientific requirements *case study research* and *network theory* could be used. Many universities accept the use of case study research in marketing while others consider statistical techniques, such as surveys, to be more scientific. The weakness with the statistical techniques is that they cannot handle the complexity of service systems and the new service marketing.

Network theory offers a way of thinking in relationships and interaction but also techniques for addressing complexity, context and change. It can be used with different degrees of sophistication: a verbal treatise (discussion or text), graphics (from sketches of nodes and links to computer generated diagrams) and mathematical processing. In marketing, network theory has mainly been applied to B2B but has equal potential for B2C/C2B and consequently to marketing in general. Marketing is part of or a perspective on management and to become efficient marketing should be seen in a management context; it's marketing-oriented management rather than marketing management. Combining case study research with network theory can resolve much of this conflict. In practical marketing complexity has to be handled whether it fits our preconceived ideas or not. It is about survival.

Service systems quickly become complex. Even the simple micro service system of buying a ticket consists of many parts that must work smoothly together. Service delivered through machines is often very simple and can be performed by unskilled labour. All the same it took 50 or more years to design the service system that makes up a washing machine. It required herds of engineers, high-tech and low-tech, electro-mechanics and IT, to eventually assemble this household appliance into a reliable and efficient service provider. But the service is co-created with the consumer who has to feed and instruct the machine and then has to continue the service process after the washing and perhaps drying; the machine cannot handle the whole process.

There are also supportive macro service systems – infrastructure – making it possible for people and companies to function. The national and global financial systems are part of an infrastructure which is beridden with problems, the major one being that it is complex, dynamic through transactions every split second 24/7, and that it is non-transparent and can be tampered with by insiders. In 2008 the world economic system started to break down and the fragility of the financial infrastructure became visible to everyone. More stability is found in the almost 200-year-old railway infrastructure that is constantly being upgraded to fit new customer demands of comfort, speed and environmental considerations. The European Union, EU, is an economic and political infrastructure. Through the implementation of its 'four freedoms' – free movement of goods, services, people and money across the national borders of member states – gradually new opportunities open up for marketers.

New infrastructures do not emerge often but they have a major impact on society, business and marketing. The newest is of course IT. Its interactive C2C part, the social media, is currently growing rapidly. As stated in a newsletter from the service science programme (SSME, May 15, 2009):

> **Social media refers to a conversational, distributed mode of content generation, dissemination, and communication among communities. Recent years have witnessed tremendous growth of social media through platforms and applications enabled by the Web and mobile technologies (for example, weblogs, microblogs, online forums, wiki, podcasts, lifestreams, social bookmarks, Web communities, social networking, and avatar-based virtual reality). Social media is a tremendous asset for understanding various social phenomena and has found applications in a wide spectrum of problem domains, including business computing, entertainment, politics and public policy, and homeland security.**

It offers a new social and market order.

Social sciences, including marketing, management and economics, dodge complexity by straightening out the road they travel. Research and practice in marketing can be compared to driving a wreck on a dirt road but social sciences behave as if they were driving a new Lexus hybrid on a straight and empty highway under perfect weather conditions. This means that curves, loose gravel, holes in the road, wet or icy spots, crossing animals, imperfections of the car, and not least other cars, are largely disregarded. Practitioners have to take the consequences while marketing theorists don't; book-smarts aren't enough. Driving the wreck requires street-smarts to handle unforeseen situations by using experience, common sense, intuition, hunches, gut feelings, reflexes, wisdom, insight and sound judgement. Book-smarts and street-smarts should not be too far apart, and better book-smarts could help avoid the pitfalls of spur of the moment street-smarts.

Network thinking and many-to-many marketing has ramifications for organizing marketing. In American terminology a company is led by a Chief Executive Officer, CEO, and the former Marketing Director is now called Chief Marketing Officer, CMO. It does not fit the view of the new service marketing. My suggestion is instead that they are renamed *Network Executive Officer*, NEO, and *Network Marketing Officer*, NMO, thus establishing that interacting in networks of complex relationships is their main task. That's what they do in practice anyway.

Connecting the drivers

S-D logic, service science and many-to-many marketing are viable syntheses and additions on the way to marketing theory on a higher level of generalization and abstraction – grand theory. The new developments draw on lessons from G-D marketing management, services marketing and relationship marketing. The three drivers are interdependent and they should be treated in an integrative spirit. S-D logic dissolves the divides between goods/services and supplier/customer into co-created service and value. It offers a philosophy for service science and its application in education, research and practice in its effort to create hassle-free, innovative service systems. Network theory is a systemic way of thinking, a methodology to go beyond fragmented research in management and marketing, and to address complexity and context for application on service systems.

The following case study offers a flavour of how the three contributions may appear in a real-life situation (based on Gummesson, 2010).

Case study 19.1

Eighty-two-year old Anna has 23 age-related disorders including fatigue, pain, memory loss, and reduced eyesight and hearing. She has been through 11 different therapies encompassing 41 components. During one year she was exposed to 7 types of therapies performed by 55 specialists. From 5 doctors she has been prescribed 9 types of medication to be consumed daily, and 2 to be used on demand. She regularly goes to massage and physical exercise, and twice a week a social assistant comes to her home to help. Assistants stay for only short periods on the job and new ones appear constantly. Anna is also dependent on social insurance people – who also come and go. Apart from all these contacts with people, Anna is exposed to an endless amount of capital goods (huge hospital buildings, x-ray equipment, operating theatres) and disposable products (pills, food, syringes). During a year she is perhaps in contact with 100 different healthcare representatives. To get 23 disorders, 11 therapies, 9 + 2 pills and other products, and 100 people together to co-create value and service requires advanced systems and network management.

Anna is a customer of the healthcare sector, a subcategory of what is conventionally called the service sector. But healthcare is not about sectors; it is about thousands of health-related value propositions of excessively diverse kinds. She is exposed to value propositions from a large number of people, and these are only loosely and haphazardly coordinated into a service system. Each may be an efficient system within the supplier value chain, but they do not concur with Anna's value network; they are not customer-centric. In healthcare, the necessity of co-creation is obvious. The patient must do her part and be active within her ability: communicate with the therapists, take her pills, eat well, rest, exercise and so on. Each therapy and other activity is a system in itself and somebody has to manage the network of systems. Would you hire Anna as network manager? No, you would say – but that's what you have already done.

Figure 19.1 shows the network of people, therapies, products, and systems in which Anna is supposed to co-create value and get service. Although the figure is simplified a little fantasy and empathy will enable you to visualize the complex context and the many-to-many relationships within which Anna lives. If there is one thing that Anna needs in her situation it is certainly not complexity. She needs simplicity. Each therapeutic system by itself may have the good intention to provide just that, but first, each system is too provider-centric, and second, it is operating within the logic of its speciality, career system, organization, budget, locations, and so on, with sparse co-creation between the systems.

Where does marketing enter this network? Anna's service is a combination of government service (which can be a free citizen's right paid through taxes), private insurance, and service and value propositions from enterprises. Healthcare offers opportunities to sell to government organizations like hospitals and laboratories, and to private doctors and other therapists. Anna herself may be in the market for health food, vitamins, minerals, medication, eyeglasses and so on. She may listen to family and friends, television and radio programmes and read, all of this forming an information network affecting her behaviour as a consumer. Among the providers to hospitals are pharmaceutical companies, suppliers of equipment and disposable goods, computer and software consultants, building and construction firms, catering firms and cleaning firms. So the healthcare systems for the elderly are replete with marketing opportunities. It is a many-to-many marketing situation where networks meet networks and where the simple supplier–customer relationship is too limited to explain what happens.

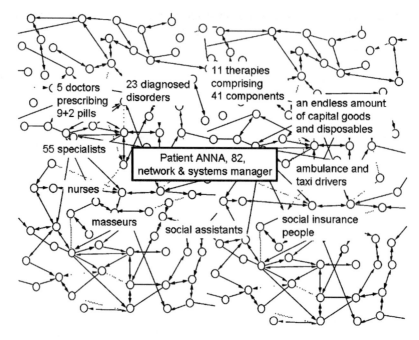

Figure 19.1   A sketch of Anna's healthcare network (© E. Gummesson, 2010)

In conclusion, S-D logic, service science and many-to-many marketing have broadened the service encounter to all aspects of co-creation of value and all aspects of value propositions. It is important to note that co-creation is not just interaction in a service encounter. In designing value propositions the following questions therefore must be answered:

- Who are the customers and who are the suppliers?
- What do suppliers do best?
- What do customers do best?
- What do third parties do best?
- What should be one-party (individual) action?
- What should be two-party (dyadic) interaction?
- What should be multi-party (network) interaction?
- What should be C2C interaction?
- What should be face-to-face interaction, ear-to-ear interaction, e-mail interaction, internet interaction, text messaging, and interaction with automatic machines?
- What do human beings do best?
- What does technology do best?
- Is there a no-man's land where service is neglected?

In the new service marketing the customer and supplier roles have merged, although they perform different tasks. The following categories of suppliers are found in the market:

- business enterprises
- governments on a national, regional and local level and increasingly on a mega, supra-national level, such as the EU
- NGOs which arise where the first two have failed, or act as supplementary to them.

In B2B, suppliers are also customers. In B2C/C2B we find:

- consumers
- citizens.

These are traditionally referred to as end-users. In many-to-many marketing the roles have broadened from a single individual consumer to social networks of family, friends, neighbours, and others. Being a citizen goes beyond the commercial consumer role; a citizen has certain rights and should primarily be served by the government sector. In the new service marketing with co-creation as a foundational premise, consumers are also suppliers of value. Therefore, consumers and citizens assume both the role of customer and supplier.

The future

In the 1990s I wrote that all organizations produce and sell both goods and services but in varying proportions; that the customer is buying utility and need satisfaction, not goods and services as such; that we know no more about services today than people knew about iron in the Iron Age and that we now have to understand the atoms and molecules and genes to create a generic theory of value-creating offerings (Gummesson, 1991, 1994). This is what has happened during the past few years. That it would materialize in 2004 as S-D logic and service science was not expected by me. My own line of thinking, complex networks actualized in many-to-many marketing, was of course known to me and my first book on the topic was published in 2004 (see further Gummesson, 2008).

Instead of making predictions that will probably prove wrong anyway, I will stick to expressing preferences. We should continue to work along the lines expressed by the new service logic and the new service marketing. It will take us places that we did not know existed. Some of the contributions will be viable and others will be less so, and may even lead us astray. There is no certainty in basic research and new discoveries. There will be discontinuities when something new and unexpected takes the lead and changes the world forever. Just think of a recent discontinuity, the internet. Columbus thought he was eastbound to India but instead went west and discovered America. This is called serendipity; you search for one thing and discover another which turns out to be useful.

Not so long ago I stated that '… marketing theory must reinvent itself and be refined, redefined, generated, and regenerated – or it will degenerate' (Gummesson, 2005: 317). There is now a call for basic research and theory on a higher level of abstraction – grand marketing theory. We need to take further steps up the marketing ladder. Marketing of services over the past decades offered middle-range theory. The new service marketing is taking us to the next rung of the marketing ladder, but I don't know how many rungs there are before we reach the top.

Recommended further reading

Readers are advised not to consult earlier editions than those referred to below.

Ballantyne, D. and Varey, R.J. (2008) 'The service-dominant logic and the future of marketing', *Journal of the Academy of Marketing Science* 36(1): 11–13.

Edvardsson, B., Gustafsson, A., Kristensson, P., Magnusson, P. and Matthing, J. (eds) (2006) *Involving Customers in New Service Development*, London: Imperial College Press.

Fisk, R.P., Grove, S.J. and John, J. (eds) (2000) *Services Marketing Self-Portraits*, Chicago, IL: American Marketing Association.

Grönroos, C. (2007), *Service Management and Marketing*, 3rd edn, Chichester, UK: Wiley.

Gummesson, E. (2007) 'Exit services marketing – enter service marketing', *Journal of Customer Behaviour* 6(2): 113–41. Also in Baker, M.J. and Hart, S.J. (eds) (2008) *The Marketing Book*, Oxford, UK: Butterworth-Heinemann/Elsevier. pp. 451–71.

Gummesson, E. (2008) *Total Relationship Marketing*, 3rd edn, Oxford, UK: Elsevier/Butterworth-Heinemann.

Lovelock, C. and Gummesson, E. (2004) 'Whither services marketing? In Search of a Paradigm and Fresh Perspectives', *Journal of Service Research* 7(1): 20–41.

Maglio, P.P. and Spohrer, J. (2008) 'Fundamentals of service science', *Journal of the Academy of Marketing Science* 36(1): 18–20.

Palmer, A. (2008) *Principles of Services Marketing*, 5th edn, London: McGraw-Hill.

Vargo, S.L. and Lusch, R.F. (2008) 'Service-dominant logic: continuing the evolution', *Journal of the Academy of Marketing Science* 36(1): 1–10.

References

Gummesson, E. (1991) 'Service quality – a holistic perspective', in S.W. Brown E. Gummesson, B. Edvardsson and B. Gustavsson (eds) *Service Quality: Multidisciplinary and Multinational Perspectives*. Lexington, MA: Lexington Books.

Gummesson, E. (1994) 'Service management: an evaluation and the future', *International Journal of Service Industry Management* 5(1): 77–96.

Gummesson, E. (2005) 'Qualitative research in marketing: roadmap for a wilderness of complexity and unpredictability', *European Journal of Marketing* 39(3/4): 309–27.

Gummesson, E. (2008) *Total Relationship Marketing*, 3rd edn, Oxford, UK: Elsevier/Butterworth-Heinemann.

Gummesson, E. (2010) 'The future of service is long overdue', in P.P., Maglio C.A. Kieliszewski and J. Spohrer (eds) *Handbook of Service Science*, New York: Springer.

Maglio, P.P. and Spohrer, J. (2008) 'Fundamentals of service science', *Journal of the Academy of Marketing Science* 36(1): 18–20.

Vargo, S.L. and Lusch, R.F. (2008a) 'Service-dominant logic: continuing the evolution', *Journal of the Academy of Marketing Science* 36(1): 1–10.

Vargo, S.L. and Lusch, R.F. (2008b) 'Why "service"?', *Journal of the Academy of Marketing Science* 36(1): 25–38.

Vargo, S.L., Maglio, P. and Akaka, M.A. (2008) 'On value and value co-creation: A service systems and service logic perspective', *European Management Journal* 26(3): 145–52.

Index

Research Methods Books from SAGE

DISCOVERING STATISTICS USING SPSS THIRD EDITION

ANDY FIELD

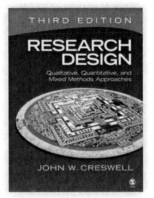

THIRD EDITION

RESEARCH DESIGN

Qualitative, Quantitative, and Mixed Methods Approaches

JOHN W. CRESWELL

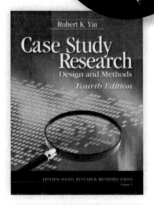

Robert K. Yin

Case Study Research

Design and Methods

Fourth Edition

APPLIED SOCIAL RESEARCH METHODS SERIES

Second Edition

QUALITATIVE INQUIRY & RESEARCH DESIGN

Choosing Among Five Approaches

John W. Creswell

Doing a Literature Review

Chris Hart

STATISTICS for People Who (Think They) HATE STATISTICS

3rd EDITION

NEIL J. SALKIND

SECOND EDITION

InterViews

Learning the Craft of Qualitative Research Interviewing

Steinar Kvale
Svend Brinkmann

THE **QUALITATIVE RESEARCHER'S COMPANION**

A. MICHAEL HUBERMAN
MATTHEW B. MILES

Basics of **QUALITATIVE RESEARCH** 3e

Juliet Corbin
Anselm Strauss

www.sagepub.co.uk

The Qualitative Research Kit

Edited by Uwe Flick

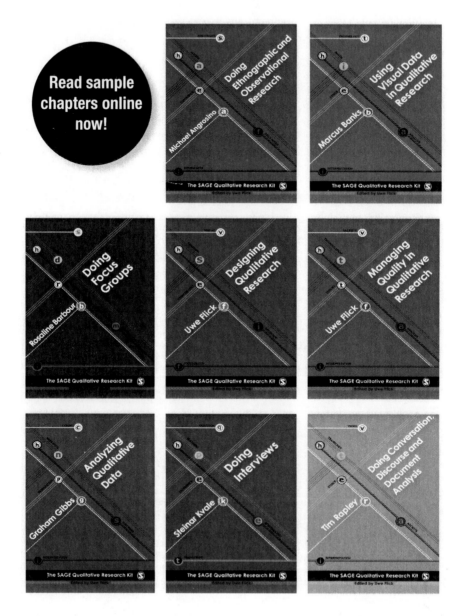

Read sample chapters online now!

Doing Ethnographic and Observational Research — Michael Angrosino — The SAGE Qualitative Research Kit — Edited by Uwe Flick

Using Visual Data in Qualitative Research — Marcus Banks — The SAGE Qualitative Research Kit — Edited by Uwe Flick

Doing Focus Groups — Rosaline Barbour — The SAGE Qualitative Research Kit

Designing Qualitative Research — Uwe Flick — The SAGE Qualitative Research Kit — Edited by Uwe Flick

Managing Quality in Qualitative Research — Uwe Flick — The SAGE Qualitative Research Kit — Edited by Uwe Flick

Analyzing Qualitative Data — Graham Gibbs — The SAGE Qualitative Research Kit — Edited by Uwe Flick

Doing Interviews — Steinar Kvale — The SAGE Qualitative Research Kit — Edited by Uwe Flick

Doing Conversation, Discourse and Document Analysis — Tim Rapley — The SAGE Qualitative Research Kit — Edited by Uwe Flick

www.sagepub.co.uk